FACING EXTINCTION

THE WORLD'S RAREST BIRDS AND THE RACE TO SAVE THEM

PAUL F. DONALD
Principal Conservation Scientist, Royal Society for the Protection of Birds

NIGEL J. COLLAR
Leventis Fellow in Conservation Biology, BirdLife International

STUART J. MARSDEN
Reader in Conservation Ecology, Manchester Metropolitan University

DEBORAH J. PAIN
Director of Conservation, Wildfowl and Wetlands Trust

CHRISTOPHER HELM
LONDON

BirdLife
INTERNATIONAL

PREVENTING EXTINCTIONS

All royalties from sales of this book will be donated to
BirdLife International's Preventing Extinctions Programme,
which aims to prevent the loss of the world's rarest birds.

Published 2013 by Christopher Helm, an imprint of Bloomsbury Publishing Plc, 50 Bedford Square, London WC1B 3DP.
First edition published 2010.

www.bloomsbury.com
www.bloomsburynature.com

ISBN (print) 978-1-4081-8966-5

A CIP catalogue record for this book is available from the British Library.

This book is produced using paper that is made from wood grown in managed sustainable forests. It is natural, renewable and recyclable.
The logging and manufacturing processes conform to the environmental regulations of the country of origin.

Commissioning Editor: Nigel Redman
Project Editor: Jim Martin

Design by Julie Dando, Fluke Art

Printed in China

10 9 8 7 6 5 4 3 2 1

Front cover: Spoon-billed Sandpiper *Eurynorhynchus pygmeus* by Baz Scampion
Frontispiece: Ivory-billed Woodpecker *Campephilus principalis* by Jan Wilczur
Spine: Forest Owlet *Heteroglaux blewitti* by Jayesh Joshi
Back: Sociable Lapwings *Vanellus gregarius* by Paul F. Donald/RSPB

Visit bloomsburywildlife.com to find out more about our authors and their books.

Main Contents

*We dedicate this edition to the memory of Don Merton (1939–2011),
whose pioneering work led to extraordinary successes in saving many
of New Zealand's most threatened birds and has informed and inspired
a generation of conservationists around the world.*

Acknowledgements

We are indebted to many people for their help during the writing of this book. For their comments on one or more of the chapters or case studies, we are very grateful to Roberto Azeredo, Thomas Bodey, Chris Bowden, Mike Brooke, Graeme Buchanan, Nicola Crockford, Richard Cuthbert, Peter Cranswick, Rhys Green, Jim Groombridge, Geoff Hilton, Josep del Hoyo, Baz Hughes, Farah Ishtiaq, Nigel Jarrett, Johannes Kamp, Ivana Lamas, Livia Lins, Huw Lloyd, Aldrin Mallari, Nial Moores, Darren Oakley-Martin, Steffen Oppel, James Pitt Simpson, Danny Rogers, Lily-Arison René de Roland, Phil Round, Geer Scheres, Rob Sheldon, Andrew Terry, Russell Thorstrom, Rick Watson, David Waugh, Glyn Young and Christoph Zöckler. We are particularly grateful to Stuart Butchart for detailed comments on a number of chapters and for providing much useful information, and to Graeme Buchanan, Geoff Hilton, Ian May, Peter Creed, Phil Taylor and in particular Mark Balman for producing some of the maps. We thank Jim Martin and Nigel Redman at A&C Black for advice throughout, Ernest Garcia for his expert editing and Jan Wilczur for his marvellous vignettes. The many photographers who contributed their work are individually acknowledged in the text. We are grateful to the Western Foundation for Vertebrate Zoology for allowing us to reproduce the photograph of Eskimo Curlew. Thanks also to Gina Pfaff, Ade Long and Nicola Crockford for helping to source the photographs. Paul Donald acknowledges the RSPB for granting him a sabbatical to write part of this book. Chapter 13 is adapted with permission from an article originally published in *British Birds*.

For their help and support in countless ways, we would like to thank Fiona Roberts, Jo Wright, Amy and Katie Marsden and Duncan McNiven.

Preface

In 1866, a single flock of perhaps more than three billion Passenger Pigeons *Ectopistes migratorius* was recorded passing overhead in Ontario, Canada. Less than fifty years later, the last ever Passenger Pigeon, named Martha, died in an aviary in Cincinnati Zoo. Intense hunting pressure and unprecedented changes to the landscape had brought about the extinction of what had been perhaps the world's most numerous bird. Four years after the death of Martha, the world's last Carolina Parakeet *Conuropsis carolinensis* lay dead in the very same aviary. Collapsing populations of Passenger Pigeons in the 1880s and 1890s caused professional hunters to train their guns instead on another abundant bird, the Eskimo Curlew *Numenius borealis*. The last confirmed record of this species was in Barbados in 1963 and it is now almost certainly extinct. Abundance, even superabundance, is clearly no guarantee against extinction. While human activities can benefit some species, there have been far more losers than winners. It is estimated that the total number of birds on the planet may have fallen by around a quarter, a loss of at least 25 billion individuals, since pre-agricultural times. Of the 10,000 or so bird species currently recognised, 12% are classified as threatened with extinction according to the 2010 IUCN Red List. Nearly 200 species are listed as Critically Endangered, the highest category of threat for a bird species living in the wild. Without current or future action to save them these species face a high chance of disappearing in the next few decades. They are the world's rarest and most threatened birds and form the central subject of this book.

Rarity in nature can be defined in a number of ways. Perhaps most obviously, a bird is rare if its total world population is small. Certainly, the list of Critically Endangered birds includes many species, such as the Madagascar Pochard *Aythya innotata*, whose population in the wild, at the time of writing, is thought to comprise fewer than 50 individuals (and just 19 in the case of the pochard). But the category also includes some species whose rarity is a reflection of their tiny ranges rather than tiny populations. Birds on islands or mountaintops often fit this pattern and many have ranges and populations that are both tiny. Having a small range but a large population is less common but the ranks of Critically Endangered birds include the Waved Albatross *Phoebastria irrorata*, which although still relatively numerous occurs on only a handful of small islands around the Galápagos. Other Critically Endangered species occupy large or even huge ranges, and yet are rare because they occur at such low population densities. The White-bellied Heron *Ardea insignis* perhaps numbers fewer than 250 individuals, spread thinly across Bhutan, India, Bangladesh, Burma and possibly parts of Tibet and China. The list of Critically Endangered birds also includes species like the Asian *Gyps* vultures, which are not yet rare in the sense that they have neither small ranges nor particularly small populations, but which are declining so rapidly that, unless something is done very quickly, their populations will plummet to extinction in a few years.

This book opens with chapters on the nature and measurement of rarity, and the causes and distribution of extinction risk across geographic areas and taxonomic groups. A disproportionate number of island bird species have become extinct in historic times and many island birds – both landbirds and seabirds – are currently on the Critically Endangered list. Because of this importance, a whole chapter is devoted to the challenges faced by the world's island birds. Yet extreme rarity is not a terminal condition. A chapter on what can be done to save the world's rarest birds from extinction shows that, no matter how small a bird's population, it is often possible to prevent its disappearance. For a number of species, however, it is not even known whether any individuals survive or not. Birds like the New Caledonian Owlet-nightjar *Aegotheles savesi* are so poorly known, and inhabit (or perhaps used to inhabit) such inaccessible areas, that it is not surprising that they are seldom if ever seen. There is understandably more hope for these species than for others, such as Ivory-billed Woodpecker *Campephilus principalis*, a species that has been the subject of greater search efforts. These species, which appear to hover between survival and extinction, are covered in a further chapter. If we are to be proactive rather than reactive in our fight to save the world's threatened birds, we need to be able to see into the future and identify emerging threats and act against them before they can wipe out further species. A final chapter examines how threats to the world's birds are shifting. Human population growth, climate change and totally new and unpredicted threats will create major challenges to birds, and those trying to protect them. We are now, at least, in a better position to face these challenges than were the conservation bodies of the 1970s. Yet resources are insufficient and birds still rely on the skill, imagination and perseverance of a relatively small number of dedicated organisations and individuals for their survival.

All but the first and last general chapters are followed by case studies, twenty in all, that illustrate the issues raised in the preceding synoptic chapter. The majority of the species covered in these case studies are listed as Critically Endangered, although the list does include two species that are already Extinct in the Wild, one that is Extinct and one listed as Endangered.

On a few beaches on the island of Madagascar, you can still pick up shell fragments of the huge eggs laid by elephant birds *Aepyornis* hundreds of years ago. This may seem amazing enough to ornithologists but imagine how wonderful it would be if elephant birds, dodos, moas and the hundreds of other species never seen alive by the naturalists of today still roamed the planet. Our species was responsible for their extinction and, unless cloning advances beyond all current expectations, we can never bring them back. Now imagine the world without the delight of the large, flightless, slightly smelly but enduringly endearing Kakapo *Strigops habroptila* – the world's largest parrot; without the albatrosses, sentinels of our wild untamed oceans; or without the unique Spoon-billed Sandpiper *Eurynorhynchus pygmeus*. Whether or not as individuals we ever get a chance to see these species, most of us would surely agree that the world would be a poorer place without them.

The unhappy history of the extinction of so many species through human agency makes sobering and depressing reading. However, we hope to show in this book that even species on the brink of extirpation can be saved provided conservation measures are implemented in time. Our case studies show how an increased awareness of what may be lost is leading to successful conservation measures across the planet, often with the enthusiastic collaboration of local people. There is real cause for optimism.

Our central message is that it is wholly within our power and ability to prevent the world's rarest and most threatened species from joining the Passenger Pigeon in extinction, as numerous recent and often dramatic successes demonstrate. We hope that this book inspires you to play your part. By buying it you have already made a start, as all royalties are being donated to BirdLife's Preventing Extinctions Programme, a major initiative set up to help ensure that world's most threatened birds receive the necessary conservation action. If you can do more to support this programme, or any of the initiatives set up to help threatened birds, please visit http://www.birdlife.org/extinction/.

In the three years since the first edition of this book appeared, the stories of some of the world's rarest birds have changed dramatically, either because of better knowledge of their status and threats or because of new developments in the race to save them. Efforts to prevent the extinction of the Spoon-billed Sandpiper (Chapter 4), the Asian *Gyps* vultures (Chapter 17) and Madagascar Pochard (Chapter 21) have seen some startling and generally positive developments that have required substantial updating of the original accounts. Recent research has revealed a great deal about the reasons for the imperiled status of the Sociable Lapwing (Chapter 3), the complex taxonomic history and peculiar distribution of the Liben Lark (Chapter 8) and the volatile population dynamics of the Raso Lark (Chapter 13). We have also taken the opportunity of a new edition to update or expand some sections of the thematic chapters. Unfortunately, no updates are required to the stories of the Po'ouli (Chapter 14) or Slender-billed or Eskimo Curlews (Chapter 25), since the last few years have produced no new evidence of their continued existence.

Chapter 1
The nature of rarity and the rarity of nature

Visitors to zoos behave in an interesting way. A series of carefully controlled experiments undertaken at the famous zoo in the Jardin des Plantes in Paris showed that members of the public spent longer looking at rare species than at common ones, they were happy to pay more money to see rare species, and they were prepared to walk further and to suffer more physical discomfort to do so (Angulo *et al.* 2009). They even took greater risks when trying to steal rare species, in the form of seeds placed tantalisingly within reach behind a fence. This fascination with rare species could not be explained by any characteristics of the animals themselves, which on average were no more physically attractive or entertaining to watch than common species. Indeed, the researchers periodically switched the information panels, so that half the time visitors were looking at common species that the panels told them were rare, and vice versa. In each case, visitors spent more time looking at the species that they *thought* were rare.

Rarity, therefore, appears to carry its own intrinsic value. Perhaps recognising the financial benefits of this attraction, zoos have greatly increased the number of rare species they hold in their collections (Whitfort & Young 2004). The same preoccupation with rarity is reflected in people's responses to wild animals and plants; as species become fewer in number, so people are prepared to go to greater lengths to see them, protect them, possess them, hunt them, steal them, wear them or eat them (Courchamp *et al.* 2006). Many birdwatchers spend a disproportionate amount of the time, money and effort they invest in their hobby looking at, and for, rare species. The same is true of the collectors of eggs, orchids, mammals and other wildlife, who are prepared to take increasingly high risks to obtain rare specimens. The international conservation community dedicates a high proportion of its resources to protecting rare species, investment often being greatest for those species that have the fewest remaining individuals (Garnett *et al.* 2003). These conservation investments are sometimes threatened by the greatly inflated economic premium that rarity carries in the international trade in endangered species (Courchamp *et al.* 2006). Conservationists face the problem that simply promoting a species' rarity as a justification for saving it might unleash a range of new pressures on it. For example, the elevation of the Javan Hawk-eagle *Spizaetus bartelsi* to the status of the national bird of Indonesia, a step encouraged by conservationists in the hope that it would draw attention to the species' plight, instead resulted in an increase in illegal trapping pressure as news of its rarity spread among aviculturists (van Balen *et al.* 2000). The description of a rare new species can stimulate the demand for specimens for museums, private collections or zoos (Stuart *et al.* 2006). Our fascination with rarity is not confined to the natural world, as the enormous prices commanded by rare stamps, coins and other antiques demonstrate. The psychological basis of this preoccupation remains unclear, but may be connected with social status (Angulo *et al.* 2009).

Rarity in the natural world clearly holds a peculiar fascination that can express itself in a number of different ways. One of these, we hope, is a desire to ask questions about the natural history and conservation of rare species. Why are some species rare and others not? Where do rare species occur? What can be done to prevent rare species from slipping over the brink to extinction? And where will rarity occur in the future? Answering these questions requires first an appreciation of the nature of rarity itself.

Unless it is measured globally, rarity is often relative: it is perhaps natural that many people perceive rarity as a measure relating to their own experience. For example, it might be that in a high proportion of the countries within which even a common species occurs it is rare in a national sense, simply because those countries capture only a small part of that species' range and population (Rodrigues & Gaston 2002). In the United Kingdom, lying at the western fringes of Eurasia and separated from it by a narrow stretch of sea, many breeding birds that are rare at the national level, and so benefit from high conservation investment, for example the Eurasian Nightjar *Caprimulgus europaeus*,

Only one of the 200 or so species listed as Critically Endangered breeds in Europe, the Balearic Shearwater Puffinus mauretanicus *(Richard Stonier).*

are often not rare at a European or global level. The disparity between perceived rarity and true rarity is greatest in the case of the vagrant birds that reach the UK each year from North America or Asia, the interest they attract from rarity-hunters being out of all proportion to their rarity in any global sense. Ironically, the majority of such vagrants originate from regions in which they are among the more common species, their sheer numbers making it more likely that a few wind-blown or disoriented stragglers will reach distant shores. In contrast, the only species that birdwatchers in Britain are likely to encounter that is listed as being rare in a truly global sense is the Balearic Shearwater *Puffinus mauretanicus*, currently listed as Critically Endangered, although it occurs sufficiently regularly to excite relatively little interest. Rarity, therefore, is a concept that is often applied subjectively and parochially.

THE NATURE OF RARITY

Rarity has many causes. Some species are naturally rare and probably always have been, limited for example by the size of the island on which they evolved, by their reliance on a particularly scarce resource or restricted habitat or by their position in a particular food chain. Others have become rare through natural processes; after all, the average evolutionary lifetime of a species is only a million years or so, rather less on islands, and the necessary prelude to natural extinction is a period of rarity (Williamson *et al.* 1989). Some species, and an increasing proportion of them, owe their rarity largely or wholly to human activities. In other words, some species are born rare, some achieve rarity and others have rarity thrust upon them.

However, classifying rare species neatly into one of these three groups is both difficult and potentially misleading, as the pressures acting on each are not independent. For example, naturally rare species are likely to be more heavily impacted by the activities of people than naturally common ones, simply because they are more likely to be severely affected by changes taking place in small areas; the great wave of extinction that has wiped away many of the world's island species has resulted from changes that affected a tiny proportion of the planet's total land surface. Species nearing the end of their evolutionary roads may be less well adapted to face the increasing threats we place on them (Meijaard *et al.* 2008). Furthermore, it is sometimes difficult to separate natural rarity from that imposed by our own actions. Species that appear to be naturally rare, for example those confined to small islands or mountaintops, may once have had a far larger distribution from which they were wiped out before the scientific recording of birds began.

Rarity in the natural world has been defined as 'the state of having a low abundance and/or a small range size' (Gaston 1994). If we accept this definition for the moment, there are three important and strongly inter-related patterns in nature that help us to describe rarity at different scales. The first is one that any naturalist will be aware of from their own observations, which is that within the broad distribution of any particular species it is common in some places and rare or absent in others. More specifically, a species tends to be more abundant within the centre of its range, where conditions are optimal, and becomes increasingly rare towards the edges of its range as the environment becomes less suitable before finally petering out altogether at the boundary of its distribution (Brown *et al.* 1995). This means that even abundant species might occur at low densities across much of their geographical ranges.

A second general pattern in nature is that, when plotted on a graph of increasing abundance or range size, most species fall towards the rarer end of the scale; in other words, at any particular location or in any community, most species are relatively rare and only a small number are extremely abundant or widespread. This initially surprising pattern is, in fact, one of ecology's oldest and most general laws and holds for most groups of animals in most habitats, although quite why it does so remains the subject of considerable debate (McGill *et al.* 2007).

The third pattern, known as the 'abundance-occupancy relationship', is less immediately apparent (Lawton 1993). It might seem obvious that species with very large geographical ranges tend to have larger populations overall than species with very small ranges, but the abundance-occupancy relationship shows that species with large distributions tend to be common within them, whereas species with small geographical distributions tend to be scarce wherever they occur (Bock & Ricklefs 1983, Brown 1984, Blackburn *et al.* 1997). In other words, there is a strong positive relationship between the size of a species' range and the density at which it occurs within that range. For example, in the mountain forests of Costa Rica, bird species occurring at few sites also have low abundance, and many are endemic to the Costa Rican and Panamanian highlands, whereas birds occurring at many sites are common at those sites and have ranges that extend well beyond that region (Jankowski & Rabenold 2007). To look at this another way, the abundance-occupancy relationship predicts that few species have very large populations crammed into small ranges and few have tiny populations that are smeared thinly over huge areas. These predictions are generally supported by observations in nature but hold less well for island species, which often occur at relatively high densities within their confined distribution. The relationship between range size and local abundance is so strong that it is possible to make a reasonable prediction about the range sizes of different species recorded at a particular location based solely on their relative abundance there.

These three general rules help us to describe patterns of rarity in nature, but they do not explain why certain species are naturally common and others rare. Species endemic to small islands will inevitably be rare in a global sense, even if they occur at high densities on the island, as their populations are limited by the area available to them. The Raso Lark *Alauda razae* of the Cape Verde islands, for example, occupies one of the smallest ranges of any bird, yet within that range its population density is high, particularly for a lark (Chapter 13). However, this is not the whole explanation for natural rarity: as the second pattern described above shows, many mainland species also have relatively small ranges and populations. An intriguing explanation for the evolution of natural rarity, discovered through work on island species but likely to apply more generally, is the 'taxon cycle' (Ricklefs & Bermingham 2002), which predicts that species go through a cycle of expansion, colonisation, specialisation and contraction before their eventual extinction. Birds arriving in a new area tend to start life in their new homes as generalists, as they are not adapted to exploit the more specialised niches available to them. In due course, however, they become increasingly well adapted to exploiting the area's scarcer resources and may become increasingly reliant upon them as competition from the expanding populations of more recent arrivals increases. An increasing reliance on rare resources will inevitably lead to increasing rarity. Over evolutionary time, they tend to start as common generalists, then range-restricted subspecies with more specialised foods and habitats, then endemic species that rely largely on rare resources, and finally relics doomed to natural extinction. The small ranges of naturally rare species might indicate that some at least are rare because they are coming to the natural end of their evolutionary lifespans, since as species age so their ranges tend to shrink (Webb & Gaston 2000). The taxon cycle is useful not only in explaining current patterns of rarity but also in predicting future rarity and extinction (Chapter 26).

THE CHARACTERISTICS OF RARE SPECIES

Naturally rare species exhibit a number of distinctive characteristics. Species high in the food chain, such as large predators like the Philippine Eagle *Pithecophaga jefferyi* (Chapter 18), require large areas to feed and so occur at very low densities. This is because of the inefficiency of food metabolism; only around a tenth of the food ingested by an animal will be converted into its own biomass, so animal biomass reduces by a factor of ten at each level of the food chain (Colinvaux 1980). But not all naturally rare species are top predators. Many are rare because they are specialised, using a narrower range of resources within their environments than common species (Kattan 1992). In particular, this specialism is characterised by the use of rarer resources, rather than the use of a narrow range of common resources (Gregory & Gaston 2000, Walker 2006, Lollback *et al.* 2008). In Australia for example, the uncommon Black-chinned Honeyeater *Melithreptus gularis* feeds in the same trees as the much more abundant Fuscous Honeyeater *Lichenostomus fuscus*, but obtains a far higher proportion of its food by probing between leaves that are bound together by certain uncommon insect larvae, whereas the Fuscous Honeyeater takes a wide range of common foods (Lollback *et al.* 2008). Because of this reliance on scarce resources, naturally rare species tend to be more vulnerable to habitat degradation or fragmentation (Lloyd 2008, Hockey & Curtis 2009), whereas more generalist species are able to occupy even the most degraded habitats, such as urban areas, are more flexible in their use of different resources and can tolerate a wide range of environmental conditions (Bonier *et al.* 2007).

Overlying these natural patterns of rarity, and indeed often swamping them completely, are the impacts that mankind has visited upon the planet. The massive environmental changes brought about through the destruction of natural habitats, the spread of agriculture, alien predators and competitors, herbivores and diseases, hunting, illegal trade and many other of the activities required to feed, nurture and entertain seven billion large and resourceful primates on a small planet have changed natural patterns of distribution and abundance out of all recognition. One conservative estimate suggests that the total number of individual birds on the planet has fallen by at least 25 billion since pre-agricultural times, representing a reduction in the carrying capacity of the planet for birds of up to a quarter (Gaston *et al.* 2003). This is not to say that there have been no winners among the world's birds, and some species have benefited from the changes brought about by human alteration of the world's environments.

MEASURING RARITY AS EXTINCTION RISK

The main practical reason for quantifying rarity in nature is to identify priorities for conservation and to track the changing fortunes of the world's most vulnerable species (Mace *et al.* 2008). The definition of rarity as being the 'state of having a low abundance and/or a small range size' is a useful starting point, because both abundance and range size can be estimated from field surveys. However, simply using population and range size as estimates of the degree of threat misses other important factors that can affect the likelihood of a species becoming extinct. For example, they say nothing about the trajectory of a population, or about its reproductive potential. A declining population of ageing individuals with low reproductive output in a fragmented range is clearly more at risk of extinction than an increasing and reproductively active population of the same size.

Before 1994, the International Union for Conservation of Nature (IUCN), the international authority on the conservation status of the world's wildlife, classified all species according to a number of categories based largely on expert opinion. An influential article published in 1991 suggested an alternative approach, which was to classify species according to their risk of extinction (Mace & Lande 1991). This incorporated measures of population and range size but then added new components, including the rate of change in population size and the degree of fragmentation of the range. By adding these new dimensions, species that did not qualify for threatened status by having small populations or ranges could now qualify if their populations were declining or ranges fragmenting at a rate likely to threaten their future survival.

In 1994, having greatly elaborated the 'Mace-Lande criteria', IUCN adopted a new set of quantitative Red List thresholds that could be applied to all forms of life on earth except micro-organisms, and although various refinements have been added over the years, these remain the basis for classifying rarity and quantifying threat in the natural world (Mace *et al.* 2008). Birds were the first group of animals to be classified using these new criteria (Collar *et al.* 1994), because they were, and remain, the best-known group of animals. The IUCN criteria (Fig. 1.1) have now been used to assign over 65,000 of the world's plant and animal species to a category on the IUCN Red List, and as information becomes available for more groups, the proportion of the world's species that are categorised in this way is increasing (Vié *et al.* 2009). The IUCN Red List is regarded as the most robust and objective system for classifying extinction risk (de Grammont & Cuarón 2006), and can be applied at national as well as global scales (Szabo *et al.* 2012a).

Five criteria with quantitative thresholds are used to assign species to one of seven IUCN categories of extinction risk. In increasing order of threat, these categories are Least Concern (LC), Near Threatened (NT), Vulnerable (VU), Endangered (EN), Critically Endangered (CR), Extinct in the Wild (EW) and, finally, Extinct (EX). Species in the categories Vulnerable, Endangered, and Critically Endangered are together referred to as 'globally threatened'. The five criteria used to assign species to the categories from Least Concern to Critically Endangered relate to: the population trend over a window of ten years or three generations (Criterion A); a combination of the size and trend of the population (Criterion B); the size and changes in it of the species' range (Criterion C); and the size of the range or population irrespective of changes in them (Criterion D). A fifth criterion (E) allows a species to be assigned to a category of threat if sufficient data exist to predict its extinction risk using quantitative methods, such as statistical population modelling, although sufficient data exist for very few species to be classified in this way. The IUCN Red List rules require that a species be listed in the highest category triggered by the criteria it meets, although it may also trigger criteria for lower categories. If a species triggers none of the threat criteria, it is listed as Least Concern, but if it comes close to triggering one or more it is listed as Near Threatened. Species for which a paucity of information precludes reliable assessment are as classed as Data Deficient (DD).

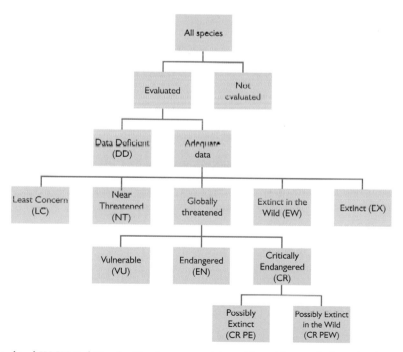

Figure 1.1. The hierarchical IUCN Red List classification system. Adapted from Mace et al. *(2008). The categories CR PE and CR PEW were added following the criteria of Butchart* et al. *(2006b).*

It is possible that the extinction risks as captured by the current IUCN criteria are overly pessimistic, since many fewer Critically Endangered species have taken the final fall into oblivion than predicted by their estimated extinction risk, a discrepancy that can only partly be explained by the positive impacts of conservation action (Brooke *et al.* 2008). However, the Red List is important in that it provides conservationists with a comparison of extinction risks between different species, allowing the identification of those in most immediate need of conservation action, and it is of fundamental importance in conservation planning, management, monitoring and decision-making (Lamoreux *et al.* 2003, Rodrigues *et al.* 2006, Vié *et al.* 2009). The birds forming the central subject of this book are those falling into the categories Critically Endangered and Extinct in the Wild.

THE RARITY OF NATURE

When the IUCN Red List criteria are applied to the world's birds, an interesting pattern emerges. As the scale moves from the species considered to be least threatened to those considered to have the highest risk of extinction, so the number of species falling into each category declines (Fig. 1.2). The species classified as Critically Endangered make up less than 2% of all the world's birds. In other words, the condition of rarity in birds, as defined by extinction risk, is itself a rare phenomenon. The same is not necessarily true in other vertebrate groups, particularly the amphibians, for which the number of globally threatened species is close to the number of species listed as Least Concern (Fig. 1.3). Indeed, across all the world's plant and animal groups, birds contain the lowest proportion of threatened species, with the possible exception of dragonflies. Around 12% of the world's species of bird are listed as Vulnerable, Endangered or Critically Endangered, compared to equivalent figures of nearly 25% of mammals, reptiles and freshwater fish, around 35% of corals and freshwater crabs, around 40% of amphibians and a staggering 55% of the ancient plant group known as cycads (Hilton-Taylor *et al.* 2009). This is likely to reflect the adaptability of birds to environmental change, most obviously manifested in their ability to move long distances and their relatively large ranges compared to other taxa, but also to a lesser extent the popularity of birds and consequently the greater resources available for their conservation. However, it might also partly reflect the far better information we have on birds, since it is sometimes the case, in birds at least, that increased knowledge of a species' status shows it to be less threatened than previously thought, as the example of Gurney's Pitta *Pitta gurneyi* (Chapter 23) so dramatically illustrates.

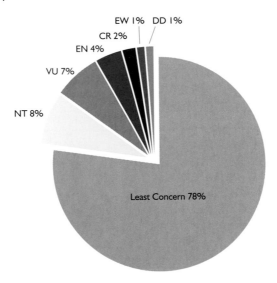

Figure 1.2. Extinction risk in the world's birds for 2011, as indicated by their categories on the IUCN Red List (BirdLife International). NT = Near Threatened, VU = Vulnerable, EN = Endangered, CR = Critically Endangered, EW = Extinct in the Wild, DD = Data Deficient.

Birds have a far lower proportion of species listed as Data Deficient than do the other groups, a further indication of the popularity of birds as study species. Of the 63 bird species listed by IUCN as Data Deficient in 2009, the majority appear likely to fall into categories of relatively low extinction risk when sufficient information becomes available to classify them (Butchart & Bird 2009). Improved knowledge for species in other animal and plant groups might in many cases lead to a more positive assessment of their conservation status. Even for birds, knowledge of the rarest species is generally less than complete, and there is a general precautionary principle in IUCN listing, in which a species is classified as threatened until further information proves otherwise. This is a pragmatic approach which stimulates the collection of the additional information required for better future assessment.

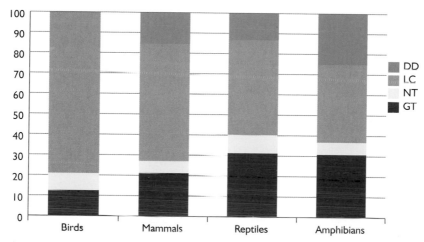

Figure 1.3. The distribution of species (percentage of living species) among IUCN Red List categories of extinction risk across the four terrestrial vertebrate groups in 2008. GT = globally threatened (which includes the categories Vulnerable, Endangered and Critically Endangered), NT = Near Threatened, LC = Least Concern, DD = Data Deficient. Estimates for reptiles are based on a randomised sampling approach. From data in Hilton-Taylor et al. (2009).

THE CHANGING STATE OF RARITY

Extinction risk categories based on standardised criteria that consider population and range size, and trends in them, have the benefit that they can be compared across species to detect changing patterns of extinction risk over time, or broken down by habitat, region or type of threat (Butchart *et al.* 2004, Butchart *et al.* 2007, Butchart 2008). 'Red List Indices' generated by the movement of species between the IUCN Red List categories provide one of the most powerful tools available to measure the success or failure of global conservation efforts, such as the Convention on Biological Diversity (Butchart *et al.* 2005b, Butchart *et al.* 2006a). They have now been adopted as one of the indicators used to measure progress against the United Nations Millennium Development Goals, in recognition of the fact that biodiversity conservation is integral to sustainable development. Species are moved between Red List categories when the Red List is updated each year in response to new information on their populations and threats. For example, seven bird species were uplisted to the Critically Endangered category in 2009, from a diverse group including the Waved Albatross *Phoebastria irrorata*, Red-headed Vulture *Sarcogyps calvus* (Chapter 17), Liben Lark *Heteromirafra sidamoensis* (Chapter 8) and Gough Bunting *Rowettia goughensis* (Chapter 12). In the same year, six species were removed from the category Critically Endangered and reassigned to lower categories of threat. These included Lear's Macaw *Anodorhynchus leari* of Brazil, Chatham Petrel *Pterodroma axillaris* of New Zealand and Mauritius Fody *Foudia rubra*, all of which have benefited so much from dedicated conservation actions that they are now considered at lower risk of extinction. In 2010, three species were removed from the list of Critically Endangered species (Chatham Albatross *Thalassarche eremita*, Yellow-eared Parrot *Ognorhynchus icterotis* and Azores Bullfinch *Pyrrhula murina*) and three added (Zapata Rail *Cyanolimnas*

Azores Bullfinch Pyrrhula murina *was one of three species removed from the list of Critically Endangered birds in 2010 (John O'Sullivan, RSPB).*

cerverai, White-bellied Cinclodes *Cinclodes palliatus* and Black-winged Starling *Acridotheres melanopterus*). In many cases, re-categorisations result from improved knowledge of the status of each species and the threats they face. In others, taxonomic rearrangements lead to revisions in Red List categories. But some species are uplisted owing to genuine deterioration in status, or downlisted owing to genuine improvement in status, usually because of successful conservation action. The Red List Index integrates just these latter two types of category change in order to show the net genuine fluctuations in the aggregate extinction risk of the world's birds.

Unfortunately, patterns over time suggest a general worsening of the status of the world's threatened birds (Hilton-Taylor *et al.* 2009). Between 1988 and 2008 there was a clear trend towards species being moved into higher categories of extinction risk (Fig. 1.4). During this period, and excluding species reclassified simply on the basis of better information on their numbers, 230 species were moved to higher threat categories, while just 38 were moved to lower categories, almost all as a result of intensive conservation action (BirdLife International, unpublished data). However, the majority of the species being downlisted to lower threat categories started out in the highest category, Critically Endangered. Indeed, in the last few decades more species have been removed from the Critically Endangered list because their status improved sufficiently for them to be moved to lower classes than were removed because they became extinct. So while the overall trend is worrying, there is at least some heartening evidence that our ability to restore populations when they reach critically low levels is sufficient to prevent an even higher rate of extinction (Butchart *et al.* 2006b, Brooke *et al.* 2008). Unfortunately, our efforts to protect less threatened species appear rather less successful, not least because there are many more species to look after or consider, and resources tend to be channelled towards the rarest species. Within the categories of Near Threatened, Vulnerable and Endangered, many more species have moved into higher threat categories than have been downlisted to lower categories.

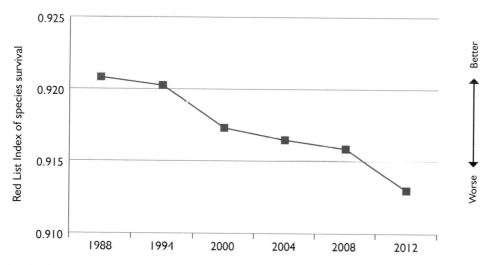

Figure 1.4. Red List Index for birds, 1988–2012. This index records the average extinction risk of the world's birds. If all the world's birds were listed as Least Concern, the index would have a value of 1. If all the world's birds went extinct, the index would have a value of zero (updated from BirdLife International 2008a).

THE WORLD'S RAREST BIRD

At least three books, each covering a different species, describe efforts to save what is claimed in their titles to be the world's rarest bird (Butler & Merton 1992, Juniper 2002, Powell 2008). It is entirely possible that each claim was indeed true at the time. The Black Robin *Petroica traversi* of New Zealand (Chapter 15) was at one point reduced to just five birds, but a spectacularly successful recovery project has allowed the population to increase to around 300 birds, all descended from a single female, and the species has now been downlisted to Endangered. The Po'ouli *Melamprosops phaeosoma* (Chapter 14) of Hawaii unfortunately never recovered from its last known population of three individuals and is now almost certainly extinct (Powell 2008). Spix's Macaw *Cyanopsitta spixii* (Chapter 20) of Brazil was for many years known to be represented in the wild by a single individual and it is almost certainly now extinct in the wild. Its future relies on a captive population, which in June 2009 numbered 68 birds. None of these therefore has a claim to be the world's rarest bird now. In fact, it is impossible to identify the true holder of this unenviable title. A number of Critically Endangered species are so poorly known that they have no known occupied sites, so it is impossible to estimate their numbers or even to be sure whether they still exist. Of the species that are known sufficiently well for reliable population estimates to be generated, perhaps the rarest in purely numerical terms is the Madagascar Pochard *Aythya innotata*, with fewer than 20 individuals known in 2009, only six of them females, although emergency conservation efforts to save this species from extinction are already proving successful (Chapter 21). In 2008, the Black Stilt *Himantopus novaezelandiae* of New Zealand, the focus of another major conservation initiative, numbered just 20 breeding pairs together with a similar number of non-breeding birds, many of them released from a captive breeding programme. The Sulu Hornbill *Anthracoceros montani*, now probably confined to the island of Tawitawi in the Sulu Archipelago of the Philippines, may number fewer than 20 pairs. Other species that reasonably reliable population estimates suggest number fewer than a hundred individuals in the wild include the Cerulean Paradise-flycatcher *Eutrichomyias rowleyi*, Bali Starling *Leucopsar rothschildi*, Puerto Rican Amazon *Amazona vittata*, Tahiti Monarch *Pomarea nigra* and Floreana Mockingbird *Mimus trifasciatus*. It remains entirely possible, of course, that the world's rarest species is one that is not even known to science. When populations reach such low levels, even small changes in their numbers mean that the world's rarest species is likely to change frequently; the death of a single bird or a single successful nesting attempt might be sufficient to relegate or promote a species from this unfortunate status. For nearly a fifth of all the bird species listed as Critically Endangered, the most pressing question is not about how many birds there are, but whether the species still exists at all.

Species with fewer than 100 remaining individuals include Puerto Rican Amazon Amazona vittata *(left) (Kevin Schafer) and Black Stilt* Himantopus novaezelandiae *of New Zealand (above) (Marcus Lawson), both the subject of ongoing conservation programmes.*

THE SIGNIFICANCE OF RARE SPECIES

The world around us is shaped, by and large, by common species (Gaston & Fuller 2008). Common species do most of the herbivory, the pollination of plants, the dispersal of seeds, the transmission of disease and the predation of other species. There are relatively few Critically Endangered bird species, and by definition they have small populations, so these species account for a vanishingly small proportion of all the individual birds on the planet. Rare species therefore tend to contribute relatively little to the functioning of the planet's ecosystems, although there are some notable exceptions (Sekercioglu *et al.* 2004). Their small numbers mean that they often do not feature among the most important predators, prey, pollinators or seed-dispersers in the ecosystems they inhabit, at least on continental landmasses. In many parts of the world, rare species contribute little to patterns of overall bird species richness and virtually nothing to the number of individual birds present (Lennon *et al.* 2004, Sizling *et al.* 2009).

This does not mean, however, that rare species are biologically insignificant or unworthy of conservation. Some species listed as Critically Endangered, such as the Asian vultures (Chapter 17), once fulfilled far more ecologically important roles than they do now that their populations have been brought so low. Conservation efforts to protect rare species often have the added benefit of conserving a swathe of other important wildlife (Lawler *et al.* 2003). But even naturally rare species that provide no obvious ecosystem function can have a significance out of proportion to their abundance. The term 'biodiversity' is now used as common currency in conservation circles, and is generally taken to refer to the diversity of life at all taxonomic levels and at a range of scales, from the level of ecosystems to the level of genes. The extinction of any species will clearly reduce the diversity of the ecosystem it previously inhabited, but if it represents a distinct lineage its disappearance will have a disproportionate impact on the planet's genetic diversity. The extinction of a species belonging to a family with many closely related species, while certainly something to be avoided at all costs, will represent less of a loss of evolutionary history than that of a species that is the sole representative of its evolutionary ancestry (Mace *et al.* 2003, Driskell *et al.* 2007).

Unfortunately, the world's rarest birds are not distributed randomly among different taxonomic groups but are concentrated in families that are of greater evolutionary age and in families or genera (sub-families) that contain very few species (Gaston & Blackburn 1997, Hughes 1999, Brooks *et al.* 2003, Redding & Mooers 2006). The extinction of rare species will therefore result in a disproportionate loss of evolutionary history and genetic diversity (Russell *et al.* 1998, Heard & Mooers 2000, Purvis *et al.* 2000, von Euler 2001). The demise of the Po'ouli and of the Stephens Island Wren *Xenicus lyalli* (Chapter 11), both the only known representatives of their respective genera, marked the permanent loss of a breadth of unique genetic diversity. A number of Critically Endangered species, including the Forest Owlet *Heteroglaux blewitti* (Chapter 24), Philippine Eagle *Pithecophaga jefferyi* (Chapter 18), Spoon-billed Sandpiper *Eurynorhynchus pygmeus* (Chapter 4) and Kakapo *Strigops habroptila* (Chapter 16), are the only representatives of their respective genera. The concentration of threatened species on the islands of Indonesia puts at risk over 500 million years of evolutionary heritage (Mooers & Atkins 2003). Furthermore, the extinction of rare birds might influence the extinction rates of other species. Birds are relatively large animals and harbour parasites and pathogens that may be found on no other species; indeed, in the days before genetic analyses, superficially similar species of bird would often be separated by taxonomists on the basis of similarities in their feather lice. For each bird that becomes extinct, a range of smaller organisms that are dependent on them will also disappear; this 'co-extinction' might indeed represent the greatest cause of biodiversity loss on the planet (Dunn *et al.* 2009).

As is the case with a high proportion of globally threatened species, the stunning Asian Crested Ibis Nipponia nippon *(Endangered) is sufficiently distinctive from its closest relatives to warrant being placed in its own genus (Deborah J. Pain).*

Chapter 2
The distribution and causes of rarity

Nearly 200 bird species are currently classified as Critically Endangered. They come in all shapes and sizes, from the California Condor *Gymnogyps californianus* (10kg) to the tiny Short-crested Coquette *Lophornis brachylophus* (2g). They inhabit every continent except Antarctica, and habitats as diverse as tropical forests and arid tundra. The Mangrove Finch *Camarhynchus heliobates* of Galápagos has a range of just one square kilometre; the Tristan Albatross *Diomedea dabbenena* ranges over 14 million square kilometres of ocean. Most have very small populations, but at the time of writing the Indian Vulture *Gyps indicus* may still number in the thousands. However, the birds identified by the IUCN Red List as being those at greatest risk of extinction do not represent a random subset of the world's species. Instead they are concentrated within certain families (Bennett & Owens 1997), regions and habitats. This partly reflects the facts that the threats they face are not randomly distributed, and that different types of bird are more vulnerable to certain types of threat than others.

WINNERS AND LOSERS IN THE EXTINCTION RISK LEAGUE

Among the more speciose families, those among the seabirds (albatrosses, penguins, shearwaters and petrels, shags, storm-petrels and auks), waterbirds (grebes, rails and ibises) and larger-bodied birds (storks, megapodes, guans, cranes and bustards) hold a disproportionately high number of threatened species (Table 2.1). Some very small families (not included in Table 2.1) contain an even higher proportion of threatened species, and six contain *only* threatened birds: the Shoebill *Balaeniceps rex* of Africa, Plains Wanderer *Pedionomus torquatus* of Australia and the Kagu *Rhynochetos jubatus* of New Caledonia are the sole representatives of their respective families and each is globally threatened, as are both species of African rockfowl (Picathartidae), both of the Australian scrub-birds

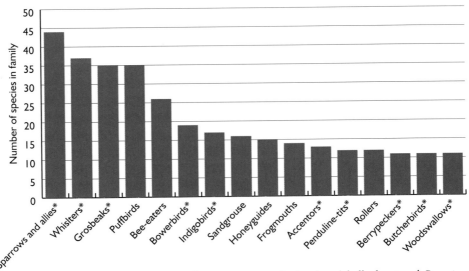

Figure 2.1. The 16 bird families of ten or more species that contain no species listed as globally threatened. Passerine families are marked with an asterisk. Figures are based on the 2009 Red List.

18

(Atrichornithidae) and all three of the Madagascan mesites (Mesitornithidae). There are also differences between families in the proportion of threatened species that appear in the Critically Endangered category of threat. Many species from groups such as penguins, storks, vangas and grouse are threatened, but very few, if any, are listed as Critically Endangered. On the other hand, groups such as grebes, ibises, spoonbills and mockingbirds may not have a great proportion of their species threatened, but those that are tend to be very threatened. At the other end of the scale, 16 families of bird containing more than ten species do not contain a single threatened species (Fig. 2.1).

Table 2.1. The 25 bird families containing the highest percentage of globally threatened species, also showing the percentage of species listed as Critically Endangered. Families are listed in descending order of the former. Families containing fewer than ten species were omitted, since percentages can become misleading with such small numbers. Passerine (songbird) families are marked with an asterisk. Figures are based on the 2009 Red List.

Family	Number of species in family	% globally threatened species	% Critically Endangered species
Albatrosses	22	82	18
Cranes	15	67	7
Penguins	18	61	0
Petrels and shearwaters	80	44	10
Megapodes	21	43	0
Barn Owls	14	43	0
Guans and allies	50	36	6
Grebes	20	30	10
Cormorants and shags	33	30	3
Pittas*	31	29	0
Parrots	355	27	5
Storks	19	26	0
Rails and allies	133	26	2
Vangas*	21	24	0
Ibises and spoonbills	34	24	12
Grouse, pheasants etc.	178	22	1
Storm-petrels	18	22	11
Auks	23	22	4
White-eyes*	97	21	6
Buttonquails	15	20	0
Bustards	25	20	4
Doves and pigeons	304	20	3
Broadbills*	15	20	0
Monarchs*	95	20	5
Mockingbirds*	35	20	9

The reasons for this disparity in extinction risk across families are not always clear. In some cases, the same threats might affect a high proportion of species in the group. Many of the albatrosses and petrels, for example, are under threat due to long-lining and other damaging fishing practices and/or the widespread impacts of introduced predators. Many of the parrots have been adversely affected by over-exploitation for the cagebird trade. The white-eyes are very successful colonists of small and remote islands, but the host of problems besetting island birds have brought some, such as Mauritius Olive White-eye *Zosterops chloronothus*, Sangihe White-eye *Z. nehrkorni* and White-chested White-eye *Z. albogularis*, to the brink of extinction (the latter two may already be extinct). Other

White-necked Picathartes Picathartes gymnocephalus, *one of two species in its West African family; both are globally threatened (David Monticelli).*

families containing large numbers of island species, such as the rails, vangas, monarchs and mockingbirds, also feature prominently. Families that suffer high rates of hunting or exploitation, often associated with the loss and fragmentation of their habitats, such as the guans, curassows and chachalacas of South America, the megapodes of Australasia, the bustards and the doves and pigeons, also contain many threatened species. Yet this is only part of the explanation for the huge differences between different families in extinction risk. Some of the least threatened families, such as the puffbirds of Central and South America, the berrypeckers of New Guinea, the frogmouths of Asia and the bowerbirds of Australasia, are also often associated with habitats that have come under considerable pressure yet have not been affected to anything like the same extent. An additional risk appears to be body size: the cranes, storks, ibises and bustards are all large species with high overall rates of extinction risk. Large body size, with the associated traits of low reproductive output, low population density and poor dispersal ability, are features that make some birds more vulnerable to environmental change and less able to bounce back from population declines than others (Gaston & Blackburn 1995, Bennett & Owens 1997, Gillespie 2000, Kean & Barlow 2004, Cofre *et al.* 2007). This may be especially important in some large-bodied birds that are hunted or otherwise exploited. Only six of the 25 families containing the highest proportion of threatened species are songbirds, yet the passerines comprise around half the world's bird families. In contrast, of the 16 least threatened families, ten are passerine. However, even within the families of larger birds, many remain common and widespread, so clearly extinction risk is the product of a complex interaction between intrinsic vulnerability and external threat (Purvis *et al.* 2000).

HOTSPOTS OF RARITY AND EXTINCTION RISK

The distribution of the world's threatened birds is as concentrated in certain regions as it is in certain families (Fig. 2.2). Most striking, islands hold a very high proportion of the world's rarest and most threatened birds, and were home to an overwhelming majority of species that have become extinct in the last 500 years (Table 2.2). Islands are so important in the story of the world's rarest birds that they are treated separately in Chapter 10. If we set islands aside for a moment and look at the distribution of rarity on continental landmasses, it is striking that so few Critically Endangered species occur in Africa, Asia and Europe, continents that have suffered longest from man's presence. Mainland Africa, for example, supports only nine species listed as Critically Endangered, whereas mainland South America, a continent just over half its size, holds over 40. No mainland breeding species in Europe is listed as Critically Endangered, although the Balearic Shearwater *Puffinus mauretanicus* and, until its removal from the Critically Endangered list in 2010, the Azores Bullfinch *Pyrrhula murina* are endemic to European islands. Even more remarkable, no confirmed bird extinctions have occurred on the continental landmasses of Europe, Africa or Asia in the last 500 years, although a number of species, particularly in Asia, continue to be listed as Critically Endangered even though they might already be extinct. The seven known mainland extinctions in the last 500 years have occurred in the Americas (Passenger Pigeon *Ectopistes migratorius*, Labrador Duck *Camptorhynchus labradorius*, Carolina Parakeet *Conuropsis carolinensis* and Slender-billed Grackle *Quiscalus palustris* in North America, Atitlán Grebe *Podilymbus gigas* in Guatemala and Colombian Grebe *Podiceps andinus* in South America) and Australia (the exquisite Paradise Parrot *Psephotus pulcherrimus*). Of these, the two grebes could also be considered as island species, both once confined to single islands of water in an ocean of land. It might be no coincidence that the landmasses occupied by mankind for longest have suffered the fewest recent extinctions, as the birds there either became extinct long ago due to the actions of early humans, or perhaps had longer to adapt alongside early humans as their impacts grew. The explosion of environmental changes brought about by European colonisation of the Americas and Australia has had a disproportionate effect on a range of mainland species unprepared for such rapid transformation of their environments, as the story of the Eskimo Curlew *Numenius borealis* (Chapter 25) so vividly demonstrates.

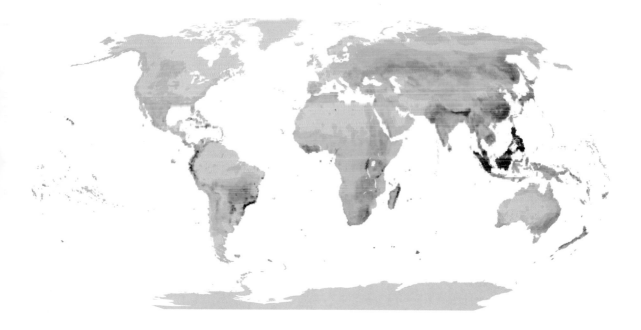

Figure 2.2. The distribution of the world's globally threatened (Vulnerable, Endangered and Critically Endangered) birds. The redder shading indicates the presence of greater numbers of threatened species (BirdLife International 2008a).

Table 2.2. The distribution of bird species classified by BirdLife/IUCN as Critically Endangered and Extinct (in the last 500 years) or Extinct in the Wild by geographical location, based upon the 2012 listings. Numbers in brackets in the central column indicate the number of Critically Endangered species that are additionally considered by BirdLife International to be Possibly Extinct. The few species recorded from more than one continental landmass are recorded under that in which they breed (or bred) in greatest numbers. Islands (the largest of which is Madagascar, by our definition) are treated separately irrespective of whichever continent they are part of politically. North America includes Mexico.

	Critically Endangered (Possibly Extinct)	Extinct (Extinct in the Wild)
Continental landmasses		
Africa	8	0
Asia	21	0
Australia	2	1
Europe	0	0
North America	7 (3)	4
Central/South America	42 (2)	3 (1)
Islands	117 (9)	126 (3)
Total	197 (14)	134 (4)

Another striking aspect of Figure 2.2 is that areas of extraordinarily high biodiversity, such as the basins of the Amazon and the Congo, hold relatively few threatened species. Indeed, huge areas of Africa and South America support a density of threatened species that is no higher than that across much of Europe and North America, despite the far greater number of species that are found in the tropics. The Amazon Basin supports the greatest concentration of species anywhere on the planet, and the bird lists of tourist lodges in places like south-east Peru or eastern Ecuador attest to the remarkable diversity of the region. Almost 600 bird species, many more than breed in the whole of Europe, have been recorded at Explorer's Inn, a lodge for birdwatchers on the Tambopata River in south-east Peru; it was here that Scott Robinson and Ted Parker recorded an astonishing 331 bird species in a single day in 1982, still the world record for the number of species seen on one day by birders on foot. The reason for the low diversity of globally threatened species in the Amazon and Congo basins is the great size of these forests and the relatively large and intact ranges of the birds they harbour. Although forest has been lost in both, enough remains so that few of the species living there currently trigger the IUCN threat criteria (Asner *et al.* 2009); it is a remarkable fact that not a single Critically Endangered or Endangered species features on the immense list of birds seen around Explorer's Inn.

There is not, therefore, always a strong positive correlation between hotspots of species richness and the distribution of threatened birds, and many of the world's rarest species are actually found in areas of relatively low diversity (de Klerk *et al.* 2002). Instead, the centres of rarity are far more concentrated, for example along the Atlantic coasts of Brazil and Argentina, the northern Andes, Madagascar, Hawaii, the Albertine Rift and Eastern Arc mountains of Africa, the eastern Himalayas, eastern China and, the hottest hotspots of all, Sundaland and the Philippines (Buchanan *et al.* 2011). These are all areas of exceptionally high endemism containing many species with restricted ranges that are coming under increasing pressure from a range of threats, particularly so in the Asian archipelagos.

With such an uneven distribution of biodiversity and rarity across the planet, conservationists have invested considerable effort in trying to identify those sites or regions where their limited resources would have the greatest impact (Brooks *et al.* 2006). At least nine different global sets of regions or sites have been recognised using quantitative approaches that include consideration of the uniqueness of the wildlife found within them, their importance to different groups of animals and plants and the degree of threat they face. Two of these, the Important

Bird Areas (IBAs) and Endemic Bird Areas (EBAs) analyses, both the products of work by BirdLife International, focus exclusively on birds and use information on the ranges of species, their numbers and extinction risk, in order to identify those parts of the world whose conservation is of particular importance. The 218 EBAs identified to date (the number continues to grow as new species are recognised) are regions where the distributions of two or more species with ranges of 50,000 km² or less overlap, and so they are rich in endemic ('restricted-range') species compared to other parts of the world (Stattersheld *et al.* 1998). While EBAs contain over 90% of the world's restricted-range bird species they cover just 4.5% of the earth's land surface, and are therefore priority areas for broad-scale ecosystem conservation.

IBAs, by contrast, are small enough to be amenable to site-based conservation and qualify if they fulfil one or more of a number of criteria, one of which is the presence of restricted-range (EBA) species and another of which is the presence of globally threatened species (Fig. 2.3). In effect, therefore, they represent a spatial reflection of the IUCN Red List criteria; the Red List identifies those species that are most in need of conservation action, and the IBA scheme identifies the key areas where those species occur. So far, nearly 11,000 IBAs have been identified globally, including 4,000 IBAs in Europe, 1,230 in Africa, 2,293 in Asia and over 2,500 in the Americas. Not only do IBAs identify areas of importance for birds, but they can also capture the ranges of other groups of threatened species, as has been shown in Uganda's forest IBAs (Pain *et al.* 2005) and East African IBAs generally (Brooks *et al.* 2001).

The Alliance for Zero Extinction (AZE), a global partnership of conservation organisations, works to prevent species loss by identifying and safeguarding sites of crucial importance for the survival of the world's most threatened animals and plants (Ricketts *et al.* 2005). These sites are the only ones where a Critically Endangered or Endangered species occurs, or contain the overwhelmingly significant part of the population for at least one part of its life history. These are not large sites, having an average size of just over 100km². Examples include the Estribaciones Occidentales del Pichincha (100km²) in Ecuador, home to the Black-breasted Puffleg *Eriocnemis nigrivestis* (Critically Endangered), and the Forêt du Day, a 145km² unprotected site holding perhaps the only viable population of the Djibouti Francolin *Francolinus ochropectus* (Critically Endangered). Unfortunately, many IBAs and AZE sites do not have any formal protection.

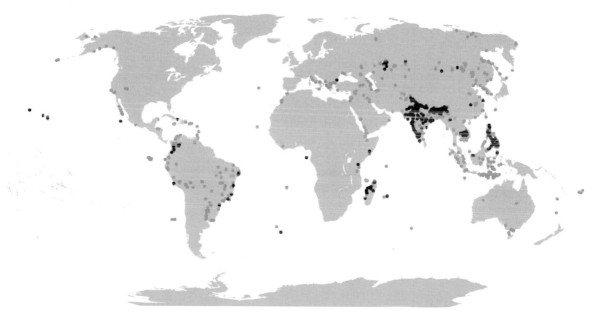

Figure 2.3. Important Bird Areas (IBAs) holding Critically Endangered species. Sites marked in red support more than one such species: the high density of such sites in South and South-East Asia reflects the distribution of several broad-ranging Critically Endangered vulture species that co-occur at many IBAs in these regions. IBAs have not yet been identified for Critically Endangered birds in New Zealand, the Northern Mariana Islands and the Federated States of Micronesia (BirdLife International 2008b).

THREATS TO THE WORLD'S RAREST BIRDS

Almost without exception, the world's Critically Endangered birds owe their precarious status to the actions, either direct or indirect, of people (Fig. 2.4). Even in the case of the small number of species that owe their high risk of extinction to natural disasters, such as volcanoes or hurricanes, it is generally the case that they have also suffered severe declines in numbers and range through hunting or habitat loss, making them more vulnerable to other threats. Between them, the spread of agriculture into natural habitats and the wholesale felling of tropical forests for timber contribute to the extinction risk of many of the world's Critically Endangered species, not least because forest loss has been greatest in areas of high biological importance (Balmford & Long 1994). Many species, particularly those on islands, owe their rarity to the ravages of a range of introduced predators and competitors. Hunting and trapping, urbanisation, pollution and a range of other activities associated with the exploitation by people of the planet's resources, and the consequences thereof, contribute to the worsening status of the world's rarest birds, and new threats are emerging all the time.

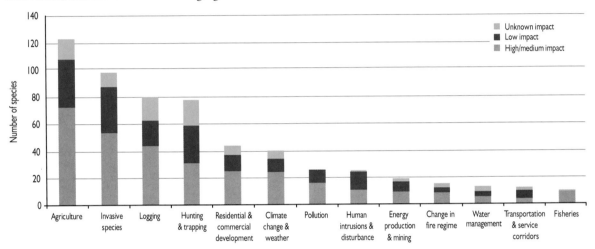

Figure 2.4. The main threats to the world's Critically Endangered birds, with the number of species (out of 194 listed in 2009) affected by each. Many species suffer from more than one threat (BirdLife International 2008b).

AGRICULTURE, HABITAT LOSS AND FRAGMENTATION

The loss of forests in the tropics represents the most important single threat to the world's rarest birds, and around three quarters of the world's Critically Endangered birds are tropical forest species. Around 1.4% of the world's forests were lost between 2000 and 2005, and by 2005 around half of the world's tropical forest biome contained less than 50% tree cover (Asner *et al.* 2009). The main drivers of deforestation are clearance of land for agriculture and the commercial logging of valuable trees, the two often operating in concert. The size of the world's human population has risen exponentially in the last two centuries, and is likely to continue to do so until at least 2050. Above all else, this burgeoning mass of people requires food and fuel, and many of the world's natural habitats have suffered as a result of clearance for the spread of agriculture. Cultivation has spread with particular speed into areas of high importance for threatened birds (Scharlemann *et al.* 2004). In EBAs, the area of agriculture is a better predictor of the threat status of range-restricted birds than is human population size (Scharlemann *et al.* 2005). To this is added the fact that at least 20% of the humid tropical forest biome was undergoing some level of commercial timber harvesting between 2000 and 2005 (Asner *et al.* 2009). The drivers of deforestation are changing. From the 1960s to the 1980s much of the world's deforestation resulted from the activities of small-scale subsistence farmers, whereas from the 1980s onwards globalisation has led to the growth of large-scale ranching, logging on industrial scales and the spread of plantations to supply distant markets (Rudel *et al.* 2009). However, even in the

The loss of tropical forests (as here in Sumatra) for agriculture, commercial logging or both, and the fragmentation of what remains, represents one of the greatest threats to birds (Jeremy Lindsell, RSPB).

most austere and remote environments, low levels of habitat disturbance are having serious impacts on species like Royal Cinclodes *Cinclodes aricomae* (Chapter 6).

The impacts of forest degradation or loss on bird communities are well documented and a number of general patterns have been identified (Sodhi *et al.* 2009). Habitats altered by people almost always contain fewer bird species than the original forest. This results in the loss of what is termed α (alpha) diversity, which is often also associated with an increased dominance by the commonest species: a few species become superabundant while the rest become rarer or absent. There is also a turnover of species when forests are degraded: large, rare and range-restricted species are replaced by small, common and widespread ones. Certain guilds of bird, such as terrestrial, understorey and bark-gleaning insectivores and frugivores, disappear, to be replaced by species such as seed-eaters and canopy insectivores that are able to exploit the new habitats available. Habitat loss and degradation therefore fundamentally alter bird populations in a number of ways, almost always to their detriment (Thiollay 1997, Aratrakorn *et al.* 2006, Scales & Marsden 2008, Maas *et al.* 2009, Sodhi *et al.* 2009). Furthermore, the effects of deforestation may be felt far away as the loss of trees fundamentally affects whole river catchments, a particular problem for the Brazilian Merganser *Mergus octosetaceus* (Chapter 5).

A high proportion of the world's most threatened birds owe their precarious status to the felling or degradation of their forest habitats. The Flores Hawk-eagle *Spizaetus floris* is dependent on large blocks of pristine forest, and has suffered a precipitous recent decline on three Indonesian islands owing to forest clearance (Gjershaug *et al.* 2004). In Japan, the Okinawa Woodpecker *Dendrocopos noguchii* requires old-growth subtropical forest to survive and what is left of this habitat is being slowly eaten away by logging, infrastructure building, agricultural expansion and golf course construction. The Rufous-headed Hornbill *Aceros waldeni* of the Philippines, Cerulean Paradise-flycatcher *Eutrichomyias rowleyi* of Indonesia and São Tomé Grosbeak *Neospiza concolor* are just a few of the world's Critically Endangered species whose main threat is loss of habitat.

Okinawa Woodpecker Dendrocopos noguchii *is Japan's only endemic Critically Endangered bird, and is threatened by loss of its preferred old-growth forest habitats to forestry, agriculture and golf courses (Pete Morris).*

However, a small number of threatened species may benefit from human land-use change when such change simulates the environment to which a species is adapted and thus fulfils their requirements. The recently discovered Munchique Wood-wren *Henicorhina negreti* has a tiny range in the western Andes of Colombia, but it is no 'pristine forest' bird (Salaman *et al.* 2003) and it may well be that certain forest changes that mimic the naturally disturbed habitats the species prefers would actually benefit it. Similarly, the Long-billed Tailorbird *Artisornis moreaui* of Tanzania and Mozambique prefers edges, glades, canopy gaps and degraded areas of forest (McEntee *et al.* 2005). Recent research on Gurney's Pitta *Pitta gurneyi* has shown that it prefers disturbed to pristine forest (Donald *et al.* 2009). It is not just forest species that might benefit, to some extent, from human habitat alteration. The Sociable Lapwing *Vanellus gregarius* (Chapter 3) now relies to a large extent on changes to steppe habitats brought about by domestic livestock (Kamp *et al.* 2009). However, conservationists are rightly cautious about classifying threatened species as 'tolerant of human-altered habitats'. What we see at present is a snapshot of a species in time, in a period when very little, if any, pristine forest remains within the ranges of some species. Thus, it may be difficult to assess what is the true habitat preferred by a threatened species. The Araripe Manakin *Antilophia bokermanni* is a stunning species described as recently as 1998 from a few localities in Ceará state, north-eastern Brazil. Its habitat preferences are recorded as '…tall, second growth forest (where there is an abundance of vines), edge and adjacent clearings….' (Coelho & Silva 1998). While this may be the case now, one must wonder if, in an area so decimated of its primary forest, these are really the optimal habitats of the species or simply the only ones available to it. Tolerance of or even preference for anthropogenic habitats may serve some threatened species well, but land use change has driven and continues to drive many more species towards extinction.

An almost inevitable consequence of habitat loss is that the remaining habitat becomes broken up into smaller patches, often surrounded by a sea of agriculture or built development. The species trapped inside these habitat islands then face threats that are additional to the habitat loss itself (Simberloff 1995, Fahrig 2003). For one thing, the population density of birds in habitat fragments is generally lower than it is in areas of continuous habitat. The Taita Thrush *Turdus helleri* of southern Kenya now only occurs in four forest fragments (Brooks *et al.* 1998),

The stunning Araripe Manakin Antilophia bokermanni *was discovered in 1996 and formally described in 1998, since when it has joined a number of other Brazilian Atlantic Forest species on the Critically Endangered list (Luiz Claudio Marigo).*

where population densities are far higher in the largest fragment than in smaller ones. However, small patches of habitat support not only fewer individuals but also fewer species than larger patches (Castelletta *et al.* 2005). As well as isolating populations, fragmentation often also leads to a decline in habitat quality, for example though tree mortality caused by desiccation or increased incidence of fires, further reducing the number of birds able to survive there (Saunders *et al.* 1991).

The reasons that small fragments support so few species and such low densities of many birds are complex, but fragmentation appears to impact on them in a number of ways. Birds clinging on in small patches of habitat suffer higher mortality, lower breeding success and even greater asymmetry in body measurements, a measure of environmental stress, than birds in large fragments or in continuous forests (Robinson *et al.* 1995, Lens *et al.* 1999, Ruiz-Gutiérrez *et al.* 2008). Fragmentation may impede the flow of genes between isolated populations of a species (Bates 2002) and promote the flow of predators from surrounding habitats, as the example of Gurney's Pitta (Chapter 23) shows. Some habitat patches may simply be too small to support even one pair of a very large raptor such as the Harpy Eagle *Harpia harpyja* or Philippine Eagle *Pithecophaga jefferyi* (Chapter 18), which require large areas of forest, or for frugivore specialists that require large home ranges to search for their food sources; and even small species may require relatively large patches to breed successfully (Butcher *et al.* 2010). Where the top predators are excluded by the small size of a habitat fragment, smaller predators can proliferate with consequent impacts on bird populations (Crooks & Soulé 1999). Even if a pair of the threatened species manages to breed successfully in a habitat fragment, its offspring will need to disperse across wide areas of potentially hostile habitats to find somewhere they themselves can breed. As a result, even suitable patches of habitat might not be colonised. Research on the Mauritius Fody *Foudia rubra* (Endangered) has shown that rampant habitat destruction between 1950 and 1975 caused the disappearance of the bird not only in areas where the forest was lost but also in areas where apparently suitable habitat still remained. This is because patches that were too small to support self-sustaining populations (termed 'sinks') were no longer being supplied with birds by more productive 'source' areas (Safford 1997b).

Belding's Yellowthroat Geothlypis beldingi *has a fragmented range in small and widely scattered marshes in Baja California, Mexico, and is listed as Endangered (Pete Morris).*

Dusky Starfrontlet Coeligena orina *is listed as Critically Endangered because it survives in tiny numbers in high-altitude elfin forest in north-west Colombia, which is coming under increasing pressure from habitat loss and mining (Jon Hornbuckle).*

Perhaps nowhere are the effects of fragmentation more acute than in the Atlantic Forests of coastal South America, which support no fewer than fifteen Critically Endangered species and hold one of the greatest concentrations of threatened birds found anywhere today (Brooks *et al.* 1999). Birds in this region are characterised by small populations, small ranges and high degree of habitat specialisation, making them inherently vulnerable to habitat change (Goerck 1997). This vulnerability has been severely challenged by high levels of habitat loss and extreme fragmentation (Ribeiro *et al.* 2009). There seems to be little cause for optimism for many seriously threatened species, especially those such as Alagoas Foliage-gleaner *Philydor novaesi* and Alagoas Antwren *Myrmotherula snowi* that inhabit the tiny forest remnants of the north-eastern states, and for the tiny Kinglet Calyptura *Calyptura cristata* of the southern forest region around Rio de Janeiro. No Atlantic Forest species has yet become globally extinct, but the Alagoas Curassow *Mitu mitu* (Chapter 19) is now Extinct in the Wild, the Kinglet Calyptura has not been seen since 1996 despite extensive searches and it is likely that many others have already gone beyond the point of no return but have yet to disappear because of the phenomenon known as the extinction debt (p.272).

The spread of agriculture has had no less an impact on the world's natural grasslands, which are particularly amenable to conversion to farmland. The wholesale loss of grasslands represents the greatest threat to species such as the Bengal Florican *Houbaropsis bengalensis* (Chapter 7) which require large areas of undisturbed natural grassland. Grassland birds have evolved to exploit very specific niches in what might appear to human eyes to be relatively uniform habitats, and even relatively small changes in grazing pressure or grassland management can have severe consequences for the birds that live there, as the example of the Liben Lark *Heteromirafra sidamoensis* (Chapter 8) demonstrates. Even coastal habitats are not immune to reclamation for the spread of agriculture, a process which has resulted in the loss of intertidal mudflats in eastern Asia vital to a range of threatened species such as the Spoon-billed Sandpiper *Eurynorhynchus pygmeus* (Chapter 4).

DIRECT EXPLOITATION

The taking of wild birds for food, for sport, for trade and for social reasons has long been both a culturally and an economically important activity in many parts of the world, particularly for rural communities. Some cases of bird exploitation or 'harvest' are traditional and sustainable, but when markets expand, sometimes driven by local factors and sometimes by international trade, levels of exploitation can rapidly become unsustainable, affecting the livelihoods of local communities and threatening the very existence of the exploited species. Overexploitation has already driven once-numerous bird species to extinction, as illustrated by the Great Auk *Pinguinus impennis* and the Carolina Parakeet *Conuropsis carolinensis*, hunted to extinction in the mid-1800s and early 1900s respectively. Although most of the world's rarest birds are today protected to some extent in law, many still suffer the effects of unsustainable hunting and trapping, with nearly 30% of all globally threatened birds experiencing overexploitation.

Hunting is the main or a major contributing factor in the declines of a number of Endangered or Critically Endangered species, especially some of the larger species including some Galliformes, which are often hunted for their flesh and sometimes feathers. Hunting is considered to be the primary cause of the Endangered status of the Green Peafowl *Pavo muticus* in Indochina. The species was once widespread but it has undergone a serious decline, with the only substantial regional populations remaining in northern and eastern Cambodia, adjacent parts of Vietnam and Laos, and in Burma. Green Peafowl occupy edge and open forest habitats that are subject to heavy human use, and as the species has no source populations in the centres of large areas of dense forest it appears to be more susceptible to the direct impacts of hunting than galliform species that use dense evergreen forests in the region (Brickle *et al.* 2008). Hunting for food was also reported to be affecting the population of the endemic Trinidad Piping-guan *Pipile pipile* more than a century ago when Chapman reported in 1894 that 'the flesh of this species is deservedly esteemed, and through the persecution of hunters it is rapidly becoming a rare bird.' Although hunting of the species has apparently declined in recent decades, thanks to public education campaigns, the population is estimated at possibly fewer than 100 and not more than 200 birds, so all persecution has to be stopped and any further loss of the large canopy trees that the guans prefer must be prevented (Hayes *et al.* 2009). It is becoming increasingly clear that hunting is a major threat to several species not previously thought to be particularly heavily targeted, such as the Sociable Lapwing and the Spoon-billed Sandpiper.

Trinidad Piping-guan Pipile pipile *is listed as Critically Endangered largely because of unsustainable hunting pressure (Kevin Schafer).*

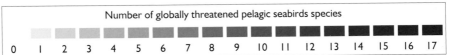

Figure 2.5. The at-sea distribution of globally threatened pelagic seabirds (excluding penguins), assessed by fitting birds with tracking devices. The deeper colours indicate regions with higher numbers of globally threatened species. Most are threatened by unsustainable fishing practices and by invasive species at their breeding sites. Map produced by BirdLife International from many sources.

Hunting, mainly for food, also threatens more than three quarters of threatened pigeons and doves, most significantly in Asia, Australasia and Oceania where bushmeat is often a preferred source of protein, especially on some of the islands (Walker 2007). In many cases this threat is only likely to be significantly reduced where local communities are helped to develop sustainable livelihoods through agriculture and other activities. In addition to hunting, egg theft seriously threatens some species including the Chinese Crested Tern *Sterna bernsteini* (Critically Endangered). Surveys between 2003 and 2007 found only two colonies within the species' potential breeding range, and estimated the total population to be no more than 50 birds. The collection of seabird eggs for food is common across these breeding areas and rapid economic development in the region is believed to have driven increased harvest rates to supply the tourist industry (Chen *et al.* 2009). Egg collection could have resulted in breeding failure in 2001, 2003 and 2005; sadly, in 2004, while the mixed breeding colony at one site re-laid after the first clutches were harvested, the colony was subsequently destroyed by two severe typhoons (Chen *et al.* 2009).

The taking of birds for pets and collections threatens many species. Parrots are a particularly heavily traded group and trade was a major factor in the declines of the Yellow-crested Cockatoo *Cacatua sulphurea* (Chapter 9) and Spix's Macaw *Cyanopsitta spixii* (Chapter 20). Inadvertent exploitation also threatens some species, with albatrosses of particular concern. Albatrosses and other seabirds (see Figure 2.5 above) are attracted to baited longlines used by commercial fishing fleets, and large numbers of birds consequently drown each year (Chapter 12).

A SUPPORTING CAST OF PROBLEMS

Together, habitat change, fragmentation and persecution make up the main problems for the vast majority of threatened species except on islands, where birds face an additional range of difficulties posed by introduced species. These are far from the only threats faced by the world's rarest birds, but they are perhaps the most easily measured. Disease, for example, is likely to be greatly underestimated as a driver of rarity and may have caused or contributed to a number of past extinctions (McCallum & Dobson 1995, Lafferty & Gerber 2002, Smith *et al.* 2006). The extent to which disease can contribute to rarity and extinction is particularly apparent in the loss of Hawaii's native forest birds (Chapter 14). Climate change is probably already having an impact on a number of the world's rarest birds, and will certainly do so in the future, although its impacts are very difficult to assess. Human disturbance is another particularly difficult threat to evaluate, not least because the observation of bird behaviour by scientists itself generates some level of disturbance, making it hard to assess how birds behave in the absence of people (Gill 2007). Perhaps more importantly, observations of the reaction of birds to disturbance do not indicate the ecological effects in terms of, for example, increased mortality or decreased nesting success. The island of Tiritiri Matangi off New Zealand's North Island offers visitors just about the only chance they will ever have of seeing some of the world's rarest birds in the wild, as access to other predator-free refuges for species like the Saddleback *Philesturnus carunculatus* and the Stitchbird *Notiomystis cincta* is strictly controlled. On Tiritiri at least, there is no evidence of a negative impact of human disturbance, since birds do not avoid nesting near pathways and nests near nature trails are no less successful than nests elsewhere (Lindsay *et al.* 2008). In Cambodia, research on Bengal Florican demonstrated no discernible impact on the species' distribution of low levels of human disturbance (Gray *et al.* 2007). For species that suffer persecution, however, approach by people, even those with the species' best interests at heart, might represent a significant problem. The unexpected discovery in Syria in 2004 of a tiny relict population of Northern Bald Ibis *Geronticus eremita* (Critically Endangered) has led to intensive conservation efforts to protect it, and as a consequence the species may have suffered from human disturbance around the time the birds are prospecting for nest sites (Serra *et al.* 2009). The rather larger population of the species in Morocco also suffers high levels of human disturbance, which during nesting can drive birds from the nesting colony and allow predators to attack eggs and young (Bowden *et al.* 2008).

Contaminants, whether pesticides or other agricultural pollutants, toxic metals, or even pharmaceuticals, affect a wide range of globally threatened species. Once-common large vultures in Asia became Critically Endangered as a result of exposure to the drug diclofenac in the tissues of livestock treated with it shortly before death (Chapter 17). Also, many bird species are exposed to fragments of lead from ammunition, either through ingesting spent lead gunshot directly while feeding (Mateo 2009) or, in the case of predators and scavengers, while feeding on game or other shot species carrying lead in their flesh (Fisher *et al.* 2006, Pain *et al.* 2009). Lead poisoning from ammunition sources was a major factor in the decline of the Critically Endangered California Condor, which at one

Hopes for the survival of the Northern Bald Ibis Geronticus eremita *were raised in 2004 when a previously unknown population was discovered in Syria, but a range of problems including hunting, disturbance and collision with power lines, saw this population reduced to just a single pair in 2012 (Chris Gomersall, RSPB Images)*

stage became extinct in the wild, and it has seriously hampered reintroduction efforts (Green *et al.* 2008). Pesticides can be an important mortality factor and are believed to have played a part in the declines and local extinctions of the Mauritius Kestrel *Falco punctatus* (once down to four known individuals but now listed as Vulnerable with a population of 600–700 birds) and the Mauritius Cuckooshrike *Coracina typica* (with 260 pairs in 1993, but now Vulnerable with 300–350 pairs), both of which showed declines and subsequent increases temporally and spatially coincident with patterns of use of organochlorines (Safford & Jones 1997). Light pollution may be a threat to the Mascarene Petrel *Pseudobulweria aterrima* (Critically Endangered) of Réunion Island. Urban street lights and lights from sports complexes are thought to be the main cause of 'downing' of inexperienced juvenile petrels, a serious issue in such a rare species. In a three year study on Réunion, 2,348 seabirds, 94% of which were juveniles, were attracted to lights with often fatal consequences (Le Corre *et al.* 2003).

The great majority of the world's most threatened birds face not a single threat but many. BirdLife International maintains a database of the threats recorded for each species, and for some the list is depressingly long. For example, the Northern Bald Ibis is considered to be at risk from illegal building, changes in farming practices, hunting, overgrazing, the collection of firewood, disturbance due to construction, mortality during migration, hunting, loss of eggs to predators, nestling starvation and disease. Assessing which is the most important for each species is difficult, not only because detailed information is often lacking but also because threats can operate together in complex ways, the presence of one making the impacts of another more severe in some cases (Laurance & Useche 2009). Parrots, for example, become less able to withstand capture for the cagebird trade when their nesting trees are lost. Other pairs of threats that are likely to act in a synergistic way are habitat fragmentation and genetic isolation, agricultural expansion and persecution, and possibly climate change and disease. This makes it very difficult for conservationists to assess which is the main threat to address. There is the added problem that some threats are more visible and easily recorded than others. Habitat degradation, poaching and fire may be more eye-catching and easily measured than the genetic effects of fragmentation, human disturbance or increased nest predation due to an introduced predator, leading perhaps to an overestimation of the importance of the former.

SMALL POPULATION SIZE AND SELF-PERPETUATING RARITY

As populations become smaller, they become vulnerable to a whole range of new threats to their survival that arise simply because numbers are so low. For example, as populations fall, it becomes increasingly difficult for birds to find potential mates (Gascoigne *et al.* 2009). Species that nest in colonies or live in flocks might rely on the defensive actions of their neighbours to prevent their nests or themselves from being predated but the population can quickly collapse if numbers fall below the critical size needed to deter predators (Gascoigne & Lipcius 2004). As populations decline, so too does the intensity of sexual selection, a process responsible for maintaining the genetic vigour of a population (Møller & Legendre 2001). Mating strategies that are highly advantageous when numbers are high, such as the habit of individual birds to be reproductively active during only part of the species' full breeding season, might prove disastrous when populations fall below a critical level (Calabrese & Fagan 2004).

These additional problems faced by species when their populations reach very low levels, causing the reproductive success of surviving birds to fall as numbers fall, are called 'Allee effects' after the ecologist Warder C. Allee. Their importance in driving the final stages of extinction has only been recognised in the last two decades (Courchamp *et al.* 1999a, Stephens & Sutherland 1999). Two or more Allee effects can operate within the same very small population, greatly increasing its extinction risk (Berec *et al.* 2007). In very small populations it becomes increasingly hard for a bird to find a mate, and when it does so there is a higher chance that the prospective mate is a close relative. Small populations, particularly those that fluctuate greatly from year to year, are also extremely vulnerable to chance, or 'stochastic', events (Hilker & Westerhoff 2007). It could be that in a tiny population of breeding birds the chicks produced in one generation are, just by chance, all of the same sex (just as it is more likely that the flip of a coin five times will produce an outcome of all heads than will the flip of a coin fifty times). Thus, in a short-lived species, a single generation dominated by one sex might seriously compromise its survival (Engen *et al.* 2003). External factors can also be subject to chance; a series of breeding seasons might be ruined by bad weather or an increase in numbers of natural predators might bring a small population to the edge of extinction much sooner than it would a large population (Pimm *et al.* 1993, Vucetich *et al.* 2000). Because birds with small populations also tend to have small ranges, even a relatively localised event such as a hurricane, forest fire or volcanic eruption can threaten the survival of an entire species. Added to this is the problem that species with very small populations may have reduced genetic diversity, making them less able to develop immunity to disease or to adapt to other environmental pressures (Spielman *et al.* 2004, Evans & Sheldon 2008), although this now appears to be less troublesome than once thought.

Some of the additional threats faced by tiny populations are only now becoming apparent. For example, it now seems that as species drift towards extinction, the number of females in the population falls at a faster rate than the number of males. Common bird populations often have sex ratios that are skewed towards males, but as one progresses through the various threat classes of Near Threatened, Vulnerable, Endangered and Critically Endangered, so the adult sex ratio becomes increasingly skewed (Donald 2007). In the case of the Raso Lark *Alauda razae* (Chapter 13), for example, males sometimes outnumber females by two to one. At the extreme end of this continuum towards extinction, there are a number of recorded cases in which just prior to the point of absolute extinction there was a period of functional extinction, during which all the remaining birds were males. Thus, the last six Dusky Seaside Sparrows *Ammodramus maritimus nigrescens* were all males, the last ten Heath Hens *Tympanuchus cupido cupido* were all males, the last 18 Kakapo *Strigops habroptila* on mainland New Zealand were all males (although fortunately in the last case an offshore island population was discovered to contain females and extinction was averted just in time: Chapter 16) and so forth. The reasons for this pattern are not yet clear, but it might result from the greater predation suffered by incubating females, particularly where the species is vulnerable to introduced predators (Donald 2007). Because population estimates are often based on counts of territorial males, which may greatly exceed the number of actual breeding pairs, current estimates of what ecologists call the 'effective population size' of many Critically Endangered species may be too high, and many species may be much closer to extinction than we realise.

However, these are not the only additional pressures faced by species as their populations fall to dangerously low levels. The fascination with rarity shown by visitors to a zoo in Paris is not confined to people with the best interests of conservation at heart. As species become rarer in nature, so people increasingly want to exploit the financial premium that rarity brings, placing added pressure on already threatened species. This 'anthropogenic Allee effect' has been implicated in the extinctions of a number of species. For example, overhunting for food and feathers pushed the Great Auk to the brink of extinction, but it might have been scientists and museum collectors anxious to obtain an increasingly rare specimen that finally wiped the bird out (Fuller 1999). The anthropogenic Allee effect can be seen at work in the stories of the Kakapo, Spix's Macaw and Stephens Island Wren *Xenicus lyalli* (Chapter 11); in each case, the financial pressure to obtain specimens (alive, in the case of Spix's Macaw) increased as the species became rarer, amply repaying the extra effort required to secure them.

Once a species' population falls below a certain threshold, therefore, it becomes subject to a range of additional threats and slips into a vortex of self-perpetuating rarity, its fate practically sealed without conservation intervention even if substantial numbers of birds remain (Gilpin & Soulé 1986). Self-perpetuating declines and the vortex of extinction that follow explain why there are unlikely to be many species with populations of fewer than 50 or so birds, because when populations reach such low levels they may rapidly disappear without conservation intervention. In the absence of this help, the minimum number of birds required to avoid extinction in the long term may be considerably higher than the current populations of many of the world's rarest species (Reed *et al.* 2003, Reed & Hobbs 2004, Brook *et al.* 2006). Around 80% of birds considered to be globally threatened have estimated populations of fewer than 10,000 individuals, and 50% number fewer than 2,500 birds. Populations may need to be far higher than this if their genetic diversity is not to fall and evolutionary processes are to continue (Frankham 1999), often far higher indeed than the targets set by conservationists, which might be merely to stabilise populations or to increase them to a modest degree (Traill *et al.* 2010). The final descent to extinction once this threshold is crossed might result from factors very different to those that brought about the original decline (Brook *et al.* 2008). This has profound implications for the conservation of the world's rarest species, since not only are many species likely to be more threatened than their numbers suggest, but conservation efforts may fail if they seek to address only the long-term problems that have brought a particular species to the brink of extinction and ignore the additional pressures that rarity brings.

Chapter 3
Sociable Lapwing *Vanellus gregarius*
CRITICALLY ENDANGERED

The vast grasslands of Eurasia, often understandably known as the Great Steppe, formerly stretched over five thousand kilometres from western Ukraine to Mongolia. This huge expanse of natural grassland, with its bitterly cold winters and blisteringly hot summers, was the domain of the Mongols of Genghis Khan, whose mounted archers would have noticed relatively little change in the landscape as they raided from their capital in Mongolia as far west as Europe. The harsh climate of the steppe prevented permanent settlement until recent times, and for centuries the region was the home of nomadic pastoralists; Tashkent, Samarkand and the other great ancient cities of the Silk Road lie far to the south. This immense area started to be eroded by conversion to arable agriculture in the nineteenth century, and by 1900 much of the steppe in Ukraine and western Russia was converted to cereal production. The loss of steppe accelerated during the Soviet era, when under collectivised farming huge areas were ploughed up and planted. Further east, however, particularly in the sparsely populated hinterlands of Kazakhstan, the climate is less suitable for cereal production and enormous areas of steppe remain despite numerous attempts to cultivate it, most ambitiously during Nikita Khrushchev's 'Virgin Lands Campaign' from 1954.

This vast, wild and beautiful landscape is home to a distinctive bird community that includes many species that breed nowhere else, such as the Black Lark *Melanocorypha yeltoniensis*, White-winged Lark *M. leucoptera* and Pallid Harrier *Circus macrourus*. All these species occasionally straggle westwards to Europe, where they have always held a particular fascination among rarity-hunters. This is particularly true of the rarest and most threatened of these steppe specialists, the Sociable Lapwing. Despite its status, Sociable Lapwings turn up surprisingly frequently in western Europe, where a few birds are seen each year (de Juana 2011). This high rate of vagrancy reflects the fact that, like the nomadic peoples of the steppe, the species is something of a wanderer: it has turned up in such unlikely locations as Cameroon, the Maldives, Sri Lanka, Japan and London. Sociable might seem to be a strange adjective to describe a species that is now spread perilously thinly across the Great Steppe, but it refers to the species' habit of gathering in large flocks outside the breeding season, particularly during migration. It is now becoming apparent that this sociability has been a contributory factor in the recent decline in numbers.

The breeding grounds of the Sociable Lapwing once stretched from Ukraine to Siberia and western China, across most of the vast steppe belt. The species perhaps also bred in western Mongolia, and there are intriguing records from June 1995 and August 1998 in the far east of that country. The accounts of early naturalist explorers in these regions suggest that it was once abundant. The German naturalist and explorer Alfred Edmund Brehm described it in 1876 as 'exceptionally common' in eastern Kazakhstan, and in 1892 the Russian naturalist V. N. Plotnikov saw post-breeding flocks of up to ten thousand birds in the same area (Plotnikov 1898). Gustav Radde reported 'vast flocks' at a migration stopover site in southern Russia. Nineteenth century accounts from the wintering grounds in Africa and India also suggest that it was then a very common bird, though generally encountered in smaller flocks than when on migration.

Declines in range and population were noticed from the 1930s onwards but may well have started earlier (Ryabov 1974, Gordienko 1991, Eichhorn & Khrokov 2002). The conversion during the nineteenth century of the steppes of Ukraine into the breadbasket of what would later become the Soviet Union resulted in the loss of practically all that region's natural steppe grassland, and the Sociable Lapwing appears to have become extinct as a breeding bird in Ukraine by 1910 (Dolgushin 1962). By the 1980s, the species had disappeared from vast tracts of land west of the Ural River (Tomkovich & Lebedeva 2004). The species was duly entered on the international Red List in the late 1980s (Collar & Andrew 1988), and when the new IUCN criteria were first applied it was treated as Vulnerable (Collar *et al.* 1994). The loss to collective farming of much of the steppe of southern Russia contributed further to the species' decline, and few breeding sites were recorded in Russia after 1990. Periodic drought and a small human population meant that cereal farming was less extensive in Kazakhstan, which now holds most of the remaining Eurasian steppe. Even here, however, there have been significant changes in steppe management, relating largely to changes in grazing practices (Robinson & Milner-Gulland 2003, Kamp *et al.* 2011). These changes have profoundly affected the Sociable Lapwing, particularly since the break-up of the Soviet Union in 1991.

A male Sociable Lapwing, one of a number of specialist steppe species in Central Asia (Paul F. Donald, RSPB).

Early in the twenty-first century a series of papers signalled that the situation was dramatically worse than had been thought, and that the decline in numbers in Kazakhstan was so severe – to perhaps as few as 200 pairs – that the species merited the status of Critically Endangered (Eichhorn & Heinicke 2000, Khrokov & Buketov 2000, Eichhorn & Khrokov 2002) and the species was duly uplisted to this category in 2004. Amid fears (thankfully soon to be allayed) that the plight of the Sociable Lapwing might therefore have been overlooked in the same way as that of the Slender-billed Curlew *Numenius tenuirostris* (Chapter 25), an emergency research effort to identify the causes of the problem was initiated in the same year, involving conservation organisations and academic institutions in Kazakhstan, the UK, Germany and the Netherlands.

Initially, the research set out to assess the hypothesis that declines were due to a drop in breeding success caused by the trampling of eggs by livestock, and possibly also by high nest predation rates (Watson *et al.* 2006). This theory derived from the fact that Sociable Lapwings are not spread randomly across the steppe but are, remarkably, almost entirely clustered around the outskirts of towns and villages, where the density of grazing animals is highest and where some potential nest predators, such as domestic cats, might be commonest. This deliberately close association with man, a phenomenon known as synanthropy, is unusual in a Critically Endangered bird (Kamp *et al.* 2009) although the importance of managed habitats for threatened birds is perhaps higher than many conservationists appreciate (Wright *et al.* 2012). With vast areas of pristine steppe available, why do Sociable Lapwings choose to breed almost exclusively on the outskirts of human settlements?

By good fortune Maxim Koshkin, the energetic young researcher chosen to lead the project for the Association for the Conservation of Biodiversity in Kazakhstan (ACBK), had grown up in a town in the centre of the region of Kazakhstan thought to contain much of the remaining population, and knew the bird and the region well. In 2005, he was joined in the project by RSPB researcher Rob Sheldon, an expert on the Northern Lapwing *Vanellus vanellus*, and by a young German scientist, Johannes Kamp. Supported by funding from the UK Government's Darwin Initiative these three researchers, with a small army of assistants, volunteers and students, have elevated our understanding of this species to such a degree that in the space of a few years what was previously one of the world's least known waders is now one of the best known.

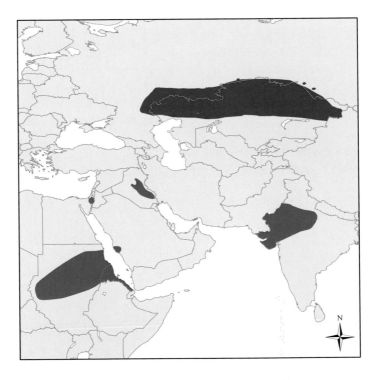

Breeding range (red) and approximate limits of non-breeding range (blue) of Sociable Lapwing.

Researcher Maxim Koshkin takes advantage of one of the many abandoned buildings that litter the steppe to gain a vantage point from which to search for nesting Sociable Lapwings (Paul F. Donald, RSPB).

ENFORCED SYNANTHROPY

Their research soon showed that the steppe is nothing like as uniform a habitat as it might at first appear to the human eye. Like the Northern Lapwing, the Sociable Lapwing prefers very short vegetation in which to nest, so that it can see predators approaching from a distance. Also like the Northern Lapwing, the Sociable Lapwing often breeds in loose colonies, and at the approach of a predator a number of birds will scramble to try to drive it away by diving on it and calling loudly. Very short vegetation is therefore a necessity for breeding Sociable Lapwings. However, with the hunting to near extinction of the formerly huge herds of native grazing animals, particularly the Saiga antelope *Saiga tatarica*, much of the heavily grazed steppe that the Sociable Lapwing needs has now grown too long (Milner Gulland *et al.* 2001, Robinson *et al.* 2003). These days, it is only around villages that still maintain traditional grazing patterns that the very short, heavily grazed steppe needed by Sociable Lapwings can be found.

By fitting cows with GPS collars that electronically record the precise location of the animal every few minutes, researchers have been able to show that as grazing pressure increases so too does the density of Sociable Lapwing nests (Fig. 3.1). Sociable Lapwings nest almost exclusively in a thin ring of the most heavily grazed steppe that surrounds only those villages with enough cattle and sheep to reduce the vegetation to the necessary height (Kamp *et al.* 2009). As a result of this heavy grazing, the steppe in such areas becomes dominated by ground-hugging and unpalatable *Artemisia* (also known as wormwood or sagebrush), and it is on such steppe that most Sociable Lapwings are found. Only a vanishingly small proportion of the Great Steppe is therefore suitable for Sociable Lapwings. This preference appears to be shared by the White-winged Lark (Kamp *et al.* 2012), and the researchers soon came to realise that a sighting of this lark was a good indication that the lapwing might also be present. So tied are Sociable Lapwings to grazing animals that up to 70% of clutches are laid in shallow scrapes on piles of dry dung, perhaps aiding concealment or helping insulation by keeping the eggs off the ground, which can still be frozen at the beginning of incubation in April. Alternatively, it may be that livestock avoid stepping on their own dung, so building a nest in a dung pile might reduce the risk of trampling. The practice is taken to extremes by the Black Lark, the females of which often build extensive pavements of dried animal dung around their nests.

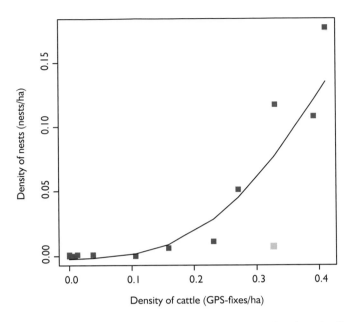

Figure 3.1. The relationship between grazing pressure, estimated from cattle fitted with GPS collars, and the density of Sociable Lapwing nests. As grazing pressure increases, so too does the number of nesting birds. Each point represents a 100m-wide ring at different distances from the centres of two villages in central Kazakhstan. The green point, where cattle spent much time but the density of nests was low, represents an area where the cattle went to drink. From Kamp et al. *(2009).*

The habit of nesting almost exclusively near villages has only been reported since 1990; before this, birds were reported as nesting in a wide range of short, open habitats from semi-deserts to saline salt pans (Kamp *et al.* 2009). Many perhaps also nested in the wake of the great migrating herds of Saiga antelope, which once grazed the steppe in their millions. Indeed, with a recovery in some Saiga populations following vigorous anti-poaching campaigns, the occasional pair of Sociable Lapwing has been seen nesting in Saiga calving areas far from human settlements (Albert Salemgareev, pers. comm.). This antelope, itself now classified by IUCN as Critically Endangered, has been hunted to near-extinction for meat and Chinese medicine (Milner-Gulland *et al.* 2001). If the Sociable Lapwing has indeed evolved to follow the unpredictable migrations of herds of grazing animals like the Saiga, this might explain the species' tendency to wander, since there is little advantage to birds in being behaviourally predisposed to return to their place of birth if the migrating herds of grazers on which they depend have taken a different route that year. Instead, it might be better simply to wander in search of suitable habitat. Moreover, Sociable Lapwings show an association not just with villages but particularly with villages along rivers, suggesting that birds follow rivers in their migration across the steppe (Kamp *et al.* 2009).

The decline in Sociable Lapwing populations and the shift in their breeding distribution towards towns and villages can both be explained to some degree by recent changes in steppe management in Kazakhstan. The old practice of putting large roaming herds of cows out on the open steppe disappeared with the collapse of communism (Robinson & Milner-Gulland 2003, Kamp *et al.* 2009), greatly reducing the area of short-grazed steppe. This has been exacerbated by an increase in poaching of Saiga, the ecosystem's most important natural grazer. Large numbers of people who voluntarily or were forcibly settled in Kazakhstan during or after the Second World War have returned to their old homelands in Russia and Germany, an exodus driven partly by the collapse of state subsidies to support otherwise uneconomical agriculture. Therefore, the already sparsely populated steppe has seen a reduction in the number of occupied villages and consequently in the number of domestic grazing animals (Kamp *et al.* 2009). The process of rural depopulation is increasing as Kazakhstan's growing oil wealth sucks people into the towns and cities. Careful searches have failed to locate any Sociable Lapwings around the many abandoned 'ghost villages' that lie scattered across the steppe. The political and social upheaval that started with the breaching of the Berlin Wall in 1989 therefore brought about significant

The Sociable Lapwing's reliance on domestic livestock is not limited to the effects of grazing: a high proportion of clutches are laid directly onto piles of animal dung (Paul F. Donald, RSPB).

changes in the distribution and population of Sociable Lapwings thousands of kilometres away on the steppes of Central Asia, a fascinating example of how human affairs can influence the ecology of birds in unpredictable ways.

Livestock numbers have increased in Kazakhstan in recent years, and it appears that populations of Sociable Lapwings are responding positively, with increases in numbers reported since 2005 at a number of carefully monitored colonies (Bragin 2006, Kamp *et al.* 2009), although at the core research sites in central Kazakhstan there was a worrying 50% decline in numbers between 2010 and 2012 (Sheldon *et al.* 2013). However, high grain prices, the development of drought-resistant varieties of wheat and a growing global demand for biofuels are likely to result in the ploughing of vast areas of steppe for cereal cultivation and the reclamation of abandoned fields. Kazakhstan's first bioethanol plant was opened in 2008 with a capacity of 350,000 tons of cereals. Not only does cereal cultivation devour steppe but communities engaged in arable agriculture tend to keep fewer livestock. Even where villages in cereal-producing areas retain some surrounding steppe, it is rarely grazed sufficiently heavily to attract Sociable Lapwings. Recent estimates suggest that with current projections of steppe conversion, the Sociable Lapwing population may decline by around 30% (Kamp *et al.* 2011).

The concentration of breeding birds around the periphery of villages appeared to support early indications that low nesting success was to blame for the observed declines (Collar *et al.* 1994, Watson *et al.* 2006). Not only are potential nest-predators such as cats, dogs and rats likely to be more abundant around villages, but numbers of tree-nesting avian predators, such as Rooks *Corvus frugilegus*, are also higher because villages contain the only large trees on the steppe. The selection by breeding birds of the most heavily grazed steppe also appeared to place their nests at considerable risk of being trampled. However, the results of the first year of nest monitoring in 2004 were not borne out by subsequent research (Sheldon *et al.* 2013). In most years nesting success is high, and productivity generally appears to be sufficient to support healthy populations. By using miniature motion-activated cameras, researchers found that predation is mostly caused by mammals that are not necessarily commoner around villages, such as Long-eared Hedgehogs *Hemiechinus auritus* and Red Foxes *Vulpes vulpes*, and trampling by livestock is surprisingly rare. Despite the close proximity of nests to villages, the cameras did not record a single instance of predation by a domestic cat, rat or dog (Sheldon *et al.* 2013).

THREATS OUTSIDE THE BREEDING AREAS

These findings all suggested that, despite profound changes to the steppe that have brought Sociable Lapwings into increasing proximity to people, it was necessary to look further afield to understand the causes of recent declines. Like most species that breed on the steppe, the harsh winters force Sociable Lapwings to move south. (The surprising exception to this autumn emigration from the steppe is the peculiar Black Lark, whose coal-black males dot the snowy wastes like the eyes of legions of melted snowmen.) Until recently, little was known of the migratory patterns of the Sociable Lapwing, although there are large numbers of historical records of non-breeding birds from eastern Africa, the Middle East and India. The Sociable Lapwing research team therefore organised and coordinated field surveys in most of the countries through which birds might migrate and fitted small transmitters to a number of birds, allowing their movements to be tracked by satellites. This has revealed a great deal about their movements, and led to the discovery of what is likely to be a serious threat to the species.

The majority of Sociable Lapwings, even it seems some of those breeding in far eastern Kazakhstan, migrate first almost due west around the northern coast of the Caspian Sea, where they turn 90 degrees south through southern Russia and cross the high mountains of the Caucasus. The relatively high rate of vagrancy to western Europe probably involves individuals that miss the southward turn and keep heading west (de Juana 2011). An early breakthrough in the study of this migration route came with the discovery of an important migration

Changes in steppe management that followed the collapse of the Soviet Union mean that breeding Sociable Lapwings are now generally confined to areas immediately adjacent to villages (Maxim Koshkin).

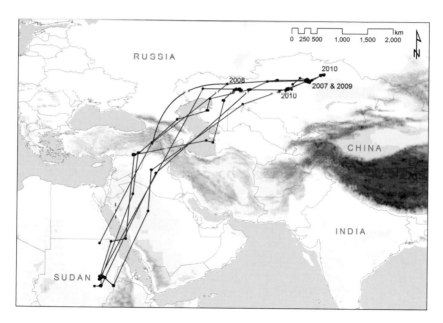

Figure 3.2. The wanderings of a male Sociable Lapwing called Erzhan. This bird was fitted with a small satellite transmitter in the summer of 2007 at a breeding colony in central Kazakhstan. Clusters of points in Kazakhstan indicate breeding territories occupied in subsequent summers (he visited two breeding colonies in 2010). The cluster of points on the border of Turkey and Syria shows this bird's stay at the extremely important migration stop-over site there, where a high proportion of the world's Sociable Lapwings gather on their way south. Erzhan wintered in eastern Sudan each winter, and was probably heading for the same area when his journey finally came to an end in autumn 2010 in northern Sudan, although perhaps his transmitter simply fell off.

stop-over location in the Caucasus, the Manych wetlands of the Stavropol region of southern Russia, where Russian ornithologist Lyubov Malovichko found nearly a thousand Sociable Lapwings in the autumn of 2005 (Malovichko 2006). This did not quite match up to the huge flocks recorded at the same site in the 1890s by Gustav Radde, but the discovery showed that the population was not as low as many had feared. On return migration in spring, Sociable Lapwings appear to retrace their route and a further major breakthrough came in March 2007 with the discovery by a team of Dutch and Syrian researchers of many hundreds of birds in northern Syria near the Turkish border (Hofland & Keijl 2008). Co-ordinated counts by researchers working for the BirdLife Partners in Turkey, Doğa Derneği, and in Syria, the Syrian Wildlife Society, later confirmed the presence of large numbers of birds on both sides of the border, counts in Turkey greatly exceeding anything recorded in that country for many years. Subsequently, these areas have been shown to be particularly important on the southward migration in autumn. In October 2007, the coordinates of a bird fitted with a satellite tag were relayed to researchers in Turkey, who immediately sent a field team to the area. On arrival, they made the remarkable discovery of at least 3,200 birds. Counts at the same site in subsequent autumns have shown that it is used by thousands of birds each year. The Turkish and Syrian stopover sites both contain small remnants of steppe, similar to the habitat used on the breeding grounds, although the birds feed largely on surrounding agricultural land.

These sites are used by birds only during migration, and the final wintering grounds were largely unknown until birds fitted with satellite tags led researchers to Sudan (Fig. 3.2). Subsequent searches by the Sudanese Wildlife Society resulted in the discovery of considerable numbers of birds in arid regions of that country, where they had not been seen for many decades. Indeed, the two birds tracked by satellites from Kazakhstan to Sudan were the first confirmed records of the species in Sudan for more than eighty years and the first in East Africa for fifty. This evidence confirms what reports and specimens suggested over a century ago, that Sudan is the most important wintering location for this species. However, small numbers of birds are recorded wintering each year far to the east, in northern India (BirdLife International 2001), where flocks of up to 90 birds were found in the state of

Gujerat. The first major migration stop-over site on the eastern flyway was found in the autumn of 2012, when between 400 and 600 birds were found beside a reservoir in the Kashkadarya Province of Uzbekistan. Originally it was thought that birds following this eastern route to India were from far eastern Kazakhstan or perhaps even from China, where the species bred historically (Kamp *et al.* 2010). However, a bird tracked by satellite from central Kazakhstan to India in autumn 2010 and another tracked from eastern Kazakhstan down the western migration flyway suggest that there may be no clear migratory divide. Quite how birds decide which route to take, whether birds can take different routes in different years and whether populations taking the two routes are reproductively isolated are all mysteries that await explanation. However, satellite technology and the sight records collected by a small army of volunteers have greatly increased our understanding of the Sociable Lapwing's migration. Satellite tracking of another steppe species, the Pallid Harrier, has shown that its migration route down to wintering grounds in east Africa is remarkably similar to that of the Sociable Lapwing (Terraube *et al.* 2011), to the extent that both species even appear to cross the Red Sea at the same point.

It appears that the Sociable Lapwing's fidelity to its wintering sites is greater than its fidelity to its breeding areas. A male Sociable Lapwing fitted with a satellite tracking device in the summer of 2007 in central Kazakhstan spent the next winter in central Sudan, the first 'sighting' (though it was not seen by human observers) in that country for many years. It then returned the following breeding season to a village in Kazakhstan several hundred kilometres west of where it had bred the previous summer (Fig. 3.2). Yet the following winter it returned to the same area in Sudan as the previous year. This time, members of the Sudanese Wildlife Society were waiting and, provided with precise coordinates from its tracking device, via a satellite and a control desk in the UK, were able to find and photograph the bird and to confirm that it was not alone. In the summer of 2009, the same individual astonished researchers by turning up right outside the town of Korgalzhyn, the home of the research team in central Kazakhstan and its third breeding site in as many years. In the autumn of 2009, the bird was back again in Sudan, and in the spring of 2010 it returned once more to Kazakhstan.

The gathering of birds in large flocks at regular sites in Syria and Turkey on both spring and autumn migration raised concerns that they might be vulnerable to hunting, and in spring 2009 there came conclusive evidence that this is indeed a major threat. In Syria, researchers reported seeing nearly 300 Sociable Lapwings shot by local hunters, and evidence of hunting pressure has also come to light in Iraq. Clearly, the trait that gives the species

Hunting of Sociable Lapwings at traditional migration stopover sites in the Middle East, such as here in Iraq, is emerging as a significant threat to the species. Three of these four birds, which have been eaten by hunters, are females (Adeeb Asaad).

Survival rates of Sociable Lapwings have been estimated from sightings of birds fitted with unique combinations of coloured rings, like this adult female. Low annual survival is likely to be linked to hunting pressure along the migration routes (Paul F. Donald, RSPB).

its common name, and its habit of using regular and predictable migration stopover sites, make it particularly vulnerable to hunting. The scale of the problem came as a shock and suggested that it is at least partly responsible for recent population declines. This suspicion was backed up by data collected on the breeding grounds, where each year researchers searched for birds marked with unique combinations of coloured leg rings. Statistical models of survival based upon the pattern of resightings of marked birds have shown that survival rates between breeding seasons are indeed too low to support a stable population, pointing the finger of guilt more clearly at the activities of hunters along the migration routes (Sheldon *et al.* 2013). As a result the population appears still to be in decline, with numbers at the intensively studied colonies around Korgalzhyn declining rapidly after 2010. Now that the problem has been recognised, however, it can be addressed, perhaps more tractably than can the problem of grazing practices across vast areas of steppe. Already the BirdLife Partners in Syria and Iraq are working hard to reduce hunting pressure through legal enforcement and education.

Through the energy and collaboration of researchers and conservationists from many nations, linked together through BirdLife International, and with considerable help from the latest electronic surveillance equipment, much has been learned of this most enigmatic species, and plans are in place to secure its conservation. In 2009, researchers and conservationists from most of the countries in which the Sociable Lapwing breeds, stops over or winters gathered in Almaty, Kazakhstan, to develop a plan of action to save the species, under the auspices of the African-Eurasian Waterbird Agreement (AEWA). At the same time, ACBK is leading a consortium of conservation agencies and the government of Kazakhstan to establish a huge network of interconnected protected areas in the steppe belt of central Kazakhstan, complete with plans to restore the great herds of natural grazers that once roamed there. However, projections of future agricultural demand, and the increasing access of farmers to high-tech agricultural machinery and new cereal varieties, suggest that the future of the Sociable Lapwing, a true flagship species of the Eurasian steppe, is likely to remain precarious.

Chapter 4
Spoon-billed Sandpiper
Eurynorhynchus pygmeus
CRITICALLY ENDANGERED

The Spoon-billed Sandpiper is the rarest wader on the Asia-Pacific seaboard and now indeed one of the world's rarest birds. Yet, 130 years ago, when an expedition led by Nordenskiöld for the first time reported the species' breeding area on the Arctic coast of Chukotka, it was sufficiently common to appear regularly on the tables of the officers (Portenko 1972). It was first described by Linneaus in 1758 as *Platalea pygmea*, placing it alongside the spoonbills (Plateinae), but this obvious wader was moved to its own genus *Eurynorhynchus* by Swedish zoologist Sven Nilson in 1821. Its spatulate bill is astonishing and quite unlike that of any other wader. One of its most extraordinary features is that the chicks are born with it, emerging from the egg sporting a disproportionately large spoon, with little to show of the rest of its bill. In contrast, the bill of hatchling spoonbills, the only other living birds with a spoon-shaped beak, is conical and only begins to flatten at the tip after about ten days. Nobody has yet been able adequately to explain its function, although several hypotheses exist. It was previously suggested that it is used like the bill of a spoonbill, swishing through the water column in order to snap up suspended animals (Piersma 1986). However, observations of birds foraging in deep water are rare, and on the west coast of South Korea most observations of foraging birds have been on wet tidal flats with a fine sand to silt substrate, foraging either with a 'run-and-peck' approach, or by vigorous rapid pecks at the substrate, called 'sewing'. This action appears to turn the top few millimetres of sediment into a slurry, and it has been proposed that this is intentional, with prey being immobilised and suspended in a 'soup', which the birds can filter with the powerful tongue and the lamellae within the bill (D. Rogers *in litt.* 2010). In South Korea the species seems to be almost entirely confined to the very outer parts of the estuaries, where this combination of sand and patches of saturated mud or silt occurs, and Spoon-billed Sandpipers on migration return to same few patches of the Geum estuary at certain stages of the tide (N. Moores, pers. comm.). Birds in Thailand have been observed using their bills like a shovel to push lumps of mud or algae ahead of them, then quickly working their bill tip around underneath them. It has been speculated that if birds deliberately search for loose bits of mud and algae, which may be scattered across mudflats, this could explain why birds seem to be so active when feeding (D. Sibley, pers. comm.). Recent research has shown that biofilm, a mucus-like substance often found on the surface of mudflats, may be an important component of the diet of small sandpipers (Kuwae *et al.* 2008, Mathot *et al.* 2010, Kuwae *et al.* 2012). Spiny structures on the tongue are probably used to help birds feed on this substance, which comprises microbes, extracellular mucus and detritus. The Spoon-billed Sandpiper may also feed on this previously unsuspected food source, although the extent to which this happens, and whether the unique bill shape aids in this, is currently unknown. There is increasing evidence from observations at migration and wintering sites that Spoon-billed Sandpipers concentrate in areas of firm substrate with a water or liquid mud layer on the surface. Here they are regularly seen to take small crabs and shrimps, suggesting that their 'spoons' may function as a sensory organ (Nigel Clark and Tong Menxiu, pers. comm).

Spoon-billed Sandpipers therefore seem to employ their bills in a variety of ways; jabbing, pecking, sweeping, shovelling and sewing, and a variety of feeding substrates are used. These vary from very wet soft mud to the drier, more elevated parts of mudflats and the tideline, and the species also captures insects on the ground or in the air (Sugathan 1985, BirdLife International 2001). Little direct dietary information is available but droppings from two birds and stomach contents from another included polychaete worms, small amphipods, microgastropods and tiny red crabs (Ali & Ripley 1968–1998, Cha & Young 1990; D. Rogers, H. Brown and Jae-Sang Hong, pers. comm.).

The bill of the Spoon-billed Sandpiper is remarkable, not least because the chicks hatch with the spoon already formed (John O'Sullivan, RSPB).

45

Spoon-billed Sandpiper in summer plumage on the breeding grounds in eastern Siberia. The species was added to the Critically Endangered list in 2008 and may now number only a few hundred birds (Baz Scampion).

A DISAPPEARING SPECIES

The Spoon-billed Sandpiper is rare, poorly known and declining at an alarming rate. It is only known to breed along the coasts of Chukotka and the extreme north of the Kamchatka peninsula, in the western Bering Sea in far north-eastern Russia. Its breeding distribution stretches along coastal lagoons over an area of 4,500km² where suitable tundra habitat exists, but its occurrence within this huge range is very patchy (Zöckler *et al.* 2008). Its migration, covering 8,000km, follows the western Pacific coast south through eastern Russia, Japan, North Korea, South Korea, mainland China and Taiwan, and forms part of what is known as the East Asian–Australasian Flyway. Important staging sites are found in the still extensive but rapidly declining tidal flats of the Yellow Sea. It winters in South and South-East Asia, ranging from India to Vietnam. Although its winter range is poorly documented, surveys since 2008 have greatly increased our knowledge. The key wintering areas are believed to be in Bangladesh and Burma, especially the Ganges Delta and East Bengali coast south to the Arakan coast in western Burma and the Bay of Martaban (Zöckler *et al.* 2006, Zöckler *et al.* 2010b). Whether birds arrive there by following the shorelines all the way around the coasts of Indochina and the Malay peninsula, or whether they cut overland further north, or indeed whether the northern and southern parts of the breeding population use the same migratory route is still unknown.

Because of its rarity, the remoteness of its breeding sites and its extraordinary bill, the Spoon-billed Sandpiper has topped the wish-lists of many world birders for decades. However, other than at a few well-known passage or wintering sites, or without the adventure of travelling to its Siberian breeding grounds, it has never been particularly easy to see. This is because it is not only scarce but also surprisingly difficult to pick out among the flocks of migrating and feeding waders with which it associates, which include Dunlin *Calidris alpina*, Red-necked Stints *C. ruficollis*, Little Stints *C. minuta*, Kentish Plovers *Charadrius alexandrinus* and Lesser Sandplovers *C. mongolicus*. Although the bill shape is unmistakable when seen head-on, the spoon is surprisingly difficult to see in profile.

Information on the Spoon-billed Sandpiper's breeding distribution and numbers was for many years based on opportunistic records of small numbers of individuals until 1972–1974, when 50–95 males were found by Alexander Y. Kondratyev on a spit of land 50km west of the mooring site of the Nordenskiöld expedition (Zöckler *et al.* 2008). It arrives on its remote breeding grounds around the second week of June and the breeding season is short, as is typical of species that nest in the far northern tundra. To capitalise on this narrow window of opportunity, breeding is initiated shortly after arrival. While the only known breeding areas lie along the sea coasts, the region is so remote and difficult to get to that researchers have understandably focused their surveys for this species in the coastal habitat where they are known to occur; the few surveys away from the coast have never found Spoon-billed Sandpipers more than 6km inland (Zöckler *et al.* 2010a). The possibility remains that other breeding areas exist, and satellite images are being used to help identify potentially suitable sites to survey further inland.

The key breeding habitat comprises sandy ridges or lagoon spits with low vegetation, such as mosses, crowberry and dwarf willow, among which the chicks find their invertebrate food (Andreyeva & Tomkovich 1992, Tomkovich 1995, Tomkovich *et al.* 2002, Zöckler 2003, Syroechkovskiy 2004). Eggs hatch from the first week of July and young fledge from late July to mid-August. Most adult birds have already left by early to mid-August, just two months after arrival, and they are shortly followed by their fledged young. Spoon-billed Sandpipers appear to be monogamous and territorial and some are site-faithful. In 2002, two individually marked birds were found on the breeding grounds only 200m and 1km from the ringing site, after 14 and 15 years respectively (Tomkovich 2003). However, it is not known whether all birds show such high site-fidelity or whether some, like the Sociable Lapwing (Chapter 3), use different breeding areas each year.

The first attempt at a population estimate was made in the 1970s, when 2,000–2,800 breeding pairs were thought to exist. This was based on breeding densities from limited distribution records, extrapolated across what was considered to be the potential coastal breeding habitat available (Flint & Kondratyev 1977). However, even at this time there were indications that parts of the population may have been declining in the northern sector of the known breeding range (Tomkovich *et al.* 2002), and the species was listed as Vulnerable (Collar *et al.* 1994, BirdLife International 2001).

Spoon-billed Sandpiper researcher Christoph Zöckler on the species' breeding grounds in Chukotka (John O'Sullivan, RSPB).

Pavel Tomkovich, an intrepid Russian scientist with a particular interest in the ecology of birds of the far north, started working on the species in the mid-1980s, and in 2000 Evgeny Syroechkovskiy of the Russian Academy of Science (Institute of Ecology and Evolution) began regular Arctic expeditions to Chukotka. Their itineraries included coastal areas that had previously been surveyed for Spoon-billed Sandpiper and some not previously surveyed. Fieldwork in Chukotka is never easy: travel into the region is by helicopter, when weather and budget allow, and when not travelling on foot (carefully avoiding the many bears that inhabit the area) dog-drawn sledges and all-terrain vehicles are needed. Results of their first expedition in 2000 raised concerns: Spoon-billed Sandpipers had declined in numbers or disappeared altogether from known breeding sites, and overall numbers of birds were low (Tomkovich *et al.* 2002).

This survey was the harbinger of the future population trend, which has shown a sharp decline in the area since the early 1990s, and perhaps much earlier. Subsequent surveys confirmed ongoing declines and as a result the species was upgraded to Endangered in 2004 and to Critically Endangered in 2008. Survey results from the 2009 breeding season suggest an extremely pessimistic outlook for the species: numbers of nests and broods declined from 39 in 2003 to just 14 in 2009 at one of the main breeding sites, Meinypilgyno, in southern Chukotka (Zöckler *et al.* 2010a). Even more worrying, no birds were reported in 2009 from Belyaka Spit in northern Chukotka, where around 50 territorial males were reported in 1986–1988 and 23 in 2002.

In June and July 2009, Zöckler, Syroechkovskiy and colleagues explored potentially suitable breeding areas along the coast on the southernmost edge of the known breeding range, in the Karaginsky Bay in north-east Kamchatka. This is an area through which the majority of migrating Spoon-billed Sandpipers pass in the spring on their way to Chukotka, and on their return migration in the autumn. The species is reported to have bred in at least two sites in this region in the 1970s, and while about 400km of coastline was surveyed, including 12 of 15 potential breeding sites (crowberry spits and lagoon coasts) identified by satellite imagery, only one briefly displaying male bird was found in an area previously considered to support between five and 50 breeding pairs (Syroechkovskiy 2004, Syroechkovskiy *et al.* 2009). No birds were found at the sites of the two previous breeding records. From these results, the feeling among researchers is that, assuming that there are no undiscovered breeding sites and that the species has not shifted its range, in early 2010 only between 120 and 220 pairs remained (Zöckler *et al.* 2010a) and the risk of extinction in the near future was thought to be very high. Surveys from 2010 to 2012 found reduced numbers at previously occupied sites. Despite widespread searches of potentially suitable but previously inaccessible and thus unsearched breeding areas, facilitated by Heritage Expeditions in 2011 and 2012, only one area was found to be occupied, with three probable territories (EAAFP 2011). Surveys of Kamchatka suggest that very few Spoon-billed Sandpipers remain in this previously important part of the breeding range. At the key site of Meinypilgyno, the number of pairs fell to fewer than ten in 2012, although a new population of as many as eight pairs was found elsewhere (EAAFP 2012a).

THREATS ON THE FLYWAY AND WINTERING GROUNDS

Records from the species' migratory staging sites and wintering areas have shown a disturbingly similar trend. Winter records from the 1980s and 1990s extend geographically from the east coast of India, through the Bay of Bengal to Vietnam. In 1989, a particularly high count of 257 individuals was reported from the Bay of Bengal (BirdLife International 2001). In recent years, recorded numbers have been far lower despite a number of dedicated searches. Records from Vietnam are now sporadic, the last observation being two birds at Quan Lan in the Red River Delta on 26 December 2008, with none seen on a survey in 2009 (BirdLife International 2009a). The species was always a rare but regular autumn migrant along the Pacific coast of Japan, although records were showing signs of decline by 2000 (BirdLife International 2001). Similarly, the famous Mai Po marshes in Hong Kong were considered a reliable site to see small numbers of birds on migration in the 1980s, but today records are sporadic (Zöckler *et al.* 2008). Small numbers of birds still winter in the saltpans of the inner Gulf of Thailand, primarily at Pak Thale and Khok Kham south of Bangkok, sites popular with visiting birders hoping to see the species.

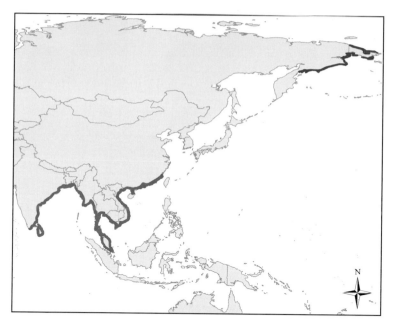

Approximate limits of the breeding grounds of Spoon-billed Sandpiper in Siberia and its wintering grounds in southern Asia. Burma and Bangladesh are emerging as the most important wintering areas.

In 2007/2008 the Bird Conservation Society of Thailand recorded 15 birds in the Inner Gulf, and ten in 2008/2009, although monitoring was less intensive in the latter period. The highest winter counts in recent years have come from Burma, on the Rakhine (Arakan) coast in the east Bay of Bengal and in the Bay of Martaban. During a survey in 2009, a total of 48 birds were recorded in the Bay of Martaban, similar to the number recorded in 2008 (BirdLife International 2009a). However, these surveys only covered a proportion of potentially suitable habitat in the Bay of Martaban, and with more extensive coverage in February 2010, survey teams reported a minimum of 71 birds, with a tentative extrapolated estimate for the whole Bay of 150–200 (Zöckler *et al.* 2010b), representing a significant proportion of the estimated global population. At Nan Thar island, Arakan, counts increased from 14 birds in 2010 to 25 in 2012 (EAAFP 2012b). Although it is almost impossible to estimate population trends when birds are spread thinly across a huge and inaccessible non-breeding range, the most recent winter counts do not appear to mirror the precipitous decline recorded at a few of the known breeding sites.

Historically, several hundred Spoon-billed Sandpipers were seen in the Nakdong estuary, South Korea (Gore & Won 1971) and, although surveys were infrequent, the species was still believed to be present there in good numbers in the 1980s (N. Moores, pers. comm.). However, numbers declined dramatically following the completion of an estuarine dam across the Nakdong river in 1990 and in recent years fewer than ten birds have been reported annually (Zöckler *et al.* 2008). The largest congregations of Spoon-billed Sandpipers observed during migration in recent decades were on the estuarine sand- and mudflat staging posts in the Yellow Sea in South Korea, especially in the Saemangeum area, where up to several hundred birds were still being reported in the late 1990s (BirdLife International 2001, Barter 2002). Since then, the largest counts at a passage site have been made along 120km of coastline at Rudong, near Shanghai, China, where 103 birds were recorded in October 2011 (EAAFP 2012a), nearly 50 in April 2012 (EAAFP 2012b) and 106 in October 2012 (Menxiu *et al.* 2013). Birds complete their moult at this site and may remain there for a month or two, making it a vitally important site for the species.

The Yellow Sea (Huanghai), named for the colour of the silt-laden water that flows into it from the Yellow River and the Hai He, is shallow and enclosed, being partially surrounded by the coastlines of China, North Korea and South Korea. It stretches about 960km from north to south and 700km from east to west, and contains some of the largest tidal flats in the world, rich in benthic invertebrates, making it of global importance for bird conservation. The entire world population of the Black-faced Spoonbill *Platalea minor* (Endangered) breeds on small islands off

Although tiny, the regular wintering population of Spoon-billed Sandpipers in the Inner Gulf of Thailand offers most birdwatchers the best opportunity to see the species. This species has become a flagship for protecting the Gulf's important bird populations (Paul F. Donald, RSPB).

the west coast of the Korean peninsula and off neighbouring Liaoning in China. The entire population of Saunders's Gull *Larus saundersi* (Vulnerable) nests in coastal saltmarshes at a few sites off the Chinese coast and South Korean Yellow and Bohai Sea coasts. Also, most of the global population of the Chinese Egret *Egretta eulophotes* (Vulnerable) breeds on small islands off the west coast of the Korean peninsula and off Liaoning. Many other globally threatened bird species migrate through or winter at or near the Yellow Sea coasts, but it is perhaps as a vital migratory staging post and feeding area for massive numbers of waders that the Yellow Sea is most renowned.

Surveys conducted in China and Korea from the late 1980s through to the 1990s demonstrated the international importance of the coastal wetlands of the Yellow Sea. An estimated two million waders, representing 40% of all waders in the East Asian–Australasian Flyway, use the region during their northwards migration, and one million during their return migration. The Yellow Sea supports more than 90% of the whole flyway breeding populations of six wader species during their northwards migration: Great Knot *Calidris tenuirostris*, Bar-tailed Godwit *Limosa lapponica*, Grey Plover *Pluvialis squatarola*, Kentish Plover *Charadrius alexandrinus*, Far Eastern Curlew *Numenius madagascariensis* and Eurasian Curlew *N. arquata* (Barter 2002). The crucial importance of the area is demonstrated by the Bar-tailed Godwit, which undertakes one of the most remarkable migrations of any bird. A recent study that used small satellite transmitters fitted to birds has shown that godwits fly an amazing 10,300km non-stop, taking eight days, from their wintering grounds in New Zealand to their refuelling sites on the Yellow Sea coast before continuing to their breeding grounds in the Arctic. The energy reserves of godwits leaving New Zealand are only just sufficient to make this journey and require that the birds are wind-assisted (Battley & Piersma 2005), highlighting the vital nature of this staging post. Yellow Sea intertidal areas also support more than 30% of the estimated flyway breeding populations of another 12 wader species during their northward migration. The majority of the world populations of the Spotted Greenshank *Tringa guttifer* (Endangered) and Spoon-billed Sandpiper use the Yellow Sea during both their northward and return migrations (Barter 2002).

In addition to its abundant wildlife, about 600 million people, around 10% of the world's population, also live in the river catchments draining into the Yellow Sea, exerting enormous pressure on the region's natural resources. There has long been concern that the destruction and degradation of wetlands in the Yellow Sea could, at least in part, lie behind observed declines in the populations of waders using the East Asian–Australasian Flyway. Intertidal wetlands have been lost to land reclamation projects for agricultural, urban and industrial development on a massive scale in recent decades, and some of the waters draining into the Yellow Sea are heavily polluted. By the beginning of this century, 37% of the intertidal areas existing in the Chinese portion of the Yellow Sea in 1950 had been lost to reclamation, along with 43% of the intertidal areas that existed in the South Korean part in 1917 (Barter 2002), and China was planning to reclaim a further 45% of its remaining intertidal sand- and mudflats and South Korea an additional 34%. This reclamation has continued apace over the last decade.

The most worrying recent example of intertidal land reclamation is that of the Saemangeum wetlands in South Korea. Saemangeum is an area of 400km², of which about 280km² was exposed at low tide, formed from the estuaries of the Mangyeung and Dongjin rivers on South Korea's west coast. It was one of the most important staging posts in the world for the Spoon-billed Sandpiper, on both spring migration and especially in autumn, with up to 280 birds reported in the late 1990s (BirdLife International 2001, Barter 2002). Numbers of birds at this site built up from late August to the end of September. Nial Moores, Director of Birds Korea, gave an account of seeing a large flock in the late 1990s:

> My own personal count at that time included a single flock of up to 76 at Okku, all stretched out in a line, most rusty-necked and speckle-breasted, with paler heads and greyer mantles, curiously swaying their heads nervously from side-to-side as the first patches of mud appeared on the falling tide. Unforgettable.

Unforgettable, and unfortunately unrepeatable. By the late 1980s the Korean government had conceived a plan to separate the wetlands of Saemangeum from the sea by building a dyke 33km long to keep the sea out. This project aimed to use the reclaimed tidal flats as agricultural and industrial land and the remainder as a freshwater reservoir. The 15-year project to build the seawall was carried out despite major campaigns by conservationists and local communities, horrified by the potential destruction of this irreplaceable wetland, and the impact that this might have on both wildlife and the livelihoods of an estimated 20,000 people who depended upon the area's natural resources. The dyke was completed and the seawall closed on 21 April 2006. Many planned land claim projects in South Korea have been opposed, and doubt was even expressed by some government ministries about the validity of land reclamation projects in general (BirdLife International 2001). Meanwhile, the tidal range at Saemangeum declined after the seawall was closed and continued to decline as this was consolidated, with tidal habitats deteriorating between 2006 and 2008. Birds Korea and the Australian Wader Studies Group monitored wader numbers on the northward migration through Saemangeum in 2006, 2007 and 2008 (Moores *et al.* 2008). Peak counts of waders declined by 74% over this short period, from 176,955 in 2006 to 46,018 in 2008. This overall trend was mirrored by numbers of Spoon-billed Sandpipers, with counts declining from 34 in 2006 to just three in 2008. Land claim behind the 33-km sea wall has not progressed rapidly, and surveys by Birds Korea in 2010 found that Saemangeum remains a key site in South Korea for southwards shorebird migration, albeit with much reduced numbers. Maintaining some of the value of this key site will necessitate keeping the sea-gates open at Saemangeum, allowing regular tides.

Proponents of land claim suggest that such projects simply result in a redistribution of waders to other coastal wetlands, and indeed numbers of some waders did increase in the neighbouring Geum estuary and Gomso Bay. However, these increases were far smaller than the dramatic declines reported in Saemangeum. Over the entire study area monitored, including these neighbouring sites, the wader count was down 41% between 2006 and 2008. Nor was there evidence that displaced birds had redistributed to more distant sites. In 2008, a national wader survey was conducted at important sites outside of the Saemangeum area, repeating one from a decade before, with no evidence of increased numbers. The Saemangeum surveys also rang alarm bells for the Great Knot, another species endemic to the East Asian–Australasian Flyway. Almost a quarter of the estimated global population of this species was recorded in peak counts at Saemangeum in 2006, but numbers declined from 86,288 birds in 2006 to only 12,406 in 2008 (Moores *et al.* 2008). There were no reported increases in Great Knot at several other important sites in the region (in China or Japan) between 2006 and 2008, and reported numbers declined sharply between 2005 and 2006 on the Australian non-breeding grounds, suggesting that the Saemangeum project may have had a permanent negative impact on the population of this species. It is not hard to imagine the cumulative impacts of the loss and degradation of huge swathes of intertidal habitat around the Yellow Sea. Many displaced waders may simply have nowhere to go and competition for resources will be greatly increased. No Spoon-billed Sandpipers were reported from Saemangeum in 2009 and only small numbers in 2010. Following the degradation of Saemangeum, the neighbouring Geum estuary has become the most important site for the species in South Korea (Moores *et al.* 2007), but there is little hope that this estuary, which has already been altered by previous partial reclamation projects, is likely to be managed in a more sympathetic fashion in future; in 2009 the South Korean government launched the 'Four Rivers Project', which includes major construction on four of the nation's five major rivers, including the Geum. Within this project there are plans to build 16 new dams and rebuild two estuarine barrages, and South Korea's estuarine areas will be further degraded.

Unfortunately, it is not only in the Yellow Sea that the tidal flats used by the Spoon-billed Sandpiper have been reclaimed or degraded; similar impacts have occurred off the coasts of Japan, China, Vietnam, Bangladesh and other sites all along the flyway (BirdLife International 2001). For example, it is estimated that more than 70% of Japan's intertidal areas have already been reclaimed. The main objective of most reclamation projects is the provision of land for agriculture or aquaculture, and intertidal areas are being lost both to large-scale projects such as Saemangeum and to small-scale dyking for saltpans or shrimp farms, for example in Bangladesh and the Arakan region of Burma (Zöckler 2006), especially as the global demand for shrimp has increased significantly. Other types of development also threaten these key coastal wetlands. Sonadia Island in Bangladesh, an important wintering area for the Spoon-billed Sandpiper where twelve birds were counted in January 2009, is threatened by plans for a deep-water sea-port. This would dramatically alter the area's suitability for Spoon-billed Sandpipers, marine turtles, dolphins and other coastal and marine wildlife, and also have a dramatic impact on the livelihoods of the large numbers of people that depend on marine resources in the area. As the human population has rapidly increased, so has coastal development for housing, industry and tourism right across the migratory and wintering range of the Spoon-billed Sandpiper, and coastal areas are increasingly being reclaimed, degraded, and lost for this and a suite of other migratory species (Zöckler *et al.* 2008).

The challenges of land claim along the East Asian-Australasian Flyway are significant, but work is underway to tackle them. In 2011, a group of conservation organisations from within and outside the region wrote to the International Union for the Conservation of Nature (IUCN) expressing their concern over the environmental and social impacts of intertidal habitat loss along the flyway. Consequently, IUCN commissioned an independent report to assess the state and condition of these intertidal habitats. The report, published in advance of the IUCN World Congress in Jeju, South Korea in September 2012, found that essential ecological services and fisheries are collapsing and that rates of decline of waterbirds using the Flyway are among the highest in any ecological system on the planet. The area around the Yellow Sea was identified as being of greatest concern. Six of 16 key areas for waterbirds along the Flyway occur around the Yellow Sea, and these have seen a massive loss of on average 35% of intertidal area since the early 1980s (MacKinnon *et al.* 2012). Measures must be found to balance economic development in the region with conservation of the environment and those very services that underpin truly sustainable development. At the IUCN World Congress, Resolution 28 was unanimously passed to improve the Conservation of the East Asian-Australasian Flyway and its threatened waterbirds, particularly around the Yellow Sea. The way that governments along the East Asian-Australasian Flyway view these habitats seems to be changing, but stemming their loss remains one of the biggest challenges that conservationists face.

HUNTING – THE BIG ISSUE?

Habitat loss is not, however, the only threat the species faces. Collectors seeking museum specimens have been reported to take eggs and skins from the breeding grounds, and although this illegal activity is difficult to quantify, collecting activities have been reported from at least seven sites, and as recently as 2006 (Zöckler *et al.* 2010a). Fisheries activities have led to local increases in gulls, skuas and crows, and these predators may have affected some breeding colonies. Inadvertent disturbance could have affected the species throughout its range. A further threat to the Spoon-billed Sandpiper is climate change, although if the species' current population trajectory

Children in the Gulf of Martaban, Burma, release a wintering Spoon-billed Sandpiper caught by bird trappers. Trapping on the winter grounds is now emerging as a significant threat to the species' survival (Rob Robinson, BTO).

continues it could disappear before the impacts of climate change are felt. Some of the most profound effects of climate change are predicted to occur in the Spoon-billed Sandpiper's breeding range (Grebmeier *et al.* 2006, Wang *et al.* 2010); already the Bering and Chukchi seas are experiencing changes in sea-surface temperature and increases in melt-season length (Hare *et al.* 2007, Markus *et al.* 2009). Ironically, the construction of dams like Saemangeum destroys the very habitats and natural processes that could otherwise provide a cost-effective buffer from the impacts of climate change.

However, it increasingly appears that hunting (both shooting and trapping) may be a particularly significant cause of mortality across the species' range. In villages in the Karaginskiy region of Kamchatka, the hunting of small waders is relatively common and with an estimated 600 active hunters in the region mortality from this cause could be significant. This is in contrast to observations from other parts of the breeding range, such as Chukotka, where hunting pressure appears to be low (Zöckler *et al.* 2008). There is certainly evidence of hunting and trapping outside of the breeding areas (Tomkovich 1992). Wader hunting is popular in several parts of Prymorie and Sakhalin, and it is unlikely that many of the estimated 80,000 or so hunters in the coastal areas of the southern Russian Far East are aware of the rarity and protected status of Spoon-billed Sandpipers. Meanwhile, startling new evidence has emerged that wader trapping at the key wintering sites of Nan Thar Island and the Bay of Martaban in Burma seriously threatens the species, and indeed may be the most significant threat to it. Surveys at Nan Thar have found individual hunters catching large numbers of shorebirds and terns, sometimes more than 100 in a single night, including many small waders (Zöckler *et al.* 2010b). Fortunately, prompt action appears to have stopped bird trapping on Nan Thar; since 2009 the island has been guarded by local people who support the conservation of the wintering site and its birds, encouraged by foreign tourists who are prepared to pay a small entry fee. Although this apparent local success is a positive sign, far more needs to be done. A survey team visiting the Bay of Martaban in February 2010 found bird hunting and trapping to be common right across the bay, and concluded that trapping is a major threat to Spoon-billed Sandpipers and other waders – a Spoon-billed Sandpiper was even caught by trappers during one of the survey team's visits (Zöckler *et al.* 2010b). Wader trapping in these areas is largely for food, and work engaging with local communities to develop alternative livelihoods in these areas is urgently needed if this activity is to be controlled (Zöckler *et al.* 2010b).

Fortunately, tackling trapping on the wintering grounds appears to be far more tractable than preventing the loss of intertidal habitats along the migration routes. Work is already underway in the Bay of Martaban and on Nan Thar to engage with local communities and develop alternative livelihoods (Zöckler *et al.* 2010b). Of 37 bird hunters identified and interviewed on the west coast of Martaban in 2011, 30 had already ceased hunting shorebirds and the remaining seven were persuaded to do so in exchange for fishing gear and livestock, although at a rough estimate these 37 hunters had between them taken over 80 Spoon-billed Sandpipers since 1989 (EAAFP 2011). A similar approach to exchange livelihood support for agreements to cease hunting has also been undertaken at the important wintering site of Sonadia in Bangladesh, where 25 hunters signed pledges to stop trapping shorebirds in 2011 (EAAFP 2012a). Preliminary indications suggest that these actions have been successful and, although more work is needed, the signs so far are positive.

Recent support from BirdLife's Preventing Extinctions Programme (BirdLife International 2009a) has been used to help establish local support groups in the breeding range, and engage with local communities in areas where hunting is a problem. Only 17% of the total area of the known sites used across the species' non-breeding range is protected (Zöckler *et al.* 2008), and few are listed as Ramsar sites. All Spoon-billed Sandpiper range countries are signatories to the Convention on Biological Diversity, and all but North Korea are parties to the Ramsar Convention on Wetlands of International Importance. These international treaties provide a mechanism by which countries can be encouraged to designate important sites, and be held to account for unsustainable management of their wetlands and biodiversity; while not perfect they are an important lever. Awareness-raising of the plight of the Spoon-billed Sandpiper and of waders using the East Asian–Australasian Flyway in general is key to improving implementation of these treaties, and this is required at all levels from governmental to local.

Despite ongoing conservation activities, the species remains at high risk of extinction. The relative importance of the various plausible causes of the Spoon-billed Sandpiper's decline is difficult to determine, but hunting and trapping on the wintering grounds in Burma appear now to be particularly significant. Efforts to reduce hunting pressure and the loss of wetland habitats are needed to protect the species, but given the current rate of decline, these conservation activities alone could prove too little, too late. In 2010, conservationists working on the species decided that the chances of the species becoming extinct before these activities started to have an effect were so high that something truly extraordinary had to be attempted.

A DESPERATE THROW OF THE DICE

Data collected by researchers on the breeding grounds suggested that the population decline is likely to have been driven largely by low survival of young birds between leaving the breeding grounds and returning there to breed for the first time. Young birds might be more vulnerable to hunting on the species' non-breeding grounds since they remain in areas of potentially high hunting pressure during their first year before returning to the breeding grounds in their second year of life, although it is also possible that some other adverse changes, such as habitat loss, might affect immature birds disproportionately. Despite the early promise of anti-hunting efforts in Burma and Bangladesh, something more needed to be done to ensure the species' survival. Population modeling suggested that if the primary cause of the recent decline had been correctly identified as trapping on the non-breeding grounds, and if this could be addressed rapidly and effectively (with a halving of winter mortality every five years from 2011), the population would still remain at an extremely low level and highly vulnerable to extinction for more than a decade (Pain *et al.* 2011). Even these assumptions were, however, optimistic. Provision of sustainable alternative livelihoods for hunters over a large area is a lengthy process, so reducing the impact of hunting at known wintering sites might take longer than hoped. Some Spoon-billed Sandpipers may winter or occur on passage at sites where they are hunted but where surveys have not detected them or where the hunting has not been identified and countered. In addition, several factors other than hunting may be contributing to the declines. In 2010, therefore, conservationists started to consider the possibility of establishing a captive population of breeding birds to produce a reliable flow of young birds for release back to the wild and to ensure that if the wild population became extinct, the world would not have entirely lost one of its most remarkable species. Establishing a conservation breeding project for a small, highly migratory Arctic wader is not as far-fetched an idea as it might first sound. Arctic-breeding waders of around the same size have been kept and bred successfully in captivity by numerous zoos and other bird keepers. A few wader species have also been reared or bred in captivity from wild-collected eggs and chicks, and successfully released into the wild as part of conservation initiatives. These include the Shore Plover *Thinornis novaeseelandiae* (Endangered) and Black Stilt *Himantopus novaezelandiae* (Critically Endangered) in New Zealand and the migratory Piping Plover *Charadrius melodus* in North America (Powell *et al.* 1997, van Heezik *et al.* 2009, Pain *et al.* 2011). Although not a wader, there is also a useful recent precedent in the reintroduction of another long-distance migrant. Chicks of Corncrakes *Crex crex* taken from stock that had been in captivity for at least ten generations in Germany were reared and released in Cambridgeshire, southern England, where the species had been extinct as a breeding bird for about 80 years. Corncrakes are long-distance migrants, wintering in sub-Saharan Africa, and released birds both retained their innate ability to migrate and were found to have similar return rates and subsequent survival as adults to wild-bred young birds (R. E. Green, pers. comm.). Like Corncrakes and the young of many small waders, Spoon-billed Sandpipers do not take migratory cues from the adults but leave their breeding grounds in groups of immature birds after the adults have departed. There is no reason to suspect that this ability would be lost in birds bred for several generations in captivity, or in their progeny when eggs or chicks were reintroduced to their Arctic Russian breeding grounds. Based upon what was known of the breeding population, simulation models predicted that taking as many as 10 clutches of eggs or chicks in 2011 would have negligible effects on the wild population, since their chances of survival in the wild were so low anyway. As part of the planning process, staff of the Wildfowl & Wetlands Trust (WWT) and the Royal Society for the Protection of Birds (RSPB), two UK organisations supporting the conservation of the Spoon-billed Sandpiper, took eggs under licence from Dunlin *Calidris alpina* nests on a north-west Scottish island in 2010 and transported them by boat and car back to the WWT's headquarters at Slimbridge in western England. Hatching and rearing success was good, which further increased confidence in the possibility of a conservation breeding mission succeeding.

There therefore appeared to be no reason why conservation breeding should not succeed in theory and the compelling and urgent case for establishing a conservation breeding programme resulted in a partnership being developed between the WWT, Birds Russia, RSPB and Moscow Zoo, with the support of the Spoon-billed Sandpiper Task Force, the British Trust for Ornithology (BTO) and many other organisations and individuals. Their ambitious aim was to attempt an emergency rescue mission for the species in 2011. However, the logistical problems that would need to be overcome were staggering. The winters in Arctic Russia are too harsh for a captive breeding programme, which requires specialist care around the clock in a carefully controlled environment; a power cut would quickly prove fatal. The decision was therefore taken to attempt one of the boldest conservation actions ever undertaken: to move eggs or chicks collected in Arctic Russia half way around the world to the WWT's headquarters and, more important, conservation breeding facilities and expertise, at Slimbridge (Pain *et al.* 2011). By January 2011, the bird conservation community was fully supportive of the need for intensive management. It was decided that with good planning, and a great deal of luck, an expedition to collect chicks in Russia's far east and move them through several quarantine barriers to the UK in a controlled environment with round-the-clock veterinary care might just be possible. What was to follow was an emotionally and physically demanding six months. This started with a somewhat frantic planning period to obtain the necessary permits and move experts and their sophisticated equipment to the town of Anadyr, the regional capital of Chukotka, and then over the last but most difficult 250km south to the breeding grounds at Meinopylgino. The team arrived in Anadyr on 16 May 2011, and a two week wait ensued until weather conditions allowed the helicopter to fly to Meinopylgino, where the search for birds and nests began. The first bird, a displaying male, was seen on 2 June, just a couple of days after the necessary permits to collect eggs had arrived. Over the next few days, more males were located on territories, but unfortunately these were flooded out by meltwater and the first nest subsequently visited proved to have been attacked by a predator, containing only a dead female and eggshells. Fortunes changed, however, and by 3 July twenty eggs had been collected from six clutches and were being artificially incubated. The first clutch of Spoon-billed Sandpipers ever to be held in captivity hatched on 5 July, the second following two days later. Given the unpredictability of the weather and thus helicopter transport, the team planned to move the eggs and/or chicks by sea to Anadyr on the ship *Spirit of Enderby* courtesy of the Heritage Expeditions tour company on 7 July. By this point, the experts looking after the birds had hoped that their charges would be either all eggs or all chicks, to make looking after them easier. However, they had to contend with eight newly hatched chicks and 12 eggs when they moved onto the boat on 7 July, with five of the eggs hatching during the rough journey. The chicks and remaining eggs arrived in Anadyr on 10 July where they were reared in the only space available – a very cramped bedsit. Here, one egg failed to hatch and two chicks died without feeding, but at between five and ten days old the surviving 17 chicks were transferred to a rearing facility built on the tundra next to a former army base until they reached fledging age. Birds were then considered sufficiently robust to withstand the 17-hour flight to Moscow, where they would need to be held in quarantine in Moscow Zoo for 30 days before their onward journey to a purpose-built facility at Slimbridge. Unfortunately one chick died before the remaining 16 chicks were transported to Moscow Zoo on 18 August. Quarantine is a stressful time for any animal, and the holding period had to be extended to 87 days due to a case of the disease psittacosis in another bird being held at the zoo, which resulted in temporarily restrictions on all bird movements. Despite excellent care in Russia, a further three chicks died during this period, but the remaining 13 chicks were flown to the UK on 11 November for a further period of 30 days of quarantine before being moved to their high-tech aviaries at Slimbridge on 15 December. Here, aviculturists simulate the day-length and temperature that birds would be subject to in the wild, provide a wide variety of foods and monitor the weights and health of the birds on a regular basis. Rearing 13 chicks from twenty eggs was a remarkable achievement, given the logistical problems that had to be overcome and the fact that nothing similar had ever been attempted with Spoon-billed Sandpipers before. In the wild, only around 3 birds would be likely to fledge from 20 eggs.

Newly-hatched Spoon-billed Sandpiper chicks at the WWT's conservation breeding centre in western England (Tim Ireland, WWT).

Not content with this extraordinary success, the team decided to attempt an even more challenging collection method for the second batch in the summer of 2012, designed to minimize loss of chicks and stress for the young birds. The aim this time was to collect eggs at Meinopylgino and, rather than hatch and rear them in Russia, to fly the eggs directly back to the UK and hatch them there, much reducing quarantine times (Hughes 2012). However, the success of this was entirely contingent upon collecting enough eggs at a stage of incubation that would allow them to be flown to the UK without hatching en route and doing so by 26 June, the date on which a helicopter had been chartered to take them on the first stage of their journey from Meinopylgino to Anadyr. As weather can delay helicopter flights by weeks in this region, this was a gamble and the fallback position was a repeat of the methods used in 2011. Thankfully, good weather allowed the multi-national field team of nest-finders to reach the breeding grounds in record time. The first birds were seen on 30 May and the first nest found on 15 June. These were taken immediately, to give the birds the best chance of laying a replacement clutch. Twenty eggs were collected in the nick of time and, despite bad conditions the preceding week, again the weather blessed the team; the helicopter landed on schedule and the 20 eggs started their long journey to the UK. Thanks to considerable help provided by Captain Jerry Woodham and other British Airways staff, the eggs arrived at Slimbridge on 5 July, with the first egg hatching just six hours later, an indication of the tiny margin of error the team had. More eggs hatched over the ensuing days and a total of 17 chicks, half of them precious females, were added to the birds from 2011, of which very few were females. In time, it is hoped that these birds will breed and produce as many as 40 eggs per year that can be returned to Russia to reintroduce birds to areas from which they have disappeared and augment the wild population to help its recovery.

In addition to the conservation breeding initiative, additional eggs were collected in 2012 to attempt a technique called 'headstarting'. This involved taking eggs from the wild, rearing them in incubators and chick brooders in Meinopylgino next to the breeding area, and then putting them back onto the arctic tundra in large aviaries, protected from predators, until they could fly. The aviaries were then opened, allowing the birds to leave as they wish, with provision of small amounts of supplementary food continuing near the aviaries for a few days. This technique has been used successfully with the Piping Plover in North America, and has the potential to boost the wild population. This is a numbers game; high levels of predation result in each pair in the wild only fledging 0.6 chicks per year, but conservationists can do five times better than this, with an average of more than three young per clutch reared to fledging. In 2012, 11 eggs were collected for head-starting, nine of which were hatched, reared, marked with individually numbered leg-flags and released successfully. Post-release monitoring showed that these birds behaved normally and seemed to migrate without problem, leaving the release site within 13 days. It is not yet known how well these birds survived on migration, though their survival would have to be astonishingly low for the five-fold advantage in productivity to be nullified. This management technique therefore shows great potential to help boost the wild population, and can be evaluated by monitoring the return rate of tagged young. It will also help aviculturists hone the methods that will be needed for reintroduction of captive bred birds, and the individually marked birds will aid monitoring.

The astonishing dedication of a multinational team that attempted the almost impossible appears to have thrown the Spoon-billed Sandpiper an unexpected lifeline. This alone will not be enough of course; trapping on the non-breeding grounds and the loss of critical inter-tidal habitats must be dealt with as a matter of urgency. However, the Spoon-billed Sandpiper Task Force and a wide range of organizations from across the East Asian-Australasian Flyway and beyond are working hard to raise the profile of the Spoon-billed Sandpiper and promote the measures needed to conserve it and the many other threatened waterbirds that share its flyway. With luck, the combined activities of this group of committed individuals and agencies will be enough to prevent the loss of one of the world's rarest and most remarkable birds.

Chapter 5
Brazilian Merganser *Mergus octosetaceus*
CRITICALLY ENDANGERED

Six species of wildfowl are listed by IUCN as Critically Endangered. Two of these, the Pink-headed Duck *Rhodonessa caryophyllacea* and the Crested Shelduck *Tadorna cristata*, are probably extinct. The Pink-headed Duck of north-eastern India, Bangladesh and Burma was last seen in 1949. Numerous attempts to find the species since then, including six expeditions to Kachin state, Burma, between 2003 and 2008, have failed to relocate it, though a tantalising sighting of what might have been this species was made there in 2004 and a trickle of reports from local fishermen keep alive hopes that the species still survives (Tordoff *et al.* 2008). The last reliable sighting of the Crested Shelduck, formerly known from eastern Russia, South Korea and perhaps north-eastern China, was made in 1964, but there is a record from 1971, when two males and four females were claimed at the mouth of River Pochon-gang, north-east North Korea (Kear 2005). Despite extensive publicity campaigns in Russia, China and North and South Korea, there have been no subsequent confirmed observations. However, another of the six Critically Endangered wildfowl species, the Madagascar Pochard *Aythya innotata* (Chapter 21), was also considered likely to be extinct until its rediscovery in a remote part of northern Madagascar in November 2006, giving hope that the previous two species may yet hang on in remote and unvisited parts of their ranges.

Action has been taken by the New Zealand Department of Conservation to improve the status of the Campbell Island Teal *Anas nesiotis*. This species had a tiny breeding population for many years, with a total estimated population of 48–100 individuals. A captive breeding and reintroduction programme was completed in 2006 and has established a second population, which at present appears to be increasing. A similar increase in sites has helped the Laysan Duck *Anas laysanensis*, which has a larger (600–700) but fluctuating population and was confined to Laysan atoll in the Hawaiian islands until birds were successfully translocated to the two islands of Midway Atoll National Wildlife Refuge in 2004 and 2005 (Reynolds *et al.* 2008).

One of the many threats facing the Brazilian Merganser is the very low survival of young birds, the great majority of which never reach adulthood (Adriano Gambarini).

So far, the Brazilian Merganser has not been subject to the same level of intensive conservation management. Although birds have been recorded at new sites since its status was comprehensively documented for the first time in the early 1990s (Collar *et al.* 1992), it nonetheless remains highly threatened and has a small and fragmented population. Although once far more widespread, it may always have been relatively rare and widely scattered across its range. This shy and elusive bird, with its barking dog-like call, occupies remote and beautiful habitats but is at risk from a wide range of threats. It is the only Critically Endangered waterfowl species to be confined to rivers and large streams, a condition which greatly restricts its population: species with linear distributions (along shorelines and rivers) inevitably have highly limited habitat in which to feed and breed, and each pair or family party of mergansers requires nine to 14 kilometres of river (Silveira & Bartmann 2001), so densities are extremely low. Moreover, rivers are less amenable to conservation through protection, because only small stretches can generally be secured within reserve boundaries and even then they are susceptible to upstream mismanagement. The Brazilian Merganser is a very intriguing species, and its conservation presents some complex challenges.

SHRINKING RANGE AND NARROW NICHE

Historically the Brazilian Merganser occurred in parts of Argentina (Misiones province), eastern Paraguay (Alto Paraná) and south-eastern Brazil (Carboneras 1992), although today the majority of the known population is found in Brazil. There have been few sightings in Paraguay since 1984 (Collar *et al.* 1992, Giraudo & Povedano 2005, Lamas & Lins 2009), and fears have been raised that little suitable habitat remains there (Hayes 1995, BirdLife International 2000). Only a few single birds have been reported from Argentina in recent years (Collar *et al.* 1992, Benstead *et al.* 1998, Bosso & Gil 2000, Giraudo & Povedano 2005, Hughes *et al.* 2006).

Within Brazil, mergansers occurred in the states of Goiás, Tocantins, Minas Gerais, São Paulo, Rio de Janeiro, Paraná and Santa Catarina (Collar *et al.* 1992, Lamas & Lins 2009). Today, the species has been lost from many of its historic sites and it is considered extinct in Rio de Janeiro, São Paulo and Santa Catarina. The largest known and best-studied Brazilian Merganser population occurs in and around the Serra da Canastra National Park (SCNP) in Minas Gerais, at the headwaters of the rio São Francisco, a river of major importance in Brazil uniting the south-east and north-east of the country, known as 'the national river of integration'. Results of recent surveys estimated that 65-100 territories exist in this area, with around 130-200 individuals, rather more than the 60 pairs previously thought to be present in the region of the Park (Livia Lins, pers. comm.). Elsewhere in Minas Gerais, a bird was recorded recently near Ouro Preto city (De Paula *et al.* 2008), in a transition zone between cerrado (woodland-savanna) and Atlantic Forest. However, it is possible this individual was a vagrant as no other birds have so far been found in the area. In 2008, three individuals were observed in Patrocínio municipality, in the western part of the state of Minas Gerais, thus confirming its presence 30 years after the first report in that locality (Lamas *et al.* 2009). Over the last decade, birds have been reported in Goiás state on the tributaries of the rio Tocantins in the north, including within and around the Chapada dos Veadeiros National Park (Bianchi *et al.* 2005, Hughes *et al.* 2006). Birds have also been recorded in Tocantins state on the Novo river near Mateiros, where a 55-km stretch of the Rio Novo was surveyed in six expeditions in 2007 and 2008 with three breeding pairs located (Barbosa & Almeida 2010), and in the Jalapão State Park and the eastern part of Tocantins state, where a significant population may exist (Pacheco & Silva e Silva 2002, Braz *et al.* 2003). Although birds were recorded on the rio Tibagi in Paraná state in 2001, a six-month expedition to this area in 2005 failed to find the species (Hughes *et al.* 2006). More than 30 birds were reported from tributaries of the São Francisco in western Bahia (Pineschi & Yamashita 1999), although subsequent surveys have failed to confirm the species in that area, and most of the riverside vegetation has been removed for agriculture (Olmos & Silva e Silva 2003, Hughes *et al.* 2006, Silveira 2008).

Recent estimates put the population size at 43–75 pairs in Brazil, and fewer than 250 individuals in all (Hughes *et al.* 2006), although these could be underestimates as recent surveys, which require confirmation, show possibly 65-100 pairs in SCNP alone. Although no complete census has been conducted since a population estimate of 250 individuals in 1992, threats continue and the current population could be lower; BirdLife International currently places the species' population within the band of 50-249 mature individuals. While recent surveys and discoveries of birds at new sites leave room for hope that the population size may be larger than previously thought, insufficient information exists to estimate population size any more accurately.

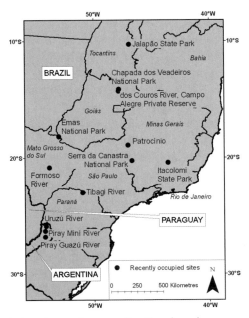

Distribution of Brazilian Merganser in interior south-eastern Brazil and north-westernmost Argentina.

A family group of Brazilian Mergansers. The species requires clear water, and is threatened by turbidity caused by deforestation (Adriano Gambarini).

The Brazilian Merganser is almost exclusively confined to clear, fast-flowing and rocky-bedded rivers and streams, often interspersed with calm pools and waterfalls, in remote areas of subtropical forest and cerrado. It frequently occurs on upper river tributaries with rapids, steep escarpments and valleys with gallery forest up to elevations of about 1,300m (Collar *et al.* 1992, Hughes *et al.* 2006). A survey of mergansers at SCNP between 1996 and 2000 found that areas occupied by the birds had clear water, were more than 1m deep and 3m wide and had exposed rocks where the birds roosted, although when rivers became turbid after rains the birds moved temporarily to much smaller tributaries with clearer water (Silveira & Bartmann 2001). Although gallery forest provided nesting habitat, continuous forest did not appear essential. While some pairs had territories that included areas near camp sites, roads and towns, birds flew to areas of riverine vegetation with few people when disturbed; it is possible that birds will tolerate some level of human presence if they have a suitable refuge of preserved habitat (Lamas 2006). Occupied areas of the rio Novo in Tocantins were around 50m wide, characteristically had clear water, rapids, waterfalls and many exposed rocks, but had only very narrow gallery forest surrounded by open cerrado, suggesting that the birds are not only found on well-forested rivers (Braz *et al.* 2003). From the evidence available, fast-flowing clear water may be more important than the structure and density of adjacent forest (Antas 1996), although some level of fringing forest or similar vegetation appears to be very important, be it the tall dense forest characteristic of the Atlantic Forest biome, gallery forest of cerrado, or other types of well preserved 'gallery forest' that borders rivers in some grassland areas.

In Brazil, the species is found largely in areas of plateaus or 'chapadas', and many of the birds remaining in Brazil are found within and around protected areas such as state or national parks. This may be partly because areas of suitable riverine vegetation, such as gallery forest, have been retained (Silveira & Bartmann 2001), there is relatively less disturbance, and rivers have better water quality than those outside protected areas.

Before 1990, little was known of the species and few studies were undertaken (Partridge 1956, Bartmann 1988), but more recently the investigations of Lamas, Silveira, Bartmann, Bruno, Lins and colleagues have added considerably to our knowledge, although many questions remain about the ecology of this shy and rare species. Until 2002, the only documented record of nesting was in a tree-hole and it was assumed that the species relied on riverside trees during the breeding season (Partridge 1956). Nest site availability following widespread deforestation was therefore considered to be a key, and potentially limiting, factor. However, in 2002 a nest was found in a depression in a rock crevice, with seven eggs laid on a thin layer of sand and soil, 10.5m above a watercourse in SCNP (Lamas & Santos 2004). Since then other nests have been recorded in tree holes, rocks in river banks and disused armadillo burrows (Hughes *et al.* 2006, Andrade *et al.* 2009, Lamas & Lins 2009). Although a lack of nest sites may not be as significant a problem as previously believed, little is known of nest site preference or success rates, and it remains possible that nest sites could be limiting in some situations. There are many potential competitors for large nest holes, including Muscovy Ducks *Cairina moschata*, Red-breasted and Toco Toucans *Ramphastos dicolorus* and *R. toco*, parrots, and mammals such as opossums *Didelphis* spp. (Silveira & Bartmann 2001).

Nesting takes place from May to October (Lamas & Santos 2004, Bruno *et al.* 2006), with the peak of incubation in July and hatching in August, although there may be some geographical or annual variation in seasonality. This is the dry season in the Serra da Canastra region, when rivers are at a low level with clear calm waters. The species has a relatively small clutch of up to eight eggs compared to 7–12 eggs for other *Mergus* species (Carboneras 1992, Bruno *et al.* 2010). This is not unexpected as species in temperate environments, especially the northern latitudes occupied by other *Mergus* spp., frequently have larger clutches than their tropical counterparts (Jetz *et al.* 2008). Insufficient demographic information exists to evaluate the population significance of reported productivity levels. An annual mean brood size of 1.58 was reported for pairs observed in six territories from 1996–2000 (Silveira & Bartmann 2001), and of 3.7 for pairs observed in four territories between 2001 and 2005 (Bruno *et al.* 2006). These annual averages include some years when no ducklings were observed with a pair of adults. There is no published information on the number of young that survived to independence and some of the broods will have been detected at different stages. Young have been observed to stay with their parents for about six months, and some as long as 8–10 months (L. Lins, pers. comm.). Many young die in the first months of life (Lamas & Lins 2009). Adults appear to tolerate their young until at least April, prior to the next breeding season. Very little is known of dispersal or the fate of the young after they leave their parents' territory, but Ribeiro *et al.* (2011) published the first information on dispersal and first date of sexual maturity after they caught and marked a male a few months old on the São Francisco river in September 2010. The bird was seen on the river until the end of the following April but less than 2 months later was found nesting nearly 20 km away on Santo Antonio river on the opposite side of the Canastra plateau, suggesting reasonable dispersal abilities.

Brazilian Mergansers appear to feed mainly on small fish (up to 20 cm) and aquatic invertebrates (Partridge 1956). They dive to about 0.5m to feed, largely in pools of slower-flowing water, although the species also frequently feeds in rapids (Silveira & Bartmann 2001). The birds loaf and roost on rocks, often in the middle of the river (Silveira & Bartmann 2001), presumably to reduce the risk of predation by land predators.

A WATERBIRD THREATENED BY DEFORESTATION

Habitat loss and degradation are considered to be the main causes of the historic population decline. The driving factors are expanding and unsustainable agricultural practices, mining activities, the construction of dams for hydroelectric power generation, expansion of human habitation, clearance for forestry plantations, tourism and other forms of development (Silveira & Bartmann 2001, Hughes *et al.* 2006, Lamas 2006). Water quality has been severely compromised in many areas, especially from the increased sediment loadings and turbidity due to erosion from the massive deforestation and poor land management that have occurred throughout large parts of the range, e.g. in Misiones, Argentina (Collar *et al.* 1992). In Paraguay, where deforestation occurred, gallery/riverine forest was often left to provide shade for cattle, and there is a legal requirement to retain a margin of forest bordering watercourses. However, a recent increase in soybean farming has resulted in removal of many remnants of gallery forest to maximise the area under cultivation (Hughes *et al.* 2006). The requirement to retain a margin of riverine gallery forest also exists in Brazil although, again, compliance appears poor. The construction of dams has destroyed large areas of suitable or potentially suitable merganser habitat, both directly, through the removal of forest, and indirectly, through the resulting hydrological changes. Large areas were flooded by the construction of dams on the arroyo Urugua-í in Misiones, Argentina, and on the Itaipú, Acaray and Yacyreta in Paraguay. In Brazil, plans appear to be underway to develop hydroelectric energy plants on several of the rivers from which mergansers have been reported, the rios Tibagi in Paraná, Paraná in Goiás, Novo and Tocantizinho in Tocantins, and Samburá in Minas Gerais, and this represents a serious ongoing threat to the species' habitat (de Luca *et al.* 2006, Hughes *et al.* 2006).

In SCNP, mining activities in the 1980s and 1990s appear responsible for the loss and degradation of much merganser habitat, with clear-felling of gallery forest, and waterways affected by siltation from soil erosion; areas previously used for mining have not been restored and soil erosion continues (Silveira & Bartmann 2001). Although commercial diamond mining was banned in SCNP in 2006, following a visit to the park by the former President of Brazil, Fernando Henrique Cardoso, the area remains threatened by new mining enterprises (Hughes *et al.* 2006). Despite the Park's importance, Brazil's Chamber of Deputies approved two bills in 2010 aimed at reducing SCNP's official boundaries and transforming some of its parts into an Environmental Protection Area (EPA). Unless these bills are refused at the Federal Senate, this will probably increase the risks to Brazilian Mergansers from mining activities in SCNP (Bueno *et al.* 2011). Traditional farming practices in the region include slash-and-burn agriculture and, while fire is an important natural feature of cerrado ecosystems (Coutinho 1982), uncontrolled burning by farmers has become common in Brazil. This results in the destruction of native vegetation and increasing soil erosion which reduces water quality both for the mergansers and local people. Siltation resulting from all of these activities is believed to have affected mergansers by reducing fish populations and by increasing water turbidity, thus reducing underwater visibility and hampering the birds' feeding activities. Longer-term changes to waterways also result, although these are less predictable (Hughes *et al.* 2006). Tourism represents an increasing problem at SCNP and possibly in other parks and their surrounding areas, including the Jalapão State Park and Chapada dos Veadeiros National Park. SCNP is a stunningly beautiful place, with clear pools and numerous waterfalls, but with ever-higher numbers of tourists using the area for watersports. Such activities, often labelled as 'ecotourism' or 'green tourism' have not generally been managed in an environmentally sustainable way. The main facilities built to attract and support tourists include camp sites, barbecues and swimming pools along the riverbanks, with obvious habitat destruction, disturbance and water pollution implications for mergansers (TBI 2006).

Potential predators and their impacts are virtually undocumented. Many mammal species, including the Ocelot *Leopardus pardalis*, the Crab-eating Fox *Cerdocyon thous* and the Neotropical River Otter *Lontra longicaudis*, are potential Brazilian Merganser predators, along with numerous species of raptor (Lamas & Santos 2004). A Great Black-hawk *Buteogallus urubitinga* was observed stooping over a merganser at SCNP by Lívia Lins and colleagues (Lamas & Santos 2004) and the Black-and-white Hawk-eagle *Spizastur melanoleucus* was considered to be an important predator of Brazilian Mergansers in Argentina (Partridge 1956). Carnivorous fish such as the Dourado *Salminus maxillosus* could take ducklings, and domestic or feral dogs could also present a risk (Lamas 2006). Introduced invasive species have not been well studied in the region but the largely piscivorous peacock bass *Cichla* sp. and other species introduced to watercourses will alter the dynamics of the native river communities and could affect the merganser's food supply (Lamas & Santos 2004). The impacts of introduced fish are believed to have played an important role in the declines of many bird species, for example the Madagascar Pochard (Chapter 21). Although there is no evidence that hunting for food currently presents a significant threat to Brazilian Mergansers, its past and present significance is difficult to evaluate (Lamas & Lins 2009). Hunting can dramatically affect small and sedentary populations, and baited traps used to catch other animals have been reported along the rio São Francisco, so vigilance and public awareness activities to counter this threat are essential.

Overall, it is likely that both habitat loss and habitat degradation, through the sedimentation resulting from poor land management and deforestation, played the most significant parts part in the species' decline across its range. Other factors may be locally important.

PLANNING THE RECOVERY

Many conservation measures have been undertaken and more are required to ensure the long-term persistence of the Brazilian Merganser, which is already legally protected throughout its range. Although in Brazil a large proportion of the Brazilian Merganser population occurs within six national or state parks, it is necessary that newly discovered populations receive effective protection (Hughes *et al.* 2006). This could, where possible, involve expansion of the boundaries of existing parks to encompass new areas, alongside the development of effective special protection measures for watercourses and their borders; existing measures for the protection of gallery forest have failed in many areas. Activities such as agriculture and ecotourism, both within protected areas and throughout the watersheds in which they occur, need to be practised in a sustainable fashion to maintain water quality. Even within protected areas, active management is sometimes necessary to conserve the integrity of riverheads and essential merganser habitat. For example, the lack of restoration of areas historically degraded by mining in SCNP is likely to result in continuing upstream soil erosion that can compromise water quality downstream. Although gallery and other riverine forest is not the only nesting habitat, it is nonetheless important both for nesting and as a refuge from disturbance. It may also contribute to better river habitat through shading and helping to mitigate soil erosion, and its long-term conservation has to be a priority. This requires active engagement with the local communities, as passive protection, such as legislation alone, rarely works in the absence of effective community engagement. In SCNP for example, gallery forest continues to be illegally destroyed (Lamas & Santos 2004). In addition to deforestation, lack of fencing of land grazed by cattle results in trampling of the understorey and soil compaction, which inhibit gallery forest regeneration. Many damaging activities probably occur because local land managers and other stakeholders are not aware of the threatened status and needs of Brazilian Mergansers, and of options for practising alternative, less damaging activities. The situation in and around SCNP is an excellent example of the need for conservationists to work constructively in partnership with local stakeholders to develop solutions.

In recent years a local NGO, the Terra Brasilis Institute, has been working at SCNP to help sensitise both local communities and the public, including tourists, to the plight of the species and its habitat. Their work also aims to help develop a sense of local ownership of the species and responsibility for its maintenance (TBI 2006). Activities have included a campaign, 'Wanted Alive', with questionnaires focused on both providing information and obtaining records of observations, along with lectures at schools. Local farmers have an essential role to play and Terra Brasilis are conducting a pilot study with them on the rio Peixe, a tributary of the São Francisco (which originates in SCNP), to investigate the impacts and conservation implications of existing farming practices. The intention is that best practice farming methods will then be developed with, and disseminated by, the local farmers. Tourism activities in protected areas also need to be regulated to ensure that they take place in a way that is compatible with the needs of the merganser and its habitat, and to be carefully monitored.

Both people and biodiversity will ultimately benefit from sustainable management of the resources in and around SCNP. For example, water quality has major implications for human wellbeing in the region. Turbid water is costly to clean for domestic purposes, it has impacts on fisheries management, it reduces aesthetic appeal and thus tourism, it can contribute to flooding and it has an impact on the functioning of hydro-dams. The Brazilian Merganser is therefore an excellent flagship for the promotion of environmentally sustainable soil management, something that would be of massive benefit to people in the region.

As only basic ecological information exists, research and monitoring remain key priorities. Regularly monitoring of birds in SCNP and at other sites where they have recently been recorded is important, as are additional surveys of potentially suitable habitat within the species' historical range in Brazil, Argentina and Paraguay. One priority is to establish the status of recently discovered populations, and some authors consider that others may remain in the extensive river systems of Misiones in Argentina (Lamas & Lins 2009).

While the ecological research undertaken in recent years has advanced our knowledge of the species, much information is still needed to inform conservation management and ensure that it is effective. This would best be done through detailed systematic studies involving colour-marked birds so that productivity and survival can be related to environmental factors. Priorities for research include determining the factors that influence productivity, confirming territory size and how this relates to environmental factors, investigating daily and seasonal movements, and establishing the fate of independent young.

In April 2008, the Terra Brasilis Institute, with support of The Wildfowl & Wetlands Trust (WWT) and the Instituto Chico Mendes de Conservação da Biodiversidade (ICMBio), started a programme to mark and monitor Brazilian Mergansers at Serra da Canastra. The team successfully caught, colour-ringed and radio-tagged three mergansers – the first time that this has been undertaken. Seventeen more birds have been caught subsequently (Lins *et al.* 2010) and this ongoing study should help fill many gaps in our knowledge; for example radio-tagging should provide information on habitat use and dispersal, and colour ringing will help confirm what is currently assumed about monogamy, territoriality and territory sizes. Terra Brasilis continued to monitor the mergansers throughout 2009, including three of the pairs ringed in 2008, which produced 17 ducklings.

Although Brazilian Mergansers will use holes in trees, rock crevices and burrows to nest, only limited data exist on their nest site preferences and nesting success. We do not know if nest site availability and type limits any populations but it would be simple to assess whether artificial nest site provision could boost productivity and/or improve carrying capacity in areas with few apparent nest sites. Another globally threatened (Endangered) sawbill duck, the Scaly-sided Merganser *Mergus squamatus*, also uses fast-flowing streams and nests in tree holes in riverine forest. This strikingly beautiful species, with its scaly-patterned flanks and shaggy crest, is suspected to be undergoing a sustained decline. It breeds primarily in the Primorye region of south-east Russia, but also in North Korea and north-east China, where it is found in areas of tall riverine forest, especially primary forest with abundant nest holes. In Primorye, deforestation seriously threatened this species historically and continues to do so. Between 2001 and 2009, a programme of artificial nest provision in south and central Primorye, using both boxes and nest tubes, has proved very successful. Over this period, where 180 artificial nests were provided along 11 rivers, the breeding population on one of the rivers increased from 30 pairs to 50–70 pairs. Nest success was 88% in artificial nests compared with 81% in natural cavities, and nestbox occupation rates were significantly higher along logged than along unlogged rivers, suggesting that tree hole nest sites are limiting along logged rivers (Solovieva *et al.* 2010).

Captive breeding of mergansers is an option that could reduce the species' extinction risk and a conservation breeding programme was initiated in 2011 at the Poços de Caldas Breeding Center in Minas Gerais, with two young successfully reared by 2012 (Livia Lins, pers. comm.). In general ducks, including mergansers, breed readily in captivity. If artificial nest sites were used by wild birds then clutches would be relatively easy to locate and there would be a good chance of females relaying if the eggs were taken sufficiently early. However, reintroduction would require the initial causes of decline to have been adequately addressed, and research is still needed to pin down these causes. Some authors consider that large areas of potentially suitable habitat may still occur in southern Brazil and Misiones in Argentina (Silveira & Bartmann 2001, de Luca *et al.* 2006), although we do not currently know why the species is absent from some areas that appear to be suitable. Nonetheless, captive breeding and reintroduction has been successfully used as one of a suite of necessary conservation measures for other Critically Endangered ducks, including the Laysan Duck and Campbell Island Teal, and it will be critical for the future of the Madagascar Pochard.

In 2006 a species action plan was produced for the Brazilian Merganser, with participation from national and regional government and all relevant local and international stakeholders (Hughes *et al.* 2006), with a Brazilian Merganser Recovery Group initiated to make progress with the essential actions. The current level of enthusiasm and both national and international cooperation may enable populations of this shy and elusive species, a perfect indicator of sustainable watershed management, to be maintained and enhanced over the next decades.

The *Scaly-sided Merganser* Mergus squamatus *of eastern Asia faces many of the same problems as the Brazilian Merganser (Peiqi Liu).*

Chapter 6
Royal Cinclodes *Cinclodes aricomae*
CRITICALLY ENDANGERED

It takes just three hours or so to drive from Peru's capital Lima, at sea level, to the páramos of the high Andes at a heady 4,500m above sea level. Many birdwatchers make this journey because this area is one of the world's most accessible sites for such high-altitude ornithological challenges as the Puna Tinamou *Tinamotis pentlandii* and the Diademed Sandpiper-plover *Phegornis mitchellii*, the latter claimed by many to be the world's most attractive wader. Most visitors arrive with thumping headaches caused by the rapid ascent, some even having to be carried the last few metres and propped up in front of their telescopes. There are of course many other special birds of the high Andes of Peru and a surprising diversity of habitats. The most remarkable of these is a woodland that is on the edge, in terms of both the climatic conditions suitable for tree growth and its continued survival.

As one climbs through the Andes, the native evergreen trees and planted eucalyptus plantations give way to shrubs and occasional flowering bushes such as *Nicotiana* (tobacco plants), attended by Giant Hummingbirds *Patagona gigas*. Even at these relatively modest altitudes conditions can be tough, and Giant Hummingbirds save energy at night by entering a state of torpor. Above 3,000m, the first páramos (alpine grasslands) start to appear. At 4,000m, conditions are extreme and birds adapt to them in unpredictable ways: the Olivaceous Thornbill *Chalcostigma olivaceum*, a species of hummingbird, walks around on the ground, while the Stripe-headed Antpitta *Grallaria andicolus* and the Tawny Antpitta *G. quitensis*, members of a notoriously elusive family, bounce about in the open for all to see.

Unfortunately, extreme altitude and low human population density are no safeguards against extinction risk. Among the Alpacas *Vicugna pacos* and seedsnipe (Thinocoridae) live many bird species of the family Furnariidae, more commonly called the ovenbirds after the clay nests built by a few species in the group. This huge songbird family is restricted to South and Central America (confusingly, the Ovenbird *Seiurus aurocapillus* of North America is not related to the true ovenbirds) and includes bird groups with such engagingly busy names as foliage-gleaners, woodcreepers, leaftossers, miners, firewood-gatherers, streamcreepers and treerunners. Two highly threatened ovenbirds inhabit the central Peruvian Andes. Both are cinclodes, members of a genus of a dozen or so stout-bodied, ground-dwelling birds that inhabit South America's open country habitats such as high mountains and seashores. One species, the White-bellied Cinclodes *Cinclodes palliatus*, lives on open treeless boggy grasslands above 4,500m to the east of Lima. It is known from just a handful of sites in Peru, all within an area of around 24km², where extraction of peat, used as compost for growing mushrooms in the country's capital, is a major threat. In 2010, the White-bellied Cinclodes was added to the list of Critically Endangered birds. The range of the other cinclodes lies further south in Peru, around the splendid city of Cusco, where it inhabits the highest woodlands found anywhere in the world. This woodland, dominated by trees of the genus *Polylepis* (Rosaceae), sometimes with *Gynoxys* shrubs, has for some twenty years or so been recognised as one of the world's most endangered ecosystems (Fjeldså 1987). Growth rates are extremely low at such high altitudes and trees can take 80 years or more to reach heights of just a few metres (Suárez *et al.* 2008). Plant diversity is low in these woodlands, with only around 30 species (many of them ferns) being found in some woodland patches (Terrazas & Stahl 2002). Few shrubs can survive under the heavy shade of a full *Polylepis* canopy and the woodland floor is often just moss-covered earth, rock or fallen trees. This is the home of the Royal Cinclodes.

The Royal Cinclodes was described in 1932 under the name *Upucerthia aricomae*, based on a specimen collected near the Aricoma Pass, in the Puno department of southern Peru (Carriker 1932). There is, however, a specimen in the British Natural History Museum that pre-dates the type specimen by more than 50 years, and, strangely, this specimen was collected in the department of La Paz, Bolivia (Fjeldså *et al.* 1987), a region from which there have been only a handful of subsequent records (Valqui 2000, Witt & Lane 2009). The Royal Cinclodes spent many of its early taxonomic years listed as a subspecies of the more widespread Stout-billed Cinclodes *Cinclodes excelsior*, an open country species of the high Andes further north in Ecuador and Colombia, but it was finally recognised as a distinct species in the 1980s (Fjeldså & Krabbe 1990). By then it was, as it is now, *Cinclodes aricomae*, the Royal

Royal Cinclodes is under threat from loss of Polylepis *forests and now has a highly fragmented range (Fabrice Schmitt).*

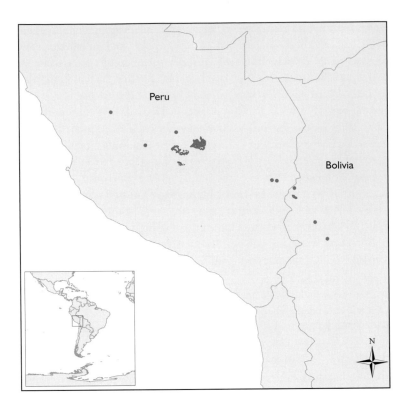

Distribution of Royal Cinclodes.

Cinclodes, named not for its majestic appearance but rather as a reference to the Cordillera Real (Royal Mountains) that make up most of its range.

To understand the plight of the Royal Cinclodes and other threatened bird species of the *Polylepis* woodlands of the high Andes, it is first necessary to understand what makes these woodlands themselves tick: what determines their distribution, what services they provide to animals and people alike, and what threats they face. In addressing these issues, a rather important debate has emerged, the resolution of which will have a profound effect on the way we view the current health and future of this habitat.

Polylepis woodland is found over much of the Andes from Venezuela to Argentina, although most of the important sites for birds are in Ecuador, Peru, Bolivia and Argentina. It often occurs as near-monotypic stands, that is, nearly all trees are of just one or a few species. Which of the 22 species of *Polylepis* species dominate in a particular stand varies with latitude: *Polylepis sericea* is the main species in Venezuela, while several co-occur in Peru and Bolivia, and *P. australis* dominates in Argentina. *Polylepis* is found at or above the usual treeline; in Peru this means at elevations of 3,500–4,500m. Unlike the forests at lower altitudes that are, or rather were, more or less continuous, *Polylepis* exists in scattered, rather small patches, interspersed by a matrix of puna grasslands or rock-scree (Lloyd & Marsden 2008). There is much debate over the 'original' extent of the woodland, although its extent has been quite dynamic and will be probably shift again with climatic change, probably more to do with drying at this altitude than warming. At present, however, most remnants are restricted to rocky outcrops where livestock grazing pressure is lower and where frequency of burning not so great (Fjeldså 2002).

Jon Fjeldså has studied the birds of *Polylepis* woodlands longer than anyone. He estimates that around 670 Andean bird species occur within the current and historical range of *Polylepis* woodlands. However, many of these are grassland rather than woodland birds and others are not *Polylepis* specialists. The latter group include many cloud-forest birds from lower elevations that sometimes occur in *Polylepis*, or generalists such the House Wren *Troglodytes aedon*. Only around 50 bird species are really characteristic of, and dependent upon, *Polylepis* (Fjeldså 2002). These *Polylepis* specialists form two main centres of endemism, both in Peru, with a smaller centre of endemism along the northern edge of the Cochabamba basin in Bolivia, and several other areas where one or two endemics are found. The two main centres of endemism in Peru are the Cordillera Blanca and the mountains around Cusco and Apurimac, which are home to the Royal Cinclodes. These two centres of endemism will protect the majority of *Polylepis* bird species if conserved properly. The analysis of patterns of endemism has become increasingly popular among conservationists as it allows identification of the most important areas for protection: since it will not usually be possible to preserve every last patch of habitat, it is vital to choose the right ones on which to concentrate conservation resources (Balmford 2002). This usually requires conservationists to consider two parameters. The first is representativeness – how well does the chosen area represent the species that are present in the wider area? The Cordillera Blanca and the mountains around Cusco and Apurimac certainly do this, as they hold many species of *Polylepis* and some local endemic birds as well. The second consideration is complementarity, which relates to the choice of further areas: if one area is protected, where could another reserve be established that would protect the highest number of species not already benefiting from the first? Again, it is necessary to protect *Polylepis* in both the Cordillera Blanca and the Cusco/Apurimac mountains, as both hold a very different complement of bird species.

FOREST ON THE EDGE

Polylepis woodland does not hold a high diversity of bird species but the ones it does support are important and many are rare (Rios *et al.* 2011). Table 6.1 shows 19 *Polylepis*-restricted bird species within a site in the mountains around Cusco, Peru (Lloyd & Marsden 2008). The list includes three globally threatened species, four Near Threatened species and a further eight species that have very restricted ranges. That leaves only five species for which there is currently little conservation concern. Such is the tiny size and extreme fragmentation of remaining *Polylepis* blocks in this region of Peru that the future may be bleak, not just for the Royal Cinclodes but for a number of other *Polylepis* specialists. Birds such as the restricted-range Rusty-fronted Canastero *Asthenes ottonis* occur at very low densities of around one bird per square kilometre, and several others have densities of less than five birds per square kilometre. Given the tiny sizes of the remaining patches and these low densities, the populations of these species must be very small indeed. Individual *Polylepis* patches or small clusters of patches typically contain as few as 10 to 50 individuals of each species (Rios *et al.* 2011).

As well as their importance for birds and other wildlife, *Polylepis* woodlands also provide a range of ecosystem services for local people (Aucca & Ramsay 2005) and for the wider Andean environment. *Polylepis* trees soak up water from the frequent mists and, more importantly, they regulate water supply into rivers, an important service during periods of drought. With Andean glaciers undergoing a period of rapid retreat, there is concern for future water supplies across many areas of the dry western Andean slopes of Peru and Chile, so the beneficial effects of *Polylepis* patches on hydrology might be felt well away from the highlands. Another important service provided by *Polylepis* is the creation of soils and a reduction in soil erosion during heavy rain. This last function is important because the loss and degradation of *Polylepis* stands through excessive grazing and burning destroys the soil, thus making it more difficult for *Polylepis* seeds to germinate (Renison *et al.* 2004). Local people have many uses for *Polylepis* and have been exploiting it since Inca times, when the trees had a significant cultural and religious importance, as a consequence of which they are thought to have been used sustainably by pre-hispanic peoples (Capriles & Bedregal 2002). Perhaps most importantly, they provide fuel for local people. This is a significant concern for conservationists and one that has catalysed a rather unusual conservation action: in seeking to reduce the pressure on *Polylepis* woodland, conservationists are actually encouraging local people to plant exotic trees.

The Royal Cinclodes is, like so many other Critically Endangered species, very poorly known. This is perhaps understandable – ecological work at altitudes over 4,000m is difficult in the extreme. Nevertheless, Huw Lloyd managed to complete his PhD on the *Polylepis* birds of Cordillera Vilcanota in Peru in 2007 (Lloyd 2008a,b, Lloyd & Marsden 2008). He found that the Royal Cinclodes occurs at extremely low densities in *Polylepis* patches, estimating numbers in the larger patches at just 2–3 individuals per square kilometre. This is extremely low for a songbird, but an even more worrying finding was that its density dropped in smaller patches to less than one bird per square kilometre. If such estimates are reliable, then the global population of the cinclodes is extremely low, perhaps as low as the 50–250 birds estimated by BirdLife International. So little *Polylepis* woodland remains, and those patches that survive are so distant from each other, that there is a very real chance of the species becoming locally extinct and perhaps never recolonising, since with such a fragmented range it must be difficult for dispersing birds to reach new woodlands and find new and unrelated mates. Perhaps a reason for the difference in density between larger and small patches was that habitat quality was higher in the larger patches (Lloyd 2008b). The species was found to prefer areas towards the lower limit of the range of altitude within which *Polylepis* grows, and it selects patches with large, old *Polylepis* trees. Ideal areas hold a high density of large trees forming a closed canopy under which the species forages on the ground and over moss-covered boulders and fallen trees. Extraction of *Polylepis* trees breaks up this canopy, allowing grasses to move in; such areas are used by other cinclodes species but seldom by the Royal Cinclodes.

Table 6.1. Polylepis-restricted bird species from the Cordillera Vilcanota, Peru, with their IUCN threat status or, if not threatened, indicating those that have restricted ranges or that are currently ranked as Least Concern (from Lloyd & Marsden 2008). Restricted-range species have ranges under 50,000km² (see p.23).

Species	Conservation status
White-tufted Sunbeam *Aglaeactis castelnaudii*	Restricted-range
Royal Cinclodes *Cinclodes aricomae*	Critically Endangered
White-browed Tit-spinetail *Leptasthenura xenothorax*	Endangered
Tawny Tit-spinetail *Leptasthenura yanacensis*	Near Threatened
Creamy-crested Spinetail *Cranioleuca albicapilla*	Restricted-range
Rusty-fronted Canastero *Asthenes ottonis*	Restricted-range
Line-fronted Canastero *Asthenes urubambensis*	Near Threatened
Stripe-headed Antpitta *Grallaria andicola*	Restricted-range
Puna Tapaculo *Scytalopus simonsi*	Restricted-range
Ash-breasted Tit-tyrant *Anairetes alpinus*	Endangered
Tufted Tit-tyrant *Anairetes parulus*	Least Concern
Rufous-breasted Chat-tyrant *Ochthoeca rufipectoralis*	Least Concern
Great Thrush *Turdus fuscater*	Least Concern
Cinereous Conebill *Conirostrum cinereum*	Least Concern
White-browed Conebill *Conirostrum ferrugineiventre*	Restricted-range
Giant Conebill *Oreomanes fraseri*	Near Threatened
Tit-like Dacnis *Xenodacnis parina*	Restricted-range
Black-throated Flowerpiercer *Diglossa brunneiventris*	Least Concern
Thick-billed Siskin *Carduelis crassirostris*	Restricted-range

Until the 1980s, there was no easily accessible site where birdwatchers could see a Royal Cinclodes. However, in the 1990s the species was discovered at Abra Málaga, a pass above the town of Ollantaytambo, where many tourists start their trek along the Inca trail (Engblom *et al.* 2002). In fact, there is a link between the Inca trail – and perhaps tourism generally – and *Polylepis* destruction. During trips to Abra Málaga in 2000, Lloyd witnessed firsthand the destruction of *Polylepis* woodland fragments. On one occasion he noted 'five horses loaded with freshly cut *Polylepis* wood, and the cutting continued the next day, with local farmers in the process of felling some of the largest *Polylepis* and *Gynoxys* trees within the area occupied by the Royal Cinclodes'. Apparently, the cutting at Abra Málaga was carried out by a single family, who sold the wood to hotels in Urubamba and Ollantaytambo where it was burned to warm tourists. There are just a handful of Royal Cinclodes left in the tiny remnants of *Polylepis* at Abra Málaga.

This paints a grim picture of the Royal Cinclodes's chances of survival, but there is scope for cautious optimism. Better preserved *Polylepis* patches, such as that at nearby Cancha Cancha, have recently been found, and their remoteness may play a role in protecting them. A significant recent development has been the discovery of a single Royal Cinclodes in an area some 300km north-west of the species' previously known range (Witt & Lane 2009). As the previously known range of the Royal Cinclodes only spanned 580km, this single record adds something like 50% to its extent of occurrence. Even more surprisingly, the bird was observed in a remnant patch of high-altitude elfin forest that lacked *Polylepis* altogether. This record, backed up by photographic evidence, is both puzzling and encouraging, although it is not known whether the individual was a transient, one of the last of an almost lost population, or one of several or many birds living happily outside the known range and habitat. There may be other undiscovered populations in Peru (Witt & Lane 2009), giving hope that the species may not be so close to extinction as current estimates suggest. While the recent outlying record calls into question our understanding of the true range and habitat of the Royal Cinclodes, there is an ongoing and fundamental debate about the original distribution of *Polylepis* woodland itself.

POLYLEPIS: NATURALLY PATCHY OR RELICTS OF DEVASTATION?

The *Polylepis* patches that support the greatest number of endemic and threatened bird species are those found close to the ancient centres of civilisation of the Inca and other cultures (Fjeldså *et al.* 1999). A possible explanation for this is that these areas were those that had relatively stable climates, providing optimal environments for both human agriculture and wildlife. This presents an interesting paradox, since logic would dictate that if *Polylepis* woodlands have been lost and degraded by human actions, the best remaining patches should be well away from areas of high human population density. Could it be possible then that the patchy distribution and restricted extent of *Polylepis* woodlands over much of the Andes are not the result of human activity? An important shift in belief over the natural ecology of *Polylepis* woodland has taken place in recent decades. Originally it was thought that *Polylepis* was naturally very patchy in its distribution, on the basis that in order to grow at such altitudes it needs a special combination of climatic and ecological conditions, explaining why it occurs largely in ravines and on rock slopes. However, more than half-a-century ago an alternative scenario was proposed, which suggested that human activities, especially burning, timber cutting and livestock grazing, have been responsible for the reduction of *Polylepis* in most areas to a fraction of its original extent (Ellenberg 1958). In effect, we now see *Polylepis* only in ravines and on rock slopes because those difficult terrains are the only places in which it has managed to survive. Today, most conservationists are convinced of Ellenberg's thesis. Current *Polylepis* cover may represent around 10% of its original range in Bolivia and no more than 2–3% in Peru (Fjeldså & Kessler 1996).

But when did this destruction take place and how did it happen? Pollen analyses in the Lake Junín area of central Peru (home to the Critically Endangered and flightless Junín Grebe *Podiceps taczanowskii*) have shown that much loss of *Polylepis* woodland occurred around 10,000 years ago. As this was a period of major environmental change brought about by both climate and the activities of people, distinguishing between the two effects is difficult. Some believe that it was the use of fire by early hunter-gatherers that caused the woodland to contract at this time (Fjeldså 2002), others that this was due to natural climate change (Hansen *et al.* 1994). It may, of course, have been a combination of the two, but what becomes clear is that recent depletion of *Polylepis* is just the most recent chapter in a very long history of depletion. By two thousand years ago, *Polylepis* woodland seems to have disappeared from many areas of the Andean uplands. From then on, right through until the Spanish colonial period in the middle of the last millennium, the woodland's extent may have declined very little (Fjeldså 2002), but with the arrival of Europeans there is ample evidence of a resumption of high pressure on the woodland remnants. Agricultural changes and timber felling for the mining industry both had major impacts on high-altitude woodlands.

Polylepis *forest occurs at higher altitudes than any other forest type and supports a unique and threatened bird assemblage (Huw Lloyd).*

Very recently, however, evidence has emerged that further alters our perception of recent rates of *Polylepis* loss, and it now appears that some regions have lost *Polylepis* whereas others have not. In the midst of serious conservation concern for this rapidly disappearing habitat (Herzog *et al.* 2002) come some rather surprising findings. A recent study assessed changes in *Polylepis* patches in the Cordillera de Vilcanota, Peru, over a 50-year period, using aerial and ground photographs, and interviews with local people (Jameson & Ramsay 2007). The results showed that very few patches had been lost completely in that time, and indeed few patches had changed in size. There were some changes in canopy densities in about one in ten patches but, in general, losses of *Polylepis* were very modest. Even more surprising were analyses of aerial photos of the Cordillera Blanca from the 1930s and late 1990s that showed no decline and perhaps even an increase in *Polylepis* cover in most valleys (Byers 2000). Clearly, we do not know as much as we should about the history of this fascinating woodland, but we do know that the future of its threatened bird species is tied to maintaining or preferably extending what *Polylepis* currently remains.

SAVING *POLYLEPIS*

Hope for the Royal Cinclodes, and, indeed for Peru's *Polylepis* woodlands, rests largely with ECOAN (Asociación Ecosistemas Andinos), a non-governmental organisation founded by biologists in Cusco in 2000. ECOAN works only in the high Andes, and makes the crucial link between biodiversity conservation and the livelihoods of local people (Aucca & Ramsay 2005), both of which are very fragile in this most inhospitable of environments. ECOAN recognised that local people need *Polylepis* wood, and indeed have needed it for centuries, for heating and cooking, for construction materials and for making charcoal. Therefore, to preserve the *Polylepis*, the obvious step was to provide people with an alternative. Local management agreements were set up with communities, after thorough consultation, which control grazing, firewood collection and burning of pastures. In return, ECOAN, with the help of the American Bird Conservancy (ABC) and other agencies, was able to provide resources that would help improve the quality of life of local communities (Aucca & Ramsay 2005). The use of energy-efficient stoves, diversification of agriculture through the conversion of abandoned stone buildings into greenhouses, and donation of medical supplies have all been implemented. Over 30,000 *Polylepis* trees have been planted, with an emphasis on connecting fragments of existing woodland. It may seem unusual for a conservation organisation to be promoting the planting of non-native trees but ECOAN is pragmatically also planting fast-growing eucalyptus in order to provide an alternative source of firewood to *Polylepis*. Given the environmental damage caused by the introduction of exotic species into other fragile ecosystems, the use of non-native trees may intuitively appear inappropriate, but if it is seen as a bridging strategy in a developing emergency it appears as sensible as the protection and planting of *Cryptomeria* conifers as a nesting substrate for Mauritius Fodies *Foudia rubra* (p.112).

The poor conservation status of Peru's *Polylepis* birds is an exception to the general pattern that high-elevation bird species are not as threatened as their relatives in the lowlands. The vast majority (in fact all but two or three) of the world's Critically Endangered bird species are found below altitudes of 4,000m. The reasons for this are clear in most cases. More people live at low altitudes because lower-lying areas are warmer, better for agriculture and more productive in terms of timber. In fact, most of the world's human business is conducted at lower altitudes, just as it is done away from extreme latitudes. But there are a few highly threatened bird species at very high altitudes and there is every reason to assume that not only will these species become more threatened, but that more high-altitude species will join them on the Red List. Concern for mountain species has risen in recent years due to what has been termed the 'escalator effect', in which warming climates force species adapted to cooler conditions to move uphill (Wilson *et al.* 2005). That poses a serious risk to species trapped on the escalator, because the areas of land in each altitudinal band get smaller and smaller the higher one goes. For those species that already occupy the summits of mountains, the prognosis is particularly dire. Here the escalator runs out and species literally have nowhere to go; it is no coincidence that the world's first extinction that can reasonably be attributed to climate change was that of the beautiful Golden Toad *Bufo periglenes* of Costa Rica, which was confined to the top of a high-altitude cloud forest (Pounds *et al.* 1999).

Most threatened species at extreme altitudes fall, at present, in the Endangered and Vulnerable categories, with the roll call dominated by Andean species. These include such birds as Violet-throated Metaltail *Metallura baroni* of Ecuador; the Perija Metaltail *M. iracunda* and the Perija Thistletail *Schizoeaca perijana*, restricted to tiny highland areas on the border of Colombia and Venezuela; the Cochabamba Mountain-finch *Poospiza garleppi* of Bolivia; and the Ash-breasted Tit-tyrant *Anairetes alpinus* of Peru's *Polylepis* woodland. If predictions of the escalator effect are correct, then the situation for these species may well deteriorate, and they will be joined on the Red List by perhaps an additional 300–400 highland bird species that are not currently at risk (Sekercioglu *et al.* 2008). If fortunes turn so badly for so many of the world's highland birds, then the future is very gloomy indeed for the Royal Cinclodes, which seems already to be struggling to cope with life in a woodland at the edge.

The understorey of Polylepis *forest, habitat of the Royal Cinclodes, comprises largely mosses, with very few shrubs (Huw Lloyd).*

Chapter 7
Bengal Florican *Houbaropsis bengalensis*
CRITICALLY ENDANGERED

The bustards are a family of birds whose fate is inextricably tied to that of grasslands. Africa is the home of the world's largest tropical grasslands and of 18 of the 25 species of bustard. Of the seven remaining species, three are endemic to the Palearctic, three to the Oriental region and one is confined to Australia and southernmost New Guinea. Their wide geographic spread, large size and use of wide-open spaces do not, however, make bustards well known animals. Being among the largest of grassland birds, they are attractive to both natural and human hunters. Prudence is therefore a cardinal virtue for bustards, and through a combination of cryptic plumage, vigilance and stealth, and keeping their distance from everything that might be a threat, they have found a surreptitious pathway through thousands of years of hunting and predation that has led them down to the present without any known extinctions. However, human demands on open space are such that six species are listed by IUCN as globally threatened and six as Near Threatened, a higher proportion than the average across all bird families.

In conservation's entirely understandable and necessary race to secure for the future as many tropical forest and wetland areas as possible, the big loser has been grasslands. Inevitably, a habitat that is structurally rather simple is less rich in animals than one with greater complexity and this may contribute to the disappointing scarcity of conservation interest in the world's natural grasslands. Grasslands are the easiest places to convert into farmland, and in the human drive to settle the planet it has been grasslands that have soonest been targeted for cattle-rearing and agriculture. This is not something that conservationists have been well equipped to counter, partly because the human need is too strong and partly because the impact of farming on the original habitat is not always easy to assess.

The sensitivities of grassland-dwelling species to even subtle changes in habitat structure vary greatly. For example, the Sociable Lapwing *Vanellus gregarius* (Chapter 3) needs extremely heavily grazed steppe grassland whereas the Liben Lark *Heteromirafra sidamoensis* (Chapter 8) can survive alongside pastoralists only where grazing pressure is relatively low. The transformation of the North American prairies to cropland may have dealt a fatal blow to the Eskimo Curlew *Numenius borealis* (Chapter 25). On the other hand, some species have actually profited from the human creation of farmland, occupying deforested areas as if they were natural grasslands. Two bustard species, the Great Bustard *Otis tarda* and the Little Bustard *Tetrax tetrax*, are among the best examples of this kind of agricultural camp-following, for their spread into Europe appears to have resulted almost entirely from human deforestation of the landscape. Current worries about recent severe declines in the populations of these and other farmland birds in Europe concern a group of species that would not be anything like as widespread and abundant as they are even now were it not for the spread of agriculture into largely wooded landscapes that started around ten thousand years ago. The livestock pastures and fallow fields of the early cultivators would have been very similar in structure and composition to the original steppes and rangelands of Asia and North Africa, the ancestral homes of these species. Now, however, Great and Little Bustards are in rapid retreat as farming intensifies (Inchausti & Bretagnolle 2005, Martínez 2008), and the ranges and populations of bustards in Africa are similarly diminishing (Moreira 2004).

As with many animal species that have found low-intensity farmland to be an acceptable substitute for grassland, there is clearly a tipping point in the degree to which their habitats are managed and disturbed, and the birds that are everywhere so adept at vanishing from sight are now beginning to vanish completely. In Asia, where 60% of the human population of the planet (the great majority of them farmers) is concentrated, the three endemic species of bustard have some of the most restricted ranges of any in the family, and all three are in the highest categories of threat. The Lesser Florican *Sypheotides indicus* is listed as Endangered and the Great Indian Bustard *Ardeotis nigriceps* and the Bengal Florican are the only species in the family to be listed as Critically Endangered.

The Bengal Florican is one of the most elusive of bird species and has a remarkable distribution, occurring in two widely separated and declining populations (Markus Handschuh, ACCB).

Not only is the Bengal Florican the world's most threatened bustard but it also has by far the most unusual distribution of any (BirdLife International 2001). Although its area of occupancy (the area of land actually used by the species) is extremely constrained, its extent of occurrence (the area defined by the shortest imaginary boundary encompassing all its known sites) is not. It is (or was) present from India just west of Nepal right through the Nepalese lowlands back into India's north-eastern reaches up the Brahmaputra valley. It then reappears much further east in Indochina, in Cambodia around the Tonle Sap and (at least formerly) in the Vietnamese lowlands around the Mekong delta. With the possible exception of the Kori Bustard *Ardeotis kori*, no other bustard has anything remotely comparable in terms of a naturally fragmented distribution. The Kori's disjunction, in any case, is far more easily explained: its two populations, one in southern Africa and one in eastern Africa, were one until relatively recently; when the planet was drier and cooler, the forests of Africa retrenched and its grasslands connected. It is not at all clear that the Bengal Florican has experienced a similar expansion and contraction. As the only bustard in South-East Asia, its presence in Indochina is something of a biogeographical surprise. It is also a rather recent one, since it was only discovered in the region in 1927, almost 140 years after the species was originally described from Bengal.

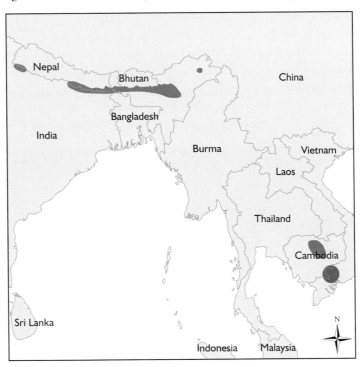

The peculiar distribution of the Bengal Florican. Outside the breeding season, the Cambodian population may range (or once have ranged) south into the area indicated by the blue circle.

This very late discovery of the Bengal Florican in what historically has been a well-watched and well-researched region supports the view that, in terms of sheer reclusiveness, the species out-bustards all other members of its family. Apart from the period when the males leap into the air in a dipping display-flight to compete among themselves for females, at which time they make the most of their all-black head, neck and belly and white wings, this species is among the most cryptic and retiring of birds, particularly so for its size. One only has to look at the distribution of records (both sightings and museum specimens) across its entire range by month, as documented in a comprehensive account of the species (BirdLife International 2001), to see that something remarkable is going on (Fig. 7.1). These figures cannot be entirely exhaustive and include a degree of observer bias, with more study being focused on the time when the species is displaying in the spring. Nevertheless, it is still extraordinary to consider that up to the start of the present century it was only ever recorded on a single occasion in the each of the months from September to November.

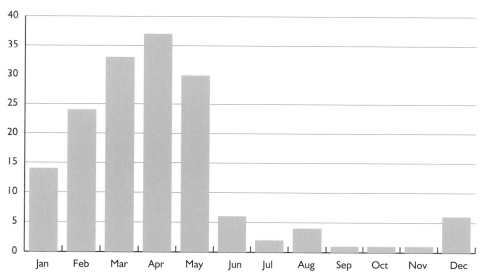

Figure 7.1. Distribution by month of all known records of Bengal Florican prior to 2001, based on data compiled in BirdLife International (2001).

The only time it is easy to see Bengal Floricans, and therefore assess their population, is during the period in which the males make their remarkable aerial displays (Laxman Poudyal).

PARKS AS ISLANDS: THE SUBCONTINENT'S SOLUTION

Running in a thin strip along the feet of the Himalayas, from Uttarakhand in the west deep into Assam in the east, is a distinctive tall grassland habitat called the 'terai'. Rainfall is low but flooding annual, bringing silt loads from the high mountains and making the soil very fertile and productive. Patches of woodland intersperse the grassland, making for a mix that is particularly rich in wildlife. Various natural effects, including flooding, fire, grazing and trampling, keep the height of the grass and the species diversity of the animals that inhabit it variable. In places the grass reaches much higher than a person. Thus the grasslands of the terai give cover not only to Tigers *Panthera tigris* and deer but also harbour a wonderful community of animals found nowhere else on earth, including the Indian Rhinoceros *Rhinoceros unicornis*, Pygmy Hog *Porcula salvania*, Hispid Hare *Caprolagus hispidus*, Swamp Francolin *Francolinus gularis*, Manipur Bush-quail *Perdicula manipurensis* and Slender-billed Babbler *Turdoides longirostris*.

Unfortunately, these endemic animals are all threatened by loss of habitat as the grasslands have been swallowed up by cultivation. They survived well into the twentieth century largely because they were, in season, virulently malarial. Jim Corbett's story 'The Talla Des Man-eater' begins with a hunt from elephant-back in one such area of grassland in Kumaon, the eastern division of Uttarakhand. The date was February 1929, only two years after Jean Delacour had first found the Bengal Florican in Indochina. 'Shooting from the back of a well-trained elephant on the grasslands of the Terai', he wrote, 'is one of the most pleasant forms of sport I know of. No matter how long the day may be, every moment of it is packed with excitement and interest.' On that morning, the last game animals that his party got, as it worked its way along the bank of a stream for a mile or so, were 'five more peafowl, four cock florican – hens were barred – three snipe, and a hog deer with very good horns'. Four Bengal Floricans in a mile seems extraordinary today, but clearly from the way Corbett lists them, this was nothing exceptional at the time. Wherever that magical place was, it will all now be under crops. Control of the mosquitoes of the terai in the 1950s and 1960s with the environmentally harmful insecticide DDT precipitated the descent into the region of settlers who immediately dispossessed the sparse malaria-resistant indigenous population and began ploughing and planting up the grasslands. The terai was so narrow (the patch of grassland in Corbett's story was 'some twelve miles long and ten miles wide') that its conversion took only a few years.

At least some and perhaps all the species that might now be characterised as terai specialists originally ranged rather more widely than this narrow belt of land, being found in patches of suitable habitat in the Gangetic plain and often extending down through much of what is now Bangladesh, particularly along the Brahmaputra River. For example, maps of the historic distributions of the Bengal Florican, Swamp Francolin and Slender-billed Babbler show that they extended well to the south of their current chain of sub-Himalayan sites (BirdLife International 2001). In terms of extent of occurrence, all three have lost something in the order of 75% of their ranges in the past 150 years. In terms of area of occupancy, the loss may be as high as 95%. Nevertheless, their heartland was the terai, and it is in the fragments of the terai that they make their last stand. Indeed, almost all that now remains of the terai's original vegetation and wildlife is what can be found in a handful of protected areas, strung out in a broken chain across the base of the Himalayas like small islands in a volcanic archipelago. These crucial reserves serve as the last bastions against a human tide that has otherwise swept away the riches of the region's environment.

However, often only very small areas in these reserves are suitable for Bengal Floricans. For example, Bardia in Nepal covers 968km² but perhaps only two to three square kilometres are suitable for the species, while only 20% of Chitwan's 932km² are grassland. As these reserves come under increasing pressure (Table 7.1), the area of suitable habitat is likely to shrink further. Furthermore, many of the reserves are so isolated that it is by no means certain that the birds they hold have the capacity to exchange genes with birds in other reserves, which inevitably means that over time each reserve will be harbouring increasingly inbred populations with a high risk of local extinction.

For Nepal, the population estimates in Table 7.1 are the latest in a series of extrapolations from studies and surveys. The country's Bengal Floricans were first surveyed in 1982 (Inskipp & Collar 1984), with follow-up work in all or some of the protected areas in 1990, 2001 and 2007 (BirdLife International 2001, Baral *et al.* 2003a,b, Poudyal *et al.* 2008). Depressingly, the pattern for three of the four parks harbouring the species has been the same, the number of males falling over the 30-year period from 29–41 in 1982 to 11 in 2012 (Table 7.2). The happy exception is at Koshi Tappu, where it was assumed that the species had disappeared following the loss of much of the grassland there in the early 1980s and the park was omitted from subsequent surveys of the species in Nepal. However, improved grassland management, including the exclusion of cattle from parts of the sanctuary, perhaps coupled with heavy monsoonal rain and changes in hydrology have allowed the recovery of grassland in the area and a survey in 2011 estimated at least 8 to 12 pairs (Baral *et al.* 2012). More extensive surveys in 2012 within and around the sanctuary counted at least 29 males and the population may be much higher (Hem Sagar Baral, pers. comm.). Despite this, the likelihood of the species' extinction in the country within the next 25-year period is all too apparent. However, the factor believed responsible for all these declines, inappropriate grassland management resulting in the loss of short-grass habitats, could easily be remedied (Peet *et al.* 1999).

Table 7.1. Estimated numbers of Bengal Floricans in reserves in India and Nepal, along with some threats to the areas. *1–5 is an estimate based on records of single birds or what were simply described as 'recent reports'; — = no information. NP = National Park, WS = Wildlife Sanctuary, WR = Wildlife Reserve. (Data from BirdLife International 2001, Poudyal et al. 2008 and other sources).

Protected area	Number of floricans estimated	Year of estimate	Threats
Dudhwa NP & Kishanpur WS	40–60	1998	Encroachment
Sukla Phanta WR	16–18	2007	Encroachment, cattle
Bardia NP	2–4	2007	Grassland mismanagement
Chitwan NP	10–14	2007	Grassland mismanagement, disturbance
Koshi Tappu WR/barrage	>50	2012	Overgrazing, disturbance
Jaldapara WS	10	1990	Heavy overgrazing
D'Ering Memorial WS	1–5*	2001	—
Dibru-Saikhowa NP	9–12	2000	Invasion, overgrazing, cultivation, floods, erosion
Nameri NP	1–5*	2000	—
Sonai-Rupai WS	4–8	2000	—
Manas NP	80–100	2000	Security problems, overgrazing
Orang NP	35–45	2000	—
Kaziranga NP	50–80	2000	Floods, erosion
Burachapori/Laokhowa WS	20–34	2000	Encroachment, cultivation, disturbance, cattle
Pobitora WS	2–6	2000	Floods, disturbance, grass exploitation
TOTAL POPULATION	280–401		

Table 7.2. Numbers of male Bengal Floricans counted in four protected areas in Nepal from 1982 to 2012 (Baral et al. 2003a, Poudyal et al. 2008 and other sources). These are records, not estimates, and of one sex only: hence the disparity with figures for the same reserves in Table 7.1.

Protected area	Number of male Bengal Floricans counted				
	1982	1990	2001	2007	2012
Sukla Phanta	13	14	12–14	8–9	4
Bardia	8–9	5	3	1	—
Chitwan	8–19	—	3	5	7
Koshi Tappu	2–5		—	—	29

There is no easy solution to the species' problems in India. India's terai grassland protected areas appear to hold (or to have held) rather higher overall numbers than those in Nepal, but the threats within their borders are rather more intractable (Table 7.1). Human invasions and high numbers of livestock represent a far greater challenge to which the park authorities have to rise, and in many cases the situation requires a political solution to the problems of landlessness that protected area staff cannot be expected to negotiate.

Clearly, it is imperative that more is done within protected areas in India and Nepal in order to enhance the status of the Bengal Florican. The total population of birds is now so low and so clumped, with probably fewer than 400 individuals divided between 15 widely scattered protected areas (Table 7.1), that conservationists should be moving at top speed and in concert to increase that number as soon as possible. As Figure 7.1 indicates, the birds effectively disappear after the breeding season and their whereabouts are practically unknown for roughly half of every year. It is still unknown whether the birds simply melt away into the comparative safety of the protected areas in which they breed, keeping their heads down until the next breeding season, or whether they move elsewhere, as in some cases it seems they must, in response to flooding, or for other reasons. If they do move, we have no information at all on the threats they face at that time of year, or whether their movements serve to exchange individuals between different breeding populations. Further research is urgently required.

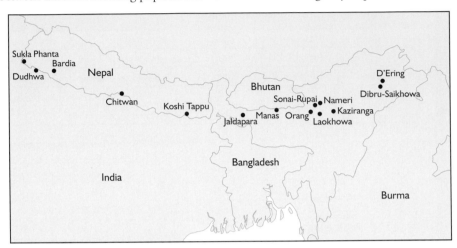

Protected areas in Nepal and India holding Bengal Floricans, either now or in the past.

NOWHERE TO HIDE: THE INDOCHINESE EXPERIENCE

Not only did it take 140 years after the discovery of the species in India to find the Indochinese population (separated taxonomically by Delacour as *blandini* on account of its richer colour, shorter black ornamental feathers of the male, shorter wings and broader, flatter bill), it took a further 70 years before it was realised that this population was of any significant size and not just a baffling relic on the brink of extinction. As recently as 1996, this population was described as 'extremely poorly known, with as few as four birds recorded in recent years, in Vietnam, on land under development' (Collar 1996a).

That the species occurred in Indochina at all could have been revealed to the world as long ago as 1880, since two mounted specimens bearing that date and labelled as from Tonkin (Vietnam) were found languishing in the Paris Museum by Delacour while he was searching for material with which to compare his 1928 specimens. During his explorations in the late 1920s, Delacour had been tipped off by a colonial administrator in southernmost Cambodia that bustards of an unknown species appeared seasonally in the region. To prove it, the administrator found a local person who was keeping a live female in captivity, and in June 1928 he cabled to tell Delacour that the birds were now arriving in his area; a collector was despatched to bring back specimens. Soon after, the species was found slightly to the east in Vietnam, and a decade later birds were observed in the far north-west and far south-west of Cambodia. This small scatter of records made for a large triangle of land to search for further populations: and almost all populations found subsequently fall within it. However, war and political conflict blighted southern Indochina for the half-century after 1939 and thwarted any notions of biological research there.

In 1990, the species was discovered in Tram Chim Nature Reserve in Vietnam, close to the Cambodian border, and it was later found on the Ha Tien Plain in the Mekong Delta. In both cases local farmers reported that birds bred at these sites, but these claims were never substantiated. Meanwhile, such was the speed and intensity of agricultural development, which took with it most of the small (76km²) Tram Chim reserve, that hopes for the species' continued survival in that country have faded and attempts to conserve it stalled. This was less defeatism than pragmatism, in part because conservationists had many more immediate challenges in Vietnam, and in part because the news beginning to emerge from Cambodia appeared to be rather promising.

In 1999, the Oriental Bird Club gave a small grant to Sam Veasna (Sam being his family name) to survey Sarus Cranes *Grus antigone* and other rare species in part of the eastern flank of Tonle Sap, the great lake at the geographic and economic heart of Cambodia. Because of the appalling Khmer Rouge regime of the 1970s, Cambodia had fallen far behind in agricultural investment so that, by comparison with its neighbours, the country was relatively rich in wildlife and possessed the last significant populations of many species in Indochina or indeed the world. While undertaking his survey Sam, a courageous and utterly committed wildlife officer who was tragically to die later that year of cerebral malaria (he is fittingly commemorated in the scientific name of the Mekong Wagtail *Motacilla samveasnae*), made an astonishing discovery. On finding some Bengal Floricans at Kruos Khraom in Stung Sen district, he began making inquiries of local people there, and was told that every year no fewer than 30–60 birds were shot in the area. Two separate reports reached Sam of two hunters each shooting 200 birds earlier that year. Further enquiry suggested that between 300 and 600 birds were being traded annually, either alive or as fried food, from 15 stalls at one market in Srayov commune. A population of Bengal Floricans of international significance had been found at the Tonle Sap floodplain grasslands (Goes & Sam 1999).

The Tonle Sap is a remarkable phenomenon. A riverine lake that flows into the Mekong at Phnom Penh, it is fed from two sources. For most of the year it receives the normal inflow of rivers on its western, northern and eastern shores. However, from May to September floodwater backs up as monsoon rains combine with the Mekong's glacial meltwater to reverse the flow of the lake, so that it fills and spreads to flush across a huge area of land. At its lowest, in spring, the lake is only a metre deep and 3,000km² in area; at its highest, in late summer, it is nine metres deep and covers 16,000km². Fish thrive on the nutrients of the floodwaters, and Cambodians thrive on the fish: no less than 70% of Cambodia's protein intake originates in the Tonle Sap (Bonheur & Lane 2002). Moreover, the floodwaters allow the many human settlements that ring the lake to grow rice – widely dubbed 'deepwater rice' – in the wet season. The stubbles and grains that remain when the waters begin to recede after October provide food for huge numbers of rodents and wintering songbirds, and hence for high densities of birds of prey. Waterbirds, many of them globally threatened, follow the shifting margins of the lake in good numbers, and where longer and shorter grasses form a mosaic (typically the result of human burning) the Bengal Floricans come to display and breed every spring, starting in February. It was at this time that birds were being shot and caught.

New York's Wildlife Conservation Society (WCS) had established a programme in Cambodia some years before Sam's discovery, and a campaign was rapidly rolled out to eliminate the hunting of floricans for food in the area he had surveyed. Large-scale trapping of the species perhaps only began in the 1990s, as it is inconceivable that such high numbers of birds could have been taken from the wild for any extended period, and the political turmoil of earlier decades may have precluded such activity. Even so, the damage of such persecution was clearly severe and unlikely easily to be reversed. At the start of the twenty-first century, the number of Bengal Floricans in Cambodia was estimated to be around a thousand, but already drainage was replacing persecution as the greater threat to the species. A two-pronged initiative was launched to implement practical conservation measures, including the identification and establishment of Important Bird Areas (IBAs), and one to research the ecology of the species so as to determine as clearly as possible what conditions and management it needs to maintain its numbers and range.

The research, under the direction of Paul Dolman at the University of East Anglia in the UK, has revealed much about the species' habitat use, population density and movements (Davidson 2004, Gray *et al.* 2009a). Displaying males prefer shorter-grass areas, whereas breeding females prefer taller cover, so a mosaic of different grassland types is needed (Gray *et al.* 2009b). Densities are low, with around one displaying male per five square kilometres (Gray *et al.* 2009a). All these lines of investigation have contributed vital information for the conservation effort (Gray *et al.* 2007). More recently, research that involved catching floricans and fitting them with satellite tags has revealed a great deal about the movements of the birds of Tonle Sap. This technology has answered the mystery of where the birds go when rising flood waters inundate the area in the wet season (Packman 2011). When the flood waters do not rise too far, some birds are able to survive in the drier parts of Tonle Sap, but in wetter years most birds are forced into thicker savanna woodland habitats up to 40 km from their breeding sites. Unfortunately, most of these non-breeding areas fall outside existing protected areas and are as threatened with conversion to agriculture and plantations as the grassland itself. Clearly, the conservation of Cambodia's Bengal Floricans will require considerably more than just the protection of the flooded grasslands of Tonle Sap.

This male Bengal Florican has its plumage ruffled as part of its display (J.C. Eames).

The single most vital discovery of all this research was the terrifying rate of land-use change on the floodplain particularly after 2005 (Gray *et al.* 2009a, Packman *et al.* 2013). That year, massive machines appeared across the grasslands for digging water-retaining walls and irrigation dykes. Investors from Phnom Penh, backed by money believed to be coming from outside the country, had realised that by damming the seasonal floodwater enormous areas of the plain could be converted to dry-season rice production. In the course of a year a formerly intact block of grassland of 180km² was converted almost entirely to rice. By June 2006, 50% and 90% respectively of the IBAs identified for Bengal Floricans at Stoung Chikreng and Veal Srangai had been lost (Gray *et al.* 2009a). The area of dry-season rice production on reclaimed grassland increased from 50km² in 2005 to nearly 400km² in 2009 (Packman *et al.* 2013). Of the grasslands surviving to 2009, only around a quarter were under some form of protection, and by 2011 over 25% of the grassland in these protected areas had been lost (Mahood *et al.* 2012). The speed of the calamity recalled that which befell the terai after DDT was used to rid it of malaria. The fact that this appropriation of traditional rice-growing land was taking place without the consent or wish of the local communities prompted WCS to propose a suite of 'Integrated Farming and Biodiversity Areas' (IFBAs), which would demarcate tracts of grassland on which no development would be permitted. The idea was taken up with enthusiasm in a project involving WCS, BirdLife International in Indochina and Cambodia's Forestry Administration, and IFBAs were established as early as August 2006 in several areas being targeted by private commercial investors. Altogether five such areas, covering some 350km² of grassland, were designated for the protection of biodiversity and local livelihoods within the floodplain.

This did not mean that the spectre of extinction had vanished. Not all the grasslands of the floodplain could be designated as IFBAs, and the land-grab continued. Between January 2005 and March 2007, 28% of the grassland cover was lost from a sample of plots being monitored by the researchers. When extrapolated to the entire floodplain, the number of male Bengal Floricans was estimated to have fallen from 416 to 294 in that two-year window (Gray *et al.* 2009a). Worse, many private commercial investors in Cambodia have not been greatly troubled by the law. In 2007 they made land-grabs within some of the IFBAs and simply converted them to dry-season rice and they have been continuing to do so, in clear contravention of legal proclamations, ever since. In a matter of just ten years, the Tonle Sap floodplain has gone from a haven for wildlife to something far too rapidly approaching what Philip Round, contemplating the chemically treated, birdless rice-paddies of Thailand, has memorably referred to as 'a bright green, poisoned landscape'. The race to save the Bengal Florican still has long to run.

Chapter 8
Liben Lark *Heteromirafra archeri*
CRITICALLY ENDANGERED

The larks in the peculiar African genus *Heteromirafra* have long interested taxonomists and conservationists. In structure they are quite unlike any other larks, their long legs and necks and small, almost triangular heads giving them a most distinctive appearance. Their ranges are tiny and fragmented, suggesting that the genus is a relic of an ancient group that was formerly more widespread. Indeed, these birds might be the most primitive of larks, perhaps ancestral to all others in the family (de Juana *et al.* 2004). The weak fluttering flight, soft flight feathers, pencil-thin tails and brief aerial song display, during which the bird seems barely able to retract its long legs, all suggest birds with limited powers of travel (Collar *et al.* 2008). As so often, taxonomic distinctiveness walks hand in hand with rarity, and both species in the genus are globally threatened. Rudd's Lark *H. ruddi* inhabits the high veldts of eastern South Africa, where it is rare and threatened by changes in grassland management (Maphisa *et al.* 2009). It was once listed as Critically Endangered but research showing it to be more widespread than previously thought resulted in its downlisting to Vulnerable. The other species in this genus has a complex taxonomic history that has only recently been disentangled (Spottiswoode *et al.* 2013). Between 1918 and 1920 Geoffrey Archer, governor of British Somaliland, collected at least 18 specimens of a new species of lark at the Wajale Plain, close to the border with Ethiopia, in an area of tussocky grassland that has since been greatly degraded. This new species was eventually named after him as Archer's Lark and given the scientific name of *Heteromirafra archeri*. Despite numerous searches of the area between 1970 and 2010, Archer remains the only ornithologist ever to have seen the species in Somaliland, and the population of birds he found appears to have been lost. In 1968, some 600km to the southwest of the locality of Archer's Lark, Christian Érard collected a specimen of a strange lark from the

The Liben Lark, as with the other member of the peculiar and perhaps ancient genus Heteromirafra, *has a characteristic small-headed, upright appearance with a long, thin tail (Paul F. Donald, RSPB).*

Liben Plain, near the town of Negelle in a region of southern Ethiopia inhabited by the Borana tribe of the Oromia peoples (Érard 1975). A further specimen was collected there by John Ash in 1974, before the first had been described or was known about (Ash & Olson 1985). At the time, neither Érard nor Ash realized the importance of their discovery, so they paid little attention to its population or habitat. When in 1975 the importance of their specimens was recognized, this lark was described as a new species, the Sidamo Lark *Heteromirafra sidamoensis*. The species has never been seen anywhere else in southern Ethiopia. In 2009, in order to help engender local support for the species' conservation and to reflect changes in administrative regions, which meant that Sidamo Province ceased to exist after 1995, the English name of the species was changed to Liben Lark (Collar 2009). Thus it appeared that there were two species of *Heteromirafra* larks in the Horn of Africa, Archer's Lark in Somaliland and Liben Lark in Ethiopia, both with tiny ranges. The two were certainly known to be very similar indeed, differing only in subtle shades of colour (and colour in larks is known to vary within species to match the colour of the local soils), but with the apparent loss of Archer's population it was impossible to compare the two in terms of their ecology, song or behaviour. However, sightings of what appeared to be a *Heteromirafra* lark near the town of Jijiga in north eastern Ethiopia, only around 50km from the Wajale Plain in Somaliland, raised hopes that Archer's Lark was not lost. In early 2011, a visiting birdwatcher photographed a lark near Jijiga that was clearly a *Heteromirafra*, and, to researchers studying the Liben Lark far to the southwest, the similarity to that species was remarkable. An expedition to the Jijiga area a few months later succeeded in capturing several birds, taking blood samples and recording the song. Using a range of analyses, including extraction of DNA from the foot pads of some of Archer's old museum specimens, it became clear that the birds at Jijiga are indeed the same as those found by Archer over the border in Somaliland, and, perhaps more important, they are also identical in all respects to the birds on the Liben Plain (Spottiswoode *et al.* 2013). In other words, the Horn of Africa supports only a single species of *Heteromirafra* (for which the scientific name *archeri* has priority, but which retains the English name Liben Lark). Although extremely similar in plumage and structure, Rudd's Lark of southern Africa is genetically distinct and has a very different song display.

Statistical models of distribution suggest that the small fragments of grassland near Jijiga and on the Liben Plain are the only home of this species, although there may be other populations of the species still to be discovered if it also occurs in other habitats. It is likely that these fragments are the remnants of a formerly much larger range that spread continuously from Somaliland to southern Ethiopia, and indeed the genetic analyses suggested that the Liben and Jijiga populations have not long been separated (Spottiswoode *et al.* 2013).

MAINLAND AFRICA'S FIRST BIRD EXTINCTION?

The discovery of a second population of the Liben Lark at Jijiga gave scant comfort to conservationists working to save what had been until then the only known population of the species on the Liben Plains. The species' survival in two small remnant populations at the ends of what had once must have been a far larger range attested to decades of decline. Both remaining populations are small and, certainly in the case of the Liben population, declining rapidly. When in 1975 the Liben Lark was recognised as a new species, its threat status was not known, so it was placed in the old IUCN category Indeterminate (Collar & Stuart 1985). In 1994, concerns that its habitat might be deteriorating led to its uplisting to Endangered, but this change coincided with the first observation of the species alive in the field, along with some reassuring evidence that the pressures on the grasslands of the Liben Plain were not as great as previously thought (Robertson 1995, Collar 1997a). Thereafter the species became one of many for which little information existed but for which no particularly severe threat was recognised, and it was subsequently downlisted to Vulnerable (BirdLife International 2000). It only became apparent after visits in 2006 by Claire Spottiswoode and colleagues that the species required serious study and rapid re-evaluation. This led to a series of visits to the Liben Plain in 2007 (the first population survey), 2008 (to assess the degree of agricultural encroachment on the plain) and 2009 (a second population survey), undertaken by teams of Ethiopian, British and Kenyan researchers under the aegis of the Ethiopian Wildlife and Natural History Society, the local BirdLife Partner, led by Mengistu Wondafrash. Unfortunately, the common pattern that improved knowledge of a species proves it to be less threatened than previously thought was not repeated, since these surveys have shown that the Liben population appears to be sliding rapidly towards extinction. The species was consequently uplisted to Critically Endangered in 2009 and, unless something can be done to stem a complete collapse in its population, the Liben Lark seems set to become Africa's first-ever recorded mainland bird extinction.

Liben Lark fly-catching while in song-flight, a very unusual behaviour in larks. The extremely long hindclaws suggest that the structure of the grassland currently found on the Liben Plain is unsuitable for the species, which is poised to become Africa's first mainland bird extinction (Andy and Gill Swash, worldwildlifeimages.com).

Increasing areas of bare ground on the Liben Plain favour larks with short claws, such as this Somali Short-toed Lark Calandrella somalica: *in contrast, the long hindclaw of the Liben Lark suggests an affinity for higher grass cover (Paul F. Donald, RSPB).*

The first population survey in 2007 confirmed suspicions that the species was seriously threatened. Its range, previously thought to be roughly 750km², was found to be less than one twentieth that size and the population, previously judged to be around two thousand birds, was estimated at between just 90 and 256 individuals; moreover, there was a strong suspicion that the majority of these might be males (Spottiswoode *et al.* 2009). Measurements of grass height and cover in occupied and unoccupied parts of the Liben Plain showed that the Liben Lark strongly prefers taller grass and avoids bare ground. When the population survey was repeated in 2009, researchers were dismayed by the speed with which the grassland had deteriorated. In just two years, the grass had become significantly shorter, the area of bare ground had almost doubled, and much grassland had been lost to arable cultivation, which the larks appear to avoid completely. As a result, the number of birds recorded along transects fell by over 40% (Donald *et al.* 2010), a rate of decline which, if not arrested, will result in extinction within a very few years. Moreover, grassland degradation was found to have been greatest in areas that had held the most birds two years previously. Even more worryingly, almost all records were of single males; indeed, only two definite females were seen in 2009. Although males are inevitably more easily detected than females because of their song flights, researchers followed a number of male birds for long periods without seeing them encounter a female. It is very likely, therefore, that males greatly outnumber females, a common pattern in endangered species (see p.33), including other threatened larks such as the Raso Lark *Alauda razae* (Chapter 13) and Dupont's Lark *Chersophilus duponti* (Suárez *et al.* 2009). This imbalance might result from predation of females at the nest, which is more likely to occur when nesting cover is much reduced. Up to the end of 2012, only four nests of the Liben Lark had ever been found on the Liben Plain, and of these two were placed under isolated plants that stood out against the short sward of the plain, making it easy for predators to search from plant to plant for nests. Predators destroyed both nests, and at one the female was killed (Collar *et al.* 2008). If only a few females survive, the species may be even closer to extinction than the dwindling counts of singing males might suggest.

No detailed information on the Liben Lark's habitat was collected prior to recent surveys, but there is ample evidence that the grassland of the Liben Plain has suffered severe degradation that has accelerated in recent times. Almost forty years after making his discovery, Christian Érard recalled that the habitat from which his specimen was collected was waist-high grass, of which there was much in the vicinity though it was by no means continuous (Collar *et al.* 2008). When John Ash collected the second specimen, he described the Liben Plain as having much new grass but also 'extensive areas of tall dead grass, some of it forming tussocks'. References to the presence of long grass on the Liben Plain, and the bird's association with it, were made by visiting ornithologists until as recently as 1997 (Robertson 1995, Francis & Shirihai 1999, Collar *et al.* 2008). Local people recall that the grass on the plain was so high that until recently children used to make temporary rain shelters simply by tying together the tops of standing grasses. Today, however, the grassland on the Liben Plain is very different, and nothing resembling tall-grass habitats has been seen during recent surveys. So heavily grazed is it by cattle that no grass over a few centimetres tall remains. Furthermore, surface erosion has created extensive patches of bare soil between the remaining clumps of grass. Far less is known about the population size and trends of the recently discovered population of the species at Jijiga, due partly to security problems in the area, but brief visits to the area suggest that the same problems may be occurring there. Indeed, measurements of grass height at both sites in May 2011 suggested that the grassland fragments at Jijiga were in even poorer condition than the Liben Plain. As on the Liben Plain, the birds at Jijiga were found in areas of higher than average grass cover (Spottiswoode *et al.* 2013).

A further indication of the species' historically preferred habitat can be found by examining its morphology. Not only does it possess relatively long legs and neck, but it also has a very long hindclaw on the foot, a feature of larks using thick grass habitats, since it helps them to walk over dense mats of vegetation (Green *et al.* 2009). In contrast, the Somali Short-toed Lark *Calandrella somalica*, which is abundant on the Liben Plain, has as its name suggests the short claws of species associated with bare ground. Grassland changes that have brought the Liben Lark to the verge of extinction appear to have favoured the far more common and widespread *Calandrella*. Further clues to the Liben Lark's preferred habitat can be found by looking at the other species in this strange genus. As with the Liben Lark in Ethiopia, an increase in the extent of bare ground has been implicated in local losses of Rudd's Larks in South Africa (Maphisa *et al.* 2009). Rudd's Lark also shows a preference for lightly grazed grass that has been recently burned; nesting starts earlier and lasts longer on grassland burned shortly before the start of the breeding season. The loss on the Liben Plain of an annual grass burning regime, which not only prevents scrub encroachment but also provides a patchwork of open areas for feeding and taller, denser grass for nesting, might also therefore have affected the Liben Lark.

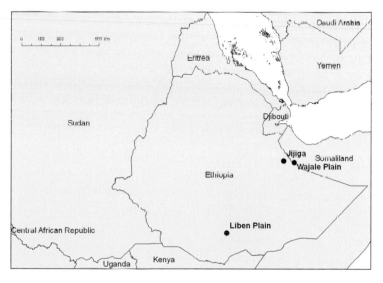

The three known locations of Liben Lark, showing the species' highly fragmented distribution. The population at Wajale is probably extinct.

GRASSLAND ON THE POINT OF COLLAPSE

It seems certain that the tiny population of the Liben Lark is declining due to degradation of its grassland habitat. Until recently, the rangelands of southern Ethiopia were among the most productive pastures in Africa because of the highly effective traditional 'Geda' system of grassland management practised there (Angassa 2002). This involved the movement of cattle around the landscape in response to rainfall and the careful avoidance of overgrazing. Traditional communal management of grazing lands by pastoralists not only maintains the quality of the grassland, but is also a better system than ranching for helping people and cattle to survive periods of drought (Angassa & Oba 2007). A good rangeland from a pastoralist's perspective is also a good rangeland for wildlife, and there is a strong positive correlation between the condition of rangelands as measured by pastoralists and their biodiversity as measured by scientists (Oba *et al.* 2008). Traditional Borana grazing practices are still recognised by local pastoralists as essential for sustainable rangeland management, but pastoralism is coming under increasing pressure, through incentives to reduce the seasonal movements of people with their livestock and the selling off of common land to individuals or businesses (Angassa & Beyene 2003). The construction of watering holes for cattle has encouraged the permanent settlement of people and their cattle, and a consequent rise in livestock density (Angassa *et al.* 2006). This loss of transhumance (the seasonal movement of livestock and their herders) has been a common trend in other parts of Africa and has severe impacts on wildlife (Western *et al.* 2009). Changes in land management and land ownership throughout the Borana zone have intensified the pressure on the remaining communal grasslands of the Liben Plain, as pastoralists from an increasingly wide area around it are now forced to bring their cattle to these dwindling commons. News in August 2009 of a herd of perhaps 200,000 cattle being driven northwards into southern Ethiopia to escape drought in Kenya raised yet further concerns for the survival of the grassland of the Liben Plain and its endemic lark, although on this occasion this super-herd did not reach the plain.

Not only is the grassland of the Liben Plain declining in quality, it is also declining in area. The loss of native browsing animals and the cessation of traditional fire management have allowed acacia scrub to encroach from the edges of the plain, a common problem in poorly managed rangelands across Africa, since grazing by cattle alone is not sufficient to prevent encroachment (Roques *et al.* 2001, Angassa & Oba 2009). Scrub invasion is likely to accelerate, since overgrazing leads to a reduction in the long grasses that fuel natural fires, and a reduction in fire leads to increased woody growth. Over the millennia, the areas of the world's grasslands have contracted or expanded depending on whether the climate favours herbaceous vegetation, with the biomass largely below ground,

The Liben Plain has suffered severe habitat degradation because of overgrazing and soil erosion (Paul F. Donald, RSPB).

or woody species whose biomass is largely above ground. Rising atmospheric carbon dioxide concentrations and changes in the shape of the Earth's orbit promote climatic conditions that favour the development of woody vegetation over grass, and the planet's grasslands appear to be suffering a long period of higher than average encroachment (van Auken 2009). Within the lifetimes of local village elders currently residing around the Liben Plain, four of seven villages formerly located in open grassland have become surrounded by thick scrub. The open grassland that remains on the plain, now covering less than 35km², represents the last remnant of an ecosystem that formerly spread across much of the Borana region. Fennel and other plants are also invading the plain, although there is no evidence that they are yet having an impact on the Liben Lark.

SEEKING A RANGELAND REVIVAL

Despite its desperate plight, the Liben Lark is not a hopeless case, since the conservation actions it requires have the full and active support of many local people. Pastoralists around the Liben Plain are increasingly worried about the worsening condition of their grasslands, especially as some townsfolk are unilaterally appropriating some of it for arable agriculture, further reducing the area of remaining grassland. The milk yield of cattle on the plain has fallen to just 2% of its previous level (Spottiswoode *et al.* 2009), and worries about the effects of drought on their cattle weigh heavily on pastoralists, who depend on them entirely. Sustainable use of Ethiopia's rangelands in the future will require a greater focus on regulating crop farming and ranching, as well as reintroducing fire where necessary to control the expansion of bush cover (Angassa & Oba 2008). If the Liben Lark's extinction is to be prevented, substantial areas of the Liben Plain need to be temporarily closed off to grazing cattle to promote grassland recovery, provide suitable feeding and breeding habitat for the lark and reduce surface soil erosion. Such exclosures have been established by international aid agencies near the Liben Plain and have resulted in grassland recovery within as little as a year. The restoration of the Liben Plain already enjoys strong local support from an association of village elders, local authorities and development organisations, who in May 2009 unanimously requested the help of conservationists to achieve this aim (Donald *et al.* 2010).

Diminished grazing resources and political instability have helped transform the Borana region from one of Africa's richest rangelands into an area blighted by famine and ethnic clashes (Coppock 1994). A problem whose social dimensions have preoccupied agronomists and development agencies for decades could be addressed, at least in a small way, by actions taken by the international conservation community to protect a small brown bird from extinction, showing that conservation and social development are not incompatible. A longer term aim of the current conservation strategy for this species, and one that will again bring considerable benefits to local people, is to clear encroaching acacia thorn scrub and so increase the area and quality of land available for both birds and grazing livestock. Field surveys undertaken in 2012 indicated that the removal of encroaching scrub on part of the Liben Plain led to rapid recolonisation of the area by breeding Liben Larks, and further scrub clearance is planned. Conservationists are testing other, less conventional, ways to help the Liben Lark. Spotted Hyenas *Crocuta crocuta* sometimes cross the Liben Plain, leaving the occasional pile of dung behind them. Hyena dung appears to deter cattle from grazing nearby, and small patches of taller grass grow as a result. Ethiopian researchers are now assessing the use of lion and hyena dung to provide small oases of longer grass for Liben Larks. However, such patches of good habitat might also attract predators, so the researchers are also using artificial nests filled with eggs made out of modeling putty to collect imprints of the teeth of predators and so work out which ones might take nests. Whether or not these ingenious methods will help to prevent the Liben Lark from becoming Africa's first recorded mainland bird extinction remains to be seen.

Chapter 9
Yellow-crested Cockatoo *Cacatua sulphurea*
CRITICALLY ENDANGERED

Driving through the suburbs of Sydney or looking over agricultural landscapes elsewhere in Australia, it is difficult not to be impressed by the sheer abundance of cockatoos. Species like the Little Corella *Cacatua sanguinea* form vast flocks that can reach almost plague-like proportions. However, the abundance of cockatoos is, or rather was, not just an Australian phenomenon. On visiting the Indonesian island of Sumba at the end of the nineteenth century, the American entomologist and bird collector William Doherty remarked 'cockatoos are so numerous that I have seen the trees white with them!' (Hartert 1896). These were exciting times for Doherty, who on leaving Sumba travelled to Bali where he came face-to-face with a tiger. One hundred years later the tiger was a distant memory in Bali, and excessive trade had seemingly reduced the distinctive Sumba endemic *citrinocristata* race (with a flaming orange rather than sulphur-yellow crest) of Yellow-crested Cockatoo to just a handful. By then, the cockatoos were in trouble not just on Sumba but on all the islands of the East Asian archipelagos: populations of Yellow-crested Cockatoo were in freefall throughout its native Wallacea, while the Salmon-crested Cockatoo *C. moluccensis* on Seram, the White Cockatoo *C. alba* from the north Moluccas and the Tanimbar Corella *C. goffiniana* (Tanimbar islands) were all extremely heavily traded and presumed to be declining. Further to the north the Philippine Cockatoo *C. haematuropygia* was being decimated across its native islands.

Being attractive, intelligent and long-lived birds, parrots are very popular as pets, and cockatoos have a particular allure. Their separate family status within the parrot order Psittaciformes is based on several major points of difference: unlike other parrots they have a gallbladder, distinctive skull and arterial structures, downy young and, more to the point for pet lovers, striking crests and a complete absence of blues and greens in the plumage. The great majority of cockatoos are thus either greyish-black or pure white in body plumage, albeit with flashes of red, pink or yellow in the crests or tails. In terms of popular appeal, the white ones are especially alluring, perhaps in part because all-white birds in nature are rare (at least outside the heron family). The cockatoos of Indonesia and the Philippines are all white, but comprise three types: Yellow-crested has a long crest that curls forward, Salmon-crested and White have long crests that curl back, and Tanimbar Corella and Philippine Cockatoo have small, backward-curving crests. Unsurprisingly, the cockatoos inhabiting islands with the highest human populations have been the most heavily exploited and depleted: the Yellow-crested and Philippine Cockatoos are consequently both Critically Endangered, while the White Cockatoo on the more sparsely settled islands of the north Moluccas is Vulnerable, and the Sulphur-crested Cockatoo *Cacatua galerita* of New Guinea and Australia is not threatened.

THE GROWTH OF INTERNATIONAL TRADE

Trade in wild-caught parrots is not a new phenomenon: an amazon parrot was the first acquisition Columbus is believed to have made in the New World. Cockatoos, too, have been kept as pets as long as people have had access to them. Birds started to arrive in Europe early, presumably with the return from the East Indies of some of the first spice traders, and from the Philippines, where Spain established a colony in 1565. Joseph Wright's celebrated oil painting 'An Experiment on a Bird in the Air Pump' (1768) depicts an unfortunate cockatoo (in size and coloration perhaps a Philippine Cockatoo) being deprived of oxygen, its near-sacrifice (the experiment is not necessarily intended to kill, merely to demonstrate an effect) suggesting that even at this time many tropical birds were not only readily available but also relatively affordable in western Europe. Two centuries later, however, the scale of such trade had changed beyond recognition. The rapid growth in international jet air transport in the 1960s, coupled with ever-expanding commercial maritime networks, provided the basis for an entirely new dimension for the pet industry in which living animals and plants could be moved in a remarkably short time from one part of the planet to another. Consequently, concern steadily grew about the over-exploitation of animals, on the grounds of both conservation and compassion.

In the 1980s, a high proportion of the entire global population of Yellow-crested Cockatoos was taken to supply the trade in caged birds (Stefan Behrens).

In response to these concerns, the Convention on International Trade in Endangered Species of Wild Fauna and Flora (CITES) came into existence in 1975, as the policy response intended to ensure that global wildlife trade did not threaten the survival of any species. CITES signatory countries (175 states in all) have a duty to monitor wildlife trade to make sure that 'harvests' of animals and plants are 'non-detrimental'. The main instrument in CITES is the inclusion of species on its appendices: listing on Appendix I means that international trade is illegal and banned, while listing on Appendix II means that trade in species is strictly controlled through a quota system. Today, over 40,000 species of plant and animal have been placed on these appendices. It would be hard to overstate the importance of CITES and its achievements but it has, nevertheless, several serious drawbacks. First, it can only monitor and seek to regulate trade among its signatories – nations that do not join are free to trade as they please, either as exporters or as importers (although signatory countries are not supposed to deal with them). Second, it has no power to control domestic trade, the volume of which may be several times that of international trade in countries like Indonesia and the Philippines. Third, it depends on its signatories establishing strong enough customs controls and specialist police to be able to enforce the law to which they have committed themselves. In developing countries, especially those with dozens of islands and multiple exit points ('porous borders'), the challenge in terms of facilities, training, conflicting cultures and local political will is often beyond local capacity.

Certainly in recent decades the scale of global wildlife trade has been, and indeed remains, alarmingly high. In the early 1990s, TRAFFIC, the wildlife trade monitoring network of IUCN and WWF, estimated that legal commerce in animal and plant products was worth around £100 billion per year (www.traffic.org/trade), equivalent to the gross domestic product of countries such as Chile, Egypt or the Philippines (figures from the World Bank in 2008). CITES itself reported in excess of 1.5 million live birds being traded annually during the period 1995–1999. Of course, this trade is legitimate and perhaps often sustainable, in the sense that the harvest does not have a negative effect on wild populations. On the other hand, it is perhaps not surprising that in 2008 one-third (408 species) of all globally threatened birds were thought to be affected by overexploitation for food or trapping for the cagebird trade (BirdLife International 2008a). What the TRAFFIC and CITES figures show is that there is an enormous demand among peoples around the world for animals as pets and plants as ornaments or food. What the figures from BirdLife show is that legal supply, even at these high rates, simply cannot keep up. Consequently and inevitably, therefore, a great deal of additional supply comes from smuggling.

Indonesia has always found the management of its parrot trade problematic. To begin with, it has so many species within its borders: 77, many of them occurring as distinct subspecies on different islands. It also has a deep cultural tradition of catching and keeping birds in captivity, so there is a huge inbuilt national skill-base in the capture, movement and marketing of parrots. Furthermore, its very porous borders and proximity to the major international trading cities of Singapore and Hong Kong present enormous difficulties for those trying to control illegal trade and to enforce CITES. Since 1981, CITES has placed virtually all parrots on Appendix II, but the trade in the 1980s from Indonesia was so great that in 1984 alone CITES signatories reported importing no fewer than 41,000 of the country's cockatoos (Inskipp *et al.* 1988). More than 28,000 Yellow-crested Cockatoos were traded internationally in the five years between 1981 and 1985, a staggering figure considering that the two largest populations remaining to be conserved some twenty years later were those on Sumba (3,200) and Komodo (600) (BirdLife International 2001). Even more disturbing is that these trade figures included only those birds that survived the rigours of capture, storage and transport under often dreadful conditions. The numbers of birds that were taken from the wild but died before they could be traded might easily have been as many as those that survived, and sometimes more (Edwards & Nash 1992). For example, one shipment of 56 cockatoos inspected in Sumba's capital Waingapu in 1989 were being held in awful conditions: two days after their arrival in Jakarta a week later, only one bird in five was still alive.

Smaller parrot species such as lories (*Eos* and *Trichoglossus*) were also appearing in trade in large numbers. During the 1980s, up to 8,000 Rainbow Lorikeets *Trichoglossus haematodus* and more than 12,000 Red Lories *Eos bornea* were being exported from Indonesia every year (Inskipp *et al.* 1988). Trade also included species such as the Eclectus Parrot *Eclectus roratus* (despite its protected status under Indonesian law). Prices for parrots at markets within Indonesia ranged from *uang rokok* ('cigarette money') for a Red Lory *Eos bornea* to over $30 for a Yellow-crested Cockatoo (Marsden 1995). Of course, these were the prices paid to the trappers, usually indigenous young men who caught parrots using snares (often using decoy birds) or, more riskily, by climbing the large trees used for nesting and taking young from cavities. Sumba is home to many men who have fallen from trees and broken their backs while trying to catch young cockatoos; without formal health insurance, they are left with no means of supporting themselves. The money these people received did not reflect the prices paid by dealers and collectors for rare cockatoos in Europe and North America, where a cockatoo was priced at around £400 in 1995. This 'Western' price itself rose during the 1970s and 1980s as birds became rarer, a reflection of what conservationists call the 'anthropogenic Allee effect' (p.32).

HABITAT LOSS – A THREAT TO RIVAL TRADE?

At the same time as Indonesia's parrots were coming under growing pressure from bird trappers, the more pervasive threat to wildlife of tropical forest loss was also accelerating. This was driven by the conversion of huge areas of lowland forest to farmland, including plantations of sago and the first oil palms, burning of forest for pasture and, most important in terms of land area, selective logging – a process by which the most commercially valuable trees are harvested from forests which are thereafter left to regenerate. Many species of birds and other animals and plants were believed to be under threat from these habitat changes, although there was relatively little information on which species might be most affected, and to what extent forest loss or change might threaten species with extinction. The problem lay in the complexity and diversity of the Indonesian archipelago itself. While the western Sundaic islands of Sumatra, Java and Borneo were relatively well known, the situation on Sulawesi was less understood, and the many smaller islands of Wallacea such as Seram, Buru, Halmahera, Flores and Timor were practically or even actually unvisited by ornithologists since Doherty's day. No field guide existed, transport was uncomfortable, slow and undependable (or if none of these things then expensive), language problems for foreign visitors were significant, and many of the best areas were remote, sometimes dangerous and difficult to reach. Ornithological discoveries emerging from Indonesia were mainly of a descriptive nature: new species or subspecies for science, lists of species in certain protected areas and new bird records on individual islands. Almost nothing

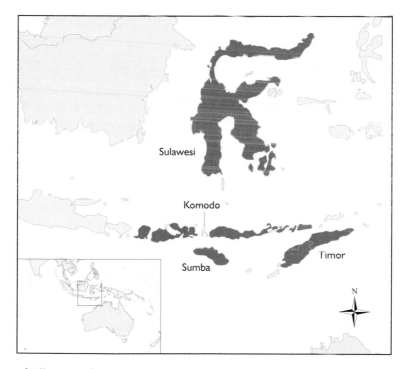

Original distribution of Yellow-crested Cockatoo.

was known about the conservation biology of parrots or any other species: their total populations, their tolerance of habitat change, even whether they were very common or hurtling towards extinction, were all unknown. For traded species such as the white cockatoos, in particular, it was unclear whether trade or habitat loss represented the greater threat, and it was time to find out.

The first step in addressing this problem was to gather baseline data on the abundance of parrots on several islands, and indeed to assess whether there were even any birds remaining. Reports from Seram (Bowler & Taylor 1989) suggested that the Salmon-crested Cockatoo was on the brink of extinction. It was estimated that 8,000–9,000 cockatoos were exported illegally from Seram each year from the north coast alone, and not more than 20 individuals were recorded in the wild during 40 days of fieldwork deep inside Manusela National Park, where the cockatoo should in theory and in law have been safe from trappers (Bowler & Taylor 1989). With commendable speed, the species was uplisted to Appendix I of CITES, banning all international trade, in 1989. On Sumba, a survey in 1989 recorded an 80% decline since 1984 in numbers of the 'Citron-crested Cockatoo', the *citrinocristata* subspecies of the Yellow-crested Cockatoo. Visitors to other islands reported that cockatoos were becoming very scarce. This rarity was a far cry from casual reports of even ten years before, let alone the great flocks that delighted Doherty in the nineteenth century. Parrots were found to be generally rare close to habitation, and common sense suggested that they were now restricted to the remotest areas, furthest away from trappers. Cockatoos were rare in logged forests, which were made easily accessible to trappers by logging roads. Prices of parrots within Indonesia were increasing steadily, and local people reaffirmed conservationists' fears that cockatoos had become extinct in many areas. The data were suggestive of species on the brink of extinction, but inexplicably there were still reports coming from local people in Indonesia of cockatoos being a pest and raiding farmers' crops (Jepson *et al.* 2001). Surely there were not enough cockatoos left to be considered an agricultural pest?

In the early 1990s, concerted efforts were made to examine the problem of trade and this time ecologists were armed with a new bird survey method called distance sampling, which allowed them to estimate the size of bird populations in a wide range of different habitats, including thick tropical forest. This was something of a breakthrough; with distance sampling, conservationists would now be able to relate the size of parrot populations in the wild to the numbers that were appearing in trade each year. Martin Jones of Manchester Metropolitan University (MMU) in the UK led a team to support the Indonesian Directorate General of Forest Protection and Nature Conservation (PHPA) on Sumba and Buru in 1989, while two researchers primed in distance sampling techniques visited Seram, Halmahera and other north Moluccan islands in 1991–1992, and a PHPA/BirdLife team visited Tanimbar in 1993.

The good news that emerged from these surveys was that no cockatoo appeared to be on the edge of extinction; in fact, there appeared to be more cockatoos left on the islands than had been thought. These are big places after all: Seram covers 17,000km², a little smaller than Wales and twice the size of Puerto Rico. So there is a lot of forest in which a cockatoo can live undetected, and many more survived there than the handful recorded by previous surveys. In the case of the Salmon-crested Cockatoo, there were even individuals present on the populous island of Ambon, just a bus ride away from the main city of the Moluccas, and flocks occurred quite close to villages, although only where good forest remained (Marsden 1992). In the north Moluccas, the results were not so encouraging – the global White Cockatoo population was estimated at around 50,000 birds, and the minimum number captured in 1991 was thought to be around 5,000 (Lambert 1993). So trade might have taken one or more in every ten birds each year, figures that were clearly unsustainable for a species that breeds slowly. The situation on Tanimbar, where the corellas were still said to be major crop pests, was different again (Jepson *et al.* 2001). Here the team reported population densities of almost 100 birds per square kilometre of forest – a huge figure, and quite possibly an overestimate, but still one suggesting that the corella remained relatively common despite pressure from trappers.

The situation appeared to be far worse in the Lesser Sundas – the chain of islands that stretches from Bali and Lombok to Timor – and Sulawesi. Yellow-crested Cockatoos had disappeared from most of their range, snuffed out on island after island, or clinging on in tiny numbers that offered little scope for effective conservation. Sulawesi was particularly badly hit: teams of trappers from Makassar travelled all over the island in the 1980s to capture birds at their roost sites (BirdLife International 2001). By the end of that decade the two strongholds appeared to be the well-wardened Komodo National Park (the 'dragon' being such a tourist money-spinner), where 'healthy numbers', including flocks of up to 20 birds, were reported in the early 1990s, and the rather isolated and culturally distinct Sumba, where there were reports that the endemic citron-crested race was apparently holding on. In 1989 and again in 1992, the MMU/PHPA teams estimated the total population of cockatoos on Sumba to be in the region of 3,200 individuals (Jones *et al.* 1995). A later study of the workings and volume of the parrot trade on the island indicated that perhaps around 1,600 Citron-crested Cockatoos had been exported each year from the island in the late 1980s and early 1990s, a level that clearly could not be sustained by the wild population (Cahill *et al.* 2006). That the trade continued on the island was not in doubt; two cockatoos were found in a box under the seat of a bus on which Jones's research team was travelling! A shipment of 26 birds was confiscated by wildlife officials from PHPA during their stay on the island. These birds were later released in a patch of forest on the island.

The conservationists were now armed with some hard data on the remaining numbers, distribution and habitat use of the Yellow-crested Cockatoo. The next question that needed to be addressed concerned the numbers that were being caught from the wild, arguably as difficult a task as getting information on population sizes in remote areas. CITES records showed that no fewer than 96,785 Yellow-crested Cockatoos had been exported legally from Indonesia between 1981 and 1992. However, getting information on the origin of these birds was not easy. It was not even known what proportion of them consisted of the distinctive citron-crested subspecies. The other thing that conservationists did not know was the extent to which the numbers of imported birds, reported through CITES, matched the numbers leaving the forest. As already noted, only birds traded openly and internationally are recorded in CITES data, so the figures exclude any birds that are for the domestic market within Indonesia, or which are smuggled to nearby countries, or which have already died between capture in the forest and clearing import customs.

TRADE CONTROLS AND BANS

With huge numbers of birds appearing in trade, and perhaps even larger numbers disappearing in trade, there was a clear need for action. With the exception of the Salmon-crested Cockatoo, already on Appendix I, all Indonesian cockatoos were listed on CITES Appendix II, thereby requiring Indonesia to ensure that the number it allows to be traded internationally is sustainable (or 'non-detrimental' in the language of CITES). To do this, the government issues harvest quotas, which are effectively licences to trade cockatoos. Of course, the system carries the risk (frequently fulfilled) that quotas will be accidentally or deliberately set too high, not enforced and generally ignored. It was, in effect, as easy as adding a zero on the end of 32 (in matching writing of course) to make the quota 320. This could not be allowed to continue. The Tanimbar Corella was next to be uplisted to Appendix I, at the eighth meeting of the CITES Conference of Parties held in Tokyo in 1992. This was controversial, and there is bad feeling to this day about the way that western CITES parties pushed it through despite having no evidence on which to base their arguments. In the event, the Tanimbar Corella remained quite common, and local communities were dealt a double blow: first, they were not allowed to gain important revenue from trading the cockatoos; second, the cockatoos remained common and responsible for serious damage to crops. A moratorium on the capture and trade of the Yellow-crested Cockatoo was put in place in 1994, so CITES signatories left it until the thirteenth CITES meeting in 2004 before uplisting the species to Appendix I.

These measures have certainly reduced the numbers of cockatoos reported in international trade. For Citron-crested Cockatoos, CITES figures for birds exported from Indonesia have been reduced from around 1,000 per year in the early 1990s down to a few hundred in the mid-1990s to almost none since then (Cahill *et al.* 2006). There is a slightly worrying increase in dubiously 'captive-bred' birds but the volume is not great in comparison to the 1980s. CITES has been helped by consumers in the west, who have becoming increasingly sensitised to the plight of cockatoos and other traded species. However, there is no evidence that domestic trade pressure has altered, or that new markets might not emerge. Furthermore, it is impossible to quantify the volume of illegal trade, as smuggled birds do not get reported. Thus a reduction in legal trade may simply have been replaced by an increase in illegal trade. Rumours of organised smuggling operations using fishing boats bound for Singapore are certainly worrying.

So the trade bans certainly appear to be have had an effect, but it was not clear whether this in turn led to increases in wild populations of cockatoos. In 2002, a team from the UK was able to revisit Sumba to undertake a repeat survey of the Citron-crested Cockatoo (Cahill *et al.* 2006). The team surveyed some of the forests visited in 1992 and even repeated some of the transects originally walked, using the same methods. What they found was encouraging. The amount of forest cover within the patches was similar to that in 1992 and cockatoos were recorded in bigger groups than ten years previously. Cockatoo densities at two forest sites had increased considerably, and at another site the population was at least stable. Less encouraging was that cockatoo numbers had decreased in one small forest patch, making extinction at this site imminent (and again showing how important habitat protection and management might be). The repeat survey was significant as, although measures such as the guarding of nest are effective in reducing parrot capture (Wright *et al.* 2001, Pain *et al.* 2006), this was one of the first occasions when ecologists sought to demonstrate the effects of a trade ban. It was immensely encouraging that the ban, coupled with the excellent educational work that has been conducted on Sumba for over a decade by Burung Indonesia (the BirdLife Partner in Indonesia), was indeed having a noticeably beneficial effect on the species' population (Cahill *et al.* 2006). Overall cockatoo density had increased from around two birds per square kilometre in 1992 to over four per square kilometre by 2002.

In 2005 there was a further twist in the trade-control tourniquet. In October of that year, the British government announced that imported birds housed in a quarantine centre in Essex had tested positive for the highly pathogenic H5N1 strain of avian influenza. There followed an almost immediate ban on the importation of wild-caught birds into the European Union. This ban was made permanent at the EU's chief veterinary officers' meeting in Brussels in July 2007. Many from the conservation world were delighted, regarding it as particularly good news for species such as the African Grey Parrot *Psittacus erithacus*, of which, according to CITES, over one-third of a million were legally traded across national borders between 1994 and 2003. Others were less enthusiastic, suggesting that a blanket ban on bird imports was inequitable and unlikely to reduce the problem (Cooney & Jepson 2006).

HOPES FOR THE FUTURE

The population of Sumba's Citron-crested Cockatoos has made a modest recovery, but densities remain low compared to cockatoo populations elsewhere, and there is a long way to go before the trees are again white with cockatoos. There is an argument that it would be unwise for conservationists to aim for such abundance in Indonesian cockatoos anyway, as some species are no doubt serious pests of maize and other crops. The population certainly has not recovered quickly and this pattern is mirrored by that of the Salmon-crested Cockatoo in Seram. There, scientists from the Wildlife Conservation Society looked at abundance around nine years after the CITES ban on export of the species, finding only a modest increase in the population even after this long period of apparent protection (Kinnaird *et al.* 2003). Perhaps this, and the slow rate of recovery in Citron-crested Cockatoos, tells us something about the current stresses and strains on cockatoo populations within Indonesia, something that was largely ignored during the 1980s. So much of the natural forest of Indonesia has been changed by people, either cut down completely to make way for plantations or agriculture or altered through selective logging, that the ecological niches of earlier times have been lost or greatly constrained; in this regard, parrots have often been among the biggest losers.

One of the main findings of research on the Indonesian cockatoos is that they need trees of a particular size, age and type in which to breed; on Sumba, for example, birds nest in cavities in very large trees, and in trees of only a handful of species (Marsden & Jones 1997). This finding is mirrored in several other parrot species around the world (Monterrubio-Rico *et al.* 2009). Holes suitable for large birds to use as nest cavities only generally form in trees of a type which, as they mature, develop fissures in their trunks or major limbs, often as a result of losing a large branch in a storm. However, in many places these are the very trees that are most sought after for their volume of timber. The consequence is that parrot populations, in particular cockatoos, have been seriously compromised in their breeding rates by the absence of suitable nest-sites. The birds can find food easily enough, and survive for many years, but their reproductive output may be too small to sustain the population in the long term. This might now be the most significant factor, over and above trade pressure, in the decline and disappearance of the Yellow-crested Cockatoo on many of the Sundaic islands where it once flourished.

Certainly on Sumba numbers of parrots in different patches of forest on the island proved to be strongly related to the number of likely nest sites (suitable big trees) in those forests (Marsden & Jones 1997). This was true not only for the cockatoo but also for little-traded species, meaning that parrot numbers were not just influenced by trade but also by habitat quality. However, on Sumba, at least, many large trees have been left purposely by local people precisely because they contain cockatoo nests (some trees contain three or four nests of more than one hole-nesting parrot or hornbill) and thereby offer the chance of a continuing source of income from trade. Some of the nesting trees are enormous, and the cockatoo nest cavities can be too high up even for the brave (or reckless) men of Sumba to reach. As well as being protected from raiders by height, some cockatoo nests are spared for other reasons. Areas held sacred are avoided, although outsiders might come in and take cockatoos, and one breeding pair of cockatoos at least was protected by a nest of ferocious hornets.

There are perhaps some glimmers of hope for the long-term survival of the Yellow-crested Cockatoo. The species remains listed by IUCN as Critically Endangered, but there is every possibility that it might drop to a lower category in the near future. In 2008, the Indonesian Parrot Project and Konservasi Kakatua Indonesia 'rediscovered' the *abbotti* subspecies of Yellow-crested Cockatoo on tiny Masakambing Island (just 500ha) in the Java Sea, where ten individuals were found. More importantly, conservationists now recognise that the 'hearts and minds' strategy of developing community relations and livelihoods can be just as effective as the 'shock and awe' of global trade bans. On Sumba, some excellent awareness programmes are being run by Burung Indonesia, modelled in part on the environmental education work of Paul Butler and RARE on Caribbean parrots many years before (Butler 1992). Coupled with these imaginative environmental education initiatives are robust actions against trappers and traders. Some trappers are finally being convicted: one was sentenced to seven months in prison. On the other hand, the latest data from Komodo National Park, the stronghold of Yellow-crested Cockatoo away from Sumba, is worrying. A recent survey of this apparently well-protected population has suggested that numbers have more than halved between 2000 and 2005, a rate perhaps more rapid than any population decline in the 1980s (Imansyah *et al.* 2005). What has caused this apparent decline is not known. Illegal trade is a distinct possibility, and other candidate explanations include disease, predation by young Komodo Dragons *Varanus komodoensis*, introduced predators, famine and the steady failure of recruitment to match mortality as a result of insufficient number of nest-sites.

That significant positive changes to the status of cockatoos, and to the mindsets of local people, can be brought about is further illustrated by the work of the Katala Foundation in the Philippines (Widmann & Lacerna Widmann 2008). The Philippine Cockatoo was once distributed throughout the Philippine archipelago and recorded from 52 islands as far north as Manila (BirdLife International 2001) and in many places it was common, but it was trapped out during the course of the twentieth century, and with particular intensity after 1980, leaving only two island groups where small but significant numbers survived: Palawan and related islands and Tawitawi and related islands (Lambert 1994). The latter have proved simply too dangerous for foreign conservationists to work there, but Palawan represented a real opportunity, and the Katala Foundation seized it. A tiny inshore island, Rasa, was home to some 25 cockatoos in 1998, but the population was being persistently poached and steadily reduced. The Katala strategy was to convert the poachers to wardens, and to make Rasa the focus of a small-scale tourism venture. Little could they have suspected that ten years later the Philippine government would identify the island as one of the top twelve birdwatching sites in the country! Numbers of birds on Rasa have steadily increased: in July 2008 there were 200 cockatoos at roost there and the foundation's portfolio of activities has expanded to other sites in the country. Always the basis for its work is the provision of alternative livelihoods, with ex-trappers being given discounts on agricultural tools, training to improve agricultural practices and low-interest loans to buy crop seed. However, as on Sumba, the steady building of local people's pride in their unique wildlife has also been a crucial dimension to the work, and is surely a vital means of ensuring the long-term success of the conservation endeavour.

Chapter 10
Rarity and extinction on islands

In the last five hundred years around 140 species of bird, and a similar number of subspecies, are known, with a reasonable degree of certainty, to have become extinct (Butchart *et al.* 2006b, Szabo *et al.* 2012b). These extinctions have been far from random in their geographical spread (Fig. 10.1). Most strikingly, 90% of them have been of species confined to islands, despite the fact that island birds make up less than one fifth of the world's species (Manne *et al.* 1999, Butchart *et al.* 2006b). There have been no confirmed extinctions of birds in the last 500 years on the continental mainlands of Europe, Africa or Asia, but nearly 30 on the islands of Hawaii alone. The number of extinct species on continents is likely to be greatly underestimated, since it is more difficult to be confident that a species has died out on a large landmass than on a small island; but even if the species that are possibly extinct on continents are included in the calculation, islands still show an extinction rate hugely in excess of that on continents (Butchart *et al.* 2006b, Pimm *et al.* 2006). Native island mammal populations have shown the same elevated rate of extinction (Alcover *et al.* 1998). A disproportionally high number of today's bird species that are listed on the IUCN Red List as Critically Endangered are also restricted to islands; when all the world's countries and other geopolitical states are ranked according to the proportion of their bird species that are globally threatened, the top twenty are all islands (Hilton-Taylor *et al.* 2009). Clearly, islands are of particular concern to conservationists and the birds on them face a range of threats that makes them uniquely vulnerable. The story of the world's rarest birds is therefore intimately linked to the fate of birds on islands.

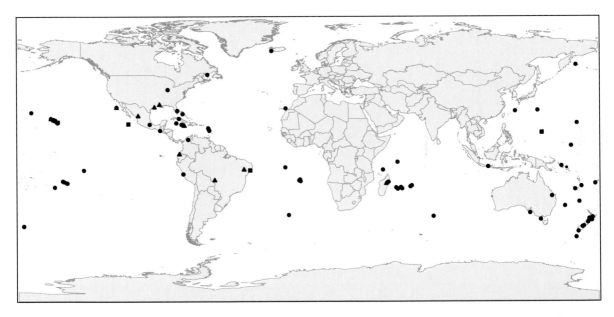

Figure 10.1. The localities of the last sightings of the 150 bird species that have become extinct in the last 500 years. The species include those listed by BirdLife International/IUCN as Extinct (circles), Extinct in the Wild (squares) and Critically Endangered (Possibly Extinct) (triangles). The great majority are on islands and Hawaii alone accounts for nearly 30 extinctions. From Butchart et al. *(2006b).*

ISLANDS AND THEIR BIRD COMMUNITIES

Alfred Russel Wallace (1823–1913), the father of biogeography and co-proponent of the theory of evolution by natural selection, presented in his book *Island Life* a classification of the world's islands that is still in use today (Whittaker & Fernandez-Palacios 2007). This divided them into three groups according to their geological mode of origin.

Continental islands (or land-bridge islands), such as the British Isles, Newfoundland, Sri Lanka, New Guinea, Borneo and Trinidad, are corrugations at the edges of continental plates, separated from their parental continents by shallow and generally narrow seas. Changing sea levels mean that on occasion these seas dry out and reconnect the island to the mainland. Because of these periodic reconnections, and similarities in geology, landscape and climate, bird communities of continental islands are sometimes very like those of the adjacent mainland, although certain species may be missing. Thus the bird community of Ireland resembles that of Britain but a number of species, for example the woodpeckers, are absent. In turn, a few species are absent from or rare in the UK that are found commonly in adjacent areas of continental Europe. Continental islands vary greatly in their complement of endemic species. Some, such as the British Isles and Newfoundland, support few if any. Others, particularly larger ones such as New Guinea, Borneo and Sri Lanka that have been isolated for longer from their continental mainland, can support many. The Chatham Islands, lying at the edge of the New Zealand plate and hence strictly continental islands, despite the great distance of ocean that separates them from New Zealand, once supported many endemic species but most are now extinct.

Continental fragments, also known as ancient continental islands or microcontinental islands, are chunks of land that became detached from continental landmasses through rifting during or since the break-up of Gondwanaland, which started around 160 million years ago. They continue to drift until they collide with a continent, as India did (a process that created a surge of evolution of new species, many now endangered, through the formation of the Himalayas). Examples of continental fragments include New Zealand, New Caledonia, Madagascar, Jamaica, Cuba and Socotra. A high proportion of the birds present on them are endemic because these islands have been isolated for a long time, sometimes far from other land; because they are often large, and so contain a wide range of habitats; and because they sometimes retain the descendants of ancient lineages. Continental fragments now support bird communities that are composed of species with at least four different modes of origin: the ancestors of species trapped on the island when it split off, the ancestors of species that arrived later and evolved into new forms, species that arrived unaided but did so too recently to evolve into new forms and species that have been deliberately or accidentally introduced by humans in recent times (Trewick & Gibb 2010).

Oceanic islands, such as Hawaii, the Galápagos, Mauritius, Montserrat, Cape Verde, the Canaries and most of the other small and isolated specks of land – sometimes merely coral atolls – that lie scattered across the world's oceans, were formed by submarine volcanic activity and so have never been connected to a continental landmass. Because these islands were initially sterile, the native bird communities of these islands are composed entirely of immigrants and their descendants. The more isolated the island, then the greater is the time gap between each successful bird colonisation, so the number of species present tends to be smaller and the proportion of endemics higher. Each colonisation can lead to the evolution of new forms that fit the particular conditions of their new homes, so many of the species found on oceanic islands are unique to them; indeed, much of what is known about the origins of the planet's biological diversity stems from research on island birds (Grant 2001). The degree of endemism on oceanic islands varies greatly and depends in large part on the isolation, size and age of the island. Small and geologically young islands formed relatively close to a continental landmass, such as the Azores and Canaries, have relatively few endemic species, whereas the bird communities of remoter, larger and older island groups, such as Hawaii and Galápagos, are made up almost entirely of endemic species. Clusters of islands tend to hold higher numbers of endemic species for their area than isolated islands, since a single colonisation event can lead to rapid speciation on each island. Hawaii's native bird fauna at the time of Polynesian colonisation contained only three species not endemic to the islands: Short-eared Owl *Asio flammeus*, Common Moorhen *Gallinula chloropus* and Black-crowned Night Heron *Nycticorax nycticorax*; all the passerines were endemic. Because even relatively large oceanic islands (the largest is Iceland) are geologically short-lived, surviving perhaps a few million years before being levelled by erosion or by volcanic upheaval, their endemic birds tend to have arrived relatively recently in geological

Island species, particularly those confined to small islands in the Pacific, have suffered high rates of extinction, and many of the world's rarest species today are confined to islands. For example, Polynesian Ground-dove Gallicolumba erythroptera *and Tuamotu Kingfisher* Todiramphus gambieri *of French Polynesia are both listed as Critically Endangered (Pete Morris).*

time and so often show fairly clear affinities to species still found at the source of colonisation. In contrast, some of the birds of ancient continental fragments like New Zealand have evolved into forms so different from any others that it is difficult to speculate what their ancestors were, even using modern genetic analyses (Trewick & Gibb 2010).

Rates of natural extinction on islands are high, especially on oceanic islands, as new colonists arrive to oust established ones, as chance events drive small populations to extinction and as islands move, grow old, erode and die (MacArthur & Wilson 1967, Williamson *et al.* 1989, Whittaker & Fernández-Palacios 2007). Furthermore, rates of evolution on islands are high because they have less complex and more changeable environments than continental landmasses, meaning that new arrivals have to adapt rapidly, so new species are quickly replaced by newer ones. Superimposed on this natural pattern of the birth and death of species on islands is that of human-driven extinction and human-aided colonisation, which have altered the natural communities of islands out of all recognition (Milberg & Tyrberg 1993). Some species, such as the Stephens Island Wren *Xenicus lyalli* (Chapter 11), have disappeared so rapidly that they are known only from bones or a few skins.

However, some patterns have been observed frequently enough to make possible a few generalisations about the nature of island bird communities (Whittaker & Fernandez-Palacios 2007). First, island communities tend to comprise fewer species than equivalent areas on continents. This is particularly true for oceanic islands and continental fragments that are distant from continental landmasses, and for less dispersive groups of animals, such as mammals and reptiles. Furthermore, smaller islands have fewer species per unit area than do larger islands. The reasons for this poverty in species are likely to relate to the high natural extinction rates and turnover of island species, particularly on smaller islands (Azeria *et al.* 2006), the reduced number of niches and resources available on small islands, the inability of a high proportion of the pool of potential colonists on adjacent continents to reach islands, and of course the ravages brought about by humans and their ragbag of camp followers (Whittaker & Fernández-Palacios 2007).

A second general pattern is that island bird communities tend to contain a higher proportion of endemic species with restricted ranges than do continental communities. Larger, more remote and more topographically diverse islands support more habitats and a wider range of environmental conditions than smaller ones, and so hold particularly high numbers of endemic species. One explanation for this is that when a species reaches a new island, particularly one that few if any others have yet reached, a process of adaptive radiation occurs by which increasing specialism on different resources by different subpopulations of the colonist species, perhaps aided by their isolation on different islands in the same group, leads to the formation of new species found nowhere else. The Galápagos (or Darwin's) finches and the Hawaiian honeycreepers (Chapter 14) are classic examples of this process; it is likely that these groups each evolved from a single ancestral species. However, adaptive radiation is not the only reason for the high frequency of endemism on islands. For example, islands may provide the final refuges for species formerly found over much larger areas.

A third general pattern is that islands support a higher proportion of rare and threatened species than do equivalent areas of adjacent continents. It is clear that, as in the case of extinctions, this is to a large extent the result of a number of changes in island environments brought about by humans. However, some island species are naturally rare because they occur on small islands that could never support large populations. Islands, and particularly oceanic islands, are often volatile and short-lived environments and natural disasters can bring small populations to the edge of extinction. However, while island species may be rare in respect of the tiny ranges they occupy, they are not necessarily rare within these ranges in terms of their population density, and many island birds, such as the Raso Lark *Alauda razae* (Chapter 13) occur at relatively high densities. This is a product of what ecologists call ecological release, a process whereby species on islands occupy wider niches than on mainlands and utilise a wider range of resources because of reduced completion in environments that may contain few other species.

Island bird communities may be characterised by a paucity of species, but the high rate of endemism and the huge number of islands that dot the world's oceans mean that islands actually support a very large number of species for their collective land area. Despite occupying only a tiny proportion of the planet's land surface, islands support over 1,750 species not found on continental landmasses, nearly 20% of the total number of known birds (Johnson & Stattersfield 1990). This makes them very important in the conservation of the planet's biological diversity, and islands feature heavily in attempts to prioritise the world's regions on the basis of the uniqueness and rarity of their wildlife.

THE VULNERABILITY OF ISLAND BIRDS

A striking and well documented example of the vulnerability of island birds is the ecological devastation of Guam, a self-governing US island territory in the western Pacific. Until 1950, Guam supported a number of endemic species that had survived numerous waves of human colonisation by different cultures, not to mention intense naval bombardments and the levelling of most of the island's forests during fierce fighting in the Second World War. It is not known when the first Brown Tree-snake *Boiga irregularis* arrived on the island, or how it got there, although it probably arrived between 1945 and 1952 as a stowaway in the hold of a cargo ship. The war-torn landscape of Guam, with its many rats and cockroaches, might have provided an ideal initial hunting ground for the snake. The first documented report was made near the main harbour in the south of the island in 1953. This was followed by a rising tide of reports as the snake spread rapidly across the island at a rate of around two kilometres per year. By 1968 it had reached the island's north coast and was almost ubiquitous. During the 1970s and 1980s the population continued to grow and the first reports were received of severe declines in native wildlife (Savidge 1984). The island's fauna was not adapted to predation by snakes, but the snakes were extremely well adapted to preying upon birds and their eggs. As a result of snake predation, largely of eggs and chicks, all of the island's native bird species have been greatly reduced in numbers or wholly extirpated; declines of over 90% in less than ten years were observed in many species (Wiles *et al.* 2003). Guam has lost all its breeding seabirds, ten of its original thirteen native forest birds, two of three native mammals and six of around ten native reptiles. The Guam Flycatcher *Myiagra freycineti* was common in the 1970s but was extinct by 1983. The last Guam Rail *Gallirallus owstoni* in the wild was seen in 1987, although thankfully a captive population was established just in time to prevent its complete extinction through the heroic efforts of the late Bob Beck, the leading conservationist on the islands. The species now survives in snake-proof enclosures on Guam and in a number of zoos in the USA, and a small population released onto the neighbouring island of Rota appears to be viable. The Mariana Crow *Corvus*

One of the many victims of the introduction of Brown Tree-snakes to Guam is the Nightingale Reed Warbler Acrocephalus luscinius, *which was wiped out from Guam in the 1960s and survives now only on Saipan and Alamagan; it is listed as Critically Endangered (Jon Hornbuckle).*

kubaryi (Critically Endangered) has been wiped out from Guam and survives in dwindling numbers only on Rota. In contrast, introduced bird species fared rather better, as they originated in regions where snakes were always present and so were better adapted to cope with them. Even so, snakes may now outnumber birds on Guam by around four to one.

The full extent of the ecological damage wrought by the snakes is still becoming apparent. Trees pollinated by birds are starting to suffer as their seed production is dwindling. Birds are also important seed dispersers, and their loss means that the reduced numbers of seeds now being set are likely simply to fall in the shade of the parent tree and not germinate or spread (Mortensen *et al.* 2008). The loss of birds and native bats, important predators of insects, raises fears that insect-borne diseases might become more prevalent. The island's human residents are plagued by power cuts caused by snakes trying to cross overhead power lines. Guam is an important maritime hub with a busy harbour and military airbase and snakes have already been accidentally exported from there to other islands in the region, whose environments are now starting to suffer as Guam's did. Snakes from Guam have reached as far as Hawaii and Texas, hiding in cargo crates on ships or dropping onto tarmac runways from the wheel housings of aircraft. In 1994, a Brown Tree-snake was found in a cargo container from Guam on the tiny island of Pohnpei, home of the Pohnpei Starling *Aplonis pelzelni* (Critically Endangered) and several other endemic birds.

The devastation of Guam's birds, and those of many other islands around the world, raises the question of why it is that island birds are so vulnerable to introduced predators. Part of the answer lies in the fact that islands are often poor in resources, so there is strong pressure on birds to evolve ways to reduce their energy expenditure (McNab 2002, McNab & Ellis 2006). Flight is clearly very energy demanding, not just in terms of the aerobic exertions of flapping but also for the growth and maintenance of sufficiently large wing bones, muscles and flight feathers to make it possible. Because of this, flightlessness is an extremely effective strategy for surviving on islands without predators and it has arisen independently many times in a wide range of bird families (Slikas *et al.* 2002). Loss of flight can occur very rapidly in island species, not over millions of years but over a relatively small number of generations; indeed the flightless condition might evolve even before reproductive isolation between species is complete (Kirchman 2009). A small number of species alive today, such as the White-throated Rail *Dryolimnas cuvieri* of Madagascar and other Indian Ocean islands, have both flying and flightless subspecies. The rapidity with which birds of many different families have evolved a flightless condition after arriving on predator-free islands indicates its success as an adaptation for surviving on islands and suggests that perhaps flight in birds originally evolved primarily as a way of avoiding predators. The success of flightlessness as an adaptation to surviving island life can be appreciated by considering that in prehistoric times perhaps as many as 10% of all the bird species on the planet were flightless rails (Steadman 1995). Superb island adaptation as it might be, defencelessness often proved disastrous when the first canoes or galleons appeared over the horizon. Flightless birds account for only a small proportion of recorded recent extinctions on islands, but the vast majority of prehistoric ones (Steadman 1995). This does not to imply that island species are wholly defenceless, since they retain the ability to avoid their natural predators; the Laysan Duck *Anas laysanensis* (Critically Endangered) of Hawaii does not fly when it is alarmed as most ducks do but instead freezes, an excellent way to avoid detection by its natural avian predators but a suicidal tactic to adopt when it is being pursued by an introduced mammalian carnivore (Moulton & Marshall 1996).

Another way for island birds to save energy is to change their metabolism, and many have evolved a low metabolic rate and therefore a poor ability to respond to new threats, such as escaping from predators (Blondel 2000, McNab 2002). The flightless kiwis of New Zealand are a classic example of this, having a metabolic rate and body temperature closer to that of mammals of equivalent size than to the higher rate of other birds. One result of such a change is that, while such birds might live longer, their reproductive output is low, both in terms of the number of eggs laid in a clutch and the frequency with which they breed, contributing to their inherent vulnerability to predators (McNab & Ellis 2006).

Birds that evolve characteristics that make them supremely able to exploit predator-free environments may become not just physically but also behaviourally incapable of escaping from predators when they arrive; the extreme tameness of birds and other animals on islands was noted with amazement by early naturalists and with glee by hungry sailors. The physiological basis of this tameness is little studied in birds, but research on Marine Iguanas *Amblyrhynchus cristatus* on the Galápagos Islands has shown that when animals that are not used to

The Laysan Duck Anas laysanensis *of Hawaii does not fly when alarmed but freezes, a successful tactic in evading its natural avian predators but highly risky when it comes to avoiding introduced mammals (James Breeden).*

predators are first chased by human researchers, they do not produce corticosterone, the hormone that allows animals to react appropriately to threat (Rodl *et al.* 2007). As a result, the lizards were easily captured, just as Dodos *Raphus cucullatus* once were. However, New Zealand Robins *Petroica australis* living in areas where introduced Stoats *Mustela erminea* are present react strongly to them, whereas birds living in places where Stoats are absent do not react to them initially, but quickly learn to do so (Maloney & McLean 1995). It seems likely, therefore, that the poor response of many endemic species to introduced predators is partly behavioural and partly physiological. The ability of some species to survive and sometimes even thrive alongside introduced predators may result from their faster learning response to the new threat; this might explain why New Zealand Robins have not suffered the fate of many other New Zealand species. Why some island birds and not others are able to do this is unclear, but it may be related to the length of time for which a species has been isolated from predators (Blumstein 2006). Niche may also matter: presence or absence of predators may decide songbirds whether or not to nest on the gound (Peluc *et al.* 2008), but on Abaco in the Bahamas a lack of tree-holes has forced the Cuban Amazon *Amazona leucocephala* to nest in limestone sink-holes, where now it falls inevitable prey to introduced cats (Stahala 2005). For vulnerable species, indeed, there is no sign of a reduction over time in the danger posed by introduced predators; on New Zealand, these have been the greatest single threat to native birds since the arrival of Europeans, and continue to be the most important limiting factor to the birds surviving there today (Innes *et al.* 2010).

Island bird species also suffer from the impacts of introduced grazing animals. As with endemic birds, island plants and trees have also evolved a degree of defencelessness. In the absence of grazing mammals, plants on remote islands have had no need for the energetically expensive production of toxic chemicals or sharp spines that mainland plants rely on to deter grazing animals. The arrival of goats and other grazing animals was therefore catastrophic for native island vegetation, as these new arrivals feasted preferentially on the succulent and defenceless native plants. The rapid loss of native vegetation has added much to the woes of island birds. It is possible for example that the extinction of several species of Hawaiian honeycreeper that had long, decurved bills for extracting nectar from deep within flowers was precipitated by the arrival of goats and the rapid extinction of many of Hawaii's native plants that swiftly followed.

ISLAND EXTINCTIONS

The tragedy of Guam has been repeated many times over, particularly on the islands of the Pacific. Of the species listed by BirdLife International as having become extinct in the last 500 years, 11 were lost from islands in the Atlantic, including seven from St Helena; 12 from Islands in the Caribbean; 31 from islands in the Indian Ocean, particularly Mauritius, Réunion and Rodrigues; and 70 from islands in the Pacific, including 14 from New Zealand and its associated islands and a staggering 30 or so from Hawaii, many of them within the last century. Only the Galápagos have retained their entire endemic avifauna, a remarkable survival in a wildfire of Pacific island extinctions but perhaps only a temporary one, as the islands support four species now listed as Critically Endangered. One of these, the Mangrove Finch *Camarhynchus heliobates*, has a tiny and declining population confined within perhaps the smallest range of any living bird species.

The scale of recent island extinctions is staggering, but is dwarfed by the losses that occurred previously. One estimate, based on archaeological remains, suggests that in the Pacific alone two thousand bird species, equivalent to a fifth of all today's living species, were driven to extinction by people in prehistoric times, perhaps half of them flightless rails (Steadman 1995). Prehistoric Polynesian peoples are likely to have wiped out at least half the bird species in each island group they reached (Pimm *et al.* 1994), and their impacts were apparent on large as well as on small islands (Steadman *et al.* 1999). The Pacific (or Polynesian) Rat *Rattus exulans* that they carried with them, previously regarded as a relatively innocuous little rodent, is now thought to have had impacts on native and naive wildlife that are comparable to those of the larger and more aggressive Black Rat *R. rattus* and Brown Rat *R. norvegicus* that later European island colonists spread (Jones *et al.* 2008, Towns 2009). However, care must be taken when ascribing extinction to a particular culture or colonisation event; were it not for the accidental discovery of living Po'ouli (Chapter 14) in 1973, the fossil record might have suggested that its extinction was the result of Polynesian, rather than European, colonisation (Pimm *et al.* 1994).

The majority of island extinctions, particularly those on small and remote islands, can be attributed partly or wholly to the impacts of introduced species, among which cats and rats have taken the greatest toll (Courchamp *et al.* 2003, Blackburn *et al.* 2004, Towns *et al.* 2006, Howald *et al.* 2007, Hilton & Cuthbert 2010, Tennyson 2010)

Following a wave of extinctions on St Helena, the St Helena Plover (or Wirebird) Charadrius sanctaehelenae, *is the last surviving endemic bird of this South Atlantic island, and was uplisted to Critically Endangered in 2007 (Andrew Darlow, St Helena Nature Conservation Group).*

Table 10.1. *Critically Endangered and Extinct species on Caribbean islands, showing the relatively low impact of predation by invasive species on islands that hold native mammals and snakes. An estimate of population and range size is given for extant species, with question marks indicating species with no known populations and blanks for species listed as Extinct. The main supposed threat or cause of extinction is indicated. CR = Critically Endangered, PE = Possibly Extinct, EX = Extinct.*

Species	Population	Range (km²)	Last sighting	Main threat or cause of extinction
Trinidad Piping-guan (CR) *Pipile pipile*	70–200	150		Hunting
Jamaica Petrel (CR-PE) *Pterodroma caribbaea*	?	?	1879	Predation
Cuban Kite (CR) *Chondrohierax wilsonii*	50–249	3,900		Habitat loss
Ridgway's Hawk (CR) *Buteo ridgwayi*	160–240	210		Habitat loss
Jamaican Red Macaw (EX) *Ara gossei*			1765	Hunting (?)
Dominican Macaw (EX) *Ara atwoodi*			1791	Hunting (?)
Jamaican Macaw (EX) *Ara erythrocephala*			c.1800	Hunting (?)
Lesser Antillean Macaw (EX) *Ara guadeloupensis*			c.1800	Hunting (?)
Cuban Macaw (EX) *Ara tricolor*			1865	Hunting
Guadeloupe Parakeet (EX) *Aratinga labati*			c.1775	Hunting
Guadeloupe Amazon (EX) *Amazona violacea*			c.1800	Hunting
Martinique Amazon (EX) *Amazona martinicana*			c.1800	Hunting
Grenada Dove (CR) *Leptotila wellsi*	70–120	8		Habitat loss
Puerto Rican Amazon (CR) *Amazona vittata*	30–35	160		Habitat loss
Jamaican Pauraque (CR-PE) *Siphonorhis americana*	?	?	1860	Predation
Puerto Rican Nightjar (CR) *Caprimulgus noctitherus*	>1,400	60		Habitat loss
Brace's Emerald (EX) *Chlorostilbon bracei*			1877	Unknown
Ivory-billed Woodpecker (CR) *Campephilus principalis*	?	?	1987	Habitat loss
Grand Cayman Thrush (EX) *Turdus ravidus*			1938	Habitat loss
Semper's Warbler (CR) *Leucopeza semperi*	?	?	1961	Predation
Montserrat Oriole (CR) *Icterus oberi*	500–5,200	10		Volcano

Feral cats on islands are responsible for at least 14% of global extinctions of birds, mammals and reptiles, and native birds form a large part of their diet on almost all of the islands to which they have been introduced (Bonnaud *et al.* 2011, Medina *et al.* 2011). Where rats and cats are absent, mice can sometimes fill the predator-gap and have the same devastating impacts on native species (Angel *et al.* 2009), as the bizarre story of the Tristan Albatross *Diomedea dabbenena* illustrates (Chapter 12). The problem of introduced predators is not restricted to a few islands; rats have reached and become established on at least 80% of the world's island groups (Caut *et al.* 2008). Invasive species are the dominant threat to endangered species on islands today, particularly those with small ranges; 75% of the world's threatened birds that are confined to islands face severe threats from introduced species (BirdLife International 2008a). This contrasts with the situation on continental landmasses, where habitat loss is the dominant threat (Clavero *et al.* 2009). Even where introductions took place thousands of years ago, such as on the islands of the Mediterranean, evidence of their impacts can still be detected in the numbers of birds breeding there today (Martin *et al.* 2000). Despite the removal of mammalian predators and grazers from many of the world's islands, the impacts of invasive species on birds and other groups of animals and plants appear to be strengthening (McGeoch *et al.* 2010). Increasing awareness of the problems caused by invasive species and improved efforts to prevent further colonisations have not yet resulted in a decline in the number of introductions to some of the world's most sensitive island ecosystems (Tennyson 2010).

The extreme vulnerability of birds that evolved on predator-free islands to the arrival of invasive animals is illustrated by the fates of island birds that evolved alongside native predators. The islands of the Caribbean have suffered a rate of extinction and threat comparable to that on any other island group, but because they form a chain that in places lies close to two major continental landmasses, most support populations of native mammals and snakes, many of which are themselves endemic. As a result, native birds were generally better able to cope with introduced mammals when they arrived. The ecological havoc wrought by early human settlers drove many to extinction, but in only a few cases was predation by invasive species the main cause (Table 10.1). In the same way, the threat status of birds on the islands of the Philippines and Indonesia can be predicted almost perfectly by the deforestation of their ranges, and far less well by the spread of invasive mammals (Brooks *et al.* 1997).

In each of the world's oceans, most bird extinctions in the last 500 years have occurred predominantly on what Wallace termed oceanic islands (Fig. 10.2), the class of island that includes the smallest and most remote specks of land. The only continental fragments with recent bird extinctions are New Zealand, New Caledonia, Cuba and Jamaica, and the only continental islands suffering extinctions are a small number lying off the coasts of Australia, Madagascar and New Zealand; some of these, like the Chatham Islands, are as small and isolated as oceanic islands. Extinctions, then, have occurred primarily on the world's smallest and most isolated islands, whatever their geological origins (Biber 2002, Karels *et al.* 2008). There are a number of reasons for expecting this to be the case. First, smaller islands can support only low populations, and small populations are at greater risk of extinction (O'Grady *et al.* 2004). Second, small and isolated islands are less likely to support populations of native mammals or snakes, meaning that their native bird communities are less well prepared to cope with introduced predators when they arrive. Remote islands are also likely to be free of insect disease vectors, and their residents are more susceptible to disease when it arrives as they have poorer immune responses (Matson 2006): the Po'ouli and many other Hawaiian species have been particularly hard hit by introduced diseases (Chapter 14). Third, remote islands may have been colonised later by people; perhaps counter-intuitively, islands on which people settled first have suffered lower rates of extinction than islands that have been colonised in modern times (Biber 2002), although as Table 10.2 shows there are plenty of exceptions. Early human colonisation might have led to the introduction to islands of relatively few predators, giving the species on these islands more time to adapt to living in their presence (Biber 2002). Alternatively, it might be that early extinctions are under recorded relative to later ones and the pattern reflects the fact that the remaining species on islands colonised early are simply those that are better able to adapt (Pimm *et al.* 1994).

The world's recently extinct island species are randomly distributed neither geographically nor taxonomically. Of the recently extinct island species, 16% were rails or crakes, 14% were parrots and 10% were doves or pigeons, yet these families make up a far smaller percentage of living birds today. Why are these groups so over-represented in the list of extinct species? Part of the answer lies in another interesting characteristic of island bird communities, which is that they are 'disharmonic' – they tend to differ in terms of taxonomic composition from mainland

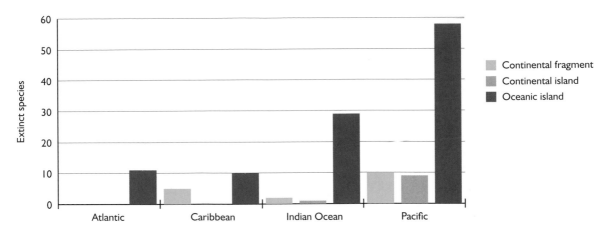

Figure 10.2. The geographical distribution by island type of island species that have become extinct since 1500. This includes all 133 island species listed by BirdLife International in 2009 as Extinct or Critically Endangered (Possibly Extinct).

communities. This does not mean they are in any sense unnatural, but some families of birds tend to be over-represented compared to mainland communities, and others are under-represented. This is reflected in the seemingly skewed patterns of extinct birds on islands and indeed in island bird communities today. Rails, parrots and pigeons appear to be surprisingly good at colonising remote islands, so it is to be expected that they feature heavily in the list of extinct species: rails in particular appear to be remarkably quick to evolve flightlessness (Diamond 1991, Slikas *et al.* 2002). The number of prehistoric extinctions of rails might run to well over a thousand species in the Pacific alone (Steadman 1995).

This is not the complete explanation, however, as there is another pattern overlying this, which is that larger, long-lived species with low reproductive rates tend to be more prone to extinction than smaller, faster-breeding species (Gaston & Blackburn 1995, Butchart *et al.* 2006b, Kelly & Sullivan 2010). Less than a third of recorded island extinctions were of passerines, yet these generally small birds make up over half the species alive today. Smaller species are less prone to extinction through human impacts because they tend to suffer lower hunting pressure, occur in higher numbers, are less visible, have lower rates of flightlessness and have a higher potential reproductive output (Cardillo 2003). Colonisation of New Zealand by the Maori around 800 years ago led to a wave of extinctions that preferentially selected larger-bodied species, most famously the moas (Dinornithidae), which were hunted to extinction for food (Duncan *et al.* 2002, Duncan & Blackburn 2004, Tennyson 2010). The elephant birds (Aepyornithidae) of Madagascar met a similar fate at around the same time. Today, huge piles of moa bones, many bearing signs of butchery, continue to be unearthed across New Zealand. All ten or so moa species were probably hunted to extinction before the year 1500, and possibly before 1400, just a century or so after the arrival of the Maoris. Their extinction ensured that of their only known natural predator, Haast's Eagle *Harpagornis moorei*, by far the largest bird of prey ever to have lived, though it was still only one fifteenth the weight of its moa prey. This predatory giant provides an interesting insight into the evolutionary changes that can take place when new species arrive on islands, as genetic analyses show that it probably evolved from one of the world's smallest eagles (Bunce *et al.* 2005). Only an ecological ghost of the moa and the elephant birds remains, in the form of the large number of surviving plants on New Zealand and Madagascar that still show morphological adaptations to reduce browsing pressure by these giant birds (Bond & Silander 2007, Lee *et al.* 2010). Later colonisation of New Zealand by Europeans, who brought with them a range of predatory species not associated with Maori culture, precipitated a further wave of extinctions across New Zealand that affected primarily smaller species (Bromham *et al.* 2012). In Hawaii, fossil evidence reveals a similar wave of extinctions of large-bodied species after the arrival of the early Polynesians followed by a second wave of extinctions of smaller species following European colonisation (Boyer 2008). The later arrival of people to the islands of the Caribbean resulted in the hunting to extinction of a number of larger species, particularly parrots, whereas the majority of smaller species have survived (Table 10.1), probably because, as noted above, they evolved in the company of native snakes and mammals.

Clearly, larger-bodied species on smaller and more remote islands, particularly flightless species, have suffered extinction disproportionately; the Dodo's disappearance was not a chance event but practically an inevitability.

RARITY ON ISLANDS TODAY

The distribution of the world's rarest birds today shows a similar but less strong insular tendency (Ricketts *et al* 2005), with around 60% of species currently listed by BirdLife International on the IUCN Red List as Critically Endangered being confined to islands (Fig. 10.3). The effect of island size is still apparent for, as with extinct birds, smaller islands hold a higher proportion of endangered species than do large islands (Biber 2002), although the overall number of threatened species is higher on larger islands (Trevino *et al.* 2007). The island groups with high numbers of recorded recent extinctions continue to hold high numbers of Critically Endangered species today (Table 10.2). Thus Hawaii, with over 20 confirmed extinctions in the last few centuries, today holds 14 endemic species listed as Critically Endangered, at least five of which are probably already extinct, as well as one species that now survives only in captivity. New Zealand, with 15 extinctions since 1500 (all but two of them since 1800), has eight endemic Critically Endangered species and a further 24 species listed as Endangered, many of them seabirds. Although the majority of recent extinctions of island birds were caused by introduced predators, a number of other threats to rare species, such as habitat change, also exist on islands. Therefore islands are important today in terms of the number of extremely threatened species they support, but the reason for these species' rarity is not always linked to introduced predators. Whether or not island species are now more threatened than mainland species is open to question. Certainly, a higher proportion of island species are threatened with extinction than mainland species, but this might simply reflect the fact that island species tend to have smaller populations and smaller ranges to start with, key components of the IUCN Red List classification. When range size is allowed for, continental species, particularly those inhabiting the lowlands of the tropics, may now be more threatened on average than island species (Manne *et al.* 1999, Manne & Pimm 2001).

*Table 10.2. The contrasting fates of birds on four Pacific island groups. *Includes five Hawaiian species listed as 'Critically Endangered (Possibly Extinct)' or 'Extinct in the Wild'. It is not clear whether the New Caledonia Gallinule* Porphyrio kukwiedei *survived into the nineteenth century.*

	Hawaii	Galápagos	New Zealand	New Caledonia
Land area (km²)	20,311	7,880	268,680	18,575
Human population (thousands)	1,288	40	4,316	249
Population density (people/km²)	45.5	5.1	16.1	13.4
Approx. number of years of permanent human habitation	2,300	<200	>700	3,500
Island type	Oceanic island	Oceanic island	Continental fragment	Continental fragment
Endemic bird species surviving	48	21	78	22
Number of Critically Endangered species	9	4	8	4
Number of endemic bird species extinct since 1800*	27	0	13	1(?)

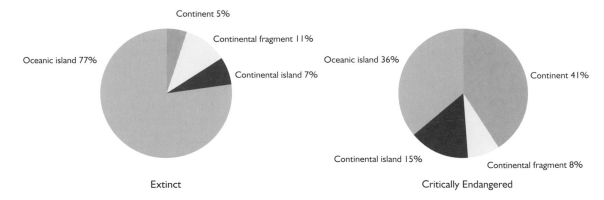

Figure 10.3. Geographical distribution by continent or island type of the 131 species of known provenance that have become extinct in the last 500 years (left) and the 192 species listed as Critically Endangered in 2009 (right).

The arrival of people on pristine islands often leads, paradoxically, to an increase in the number of species found on an island, since the number of introduced species often exceeds the number of extinctions of endemic birds (Sax *et al.* 2002), and habitat changes brought about by people allow other species to colonise. Human alteration of habitats in New Zealand has permitted the natural colonisation from distant Australia of a number of species that could not previously have survived there, and homesick British settlers on the islands formed Acclimatisation Societies, one of whose main roles was to introduce, quite deliberately, a wide range of common European species (Wilson 2004). On the remote Juan Fernández Islands off Chile, famous for being the home for four years of the castaway Alexander Selkirk, the inspiration for Robinson Crusoe, the number of regularly breeding terrestrial birds has increased from seven to eleven since the islands were first colonised by people in 1574 (Hahn *et al.* 2005). However, six of the original seven species are endemic and, while none has yet become extinct, each is now confined to a single island and all are threatened. The Juan Fernández endemic birds exhibit another pattern that appears to be common on heavily altered islands, which is that they have smaller range sizes and populations and occupy a narrower range of habitats than do the recent colonists. The endemic species are largely confined to native vegetation, whereas more recent arrivals thrive best in altered habitats. On the island of Puerto Rico, for example, endemic species survive in greatest numbers in upland habitats that have been less altered by humans, whereas lowland and heavily degraded habitats are dominated by introduced species or recent colonists (Acevedo & Restrepo 2008). This pattern is repeated on islands all over the world (Jones *et al.* 1987, Case 1996); it seems that the physical and behavioural adaptations that allow endemic island species to survive under natural conditions reduce their ability to respond to the habitat changes brought about by the arrival of people, but they can often hold their own against avian invaders in pristine habitats.

THREATS TO ISLAND BIRDS

Island birds face many of the same threats as are faced by birds on continental landmasses, such as habitat loss, disease, hunting and unsustainable exploitation. However, they may be particularly susceptible to such threats because they often have small populations and limited or no ability to move elsewhere. They also face a range of additional threats, accounting for the over-representation of island species on lists of extinct or threatened birds. Foremost among these, as we have seen, is the introduction of non-native species, which have a particularly severe impact on endemic species (Berglund *et al.* 2009). Introduced mammals remain the greatest threat, affecting over a third of all Critically Endangered birds, although other groups of introduced flora and fauna also affect a large number of the world's rarest species (Fig. 10.4). The importance of mammals as a threat to island birds stems from their particular success in colonising new islands (Jeschke 2008), perhaps a result of their ability to exploit new sources of food, as illustrated by the albatross-eating mice of Gough Island (Chapter 12).

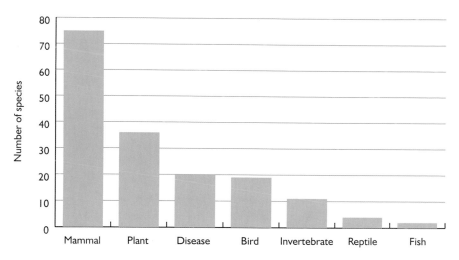

Figure 10.4. The number of Critically Endangered birds threatened by different types of alien invasive species (BirdLife International 2008b).

The impacts of introduced predators may become even more devastating to native wildlife where they occur in the presence of populations of introduced prey species, through a process known as 'hyperpredation' (Courchamp *et al.* 2000). High densities of introduced prey species, for example rabbits or mice, can support higher numbers of introduced predators than could survive on endemic prey species alone, with consequently greater impacts on native wildlife. When the introduced prey species is itself capable of causing damage to native wildlife, as is the case with introduced mice and rats, the removal of the top predator can lead to a population explosion of the predator lower in the food chain, which can have just as serious an effect on native wildlife as did the original predator. The likelihood of ecological damage increases with the number of different predator species introduced to an island, since each predator has its own unique hunting behaviour and prey spectrum; a native species that is relatively immune to the impacts of one predator might be susceptible to the ravages of another (Blackburn *et al.* 2005). For example, monarch flycatchers appear to be relatively immune to the presence of the Pacific Rat, which was spread across the Pacific by prehistoric Polynesian settlers and is the likely cause of many prehistoric bird extinctions, but they are extremely vulnerable to the larger and more aggressive Black Rat brought by Europeans (Thibault *et al.* 2002).

Introductions can impact on native birds in wholly unpredictable ways. The Guam Swiflet *Collocalia bartschi* (Endangered) managed to survive the wave of extinction that followed the arrival of the Brown Tree-snake but now faces threats from two introduced insects, a cockroach that feeds on the dried saliva that the birds use to stick their nests to the walls of caves, and a wasp that builds its heavy nests on the underside of the swiftlets' fragile nests and nest clusters, both causing the nests to fall from the cave wall. On the Galápagos Islands, the arrival of a type of fly that has blood-sucking larvae has increased the nestling mortality of the Medium Tree-finch *Camarhynchus pauper* to the extent that the species is now listed as Critically Endangered, threatening the integrity of the Galápagos avifauna that has thus far survived intact (Huber 2008). Predictably, as an island species, the finch seems to have little natural resistance to this new parasite and infestation rates in native birds on Galápagos greatly exceed those recorded anywhere else. The accidental introduction to Christmas Island of the Yellow Crazy Ant *Anoplolepis gracilipes* has caused a complete meltdown of the island's ecology (O'Dowd *et al.* 2003). On the forest floor, the ants extirpated the land crabs that were the primary consumers there, leading to an explosion in the number of tree seedlings and a change in the structure of the forest. In the canopy, the ants formed a protective association with introduced honeydew-secreting scale insects, leading to a proliferation of the scale insects, the spread of tree diseases and a die-back in the tree canopy. This in turn has had serious effects on Abbott's Booby *Papasula abbotti* (Endangered), which nests in the canopy, although thankfully there have been no observations of ants attacking birds or nestlings directly. The ant invasion has also led to significant changes in the distributions and feeding patterns of a number of other bird species on the island, some positively and some negatively (Davis *et al.* 2008). Frantic attempts to combat the supercolonies that the ant forms have had some success and parts of the island are once more ant-free, although keeping the ants under control is a major ongoing challenge. The introduction to the Aleutian Islands of the Arctic Fox *Alopex lagopus* led to a reduction in seabird numbers through predation, but an unexpected result of this was a complete change in the vegetation of the islands, as the flow of nutrients from the sea to the land in the form of bird droppings was interrupted (Croll *et al.* 2005).

Because every nation on earth is an exporter and importer of goods and services, so every nation is a facilitator and victim of the invasion of alien species (Reaser *et al.* 2007). Although the majority of rodent and cat introductions took place a century or more ago, there is no evidence of a decline in the rate at which new plant species are arriving and becoming established on islands, and therefore many more plant species are likely to be introduced to many more islands (Sax & Gaines 2008). The spread of invasive species is likely to accelerate under changing climates, presenting a range of new threats to island and mainland species alike (Walther *et al.* 2009). However, not all introductions are harmful, and in rare cases they can be beneficial. The Mauritius Fody *Foudia rubra*, a relative of the weavers, has suffered through habitat degradation and the introduction to its island home of predators, particularly the Black Rat and the Crab-eating Macaque *Macaca fascicularis*. The depredations of these species on nests of the Mauritius Fody led to a rapid decline in its population. Between 1975 and 2001, its numbers fell by more than half and the species was uplisted to Critically Endangered. Since then, however, the situation has stabilised, largely owing to the birds' use of plantations of introduced but non-invasive conifers, trees with 'continental' defences such as gum exudates and long spines that have evolved to deter continental animals like rats. Within these habitats, the fody's nest survival is much higher than nests in native vegetation and not much

In a rare reversal of fortune, the Mauritius Fody Foudia rubra *has benefited from the introduction of alien plant species, and has been downlisted from Critically Endangered to Endangered (Dennis Hansen).*

different from that of birds moved to a predator-free island (Safford 1997a, Cristinacce *et al.* 2009). Consequently the Mauritius Fody has been downlisted to Endangered and it continues to increase in numbers. In a rare reversal of fortune, a vulnerable island species has profited from one well-armed continental species in order to avoid the attacks of another.

Hunting is a threat to island and mainland species alike but island species have suffered disproportionately owing to their inability to escape, the large and meaty nature of some of them, their small initial populations and the need to provision early sailing ships. The evolutionary pressures that caused many island birds to become very large, thereby filling the role of absent mammalian herbivores, made them particularly attractive to hungry sailors. The Dodo, the Great Auk *Pinguinus impennis*, the moas of New Zealand and the elephant birds of Madagascar were all largely eaten out of existence (Duncan *et al.* 2002). Perhaps the most recent species to be hunted to extinction for food was the (predictably) flightless Wake Island Rail *Rallus wakensis*, which appears to have been hunted to extinction by starving Japanese soldiers during the Second World War; before the war the species was reported as being quite plentiful, but when the island was captured by American troops in 1945 not a single bird could be found (Mayr 1945). However, hunting today poses less of a threat to island birds than do introduced predators or disease, not least because most of the large species have already been extirpated.

Many of the world's rarest birds are endemic to oceanic islands, formed by volcanic activity that persists today. Many also occur on islands in the tropics where severe weather and seismic events occur (Tanner *et al.* 1991). The eruption of the Soufrière Hills volcano on the Caribbean island of Montserrat in 1995 destroyed more than half of the forest in the range of the endemic Montserrat Oriole *Icterus oberi* and led to severe declines in insect numbers in the rest of the species' range, causing it to be rapidly uplisted to Critically Endangered and setting in train an emergency programme of captive breeding (Hilton *et al.* 2003). The problem was exacerbated by the loss since human settlement of much of the island's forest, confining the oriole to patches of habitat immediately around the volcano. Although fairly infrequent on Puerto Rico, hurricanes appear to be the main factor limiting the population of the Critically Endangered Puerto Rican Amazon *Amazona vittata* (Beissinger *et al.* 2008). The Cozumel Thrasher *Toxostoma guttatum* was common on the island of Cozumel, just off Mexico's Yucatán Peninsula, until September 1988 when Hurricane Gilbert hit. The devastation caused by the hurricane to Cozumel's natural vegetation, and perhaps direct mortality caused by the ferocious storm, almost drove the species to extinction. When Hurricane Roxanne hit in 1995, it was feared that the species was extinct, until reliable sightings of the species were made in 2004. In 2005, however, Cozumel was battered by Hurricanes Emily and Wilma and the species has not reliably been sighted since. The species might have been further affected by the introduction of boas to Cozumel in 1971, apparently released in a typical act of thoughtlessness or, worse, indifference, when they were no longer needed in the making of a film. Island species suffer the world's environmental problems in microcosm.

THE SHIFTING SPOTLIGHT OF EXTINCTION

The spotlight of extinction risk appears to be slowly moving away from islands towards continents, where human activities are placing mainland species under increasing pressure (Ricketts *et al.* 2005, Butchart *et al.* 2006b). The spread of agriculture into natural habitats now outranks invasive species as a threat to globally threatened birds (BirdLife International 2008a, Vié *et al.* 2009). However, many of the threats faced by island birds are likely to become increasingly important for populations of mainland birds, and indeed the distinction between them is starting to blur. The ranges of many mainland species are now starting to resemble those of oceanic island birds: the destruction of natural ecosystems has led to the fragmentation of mainland species into ever smaller and more isolated islands of habitat surrounded by hostile seas of agriculture. Climate change is driving many species uphill, isolating their populations on mountaintop refuges. Rapid global warming is also likely to lead to a significant redistribution of many species' ranges, bringing mainland birds into contact with a range of predators, competitors and diseases to which their evolutionary history offers little defence. Already there is evidence of a slowing of extinction rates on islands and an acceleration in extinction rates on continents (Szabo *et al.* 2012b). Mainland birds are, in conservation terms, becoming island birds.

Chapter 11
Stephens Island Wren
Xenicus (*Traversia*) *lyalli*

EXTINCT

There can be no better illustration of the reasons for the disparity in extinction rates between islands and continents than the famous story of the lighthouse-keeper's cat. The generally accepted and often recounted version of the legend is that Stephens Island Wren was the world's only flightless songbird and the bird with the smallest range of any, and that its entire world population was wiped out by a single cat called Tibbles, owned by a lighthouse-keeper. This sad and simple tale, greatly coloured and humanised by the name of the cat and the connotation of a lonely lighthouse-keeper, has entered the conservation lexicon as a textbook illustration of the extreme fragility of island life and the impacts of introduced predators. However, a little historical detective work (Galbreath & Brown 2004, Medway 2004a) suggests that almost everything about this version of events is untrue. To begin with, there is no evidence that the cat *was* called Tibbles, and it probably did not belong to the lighthouse-keeper, who certainly was called David Lyall. The bird was not the world's only flightless songbird (although it was the last) and it did not have the smallest range of any species. Furthermore, the bird was not driven to extinction by a single cat, but by the depredations of a population of feral cats which wiped out not just the wren but every other bird on the island too (Medway 2004a). However, the true story of what happened, which has only marginally less pathos than the legend, serve as an excellent illustration of a series of events that has been played out many times, with different casts of characters, on small islands all around the world.

The Marlborough Sounds comprise a complex network of flooded valleys, islands and peninsulas that jut outwards from the northern coast of New Zealand's South Island. This creates a constriction in the Cook Strait, the body of water that separates North Island from South Island, making it a dangerous shipping lane. At the

Stephens Island, or Takapourewa, once home to the world's last flightless songbird and to a cat that was probably not called Tibbles (Paddy Ryan).

northernmost tip of the Marlborough Sounds lies tiny Stephens Island, covering an area of less than 3km². In 1891, preparations were made for the construction of a lighthouse and a farm on Stephens Island. This was no mean feat, because although it is small the island rises steeply to over 300m and was covered in thick bush through which a tramway had to be laid to transport building materials to the summit. The following year, a construction worker called F. W. Ingram reported seeing large numbers of native birds on the island, including 'two kinds of wren', the first ever mention of the Stephens Island Wren (the other species he saw was probably the Rifleman *Acanthisitta chloris*, a species that remains fairly common in New Zealand today). He later wrote an account of his experiences of Stephens Island in a local newspaper, expressing his surprise at the wealth of birdlife the island still supported, for by this stage the destruction of New Zealand's native birds was already well underway. In January 1894, the lighthouse began operation and Lyall and some sixteen other people arrived on the island, bringing with them sheep and cattle.

WHAT THE CAT BROUGHT IN

At some point, perhaps in February 1894, a single pregnant cat got onto the island. One of the offspring of this cat appears to have been taken in as a pet by the lighthouse-keepers and their families, while the rest went feral. In June, when it was old enough to hunt, the pet cat started to bring back to the lighthouse the bodies of a very peculiar little bird. Lyall, who was interested in wildlife, sent one of these via A. W. Bethune, second engineer on the government steamboat *Hinemoa*, to Sir Walter Buller; the specimen reached him in July. Buller, a native New Zealander and the country's leading authority on birds, often received specimens from Bethune, whose work took him to many remote islands around New Zealand, but he can rarely have been as pleased with anything Bethune had brought him before. Buller at once recognised the bird as a new species and prepared a description of it to put before the world's scientific community through the pages of the British Ornithologists' Union journal *Ibis*. On receiving his specimen, he wrote

> There is probably nothing so refreshing to the soul of a naturalist as the discovery of a new species. You will readily understand, therefore, how pleased I was at receiving, through the good offices of Mr Bethune, the skin of a bird from Stephens Island which was entirely different from anything hitherto known.

Having written his description, Buller sent the specimen to the famous bird artist John Gerrard Keulemans in London to prepare an illustration for the article, thereby delaying its publication. Unfortunately for Buller, Lyall had collected a few more of the little corpses that were being brought in by the cat and had sold nine of these to the Wellington naturalist and dealer in rare specimens, Henry H. Travers. Realising the value of these specimens, and with an eye to making a quick profit, Travers offered his nine specimens for sale to the wealthy English naturalist and collector Walter Rothschild, knowing that he would pay him far more than Buller could. No doubt intrigued by Travers's letter, which stated, perhaps untruthfully, that no other naturalist knew about these birds and, certainly truthfully, that there would soon be none left, Rothschild duly acquired his nine specimens in October 1894 and set to work writing his own scientific description of this curiosity. Whether or not he was aware of Buller's pending description is unclear, but Rothschild certainly wasted no time, and his description was read on Rothschild's behalf to a meeting of the British Ornithologists' Club on 19 December 1894 by the curator of his museum, Ernst Hartert. Rothschild gave the species the scientific name *Traversia lyalli*, in honour of both the finder and the procurer of his specimens. Philip Sclater, who as the editor of *Ibis* knew about Buller's as yet unpublished description, was present at the meeting and raised the matter with Hartert, but the latter replied that he had no authority to withdraw Rothschild's description, which was published in the *Bulletin of the British Ornithologists' Club* later that same month. When Buller's description of the bird was published in *Ibis* in April 1895 under the name *Xenicus insularis*, it was accompanied by a reprint of Rothschild's original article, expanded to describe the bird's rail-like appearance and its apparent flightlessness, which he deduced from the very small wings and the soft and lax plumage. The wren's flightlessness was later confirmed by skeletal analyses (Millener 1989).

As Rothschild's description was published before Buller's, the name *Traversia lyalli* was accepted and Buller's name reduced to a synonym (since then, the species has been variously placed in the genus *Xenicus* as Buller had intended and in *Traversia*). Rothschild wrote that this was bad luck on Buller, but that as he had published first, had nine specimens to Buller's one, and indeed had paid more for his specimens than had Buller, his choice of name should stand. This incident generated a great deal of rancour between Buller and Rothschild, and helped to sour a friendship during which Buller had provided Rothschild with many hundreds of specimens (when Rothschild was sent by his father to Cambridge University, he arrived with a flock of live kiwis sent to him by Buller). Rothschild came to think of Buller as a greedy dealer, rather than a serious ornithologist, and even after Buller's death continued to publish highly critical reviews of his work. The story of the lighthouse keeper's cat can be found in an article written by Rothschild on extinct and vanishing birds, and later in a book on the same subject, and it may well be that this was where the myth of Stephen's Island Wren was first propounded (Rothschild 1905, 1907).

THE LOSS OF THE WORLD'S LAST FLIGHTLESS SONGBIRD

In February 1895, Travers visited Stephens Island with three companions and spent at least five days in search of further lucrative specimens, but they failed to find the bird. In the same month, Lyall wrote to Buller that 'the cats have become wild and are making sad havoc among all the birds'. As news of the bird spread following the publication of not one but two scientific descriptions, so too did speculation on the bird's demise, perhaps fuelled by Travers's failure to find the bird in February 1895. The following month, an editorial in the *Christchurch Press* read

> There is very good reason to believe that the bird is no longer found upon the island, and, as it is not known to exist anywhere else, it has apparently become quite extinct. This is probably a record performance in the way of extinction. The English scientific world will hear almost simultaneously of the bird's discovery and its disappearance before anything is known of its life history or its habitats.

All that remains of Stephens Island Wren today are a handful of skins and mounted specimens. Even allowing for the age of these specimens, this was clearly a most unusual-looking bird (Paddy Ryan).

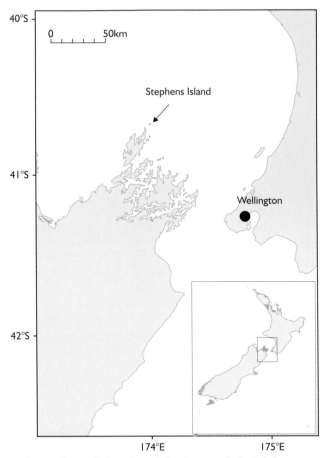

Stephens Island; projecting into the Marlborough Sounds and clearly in need of a lighthouse.

Indeed, nothing is recorded about the species in life, other than Lyall's opinion that it was semi-nocturnal and ran about in the rocks like a mouse. Lyall lived on the island for two and a half years and apparently only saw it alive twice, writing to Buller that he thought it was never common. In December 1895, Travers again visited Stephens Island, and once more met with no success. The bird probably became extinct in 1895 or 1896. In early 1895, the depredations of a growing feral cat population of the island's previously abundant bird life were apparent to everyone, and all 25 species of native land bird present when the lighthouse was being constructed were lost by the end of the century (Medway 2004a). Removal of cats in the early twentieth century led to the recolonisation of the island by 11 of the original 25 species, all of them widespread elsewhere in New Zealand, but one of the original inhabitants, the South Island Piopio *Turnagra capensis*, shared the fate of Stephens Island Wren and was probably extinct by 1910. The Piopio population on Stephens Island might have represented an endemic race (Medway 2004b), and before the arrival of cats the species was abundant there. Many years after its extinction it was realised that piopios were New Zealand's only representative of the bowerbird family (Christidis *et al.* 1996). Hamilton's Frog *Leiopelma hamiltoni*, one of the world's rarest amphibians and its most ancient frog, somehow survived the cat invasion and clings on today in tiny numbers on a single stack of rock on Stephens Island (Tocher *et al.* 2006). Nearby, North Brother Island became the final sanctuary of Gunther's Tuatara *Sphenodon guntheri*, an ancient reptile that has recently been introduced to two other islands (Nelson *et al.* 2002b). The Striped Gecko *Hoplodactylus stephensi* and the Cook Strait Click Beetle *Amychus granulatus* (which in typical island fashion has lost the ability either to fly or to click) survive still on Stephens Islands and just a handful of other places. All that remains of Stephens Island Wren, however, are 15 specimens scattered in museum collections around the world, and a number of prehistoric bones.

It seems certain that Stephens Island Wren was not wiped out by a single cat, as the legend has it. Other cats were certainly present on the island, and the small number of wrens collected by Lyall who, knowing their value, would certainly have kept all he could, is unlikely to have represented the whole population. A number of other commonly held beliefs relating to the story of the Stephens Island Wren also now appear untrue, and unravelling these myths provides further insights into the unique threats faced by island species. First, the species was not the world's only flightless songbird, although it is the only one to have survived into recent times. At least one other member of the New Zealand wrens (Acanthisittidae) and the remarkable Long-legged Bunting *Emberiza alcuveri* of Tenerife, known only from fossil remains (Rando *et al.* 1999), were also flightless, and doubtless more will come to light. More recently, two almost flightless songbirds have joined them in extinction: the Bush Wren *Xenicus longipes*, another New Zealand wren last seen in 1972, and the Chatham Islands Fernbird *Bowdleria rufescens*, the last known individual of which was shot in 1895 to furnish Rothschild's collection with a specimen. The now complete extinction of flightless songbirds mirrors the extinction of many other flightless birds, the most famous of which were the Dodo *Raphus cucullatus* of Mauritius and the moas of New Zealand.

A second inaccuracy in the most frequently recounted version of the story of Stephens Island Wren is that it had the smallest range of any bird. This might have been true in 1894 (though the range of the recently extinct Aldabra Warbler *Nesillas aldabrana*, discovered in 1967 and last seen in 1983, might have been smaller still), but it is now clear that Stephens Island Wren previously occurred across much of New Zealand, as fossil bones of this species have been found in a number of widely scattered localities on North Island. By the end of the nineteenth century, extinction on other islands, probably following the introduction by pre-Maori settlers of the Pacific Rat *Rattus exulans* around two thousand years ago, meant that it persisted only on the (then) predator-free Stephens Island. Stephens Island might therefore have been the final refuge of this formerly widespread bird for nearly two millennia. The same is true of Hamilton's Frog and Gunther's Tuatara, both of which previously occurred more widely on the New Zealand mainland (Nelson *et al.* 2002a,b, Tocher *et al.* 2006). It is likely that they were able to reach the island when lower sea levels drained the shallow waters of the Marlborough Sounds. Stephens Island Wren was therefore an example of what is called a paleoendemic, a species that is endemic to an island because its populations have been wiped out elsewhere. The majority of island endemics are likely to be neoendemic, in other words species that have evolved *in situ* and were never found elsewhere, though these terms simply represent the ends of a continuum.

The loss of Stephens Island Wren was certainly a significant one. The New Zealand wrens, which following the more recent extinction of the Bush Wren are now represented by just two living species, the common Rifleman and the much less common Rock Wren *Xenicus gilviventris*, are an unusual and ancient group whose origins are uncertain. Genetic analyses suggest that the songbirds evolved in Australia before spreading to dominate many bird communities around the world (Ericson *et al.* 2002). The New Zealand wrens, which are wholly unrelated to the true wrens (Troglodytidae), may be the remnants of a group of early songbirds that became stranded when New Zealand broke away from Gondwanaland some 85 million years ago. More likely, however, is that their ancestors arrived after New Zealand broke away, albeit at a time when the islands were closer to Australia than they are now. What is certain is that they have no close living relatives. Indeed, although undoubtedly songbirds, they are thought to form a sister group to all other songbirds (Barker *et al.* 2002, Ericson *et al.* 2002) and may be New Zealand's most ancient birds; even the extraordinarily distinctive kiwis diverged from their ancestors later than did the New Zealand Wrens. The loss of island species, many of which have no close living relatives as in the case of paleoendemics (Cronk 1997), often therefore results in a far greater global loss of genetic and morphological diversity and taxonomic history than the loss of mainland species, which are more likely to have close living relatives. Unfortunately, as New Zealand exemplifies, it is also relatively easy to achieve. The introduction of cats to Stephens Island, at a time when the devastation that they could cause was already well known, spelled doom for the world's last flightless passerine and one of the most unusual of all birds.

Chapter 12
Tristan Albatross *Diomedea dabbenena*
CRITICALLY ENDANGERED

It is a stark illustration of the ability of mankind to wreak ecological havoc in even the most pristine areas that birds inhabiting the most expansive and least populated part of the planet's surface, the open oceans, are on average far more threatened with extinction than birds that live on dry land. Indeed, seabirds as a group are more threatened, and their conservation status has worsened faster over recent decades, than any other comparable group of birds (Croxall *et al.* 2012). Today, all of the world's 22 species of albatross are listed as either Near Threatened (five) or globally threatened (17), and three of them, the Waved Albatross *Phoebastria irrorata*, Amsterdam Albatross *Diomedea amsterdamensis* and Tristan Albatross, are Critically Endangered. A further five are listed as Endangered and nine as Vulnerable. The proportion of albatross species that are listed as globally threatened is eight times the global average across all bird families. The world's petrels and shearwaters are not faring much better: of 95 species, around two-thirds are listed as globally threatened or Near Threatened, including eight listed as Critically Endangered. The high proportion of seabird species at risk of extinction and the severity of the declines in large, long-lived and formerly common birds parallel the equally catastrophic and unexpected collapse in Asian vulture populations (Chapter 17) and make this one of the most pressing issues in global bird conservation today.

THE EXTREME VULNERABILITY OF SEABIRDS

The poor conservation status of the world's seabirds stems largely from three aspects of their ecology. First, many nest only on islands, where they are exposed to all the usual threats faced by island species. In particular, introduced predators pose a significant threat due to their heavy rates of predation on seabird chicks, many of which undergo a

A male Tristan Albatross and his chick – the adult is at risk at sea from longline fishing, the chick is vulnerable on land to the most unexpected of invasive predators (Ross Wanless and Andrea Angel).

long period of maturation during much of which they are left unguarded and vulnerable while their parents forage at sea. As with so many island species, having evolved in the absence of land mammals, most seabirds have very poorly developed anti-predator capability. At least two species, the imaginatively named Large St Helena Petrel *Pterodroma rupinarum* and Small St Helena Petrel *Bulweria bifax*, became extinct soon after that island was discovered in 1502, probably as a result of introduced predators (Olson 1975, Hilton & Cuthbert 2010). The high fat and oil content of seabird chicks (a result of their rich diet of marine fish and invertebrates) coupled with their ease of capture and their often large size relative to other island species, make them extremely attractive prey to introduced predators. On Réunion Island in the Indian Ocean, for example, chicks of Barau's Petrel *Pterodroma baraui* (Endangered) form the most frequent single prey species found in the scats of feral cats, outnumbering even the abundant introduced rodents available (Faulquier *et al.* 2009). Rats also pose a serious predation threat to seabirds, particularly to smaller, burrow-nesting species (Jones *et al.* 2008). The importance of introduced predators in driving population declines in island-nesting seabirds is dramatically illustrated by the extent to which they can recover when predators are removed (Rayner *et al.* 2007).

The second ecological condition that renders seabirds particularly vulnerable is their slow reproductive rate. Some large species do not start breeding until the age of ten years or more, and then only make one nesting attempt every two years. To counterbalance this, they rely on their great longevity to produce enough chicks over their lifetimes to maintain their numbers. This means that these populations are highly susceptible to even very small reductions in their survival rates.

The third area of vulnerability lies in their feeding behaviour. Many seabirds range widely across the world's oceans in search of often unpredictable concentrations of food, particularly in the colder, more productive waters at high latitudes. People seeking fish and other marine resources behave in exactly the same way and target the same areas (Brothers *et al.* 1999), and by coincidence seabirds (of all species) and fishermen remove approximately the same tonnage of marine animals from the world's oceans each year (Brooke 2004). This shared behaviour brings many seabirds into proximity with fishing vessels. Until recently, this was not generally a problem, and there is even some evidence to suggest that discarded fish offal from trawlers, which can attract huge concentrations of seabirds from a very wide area, has contributed to increases in a few seabird populations (Votier *et al.* 2008). However, changes in fishing methods now place large numbers of seabirds at risk of a sudden and nasty death.

Longlining, a fairly recent development in fishing, is the worst culprit. Using this method, cables up to an astonishing 130km in length and fitted with tens of thousands of baited hooks, are dragged behind moving ships like the long tentacles of a predatory jellyfish. The targets of these hooks are large fish such as tuna, swordfish, halibut and toothfish, which are of course too big and swim too deep to be of interest to seabirds as food. However, seabirds are attracted to the bait on these hooks, which is often squid. Albatrosses and large petrels feed largely by scavenging dead or dying fish or squid from the sea surface, and so are attracted to fishing vessels by the smell of the bait and offal being thrown overboard (Brothers *et al.* 1999). Birds often make a grab for the baited hooks as the line is being set, particularly close to the stern of the vessels where the hooks are closest to the surface. Once snagged, they are quickly pulled under and drowned. The development of lighter, more buoyant lines that stay near the surface for longer has added to the problem (Brothers *et al.* 1999).

In the southern oceans, longlining took off on an industrial scale during the 1980s, and almost immediately declines were noticed in the populations of a number of albatross species (Croxall 2008), but it was not until the early 1990s that seabird biologists started to realise the scale of the toll that this practice was taking (Brothers 1991). At its height, the relatively small-scale longlining fishery off Peru caused the deaths of perhaps as many as 13% of the entire world populations of Waved and Chatham Albatrosses each year (Jahncke *et al.* 2001), and high seabird mortality has been found across the world's oceans wherever this fishing method is employed. Ironically, part of the stimulus for the development of longlining was that it has a number of environmental benefits over the alternative method of setting nets. It has a lower bycatch of marine mammals and of unwanted fish, reduces the fuel consumption of fishing vessels and leaves the seabed largely undisturbed (Brothers *et al.* 1999, Jahncke *et al.* 2001). Trawling with nets kills smaller but still significant numbers of birds, which become tangled in the nets and drown, or collide with the steel cables used to hoist in the nets (Zydelis *et al.* 2009a). Around 12,000 albatrosses are killed each year by collision with trawler cables in a single South African fishery (Watkins *et al.* 2008), and in some places deaths of albatrosses to collisions or entanglement with nets might even exceed deaths to longlining (Baker *et al.* 2007).

Despite spending much of their lives well away from land and often breeding only on remote, inhospitable and uninhabited islands, albatrosses present some advantages to researchers working to understand their problems: they return predictably to the same colonies to breed, where they can easily be caught, tagged and measured, and being very large birds, it is possible to fit them with a range of electronic devices that record their position and even their activity during their ocean wanderings. Furthermore, as a scientific preserve (declared through the Antarctic Treaty System), the Antarctic hosts many research centres with long standing seabird research programmes that were ideally placed to identify the causes of the declines. Satellite technology has allowed the oceanic movements of albatrosses and larger petrels to be tracked from space, making it possible to identify areas where albatrosses and longline fisheries are likely to overlap (BirdLife International 2004). Indeed, our knowledge of the movements and behaviour of seabirds is now at least as comprehensive as our knowledge of the movements and behaviour of fishing vessels. This work has shown that there is a close association between rates of longlining and population declines in a number of albatrosses and large petrels, and in many cases it has been possible to prove that these declines have been the direct result of unsuitable fishing methods (Weimerskirch *et al.* 1997, Nel *et al.* 2002, Croxall 2008). The available evidence suggests that perhaps 100,000 albatrosses are killed by longlining each year: one every five minutes. For birds that often mate for life, this creates a huge population of single adults in the population each year, many of which might never breed again.

Satellite tracking of large numbers of albatrosses has shown that due to their distribution and ranging behaviour, some species are more vulnerable than others, population declines being greatest in species whose at-sea distributions have a high degree of overlap with longlining fisheries (Fischer *et al.* 2009). Indeed, male and female albatrosses of the same species often feed in different parts of the ocean, so their mortality rates at the hands – or rather hooks – of fisheries may differ, leading to an imbalance in adult sex ratio. This might explain the discovery of same-sex 'pairs' in a number of albatross species (Young *et al.* 2008). In some albatross populations, the adult sex ratio is now heavily skewed towards males, in others towards females (Mills & Ryan 2005, Awkerman *et al.* 2007). The effects of these unbalanced sex ratios on long-lived monogamous birds will be evident for many years after the cessation of longlining. For species in which males and females are hard to distinguish, the number of true reproductive pairs might be greatly overestimated in many populations. Many albatrosses therefore face the twin threats of reduced productivity, caused directly by invasive predators, and indirectly by longlining and by reduced adult survival through deaths caused by longlining alone (Cuthbert *et al.* 2003b). Some unfortunates, like the Tristan Albatross, face both.

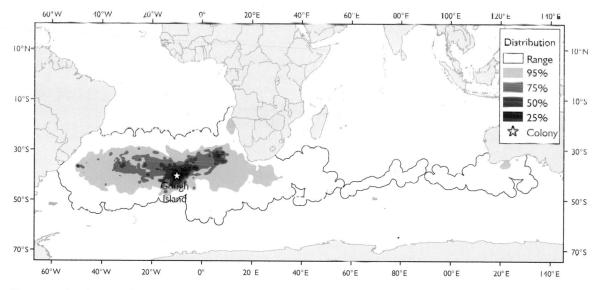

The at-sea distribution of Tristan Albatross assessed using tracking devices. The shading indicates the percentage of recorded locations, such that the darkest blue areas contain 25% of all locations, the next darkest 50% and so on. Based on data collected by Richard Cuthbert and Ross Wanless.

UNDER ATTACK ON LAND AND AT SEA

The number of recognised species of albatross has increased in recent years with the advent of genetic analyses, although there is still considerable uncertainty in the taxonomy of the group (Burg & Croxall 2004). The Tristan Albatross itself was only confirmed as a full species in 1998, when it was found to be genetically distinct from the slightly larger Wandering Albatross *Diomedea exulans* (Robertson & Nunn 1998, Burg & Croxall 2004, ACAP 2009), although it is so similar to the Wandering Albatross that certain identification requires detailed measurements to be taken (Cuthbert *et al.* 2003a) and distinguishing the two species at sea is almost impossible. The Tristan Albatross breeds only on Gough Island (a pair or two occasionally nest on nearby Inaccessible Island), one of the islands in the Tristan group in the south Atlantic. A colony was once present on the main island of Tristan da Cunha but this was driven to extinction between 1881 and 1907 by human persecution and perhaps also by invasive mammals. In 2008, the world population of the Tristan Albatross was estimated at 1,700 breeding pairs, although the large number of non-breeding birds means that the global total of individuals is in the region of 11,300 (ACAP 2009, Wanless *et al.* 2009). Estimates of productivity and survival suggest that the population is predicted to continue to decline by around 3% each year (Wanless *et al.* 2009), an alarming rate for such a long-lived bird. However, if immature birds, which wander at sea for many years before starting to breed, suffer higher longlining mortality than do adults, as seen in other species, this rate of decline is likely to be a serious underestimate.

Each breeding cycle of the Tristan Albatross lasts a full year, and individual birds breed only once every two years. The single egg is laid in January or February and hatches in March or April. There then follows a very long nestling period of eight or nine months, during much of which the chick is left alone while the adults feed at sea. When the chick finally leaves the nest and sets off to sea, it will not return for between three and seven years, and will not breed until it is about ten or sometimes even twenty years old (Cuthbert *et al.* 2004). The reproductive rate is therefore very low; the most a pair can hope for is to produce a single chick every two years, and that chick will make no contribution to the breeding population for another decade or more. Such a low rate of productivity would be unsustainable were it not for the fact that these birds are very long-lived, and so can expect to make a good number of breeding attempts during their lives. Adult annual survival is currently around 91% which, although very high compared with most birds, is not sufficient to maintain the population of a species that breeds at such low rates (Cuthbert *et al.* 2004). For its size, the Tristan Albatross has one of the lowest adult survival rates of any albatross (Wanless *et al.* 2009), probably because birds spend much of their time feeding in parts of the ocean known to support high levels of longline fishing, particularly in the seas immediately around Gough where Taiwanese and Japanese fishing fleets operate (Cuthbert *et al.* 2005).

But longlining is not the only problem facing the Tristan Albatross. Chick survival is also falling, as a consequence of a problem previously unencountered in bird conservation. The only mammalian introduction on Gough is the diminutive House Mouse *Mus musculus*, a species not generally judged to cause serious problems on other islands to which it has been introduced. It probably became established accidentally when the island was used as a base by seal hunters in the nineteenth century. In the absence of predators or competitors, however, the mice of Gough have gradually increased in size over time and are now around twice the size of mice elsewhere (Angel *et al.* 2009). When mysterious large lesions were found on dead and dying Tristan Albatross chicks, video footage revealed mice swarming over the young birds at night and literally eating them alive. At least a third of all Tristan Albatross chicks are killed by mice each year, and in one year breeding success averaged just 14% (ACAP 2009), a far lower rate of productivity than has ever been recorded in albatrosses. The mice attack the birds from behind, biting holes through the skin around the rump. These can be so deep that the intestines spill through. The albatross chicks die of these wounds and the mice feed for several days on the carcass, helped out by scavenging giant petrels *Macronectes* and skuas *Stercorarius*, which may themselves kill albatross chicks weakened by mouse attacks. Unfortunately, the chick-rearing season on Gough coincides with the period when seeds and other more usual foods of mice are in shortest supply (Cuthbert & Hilton 2004). The ability of invasive rodents to switch flexibly between different foods as they become available through the year has been a major factor in their success at colonising and surviving on islands (Caut *et al.* 2008); the mice on Gough appear to have managed this so successfully that their densities on the island

Automatic cameras set up on nests record mice attacking young albatrosses at night, generally from the rear (Ross Wanless and Andrea Angel).

are far higher than on any other in the southern oceans, and these rodents are estimated to consume about three tonnes of Gough's native plants, insects and birds each day (Parkes 2008).

The discovery that mice were effectively preying upon very large birds up to 300 times their size was truly remarkable and wholly unanticipated (Cuthbert & Hilton 2004). Even rats rarely behave this way, although the Pacific Rat *Rattus exulans* has been recorded causing very similar injuries to chicks of the Laysan Albatross *Phoebastria immutabilis* (Kepler 1967). However, the Tristan Albatross is not the only threatened species suffering from the attentions of Gough's supermice. The Gough Bunting *Rowettia goughensis* also faces extinction by the incessant nibbling of mice, and its population is in long-term decline (Cuthbert & Hilton 2004, Ryan & Cuthbert 2008), as a result of which it was uplisted to Critically Endangered in 2008. Indeed there appears to be a strong positive relationship between the breeding success of buntings and the breeding success of albatrosses, suggesting that both respond in the same way to changes in the mouse population (Ryan & Cuthbert 2008). A similar fate befalls many chicks of the Atlantic Petrel *Pterodroma incerta* (Endangered), another species that breeds only on Gough (Cuthbert & Hilton 2004, Wanless *et al.* 2012).

BYCATCH SOLUTIONS AND RODENT REMOVAL

In conservation terms, it is fortunate that what is bad for albatrosses is also bad for fishermen. Each hook that catches an albatross or another seabird is a hook that does not catch a fish, so there is a financial incentive for fishermen to reduce bycatch (Brothers 1991). The combined interests of the conservation movement and the fishing industry to reduce bycatch have stimulated the development and implementation of a range of preventative measures. Indeed, the development of methods to reduce seabird bycatch was underway within the fishing industry, particularly the Japanese tuna longline industry, well before conservationists were even fully aware of the problem (Bergin 1997, Brothers *et al.* 1999). The number of seabirds caught by a particular fishing vessel appears to depend not so much on where or when it fishes, although these can also be important, but on *how* it fishes, particularly how the longline is played out and hauled in (Laich *et al.* 2006, Dietrich *et al.* 2009). This is important, because it means that vessels can continue to fish in the same waters at the same times of year but still greatly reduce the number of birds they accidentally catch by simply changing what they do there. There are at least five measures that can be taken:

• Setting hooks at night greatly reduces bycatch, but might not in itself be enough to remove all threats, particularly when the moon is full (Jimenez *et al.* 2009). The high concentration of bioluminescent squid in the diet of Tristan Albatrosses suggests that they may spend much time feeding at night (Imber 1992).

• Reducing the discharge of fish offal reduces the number of seabirds that are attracted to the killing zone in the wake of fishing vessels (Abraham *et al.* 2009).

• In Chile, a traditional method of preventing hooked fish from being eaten by toothed whales has been found also to reduce, to practically nothing, the bycatch of seabirds (Moreno *et al.* 2008). This Mammals and Birds Excluder Device (MBED) comprises a net sleeve placed around the hooks, excluding birds and causing the line to sink more quickly.

• Adding weights to the lines to make them sink more quickly and adding streamers to deter birds from venturing into the danger zone immediately behind vessels can massively reduce seabird mortality with no reduction in fish catch (Dietrich *et al.* 2008).

• Perhaps the most effective method to reduce seabird deaths is to lay out the longline below water through a chute, completely eliminating bycatch (Brothers *et al.* 1999).

In practice, the optimal method will depend on many factors, not least the design of the vessel itself (Bull 2007). However, most methods tested so far have been shown to reduce the number of seabirds caught by at least 60% even when used in isolation (Brothers *et al.* 1999).

Developing methods to reduce seabird bycatch is only the first step to a solution. Also necessary is the implementation of policy mechanisms to ensure that all vessels are fitted with such devices. A particular problem in the conservation of the albatrosses, and indeed marine resources generally, is that they fall largely outside any national jurisdiction. The high seas, where resources are available to anyone who wants to exploit them, have suffered from particular over-exploitation through a syndrome known as 'the tragedy of the commons' (Hardin 1968, McWhinnie 2009): where the cost of over-exploitation is shared, in the short term it pays each fisherman to remove as much as possible for himself even if it spells his ruin in the long term. However, the world's governments and conservation organisations have responded effectively to this problem and a number of mechanisms are now

Albatross Task Force instructor Meidad Goren from Cape Town assembling a tori or streamer line. The streamers, made of fluorescent tubing, are suspended from the lines, creating a barrier to deter albatrosses from approaching fishing vessels too closely (Grahame Madge, RSPB Images).

in place to regulate fishing and reduce seabird bycatch. In 1996, IUCN passed a resolution calling on all nation states to act to reduce seabird bycatch to negligible levels. The following year, all albatross species were added to the appendices of the Convention on the Conservation of Migratory Species (CMS), making their conservation a legal requirement for the majority of the world's governments. The Agreement on the Conservation of Albatrosses and Petrels (ACAP) came into force in 2004 and to date has been signed by the governments of 13 countries, committing them to work together to mitigate known threats to seabirds. Regional Fisheries Management Organisations (RFMOs), which police fishing operations on the high seas, are also taking action to reduce seabird bycatch, and the United Nations' Food and Agriculture Organization (FAO) has developed a number of national action plans to guide the efforts of governments to address the problem. The voluntary sector has also been hard at work; the Albatross Task Force, established by BirdLife International in 2006, works directly with fishermen, often joining their vessels at sea, to raise awareness of the problem, monitor bycatch and demonstrate cheap but effective solutions.

Efforts to reduce the number of albatrosses killed at sea by longlining appear to be paying off. Since the mid-1990s, the greatest damage has been done by illegal, unreported and unregulated (IUU) fishing, which has resulted in the deaths of tens of thousands of seabirds each year, a high proportion of them albatrosses (Kock 2001). However, pirate fishing, which at its peak accounted for perhaps a third of all albatross deaths, has declined owing to catch certification schemes and increased patrolling by fisheries protection vessels. Moreover, prosecutions have been brought and in some cases the offending vessels have actually been scuppered. Within the vast area of the Southern Ocean managed by the Commission for the Conservation of Antarctic Marine Living Resources (CCAMLR), which includes some of the world's most important seabird colonies within its 32 million square kilometres, albatross mortality caused by longlining has been reduced within a decade to negligible levels, thanks to a combination of the development and enforcement of new fishing policies, education, and changes in fishing methods (Cooper *et al.* 2001, Dunn *et al.* 2006, Croxall 2008). Even in the Uruguayan longline fishery, previously among the most destructive to albatrosses, the capture rate of birds has declined (Jimenez *et al.* 2009). A cessation of longlining around Amsterdam Island in the Indian Ocean has given the Amsterdam Albatross a reprieve and its tiny population is now very slowly recovering (Inchausti & Weimerskirch 2001, Rivalan *et al.* 2010). In some of the world's oceans at least, longlining is posing a diminishing threat to albatrosses and petrels, and the tremendous success of CCAMLR provides a blueprint for similar successes in other seas (Croxall 2008).

Unfortunately, the range of the Tristan Albatross falls north of the well-policed CCAMLR region, and the species spends much time in seas where longlining continues to pose a serious threat. It would continue to decline because of the predation of chicks by mice, even if fisheries-related deaths were reduced to zero; equally, if mice were eradicated, the current level of adult mortality to longlining would cause the population to continue to decline (Wanless *et al.* 2009). A controversial suggestion exists to exploit the growing links between conservation practitioners and fisheries industries by establishing a system of compensation, through which the fishing industry funds island mammal eradications to offset the mortality caused to birds by longlining (Donlan & Wilcox 2008b), but, as indicated, this will achieve nothing for the Tristan Albatross without a reduction in deaths through encounters with fishing boats (Wanless *et al.* 2009). Moreover, compensation would do little to alleviate the problems caused by fisheries to marine species that are not affected by island predators (Zydelis *et al.* 2009b).

Although found only in the southern oceans, the Tristan Albatross, Gough Bunting and Atlantic Petrel are, in a political sense, endemic British breeding birds, since the Tristan group forms one of the UK Overseas Territories. These island territories, scattered across the world's oceans, hold a disproportionately high number of threatened birds (Hilton & Cuthbert 2010). Although their total area is less than one tenth of that of the UK, they hold more globally threatened birds than the whole of Europe, and many are endemic to these territories (Hilton *et al.* 2001); moreover, some of the islands have wider biological values – Gough Island itself has been described as 'a strong contender for the title of the most important seabird colony in the world' (Collar & Stuart 1985). Yet in a situation with echoes of Hawaii, where US government conservation spend is significantly lower than in mainland USA despite the islands' pre-eminence in global bird conservation (Chapter 14), the UK government's investment in the conservation of many globally threatened species that breed on the scattered fragments of its former empire is proportionally lower than its investment in less threatened species in the UK itself.

This is unfortunate, since the removal of mice from Gough Island will require considerable resources. At around 65km², Gough is nearly ten times larger than any of the thirty or so islands that have successfully been cleared of invasive mice, and mouse eradication is more difficult and more expensive to achieve than rat eradication (Howald *et al.* 2007, Parkes 2008). The only practical method is to use poison, and the impacts of the various poisons available on native wildlife and people need careful evaluation. The endemic Gough Moorhen *Gallinula comeri* (Vulnerable) is likely to be at risk from eating both the bait and dead or dying mice, and some would need to be taken into protective custody until the island was free of poison. The same precaution would need to be taken to protect the Gough Bunting. Unless almost every mouse is killed, any attempt to rid the island of them will fail. There are many caves and lava tubes on Gough within which it would be impossible to spread poison bait and which might therefore act as refuges for mice. Even so, feasibility studies suggest that eradication is a realistic proposition and plans are underway to establish trial plots on the island (Parkes 2008). This ambitious plan may be the only way to prevent one of the world's largest and most magnificent birds from being eaten away by giant mice.

Not all birds that become hooked on longlines drown. This young bird has a rusting fishhook embedded in its neck, making it one of the 'lucky' ones (Ross Wanless and Andrea Angel).

Gough Bunting Rowettia goughensis *also suffers from predation by introduced mice and was uplisted to Critically Endangered in 2008 (Richard Cuthbert, RSPB).*

Chapter 13
Raso Lark *Alauda razae*
CRITICALLY ENDANGERED

On 28 April 1897, the young English naturalist and explorer Boyd Alexander scrambled up the low cliffs that fringe the southern rim of the waterless and uninhabited island of Raso, which at 7km² is one of the smallest of the Cape Verde archipelago. Alexander had previously visited several of the other Cape Verde islands in this (at the time) Portuguese colony some 800km west of Senegal, and can hardly have expected to make the most extraordinary and unexpected discovery of his life on an island so small and inhospitable. However, after emerging onto the flat, low plain that makes up the southern half of Raso, he realised that the island was inhabited not only by abundant seabirds but also by an unfamiliar lark, which he described as being 'so tame that we could have knocked many over with sticks' (Alexander 1898). He compensated for the absence of sticks on this treeless island by shooting a good number of them instead, and these specimens still reside in the skin collections of the British Natural History Museum and the American Museum of Natural History in New York. Alexander did not realise that what he had found was actually a very close relative of the familiar and widespread Eurasian Skylark *Alauda arvensis*, and indeed the species' true affiliations were not recognised until the 1960s (Hall 1963). This is hardly surprising: the nearest populations of Skylarks lie along the coasts of North Africa, several thousands of kilometres away (Donald 2004b). Furthermore, there are marked structural differences. The Raso Lark is a smaller bird than any other member of the genus but it has a disproportionately large bill. It also shows a high degree of sexual dimorphism: males are larger, and particularly larger-billed, than females (Burton 1971, Donald *et al.* 2003). Quite why this should be is unclear but males and females tend to feed in different ways and a difference in bill size may allow the two sexes to exploit different food items, thereby reducing competition between them for scarce resources on their tiny island home (Donald *et al.* 2007a). These adaptations have so altered the original body plan that Alexander could not recognise in the Raso Lark any semblance of the Skylark, a species with which he would have been very familiar.

In years when the population is low, around two thirds of adult Raso Larks are males, like this bird. A sex-ratio skew towards males is a common pattern in small or declining bird populations, and is generally caused by higher mortality of females (Mike Brooke).

A year after Alexander's discovery, the Italian naturalist Leonardo Fea visited Raso and collected a further 30 specimens, now in the Museo Civico di Storia Naturale, Genova. (Fea was also, incidentally, perhaps the last naturalist to observe in the wild the remarkable Cape Verde Giant Skink *Macroscincus coctei*, probably endemic to Raso and nearby Branco and hunted to extinction around a century ago: Andreone & Gavetti 1998). The lark was then left in peace until 1922, when José Correia, an Azorean naturalist, collected specimens for the American Museum of Natural History. Two years later, further specimens were collected during an expedition in the sailing ship *Blossom* by the Cleveland Museum of Natural History. After another long absence from the attention of ornithologists, the Raso Lark briefly reappeared in the writings of the shadowy Richard Meinertzhagen (Meinertzhagen 1951), who claimed to have seen it when in fact he had not (see p.256). It was recorded by Bourne (1955), before the Abbé de Naurois embarked on a series of visits to the island in the 1960s (de Naurois 1994). Further specimens were collected until at least 1970, but little was recorded of the species' numbers, ecology or behaviour before a series of expeditions by researchers from the RSPB and Cambridge University, UK, commenced in 1999 (Ratcliffe *et al.* 1999, Donald & Brooke 2006, Brooke *et al.* 2012). These have already yielded fascinating information on the bird's unusual ecology and behaviour, and the Raso Lark clearly has a great deal more to tell us about adaptation to life on remote islands with harsh environments.

ORIGINS AND DISTRIBUTION

Where did the Raso Lark, closely related to the Skylark yet separated from the nearest population of that species by more than 2,000km of sea and desert, come from? One possibility is that the birds on Raso represent the last remnant of a species that was formerly far more widespread across Africa, perhaps a western counterpart of the Oriental Skylark *Alauda gulgula*, which replaces the Skylark in southern Asia today. Alternatively, it may have evolved on the Cape Verdes following colonisation by Skylarks (or their ancestors), perhaps during one of the Ice Ages, when the European fauna was pushed southwards into the area now occupied by the Sahara. As the ice retreated and the Sahara reverted to desert, some may have become stranded on the Cape Verdes to evolve into the species that survives there today.

Since its discovery, the Raso Lark has only ever been recorded on Raso (a single bird seen on the island of Sao Nicolau in March 2009 may have been a genuine vagrant, although there were rumours that some birds had been taken illegally from Raso), but recent findings from a most unexpected source have shown that it was previously more widespread in the Cape Verde islands (Mateo *et al.* 2009). It is a remarkable aspect of the ecology of birds of prey that some species may occupy the same nest sites continuously for very long periods; some Gyrfalcon *Falco rusticolus* nesting ledges in Greenland, for example, appear to have been in continual use for more than two thousand years (Burnham *et al.* 2009). During these long periods of occupation, the droppings of the raptors and the remains of their prey gradually build up in layers that can be dated by a variety of methods, giving scientists the opportunity to treat these sites as archaeological records (Houston & Nager 2009). Analyses of subfossil pellets accumulated around traditional nest sites of Barn Owls *Tyto alba* (one of them still in use today) have shown that Raso Larks were once present on at least three other islands in the Cape Verdes: Santa Luzia (35km²), São Vicente (227km²) and Santo Antão (779km²) (Mateo *et al.* 2009). The remains of the Cape Verde Giant Gecko *Tarentola gigas*, a species now confined to Raso and the smaller and almost unvegetated sea stack of Branco (3km²), and bones of the now extinct Cape Verde Giant Skink, were also found in the strata containing Raso Lark bones. Only the bones of mice were found above these older layers, however, suggesting that the extinction of the lark and the gecko on these islands coincided with the arrival of people and their associated invasive mammals. The Raso Lark is likely to have had an even larger distribution than findings of bones on other islands might suggest, since all these islands are separated by relatively shallow seas and were joined together during periods of lower sea levels into a far larger and now largely submerged island that covered thousands of square kilometres. Populations appear to have persisted on several islands after rising sea levels separated them, right down to the islands' discovery and occupation from 1462 onwards by Portuguese settlers and their accompanying cats, dogs, rats and goats. It is probably no coincidence that the Raso Lark survives on the largest island in the Cape Verdes that has never been permanently inhabited by people or cats (Donald & Brooke 2006).

Half the area of Raso comprises a low flat plain of decomposing lava and tufa, intersected by small dry streambeds ('ribeiras') with a scant cover of grasses and herbs. It is here that the majority of Raso Larks are found, although birds are not spread evenly across it. Highest densities occur along the ribeiras and the tops of the low

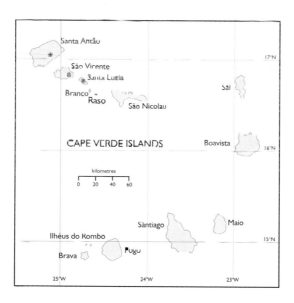

The Cape Verde Islands. The Raso Lark is currently restricted to Raso, but recent archaeological excavations of nests of the Barn Owl Tyto alba *have shown that the lark was once present on at least three other islands. The locations of Raso Lark bones from owl nests are marked with asterisks.*

131

sea-cliffs (Donald *et al.* 2005). Within these restricted areas, densities of birds are actually rather high for a lark, and the species appears generally more gregarious throughout the year than the Skylark (Donald *et al.* 2003). The rest of the island comprises hilly outcrops rising to 164m, valleys and raised plains, and is largely devoid of vegetation. Very few birds are found in this relatively barren area during the breeding season, but up to half the population moves there when birds are not breeding (Donald *et al.* 2005). At such times, all the birds present in this part of the island form a single tight flock, and are more wary and less approachable than birds elsewhere on the island, perhaps because of the presence of kestrels in the area. Less than half of Raso's meagre land area is regularly used by the larks, and the species now has one of the smallest ranges of any bird.

There is little historical information on population size (Hazevoet 1995). A visitor in 1951 said that the birds 'swarm' on the island and are 'totally fearless' (Bourne 1955). On his first visit to Raso in 1962, the Abbé de Naurois recorded 'an abundance of adults and immature birds' awaiting him, but on subsequent visits he noticed decreasing numbers, recording only approximately 50 pairs in 1965 (de Naurois 1994). By the early 1980s, the population appears to have fallen to as few as ten pairs, although these estimates were not based on systematic surveys (Hazevoet 1995). The first complete count of the species did not occur until 1998, when the population was estimated at just 92 birds (Ratcliffe *et al.* 1999). In October 2001, numbers stood at around 130 individuals (Donald *et al.* 2003), but by November 2003 this had fallen to 76–87 individuals, and in December 2004 only around 65 birds were present (Donald *et al.* 2005). However, following good rainfall in 2005, the population increased sharply and in December 2005 again numbered around 130 (Donald & Brooke 2006). After 2009, heavy rainfall led to further mass breeding and the population rocketed to over 1500 birds in 2011 (Fig. 13.1).

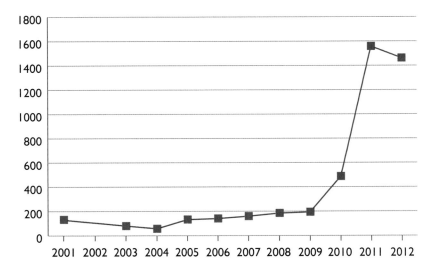

Figure 13.1. Population trend of Raso Lark, 2001–2012, showing the extraordinary effects on the population of heavy seasonal rainfall after 2009. From data in Donald et al. *2005 and Brooke* et al. *2012, with data for 2012 provided by M. de L. Brooke (pers. comm.).*

THE CHALLENGES OF ISLAND LIFE

From these population estimates, it is clear that numbers of Raso Larks fluctuate greatly and are dictated largely by rainfall, which is a prerequisite for breeding (Brooke *et al.* 2012). Catastrophic droughts lasting up to 18 years have occurred throughout the Cape Verdes' recorded history and it is unlikely that there were many breeding attempts during these long periods. Populations were extremely low in the early 1980s, following a drought of more than a decade, the number of females perhaps falling to fewer than ten. Thus after rain the Raso Lark

Raso in October 2001, following rain. The island was covered with low vegetation and most Raso Larks were breeding. In drought years, few birds can breed. The Raso Lark has one of the smallest distributions of any bird; the area shown in the photograph contained well over half the entire population of the species (Paul F. Donald, RSPB).

population increases and in drought it can fall to very low levels. This pattern is apparent even from the few existing population estimates and there is a strong positive correlation between population size in any one year and rainfall in the previous year (Donald *et al.* 2003, Brooke *et al.* 2012). Mass breeding events are probably less than annual but it may be that some pairs are capable of breeding in any year, as suggested by the presence of a recently fledged juvenile in January 2003, despite a long preceding period with no appreciable rainfall. Indeed, it is hard to imagine how the species could survive a drought of nearly two decades without some reproductive input into the population, although the birds' remarkable longevity (see below) must have been selected for as a direct response to drought. Rainfall patterns in the Sahel, which are likely to be a reasonable indicator of rainfall on the Cape Verde islands, show that rain in the region was well above average at the time of Bourne's 'swarm' in the early 1950s and of de Naurois's 'abundance' in the early 1960s. Since 1970, however, rainfall in the region has generally been below the long-term average, and until the recent boom populations may have been lower on average as a result (Donald & Brooke 2006).

Whether or not there has been any long-term population decline, the Raso Lark is clearly steering a course perilously close to extinction. Species with greatly fluctuating populations are more at risk of extinction than species with stable ones, simply because there is a higher risk of chance fluctuations reducing the population to zero or to such low levels that inbreeding effects multiply. When the population is small to start with, extinction becomes a real possibility. The problem is compounded by the fact that when populations are low, the sex ratio is greatly skewed towards males, such that before the population explosion after 2009, males outnumbered females by about two to one, greatly reducing the population's ability to survive (Donald *et al.* 2003, Brooke *et al.* 2010). However, as the population rose, so the sex ratio returned to parity (Brooke *et al.* 2012). The most likely explanation for this is that, as in many birds, male Raso Larks have slightly higher annual survival rates than females. After long periods of drought with little breeding, the average age of birds in the population increases and the small difference in annual survival rates between the sexes begins to manifest itself as a skewed sex ratio. In boom years, however, the average age of the population is too low for these small differences in survival rates to make much of a difference and the population sex ratio is closer to equality. It may be, therefore, that the adult sex ratio of any bird population might be a good indicator of whether it is increasing or declining (Donald 2007). What is less clear is why male Raso Larks live longer than females, but a possible clue lies in observing their feeding behaviour when times are tough. In years of drought, males spend much of their time excavating burrows in the sand to find tubers of a type of nutsedge *Cyperus*. These plants produce bulbs that are very rich in carbohydrates and water, and indeed nutsedges are an important 'famine food' for people facing starvation (Gupta & Kanodia 1968). Although female Raso Larks appear to be as capable of excavating these bulbs as the longer-billed males, they are generally prevented from doing so by the males, which aggressively guard their burrows and evict smaller birds from areas where the nutsedge occurs (Donald *et al.* 2007a). When female birds do manage to find a nutsedge bulb, it is often stolen from them by the males. It might be therefore that females are excluded from an important food resource and hence are more vulnerable to starvation during droughts. Whatever its causes, this skewed sex ratio clearly increases the likelihood of extinction, since natural fluctuations need only to reduce the tiny number of females to zero for the species to become functionally extinct; the males' songs might ring out over Raso for several years after the species becomes consigned to history through the death of the last female. That the Raso Lark has managed to survive for so long suggests remarkable endurance, but it must have flirted with extinction many times during its history (Donald & Brooke 2006).

Drought is not the only threat faced by the isolated little population of Raso Larks. Detailed observations of a large sample of nests suggest that predation of eggs, and possibly of some incubating females, is extremely high, with the evidence pointing to a nocturnal animal (Donald *et al.* 2003). The culprit is the near-endemic Cape Verde Giant Gecko, once also recorded as food in Barn Owl nests on other islands and now itself a globally threatened species; the eggs of one of the world's rarest birds are being predated by one of the world's rarest reptiles, in a situation reminiscent of the predation by the threatened Madagascar Harrier *Circus macrosceles* of the even rarer Madagascar Pochard *Aythya innotata* (Chapter 21). The extremely low rate of productivity would lead to rapid population decline in a short-lived species, but despite their drought-plagued environments, ongoing studies of colour-ringed birds suggest that Raso Larks are extraordinarily long-lived (Donald & Brooke 2006), with an annual survival rate of 87% for males and 74% for females (Brooke *et al.* 2012). This longevity underpins the species' ability to survive long periods of drought with little breeding, so anything that reduces adult survival, such as the accidental or deliberate introduction of predatory mammals to Raso, will lead to rapid decline or extinction. Although cats and dogs have occurred on the island in the past, they have not become established, perhaps because of the lack of fresh water, and Raso Lark remains have not so far been found in the cat and dog scats examined; these contained almost nothing but seabird remains (Donald *et al.* 2005). At least one Short-eared Owl *Asio*

In drought years, the ground of Raso is pock-marked with burrows excavated by Raso Larks, mostly males, digging for food (Paul F. Donald, RSPB).

The Cape Verde Giant Gecko Tarentola gigas *is a threatened reptile with a range almost as small as that of the Raso Lark. Although docile when handled, it has a powerful bite and may be an important predator of the eggs and chicks of Raso Lark (Paul F. Donald, RSPB).*

flammeus, a rare visitor to the Cape Verdes, has been present on the island in recent years, although again its pellets contained mostly the bones of seabirds and no remains of Raso Lark were found in the samples examined. Common Kestrels *Falco tinnunculus* of the distinctive race *neglectus* and Brown-necked Ravens *Corvus ruficollis* both breed in small numbers (one to three pairs of each) on Raso (Donald *et al.* 2003) but have probably done so for many years, and the birds infrequently hunt over the areas occupied by Raso Larks. At present, therefore, there is no suggestion that predators other than the gecko are impacting on the Raso Lark population or those of the many seabirds on the island. On nearby Santa Luzia, which has a source of fresh water but is no longer inhabited by people, cats and mice are abundant and the island is almost devoid of birds.

Permits are required to visit Raso. The Cape Verde islands are being promoted as a tourist destination and any increase in the number of unregulated visits to Raso by tourists unaware of the fragility of the island's ecosystem would pose a threat. However, many of the local boatmen now refuse to take visitors to the island if they do not have a permit so the number of visitors is more strictly regulated. It is most important that precautions are taken to prevent the accidental introduction of mammals, through appropriate packaging of food and other supplies, and to avoid crushing the holes excavated by birds burrowing for bulbs.

Increases in drought length and frequency represent another important threat. How climate change will affect rainfall patterns in the Cape Verdes is currently unclear, but other islands in Macaronesia are predicted to suffer significant losses of endemic birds. Some models predict an increase in rainfall on oceanic islands, which may bring the Raso Lark some respite, but many islands in the Cape Verde archipelago are suffering from desertification and as a result some of the larger ones are scattered with abandoned villages. The most recent models suggest that climate change is responsible for the recorded drying of the Sahel zone since 1970, which is likely to get worse in the future (Held *et al.* 2005). This would reduce the average population of the Raso Lark still further and increase the probability of its extinction. Drought is likely to have brought the species close to extinction many times in the past.

After prolonged drought, the population can decline to levels that make the Raso Lark one of the world's rarest species. Regular monitoring of the species, careful checks that mammals have not reached the island and proper management of visitors to the island are the absolute minimum conservation requirements, but the best chance of ensuring the species' long-term survival may lie in the re-establishment of a population on neighbouring Santa Luzia, where there is much apparently suitable habitat (Donald *et al.* 2005) and where the species was present before the arrival of people (Mateo *et al.* 2009). Unfortunately, although the last human inhabitants abandoned the island decades ago, Santa Luzia harbours introduced populations of feral cats and mice. Cat removal is likely to be relatively straightforward and in early 2013 funds were secured to undertake the first phase of an island restoration project on Santa Luzia. Often the removal of cats on islands that also have mice can lead to severe problems as mouse populations explode. In the absence of other land mammals, mice can become larger, more numerous and more voracious than on islands where other predators keep their numbers in check (Angel *et al.* 2009), as the example of the Tristan Albatross (Chapter 12) has shown. However, preliminary data suggest that mice are found on Santa Luzia only around camps used by fishermen. The clearance of cats from Santa Luzia and the establishment of a second and potentially far larger population of Raso Larks therefore appears to be a realistic conservation goal. Meanwhile, local conservationists are starting to become active on the Cape Verde islands, and local volunteers now occupy Raso during the seabird breeding season to prevent illegal harvesting of young shearwaters by visiting fishermen. An action plan was prepared for Raso in 2009 and momentum appears to be gathering to enforce protection of the species. That the Raso Lark has survived for so long on its tiny drought-stricken island appears miraculous but its remarkable tenacity may not be enough to see it survive a period of rising pressures without help.

As part of a long-term study of the species' population dynamics, many Raso Larks have been fitted with unique combinations of coloured rings (Paul F. Donald, RSPB).

Chapter 14
Po'ouli *Melamprosops phaeosoma*
CRITICALLY ENDANGERED
(POSSIBLY EXTINCT)

In a recent survey, the US Fish and Wildlife Service estimated that there are nearly 50 million birdwatchers in the USA, their activities contributing some $36 billion each year to the national economy (La Rouche 2009). The country boasts some of the longest-established and best-resourced conservation organisations in the world. Yet the world's wealthiest nation has an unenviable record of recent bird extinctions; and of all the world's nations, only Brazil is home to more species listed as Critically Endangered. This alarming circumstance is due largely to events unfolding on an island chain in the mid-Pacific. Mainland conservation successes like the ongoing recovery of the California Condor *Gymnogyps californianus* from what seemed like certain extinction, and long-term efforts to save the Whooping Crane *Grus americana*, are overshadowed in global terms by the ecological catastrophe of Hawaii. Perhaps more than half the world's bird extinctions in the last fifty years have occurred in the fiftieth state of the USA; were it not for the loss of so many of Hawaii's native birds, the global extinction rate of birds over the last few decades might have been no higher than at any time during the last two thousand years (Pimm *et al.* 2006). In fact, extinction rates on Hawaii have actually increased over time (Fig. 14.1). The Hawaiian Crow *Corvus hawaiiensis* was last seen in the wild in 2002 and survives now only in captivity, making it one of only a handful of bird species with this conservation status (Butchart *et al.* 2006b,c). The Palila *Loxioides bailleui* and the Akekee *Loxops caeruleirostris* have recently joined twelve other Hawaiian species on the Critically Endangered list; five of these have not been seen for over five years and are probably already extinct. Ornithologists who visited a pristine plateau on the island of Kauai in 1975 were to describe it less than twenty-five years later as a 'lost world', so rapid was the ecological collapse in the intervening period (Conant *et al.* 1998).

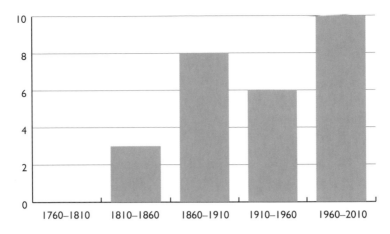

Figure 14.1. Approximate number of extinctions of Hawaiian native birds in half-century blocks, 1760–2010. The chart includes five species still listed as Critically Endangered but not seen in recent years and likely to be extinct, and one species that is now extinct in the wild but survives in captivity.

The majority of extinct and rare species belong to an amazing group of birds called the Hawaiian honeycreepers, which are actually relatives of the finches, although many look remarkably unfinchlike. This is one of the world's great island bird radiations: all 50-odd known living or extinct species are thought to have evolved from a single colonising ancestor that arrived on Hawaii, the world's most remote island group, some three to five million years ago (Cowie & Holland 2008). As a result of this common ancestry they share a number of features, not the least remarkable of which is a distinctive body odour, like that of rain on asphalt, which perhaps reflects some sort of chemical defence (Weldon & Rappole 1997); however, the differences are far more striking than the similarities. From a single ancestor, helped by the fortuitous geography of Hawaii with its originally wide range of habitats and high mountains, the Hawaiian honeycreepers have evolved a remarkable variety of colours, shapes and sizes. Particularly diverse are the bills, which range in shape from massive and parrot-like for cracking seeds and tearing wood to extraordinary long sickles for drinking nectar deep within trumpet-shaped flowers. Perhaps the most remarkable bill of all in a living species of bird is that of the endangered 'Akiapola'au *Hemignathus munroi*, which has a short, straight and stout lower mandible for chiselling holes in wood like a woodpecker, and a much longer and thinner curved upper mandible used to hook out grubs from within. Some of the extinct species had even more bizarre feeding apparatus: the shovelbills *Vangulifer*, for example, had a beak like a spoonbill, possibly for snapping insects from the air in flight. The enormous bill of one extinct species so impressed the finders of its fossil remains that they named it *Chloridops regiskongi*, the King Kong Grosbeak! Recent research has shown that not only have the Hawaiian honeycreepers radiated into a dazzling array of different forms, but that a parallel process of convergent evolution has also taken place, with some remarkable similarities evolving between species that are not particularly closely related (Reding *et al.* 2009). All this variety has arisen through evolution acting on a single species of finch. Perhaps nowhere else on earth has natural selection been so dramatically and exquisitely illustrated, but with some 70% of Hawaii's native birds now extinct this wonderful diversity has been irreversibly laid waste.

PO'OULI: LATE DISCOVERY, EARLY LOSS

The discovery and loss of the Po'ouli (also known as Poo-uli, Po'o-uli, Poouli and other variants) provide a compelling illustration of the problems facing Hawaii's birds. Remarkably, this unspectacular but highly distinctive species evaded detection until 1973, when it was discovered by a student expedition in high-altitude forests on the eastern slopes of the Haleakala Volcano on Maui, the second largest of the Hawaiian Islands (Casey & Jacobi

1974). It appears to have been unknown even to pre-European colonists, so the species' Hawaiian name had to be created for it after its discovery. The population at the time of its discovery was estimated to be around 200 birds, occupying some 13km² of forest within which all subsequent records have come (Groombridge 2009). Two specimens were collected, both later proving to be immature birds.

Although population estimates from field surveys are known to be imprecise, because of the difficulty of surveying this extremely quiet and unobtrusive species, there is evidence of a complete collapse in the population between 1975 and 1980, after which no more than a handful of birds could be accounted for in any year (Scott *et al.* 1986, Groombridge *et al.* 2004a). In 1986 two nests were found, both belonging to one pair (Engilis *et al.* 1996, Kepler *et al.* 1996); these were the first and, as it turned out, the last nests of this species ever seen. The last documented evidence of breeding activity was in 1995 (Reynolds & Snetsinger 2001). The following year, a live bird was caught for the first time, allowing a detailed description to be taken of the plumage of an adult (Baker 1998), but by this time the Po'ouli was already perhaps the world's rarest animal species, with only four known individuals remaining (Reilly 1998, Baker 2001). Efforts to protect and restore its core area by the creation of the Hanawi Natural Area Reserve, and the exclosure or removal of feral pigs and rats, failed to restore the population, and between 1997 and the last sighting in the wild in 2002 only three ringed birds were known, all in different parts of the forest. So elusive is this species that simply checking that these three birds were still present each year was a major undertaking in terms of fieldwork effort (Groombridge 2009).

In 2002, the decision was taken by the Maui Forest Bird Recovery Project to move a female bird into the territory of a male to try to stimulate breeding (Groombridge *et al.* 2004a). Enormous care was taken to prevent harm to the birds during this procedure. The methods were tested on a large number of the related but not endangered Maui 'Alauahio *Paroreomyza montana*, and white blood cell counts were used to identify the transportation method that caused the least stress to the birds (Groombridge *et al.* 2004b). A complex veterinary apparatus was devised, including an intensive care unit and an oxygenator in case of emergency. A companion compartment was provided so that if a Po'ouli needed to be held for any length of time, for example in case of injury, a surrogate 'tutor' bird of an ecologically compatible native species could be introduced to encourage the sick bird to feed. Endemic snails, on which the Po'ouli (uniquely for a Hawaiian honeycreeper) fed largely in the wild, were collected as food for

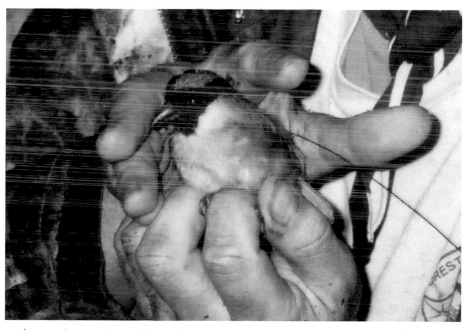

The Po'ouli was discovered as recently as 1973, and the last known bird died in captivity in 2004. This photograph, one of very few ever taken of the species and previously unpublished, records the last-ditch attempt in 2002 to create a pair in the wild by transferring one of the last three known birds into the territory of another (Jim Groombridge).

any bird that needed to be held. After these exhaustive preparations, the nets were set and on 4 April 2002, after eight days of work under extremely difficult conditions, a female Po'ouli was finally captured and carefully moved into the territory of a male. She roosted there overnight, but to the intense disappointment of the researchers who were tracking her through a tiny electronic transmitter fitted to her back, next morning she started to move back through the forest to her original home over a kilometre away, reaching it that afternoon (Groombridge *et al.* 2004a). It is unlikely that she even met the male whose territory she had been moved to.

One of the last three Po'ouli, captured on CCTV cameras in the holding cage carefully designed for it. Unfortunately, this attempt in 2002 to create a pair in the wild failed; two years later, what was probably the last Po'ouli died in captivity (Jim Groombridge).

The cause of the Po'ouli's demise is unknown, but the rapid decline that followed its discovery coincided with the invasion of its range by feral pigs and consequent habitat deterioration (Engilis 1990, Mountainspring *et al.* 1990). Efforts to save the species foundered because of a lack of agreement on what needed to be done; a wide range of conservation options were proposed, debated and rejected while the species quietly slipped away (VanderWerf *et al.* 2006, Powell 2008). In 1998, with the species already perilously close to extinction, a document with the less than urgent title *Draft environment assessment for possible management actions to save the Po'ouli* was published (Rosa *et al.* 1998). Following the valiant but sadly unsuccessful attempt in 2002 to create a wild pair, the decision was finally taken to remove the remaining birds to captivity, but only a single individual could be caught. In November 2004 this bird, which might well have been the last Po'ouli in existence, died in the Maui Bird Conservation Center. Post mortem analyses showed it to have been suffering from malaria, but it probably died simply of old age. It also showed that the bird was male rather than female as previously assessed by DNA testing, so it is possible that the sex of the translocated bird was also wrongly assessed (Groombridge 2009). If so, the last three Po'ouli might all have been males, a common pattern in the immediate run-up to complete extinction. Recent intensive surveys, supported by bioclimatic models to identify suitable areas (Porter *et al.* 2006), have failed to find any birds, but the Po'ouli is one of five Hawaiian species that remain optimistically classified in the new BirdLife status category Critically Endangered (Possibly Extinct).

Very little is known of the Po'ouli in life. It appears to have been as unassuming in its behaviour as it was in its plumage, quietly foraging alone or in mixed flocks in the lower and middle layers of the canopy and rarely calling or singing. Only towards the end did it become clear that it was a particularly unusual bird, differing from all other honeycreepers in the structure of the tongue (perhaps an adaptation to its unusual diet of snails) and lacking their peculiar body odour. Indeed, so unusual was the Po'ouli that some thought it was not a Hawaiian honeycreeper at all (Pratt 1992). More recently, however, genetic analyses have shown that it formed a unique and ancient lineage within that group, contributing more evolutionary diversity to the honeycreepers than any other species (Fleischer *et al.* 2001). With the death of the last bird, a very long branch of the extraordinary radiation of the Hawaiian honeycreepers was lost.

HAWAII'S EPIDEMIC OF EXTINCTION

The extinction crisis on Hawaii has been brought about by the usual combination of factors that have devastated island ecologies elsewhere. Indeed, the great majority of threats that impact on island bird populations around the world have come together here with devastating effect. Early Polynesian colonists, who first populated Hawaii around 500 AD, cleared virtually all forests below 500m and most of the drier forests between 500m and 1,500m, and brought with them the Pacific Rat *Rattus exulans* (Cuddihy & Stone 1990). Since Captain Cook's 'discovery' of the islands in 1778 and their subsequent colonisation by Europeans, logging and grazing have removed practically all the remaining dry forests, although much of the original high-altitude rain forests remain. European colonisation also brought with it a range of invasive predators, including feral cats, Black Rat *Rattus rattus* and the Small Indian Mongoose *Herpestes auropunctatus* (Tomich 1986), to say nothing of the influenza, smallpox and measles that decimated the islands' human inhabitants. Since becoming the most recent state of the USA in 1959, Hawaii has become the playground of America's rich, placing intense pressure on the islands' limited land area. The usual complement of introduced predators and competitors has taken its predictable toll. Feral pigs and goats have played havoc with the ecology of the islands, drastically altering the structure and function the remaining forest. In many lowland areas, native plants have been largely replaced by exotic species. Rats and cats abound. Moth larvae, an important prey for several native birds, are heavily parasitised by introduced wasps and flies (Banko *et al.* 2002). Generalist alien birds outcompete specialised native species, as in the case of the introduced Japanese White-eye *Zosterops japonicus* and the native Akepa *Loxops coccineus*, whose population has collapsed in response to competition for food and to infestations of feather-chewing lice from the white-eyes (Freed *et al.* 2008a). Such has been the pressure from the white-eye that in areas where the two coexist young Akepa have actually become smaller in body size over time, leading to reduced survival; where the white-eye has not colonised to the same extent, the native species has shown no reduction in body size (Freed & Cann 2009). The Akepa is not the only native species to be suffering in this way. Following the arrival of introduced birds at higher altitudes, there has been an explosive increase since 2003 in the number of feather-chewing lice infesting native Hawaiian birds that were previously free of them (Freed *et al.* 2008b).

Many of these problems continue to blight the biota of the world's once-rich islands, though no others have suffered the same rate of recent extinction. What makes Hawaii unique as a conservation problem is the prominent role that disease has played. Around 1830, the Southern House Mosquito *Culex quinquefasciatus* became established on Maui, possibly after larvae hatched from water barrels carried aboard whaling ships. From here it either spread or was introduced independently (Fonseca *et al.* 2000) to the other islands. Avian poxvirus, which can be transmitted by mosquitoes, appears to have become established on Hawaii shortly after, as early naturalists reported seeing tumour-like swellings on dead and dying forest birds (Atkinson & LaPointe 2009). More than a century later, birds carrying malaria, both probably Asian in origin, were introduced to Hawaii (Beadell *et al.* 2006). The combination of parasite and vector proved disastrous for Hawaii's native birds, which had evolved in a relatively disease-free environment; indeed, it might be that the remarkable radiation of the Hawaiian honeycreepers could *only* have occurred in the absence of endemic disease, since disease-mediated competition might inhibit the evolution of co-existing species (Ricklefs & Bermingham 2007). They certainly had little resistance to malaria when it arrived.

No conclusive evidence exists that disease has directly caused the extinction of any Hawaiian bird, but it has clearly contributed to many losses. All native Hawaiian birds experimentally exposed in the 1950s to disease-carrying mosquitoes died from fulminating pox or malaria. Later studies have confirmed that native birds infected with malaria typically suffer 40–100% mortality and exhibit severe clinical symptoms such as acute anaemia and a grossly enlarged liver and spleen. Infected birds eat less and rapidly lose body mass and condition. Poxvirus and the secondary bacterial infection of lesions appear to cause similarly high mortality, and birds weakened by malaria often contract poxvirus, and vice-versa (Atkinson & LaPointe 2009). Perhaps the most convincing demonstration of the impact of disease is that the distributions of birds on Hawaii appear to be determined very largely by the distribution of mosquitoes (Atkinson *et al.* 2000, Atkinson *et al.* 2001, Atkinson & LaPointe 2009). Common introduced bird species show a far greater degree of immunity to malaria than do native species (Atkinson *et al.* 1995) and proliferate in the lowlands, where mosquitoes are commonest – indeed, so immune are introduced species that the main reservoir of the malaria now lies in native species (Atkinson & LaPointe 2009). Below an altitude of 1,000m, practically all the birds now encountered in Hawaii, in terms of both species and individuals, are introduced, and the ranges of most Hawaiian species are now confined to higher elevations (Banko *et al.* 2002). Above 1,500m, where mosquito numbers are low, the development of the parasite is slow and disease transmission close to zero; birds in pristine forest reserves at these altitudes show a very low incidence of avian malaria and poxvirus (Van Riper *et al.* 2002, Aruch *et al.* 2007).

This altitudinal contraction cannot be blamed on the greater loss of native habitat at lower elevations since, even in lowland habitats still dominated by native plants, there has been a pattern of local extinctions of native bird species and their replacement by exotic species (Reynolds *et al.* 2003, Spiegel *et al.* 2006). So strong is the pressure to withdraw uphill to escape disease that many native species today confined to highland forests are likely to have been lowland species before disease arrived, and may therefore currently occupy suboptimal habitats (Burney *et al.* 2001). This was probably the case for the Po'ouli, subfossil remains of which have been found only at a number of dry lowland sites on Maui (Pratt *et al.* 1997). In the upland habitats in which it was discovered and then so quickly lost, the Po'ouli appears to have been rather thinly distributed, perhaps because birds required large territories to provide sufficient numbers of the tree snails that made up a high proportion of their diet (Pratt *et al.* 1997, Groombridge *et al.* 2006).

The concentration of native birds in a few high-altitude refuges poses a further problem, which is that these areas are those most likely to be altered by climate change (Benning *et al.* 2002). High-altitude forests that are currently free of malaria are likely to become malarial in the future, and already the disease seems to be moving uphill. A warming of 2°C is projected to lead to the loss of 57–96% of currently disease-free forests (Atkinson & LaPointe 2009). Unless the forests themselves can also migrate upwards beyond the current treeline to follow changing climate, these high-altitude refuges will become increasingly squeezed. As birds and disease-free forest move towards the summits, so the area of land available will become smaller. Furthermore, there is now little option for birds to take shelter from mid-Pacific cyclones in lowland valleys, as habitats there have been drastically altered and disease is rife (Conant *et al.* 1998). Populations of one or two native species capable of developing resistance to malaria have bounced back in recent years as strong selection pressure has acted to increase their immunity (Woodworth *et al.* 2005, Spiegel *et al.* 2006, Eggert *et al.* 2008), but lack of genetic diversity may prevent the development of resistance in rarer species (Atkinson & LaPointe 2009). It is not known what attributes of life-history or genetic makeup determine the ability to develop resistance sufficiently quickly to prevent extinction but many Hawaiian species clearly lack them (Foster *et al.* 2007).

Malaria and poxvirus appear to have been the only two diseases having population-level impacts on a wide range of species, but some Hawaiian birds have suffered from other introduced diseases and disease remains a risk even to species that appear to be well on the road to recovery (Atkinson & LaPointe 2009). In 2008, for example, an outbreak of botulism killed up to half the Laysan Ducks *Anas laysanensis* on Midway Island, setting back the long-hoped-for removal of this species from the list of Critically Endangered birds. The same species of mosquito that spread such devastating disease in Hawaii has recently appeared in New Zealand and the incidence of *Plasmodium relictum* malaria in birds there is increasing (Tompkins & Gleeson 2006). The remarkable survival of the complete endemic avifauna of the Galápagos Islands might be due to the failure of malaria and its vector to become established there (Wikelski *et al.* 2004), although there is recent worrying evidence that mosquitoes are now present and that malaria parasites of a variety known to cause high mortality in birds have infested populations of the Galápagos Penguin *Spheniscus mendiculus* (Levin *et al.* 2009).

142

SAVING HAWAII'S REMAINING BIRDS: AN UPHILL STRUGGLE

What can be done to prevent the extinction of Hawaii's remaining forest birds? The Po'ouli is almost certainly lost, but nine Critically Endangered birds and a similar number of Endangered and Vulnerable species are still there to be saved. Key to their survival is mid-elevation forest. Here disease transmission is currently at its highest, as these forests are at the zone of overlap between mosquitoes from the lowlands and native birds in their highland refuges. Young birds dispersing into mid-elevation forests from high-altitude refuges and adult birds undertaking altitudinal movements to follow changing nectar supplies are rapidly infected as they move downhill, thus maintaining the reservoir of parasites in native birds. Clearing mosquitoes from mid-elevation forests will therefore reduce parasite reservoirs in native birds and increase the amount of safe habitat for them. Relatively simple interventions could help achieve this aim. The foraging actions of pigs create hollows that fill to form pools of water used by mosquito larvae, so fencing and culling feral grazers could reduce mosquito numbers significantly. Plans are being made to eradicate rodent nest-predators and thereby boost productivity, increase populations and widen the genetic diversity needed to develop disease resistance (Kilpatrick 2006). For some species, indeed, the eradication of invasive rodents might be more important than the control of disease (VanderWerf 2009). Following the New Zealand method of creating predator-free 'islands within islands', helicopters have been used to drop rodenticide bait. Vaccines and chemotherapy could be used to maintain the health of small populations of birds in intensive conservation projects, but currently there is no effective way of delivering these to larger numbers of individuals (Atkinson & LaPointe 2009). The creation of genetically modified mosquitoes, poor vectors of malaria but strong competitors with disease-carrying insects, has also been proposed, but there are severe technical and legal obstacles to overcome (Atkinson & LaPointe 2009). Recent evidence of the effects of the Japanese White-eye (see above) suggest that its removal may be key to the survival of some native species (Freed & Cann 2009).

Clearly, the problems faced by Hawaiian birds are many and severe, yet species have been successfully restored from tiny populations in the face of overwhelming odds elsewhere. New Zealand and Mauritius have pioneered the restoration of relict and seemingly doomed populations (Butler & Merton 1992, Jones *et al* 1995). The failure of the world's wealthiest nation, where one person in five claims to be a birdwatcher, to prevent the recent extinctions in Hawaii begs an explanation. There has clearly been no lack of scientific research – since 1996 many more scientific papers and reports have been written about the Po'ouli than there were birds in existence. Much of what is known about the conservation implications of avian diseases has been generated by world-class research on Hawaii's rare birds. There has also been no lack of effort by conservationists in the field, who have had to work on an elusive bird like the Po'ouli under very difficult conditions, in thick forests on steep slopes at high altitudes and often in torrential rainfall (Phalen & Groombridge 2003, Groombridge 2009) Indeed, so dramatic were the final attempts to save this species that a whole book has been dedicated to describing them (Powell 2008).

Part of the problem facing Hawaii's remaining endemic birds appears to be that government conservation resources are not directed at the country's rarest species (Restani & Marzluff 2001). Only 4% of the $750 million spent by federal and state authorities between 1996 and 2004 on the USA's most threatened species went to Hawaii, despite its clear global pre-eminence as a conservation priority; mainland species received on average fifteen times more expenditure than Hawaiian species (Leonard 2008). This might reflect a lack of enthusiasm on the part of wildlife authorities to commit themselves to what would have to be very long-term and expensive investments. Rodent control alone costs thousands of dollars per square kilometre and, although it is successful in the short term, rat populations recover to pre-treatment levels within a year (Nelson *et al.* 2002).

Finance, however, is unlikely to be the full explanation for the catastrophe of Hawaii. Hawaiian species have been subject to the full gamut of threats that island species face, and disease, an almost intractable problem, appears to have had a greater impact on birds in Hawaii than anywhere else. Furthermore, conservation options are limited by the lack of predator- or disease-free offshore islands of appropriate size and ecology on which to establish populations of rare species, precluding a strategy used to such good effect on a number of New Zealand's most threatened birds. There may also perhaps be another contributory factor, reflecting a more systemic problem. At a crisis meeting in 2002, when only three Po'ouli remained, the representatives of seven different conservation

Captive breeding in the UK in the 1950s prevented the extinction of the Hawaiian Goose Branta sandvicensis *but captive breeding facilities were constructed very late on in Hawaii, perhaps contributing to the high extinction rate of the islands' native birds. These geese are pictured on Haleakala Volcano on Maui, the only home of the Po'ouli (Kevin Schafer).*

and research agencies failed to unite on what should be done (Powell 2008). Irresolution, perhaps because of the large number of different agencies involved, seems to have gripped the conservation process (Groombridge *et al.* 2004a, Powell 2008). Had a decision been made to take the remaining Po'ouli into captivity in the 1980s, when the species was known to be in desperate trouble, it might survive today (Powell 2008). However, captive breeding facilities were not constructed on Hawaii until the mid-1990s (Kuehler *et al.* 2001), decades after their efficacy was proved elsewhere. Indeed, one of the first species to be saved using this conservation technique was a Hawaiian endemic, the Nene or Hawaiian Goose *Branta sandvicensis*, whose extinction was prevented by a programme of captive breeding initiated by Sir Peter Scott in the UK in the 1950s followed by successful reintroduction (Black 1995).

Perhaps stung by criticisms about levels of funding and lack of incisive action, in April 2009 the US Fish and Wildlife Service announced plans to invest $14 million to save the Hawaiian Crow from extinction. Efforts to save Hawaii's other rare birds are also gathering pace, particularly in the area of intensive species management. Since 1994, the Hawaiian Endangered Bird Conservation Program, managed by San Diego Zoo, has raised hundreds of native birds to fledging in captive propagation units, and plans are in place to start reintroducing species to areas from which they have been extirpated. Watershed partnerships have been established to implement ecosystem-scale conservation, and expertise has been developed in all aspects of conserving Hawaii's birds. A small number of species appear to be responding to these efforts and it seems likely that the fortunes of other threatened species will improve. For the Po'ouli, however, time seems to have run out.

Chapter 15
Saving the world's rarest birds

By the late 1970s, it appeared inevitable that yet another island species would soon be added to the growing list of extinct birds. Habitat loss, introduced predators and the unrestricted use of the pesticide DDT had reduced the known population of the Mauritius Kestrel *Falco punctatus* to just four birds, only one of them a fertile female (Cade & Jones 1993). Even if the population could be increased, genetic theory suggested that after going through such a narrow bottleneck it would be too inbred to survive. However, Carl Jones and his colleagues in the Mauritius Wildlife Foundation did not give up hope and delighted the conservation world by bringing the species back from the brink in the most spectacular fashion (Jones *et al.* 1995, Jones & Hartley 1995, Jones & Swinnerton 1997). After three decades of conservation effort, involving captive breeding and release, nest-guarding, the provision of supplementary food, predator control and many other labour-intensive management techniques, the population of the Mauritius Kestrel now stands at around 400 birds in the wild. Additional birds are held in captivity, providing insurance against any future catastrophe on Mauritius. In 1994, the species was

The Mauritius Kestrel Falco punctatus, *one of a number of Mauritian species that has been successfully pulled back from the brink of extinction (Malcolm Nicoll).*

'Old Blue', the Black Robin Petroica traversi *that saved her species from extinction, with more than a little help from Don Merton and the New Zealand Department of Conservation (Don Merton).*

A Tomtit Petroica macrocephala *feeding young Black Robins* P. traversi. *The fostering of Black Robin chicks on to tomtits greatly increased the number of Black Robins produced each year and made a major contribution to preventing the species' extinction (Don Merton).*

downlisted to the IUCN threat category of Endangered and in 2000, as the population continued to rise, it was again downlisted to Vulnerable. Jones and his colleagues went on to prove that their success with the kestrel was not simply a matter of good luck by repeating it with no fewer than five other bird species on Mauritius and nearby Rodrigues, all previously listed in the highest IUCN risk category. As a result, the Pink Pigeon *Nesoenas mayeri*, Mauritius (or Echo) Parakeet *Psittacula eques*, Mauritius Fody *Foudia rubra*, Rodrigues Fody *Foudia flavicans* and Rodrigues Warbler *Acrocephalus rodericanus* have all been downlisted to lower categories of threat (Jones & Hartley 1995, Jones & Swinnerton 1997, Safford & Jones 1998). Mauritius now hosts only one species that is still listed as Critically Endangered, the Mauritius Olive White-eye *Zosterops chloronothos*, and there is every hope that ongoing efforts to save this bird will achieve the same success as other recovery projects on the islands. The tide of extinction on Mauritius and Rodrigues, which in the last five hundred years has taken with it not only the famous Dodo *Raphus cucullatus* but also at least 16 other bird species, has finally been turned.

At around the same time that Carl Jones was starting to achieve his first successes on Mauritius, the New Zealand conservationist Don Merton was embarking on what would become another of the world's great conservation success stories. His aim was to save from extinction the Black Robin *Petroica traversi*, by that time confined to the scrub-covered cap of a remote sea stack called Little Mangere in the Chatham Islands, over 800km east of New Zealand's South Island. Like Jones, Merton and his colleagues in New Zealand's rightly famous Department of Conservation (DOC) were faced with the seemingly impossible task of preventing the extinction of a bird whose population contained, for three precarious years, only a single fertile female. The problem was compounded by the fact that she was well past the average age for her species, and for a doubly perilous period there was only a single fertile male as well. Fortunately 'Old Blue', as the female became known from the colour of the identification ring on her leg, survived long enough to produce, with the male 'Old Yellow', enough eggs to prevent the extinction of her species.

Suffering a great deal of personal stress and risking no little physical danger, Merton and his colleagues first undertook the job of moving the few remaining birds to the larger Mangere Island, on which habitat had been restored and where for a time the species teetered on a knife-edge (Butler & Merton 1992, Merton 1992). When it became clear that translocation to a new home was not in itself going to be enough to save it, a more hands-on approach was adopted, which included the fostering of Black Robin chicks into the nests of the Tomtit *Petroica macrocephala*, another small insectivorous species on the island, so inducing the original parents to lay again. This thrilling story of hope and despair, described in a book in 1992 (Butler & Merton 1992), is required reading for conservationists the world over. Old Blue became a national icon and her picture featured on a national postage stamp; her death in late 1983 or early 1984, at an age twice that of any other Black Robin, was much lamented by the people of New Zealand and reported widely around the world (Merton 1992). Today the population of this species numbers over 250 individuals and is still rising (Bell & Merton 2002).

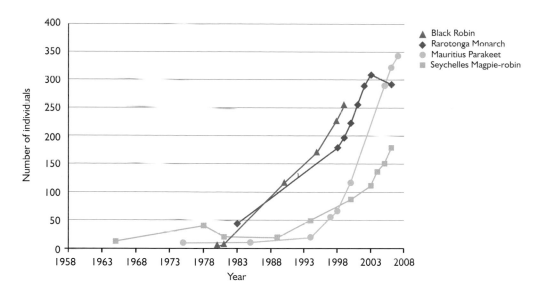

Figure 15.1. The population response of four species to intensive conservation management (BirdLife International 2008a). All have now been removed from the list of Critically Endangered birds.

INTENSIVE MANAGEMENT OF TINY POPULATIONS

The success of the last-gasp efforts to save the Mauritius Kestrel and the Black Robin has proved that it is not too late to intervene to save a rare species from extinction even when its population has dwindled into single figures (Merton 1992). The populations of at least 24 bird species, most of them confined to small islands, have been recovered from fewer than 50 individuals, sometimes to many hundreds (Table 15.1, Fig. 15.1). Initially, most of these species were saved not by using the tried and tested methods of habitat protection or legal safeguards, mechanisms that form the central pillars of conserving less threatened populations, but by developing a new set of conservation techniques and strategies designed specifically to increase populations on the very edge of extinction (Safford & Jones 1998, Bell & Merton 2002, Jones 2004). When populations reach such low levels, the likelihood of their extinction increases exponentially because of chance events and Allee effects (p.32), so conservation methods appropriate for larger populations that are in decline are rarely sufficient (Caughley 1994). Indeed, a number of successful rescue operations have been launched when the cause of the species' endangerment was not even known; the important lesson that has been learned in these cases is that it is not always necessary, at least initially, to address directly the factors that brought the species to the edge of extinction, and that protecting it from a wholly different set of threats is the first priority (Green 2002, Jones 2004).

In the fight to save the world's rarest birds from extinction, interventionist strategies often predominate over protectionist ones (Merton 1992, Atkinson 2001, Clout 2001). The successful rescue of very small populations has generally involved the use of more than one conservation technique (Table 15.2). These emergency recovery methods were often based on techniques originally developed to enhance populations of gamebirds, or used by falconers or aviculturists (Jones 2004), and they frequently had to be rapidly adapted to prevent the extinction of some of the world's rarest birds without the luxury of time to test and develop refinements on less threatened species. Sometimes, methods had to be developed that had no precedent in conservation. Don Merton's idea of cross-fostering Black Robin chicks into the nests of other species, for example, stemmed from his childhood memories of the behaviour of his grandmother's pet canary! The extraordinary Kakapo *Strigops habroptila* of New Zealand is now slowly responding to perhaps the most intensive and sophisticated conservation initiative ever

Table 15.1. *The effects of intensive conservation effort in rescuing 24 species with initial populations in the wild of fewer than 50 individuals. Only four of these (marked *) are mainland species, though the Black Stilt occurs on a very large island (South Island, New Zealand), as did the Kakapo before the whole population was moved to small offshore islands. The lowest population reached (approximate number of adult birds) and the year it was reached are given, together with the wild population estimate for 2012. Most of these species now have populations that are stable (↔) or continuing to increase (↑), although a few have fluctuating populations (↕) and one may be in decline once again (↓). Many also have sizeable populations in captivity. Data from BirdLife International and many other sources. Species are listed by lowest known population (column 3).*

Species	Location	Lowest known population (approx)	Year	Population in 2012
Mauritius Kestrel *Falco punctatus*	Mauritius, Indian Ocean	4	1974	400 ↕
Asian Crested Ibis* *Nipponia nippon*	China	4	1981	c. 500↑
Black Robin *Petroica traversi*	New Zealand	5	1980	c. 260↑
Laysan Duck *Anas laysanensis*	Hawaii, USA	7	1912	600–700↑
Magenta Petrel *Pterodroma magentae*	New Zealand	8	1994	150–200↑
Pink Pigeon *Nesoenas mayeri*	Mauritius, Indian Ocean	10	1990	360–395↕
Mauritius Parakeet *Psittacula eques*	Mauritius, Indian Ocean	11	1973	c. 580↑
Rodrigues Fody *Foudia flavicans*	Rodrigues, Indian Ocean	12	1968	1,000–8,000↑
Seychelles Magpie-robin *Copsychus sechellarum*	Seychelles, Indian Ocean	12	1965	180↑
Puerto Rican Amazon *Amazona vittata*	Puerto Rico, Caribbean	13	1975	50–70↔
Whooping Crane* *Grus americana*	USA	14	1938	c. 400↑
Rodrigues Warbler *Acrocephalus rodericanus*	Rodrigues, Indian Ocean	17	1979	>3,000↑
Short-tailed Albatross *Phoebastria albatrus*	Japan	<20	1951	c. 2,500↑
Pale-headed Brush-finch* *Atlapetes pallidiceps*	Ecuador	20	1998	c. 340↑
California Condor* *Gymnogyps californianus*	USA	22	1981	213↑
Lord Howe Woodhen *Gallirallus sylvestris*	Lord Howe Island, Australia	22	1971	c. 220↔
Black Stilt *Himantopus novaezelandiae*	New Zealand	23	1981	78↑
Seychelles Warbler *Acrocephalus sechellensis*	Seychelles, Indian Ocean	26	1968	>2,500↑
Tahiti Monarch *Pomarea nigra*	Tahiti, Pacific	27	1998	40–45↑
Rarotonga Monarch *Pomarea dimidiata*	Cook Islands, Pacific	29	1989	c. 380↔
Hawaiian Goose *Branta sandvicensis*	Hawaii, USA	<30	1952	c. 2,500↑
Norfolk Island Parakeet *Cyanoramphus cookii*	New Zealand	34	1994	<250↓
Bermuda Petrel *Pterodroma cahow*	Bermuda, West Atlantic	36	1951	c. 250↑
Kakapo *Strigops habroptila*	New Zealand	47	1994	126↑

Table 15.2. *The main management techniques used to restore the small populations shown in Table 15.1. 'Translocation' refers to the establishment of birds on islands or in countries outside the range of the donor population, though often within the species' historical range. 'Nest manipulation' includes a range of nest management techniques, including cross-fostering, clutch and brood manipulation etc. 'Predator control' includes control of invasive species and nest parasites such as cowbirds. 'Legal and policy' includes legal protection, the designation of protected areas, changes to hunting laws and fisheries regulations. The squares represent the one or two most important actions for each species. Mainland species are marked with an asterisk. Order of species as in Table 15.1*

Species	Captive breeding and release	Nest protection	Nest manipulation	Predator control	Food provision	Translocation	Habitat restoration	Legal & policy	Disease control	Other
Mauritius Kestrel *Falco punctatus*	■	●	●	●	●		●			●
Asian Crested Ibis* *Nipponia nippon*	■	●			●	●	●	■		
Black Robin *Petroica traversi*		●	■	●	●	■	●		●	
Laysan Duck *Anas laysanensis*	■			●		●	■		●	
Magenta Petrel *Pterodroma magentae*				■						
Pink Pigeon *Nesoenas mayeri*	■		●	●	■	●	●		●	
Mauritius Parakeet *Psittacula eques*	■	■	●	●	●		●		●	
Rodrigues Fody *Foudia flavicans*							■			
Seychelles Magpie-robin *Copsychus sechellarum*		●		■	●	■	●			
Puerto Rican Amazon *Amazona vittata*	■	●		●						●
Whooping Crane* *Grus americana*	●		●					■		●
Rodrigues Warbler *Acrocephalus rodericanus*							■			
Short-tailed Albatross *Phoebastria albatrus*					●	●		■		●
Pale-headed Brush-finch* *Atlapetes pallidiceps*				●			■			
California Condor* *Gymnogyps californianus*	■	●			●			■	●	
Lord Howe Woodhen *Gallirallus sylvestris*	■			■						
Black Stilt *Himantopus novaezelandiae*	■	●	●	●			●			
Seychelles Warbler *Acrocephalus sechellensis*				●		■	●			
Tahiti Monarch *Pomarea nigra*				■						
Rarotonga Monarch *Pomarea dimidiata*		●		■		●				
Hawaiian Goose *Branta sandvicensis*	■			●	●					
Norfolk Island Parakeet *Cyanoramphus cookii*	■	●		●						
Bermuda Petrel *Pterodroma cahow*		■		●			●			●
Kakapo *Strigops habroptila*		●	●	●	●	■	●		●	

attempted on a single species (Chapter 16), but one that can be traced back directly to the desperate attempts of a few conservationists who were prepared to try anything to avert extinction. Methods such as the translocation of birds to predator-free islands, captive breeding, supplementary feeding and cross-fostering continue to yield conservation benefits. What started from the ideas and passion of a few committed individuals has rapidly developed into a respected and increasingly well-researched branch of conservation science (Bell & Merton 2002, Jones 2004). As a consequence of this commitment and inventiveness, at least 16 species of bird that would otherwise have become extinct in the last two decades have been granted a reprieve (Butchart *et al.* 2006c).

CONTROL AND ERADICATION OF INVASIVE SPECIES

In just a few centuries, we have taken the world's species and shaken them together so effectively that few places on the planet still support intact and pristine natural communities of plants and animals. Even Antarctica, the most austere and least populated part of the planet, now supports a wide range of invasive species, the majority of them European in origin (Frenot *et al.* 2005). A high proportion of the world's most threatened species, and the great majority of those on islands, owe their poor conservation status partly or wholly to the impacts of introduced predators, particularly cats and rodents but also monkeys, mustelids (particularly stoats), reptiles, other birds and even insects (Courchamp *et al.* 2003, BirdLife International 2008a,b, Clavero *et al.* 2009, Hilton & Cuthbert 2010). Introduced herbivores, particularly goats, pigs and rabbits, and invasive plants have also affected native vegetation on many islands, with consequent impacts on native birds: the introduction of rabbits to Laysan Island in Hawaii and the consequent devastation of the island's natural plant cover drove three of the four endemic birds to extinction, the Laysan Duck *Anas laysanensis* only just surviving (Moulton & Marshall 1996). Invasive birds may outcompete or hybridise with native species (Muñoz-Fuentes *et al.* 2007), act as reservoirs of introduced disease and even parasitise their nests (Oppel *et al.* 2004b). Although many of the introductions to islands of invasive mammals occurred a century or more ago, there is no evidence of a reduction in the rate of establishment of new species of plant on the world's islands (Sax & Gaines 2008). The problems caused by invasive species on continental landmasses, while still far fewer than those in islands, are growing: mammals appear to be just as successful at colonising new continents as they are at invading islands (Jeschke 2008).

Not surprisingly, therefore, conservationists have invested much effort in developing methods to control or completely eradicate a wide range of invasive species, particularly from smaller islands. This may be expensive and time-consuming, but populations of native species generally recover rapidly when alien species are removed (Orueta & Ramos 2001, Courchamp *et al.* 2003, Keitt & Tershy 2003, Donlan *et al.* 2007). For example, the control of aggressive alien ants on Christmas Island (Australia) led to population increases in native birds that saw no fewer than four species downlisted from Critically Endangered in 2004 (BirdLife International 2008a). Indeed, effective ecological restoration of any damaged site is often not possible without the control or eradication of introduced mammals (Atkinson 2001). Of the bird species whose populations have been recovered from fewer than 50 individuals, predator control (though not necessarily total eradication) was the single most frequently employed conservation intervention (Table 15.2).

Methods of eradicating rodents from islands were developed in the 1970s and have become more effective as baits have improved and conservationists have developed better ways of delivering them (Howald *et al.* 2007). These improvements, in particular the development of anti-coagulant rodenticides and methods to deliver them effectively from the air, mean that ever-larger islands can now be cleared of an increasingly wide range of predators (Clout & Russell 2001, Towns & Broome 2003, Krajick 2005, Bellingham *et al.* 2010) (Table 15.3). Except in the case of mice, island size may no longer be the limiting factor for rodent eradications; rather, social acceptance and funding are the main challenges (Howald *et al.* 2007). Conservationists are therefore now in the position of being able to eradicate most invasive animal species from most oceanic islands, although the removal of invasive plants remains more difficult. Whilst rodent removal is more costly than the removal of herbivores, their importance as threats to the world's most threatened birds has led to a greater number of successful eradications. In practically all cases, rodent removal has been achieved using anticoagulant rodenticides, particularly Brodifacoum. Poisoned bait is either presented at bait stations or, on larger islands, scattered from helicopters. In some cases it is necessary to take potentially vulnerable native species into protective captivity for the duration of the eradication. Removal of larger mammals tends to be easier, allowing conservationists to rid much bigger islands of such species (Table 15.3). Control methods also differ. Cats have been successfully removed from over 50 islands, the largest of them the subantarctic Marion Island (298km²) off South Africa (Bester *et al.* 2002, Nogales *et al.* 2004). This has usually involved trapping and hunting, sometimes using dogs, although poison and disease agents have also been used (Nogales *et al.* 2004). Goats have been eradicated from around 120 islands, largely by shooting (Campbell & Donlan 2005).

Where total eradication is unfeasible, for example on the mainland of New Zealand, 'mainland islands' of predator-free habitat have sometimes been created. This method has been adopted successfully in the conservation of the Kokako *Callaeas cinerea* (Endangered), a peculiar species of wattlebird that survives in a few forests on North Island, where intermittent control of rats and possums has greatly increased breeding success (Innes *et al.* 1999, Basse *et al.* 2003). If populations of threatened species can be increased, they may become more resilient to the effects of predators, allowing predator control to be relaxed (Sinclair *et al.* 2006).

Table 15.3. The largest islands yet cleared of each of the most important invasive mammals. *Ongoing efforts are being made to clear Macquarie Island (128km²) of rabbits, mice and rats. (From Nogales et al. *2004, Lorvelec & Pascal 2005, Donlan & Wilcox 2008a, Phillips 2008).*

Introduced species	Largest Island cleared	Area (km²)
Brown Rat *Rattus norvegicus*	Campbell, NZ	113
Black Rat* *R. rattus*	Hermite, Australia	10.2
Pacific Rat *R. exulans*	Little Barrier, NZ	30.8
Rabbit* *Oryctolagus cuniculus*	St Paul, France	8.0
House Mouse* *Mus musculus*	Enderby, NZ	7.1
Goat *Capra hircus*	Isabela, Galapagos	4,588
Pig *Sus scrofa*	Santiago, Galapagos	584
Cat *Felis catus*	Marion, South Africa	298
Stoat *Mustela erminea*	Resolution, NZ	210

The financial costs of eradication depend almost entirely on the size of the island and the nature of the target species (Martins *et al.* 2006), but can be relatively low for the huge benefits they bring. For example, mammal removal on 26 islands off western Mexico cost on average just $20,000 to protect each seabird colony, or $50,000 to protect each terrestrial species (Aguirre-Muñoz *et al.* 2008). At the other end of the financial scale, the eradication of feral goats from the much larger Santiago (58km²) in the Galápagos cost over $6 million (Cruz *et al.* 2009) and the planned removal of an estimated 36,000 rats, 103,000 mice and 130,000 rabbits from Macquarie Island (128km²) is likely to cost $21 million (Anon. 2007). A global analysis of islands suggests that the greatest overall conservation benefits would accrue through the removal of non-native species from fairly large islands as different and far apart as Fatu Hiva in Polynesia, Guadalupe and Socorro in the eastern Pacific, Madeira in the north Atlantic and Chatham Island in the southern Pacific (Brooke *et al.* 2007). When cost is factored in, the greatest conservation gain per unit of financial expenditure is found to be on smaller islands, including many of the Seychelles.

Eradication or control of invasive species is not without its pitfalls, and our ability to remove predators from islands greatly exceeds our ability to predict the ecological consequences (Bellingham *et al.* 2010). The removal of predators such as cats might not always be in the best interests of endangered island birds if smaller 'mesopredators' are also present (Courchamp *et al.* 1999b). These effects can trickle down several levels, so the eradication of rats

Cook's Petrel Pterodroma cookii *declined to alarmingly low numbers after cats were removed from its island home because of an explosion in the number of rats. Successful rat eradication led to a huge increase in the petrel's breeding success and the species is now listed as Vulnerable (Ray Wilson).*

can lead to a population increase in mice, and so on (Caut *et al.* 2007, Witmer *et al.* 2007). An example of this effect, which is called 'mesopredator release' (Courchamp *et al.* 1999b), occurred when cats were removed from Little Barrier Island, New Zealand, to protect breeding colonies of the threatened Cook's Petrel *Pterodroma cookii*. Unfortunately, this led not to an increase in the petrel's breeding success as expected but to a population explosion in another introduced predator, the Pacific Rat, causing a sharp decline to dangerously low levels in the petrel's nesting success (Rayner *et al.* 2007). When the rats were removed as well, however, the petrels' breeding success soared from just 5% to 70% and the population quickly recovered.

The removal of top predators can also produce unfettered growth in the numbers of non-predator species beneath them in the food chain, which can have as devastating an effect on island ecologies as did the original predators. The eradication of cats in 2001 from Macquarie Island, a World Heritage Site lying between New Zealand and Antarctica, led to an explosion in the population of introduced rabbits, which then ravaged the island's native plant communities (Bergstrom *et al.* 2009). The alternative, removing introduced mammals from the bottom of the food chain upwards, might also create problems, as higher predators might increasingly target native species as their introduced prey dries up. Furthermore, introduced species might play important roles in ecosystem functioning when the native species that once undertook such roles have been lost. In New Zealand, for example, where many native vertebrate pollinators have been lost, invasive rats are now known to provide an important function in pollinating native plants (Pattemore & Wilcove 2012). The impacts of the removal of a particular invasive species on other invasive species and on the island's natural wildlife can therefore be very difficult to predict and might even lead to a worsening of the situation (Myers *et al.* 2000b, Zavaleta *et al.* 2001, Courchamp *et al.* 2003).

TRANSLOCATION AND SUPPLEMENTATION

Rare species tend to have very small geographical distributions and often inhabit only a fraction of their original range. The reasons for these reduced ranges might be related to invasive species, habitat loss or natural local extinction. If conditions can be improved in previously occupied areas, the potential exists physically to move species back there, a method known as translocation. In 1968, the world population of the Seychelles Warbler *Acrocephalus sechellensis* stood at fewer than 30 birds, confined to the single island of Cousin. It once occurred more widely in the Seychelles, until extensive planting with coconut palms *Cocos nucifera* in the early twentieth century destroyed its habitat. In 1968 the Royal Society for Nature Conservation and the International Council for Bird Preservation purchased the island to save the species, cleared the coconut trees and allowed the native vegetation to regenerate. The Seychelles Warbler quickly responded, and soon the island was at carrying capacity with over 300 birds. Once at saturation, subsequent habitat management did not lead to a larger number of territories, although it did improve territory quality and breeding success (Komdeur & Pels 2005). These factors reduced the species' risk of immediate extinction, but it remained potentially very susceptible to catastrophic events that might hit Cousin. Although the species is physiologically capable of flying to other islands, it does so very rarely (Komdeur *et al.* 2004): over the years, of more than 1,900 birds fitted with rings that allow them to be identified in the field, only two have successfully reached other islands unaided. In order to spread the risk, the species was therefore translocated to Aride in 1988, Cousine in 1990 (Komdeur 1994) and Denis in 2004, following predator control and habitat restoration. The population now stands at over 2,500 and the species has been downlisted to Vulnerable. The Seychelles Magpie-robin *Copsychus sechellarum*, Seychelles White-eye *Zosterops modestus* and a number of other species have also increased in numbers and range following successful translocations to predator-free islands (Table 15.2).

In many cases, it is known or assumed that the places to which birds are translocated fall within those species' historical ranges. Sometimes, however, it is necessary to move birds to places that they have never previously occupied, creating populations of biological refugees (Safford & Jones 1998). In a reversal of the usual situation, the number of rare species on such islands has therefore increased. On Mauritius, the recovery of once Critically Endangered species has been aided by the establishment of populations on predator-free offshore islands where

Two Seychelles species that have been saved from extinction by a combination of predator control, habitat restoration and translocation to other islands; Seychelles Warbler Acrocephalus sechellensis, *now listed as Vulnerable (left; Martijn Hammers) and Seychelles Magpie-robin* Copsychus sechellarum, *now Endangered (right; Jon Hornbuckle).*

153

The Saddleback Philesturnus carunculatus *of New Zealand has been rescued by the relocation of birds to predator-free offshore islands, where birds have bred so successfully that the species is now listed only as Near Threatened and plans are underway to re-establish populations on the mainland (Paddy Ryan).*

they may not previously have occurred (Safford & Jones 1998). In New Zealand, a number of threatened species such as the Kakapo and the Saddleback *Philesturnus carunculatus* owe their survival to populations established on islands outside their original distributions.

If captive stock of a dwindling species exists, or if one wild population has the capacity to supply individuals to support another, the technique of 'supplementation' can prove useful as a buffer against extinction. It has been used repeatedly in parrot conservation, probably because parrots are widely held in captivity even when highly threatened. There have been supplementation endeavours with such Critically Endangered species as the Orange-bellied Parrot *Neophema chrysogaster*, which breeds in Tasmania and winters on the Australian coast opposite, and which was supported by the addition of 105 captive-bred birds over the course of the 1990s (Smales *et al.* 2000a,b), and Puerto Rican Amazon *Amazona vittata*, the last wild population of which has been confined to Luquillo Forest in eastern Puerto Rico and bolstered by releases of captive-bred birds over many decades (Snyder *et al.* 1987, White *et al.* 2005). Carl Jones and his team on Mauritius undertook more complicated intervention with the Mauritius Parakeet *Psittacula eques*, removing young from wild nests to leave a single individual for the parents to rear (thereby actually *increasing* breeding success since larger broods often suffered total mortality from malnutrition), rearing them in captivity (some by hand, some – taking a leaf from Don Merton's book – using Rose-ringed Parakeets *Psittacula krameri* as foster-parents to establish a captive population which then reared some of its own young), and returning juveniles to the wild at the age when they would normally fledge (Thorsen & Jones 1998, Woolaver *et al.* 2000). The Mauritius Fody *Foudia rubra* has more recently received the same treatment (Cristinacce *et al.* 2008) and the technique underpins efforts to maximise population growth rate in the Madagascar Pochard *Aythya innotata* (Chapter 21). Even the release of a female Spix's Macaw *Cyanopsitta spixii*, almost certainly a wild-caught bird, to partner the last surviving male was a supplementation (Chapter 20), and wild Black-eared Miners *Manorina melanotis* in Australia (Baker-Gabb 2007) and wild Red-cockaded Woodpeckers *Picoides borealis* in the USA (Wallace & Buchholz 2001, Saenz *et al.* 2002, Holimon & Montague 2003) have been translocated between populations to increase the species' overall security.

CAPTIVE BREEDING AND RELEASE

It is a peculiar fact, but one for which conservationists are often grateful, that no matter how difficult it might be to encourage birds to breed successfully in the wild, they often do so readily in the wholly artificial confines of an aviary. For most species, the provision of ample food and freedom from predators and competitors appear to outweigh the absence of all the other ecological and climatic requirements that birds require to breed in the wild (Saint Jalme 2002). Because of this, captive breeding is one of the most frequently employed and successful conservation tools in the recovery of critically small populations (Table 15.2), and is often in this context referred to as 'conservation breeding'. Five species survive now only in captivity: Guam Rail *Gallirallus owstoni*, Alagoas Curassow *Mitu mitu* of Brazil (Chapter 19), Socorro Dove *Zenaida graysoni* of Mexico, Hawaiian Crow *Corvus hawaiiensis* and Spix's Macaw (Chapter 20) of Brazil. The future of a number of other species, such as the Bali Starling *Leucopsar rothschildi* of Indonesia and Madagascar Pochard (Chapter 21), depends to a large degree on the maintenance of captive populations. Captive breeding forms a key activity in current conservation efforts to save at least 25 Critically Endangered species. Had captive breeding been established sooner on the islands of Hawaii, perhaps some of the extinctions on those islands could have been averted. Indeed, the two Hawaiian species that have been rescued from perilously low populations (Table 15.1) owe their survival in large part to captive breeding, and the Hawaiian Crow's extinction was prevented just in time by taking all the remaining birds into captivity. Since the 1990s considerable successes have been achieved on Hawaii in developing captive breeding techniques for a range of threatened endemic species, and these are likely to underpin future conservation efforts on the islands (Kuehler *et al.* 2000, Tweed *et al.* 2006).

While many captive breeding programmes involve the last few individuals of a species, sometimes the rate of decline in a larger population prompts the decision to take birds into captivity. The continuing collapse in populations of vultures in southern Asia has led to the establishment of a number of captive breeding facilities even though the wild populations still number in the thousands (Chapter 17). Unfortunately, captive breeding

The Orange-bellied Parrot Neophema chrysogaster *breeds in Tasmania and winters along the adjacent coasts of Australia. Its wild population has been augmented by the reintroduction of captive-bred birds (Pete Morris).*

is commonly an expensive technique and poses a range of potential problems that require considerable expertise to address (Snyder *et al.* 1996). Indeed, the challenges of managing endangered species in captivity have required conservation biologists to conduct research in many disciplines, such as behaviour, physiology, endocrinology, genetics, husbandry, nutrition and veterinary medicine (Saint Jalme 2002). The construction, staffing and maintenance of captive breeding facilities represents a significant and often long-term investment: the facilities in which captive Asian vultures are held have had to be made secure against leopards, macaques and even elephants (Bowden 2009). Disease transmission, moreover, may be particularly high in captive populations, and veterinary support is often needed (Lafferty & Gerber 2002). Some species, such as the Kakapo, have breeding systems that currently preclude the use of captive breeding. Furthermore, animals kept in captivity for long periods might be less able to survive on their release, for example by losing the ability to identify predators and seek cover from them (McPhee 2004). Populations bred in captivity over many generations may lose genetic diversity, compromising their ability to establish new populations when they are released in the wild (Muñoz-Fuentes *et al.* 2008, Williams & Hoffman 2009). Similarly, because birds in captivity are not subject to the same pressures that in the wild would drive the evolution of beneficial new traits, they may be less well adapted to meet the challenges of their environments when they are released (Robert 2009). A final risk is that the removal of an entire species into captivity makes the protection of their remaining wild habitats, which is essential if they are ever to return there, more difficult to justify to competing interests for that land.

Because captive breeding is an invasive method of conservation and requires wild animals to be placed in cages, it can be controversial. Before the capture for breeding of the last few remaining California Condors *Gymnogyps californianus* in 1987, the start of a period of five years in which there were no birds at all in the wild, there was an acrimonious debate between conservationists with a background in wilderness preservation, who thought that the species should be saved by protecting and enhancing its native habitat, and conservation scientists who realised from their research that no amount of wilderness habitat could protect the species, and that more immediate measures were needed. The success of the captive breeding programme and the subsequent release of birds back into the wild

Mauritius (or Echo) Parakeet Psittacula eques *once numbered just 11 birds, but thanks to intensive conservation work the species now has an increasing population of over 500 birds, and was downlisted from Critically Endangered to Endangered in 2007 (Dennis Hansen).*

have done much to smooth over the divides between different conservation philosophies (Alagona 2004).

If captive breeding has developed into an increasingly sophisticated branch of conservation science, so too has the release of birds into the wild (Armstrong & Davidson 2006, Deredec & Courchamp 2007, Seddon *et al.* 2007, Cassey *et al.* 2008) and the subsequent monitoring of their survival (Ewen & Armstrong 2007). The success of reintroductions of animals into the wild is increasingly recognised as related to the degree of acclimatisation and training that they receive (Collar 2006, White *et al.* 2012). In the early days, 'hard releases', simply opening a cage door and letting the animals out on the assumption that they would immediately know what to do, were common. However, the use of 'soft releases', in which the animals are gradually exposed to local conditions, allowed to return to shelter at night, given a certain amount of food while they learn where in the wild to find it for themselves, and even trained to recognise predators (particularly important with the Puerto Rican Amazon), has come to dominate good practice. Considerable work is therefore frequently needed between captive breeding and final release, including such things as analysing the behaviours of the potential release animals and assessing their suitability for release (Mathews *et al.* 2005). Experimental releases might also be necessary. Not wishing to risk releasing a few precious California Condors into an environment that nobody could be sure was ready for them, conservationists instead liberated a number of Andean Condors *Vultur gryphus* from South America into the California Condor's range, using females only, to prevent the establishment of an alien species. The experiment proved successful and showed that it was possible for condors to survive, so all the Andean Condors were recaptured and released back in South America. When the time came for California Condors to be released, however, it proved necessary to give them aversion therapy to prevent them from flying into powerlines.

The release into the wild of captive-bred Mauritius Parakeets was a particularly intricate undertaking. Trials using Rose-ringed Parakeets suggested that birds should be acclimatised in special cages for two weeks, and liberated in small groups of two to five. Released birds were trained to associate the sound of a whistle with presentation of food. They were then released gradually, being allowed to spend increasingly long periods outside the release pens, which were left open and stocked with fresh food for two months until the released flock was fully self-feeding. Newly released birds learned to exploit their new environment, and to avoid predators, from previously released birds, making them less dependent on their human guardians. During this period, birds were trained to use food hoppers and were familiarised with nest boxes. The release programme allows a measure of control over the management of the wild population by ensuring that genetically important birds are represented in it (Thorsen & Jones 1998, Woolaver *et al.* 2000).

MANAGING FEEDING AND BREEDING *IN SITU*

Captive breeding allows rare species to produce more new birds than would be possible in the wild, because birds in aviaries breed more frequently, lay more eggs and have higher chick survival. However, it is not always necessary, or even possible, to take birds into captivity ('*ex situ*'), and many of the benefits of captive breeding can be replicated through adaptive management in the wild ('*in situ*'). Almost as welcome to conservationists as the willingness of birds to breed in aviaries is their tendency to replace lost eggs. Species that normally lay a clutch of, say, four can be induced to lay many more if their initial eggs are removed to an incubator, or placed in the nest of a foster species. This conveyor-belt production was fundamental to the success of the Black Robin recovery project, as Old Blue was persuaded to produce far more eggs each year than she would normally have done. The surplus eggs were then added to the nests of the closely related Tomtit and raised as their own (Butler & Merton 1992).

One of the resources provided by captive breeding programmes is carefully balanced but ample nutrition, and the supplementary feeding of populations in the wild can have equally beneficial effects. Supplementary feeding has been an important component in more than half the successful recoveries of species from small populations (Table 15.2) and it has been shown to have a number of effects: it encourages birds to breed, it allows them to lay larger clutches and rear more chicks, and it helps birds to survive for longer (Jones 2004). Working in the 1990s on the island of Frégate to save the Seychelles Magpie-robin from what at the time seemed like imminent extinction, the conservationist Neil McCullough found that by killing invasive cockroaches at night and presenting them to

Pink Pigeons Nesoenas mayeri *at a specially designed feeding station. Providing supplementary food made a major contribution to the increase in numbers that has seen this species downlisted from Critically Endangered to Endangered (Dennis Hansen).*

the birds as food the next day, he could induce the birds to breed more frequently and more successfully than they would otherwise, providing the flush of new birds needed for the highly successful establishment of populations on other islands (Komdeur 1996). Conservationists working to save the Kakapo have found that supplementary feeding helps birds to raise more chicks on the rare occasions that they breed, although the search for a food that causes birds to breed more frequently continues. On Mauritius, the successful recovery of the Pink Pigeon involved the provision of food at feeding stations that were visited by practically all the birds in the surrounding area (Edmunds *et al.* 2008). However, water may be no less important for some species: small reservoirs of fresh water built close to breeding colonies of the Northern Bald Ibis *Geronticus eremita* in Morocco have significantly improved the species' nesting success, particularly in years of low rainfall (Smith *et al.* 2008).

GENETIC MANAGEMENT

One of the many issues faced by Carl Jones and his colleagues in trying to save the Mauritius Kestrel was that, even if its population could be increased, because it had been through such an acute bottleneck the new population would be so similar genetically that it might not fare well in the long term. When populations fall to such low levels they are susceptible to a number of problems that may compromise their future survival. These include a reduced ability to cope with environmental change, an increased vulnerability to diseases, an increased frequency of genetic disorders and a reduced capacity to breed successfully. The success of the Mauritius Kestrel and Black Robin recovery projects has shown that these fears are not always realised, although there is evidence that both species have relatively low genetic diversity (Ardern & Lambert 1997, Ewing *et al.* 2008).

One perhaps unexpected reason why population bottlenecks may be less of a problem in the rescue of species with tiny populations than geneticists originally predicted is that many such species have been through such bottlenecks before. The Mauritius Kestrel is thought to have been brought to the edge of extinction several times in its evolutionary history by volcanic eruptions on the island, and the Black Robin is likely to have had a tiny and highly inbred population for perhaps a century before its recovery. Far from increasing the genetic problems associated with tiny populations, this might act to purge the population of deleterious alleles. As a result, many

Taking a blood sample from a Mauritius Kestrel chick to collect genetic information and screen for diseases (Dennis Hansen).

small populations of birds actually show a greater degree of genetic health than might be expected, though genetic diversity might still be low relative to more numerous species (Jamieson *et al.* 2006, Leberg & Firmin 2008). Species with a long history of small population size may therefore be more robust to the negative effects of inbreeding than large populations that crash to low levels (Bataillon & Kirkpatrick 2000, Groombridge *et al.* 2001).

The effects of inbreeding may be small relative to other threats facing species with small populations. The slow recovery of the Puerto Rican Amazon, a species whose population underwent a prolonged bottleneck from the 1970s into the present century, with a reduction of wild numbers to 13 in 1975, has been due more to periodic hurricanes and environmental and behavioural factors that prevented birds from nesting than to reduced breeding success caused by inbreeding (Beissinger *et al.* 2008). Nevertheless, threatened species generally have low genetic diversity compared to commoner ones (Evans & Sheldon 2008) and populations on islands have low genetic diversity compared to those on mainlands (Boessenkool *et al.* 2007). Genetic management is now an important tool in conservation, in particular in the nurturing of very small or captive populations (Ralls & Ballou 2004, Swinnerton *et al.* 2004, Zhang *et al.* 2006, Grueber & Jamieson 2008, Johnson *et al.* 2008). The increasing power and availability of molecular profiling mean that in small, closely managed populations, the genetic make-up of each individual and its relatedness to all other individuals can be quantified, allowing conservationists to encourage outbreeding. This has been a particularly important tool in the recovery of the Kakapo. As the technique of supplementation (see above) has demonstrated, the genetic health of small populations of wild animals can be improved by translocating individuals from other populations, although this brings with it the risk that adaptations to local conditions might be diluted (Bouzat *et al.* 2009). Of course, it is not only species with tiny global populations that may be genetically challenged; those whose ranges are fragmented into isolated subpopulations face similar problems.

SITE PROTECTION AND MANAGEMENT

Clever and imaginative micro-management techniques of the type developed and employed in the recovery of at least twenty species previously on the verge of extinction are necessary to prevent the loss of tiny populations, but many Critically Endangered species still occur in sufficient numbers to allow their survival simply through the adequate protection of the sites and habitats they presently occupy. Indeed, site protection and management are the most frequently identified priority activities for saving the world's Critically Endangered birds (Fig. 15.2) and threatened species in other animal groups (Boyd *et al.* 2008).

The world's network of protected areas, identified by IUCN as places 'recognised, dedicated and managed, through legal or other effective means, to achieve the long-term conservation of nature', cover around one eighth of the world's land surface (Joppa & Pfaff 2009). The world's protected areas are fundamental to the conservation of wildlife, but their effectiveness is hard to assess because very little environmental monitoring is undertaken. However, if properly sited, protected areas could do much to prevent the loss of the world's rarest animals (Knight *et al.* 2007, Brooks *et al.* 2009). For example, protected reserves in the Brazilian Amazon suffer lower rates of fire than unprotected areas, particularly near roads, where the risks of fire are greatest (Adeney *et al.* 2009). Similar positive benefits of site protection in preventing forest loss have been recorded from Colombia (Armenteras *et al.* 2009), Paraguay (Huang *et al.* 2009), Sumatra (Gaveau *et al.* 2009), India (Joseph *et al.* 2009), Burma (Songer *et al.* 2009) and Jamaica (Chai *et al.* 2009). However, many protected areas enjoy only nominal protection, being in effect 'paper parks', and many of the planet's ecosystems are insufficiently covered by the network (Brooks *et al.* 2004, Schmitt *et al.* 2009). Many protected areas comprise a high proportion of 'rock and ice' sites of little value to agriculture or forestry and so are unlikely to be at future risk even if they were not protected (Jenkins & Joppa 2009, Joppa & Pfaff 2009). Furthermore, there is relatively poor overlap between the world's protected areas and the distribution of Important Bird Areas (IBAs), and protected areas are particularly poor at encompassing the ranges of Critically Endangered species (Beresford *et al.* 2011). Over 200 Alliance for Zero Extinction (AZE) sites have been identified for birds (p.23) but only around half are legally protected. Site protection is therefore essential to the conservation of much of the planet's biodiversity, but far more is required if the world's rarest birds are to be adequately safeguarded.

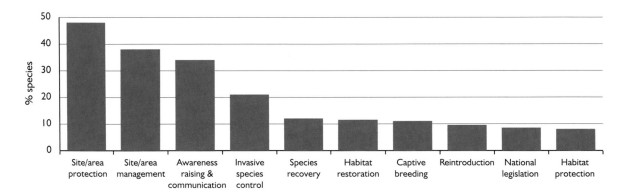

Figure 15.2. The conservation actions needed to save the world's Critically Endangered bird species and the percentage of species requiring them (BirdLife International 2008b).

Giving a site protected status is typically just the first step in saving a Critically Endangered species, since intensive habitat management within that site is also likely to be required. In 1998, the Pale-headed Brush-finch *Atlapetes pallidiceps* was rediscovered in Ecuador after an absence of records of nearly 30 years (Agreda *et al.* 1999). Within the species' tiny range, the population had fallen to around 20 birds and immediate conservation action was set in train. The bird inhabits patches of scrubby vegetation in the transition zone between arid and humid habitats in highland valleys and it might rely on patches of habitat that are regenerating after landslides. It appeared to be declining due to habitat loss and the degradation of remaining habitats from grazing by cattle and goats (Krabbe 2004, Oppel *et al.* 2004a). Under the leadership of the local conservation organisation Fundación Jocotoco, patches of the bird's fragmented range were purchased, fences erected to keep out goats and taller trees felled, after research showed that it avoids closed-canopy woodland. These managed areas now hold almost the entire population of the species. Unfortunately, the spread of agriculture into surrounding areas had attracted large numbers of Shiny Cowbirds *Molothrus bonariensis* to the abundant food that cornfields provide, and the bushy habitats produced by these conservation actions proved attractive not only to the brush-finch but also to

A cowbird chick in a Pale-headed Brush-finch Atlapetes pallidiceps *nest. This species suffers heavy parasitism by cowbirds, which are now controlled in the brush-finch's tiny range (Martin Schaefer).*

these newcomers. Cowbirds, like cuckoos, are brood parasites and the breeding success of the Pale-headed Brush-finch was consequently very low, as a high proportion of nests were parasitised; cowbird removal was therefore imperative. Intensive habitat management and cowbird removal have enabled the population to rise to well over 200 birds within six years and it is continuing to increase (Oppel *et al.* 2004b). In 2011, the species was downlisted from Critically Endangered to Endangered.

CONSERVATION LEGISLATION

The great majority of the world's rarest birds are, at least in theory, protected to some degree from persecution or disturbance by national or international legislation, and legal protection has been critical for three of the four mainland species whose populations have been recovered from populations of fewer than 50 individuals (Table 15.2). The successful captive breeding of California Condors was followed by a programme of release of captive-bred birds whose success has greatly benefited from recent laws prohibiting hunters from using lead ammunition within the species' range (Green *et al.* 2008b). The rediscovery of the Asian Crested Ibis *Nipponia nippon* in China in 1981 was quickly followed by a raft of laws protecting its habitat and banning hunting and pesticide use within its small range; in 1987, 51 nesting trees were declared state property and protected (BirdLife International 2001).

Conservationists are often sceptical about the ability of legislation, or the commitment of legislators, to protect the environment. The failure of the Convention on Biological Diversity (CBD) to achieve its target of reducing the rate of biodiversity loss by 2010 (Walpole *et al.* 2009, Xu *et al.* 2009), and the general sense of disappointment surrounding the Copenhagen discussions on climate change in 2009, provide further ammunition to those who question the ability and commitment of the world's governments to engage in a sufficiently robust way with reversing or slowing the loss of biodiversity. Nevertheless, national and international legislation can be an extremely powerful conservation tool with demonstrated benefits (Boere & Rubeck 2002, Donald *et al.* 2007b), and it has the capacity to generate a significant proportion of the resources available to protect the planet's biodiversity. For example, the US Fish and Wildlife Service, one of whose primary tasks is to enforce national environmental legislation such as the Endangered Species Act, has an annual budget of well over $2 billion, ten times that of the entire BirdLife International global partnership of non-governmental organisations (NGOs). The 1975 Convention on International Trade in Endangered Species (CITES), and the national legislation that signatories have committed themselves to adopt as a result, has made a valuable contribution to the conservation of some species that formerly were heavily traded (Wright *et al.* 2001, Pain *et al.* 2006). A number of national and international agreements, such as the Agreement on the Conservation of Albatrosses and Petrels (ACAP), introduced in response to concern about the threat to seabirds of longlining, have helped to reduce the accidental by-catch of some of the world's most threatened species (Chapter 12). A number of other multi-national conservation agreements exist, including the Ramsar Convention on Wetlands of International Importance (introduced in 1971, with 159 contracting parties in January 2010), the Convention on Migratory Species, or Bonn Convention (introduced in 1979, 113 parties) and the Convention on Biological Diversity (CBD, introduced in 1992, 193 parties). Added to these are regional agreements such as the European Union's Birds and Habitats Directives, the African-Eurasian Waterbird Agreement (AEWA), the Antarctic Treaty and the North American Waterfowl Management Plan (Boere & Rubeck 2002).

Although these agreements are signed by the world's governments and are their responsibility, much of the pressure for their implementation and the monitoring of their impacts stems from non-governmental organisations (Bowman 1999). Unfortunately, such agreements are rarely supported by adequate monitoring of the species at which they are directed, and their effectiveness is therefore extremely difficult to quantify (Ferraro & Pattanayak 2006). As a result it is often assumed, although wrongly, that an absence of evidence for their impact equates to evidence of absence. This is unfortunate, since the future of many species will increasingly depend on conservation measures operating at landscape scales, many of which can only be implemented through legislation implemented at similar scales (Boyd *et al.* 2008). Clearly, future attempts by the world's governments to prevent the extinction of the world's rarest birds will need to be accompanied by a substantial improvement in the global monitoring of their populations and habitats (Balmford *et al.* 2003b, Ferraro & Pattanayak 2006), for example through the use

Ongoing efforts to save the California Condor Gymnogyps californianus *have benefited from legislation preventing the use of lead ammunition within its range (Marcus Lawson).*

of satellite imagery (Buchanan *et al.* 2009b). Better understanding of the success, or otherwise, of these massive conservation investments will allow them to be improved, and will lead to a clearer recognition of what works and what does not (Donald *et al.* 2007b). The critical importance of legislation in the recovery of three of the four mainland species whose populations have been rescued from populations of 50 or fewer birds (Table 15.2) suggests that such an understanding will become increasingly important as the spotlight of rarity shifts from islands towards continental landmasses.

COMMUNITY INVOLVEMENT AND MUTUAL BENEFITS

Although the world's nations failed to the meet their self-imposed 2010 target to reduce the rate of loss of biodiversity, the CBD did at least bring together the governments of most countries to agree and set such a target, and thereby indicated their recognition of the need to tackle the world's environmental problems in a coherent, coordinated, top-down way. At the same time, however, conservationists have increasingly been turning towards very localised prescriptions in their endeavours to save the world's rarest birds using a more bottom-up approach, forging partnerships with local people with mutual benefits in mind (Marie *et al.* 2009). There has been a radical change in the conservation approach towards people who live around and exploit (for their own needs) sites and habitats holding threatened species, and the tendency to assume that conservation and livelihood development are necessarily conflicting ambitions has largely been replaced with the realisation that two are inextricably linked. As the case studies of the Yellow-crested Cockatoo (Chapter 9), Liben Lark (Chapter 8) and Royal Cinclodes (Chapter 6) demonstrate, preventing the extinction of the world's rarest birds might depend largely on the benefits that people living alongside them will gain as a result. BirdLife International has helped to establish Site Support Groups of local people at a number of Important Bird Areas, engaging with them in monitoring the sites' birds and habitats and helping them to develop ways of using those sites that offer the best chances of their conservation; the level of community engagement is a major determinant of the effectiveness of efforts to protect natural resources (Fiallo & Jacobson 1995, Lee *et al.* 2009b, Oestreicher *et al.* 2009). The conservation of rare species increasingly involves sharing responsibility for their future with local communities, a process to which the disproportionate recent and projected increases in human populations in areas that contain particularly rich communities of wildlife (Scharlemann *et al.* 2005, Buchanan *et al.* 2009a) lend particular urgency.

There are numerous examples of the potential benefits that can result. For example, former cockatoo catchers have become efficient nest protectors as part of a scheme to conserve the Philippine Cockatoo *Cacatua haematuropygia* (Critically Endangered) on Palawan. This project, led by the Katala Foundation, has been successful because it works by empowering local people economically to the extent that they no longer need to catch cockatoos to make a living. Such partnerships do not necessarily need to cost a lot of money but they do need knowledge of local people's lifestyles and livelihoods, requiring conservationists to develop new ways of working. One action that Katala was able to implement was to loan small amounts of money at low rates of interest to local farmers to buy rice seed, an expense that comes at a time of year when money is particularly tight. Twenty years ago, few would have made the connection between such interest rate savings and the conservation of a threatened parrot, but actions like this have certainly made a difference for the cockatoo. In Brazil, another initiative that perhaps goes against more traditional protectionist approaches is the acceptance by the non-profit organisation Parrots International that Lear's Macaw *Anodorhynchus leari* (Endangered) causes economic loss to local farmers by raiding crops in Brazil. In 2006, Parrots International dispensed around ten tons of corn to 16 farmers as compensation, the amount determined by the severity of their losses to macaws. These small sums of money, sympathy for the lot of the poor farmers and a degree of pragmatism have together greatly reduced the killing of these rare birds as they raid crops.

Partnerships with local communities can take many forms. A cooperative programme with local coconut farmers on the Pacific island of Niau was set up to protect nesting habitat for the Critically Endangered Tuamotu Kingfisher *Todiramphus gambieri*. On Réunion island in the Indian Ocean, a public appeal for help in finding, caring for and releasing young Mascarene Petrels *Pseudobulweria aterrima* that become grounded after becoming disorientated by street lighting has saved many birds (Le Corre *et al.* 2003). Efforts are now underway to conserve the Sociable Lapwing *Vanellus gregarius* by engaging with local hunters at the species' migration staging posts in Syria and Iraq. The detailed knowledge of local people about their environments may be crucial to finding and surveying threatened birds, especially species that are very poorly known, sparsely distributed or cryptic.

However, just as crucial is the need to develop a two-way educational exchange between local people and conservationists. Most efforts to save the world's rarest birds include components to provide environmental education for local communities, especially schoolchildren. In the Caribbean, such efforts have resulted in the adoption of the St Lucia Amazon *Amazona versicolor* as the national symbol of that island. The campaign, complete with reggae song about the bird, along with other conservation actions including harsh penalties for hunting, has reversed the fortune of the species (Collar *et al.* 1992). Having been reduced to as few as a hundred individuals in the 1970s, it is currently listed as Vulnerable. In India, successful community involvement in the protection of Sarus Cranes *Grus antigone* (Vulnerable) has also helped to re-establish broken cultural links between local farmers and their natural environment (Kaur *et al.* 2008).

Perhaps the most striking instance of the conservation of a Critically Endangered bird becoming central to a local community is that of the Yellow-eared Parrot *Ognorhynchus icterotis* of Colombia. This parrot was long known to be a specialist on wax palms, in particularly *Ceroxylon quindiuense*, the tallest palm in the world and the national tree of Colombia, and it once occurred down all three Andean ranges there and as far south as central Ecuador (Collar *et al.* 1992). However, deforestation in general, and over-exploitation of the wax palms in particular, caused the parrot to become so rare that for many years it was virtually invisible to ornithologists and fears for its survival were mounting. With the discovery in 1999 of a very small breeding group in the Cordillera Central

The Yellow-eared Parrot Ognorhynchus icterotis *has benefited to such an extent from a public awareness campaign within its range in Colombia that in 2010 it was removed from the Critically Endangered list (Pete Morris).*

of Colombia a long-term project was launched, backed from the start by the Loro Parque Foundation and implemented by ProAves Colombia, a recently created NGO, to attempt to bring the species back from the brink. Threats included hunting, the cutting of live wax palms for use in Palm Sunday parades, and the cutting of dead ones (often with holes for nesting) for fence-posts. Local communities were rapidly sensitised to the plight of the species through a major awareness campaign involving television advertisements, newspaper articles, radio broadcasts and poster distribution (Salaman 2006). The response has been a strong cultural swing in support of the parrot and the palms, but while a new local pride has been engendered there has also been a considerable growth in internal and international tourism to see the Yellow-eared Parrot, providing an additional reinforcement for the conservation of the species. The growth of ecotourism, driven in large part by the desire of travelling birders to see rare species, offers further opportunities for supporting conservation initiatives based around local livelihoods (Sekercioglu 2002), and it appears to be particularly successful when based on charismatic and rare species (Kruger 2005). With an almost absurd responsiveness to the new benign regime, the Yellow-eared Parrot has flourished to the point where, within ten years of the start of conservation activities, over a thousand individuals are now known in the wild (P. Salaman *in litt* 2010). In 2010, the species was removed from the list of Critically Endangered species.

THE COST OF PREVENTING EXTINCTION

The rescue of Critically Endangered bird species is a major undertaking that requires considerable financial resources; the greater the investment the greater the chances of success (Garnett *et al.* 2003). Restoring populations to levels at which they no longer need intensive conservation support can take thirty years or more (Jones 2004) and it may take even longer for the status of endangered species to improve sufficiently for them to be downlisted to lower categories of threat. For larger species, with low reproductive rates, the conservation investment may be far longer, as the slow recovery of the Kakapo illustrates (Chapter 16), although as expertise in species recovery develops success might come sooner. The resources needed to maintain conservation efforts over this length of time can be high, and one of the clearest lessons of the recent era of preventing extinctions is that it is often cheaper and simpler to conserve species before they reach Critically Endangered status than after (Drechsler *et al.* 2011). Even so, the costs of protecting the world's biological resources may be considerably lower than the costs, both economic and social, that are associated with unsustainable development (Balmford *et al.* 2002, Balmford & Bond 2005). The fight to prevent the extinction of Asia's vultures (Chapter 17), which has included major investments to diagnose the problem, develop and test solutions and construct a number of captive breeding facilities, has so far cost less than $5 million (C. Bowden *in litt.* 2010), a trivial amount in comparison to the huge financial and social problems brought about by the birds' virtual disappearance, although one that will inevitably rise as progress down the long road to recovery continues. The average cost of improving a species' status sufficiently for it to be moved to a lower IUCN threat category, based on a sample of 25 globally threatened bird species and adjusted for inflation, is around US$2 million (McCarthy *et al.* 2012), although this average masks a wide range of values. Moving some Polynesian Megapodes *Megapodius pritchardii* from what was their sole island home to another island and the establishment of a second population there, allowing their status to be improved from Critically Endangered to Endangered, cost just US$10,000. At the other extreme, reintroducing Californian Condors to the wild, so allowing their status to be changed from Extinct in the Wild to Critically Endangered, cost nearly US$50 million (Nielsen 2006, McCarthy *et al.* 2012). These two extremes exemplify a general pattern, which is that the costs of recovery are generally lower for species with smaller ranges, particularly island species, and lower for species in countries with lower GDP (McCarthy *et al.* 2012).

It was not until 2012 that the first attempt to estimate the costs of saving all of the world's threatened bird species was published. By collecting detailed data on the costs needed to reduce the extinction risk of over 200 globally threatened species and carefully extrapolating these to all 1250 such species, McCarthy *et al.* (2012) estimated that it would cost around US$1 billion a year for ten years to improve the status of all the world's globally threatened birds by one or more IUCN categories. In conservation terms, this is a vast sum of money, and indeed only around 12% of this need is currently being met. Yet looked at another way, this figure looks remarkably cheap. It is sobering to reflect that protecting billions of years of evolution by moving all the world's threatened bird species one or more steps further away from extinction would cost around the same each year as the advertising budget of a major cosmetics company, a twentieth of what Americans spend on ice-cream each year or less than one hundredth of what the world's bankers were paid in bonuses in 2011. Conserving the world's rarest species is, in the great scheme of things, cheap and affordable. This is particularly true in lower income countries, where most of the world's Critically Endangered species live, yet most conservation spend is directed internally by developed nations (Balmford *et al.* 2003a). Such efforts, entirely justifiable in a national sense, have achieved spectacular successes but the global mismatch between the distribution of threatened species and conservation resources means that they are often directed at birds that are not threatened in any global sense. Even within individual countries, the money spent on conservation may not be directed at the species most in need, as the example of Hawaii demonstrates. There can be little doubt that the future of many of the world's rarest birds will only be secured if greater resources are channelled to them from countries well outside their natural ranges. A recent initiative, BirdLife's Preventing Extinctions Programme (PEP), aims to do just this by linking people or organisations who have offered to take on responsibility for saving a species from extinction (Species Guardians) with people or organisations, generally from other countries, who undertake to provide the financial backing required (Species Champions).

A PLAN FOR SAVING THE WORLD'S RAREST BIRDS

In 2008, BirdLife International produced a ten-point plan for the conservation of the world's Critically Endangered species (BirdLife International 2008b). If this can be successfully enacted, the conservation status of a high proportion of the world's rarest birds is likely to improve.

1. Remove the veterinary drug diclofenac from the supply chain in the Indian subcontinent and South-East Asia, and prevent its veterinary use in Africa, in order to halt the catastrophic declines of several vulture species (Chapter 17).

2. Implement appropriate mitigation measures to reduce seabird by-catch by commercial longline fishery fleets in the world's oceans. This will benefit many albatross and petrel species (Chapter 12) which are declining significantly owing to incidental mortality when they get caught on baited hooks and drown.

3. Implement adequate measures to restrict the further spread of alien invasive species, and eradicate or control these on a priority suite of oceanic islands (Chapter 10), e.g. Brown Tree-snake *Boiga irregularis* in the Northern Mariana Islands; rats and cats on Niau and rats on Fatuhiva (French Polynesia); rats and cats in the Balearic Islands (Spain); cats, rats and plants in the Juan Fernández Islands (Chile); and cats, pigs, sheep and rabbits on Socorro (Mexico).

4. Strengthen the control and management of hunting and the cagebird trade (including through national laws and CITES), for example for Yellow-crested Cockatoo *Cacatua sulphurea* (Chapter 9) and Bali Starling (Indonesia), Philippine Cockatoo and Rufous-headed Hornbill *Aceros waldeni* (Philippines), Blue-billed Curassow *Crax alberti* (Colombia), Blue-throated Macaw *Ara glaucogularis* (Bolivia) and Grey-breasted Parakeet *Pyrrhura griseipectus* (Brazil).

5. Substantially scale up efforts to tackle the interlinked threats of habitat degradation, invasive species and climate change for the Critically Endangered species found only on Hawaii (USA) (Chapter 14), and for endemic species facing similar threats elsewhere, such as those in French and UK overseas territories (Chapter 12).

6. Adequately safeguard and manage the remaining forests on two island groups in Africa and one in Asia, each of which supports three endemic Critically Endangered birds: São Tomé, the Comoro Islands, and Sangihe (Indonesia).

7. In the Atlantic Forest of Brazil (Chapter 19), adequately safeguard and manage the remaining fragments, in particular those Important Bird Areas supporting Critically Endangered species, such as Chapada do Araripe (for Araripe Manakin *Antilophia bokermanni*), ESEC Murici (White-collared Kite *Leptodon forbesi*, Alagoas Foliage-gleaner *Philydor novaesi*, Alagoas Antwren *Myrmotherula snowi*), Complexo Pedra Azul/ Forno Grande (Cherry-throated Tanager *Nemosia rourei*) and Restinga de Maçambaba (Restinga Antwren *Formicivora littoralis*).

8. Protect and appropriately manage Important Bird Areas conserving tropical forest, which is increasingly threatened by inappropriate expansion of biofuel cultivation in addition to the well-established threats of clearance for agriculture and logging, e.g. in Indonesia (Chapter 9), Philippines (Chapter 18), Colombia, Ecuador, Peru (Chapter 6) and Mexico, each of which support high numbers of forest-dependent Critically Endangered bird species.

9. In Asia, strengthen wetland conservation efforts – including the protection of key tidal wetlands – under the Asia-Pacific Flyway Partnership for the benefit of species such as the Critically Endangered Spoon-billed Sandpiper *Eurynorhynchus pygmeus* (Chapter 4) and Chinese Crested Tern *Sterna bernsteini*.

10. Mount appropriately targeted surveys and searches for the suite of 'lost' and Possibly Extinct species (Chapter 22), such as Hooded Seedeater *Sporophila melanops* (Brazil), Himalayan Quail *Ophrysia superciliosa* (India), Slender-billed Curlew *Numenius tenuirostris* (Russia) (Chapter 25) and Samoan Moorhen *Gallinula pacifica* (Samoa).

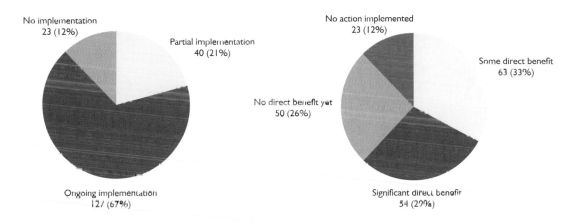

Figure 15.3. Implementation (left) and benefits (right) of the conservation actions identified as being required to save Critically Endangered birds (BirdLife International 2008b).

Most species listed as Critically Endangered are now receiving some dedicated conservation action, ranging from the efforts of committed individuals to find populations of 'lost' species to relatively expensive and extremely sophisticated long-term management by large organisations, as on Mauritius and New Zealand. Many of the necessary conservation actions identified by BirdLife International are being implemented, often with significant benefits (Fig. 15.3). Despite the enormous problems facing the world's rarest birds, there is no reason for giving up hope. Even on the Philippines, a megabiodiverse region regarded by many as a country of environmental ruin whose ecosystems are on the verge of collapse, there are encouraging signs that a combination of actions by the government and by local communities, aided by international expertise and resources, are starting to have an effect (Posa *et al.* 2008) and there is still a chance even for forest giants such as the Philippine Eagle (Chapter 18). A recent analysis suggests that although the number of animal and plant species that qualify for listing as globally threatened continues to increase, and that over 50 species of mammals, birds and amphibians move one step closer to extinction each year, this rate of deterioration would be considerably worse if it were not for the actions of conservationists (Hoffman *et al.* 2010). As one eminent conservationist has suggested, there are no hopeless cases, only expensive cases and people without hope.

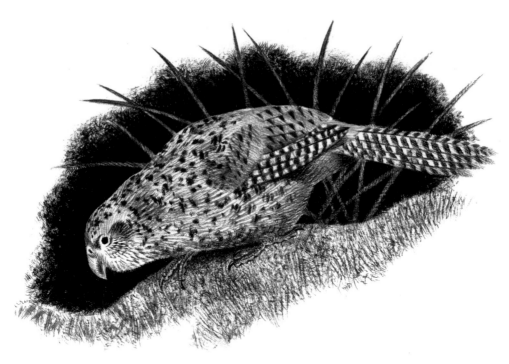

Chapter 16
Kakapo *Strigops habroptila*
CRITICALLY ENDANGERED

New Zealand's eccentric conveyor belt of evolution has produced an extraordinary bird community, moving one scientist to claim that if its mysteries could be explained, those of the rest of the natural world would fall into place around it (Nelson 1975). The origins of the peculiar avifauna of these islands continue to puzzle scientists, although recent molecular techniques suggest that the notion of New Zealand as 'Moa's Ark', a drifting lifeboat of species that were marooned when the islands broke away from the rest of the southern landmass of Gondwanaland around 82 million years ago, is unlikely to be an accurate explanation of past events. Instead, the ancestors of many or most of New Zealand's birds, perhaps even those of the kiwis, probably arrived long after the islands parted company with the rest of the southern landmass (Kelly & Sullivan 2010, Tennyson 2010, Trewick & Gibb 2010). Even so, many of these arrivals have had a very long time indeed in which to evolve into strange new forms. Although recent fossil finds show that mouse-sized mammals were present on New Zealand around 18 million years ago (Worthy *et al.* 2006), the islands have been free of them for long enough to allow birds to fill a wide range of niches normally occupied by mammals, among them that of large, generalist herbivores. Before human colonisation, New Zealand's avian herbivores dominated the terrestrial ecosystem to an extent unparalleled elsewhere (Lee *et al.* 2010).

A REMARKABLE SURVIVAL IN A WAVE OF EXTINCTION

One of the most celebrated products of this long evolutionary history, and one of the most threatened, is the Kakapo, a flightless, herbivorous, nocturnal parrot with a remarkable mating system. A male Kakapo weighs up to 3.6kg, making this the world's heaviest parrot, and it spends much of its time lumbering around on the ground with a peculiar rolling gait. Despite its size and flightlessness, the Kakapo is an agile climber, and birds will sometimes clamber to the tops of the tallest trees in search of food. For a flightless species, the Kakapo's wings are still relatively well-developed and it uses them to slow its descent from the tops of trees or bushes. The Kakapo shows many peculiarities in its anatomical structure and exhibits the greatest differences in size between the sexes of any parrot, males being on average nearly twice the weight of females (Livezey 1992). Its nocturnal habits and cryptic plumage probably evolved in response to predation by the giant and now sadly extinct Haast's Eagle *Harpagornis moorei* and other native diurnal raptors, although it is known to have featured in the diet of the Laughing Owl *Sceloglaux albifacies*, also now extinct. As with so much else about the Kakapo, its eyesight appears to be unique, being adapted in some respects for nocturnal vision but differing greatly in its visual system from other nocturnal and diurnal birds (Corfield *et al.* 2011).

The Kakapo is taxonomically important, being the only member of its genus and, together with the other two large parrots of New Zealand, the Kea *Nestor notabilis* and Kaka *N. meridionalis*, it forms a thin but very long branch of the evolutionary tree of the parrots (de Kloet & de Kloet 2005). In the absence of introduced predators, it is perhaps the world's longest-lived bird, with an average lifespan of 90 years or more. As well as having its own distinctly sweet body odour, the Kakapo has a good sense of smell, the result of a particularly diverse repertoire of olfactory receptor genes, and it has perhaps the lowest rate of energy expenditure of any bird (Hagelin 2004, Bryant 2006, Steiger *et al.* 2009). The Kakapo's owl-like face, delicate moss-green plumage and confiding and gentle nature make this a particularly attractive and endearing bird, and conservationists working with the species on a daily basis soon come to recognise that each bird has its own distinctive personality.

Kakapo (Maori bird names are the same in the singular and plural) feed on the leaves, bark, roots and seeds of a wide range of native fern, plant and tree species. The bill of the Kakapo is adapted for crushing plant material. Serrations on the inside of the upper mandible act as a file, rasping off the digestible parts of plant material and compacting the fibrous parts as a pellet, or 'chew', which is then expelled with the tongue (Butler 2006). The presence

The Kakapo is one of the most remarkable products of New Zealand's evolutionary isolation and one that, were it not for perhaps the most sophisticated and long-running species recovery programme ever attempted, would have been lost decades ago (Paddy Ryan).

of discarded chews has been used as a way of surveying the populations and movements of Kakapo. Some plants are eaten throughout the year, others only in certain seasons, and the dict appears to be flexible to the changing availability of different foods (Best 1984, Butler 2006). Birds are particularly fond of the fruits of the Rimu tree *Dacrydium cupressinum*, whose irregular masting appears to stimulate Kakapo breeding. Like mammalian ruminants, Kakapo are thought to use bacteria in their gut to help digestion. Analyses of fossilised Kakapo droppings dating back thousands of years suggest that the species has always had a wide range of plant foods, although now they may perhaps be feeding on some plants that were not previously taken (Horrocks *et al.* 2008). This catholic and flexible diet allowed the Kakapo to occupy a very wide range of habitats, from dense lowland forests to alpine moorland.

The Kakapo has one of the most unusual mating systems of any bird. Richard Henry, one of the pioneers of nature conservation in New Zealand, observed and described much of the species' intriguing social behaviour around 1900, but it was not until the 1970s that conservationists began to understand its significance. Don Merton and colleagues, working on the species in the 1960s and 1970s, finally recognised that, uniquely both for a parrot and for a flightless bird, the Kakapo is a lekking species (Merton *et al.* 1984), that is, one in which males compete against each other for the attentions of females on a communal display ground (lek). Males and females form no pair bond and meet only to mate. The problem of meeting a prospective mate in a nocturnal and flightless bird has been ingeniously solved by the Kakapo. At the start of the mating season, males walk considerable distances from their home territories to a prominent hill or ridge. The lek consists of a series of courts comprising a number of 'bowls', depressions in the ground cleared of vegetation by the males, connected by tracks that are also meticulously maintained. Kakapo are one of only a handful of lekking species that actually make their own lek structures. After a period of aggression between males to secure the best sites, during which fights can lead to injury or even death, they settle down into their respective courts, from which they perform their nocturnal displays. The most notable of these is 'booming', where the male inflates his thorax massively, until he looks like a ball with a tail, and emits a series of 15–30 booms, so low in frequency they are felt as much as they are heard, and can carry for up to 5km. These booms are often followed by a high-pitched metallic 'ching'. Booming takes place from December to March, and an individual may give 7,000 booms in a single night, moving between different bowls in his court to ensure that his booming is heard from all directions. This serenade can last for eight hours each night for several months,

A Kakapo booming bowl, constructed to amplify his self-advertising calls (Paddy Ryan).

Early writers noted the Kakapo's endearing and curious nature, but this did not save it from terrible slaughter (Paddy Ryan).

during which time the males may lose half their body weight. Don Merton gives a marvellous description of the elaborate display that has been observed at bowls, which includes 'side to side rocking movements and walking backwards while slowly raising and lowering fully extended wings – like a basking butterfly' (Merton *et al.* 1984).

Researchers wanting to know whether a particular lek is occupied need only scatter some grass or twigs along the tracks leading to the bowl and see if they are still there the next day, for the males maintain these meticulously and will quickly remove any debris placed on them. Groups of up to 50 track-and-bowl systems covering several square kilometres can occur at traditional lek sites, where females attracted by the noise move between the bowls before selecting the male of their choice. For all of this posturing and booming, visits by females are brief and infrequent, and can occur at any time during the display. Following copulation, the male plays no further part in the breeding process, and the female lays and incubates her clutch of one to four eggs in a hollow under plants or a fallen log. The remarkable display of the Kakapo is not an annual event, however, as breeding takes place only once every two to seven years, generally when there is an abundant fruiting of the Rimu or of the Pink Pine *Halocarpus biformis* (Cockrem 2006). The proportion of females attempting to breed in any particular year appears to be associated with the quantity of Rimu fruit available, and breeding females have larger territories that contain larger areas of Rimu forest than females that do not attempt to breed (Whitehead *et al.* 2012). In some years, males boom but the females do not respond, suggesting that females do not come into breeding condition every year (Cockrem 2006).

Fossil records suggest that Kakapo were once widespread and perhaps one of New Zealand's most abundant birds, but its flightlessness, confiding nature, large size and strong body odour became major disadvantages when mammalian predators arrived in New Zealand. The Maori arrived in New Zealand from Polynesia some 800 to 1,000 years ago, bringing with them domestic dogs and Pacific Rats *Rattus exulans*. They greatly valued Kakapo both as food and for ornamentation: the rotund, slow-moving, odoriferous and at times noisy birds cannot have been difficult to catch, and their feathers were turned into capes and cloaks for the tribal chiefs and their families. Some of these cloaks survive today and pay silent witness to the great number of these birds that were killed. While hunting and predation by dogs were probably the primary causes of initial declines in Kakapo populations, the rats may also have reduced productivity through predation of eggs and small chicks and competition for food. Kakapo nests are on the ground, under vegetation or in natural hollows such as between tree roots. The nests and young are cared for exclusively by the smaller female, so unguarded eggs and chicks and perhaps even brooding females would have made easy prey. Habitat destruction in the eastern and central regions of South Island may also have played a part in declines.

Despite this, Kakapo remained relatively common and widespread in the less populated parts of New Zealand right up until the late eighteenth century arrival of Europeans, who cleared huge areas of forest for agriculture and brought with them a host of other species that would drive the parrot to the brink of extinction. The early introduction of predators, such as domestic cats, and competitors for food, such as feral pigs, cattle and goats, was followed, a century later in the 1870s, by the deliberate release of ferrets *Mustela furo*, stoats *M. erminea* and weasels *M. nivalis* to control growing populations of rabbits, a move that proved disastrous for New Zealand's endemic birds, many of which were driven to extinction shortly afterwards. Added to this pressure, birds were hunted for food and sport by Europeans using dogs, and many hundreds of Kakapo were killed or captured to provide the world's museums, zoos and private collectors with specimens of this curiosity. The explorer Charlie Douglas wrote in 1899 that 'they could be caught in the moonlight, when on the low scrub, by simply shaking the tree or bush until they tumbled on the ground, something like shaking down apples. I have seen as many as half a dozen Kakapos shaken off one tutu bush this way'. As the species became rarer, so hunters and collectors intensified their efforts to obtain specimens before it became extinct, an example of the 'anthropogenic Allee effect' (p.32). However, despite this wholesale slaughter, both Maori and Europeans also valued the Kakapo as an affectionate pet. George Grey, twice Governor of New Zealand, wrote that his pet Kakapo's behaviour towards him and his friends was 'more like that of a dog than a bird'.

EARLY CONSERVATION

Although (and perhaps because) it lost a high proportion of its endemic birds in the last two centuries, New Zealand has a long history of attempting to conserve its native birds. As early as 1891, the government declared Resolution Island in Milford Sound a nature reserve, and between 1894 and 1900 the conservationist Richard Henry pioneered a radical new idea that has successfully prevented a number of extinctions. Realising the danger posed by introduced predators to New Zealand's native birds, Henry transferred hundreds of Kakapo and kiwis to Resolution Island, where they appear to have become established and started breeding. Unfortunately his efforts were in vain, because stoats reached the island in 1900 and by 1908 all Henry's good work had been undone. By this time, Kakapo probably survived only on stoat-free Stewart Island and in Fiordland, a wild and rugged region in the south-west corner of South Island. In 1950 the New Zealand Wildlife Service was formed, and dozens of expeditions were undertaken between then and 1970 to try to locate any remaining Kakapo. These focused on remote areas in Fiordland, believed by then to hold the only remaining populations. These early expeditions were undertaken by determined conservationists hiking across steep and inhospitable terrain for days on end in what is one of the wettest places on the planet. They found very few birds, but at least proved that the species survived.

Although Kakapo were known to have been held in captivity in the nineteenth and early twentieth centuries, there were no records of captive birds living for more than a year or so. However, the situation for the species was so dire that the Wildlife Service decided to attempt to breed Kakapo in captivity. Five Kakapo were caught in Fiordland in 1961 and were moved to the aviaries of the Mount Bruce Bird Reserve on North Island, but sadly all were male, and four of them died within three months while the fifth survived for four and a half years. Another male was caught in 1967 but died a year later. Although the causes of mortality might have been overcome with time and experience, captive breeding attempts were abandoned. Instead, the Wildlife Service decided to adopt the strategy pioneered by Richard Henry 80 years earlier, and to base conservation efforts on translocating Kakapo to offshore islands free of predators such as stoats and cats. This decision was reinforced by new information on the bizarre lekking system of the Kakapo, which made efforts to save the species using captive breeding appear doomed to failure (Cockrem 2002).

In the mid-1970s a new series of surveys was undertaken, spearheaded by Don Merton. Using helicopters, researchers were able to reach and search the most inaccessible parts of Fiordland. Kakapo were found by searching for their distinctive track-and-bowl display areas. Intensive searches of Fiordland between 1974 and 1977 located only 18 individuals, all of them males, clinging on in short vegetation along the treeline on the upper slopes of steep valleys where cats and stoats occurred in lowest numbers (Butler 2006). It was Merton's observation of these birds that led him to the discovery of the Kakapo's mating system. The Wildlife Service tried to reduce predator numbers in the area, but to no avail. A few birds were captured and removed to Maud Island; the rest simply disappeared. Subsequent searches for Kakapo in Fiordland, most recently in 2006, have failed to find any evidence that it survives there. For a few years, it seemed as though the species had faded to extinction.

In 1977, however, the dramatic discovery of a population of over 100 birds, including females, on Stewart Island reignited hopes that the species could be saved. Although Stewart Island was, by great good fortune, free of stoats, it did contain large numbers of feral cats, and the newly discovered Kakapo population was soon found to be in rapid decline because of predation (Karl & Best 1982). A decision was made to try to conserve the Stewart Island population *in situ*, rather than translocating birds, allowing scientists one last chance to study the behaviour and ecology of the Kakapo in its natural range (Powlesland *et al.* 1992), and in 1982 the Wildlife Service started controlling the feral cat population. The programme appeared at first to be highly successful, and annual predation rates, based on a sample of radio-tagged Kakapo, dropped from an alarming 56% (a rate that would quickly have wiped out the population) to practically nothing (Powlesland *et al.* 1995). Unfortunately, the effects of the control were short-lived, as cats quickly reoccupied cleared areas. The high cost of the work and the low productivity of the birds finally persuaded the Wildlife Service that the whole population should be translocated to more secure offshore islands. The Kakapo's distinctive smell, which had made it so vulnerable to introduced predators, worked now to its advantage, since (following Richard Henry's example) dogs could be trained to sniff them out and capture them alive for transfer to their new homes.

THE WORLD'S MOST INTENSIVE RECOVERY PROJECT

In 1987, responsibility for saving the Kakapo was transferred to the newly formed New Zealand Department of Conservation, commonly known as 'DOC', and in 1989 a Kakapo recovery plan was developed. The translocation of birds to safer offshore islands was at the heart of the plan. To provide a safe haven for Kakapo, islands had to be sufficiently large to support a viable population, they had to contain native habitats and, crucially, they had to be free, or cleared, of the major predators that had been instrumental in driving the decline on the mainland. It was also important that the islands chosen could not be easily invaded by predators, so they had to be too far from the nearest mainland for predators to be able to swim across.

Fortunately, New Zealand is well endowed with offshore islands that meet these criteria. Four potentially suitable islands were identified, although all required some form of preparatory management, involving habitat restoration or the eradication of predators. The islands initially selected were Maud Island (3km^2) in Pelorus Sound between North and South Islands (and not far from Stephens Island, home of the world's last flightless songbird – see Chapter 11), Little Barrier Island (31km^2) lying some 25km off the north-east coast of North Island, Codfish Island (14km^2), 3km off the north-west coast of Stewart Island, and Mana Island (2km^2), 3km off the south-west coast of North Island. Between 1979 and 1992, 61 Kakapo were transferred from Stewart Island to these four predator-free islands (Powlesland *et al.* 1995), most of the remaining birds on Stewart later being killed by cats. The last Stewart Island bird was found and moved to safety in 1997, by which time the island had yielded up a total of 65 birds. The majority of these birds were male, and all the last mainland Kakapo in Fiordland were also male. This pattern follows that seen in many other small and threatened populations, which tend to have a male-skewed adult sex ratio (p.33), in this case perhaps because incubating females suffer higher predation, although analyses of fossil remains suggest that a male-skewed sex ratio in Kakapo was normal even when the species was common (Trewick 1997).

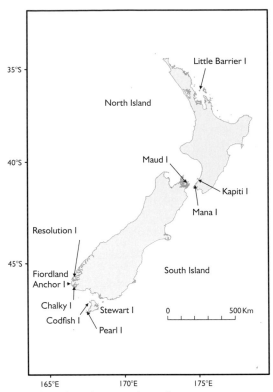

Location of offshore islands to which Kakapo have been translocated.

Codfish Island has proved to be the most suitable for introductions of the Kakapo and remains the most important site for the species, although in 1999 it became necessary to move all the Kakapo elsewhere temporarily to allow the island to be cleared of rats. Progress on other islands was even less straightforward. There were two attempts to establish Kakapo on Maud Island. Nine birds were released between 1974 and 1981, and males were heard booming twice during this period, but mortality was high and five birds were lost. When a stoat was discovered on the island in 1982, the four surviving birds were taken to Little Barrier Island and intensive stoat trapping was initiated. Between 1989 and 1991, six more birds were taken to Maud from Stewart Island and birds were given supplementary food (Powlesland & Lloyd 1994). The situation looked promising as males boomed in the summers of 1990–1991 and 1991–1992, but the females did not breed. Stoats were again found on the island in 1990 and intensive trapping on both Maud and the adjacent mainland successfully eliminated them, this time without the need for removing the Kakapo. Survival of birds translocated the second time was far higher, presumably because of enhanced predator control, better quality of regenerated forest on the island, supplementary feeding and the timing of translocation, which was latterly outside the breeding season. However, productivity remained low on Maud and efforts there were eventually abandoned.

Translocations to Little Barrier Island started in 1982 with 22 birds; 18 from Stewart Island and four from Maud. Birds were fitted with radio-transmitters to monitor survival and movements for a few months following release, and later in the programme to aid intensive management. To start with, the translocations did not appear successful. Birds lost weight and had to be fed (Moorhouse & Powlesland 1991). Although survival was high, and males were heard booming in eight of the ten summers between 1982 and 1990, no females attempted nesting until 1989, when supplementary feeding was initiated in an attempt to stimulate breeding. This appeared to work, with nesting in two of the next three years, and two male chicks were produced in 1991. However, the continued presence of rats on the island led to the evacuation of the Kakapo population in 1998. Mana Island was also evacuated and two new islands, Chalky (5km²) and Anchor (13km²), were used instead. In 2005, birds were moved from Chalky to Anchor. The current population therefore survives only on Codfish and Anchor Islands.

Soon after translocation, it became clear that this was just the first step on a long road to recovery because, while a high proportion of birds survived the move, breeding rates were so low that the number of chicks produced barely managed to replace the adults being lost (Lloyd & Powlesland 1994, Clout & Merton 1998). A more intensive management strategy was therefore developed, which included hand-rearing of chicks, the provision of supplementary food and round-the-clock protection of nests from rats (Clout & Merton 1998, Elliott *et al.* 2001). The few remaining Kakapo are perhaps the most intensively managed wild birds in the world, and exhaustive measures have been taken to ensure the population not only survives but grows. The level of information collected on each bird is extensive: one bird, for example, is known to have abnormal sperm and fathers infertile eggs. Each Kakapo receives an annual health check, during which it is screened for injury and disease. Every effort is made to prevent infection entering the population, even to the extent of monitoring disease in other species present. House Sparrows *Passer domesticus* carrying salmonella have been recorded on several translocation islands, although checks to date have shown no sign of the infection entering the Kakapo population (Brangenberg *et al.* 2003). All birds are fitted with radio tags so that they can be located and monitored at regular intervals. Static receivers called 'snarks' have been developed to record birds automatically as they pass close to them, allowing researchers to profile the type and timing of individual birds' movements. However, surprises can occur even in this small and closely monitored population. In 2009, the rangers on Codfish were astonished to rediscover, alive and well, a male Kakapo that was one of four transferred there from Stewart Island in 1987 and had not been seen since.

Supplementary feeding has been shown to increase the success of breeding females, but unfortunately it does not reduce the time between successive breeding seasons (Houston *et al.* 2007). It also carries a potential risk. In birds, females in better condition tend to modify the sex ratio of their offspring to produce more of the larger sex (Cockburn *et al.* 2002), which in the case of the Kakapo and indeed most other birds is the male. Sure enough, supplementary feeding increased the number of Kakapo males produced but not the more valuable females (Clout *et al.* 2002). This realisation led to the carefully controlled feeding of individual females in response to their body condition. Females were given sufficient food to allow them to reproduce, but not so much that their offspring were largely males. This new feeding system has increased the frequency of breeding attempts and ensures a healthy balance of the sexes in the resulting offspring (Robertson *et al.* 2006).

Researchers have shown that, in non-breeding years, Kakapo feed on a wide range of fruits and seeds, whereas in breeding years they switch their diets largely to the fruits of podocarps (Cockrem 2006, Fidler *et al.* 2008). A better understanding of this link between tree fruiting and breeding allows the recovery team to predict where and when conditions might be favourable for breeding and to manipulate the population accordingly. In 2002, all the adult female Kakapo on other islands were moved to Codfish in anticipation of an exceptional fruit crop. This triggered nesting in 95% of the females, which between them raised 24 fledglings, increasing the total population by 39% (Elliott *et al.* 2006). The success of the 2002 breeding season was a major boost for the project, as it showed that careful manipulation of the population over a long period could gradually bring the population up. However, the recovery team had to wait another seven years before the next successful breeding took the population to 124 birds in 2009 (Fig. 16.1).

Further research is attempting to understand the physiological basis for the link between the onset of synchronised breeding attempts and the availability of certain fruits, which might depend on the presence in the diet of certain plant oestrogens (Fidler *et al.* 2000, Fidler *et al.* 2008). If this link can be confirmed, it might prove possible to increase the frequency of breeding years artificially, which would be a significant step towards achieving the current target of 150 female birds. Although efforts to increase the frequency of Kakapo breeding by providing supplementary food have so far been unsuccessful, fledging success has increased significantly following the introduction of more intensive management methods.

The breeding behaviour and performance of every nesting bird has been carefully monitored (Eason *et al.* 2006). Each nest is closely guarded by an observer living in a tent nearby, who monitors progress using miniature cameras. When the female leaves the nest at night to go foraging, the guard places a small electric blanket over the eggs or chicks to keep them at the optimal temperature. Infra-red cameras detect rats around nests and small bangs and flashes are triggered to scare them away. Chicks that appear ill or fail to grow well are removed to hand-rearing facilities where they receive intensive care before being returned to the wild (Eason & Moorhouse 2006). As a

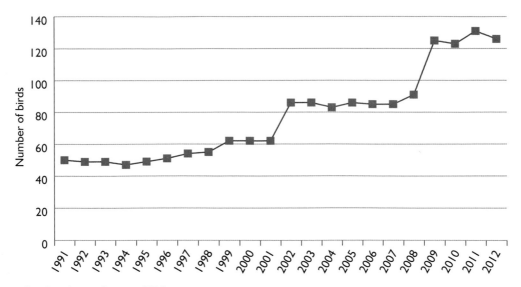

Figure 16.1. Population changes of Kakapo since 1991.

result, most chicks that hatch now survive to adulthood. Hatching success has, however, remained low, as over half of all eggs laid are infertile, perhaps because of inbreeding (Elliott *et al.* 2006). Efforts are therefore underway not only to increase the size of the population but also to improve its genetic variation. Part of the problem is that most of the remaining birds came from the same small population on Stewart Island and are genetically very similar. The last of the birds from Fjordland, called Richard Henry in honour of that pioneering conservationist, died in December 2010 at the age of perhaps a hundred years. This marked the final extinction of a population that was genetically distinct from the remaining Stewart Island stock (Miller *et al.* 2003). However, the survival of three of his progeny with Stewart Island mates means that some genetic signature of the remarkable Fjordland population still survives and might strengthen future generations. Artificial insemination is now being used to spread these birds' genes into future populations, and a tool has been developed to help assess the genetic structure of the whole population and the relatedness of every bird (Robertson *et al.* 2009).

THE OUTLOOK FOR THE KAKAPO

The problems facing the Kakapo are far from over. Thirty-five years after the current conservation plan commenced, the population is still tiny and would probably not survive for long without the intensive round-the-clock management it currently receives (Elliott 2006). Disease remains a constant risk with the potential rapidly to undo many years of hard-earned success. In 2004, three young birds died of septicaemia caused by erysipelas, a disease that had not previously been reported in Kakapo, and against which birds are now routinely vaccinated (Gartrell *et al.* 2005). Breeding remains sporadic, egg infertility is common and the population might be suffering from the effects of inbreeding. Even the most optimistic estimates of future population trends suggest that the goal of 150 female Kakapo is still perhaps twenty years away (Elliott 2006). However, the signs are encouraging: the relatively modest increase in the size of the population since birds were moved to offshore islands masks a significant improvement in the sex- and age-structure of the population, and the bumper breeding season in 2009 caused the population to leap to three figures for the first time in thirty years.

Meanwhile, the restoration of Resolution Island (208km²) and nearby Secretary Island (81km²), adjacent to the species' former stronghold in Fiordland, raises hopes that self-sustaining populations can be established there in better and more extensive habitat than that on the islands they currently occupy. The strong research component that the Kakapo recovery plan has always contained continues to pay dividends, and researchers working on the species are constantly developing new and ingenious ways to boost numbers. An average net gain of around two birds per year during a conservation programme that spans a third of a century may appear scant reward for all the effort and money that has been expended, but this is to ignore the enormous obstacles that the recovery team have had to overcome. Each and every Kakapo that has been added to the population during this time has rightly been viewed as a major success in the recovery of this species, although it rarely receives the same media attention as the occasional birth in captivity of a Giant Panda *Ailuropoda melanoleuca*, another species with a notorious disinclination to breed as often as its protectors might like.

The prevention of the Kakapo's extinction and the relatively rosy future it now faces represent one of the great achievements in global bird conservation. New Zealand has been at the forefront of developing and implementing conservation solutions for species on the brink of extinction since the pioneering efforts of Richard Henry. Perhaps only Mauritius can claim a comparable success rate in bringing species back from the brink of extinction, but even there efforts have been assisted by expertise in island restoration originally developed in New Zealand. Much of what is known today about the eradication of introduced species and the intensive management of tiny populations was first learned the hard way in New Zealand (Bellingham *et al.* 2010). The country's conservation agencies, helped enormously by a steady stream of volunteers and donors, who have invested so much time, money and effort in trying to prevent the extinction of the Kakapo and many other extraordinary birds, have earned the enduring respect of the international conservation community.

Don Merton holding Fiordland's sole surviving Kakapo, named Richard Henry after the man who first attempted translocations of the species (Don Merton). Sadly, both Don Merton and this precious Kakapo died within a year of each other, in 2011 and 2010 respectively.

Chapter 17
Asian Vultures:
White-rumped Vulture *Gyps bengalensis*, Indian Vulture *Gyps indicus*, Slender-billed Vulture *Gyps tenuirostris*
CRITICALLY ENDANGERED

Twenty years ago, it would have been difficult to think of a group of birds less likely to be brought to the brink of extinction than the *Gyps* vultures of the Indian subcontinent. Abundant and widespread species that actually benefited from the activities of a massive human population, White-rumped and Indian (or Long-billed) Vultures, together with smaller numbers of Slender-billed Vultures, filled the skies of central and northern India, Nepal, Pakistan and Bangladesh. The White-rumped (or Oriental White-backed) Vulture was considered in the 1980s to be perhaps the most abundant large bird of prey in the world (Houston 1985). Although there are no reliable population estimates for the 1980s, there were probably tens of millions of vultures in India, Nepal and Pakistan. Today, however, the skies are empty of them and all three species are listed as Critically Endangered.

Astonishing declines in numbers of over 99% have required emergency measures to be put in place to prevent the complete extinction of these formerly abundant species (Pain *et al.* 2003, Prakash *et al.* 2003, Pain *et al.* 2008). Their complete collapse represents perhaps the most unexpected catastrophe ever recorded in a bird population. Moreover, it is one that has had profound environmental, economic and social effects. The decline in vultures coincided with a sharp increase in the population of feral dogs that profited from the newly vacated food niche, and these are responsible for the high incidence of human rabies cases in India (Baral & Gautam 2007, Markandya *et al.* 2008, Pain *et al.* 2008). The future of all three *Gyps* species may now depend on the effectiveness of small populations held in emergency captive breeding facilities (Bowden 2009). Similarly dramatic but more recent

Considered in the 1980s to be perhaps the world's most abundant large raptor, the White-rumped Vulture is now listed as Critically Endangered after the most dramatic and least-expected population collapse ever recorded (Richard Cuthbert, RSPB).

This photograph, taken in 1984, gives an idea of just how common vultures were in India before the population collapse. Note the black ring of roosting vultures around the top of the buildings in the background (Goutam Narayan).

population declines have now seen the Red-headed Vulture *Sarcogyps calvus* also elevated to the threat category of Critically Endangered, and the Egyptian Vulture *Neophron percnopterus* to Endangered (Cuthbert *et al.* 2006). There is mounting evidence that some populations of the Himalayan Vulture *Gyps himalayensis* are also now in rapid decline (Acharya *et al.* 2009).

All four Critically Endangered vultures are obligate carrion-eaters. They were widespread across the countryside, and *Gyps* species were strikingly abundant around urban slaughterhouses. Photographs from the 1980s show tens of thousands of *Gyps* vultures at carcass dumps around major cities, a solid wall of waiting birds ringing the tops of all the surrounding buildings. In these macabre places, the vultures had a reliable supply of food in the form of livestock carcasses. In the 1980s, livestock numbers in India exceeded 400 million. Because many Hindus are vegetarian and cows are considered sacred, cattle tend to live relatively long lives, used as draught animals or for milking. When they become too old to be of practical use they are often turned loose to fend for themselves. Around towns and cities, dead livestock are collected and taken to specially designated dumps where skinners remove their hides for leather. Before the recent population collapse, vultures would pick a skinned carcass clean in as little as thirty minutes. The skeletons would then bake and dry in the sun before being gathered by bone collectors for the production of gum and bone meal. In rural areas, dead livestock were treated in a similar way, but were dealt with where they dropped. This was a mutually beneficial relationship: the vultures had plenty to eat, and in return they stripped the bones and provided an important environmental health service by removing rotting flesh, which might otherwise become a source of disease. Vultures were also important to practitioners of the ancient Parsi religion, who traditionally laid out their human dead in 'towers of silence' for the birds to dispose of in a way consistent with their spiritual beliefs.

In February 1995, BirdLife International convened an international workshop in Coimbatore, southern India, to compile a candidate list of species to evaluate for inclusion in *Threatened Birds of Asia* (BirdLife International 2001). Several representatives from South-East Asia attended, and they put forward the view that all Asian vultures should be considered for inclusion, since they were now so rare in their countries. The reasons for these declines were unclear, but appear to have been related to reductions in the populations of large native herbivores (Pain *et al.* 2003). The proposal that these species should be included in the Red Data book was greeted with good-natured amusement

Since the vultures disappeared, there has been an explosion in the number of feral dogs at carcass dumps, seemingly contributing to the spread of rabies (Richard Cuthbert, RSPB).

The disappearance of India's vultures has had a severe impact on people collecting bones from carcass dumps (Richard Cuthbert, RSPB).

by the subcontinent's attendees, who joked that they would be happy to set up a business exporting their surplus millions to South-East Asia to even out the situation. Despite the serious plight of vultures further east, to which everyone was sympathetic, it was clearly impossible to treat any of the species as globally threatened, given their superabundance in the subcontinent and the deep cultural traditions that meant, surely, that the situation would continue indefinitely. Many of the same attendees were still discussing the extraordinary disparity in vulture status between South and South-East Asia when they reconvened in Coimbatore for the Sálim Ali centenary conference of November 1996. Almost immediately afterwards, however, vulture researcher Vibhu Prakash of the Bombay Natural History Society (BNHS) witnessed the inexplicable disappearance of vultures from the famous Keoladeo National Park, Bharatpur (Prakash 1999), and newspapers around India started publishing ominous reports that vultures were simply vanishing. However, it was not until BNHS carried out nationwide surveys in 2000 that the extent of the declines became apparent: over 90% of vultures had been lost in just eight years, and in the last few months while the proofs of *Threatened birds of Asia* were being checked, entries were rapidly put together for the three *Gyps* vultures. Unexpectedly, the loss of vultures was found at this time to be as severe in national parks and remote rural areas as it was in towns and cities (Pain *et al.* 2003, Prakash *et al.* 2003). Similar patterns of severe decline were subsequently recorded across Pakistan (Arshad *et al.* 2009) and Nepal (Chaudhary *et al.* 2012).

THE SEARCH FOR A SMOKING GUN

These unprecedented declines attracted the attention of conservation scientists in India and around the world, and the race was on to find their cause while there was still time. BNHS, working with partners in the UK that included the Royal Society for the Protection of Birds (RSPB), the Zoological Society of London (ZSL) and the National Bird of Prey Trust (NBPT), launched what was initially a research study aimed at identifying the cause of the declines and developing expertise in emergency captive management of vultures in India. Significant funding from

181

the UK Government's Darwin Initiative allowed this to develop into a comprehensive strategy for the recovery of these species, encompassing research and monitoring, political lobbying and captive breeding. Early in this process, BNHS convened an international meeting in New Delhi to highlight the vultures' plight. This proved to be a fortuitous move, because representatives of The Peregrine Fund (TPF), a raptor conservation organisation based in the USA, were among the delegates.

Following the New Delhi meeting, TPF joined forces with the Ornithological Society of Pakistan to assess whether vultures were suffering a similar fate in Pakistan. Initial results were reassuring, with good numbers of vultures reported from a number of colonies in Pakistan. However, confidence soon gave way to concern and then to alarm as monitoring showed rapidly declining colony sizes, and large numbers of dead birds started to be reported (Gilbert *et al.* 2002, Gilbert *et al.* 2006). It seemed that vulture populations in Pakistan in the early years of the new millennium were suffering the same fate as those in India, although with a somewhat later onset. At around the same time, Bird Conservation Nepal (BCN) reported similarly worrying results in their own country.

For several years, the reason for this unprecedented collapse was the subject of increasingly frantic scientific investigation (Pain *et al.* 2008). In India, considerable collaborative efforts by conservation organisations, private laboratories and progressive and motivated individuals from several state governments were hampered by legislation prohibiting the collection of dead birds without permits. While this legislation was well-intentioned, its aim being to conserve threatened species, the very protracted process of obtaining permits made it impossible to collect and analyse all but a few of the many vulture carcasses that researchers were finding. In Pakistan, many more dead vultures were collected for analysis, but by 2003 all the researchers remained perplexed as to the cause of the declines.

The researchers had little to go on. Vultures had started declining in India around the early to mid-1990s. Declines were initially reported from the central state of Rajasthan (where the best monitoring data were available) and later elsewhere. Birds were reported as looking sick and lethargic and showed the perplexing habit of perching for long periods with their heads hanging down against their chests ('neck-drooping'), although this behaviour, considered a non-specific sign of illness (Prakash *et al.* 2003), appears also to be involved in temperature regulation (Gilbert *et al.* 2007b). The vultures would then simply fall dead from their perches. Declines appeared to be spreading, with a later

A conservationist taking a young vulture for captive breeding. The prevalence of diclofenac in the environment is still high enough to cause significant mortality to wild birds (Richard Cuthbert, RSPB).

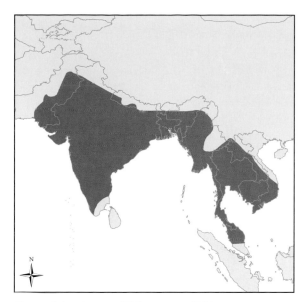

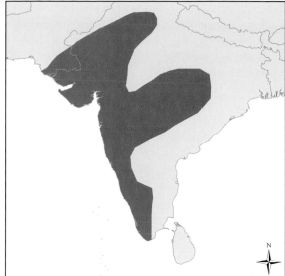

Original distribution of White-rumped Vulture.

Original distribution of Indian Vulture.

onset in Pakistan and Nepal. Examination of corpses showed that the majority of dead birds were suffering from visceral gout, an accumulation of uric acid crystals on the internal organs, indicating kidney malfunction. As far as could be ascertained, no other common scavengers at carcass dumps, such as feral dogs or crows, were declining.

Initially, research centred on the possibility that some kind of infectious disease was responsible (Cunningham *et al.* 2003). This hypothesis was supported by the observation that declines seemed to be spreading like a contagion outwards from central India (Prakash *et al.* 2003). The disease hypothesis seemed plausible because vultures are social animals, feeding and roosting in close proximity, facilitating the rapid transmission of disease from bird to bird. Furthermore, vultures are known to move many hundreds of kilometres to feed, potentially spreading the infection widely. The disease hypothesis was also favoured by the lack of any obvious alternative. The vultures' food was not thought to be a problem because no significant concentrations of the toxins most frequently responsible for the poisoning of wildlife, such as pesticides or toxic metals, were found in the tissues of dead birds, and other scavengers of dead livestock, such as feral dogs, did not appear to be affected by whatever was killing the vultures. Yet after three years of intensive research work, no candidate disease had been found. Two new vulture diseases were identified, but neither could explain the declines (Riley *et al.* 2003, Oaks *et al.* 2004a).

When all other lines of enquiry had been exhausted, Lindsay Oaks, a veterinary pathologist from Washington State University working with TPI, along with the Ornithological Society of Pakistan, returned to the possibility of a contaminated food source. In 2003 they investigated veterinary drugs in common use in Pakistan, and identified those that could possibly be associated with kidney malfunction and visceral gout. Among these were non-steroidal anti-inflammatory drugs (NSAIDs), which are in global use in human and veterinary medicine and include such commonly used painkillers as ibuprofen and aspirin. At first it seemed wholly improbable that residual NSAIDs found in dead livestock could be responsible for the vulture declines. These drugs are tested on a wide range of organisms, including birds, during their development, and any toxicity to animals would surely have been recorded. Moreover, the concentrations of NSAIDs in the tissue of treated livestock would surely be too low to produce such lethal effects. However, there are large differences in sensitivity to NSAIDs between species, and the researchers persisted with this line of enquiry.

The only NSAID in wide veterinary use in Pakistan was found to be diclofenac, a drug used to reduce pain, fever and inflammation in livestock in India since the early 1990s but, intriguingly, not available for use on livestock in Pakistan until 1998. The timing of the drug's introduction therefore seemed to fit well with the timing of declines in vulture populations, but further evidence was required to assess whether this drug could be the culprit. First, the researchers investigated diclofenac concentrations in the kidneys of fresh vulture carcasses that they had recovered. Those that had visceral gout, a symptom common to most dead birds examined, all tested positive for diclofenac. Kidneys of birds that had died without exhibiting gout, presumably of other causes, all tested negative for diclofenac. This result was highly significant and provided strong evidence for a link between diclofenac and the kidney failure that was killing the vultures (Oaks *et al.* 2004b). The link was greatly strengthened by experiments, in which researchers treated livestock with standard veterinary doses of diclofenac, slaughtered them shortly afterwards and fed their tissues to captive vultures (Meteyer *et al.* 2005). The diclofenac-contaminated food affected kidney function in the vultures. Birds that consumed more diclofenac suffered more severe effects, and birds that received the highest doses developed visceral gout and died within a couple of days. Researchers in India and Nepal subsequently analysed stored carcasses of both White-rumped and Indian Vultures for diclofenac and their results replicated those found in Pakistan (Shultz *et al.* 2004, Prakash *et al.* 2005) providing conclusive evidence that diclofenac had indeed driven the declines that had brought the formerly common and widespread vultures to the brink of extinction.

Even so, the case that diclofenac was responsible needed to be watertight to convince the authorities to take action, and many questions remained unanswered. Diclofenac is a palliative drug, relieving symptoms such as pain, inflammation and fever, but not curing the underlying cause of those symptoms. Was it likely that people in impoverished rural communities could afford palliative care for their livestock? And why had the drug's toxicity to birds not been detected during its development and testing? Furthermore, NSAIDs like diclofenac are generally metabolised and excreted very rapidly by livestock, so unless a cow were to die very shortly after being treated, its carcass would not contain more than a trace of the drug. Was it really possible that enough livestock carcasses contained enough diclofenac to drive such rapid and widespread declines? And why did other scavengers, such as dogs and crows, remain apparently unaffected? The Indian and UK research group set about answering these questions. The experimental research in Pakistan had already shown White-rumped Vultures to be highly sensitive to diclofenac, even at concentrations so low that they were unlikely to affect many mammal species, and further testing confirmed the extreme toxicity of diclofenac to other *Gyps* species (Swan *et al.* 2006b, Naidoo *et al.* 2009a,b, Das *et al.* 2011). However, Turkey Vultures *Carthartes aura*, which despite the name are not closely related to the Old World vultures, were unaffected by large doses when tested (Rattner *et al.* 2008), and diclofenac was less toxic to domestic fowl, the bird most commonly used in the testing of new drugs, than to *Gyps* vultures (Naidoo *et al.* 2007). Toxicity of different chemicals appears to vary widely and unpredictably within the bird world; for example, it appears that the Kea *Nestor notabilis*, a threatened alpine parrot of New Zealand, is poisoned by chocolate (Gartrell & Reid 2007)!

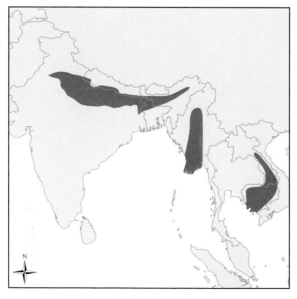

Original distribution of Slender-billed Vulture.

However, even though *Gyps* vultures were highly sensitive to diclofenac, the high rate of metabolism and excretion of the drug in mammals raised questions about how much contaminated meat the birds would have to consume to be affected. The possibility that Indian cattle might metabolise diclofenac more slowly than European cattle (a different species) was tested and quickly ruled out (Taggart *et al.* 2007a,b). In both cattle species, the drug was undetectable in tissues as little as a week after it was administered, and because many animals would be likely to survive this period, a large number would have to be treated for there to be many carcasses containing high concentrations of the drug. Further research indicated that indeed this was the case: in India alone, it was initially estimated that at least five million courses of diclofenac were used to treat livestock each year, and the true number was probably very much higher. Diclofenac is an effective drug and, importantly, out of patent, so it was being mass-produced and sold very cheaply by many companies in India. While it does not cure animals, its effective painkilling and anti-inflammatory properties may enable livestock to continue productive work, such as pulling carts and ploughs and producing milk, though many doses are likely to have been administered to animals nearing the end of their lives.

So a great deal of diclofenac was being used, but could it be enough to be killing so many vultures? Vultures are long-lived and breed very slowly, and with the frequency with which vultures feed – once every one to four days – it was estimated that less than one in a hundred livestock carcasses would need to contain lethal levels of diclofenac to drive declines at the rates observed (Green *et al.* 2004). This level of contamination seemed entirely plausible, and suddenly all the pieces of the jigsaw were falling into place. To complete the picture, the researchers needed to know the proportion of livestock carcasses in the environment that actually contained diclofenac at concentrations likely to harm vultures. They thus embarked on the unpleasant but necessary task of collecting tissue samples from carcass dumps right across India. By June 2005, nearly two thousand cattle livers had been sampled across twelve Indian states. Analysis revealed that as many as one in ten carcasses contained diclofenac (Taggart *et al.* 2007b) and enough contained concentrations at lethal levels to prove that diclofenac contamination alone was sufficient to have caused the observed vulture population declines (Green *et al.* 2007). One of the most baffling ornithological mysteries of recent times had finally been solved.

WHAT ALTERNATIVE TO DICLOFENAC?

Ever since The Peregrine Fund's breakthrough in 2003, conservationists in India had been pushing the relevant authorities towards a consensus on how to address the problem. In 2004, BNHS convened a workshop to develop a vulture recovery plan (MoEF 2006). The week started with participants airing an array of strongly held beliefs and hypotheses for the vulture declines, from shortage of food to lack of suitable nesting sites. However, as the workshop progressed it soon became evident that whatever was killing these normally long-lived animals would have to be killing adult birds, across the whole subcontinent, and all participants finally acknowledged that diclofenac had to be the major cause of the declines. All delegates, governmental and non-governmental, Indian and international, concluded that two major actions were necessary if the vultures were to survive. The first was an immediate ban on the veterinary use of diclofenac. The second was an emergency captive breeding programme to enable the species at risk to bridge the gap between a ban and its eventual implementation, and to provide a population to release into a future diclofenac-free environment.

However, diclofenac is undoubtedly a very important drug in veterinary medicine, particularly for poor rural communities that depend on their livestock for working the land, for transport and for the provision of dairy products. While a ban on the veterinary use of diclofenac was essential to save vulture populations, it soon became evident that this could not be achieved in the absence of an alternative, and so began another search. To be suitable, the drug would need to be effective at reducing pain and inflammation, out of patent to enable it to be cheaply mass-produced, and of course safe for vultures and other scavenging birds. The search was led by the RSPB in the UK. Questionnaires were sent to bird keepers and zoos across the world to discover which NSAIDs had been used to treat scavenging birds, at what concentrations and with what effects. This survey yielded two very important findings, one positive, the other deeply disturbing. The positive result was that an NSAID called meloxicam had

The future of India's vultures now rests in part on the success of a number of captive breeding facilities, here holding White-rumped Vultures (Richard Cuthbert, RSPB).

been given to *Gyps* vultures of six species and to many other species of scavenging bird with no apparent ill effects (Cuthbert *et al.* 2007). Even better, meloxicam was out of patent and already produced for veterinary use in India, albeit in relatively small amounts. The worrying finding was that several other NSAIDs, including carprofen and flunixin, had been used to treat birds that had subsequently died with kidney damage. Diclofenac may not be the only NSAID on the veterinary market that is capable of killing birds, so the catastrophe of the Asian vultures could be repeated elsewhere (Cuthbert *et al.* 2007).

Before meloxicam could be proposed as a safe alternative to diclofenac, its performance at concentrations to which vultures would be exposed when feeding on livestock in the wild had to be evaluated. All three affected Asian *Gyps* vultures had long since been uplisted by IUCN to the category of Critically Endangered, so testing a new drug on the tiny numbers of remaining wild birds was unthinkable. The few birds already in captivity were a precious resource to help safeguard the future of these species, so also could not be used for such testing. However, the closely related African White-backed Vulture *Gyps africanus* was not threatened, and good numbers of birds that could not be returned to the wild, for example because of injury, were held in captivity in South Africa. Research at Pretoria University found that meloxicam did not appear to affect the birds, even at levels higher than those that they were likely to encounter in the wild (Swan *et al.* 2006a,b). Scientists from the Indian Veterinary Research Institute worked closely with the South African researchers, and once their results indicated a very low risk of toxicity to the African sister species, they obtained permission to test meloxicam on a small number of the Asian vultures (Swarup *et al.* 2007). Again, meloxicam had no obvious adverse effects: a replacement for diclofenac had been found.

While the testing of meloxicam was underway, BNHS began a campaign to outlaw diclofenac in the treatment of animals. The authorities were kept fully informed as safety testing of alternatives progressed and, in a landmark decision in March 2005, members of the Indian National Board for Wildlife recommended a ban on the veterinary use of diclofenac. This was followed, in January 2006, by an international conference on the vulture declines convened by the Indian Ministry of Environment and Forests, coinciding with the publication of the results of meloxicam safety testing. This meeting concluded with a resolution 'to strongly recommend to the Governments of the respective countries to take immediate steps to completely phase out veterinary diclofenac'. In May 2006, manufacturing licences for veterinary diclofenac were withdrawn in India, at the behest of the Drug Controller General. The Government of Nepal took similar action in August 2006, shortly followed by the Government of Pakistan. This was a major and impressively rapid step, and one that contrasts starkly with the decades taken by the governments of countries such as the USA and UK to ban the agricultural use of DDT, despite overwhelming evidence of its disastrous environmental impacts. Responding to ongoing pressure from the BNHS advocacy programme, this measure was further strengthened by the Indian Government in 2008 when it was made an imprisonable offence to manufacture diclofenac formulations for veterinary use; measures subsequently mirrored in Nepal.

However, a ban on veterinary manufacturing is not the same as a ban on sale or use; much diclofenac remained available for purchase from stockpiles in veterinary pharmacies, and diclofenac produced for human consumption was also being used on livestock. The BNHS team monitored the incidence and concentrations of diclofenac in the tissues of livestock carcasses, and two years after the ban found little reduction in diclofenac use, although the use of meloxicam did appear to have increased (Taggart *et al.* 2009). Much therefore remains to be done before the vultures' environment is free of diclofenac. Advocacy and awareness campaigns aimed at key groups, such as veterinarians, farmers and pharmacists, are essential. A positive recent move came when the Indian government warned drug companies not to sell the veterinary form of diclofenac and directed that all human diclofenac containers must carry the warning 'not for veterinary use'. Unfortunately, however, preventing diclofenac produced for human use from being used by veterinarians constitutes a worrying gap in the measures taken so far.

The second decision taken at the pivotal recovery plan workshop in 2004 was the establishment of captive breeding facilities to tide the Critically Endangered vultures over the period during which, it was hoped, diclofenac would be removed from their food. The declines were so precipitous that had birds not rapidly been taken into captivity it may have become nearly impossible to find and capture sufficient individuals to safeguard the species

Vulture restaurants, where birds are provided with uncontaminated livestock carcasses, can be effective at protecting vultures, here largely White-rumped Vultures, from poisoning by diclofenac, but the only long-term solution to the problem is the removal of diclofenac from the environment (Richard Cuthbert, RSPB).

Long-billed Vultures in captivity; good numbers of all three Asian Gyps *species are now held in captive breeding facilities (Richard Cuthbert, RSPB).*

from extinction. Although thousands, and possibly tens of thousands, of *Gyps* vultures remain scattered thinly across southern Asia, ongoing declines and the slow rate of removal of diclofenac from their environment have justified the decision to take some into captivity (Bowden 2009). The experience gained by BNHS from as early as 2001 to care for and breed vultures in captivity gave them a head start. Today, BNHS runs three captive breeding centres, between them holding (in early 2010) over 200 vultures, and individuals of all three Critically Endangered Asian *Gyps* species. The first birds started breeding activities in 2007, with the first successful breeding of White-rumped Vultures in 2008 and of Slender-billed Vultures in 2009 (Bowden 2009). The aim of this programme is to hold 25 pairs of each of the three *Gyps* species at each of the three breeding centres; there is still some way to go, but the results so far are encouraging. If the positive moves to outlaw veterinary diclofenac prove successful, it is hoped that the environment will soon be safe for the release of the first captive-bred birds.

Neighbouring countries also have captive breeding plans, with a small centre already in existence in Pakistan (holding 14 birds in 2009), and another in Nepal (42 birds in 2009). At the same time, the provision of uncontaminated carcasses at 'vulture restaurants' has been shown in Pakistan to be effective in reducing, albeit not stopping, diclofenac poisoning (Gilbert *et al.* 2007a). Local conservation efforts in Nepal, set up around some of the few remaining breeding colonies of White-rumped Vultures, have worked to remove veterinary diclofenac from the surrounding area (replacing it with meloxicam), at the same time undertaking conservation education and providing safe food for vultures. These are also showing early and encouraging signs of protecting birds. Numbers of birds at three such sites have increased, in contrast to ongoing declines at other sites where no such actions are in place, although it is still too early to know if these increases are just due to immigration or whether such schemes are capable of protecting birds in the long term.

THE FIRST SIGNS OF RECOVERY

What now is the future for these impressive and environmentally important birds? Continued advocacy and vigilant monitoring are essential to ensure both that diclofenac is removed from the vultures' environment, and that it is not replaced by equally toxic alternatives. As long as diclofenac remains in veterinary use, the remaining wild vultures, where possible, need to be brought into captivity to boost the captive population and increase the chances of eventual successful re-establishment in the wild. In 2009 it became clear than another veterinary drug, ketoprofen, which is in increasing use as a result of the diclofenac ban and previously hoped to be harmless, is actually also highly toxic to vultures (Naidoo *et al.* 2009a). In the same year, however, came the good news that the first Slender-billed Vulture chicks had been successfully reared in the captive breeding facilities in India. Captive breeding has continued to produce a reserve of birds that are protected from poisoning and since 2009 all three critically endangered *Gyps* species have been bred successfully in captivity. Techniques in artificial incubation have been improved, allowing the birds to lay repeat clutches and so potentially double their productivity. By 2012, 61 fledgling vultures had been produced by the breeding centres in India (Prakash *et al.* 2012b). Better news was soon to follow, as systematic sampling of livestock carcasses across India showed that the percentage of animals containing diclofenac fell from nearly 11% before the ban in 2006 to around 6.5% after the ban, not enough to halt the decline of vultures but enough to reduce the rate of decline to 40% of its pre-ban level, and levels of the safe alternative meloxicam increased (Cuthbert *et al.* 2011a,c). This was backed up by counts of birds in India and Nepal, which showed that the rate of decline might have slowed or even possibly been reversed, although with populations at such low levels the accurate estimation of population trends is almost impossible (Prakash *et al.* 2012a). More good news followed, as surveys of the largest surviving vulture colony in Pakistan indicated significant increases in numbers, nest occupancy and nest productivity following the diclofenac ban (Chaudhry *et al.* 2012). Although the sale of diclofenac in pharmacies remains worrying high, largely the result of illegal circumvention of the ban on veterinary use by selling diclofenac designated for human use, the only known safe alternative drug meloxicam is now far more widely available (Cuthbert *et al.* 2011b). In February 2011 a new consortium, the happily acronymic Saving Asia's Vultures from Extinction (SAVE), was launched in Delhi and Kathmandu to provide a strategic framework through which the problems of vulture conservation can be addressed across national boundaries, regularly bringing together the key organisations engaged in their conservation. Whatever the success of ongoing conservation initiatives, it is unlikely that there will ever be a return of the tens of millions of vultures that once filled the skies of the Indian subcontinent, because new methods of carcass disposal are, of necessity, being found. However, the early indications are good and suggest that a small but committed band of researchers and conservationists are well down the road to achieving something truly remarkable in changing the practices of millions of people over vast areas to restore Asia's vulture populations to health.

Chapter 18
Philippine Eagle *Pithecophaga jefferyi*
CRITICALLY ENDANGERED

The discovery and description of the Philippine Eagle in 1896 was one of the ornithological sensations of the closing years of the nineteenth century. Apart from Sanford's Sea-eagle *Haliaeetus sanfordi*, which was formally described in 1935, all the world's large eagles and vultures had long since been found and named. Moreover, the Philippine bird was so distinctive that for more than a century it was to keep scientists guessing over what its closest relatives might be. It was also enormous, being among the two or three largest species of raptor in the world.

Its discovery was itself a stroke of the best luck directly following a stroke of the worst. Already celebrated for his many discoveries before the age of 30 in Borneo (where he was the first European to ascend Mount Kinabalu), the naturalist-explorer John Whitehead had for some years been collecting birds and mammals in the Philippines, moving from island to island in pursuit of new species and biogeographical insight. In 1895 he visited the large central island of Samar, where he spent three months diligently collecting and preparing specimens for shipping back to the British Museum in London. Within the small circle of ornithologists who frequently use museum collections, Whitehead's specimens are well known for the quality and care with which he prepared them, leaving to the world the most useful and valuable of material. In what therefore was a terrible blow not just for Whitehead and the British Museum but also for his future admirers, the consignment of skins from Samar, representing over a hundred species, was lost when the ship bearing it to England caught fire in Singapore and had to be scuttled. Poor Whitehead had to return once more to Samar and begin again.

Within a few days, however, he had discovered something he had missed in all his previous months on the island: a giant eagle. Having seen it once, he sought it for several weeks without success, until his Filipino assistant Juan shot one that was perched high in a rainforest tree. Defiant in death as it had been elusive in life, the bird fixed its talons to the branch and eventually the intrepid Juan had to climb high into the canopy to bring it down.

So heavy was the prize (females weigh about 7kg) that, emaciated by fever, Whitehead could hardly hold it at arm's length, but this time his luck held and the beautifully prepared skin duly made its way to the other side of the world, where on 16 December 1896 it was displayed to members of the British Ornithologists' Club meeting for dinner at a restaurant in Oxford Street. There it was announced that the species would be known, at Whitehead's request, as *Pithecophaga jefferyi*, 'Jeffery's monkey-eater', in honour of his father, who had financed so much of his research.

That it fed on monkeys, information that Whitehead gleaned from villagers on Samar, remained just about as much as anyone was to know about the biology of the species for 70 years (in due course it was discovered to take a wide variety of vertebrate prey, the great majority arboreal mammals and reptiles). Over this span of time, however, there was plenty of interest in it from zoos and museums eager to obtain living or dead specimens, respectively: many that went first to the zoos went later to the museums. The zoos wanted to show off the bird's extraordinary appearance: with its huge size, blue eyes, long shaggy erectile crown feathers and extraordinary deep, narrow bill (only Steller's Sea-eagle *Haliaeetus pelagicus* has a deeper one but the bill of *Pithecophaga* is much narrower) it has an appearance like no other bird of prey. The museums, on the other hand, were more interested in working out what that weird appearance meant in terms of its phylogenetic relationship to other birds. A small number of live specimens were duly shipped off to various zoos in the west, and in 1910 W. R. Ogilvie-Grant, who had made the original description of the eagle while Whitehead continued his Philippine explorations, was evidently pleased to report that studies of a new specimen, its skeleton intact, had confirmed his own assertion that *Pithecophaga* was most closely related to South and Central America's Harpy Eagle *Harpia harpyja*:

> …it has now been clearly shown by Mr Pycraft that this is undoubtedly the case, and that its affinities are not with the serpent eagles (*Spilornis*), as the late Dr Sharpe had supposed.

However, just under a century later, molecular research turned the tables on Ogilvie-Grant, by demonstrating that the link with *Harpia* is the result of character convergence in large rainforest raptors, and that indeed the closest relatives of the Philippine Eagle are, in fact, the far smaller 'serpent eagles' (Circaetinae, which includes the genus *Spilornis*) (Lerner & Mindell 2005).

Ogilvie-Grant was not wrong about everything, however. A year after he had described the species, he made a highly perceptive observation:

> That so large a raptor should have remained unknown till the present time only shows how easily these great Forest-Eagles may be overlooked. As an instance of this, it is worth mentioning that during the years Mr Salvin spent collecting birds in Central America he only once saw a Harpy Eagle… The fact is that in the dense and lofty forests where these birds make their home it is almost impossible to see them.

The truth of this commentary is not lost on the many birdwatchers who over the years have gone to the Philippines in the hope of adding the eagle to their life-list. The best chance of a sighting is probably to sit in a hide at an occupied nest and either just see the chick or wait, possibly for several hours, for an adult to pay it a visit. In the forest itself, or what remains of it, the prospects of a random encounter are too low to take seriously. Rainforest eagles are designed for life within, not above, the trees, and for the purposes of successful foraging on other animals it is greatly in their interests to be seen as little, and as late, as possible. Saving the Philippine Eagle has become one of the most compelling conservation challenges of modern times, and in part the problem revolves around the question of whether the difficulty in finding a Philippine Eagle in the wild away from its nest is because it is such a reclusive animal or because it is also genuinely rare.

Over time, records of the eagle accumulated from the two largest islands in the Philippines, Luzon in the north and Mindanao in the south, plus the two islands of Samar and Leyte that connect them in a curving line down the eastern section of the archipelago. These four islands are interesting for a suite of species that are exclusive to them (sometimes with Bohol added in), for example the Guaiabero *Bolbopsittacus lunulatus* (an unusual parrot), Sooty Woodpecker *Mulleripicus funebris*, Black-and-white Triller *Lalage melanoleuca* and Naked-faced Spiderhunter *Arachnothera clarae*. These distributions indicate a shared biogeographical history, although other birds' ranges reveal extraordinary levels of complexity in the ways the Philippines accumulated its great diversity and wealth of animals and plants. By recent taxonomic standards, 169 bird species are restricted to the Philippines (this can

The Philippine Eagle – one of the world's largest raptors (Rich Lindie).

be confidently predicted to rise to over 200 with taxonomic revisions), yet the surface area of the country is only some 300,000km², about the same as Italy, or Britain and Ireland put together. However, what unites virtually all the endemic species of the Philippine archipelago is that they are forest birds: the Philippines was originally an archipelago cloaked in trees.

THE LOSS OF PHILIPPINE FORESTS

At the end of Spanish rule, a little over a century ago, the country had just eight million human inhabitants and at least 70% (and by some estimates 90%) forest cover. This latter declined steadily but relatively slowly in the first half of the twentieth century (Bankoff 2007). However, during the twenty-one-year presidency of Ferdinand Marcos, the last fourteen of them under martial law, the nation was opened up to logging and mining on a massive scale and, as a result, suffered extensive damage both to its environment and to the institutions that are supposed to protect it. Unfortunately, such was the level of corruption in this era that the restoration of democracy in 1986 brought with it no mechanisms or powers to rein in the onslaught on the nation's forests, not even in the wake of repeated and terrible human disasters wrought by landslides following tropical rainstorms over denuded mountainsides. In the 1950s there were very roughly 100,000km² of old-growth dipterocarp forest (Kummer 1991, Bankoff 2007), the habitat occupied by the Philippine Eagle; by the end of the 1980s less than 15,000km² of this habitat remained (BirdLife International 2001). Twenty years later, with the human population now well past 100 million, the forest cover has declined even further, much of what remains is montane and very little of it is in level lowlands, which are by far the richest areas biologically.

In the early 1960s the primary threat to the Philippine Eagle was believed to be the capture of wild birds for the zoo trade, although habitat loss was certainly a concern. The well-known museum collector and naturalist D. S. Rabor, noted for his depressing (and later shown to be exaggerated) assessment of forest loss on Cebu (p.226), gained the support of the World Wildlife Fund for a study of what was then called the Monkey-eating Eagle in the years 1962–1964 (Gonzales 1968). Then, in 1965, the year of Marcos's election to office, Rabor made the first direct public expression of concern at the eagle's plight, reporting it as 'definitely on the road to extinction' and claiming that it was already lost from Samar and Leyte, with 'very few individuals left' on Luzon and some 40–50 pairs on Mindanao (Rabor 1968). The extremity of the bird's situation was a sudden and distressing revelation which catapulted the species into the first edition of the Red Data Book (Vincent 1966-1971), where its population was given as 'probably less than 100 birds' and the threats were identified as 'over-trapping for zoos' and 'local demand' for mounted specimens, which 'constitutes the most serious threat to the survival of the species'.

Rabor's strong and clearly heartfelt concerns found a sympathetic ear in Charles Lindbergh, the American aviator famous for making the first solo crossing of the Atlantic, and Lindbergh's advocacy of what he reportedly described as 'the air's noblest flier' gave the species its first strong conservation profile. Following feasibility work in 1969 funded by the International Council for Bird Preservation, a five-year project supported by World Wildlife Fund began in 1970 with the aim of creating greater awareness of the eagle among Filipinos, confiscating and releasing captive birds held in private hands, and increasing knowledge of the species' ecology and population. The hero of this early work was Robert S. Kennedy, originally a Peace Corps volunteer, who became rapidly and deeply committed to the cause of the Monkey-eating Eagle. He first studied the species on his own in the wild in the early 1970s and then in 1976 founded FREE ('Films and Research for an Endangered Environment'), a non-profit organisation whose aim was to study the bird in depth and at the same time bring film footage of it to the largest audience possible both inside and outside the Philippines. In 1978 he even persuaded Marcos to pass a presidential proclamation that the bird should henceforth be known as the Philippine Eagle.

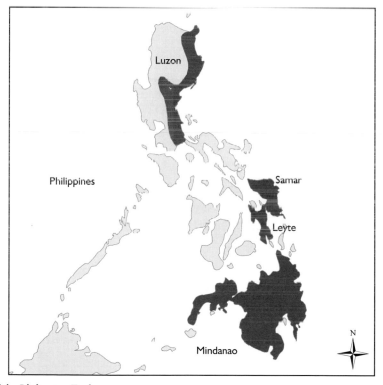

Original distribution of the Philippine Eagle.

The scientific paper that Kennedy produced from his fieldwork was the first one on the species, and indeed the only one in the entire twentieth century, to appear in a Western peer-reviewed journal (Kennedy 1977). It comprised two parts. It first provided an account of some observations at an eagle nest, allowing various comparisons with the work of Gonzales, whose study was likewise focused on a single nest (Gonzales 1968). The first part concluded with the results of an investigation into the pair's home range. Mentioning that earlier workers had judged home ranges of 31–34km² (Grossman & Hamlet 1964), 40–50km² (Rabor 1968) and 100km² (Gonzales 1968), Kennedy reported that the points of the polygon derived from his sightings covered a minimum of 6.34km², that a circle through the points furthest apart covered 12.5km², and that, allowing for the steep slopes of the terrain, the surface area of the circle might come to 25km². 'These figures suggest', he concluded, 'that the area necessary to support a pair of eagles may not be as great as formerly believed'.

The second half of the paper addressed the critical issue of the species' population size. Working in Mindanao, because of Rabor's declaration that eagles were extinct or nearly so elsewhere, Kennedy used three methods to calculate the number of birds remaining on the island, which at that time was considered to hold 29,000km² of potentially suitable habitat. First, he took the maximum home-range size from the previous estimates, Gonzales's 100km², and divided it into 29,000km² to yield a total of 290 pairs or 580 adult birds. Second, having sighted nine eagles in the 640km² of habitat found on Mount Apo (one eagle per 71km²), he extrapolated a total figure of 408 birds. Third, he added the number of records (29) by his project's various investigators to those (74) gleaned from interviewees in the area they covered in the years 1970–1973, estimated that area as about a third of the suitable habitat of the island, and multiplied 103 by 3 for a total of 309 birds. This last figure, being based on the most extensive fieldwork, he felt to be the most dependable: 'Taking everything into account, I feel that the population on Mindanao during the period of investigation was about 300 ± 100' (Kennedy 1977).

Three hundred birds in 29,000km² of forest equates to one pair every 193km² of available habitat, a far lower density than anything suggested by students of the species to this point. Yet if a pair covering 12.5km² was typical, and if all the 29,000km² of forest on Mindanao was occupied, then no fewer than 2,320 pairs could equally legitimately have been claimed, illustrating the difficulty of estimating the population of this species. Kennedy had unearthed disturbing evidence that a lot of birds were being shot as chicken-thieves; even so, if as he had concluded, eagles appeared to occupy smaller areas of habitat than previously supposed, it might have been useful to consider the home ranges offered by Grossman & Hamlet (which would result in a population estimate of 852–935 pairs) or Rabor (580–725 pairs). Furthermore, it seems unlikely that a home range, particularly one as large as 100km², would equate to an exclusive territory, or that searches for a bird that fundamentally does not want to be seen would result in the recording of each and every one present. Perhaps Rabor's trenchant views on the situation weighed heavily here: how to set his 40–50 pairs against the notion of hundreds of them? Consequently, it is possible to look at the evidence with the luxury of hindsight and speculate that in the early 1970s the numbers of eagles on Mindanao may, in fact, have been somewhat higher (Collar 1997b).

HOW TO MANAGE THE 'MONEY-EATING EAGLE'?

In conservation, there is always a precautionary disposition, in the absence of hard data, to favour the least optimistic interpretation of the evidence. Other birds for which there have been similar mismatches between presumption and reality include the Sociable Lapwing *Vanellus gregarius* (Chapter 3) and Gurney's Pitta *Pitta gurneyi* (Chapter 23). The pattern is a common one, but an initial higher sense of alarm is often an entirely appropriate reaction to a situation of great uncertainty. Moreover, there are several examples where presumption of safety has led to serious crises, perhaps most distressingly so in the case of the Slender-billed Curlew *Numenius tenuirostris* (Chapter 26), which only went on to the IUCN Red List in 1988 (Collar & Andrew 1988) when someone finally spoke up to say how rare the species had become, and when it was well past the time when useful work to understand the species was possible.

Nevertheless, the conclusion that the Philippine Eagle might number as few as 200 individuals gave crucial legitimacy to a management option that had long been contemplated, that of captive breeding. This was not one

Philippine Eagles are usually hard to see as they hunt largely below the canopy. Photographs like this of wild birds are rare (Rich Lindie).

that Kennedy saw as most relevant (Kennedy 1977): he wanted education programmes, large reserves (200km² minimum) and good forestry practices, but it soon became one that could not be ignored. In 1980 FREE, the ICBP Birds of Prey Specialist Group and the Philippines' Bureau of Forest Development drew up a plan, funded by WWF and implemented by Kennedy under the name Philippine Eagle Conservation Project (PECP). This aimed to improve population estimates across the full range of the species, to expand the small captive breeding programme that had been going for a few years using confiscated birds, to conduct a public awareness campaign, to recommend large areas as sanctuaries and to study the birds' longevity, ranging behaviour and habitat requirements on Mt Apo (BirdLife International 2001). However, within weeks of the fieldwork starting, the project camp at Apo was attacked by guerillas, seriously disrupting the field research plans. Although the team sought to redeploy to Luzon and Leyte, and some eagles were radio-tracked over many months, the detailed ecological studies never materialised. FREE's film was shown widely and 25,000 leaflets distributed, but this dimension of the work also stalled through lack of funds. The Marcos era profligacy was leaving the country in ever greater debt, causing unemployment, internal migration and forest invasion, and rendering the establishment of reserves increasingly unrealistic. Nests were no sooner found, usually by migrant peasants opening up primary forest, than the eaglets needed to be rescued for their own security. An 'adopt-a-nest' scheme, by which US$150 was donated to a local community for the successful fledging of an eaglet, foundered on intra-community jealousies. The one seemingly secure option left open to the project, which had originally planned to release confiscated birds into the wild, was to develop a major *ex situ* programme.

As early as 1977, Kennedy had charged one of his team, Ronald Krupa, with the management of the captive birds. Over the course of the next ten years, therefore, Krupa's role became increasingly central to the project effort and Krupa became its director when PECP, seeking a more permanent sense of identity and a greater stream of national support, morphed into the Philippine Eagle Foundation and established a permanent base near Davao City in Mindanao. The initial rationale of the captive breeding work was to establish a self-sustaining pool of birds from which recovering forest could be replenished, at some unspecified time in the future. The stock was originally intended to derive from confiscations or from birds found injured in the wild. However, over the course of the 1980s – which saw no successful breeding among a collection of often severely imprinted animals – the emphasis subtly shifted towards the proactive procurement of eggs and chicks from 'selected, critically threatened nest sites' in 'the doomed fragments' of forest that the Philippine government could not protect (Krupa 1989).

Given the chainsaw massacre to which Philippine forests were subjected in the 1980s, this shift is entirely understandable. However, with it came a biological judgement that is rather less easy to explain: this relates to the nature of the eagle's ability to disperse between fragments. In the years down to the mid-1980s Kennedy's work had established that Rabor had been badly mistaken about Luzon, Samar and Leyte, but in assessing the populations still remaining on these islands and on Mindanao, Krupa was concerned to lay the emphasis on their fragmented status (Krupa 1989). Using figures on forest patches and areas from an unstated source, allowing for the possibility that persecution might have left up to 60% of available habitat unoccupied, and once again applying the 100km² value – even though in 1980 Kennedy had discovered at least 15 nests on Mount Apo (which, at 640km² of habitat, yields a density of one pair per 43km²: Kennedy 1985) – Krupa estimated that Luzon held 33–83 pairs in five forest patches totalling 8,300km²; Samar held 8–19 pairs in eight forest patches totalling 1,950km²; Leyte held 1–4 pairs in two forest patches totalling 400km²; and Mindanao held 46–115 pairs in 22 forest patches totalling 11,520km². Thus in 1989 the world population of the species was judged to be 88–221 pairs, spread between 37 disjunct forested areas with a total area of 22,170km².

It is interesting how close Krupa's global total of 176–442 individuals is to Kennedy's estimate of 200–400 birds from 12 years before, even though on Krupa's figures just under two-thirds of the forest on Mindanao had in that time been destroyed and on other evidence the situation was even worse: for example, the island had only 6,678km² of closed-canopy forest remaining in 1992 (BirdLife International 2001). But in any case, things were only going to get worse. Krupa predicted that all old-growth forest within the elevational range of the eagle (an uncertain point: possibly as high as 1,450m, but probably mainly below 1,000m on Luzon and 1,200m on Mindanao) would be logged by the early 1990s and 'the entire forest wiped out as early as 2007' (Krupa 1989). Of more immediate importance was his view that the Philippine Eagle cannot disperse across open land or water over distances greater than 20km, basing this on the lack of records of the species over open country or water, its absence from other islands, and the recovery of four live birds from the sea close to shore and one from a lake. He also suggested that populations of under 50 birds could be unviable because of genetic bottle-necking, and that populations of over 50 birds might only exist in two of the 37 fragments of forest then remaining, the rest being too small.

There could hardly have been a more powerful argument in favour of captive breeding than this. It made the eagle out to be what some conservationists in the 1990s injudiciously came to call a 'basket-case'. Constitutively, it was doomed: here was a bird with a wingspan as broad as a man is tall, yet it could not cross from forest patch to forest patch. Circumstantially, it was doomed: here was a bird simply too big for the fragments of habitat that human mismanagement had bequeathed it. 'The long-term prognosis for the Philippine Eagle', Krupa concluded, 'is bleak indeed'. What he proposed by way of a response to the situation was an interchange of wild and captive-bred birds between different fragments, in order to preserve the genetic diversity of the species, and the maintenance of semi-domestic populations through intensive and constant human intervention. Clearly, while the primary goal of the Philippine Eagle Foundation remained the conservation of the eagle, its primary activity henceforward was to be the breeding of birds.

Perhaps there really was no alternative; or at least perhaps there really seemed to be none. Even so, the argument that eagles cannot traverse more than 20km of open terrain was hardly watertight. Almost certainly the five 'ditched' birds were sick or starving youngsters, down on their luck as many new-fledged eagles must inevitably be: a couple of days without food, an exhausting tussle when unsuccessfully pursuing prey and a couple more days of torrential rain could easily combine to enfeeble a bird to the point of collapse. Absence from other islands is perhaps just a reflection of the inadequacy of the habitat and prey-base to support a population. Movements of birds over open country need not be frequent anyway, and their absence from the record can confidently be attributed to no-one noticing. If some of the results of the radio-tracking in the early 1980s had been published we might have proof to the contrary, but in any case no less an authority than Kennedy described the eagle as 'a bird that frequently soars' and mentioned a record of two birds in high circling flight over a small island in the Surigao Straits in the 1940s (Kennedy 1977).

A more immediate issue at this time, however, was: where *were* the captive-bred eagles? If captive breeding was to play such a crucial role in the conservation of the species, what was the outcome of the past decade's endeavours with the various birds assembled from confiscations and recoveries in the wild? Sadly, there was nothing positive to report. Over the course of the 1980s a few eggs had been laid, but behaviourally the parents were not geared to take things any further. It was not until 1992 that a first chick was hatched, and then another, both produced by artificial insemination; and it took the rest of the decade before the feat was repeated (Tadena *et al.* 2000). This was hardly the response to the crisis that the situation required, and throughout the 1990s the uncertainties over what captive breeding could achieve for the eagle steadily multiplied. Was it a course of action that was costing a lot (jesters and sceptics called them 'money-eating eagles') and leading nowhere? Was it a necessary precaution; indeed, was it necessary at all? Was there anything else that could realistically be done for the species?

Some of the numbers emerging from government-led work in the mid-1990s looked like they were intended to rebuff these doubts: the Philippine Eagle Working Group reported that in 1995 'a total of 79 birds could be counted for the entire species', breaking down as 49 in the wild and 17 in captivity on Mindanao, 10 wild and two captive on Luzon, and one wild on Samar. Once again, however, numbers seen were being represented as numbers remaining, resulting in the implication that the situation in the wild was out of control and effectively beyond help, unless birds from captivity were to come to the rescue. In reality, of course, nobody knew how many birds were left in the wild, but there was an increasing sense that it would be good to find out. Analysis of data from the 1990s led to a computation of 82–233 pairs (Bueser *et al.* 2003), and perhaps a little suspicion that captive breeding was so centre-stage in the eagle conservation agenda that it was almost providing an excuse for the authorities not to be taking any other measures. At every turn since the 1960s, entirely well-intended assumptions based on fragmentary information had nudged the conservation of the eagle in the direction of an *ex situ* solution; but as the twentieth century drew to a close, things were changing.

NEW DIRECTIONS

This was largely because, under the new direction of Dennis Salvador, the Philippine Eagle Foundation's first Filipino leader, the *ex situ* programme began to be matched by *in situ* work, with field studies being led by Jayson Ibañez; but it was also because of growing conservation interest in the Philippines. All the major biodiversity mapping exercises of the 1990s, Hotspots (Mittermeier *et al.* 1999), Ecoregions (Olson *et al.* 2001) and Endemic Bird Areas (Stattersfield *et al.* 1998), had highlighted the cardinal importance of the Philippines, and were shortly followed by key outputs on the country's globally threatened birds and Important Bird Areas from the Haribon Foundation, BirdLife's partner organisation set up in the 1980s by none other than Robert Kennedy (*haring ibon*, 'bird king', being the name of the eagle in Tagalog, the Philippine national language). Several national governments, the European Union, the Global Environment Facility and the Critical Ecosystems Partnership Fund all responded to the overwhelming evidence stemming from these publications that the Philippines urgently needed conservation investment.

A suite of new biodiversity initiatives duly emerged, and among other developments a Philippine Eagle Alliance was forged, with different organisations shouldering responsibility for conducting research and conservation work on the species in different parts of its range. Conservation International and the World Wildlife Fund, through their respective national bodies CI-Philippines and WWF-Philippines, began major forest conservation work in Luzon's Sierra Madre, where the largest tracts of continuous eagle habitat now remain (intriguingly, the eagle may not live at such high densities there as on Mindanao, probably owing to the absence of certain key prey species such as Colugos *Cynocephalus volans* and flying squirrels). The Haribon Foundation undertook surveys in the more southerly parts of the Sierra Madre, promoted the creation of a 'natural park' in Samar and ran a forest conservation programme at Mt Hilong-hilong in north-east Mindanao. The Philippine Eagle Foundation, with its depth of expertise, took on the majority of the work in Mindanao, maintaining its captive breeding programme (Tadena *et al.* 2000), launching a strong educational campaign by targeting teachers in schools across the archipelago (vital for scaling back prejudice against the bird, which some farmers still persecute for its presumed impact on poultry), developing new field research and analysis at various sites across the bird's range (Afan *et al.* 2000, Miranda *et al.* 2000, Ibañez *et al.* 2003) and initiating community-based conservation work at two sites in Mindanao (Salvador & Ibañez 2006).

So with the financial assistance that eluded it throughout the twentieth century, the Philippine Eagle has finally become what Kennedy always hoped it would: a flagship for forest conservation throughout the Philippines, recognised and celebrated as an animal of inspirational beauty and power. Its status since 1995 as the national bird is a fitting reflection of its stature as the top predator in the islands, a species which maintains a crucial balance of forces in the ecosystem it governs (Ale & Whelan 2008). The importance of forests to the economic and human welfare of the country has become ever more evident with each dramatic cyclone and with ever greater uncertainty about the force and frequency of storms under global climate change. Moreover, the Philippine Eagle Foundation has cracked the problem of captive breeding: at the end of 2009, less than a decade after only the third bird was hatched in their aviaries, PEF held 33 eagles, no fewer than 17 of them captive-bred, and each year produces one or two new birds (J. C. Ibañez *in litt.* 2009). In 2013, the first Philippine Eagle ever produced in captivity produced her own captive offspring for the first time. It is exciting that this captive stock can now be trained for release into the wild, and experimental work on this has already begun. This confluence and coherence of developments, energies and achievements are refreshing evidence that the Philippine Eagle, one of the most extraordinary animals on earth, now has a real chance of survival.

Chapter 19
Alagoas Curassow *Mitu mitu*

EXTINCT IN THE WILD

Brazil's Amazon basin holds the most celebrated and important area of forest on earth, teeming with wildlife that still utterly defies documentation. Except at its eastern and southern fringes, it is still in relatively good condition, and the great majority of its species are currently secure. By contrast, the country's Atlantic Forest ('Mata Atlântica') has been subject to severe human exploitation ever since the European discovery and settlement of Brazil five hundred years ago. The very name of the country comes from *pau brasil*, a leguminous tree *Caesalpinia echinata* that used to grow widely in the Atlantic Forest lowlands. This was so highly prized for the colour and quality of its timber, producing a red dye and a deep shine, and perfect for making bows for stringed instruments, that it is now virtually extinct (Oldfield *et al.* 1998). All along the eastward-facing coast of Brazil, in the more temperate climate to the south, colonies became ports, which became towns, which became cities, and the forests in their hinterland became orchards, fields and pasture. Today virtually all that remains of the Atlantic Forest of Brazil, certainly in the northern and central parts, is to be found in public and private reserves and in tiny woodlots set aside on farms, holding back a human tide of consumption that has engulfed at least 85% of this habitat in the country to date (Mittermeier *et al.* 1999, Ribeiro *et al.* 2009). Today, 80% of remaining forest fragments are smaller than 50 hectares in size, half the remaining forest is within 100m of its edge, fragments are widely separated and only 1% of the original forest area is officially protected (Ribeiro *et al.* 2009).

In its pre-European condition, this forest formed a corridor that ran unbroken from the easternmost tip of South America, in Rio Grande do Norte, Ceará, Paraíba and Pernambuco, southwards to Rio Grande do Sul, and onwards and inwards into eastern Paraguay and northern Argentina. In the north the corridor was very narrow; gradually, moving south, it became a wider skirt until in some places it was several hundred kilometres deep. In many places it spread upslope towards the higher ground of the Brazilian shield, and in cooler and wetter periods in its history it penetrated the drier interior, particularly along watercourses. The various combinations of latitude and altitude contributed to the evolution of many endemic life forms within it. Some species are shared with the Amazon Forest, many like the Bearded Bellbird *Procnias averano* being found only in the north east, suggesting this region was the biological bridge between the two areas of forest. Others belong to genera that also occur in the Amazon, but many species and even genera have no counterpart in Amazonia and must have their biogeographic origins elsewhere; 6,000 plant species, 253 amphibians, 160 mammals, 60 reptiles and 73 birds are endemic to the Atlantic Forest (Mittermeier *et al.* 1999).

Some of these endemic species extend through the entire north–south belt of the Atlantic Forest, but others have remarkably restricted ranges, so that within this mega-centre of endemism can be found smaller centres of endemism (Stattersfield *et al.* 1998). Because deforestation has been so serious in the naturally already restricted northern and central parts of the Atlantic seaboard of Brazil, the endemics of these smaller centres are now among the world's most highly threatened species. The Critically Endangered birds of the north-east are the White-collared Kite *Leptodon forbesi*, Grey-breasted Parakeet *Pyrrhura griseipectus*, Pernambuco Pygmy-owl *Glaucidium mooreorum*, Araripe Manakin *Antilophia bokermanni*, Alagoas Antwren *Myrmotherula snowi* and Alagoas Foliage-gleaner *Philydor novaesi*. Those in the central (some also central-south) parts are the Purple-winged Ground-dove *Claravis godefrida*, Kinglet Calyptura *Calyptura cristata*, Restinga Antwren *Formicivora littoralis*, Stresemann's Bristlefront *Merulaxis stresemanni*, Bahia Tapaculo *Eleoscytalopus psychopompus* and Cherry-throated Tanager *Nemosia rourei*. Some of these species are desperately close to extinction. The Kinglet Calyptura, for example, went unrecorded for over a century until two birds were seen in October 1996; despite intensive searches since then, there have been no further records. But the area continues to yield surprises: one of the most notable ornithological discoveries in the second half of the twentieth century was made in 1996, when Brazilian ornithologists exploring the Chapada do Araripe, a thin strip of forested upland at the western limit of the Atlantic Forest, happened across the stunning Araripe Manakin (Coelho & Silva 1998). The species has a population of around 400 pairs confined within a small and rapidly shrinking range.

The place name that appears twice in the list of the Atlantic Forest's Critically Endangered birds is Alagoas, reflecting the high number of endemic and near-endemic species in this small state and their desperate plight. The Alagoas centre of endemism extends into coastal Pernambuco and Paraíba, and is based on the ranges of 13 bird species, all of them threatened, eight of them limited to that one centre, and most of them found in the remarkable but tiny tract of forest in Alagoas called Murici (Stattersfield *et al.* 1998, Bencke *et al.* 2006). This concentration of highly threatened birds at Murici caused it to be identified as the target of support from the British Birdwatching Fair in 1999, leading to a programme of work at the site which resulted in 2001 in the declaration of 61km² of land, half of it forested, as a government protected area (Bencke *et al.* 2006). An even better result was that the programme itself, under the leadership of Jaqueline Goerck, developed into SAVE Brasil, a national bird conservation NGO with a particular focus on the Atlantic Forest.

A PRIVATELY OWNED SPECIES

One species, however, that Murici does not contain, and which perhaps because of its altitude never did, is another species bearing the name of Alagoas, and which is now so rare that it is classified as Extinct in the Wild. The story of the Alagoas Curassow, a large bird in the family that contains the pheasants, grouse and megapodes, is remarkable, for rarely can a species have come so close to extinction and escaped it by so unorthodox a route. Even the start of the story is extraordinary. The bird was first recorded in a document published in 1648 by a German naturalist Georg Marcgraf ('Marcgrave') employed in a Dutch colony on the north-east coast of Brazil. Marcgraf's *Historia naturalis Brasiliae* contains the illustration and description, in Latin, of a bird he called 'mitu' or 'mutu' which Linnaeus went on to name *Crax mitu* in his *Systema naturae* of 1766. When the German explorer Spix later found what came to be known as the 'razor-billed curassow' of southern Amazonia, naming it *Crax tuberosa* in 1825, it became the subject of speculation whether his bird and Marcgraf's, collected from very different areas, were one and the same. The long absence of records of any similar curassow from the Atlantic Forest gradually strengthened

Alagoas Curassow, pictured with one of its saviours, Roberto Azeredo; the species is now listed as Extinct in the Wild, but were it not for the efforts of private aviculturists, the species would be lost forever (João Marcos Rosa).

the speculation that Marcgraf's bird was perhaps an individual of Spix's species that had somehow been transported from Amazonia. It took until the morning of 5 October 1951, more than three hundred years after Marcgraf's book, for the answer to be supplied, when a hunter presented the leading Brazilian ornithologist Oliverio Pinto with the body of a female curassow he had just shot in the forests they were exploring at São Miguel dos Campos in the state of Alagoas (Pinto 1952). Finally it was clear that Marcgraf's *mitu* and Spix's *tuberosa* were different, different enough, indeed, for Pinto (1952, 1954) to conclude that they were different species (Pinto 1952, Pinto 1954), although it took another forty years for this to be generally accepted (Collar *et al.* 1992).

Four species of curassow in the genus *Mitu* are now recognised where once they were all considered the same (Delacour & Amadon 1973, Strahl & Schmitz 1997). All have black plumage in both sexes and a reddish-pink bill with a strongly decurved upper mandible and pink legs. Salvin's Curassow (*M. salvini*, western Amazon) is white from belly to vent and has a white tail tip. The Crestless Curassow (*M. tomentosum*, northern Amazon), Razor-billed Curassow (*M. tuberosum*, southern Amazon) and Alagoas Curassow (*M. mitu*) are chestnut from belly to vent but the tail tip is chestnut in the Crestless Curassow, white in the Razor-billed Curassow and pale brown in the Alagoas Curassow. The Razor-billed Curassow has a very large bill in which the upper mandible is compressed upwards to form a bulbous semi-circle, a feature present but less obvious in the Alagoas Curassow. Further evaluation has shown that the Alagoas Curassow has a number of other consistent and therefore diagnostic differences from the Razor-billed Curassow, such as a dark red bill base, shading sharply to white at the tip, bare skin around the ears and all-black central tail feathers (Silveira *et al.* 2004). It has also been suggested that the calls, behaviour and egg shape of the two species differ (Nardelli 1981), and the separation of the two species has also been supported by genetic differences (Grau *et al.* 2003).

At the time of its rediscovery in 1951, there were still substantial areas of forest in the state of Alagoas, but hunters suggested that the bird was no longer easy to find, and it was clearly already very scarce (Pinto 1952, Pinto

1954). From his distant museum in New York, Vaurie thought it might already be extinct (Vaurie 1968) and, much closer to hand, Coimbra-Filho feared the same, mentioning that the forests of Alagoas were 'hoje residuais e em franco processo de devastação' ('now residual and plainly being destroyed') (Coimbra-Filho 1970). To his credit, however, he went in search of this and several other species, found there were still 85km² of forest at São Miguel dos Campos, and estimated that perhaps 20 curassows survived (Coimbra-Filho 1971). He suggested that they would be gone in perhaps two or three years, and that actions were needed immediately to prevent their extinction. He also mentioned, almost in passing, that *Mitu tuberosum* does very well in captivity.

This last observation was a seed that fell on fertile ground. The next thing the world knew of the situation came a decade later in a short taxonomic note by the great expert on Brazilian birds Helmut Sick, who still regarded the Alagoas form as a subspecies, '*Mitu mitu mitu*':

> In February 1977, I had the privilege to study a female of this subspecies which was living in the spacious aviary of Pedro Nardelli, an outstanding aviculturist in Rio de Janeiro. It had been found in Alagoas and kept in a box for several years, even once laying an egg, before it was acquired by Nardelli. Sr. Nardelli recently obtained more specimens of nominate *mitu* from Alagoas for a breeding program. In June 1979 he had four birds in Rio; they were tentatively sexed by him through cloacal examination as one male and three females… This curassow could be saved by breeding in captivity and being released in forest reserves in Alagoas. (Sick 1980)

Soon afterwards, Nardelli himself provided more context to this unexpected turn of events (Nardelli 1981, 1993). In September 1976 he undertook a private expedition to north-east Brazil in search of the curassow and spent 60 days collecting nothing more concrete than vague reports of the bird's rarity. Then on 15 November he found and bought a captive female around six years old, the same bird Sick saw. Back in Rio he tried to cross-breed it with a *Mitu tuberosum*, but it soon died. Undeterred, he returned in January 1978 for a year-long search, resulting in the collection of five birds from the wild, one of which died, and one bird, a female, found captive in the town of Maceió. The captive birds proved to comprise two males and three females, so Nardelli created a pair and a trio (Nardelli 1981). The pair fared poorly, not breeding probably because they were too young and because the female was injured. The trio, however, bred well, and between October 1979 and March 1981 they produced 24 eggs between them (17 from one female, seven from the other), nine of which hatched and with five young still alive when he submitted his report (Nardelli 1981).

At the same time, but without knowing of Nardelli's successes, a project backed by the World Wildlife Fund set out to examine the state of the forests and their fauna in north-east Brazil (Teixeira 1986, 1997). Inquiries after the curassow revealed several new locality reports for the species, but all from hunters by then in old age, and all from places by then deforested. Teixeira identified two particularly acute problems for the curassow. First, all records came from below 400m, meaning that this was a lowland bird for which forest reserves on higher ground (where almost all forest remains) would be of no value. Second, the lowlands of the north-east were the special target of the *Proálcool* programme, a 1975 government initiative to compensate for the country's lack (as then believed) of oil reserves by growing sugarcane to substitute ethanol for petrol in cars. Whatever the value to farmers of any forest patches remaining, it was no match for the value to be obtained by clearing them for sugarcane. In late 1978 three Alagoas Curassows were seen and a nest found in an area of lowland forest of some 100km² at Lagoa de Jenipapo, at Roteiro (close to Pinto's site), but within eight months the entire area had been converted to sugarcane (Nardelli 1993). This exactly parallels the loss of the largest patch of lowland forest (also 100km²) in peninsular Thailand during the search for Gurney's Pitta *Pitta gurneyi* (Chapter 23); where economic incentives favour deforestation, the rate of loss can be extraordinary.

EXTINCTION IN THE WILD, GROWTH IN CAPTIVITY

This happened just as Teixeira arrived to witness the destruction of the remaining tiny pockets. Although in 1984 he estimated that 60 birds might survive in the wild and reported that 12 were 'held by private aviculturists' (Teixeira 1986), he believed that after 1982 the fate of the curassow was already sealed by the 'sugar oligarchy'; he found some feathers of a roosting bird in 1987, but thereafter nothing (Teixeira 1997). The species appears

The future of the Alagoas Curassow relies entirely on a small number of private aviculturists. Here, eggs are reared in an incubator (João Marcos Rosa).

to have become extinct in the wild some time during the mid- to late-1980s. Moreover, he reported an alarming development in the captive population: although it was growing, the proportion of males to females had shifted from 2:3 to 13:4, and thus to the point where, to prevent inbreeding, 'the inevitable temptation' to cross-breed birds with *Mitu tuberosum* might be yielded to, which it soon was.

The male of the pair that Nardelli established proved to be too imprinted on humans and never bred (Nardelli 1993), although it was still alive in late 2003 (Silveira *et al.* 2003, Silveira *et al.* 2004). By 1990, the original trio had produced 19 young, and with five deaths among the stock the entire world population of the Alagoas Curassow in that year stood at 19 (12 males, seven females), all of them in one private collection. Thereafter, however, Nardelli decided to hybridise these birds with *Mitu tuberosum* on the assumption that one day he could back-cross them into 'pure' *Mitu mitu* (Nardelli 1993, Silveira *et al.* 2003). Although the Brazilian government's nature conservation authority IBAMA had sought to find birds in the wild for a captive breeding project of its own, no birds were encountered and the endeavour, crippled by 'excessive bureaucracy and lack of financial support', was formally abandoned in 1990 (Collar *et al.* 1992, del Hoyo 1994, Bianchi 2008). This left the fate of the species wholly in the hands of a single private collector: 'It is an extraordinary circumstance that the entire population of a species protected under national law should be held by a private bird-fancier, and even more remarkable that the agencies responsible for implementing that law have apparently developed no formal agreement for the birds' management and propagation' (Collar *et al.* 1992). By 1993 the population had reached 42 birds, at least eight of them hybrids (Nardelli 1993), but by 1999, when Nardelli's private collection was made available to IBAMA, the situation had actually deteriorated: although his facility housed 44 birds, only 12 of them were pure-bred descendants of the original trio (Silveira *et al.* 2003, Silveira *et al.* 2004).

Nardelli's birds were distributed between two well-established private breeding facilities, both in the state of Minas Gerais: Criadouro Científico Poços de Caldas (Moacyr Dias) received 20 (ten males and ten females, including one pure-bred pair) and Fundação Crax (Roberto Azeredo and James Pitt Simpson) received 24 (11 males and 13 females, three and four of them pure-bred respectively) (Silveira *et al.* 2003, Silveira *et al.* 2004), although R. Azeredo and J. P. Simpson (*in litt.* 2010), detailing their work, indicate that in fact Fundação Crax received 23 birds not 24, and that of these only 18 were likely to be capable of breeding in captivity (the other five were too old or showed behavioural problems), while half of them were considered pure individuals on the basis of their morphological characteristics. Using a technique developed from long experience, Fundação Crax quickly began breeding from this stock. The technique is to keep a male and female apart from each other but in adjacent aviaries, so that the development of their sexual condition synchronises. Just at the right moment, they are allowed together for copulation, which takes place within seconds, and then immediately separated; the operation is repeated over three consecutive days to maximise the likelihood of fertilisation and minimise the risk of injury by one bird to another. It also allows one male to be mated with as many as six different females in a single breeding season. Pure males were thus bred with both pure and hybrid females, and the offspring of the latter were again bred with pure males, so as to back-cross impure stock to be genetically and phenotypically as close as possible to the original *Mitu mitu*.

Under this regime each female generally lays two eggs four or five times in a breeding season, which can last five months, hence 8–10 eggs a year. As a result, by February 2010 Fundação Crax had increased its holdings to 90 birds, while Poços de Caldas had 40. Of the total of 130, 78 birds – exactly 60% – were judged to be pure *Mitu mitu* based on their morphological characters. In the meantime, all pure males have had semen collected and frozen for future use, artificial incubation regimes have been fine-tuned for optimal hatching success, new chick management techniques have been developed to reduce the problem of aggression, IBAMA has sampled all birds in order to assess their genetic profiles, and Fundação Crax is planning to expand its aviaries.

REINTRODUCTION: VISION AND EXPERIENCE

Since the turn of the present century, therefore, things have at last been moving in the right direction. In 2001 an intensive search was made of as many forest patches as could be found (there were 15, the largest of them covering 8km²) in the lowlands of Alagoas state: all were in poor condition, suffering logging and poaching, and none of them yielded any evidence, direct or indirect, of the survival of the species (Silveira & Olmos 2003, Silveira *et al.* 2003, Silveira *et al.* 2004). In the same year IBAMA moved to establish, as it had done earlier with Spix's Macaw *Cyanopsitta spixii* (Chapter 20), a 'Committee for the Recovery and Management of the Alagoas Curassow'. Subsequently a working group was established to carry on the work of this committee, and an action plan for the curassow was drawn up addressing public policy and legislation, protection of habitat and the species, research, captive management and reintroduction (Bianchi 2008). These developments coincide with the growth of the Instituto de Preservação da Mata Atlântica (IPMA), founded in 1996 by two sugarcane companies and a private bird breeding facility with the aim of protecting and restoring forest remnants in Alagoas and, in particular, with the ambition one day of re-establishing populations of Alagoas Curassow in these patches of habitat. The results have been encouraging. Within ten years 37 partners joined IPMA, a total of 500km² of forest (from various parts of the Atlantic Forest, most of it admittedly in the highlands where the curassow almost certainly never occurred) was voluntarily protected, a mobile school was set up and a replanting programme developed with more than two million seedlings produced (Bianchi 2008).

The issue of reintroduction has been one that Fundação Crax has long sought to address, building up experience through its work with another Atlantic Forest cracid, the Red-billed Curassow *Crax blumenbachii* (Endangered). Little of this crucial work has been published (Azeredo 1997, Simpson *et al.* 1997), but there is an important appendix to the Red-billed Curassow Action Plan (Silveira *et al.* 2005), which describes the protocols and achievements of Fundação Crax in some detail. The protocols reflect the principles of reintroduction outlined by IUCN, but they were developed long beforehand, given that Crax's first project began in 1990 at the 15km² Fazenda Macedônia (run by CENIBRA), a private reserve in Minas Gerais. Here 15 pairs of Red-billed Curassows were released in September 1991 after nine months' acclimatisation at the site, and another 15 pairs after seven months in February 1993. Despite rather high levels of predation in the first months after release, enough birds survived to breed and build up numbers, so that by 2004 no fewer than 36 offspring had been produced. Three other Red-billed Curassow reintroduction projects have grown from this work, in Minas Gerais in 1996 at the 10km² Fechos (COPASA) private reserve, in 1999 at the 6km² Peti (CEMIG) environmental station (Silveira *et al.* 2005), and in Rio de Janeiro state in 2006 at the 65km² (and constantly increasing) Reserva Ecológica de Guapiaçu

('Regua') (São Bernardo *et al.* 2008). Some of the Red-billed Curassows at Regua have been followed with radio transmitters to monitor their movements and survival, and the experience gained from this most detailed of cracid reintroduction studies should be of enormous value when it becomes the turn of the Alagoas Curassow to be re-established in the wild in its native forests.

However, deciding when a reintroduction has been successful is not always easy. There are several stages to celebrate, most notably when the released birds first breed successfully, and again when the first of the wild-bred birds themselves breed successfully. When the population reaches a given target, such as doubling the number originally liberated, is a third milestone. Saturation of available habitat, at densities similar to those found or inferred from elsewhere, is a fourth and perhaps the most significant. However, if the area is not large enough for a population to be viable in the very long term, even saturation may not be an adequate sign of success. Slowly, over time, the new population is likely to dwindle as it becomes inbred, and as chance events such as fire undercut its numbers, so that eventually it will become part of the 'extinction debt' syndrome that already affects many of the Atlantic Forest's rarest birds (p.272). The signs are good that some lowland forest in Alagoas can be rehabilitated and extended for the return of Alagoas Curassow, with the problem of hunting contained by law enforcement and local awareness campaigns. However, unless these forests are linked up through equally well-protected and well-positioned corridors, so that natural gene exchange is maximised, the signs may not be good enough. In 2009 the forest at Murici, upslope from wherever the curassow's new home will be, was showing depressing evidence of the extinction debt: Pedro Develey and Fábio Olmos, visiting on behalf of SAVE Brasil, could only find a single Alagoas Foliage-gleaner, and consider it possible that it was the very last of its kind (P. F. Develey pers. comm. 2010). This could scarcely be a more poignant reminder that, after all the work that has been undertaken on the curassow in the past decade, the viability of the future wild population must not be compromised by the constraints of scale.

Red-billed Curassows Crax blumenbachii *(male on right), some fitted with radio transmitters, being introduced into forest at Regua, near Rio de Janeiro (João Marcos Rosa).*

Chapter 20
Spix's Macaw *Cyanopsitta spixii*
EXTINCT IN THE WILD

How do animals react to being separated from other members of their species? Does the need for conspecific contact drive them into unusual patterns of signalling and movement, or do they put themselves at more risk as a result, or are they in any case at more risk? Vagrant birds can almost never have a reproductive future, but some of them survive much longer than one might expect. In the UK, for example, a Black-browed Albatross *Thalassarche melanophrys*, in due course dubbed 'Albert Ross', occupied the same ledge in the Northern Gannet *Sula bassana* colony at Hermaness in Shetland, Scotland, for 23 consecutive breeding seasons. What stress do these solitary creatures endure in never seeing or hearing one of their own kind? These are the questions a lost individual poses the longer it manages to hang on in its strange surroundings, and the greater the sympathy it elicits from its human observers. Stray animals even become the targets of public subscription to ship them home, like the disoriented Walrus *Odobenus rosmarus* ('Wally', of course) that was flown back to the arctic after floundering ashore on the east coast of England in 1981, or the Bald Eagle *Haliaeetus leucocephalus* repatriated to the USA after it reached Ireland in 1987.

How much more poignant, then, must be the plight of the last individual of its kind. Fred Bosworth's classic story *Last of the Curlews* (Bodsworth 1956), which mixed facts about the decline to extinction of the Eskimo Curlew *Numenius borealis* (Chapter 25) with a fictional and entirely unsentimental love-story about the last male and his long and seemingly successful quest to find a mate, ends with her being gunned down by a farmer just before the pair reach the tundra, and with his heart-rending return, alone, to his breeding territory. In real life, of course, there are very few cases where we are witness to the last individual of a species, and this almost only ever happens because the animals in question are either very large and slow, like Lonesome George, the sole surviving member of the race *abingdoni* of the Galápagos Tortoise *Geochelone nigra* (but see Russello *et al.* 2007), or in a cage, like Martha, the last Passenger Pigeon *Ectopistes migratorius* (died 1 September 1914 in Cincinnati Zoo) and Incas, the last Carolina Parakeet *Conuropsis carolinensis* (died 21 February 1918, by an extraordinary coincidence in the very same aviary in Cincinnati Zoo that Martha had occupied: Snyder 2004).

One thing that stands out in these cases is the high frequency with which the animals are given names, which both reflects and creates a strong if one-way bond of sympathy between themselves and their human witnesses. The trigger to such humanisation is familiarity: the animal must either have a big enough audience (as in the case of the walrus, which made every newspaper in Britain) or else be present long enough to generate that sense of honorary membership of our species that a human name bestows. For this distinction, the last Spix's Macaw never quite made the necessary grade: although a single male lived out the final decade of his life alone, he was too deep in the Brazilian outback to generate that level of public interest that would earn him a name. He was much discussed and often sought after, but rather rarely seen, perhaps because he was ranging over a much larger area than normal, ever hopeful of finding a mate or at least a foraging partner.

There was another difference in this story: the male was the last of his kind in the wild, but not in the world. There were plenty of other Spix's Macaws behind bars in Brazil and elsewhere, so public reaction to his plight was tempered by the fact that, at least in theory, something could be done for him, and indeed for the species as a whole. Certainly the conservation world was watching the people with the birds in cages with much greater interest than it was watching the one parrot still at liberty in the outback. Sadly, they still are: the story of how the male was given half a chance and missed it is long over and can freely be told, but the story of how the people with the birds in cages banded together and saved the species from extinction is still to unfold. If the Alagoas Curassow *Mitu mitu* (Chapter 19) is remarkable for having been entirely owned, for some twenty years, by a single person, Spix's Macaw, another Brazilian endemic now listed as Extinct in the Wild, is no less remarkable for being very largely owned, for similar periods of time, by a number of private individuals scattered around the globe.

The last Spix's Macaw in the wild, discovered in 1990. His disappearance in October 2000 meant that the entire population of the species then lay in the hands of a small number of private collectors (Luiz Claudio Marigo).

DISCOVERY AND REDISCOVERY

It is not difficult to see how this curious circumstance arose, but the story is nevertheless extraordinary. All the blue macaws, being birds of the Brazilian interior, were discovered relatively late and principally by means of live individuals traded back to Europe (Chapter 22). Spix's Macaw was always a very rare and little-known bird. In 1819, when the young German explorer Johann Baptist von Spix collected the first specimen (still the only one known to have come direct from the wild) near Juazeiro, up the Rio São Francisco deep inside Bahia, the Hyacinth Macaw *Anodorhynchus hyacinthinus* was itself so poorly known that he thought his bird was one. It was only seven years after Spix's premature death that a taxonomist in Munich realised the mistake and named the much smaller blue parrot for its discoverer. This was hardly an auspicious start in life, and the omens did not improve: there was no other observation of the species for the rest of the nineteenth century. However, in mid-June 1903 Reiser, another German, claimed to have seen a few birds at Lago de Parnaguá, in southern Piauí state, but with no specimens to check it is hard to judge whether his identification was correct. The general feeling these days, based in part on the absence of any other records from the area, seems to be that it was not.

Nevertheless, the impact of Reiser's testimony on the way that ornithologists regarded Spix's Macaw was probably crucial, though regrettably in a negative manner. Reiser also saw a captive bird at Remanso, in northern Bahia, near the Piauí border, and overall these two new localities created the impression that the species might be found at a scatter of sites within the dry north-east of Brazil, a sizeable and largely unexplored area. Moreover, the fact that a trickle of birds had made its way to European zoos in the second quarter of the nineteenth century and the first third of the twentieth (Collar *et al.* 1992) suggested that the species might simply live in a very remote area. This thin evidence must lie behind the fact that Spix's Macaw, like the Glaucous Macaw *Anodorhynchus glaucus* and Lear's Macaw *A. leari*, was missed off the early lists of threatened birds (Greenway 1958, Vincent 1966–1971). Even when it was finally installed in the international Red Data Book (King 1978–1979) it was only given the status Vulnerable, then as now the lowest category under which a species can be classified as threatened.

By the time King compiled his account of the species, several more pieces of relatively reassuring information had been found. One was that in 1978 there were 13 birds in captivity in Europe. Another was the confident description of the species' area of occurrence as embracing 'southern Piauí, north-western Bahia, southern Maranhão and eastern Goiás'. The third was a 'sighting of three in 1975, in north-western Bahia,… the only recent record by an ornithologist of the species in the wild'. This sighting was in 'buriti palm groves and adjacent caatinga woodland', a habitat 'not seriously threatened with destruction'. If all these assertions were true, there was no reason for placing the species in a higher threat category. The authority for the 1975 sighting was none other than the authority for all the birds of Brazil at that time, the great Dr Helmut Sick, who had been sent to the country by Erwin Stresemann in 1939 only to be stranded there for so long by the Second World War that he elected to stay forever. Sick was a brilliant naturalist who learnt the seemingly innumerable birds of his adopted land the hard way, following them in forest, scrub and marsh, learning their calls, collecting them in order to identify them, travelling where no zoologist had previously gone, and eventually pulling his lifetime's voluminous knowledge together in the book *Ornitologia brasileira, uma introdução* (1985) that opened the way for everyone who followed him.

However, the year that Sick's great work was published was also the year that the bird conservation movement finally decided that the encouraging testimony of King's Red Data Book needed the reinforcement of new evidence, and that the species had to be pinned down in the wild. The Pan American Section of the International Council for Bird Preservation (ICBP) found the money to pay Paul Roth, a young Swiss German who was studying the parrots of north-east Brazil for his PhD, to go in search of Spix's Macaw. On the first of his five expeditions, in June–July 1985, Roth met a trapper in Piauí who tipped him off that the place to look was Curaçá, a town 90km north-east of Juazeiro, near which Spix had first found the species. On the second of his expeditions, therefore, in April 1986, Roth went to Curaçá, worked the thin sleeve of gallery woodland on the Melância Creek to the south of the town, and there finally came face to face with three wild Spix's Macaws, perhaps the first ornithologist since Spix, 167 years earlier, to do so. Within a month, Roland Wirth of the Zoologische Gesellschaft für Arten- und Populationsschutz (ZGAP), a German NGO working to save the most threatened species and populations, had put up the money to hire local people to guard the birds for a year. Over the next two years, Roth made three further but fruitless journeys of exploration in pursuit of other reports of the species.

SURVIVAL IN CAPTIVITY

Things were suddenly starting to move rather faster than they had been in the previous century and a half. Word of Roth's searches and success doubtless spread just as fast in trapping circles as it did in conservation ones. It was probably no coincidence that soon after the rediscovery the remaining birds disappeared, although not so fast as to prevent two young birds being taken from a nest in February 1987, with one adult being caught that April, another that December and the third, reputedly, the following month, in January 1988. They were worth many tens of thousands of dollars to a few wealthy people and were trapped despite whatever vigilance the locals hired by ZGAP could manage. Things did not go entirely the trappers' way, however. Thanks to some nimble pursuit of leads, Juan Villalba-Macías of TRAFFIC (the global NGO that monitors trade in wildlife; the name is an acronym for Trade Records and Analysis of Fauna and Flora In Commerce) picked up the two nestlings in a raid on the house of a well-known animal dealer in Asunción, Paraguay, in March 1987, and repatriated them triumphantly to Brazil, where they were put into the care of São Paulo Zoo.

This event, coupled with the dawning realisation that there really might not be birds anywhere other than at Curaçá, was a particular stimulus for conservationists to start trying to count captive birds and identify their owners. It was fairly well known that Alvaro Carvalhães, an aviculturist at Santos, São Paulo, had kept Spix's Macaws from the 1950s to the 1970s, had bred a reasonable number ('over two dozen' in one account), and passed some of these birds to one Ulisses Moreira, who himself appeared to have bred them (Collar *et al.* 1992). But by the mid-1980s these all seemed to have died or disappeared into other hands, and the whole business of trying to work out who might possess birds inevitably had to rely on the testimony of aviculturists themselves. Some of them had knowledge they could not or would not divulge, but most were willing to part with hints and allegations, hearsay and rumour, so that the conservationists were soon groping through a world of smoke and mirrors. Thus over the course of the 1980s it was claimed (and sometimes counter-claimed) that there were up to 25 birds in Brazil, three pairs (all breeding) in the USA, and a good number in Europe, including a very prolific pair in Belgium, a pair in Germany, two females in Naples, a pair in Portugal, four birds in Yugoslavia (supposedly once owned by President Tito), two in the Canary islands, one each in France, Sweden and Switzerland, and further afield a pair in Singapore, four in the Caribbean, four in the Philippines, one in Japan and another in Thailand (Collar *et al.* 1992)!

Some of the birds in this dizzying mix existed, some did not; some *had* existed, others never; some existed, or had existed, but not in quite the time or place given; others had left multiple footprints – a bird sold on twice, for example, would leave the rumour of its existence in all three places. The birds in the Canaries were certainly real, however, and in April 1987 their owner, Wolfgang Kiessling of Loro Parque, then a large bird garden in Puerto de la Cruz in Tenerife, called a meeting with ICBP, ZGAP and the Captive Breeding Specialist Group of IUCN to develop plans for a consortium to breed and manage the birds collectively, thereby laying what should have been the first foundations of a serious international endeavour to recover the species. Back in Brazil, with the termination of Roth's fieldwork and the depressing apparent loss of the last birds in the wild, attention turned to the holders who had missed this meeting, and in September 1988 São Paulo Zoo, TRAFFIC and the CITES Secretariat drew up an agreement to which the Brazilian government duly became a party to take forward captive breeding in the country. The following month, however, at a meeting in Curitiba of the now-defunct Parrot Specialist Group, the few Brazilian holders who were prepared to attend greeted this news with something less than enthusiasm.

Nevertheless, the Brazilian government body for nature conservation, IBAMA, had major responsibilities to fulfil in this high-profile case, although with its tiny budgets and overstretched personnel it could not move with the alacrity of ZGAP or TRAFFIC. It took almost two more years before a 'Permanent Committee for the Recovery of Spix's Macaw' (CPRAA in its Portuguese acronym), its terms of reference more or less worked out, was able to meet, in July 1990. It included three holders from Brazil (São Paulo Zoo, Nelson Kawall, Mauricio dos Santos) and two from abroad (Wolfgang Kiessling and Antonio de Dios of the Philippines). A series of meetings came

Spix's Macaw survives only in captivity, mostly outside Brazil: this young bird was raised at the Al Wabra Wildlife Preservation in Qatar (AWWP).

and went: Recife in 1991, Petrolina in 1993 and 1996, Fort Lauderdale in 1994, São Paulo in 1995 and 2000, Houston in 1999, Brasília in 2001. After twelve years, however, the committee was dissolved, having endured a convoluted and sometimes agonised existence in which it struggled to maintain a coherent plan of programmatic development from one meeting (which often lacked one or more crucial members) to the next. Members of the committee, often strongly divergent in their points of view, came and went, sometimes hypersensitive, sometimes intransigent, taking unilateral decisions over one matter or another, raising and dashing hopes of cooperation and financing, forging short-lived alliances with each other or with other sources of influence, teetering on the brink of engagement but eventually, regrettably, stepping away. This is not to say that there were no moments of harmony and advance, with some useful exchanges of birds in the early stages, and in some respects the committee perhaps came closer to achieving an integrated breeding programme than the bare facts of history would suggest. But acrimony, intrigue and mistrust always cruised below the surface of these meetings, their fins sometimes showing.

The only foreign holder continuously present on CPRAA over its lifetime was Wolfgang Kiessling, who in 1994 established the Loro Parque Foundation (LPF) with a pair of Spix's Macaw as its logo and the conservation of threatened parrots as its mission. Kiessling has been the only holder to give up ownership of his Spix's Macaws and make them the property of Brazil, thereby ceding control of their management, and he has been the only holder who, through LPF, has put money into the programme (amounting to almost $750,000 over a decade). But with little funding from elsewhere and only a couple of birds in Kiessling's care (and none in his control), the 'recovery' programme could never really function. It consisted, instead, of a series of initiatives that, in the long view, have come to resemble little more than false starts. A theatre was renovated in Curaçá and painted the colours of the macaw, to serve as a centre for campaigning and education for the species, but it soon fell into disrepair (although it has now been renovated a second time). An action plan that was drafted in considerable detail was formally adopted only in March 2009 and still awaits publication. A still larger handbook detailing the history of the species in the wild and in captivity, along with a series of management prescriptions, has never been completed. Plans drawn up for a captive breeding facility on Brazilian soil have not advanced.

LOSS IN THE WILD

It may be that with no birds in the wild to serve as a focus there has been little cause for urgency in the recovery effort, but for the last decade of the twentieth century this excuse could not apply. Back in early 1990 when the CPRAA was quietly gestating, ICBP had been contacted by the Brazilian photographer Luiz Claudio Marigo with a proposal to follow up reports of Spix's Macaw in the Chapada das Mangabeiras, a range of hills in the deep interior of the Brazilian north-east. Despite the blank drawn by Roth over the three years he searched for Spix's Macaws other than at Curaçá, the possibility that a wild population was still out there somewhere was a constant source of both disquiet and hope to conservationists, and it seemed important to take this new opportunity. ICBP scraped together the money (in this story the contrast could not be starker between the cash-strapped conservationists and the cash-flush consumers: the price-tag of the rescued pair of nestlings in 1987 was reputedly $40,000!). It also volunteered one member of the team, Tony Juniper, while Marigo assembled four Brazilians, including IBAMA's macaw expert Carlos Yamashita. The search, in June and July 1990, took the team to many different parts of the north-east. The chances of success were scarcely high: 'With a potential search area of 300,000 square kilometres, a territory larger than Great Britain, to find a parrot was considerably more challenging than searching for a needle in a haystack' (Juniper 2002).

But, incredibly, they found one. It was, almost predictably, in the Melância Creek south of Curaçá. Roth's report of the last bird being captured in January 1988 had been a mistake: a single bird survived there. If the news gave a filip to the first meeting of the CPRAA, it also brought some important new insights and considerations, key among them concerning the species' habitat. Writing the first paper of the first issue of BirdLife's scientific journal *Bird Conservation International*, Juniper & Yamashita (1991) explained that the creek's gallery woodlands were largely composed of caraiba *Tabebuia caraiba* trees and that, while caraibas could be found all over the north-east, they grew tallest and densest only in a few gallery formations along these creeks south of Curaçá. There the biggest trees provided holes large enough for a mid-sized macaw to nest in, and this was almost certainly their most significant attribute (the problem of trees large enough to produce natural nest-holes is frequently crucial in the lives of threatened parrots, as for example the Yellow-crested Cockatoo *Cacatua sulphurea*: Chapter 9). Caraiba evidently once formed extensive galleries along the tributaries of the São Francisco. The great river was, however, the route by which settlement of the Brazilian north-east could proceed, and of course the settlers inevitably sourced their timber and firewood from the fringing woodland, so that all that remains today, and probably all that remained when Spix made his journey, are relics of the original, covering a mere 30km² in three separate patches (Juniper & Yamashita 1990). An attraction of this hypothesis is that it explains why the macaw has proved so rare, but if true it also suggests that most if not all of the other records of the species from elsewhere must have been misidentifications, which are surprisingly easy to make in the burning light of the parched north-east. If so, like so many of those claims of captive birds dotted around the planet, reports of wild birds in other parts of the Brazilian north-east had been a frustrating distraction; Sick's macaws were not Spix's Macaws.

The main consideration arising from the finding of the single survivor was, of course, what to do with it. ICBP made immediate recommendations, guided in part by early attempts to re-establish the Thick-billed Parrot *Rhynchopsitta pachyrhyncha* in Arizona, which showed (although many lessons have been learnt since) how vulnerable and naïve captive-bred parrots are by comparison with wild-caught birds when released (Snyder *et al.* 1994). First, therefore, the bird needed to be protected: in it was vested all the knowledge of food plants, nest sites and sheltering spots that the species had left, so it would be a vital guide and instructor for any captive-bred bird released there in the future. Second, a mate should be found for it and introduced to it as soon as possible. Third, the caraiba woodlands needed protection; after all, it was habitat destruction and not trade that was now judged the ultimate cause of the species' rarity (although capture for trade was considered the proximate cause of its extinction). Fourth, a breeding facility in the vicinity was considered a good means of promoting local support, on neutral ground and in the right climatic conditions for the birds.

Only the provision of a mate caused problems. It took the best part of two years before the idea was widely accepted in principle and another three before it was put into practice. There was, however, a real problem to

The last, lonely male Spix's Macaw (left) paired up in his last years with a female Blue-winged Macaw Primolius maracana *(right) (Luiz Claudio Marigo).*

overcome: what was the sex of the one wild bird? The consensus from photographs and observations of its behaviour was that it was male, but stronger evidence was needed. Eventually a shed feather was collected and sent, with necessary documentation, to England, where the sexing of birds by genetic analysis was being pioneered, and proof furnished that the bird was indeed male (Griffiths & Tiwari 1995). Meanwhile, in anticipation of this result, the most promising candidate for release had been found. At the start of 1992 the number of birds known in captivity was 25: São Paulo Zoo had three, Kawall a pair, dos Santos a pair, de Dios a pair and eight offspring, Kiessling a pair and J. Hämmerli (a Swiss dentist whose evidently extensive, and apparently continuing, experience with the species has never been fully documented) a pair and four offspring. Dos Santos's female was selected because she was believed wild-caught (although whether as a nestling, juvenile or adult was unclear; some thought she might actually have been the wild male's mate) and therefore most likely to be capable of surviving back in the Melância Creek.

In August 1994 she was moved to a new pre-release aviary at Fazenda Concórdia, the farm by the creek where Marigo, Juniper and colleagues had made their discovery. There she underwent seven months of acclimatisation: she was played Spix's Macaw vocalisations and learnt to select and handle local fruits and seeds. A captive male kept in a cage 200m away acted as a lure in the first weeks after release, which took place in mid-March 1995. She had her tail clipped to tell her from the wild male, but was not fitted with telemetry equipment. She took wild food from the day of her release and rapidly stopped coming to feeders. She soon assumed strong physical condition, covering up to 3km a day after one week, 15km after two weeks, and 30–40km after one month. She avoided an attack by an Aplomado Falcon *Falco femoralis* on day four. The distance to which she would let people approach her before flying off increased from a metre or so on release to 10m after two weeks and 50m by mid-May, when she finally encountered the wild male. Under the pressure of solitude, the male was paired by then with a female Blue-winged Macaw *Primolius maracana*, a species that also occupies the caraiba woodland habitat. By early June, the released Spix's Macaw had paired with the male, but to everyone's dismay within a fortnight she disappeared and the male reclaimed his former mate. She was never seen again, but four years later a local man confessed to finding her dead under some powerlines but said that he had not come forward earlier as he was a great supporter of the Spix's Macaw project and was afraid the news would undermine it. The IBAMA team had recognised the danger posed by these lines and colour-marked those which bisected areas frequented by the male, but the site where the female died was not in one of these (Collar 2006).

The male lived on another five years; he finally disappeared in October 2000. Thus, apart from a two-week honeymoon, tragically cut short in the middle of 1995, he lived alone from his species for almost 13 years. His plight caught the imagination of every parrot lover around the world, and Tony Juniper's book (Juniper 2002) ensured that his story reached into the lives of innumerable conservation sympathisers. Moreover, much was learned by the supplementation effort of 1994–1995, and indeed more was later learned when LPF, over and above its funding of the other field activities, supplied for release a group of Blue-winged Macaws at Melância Creek as a way of piloting future releases of captive-bred Spix's. Altogether the cause of conservation was served well by the solitary survivor, reminiscent of 'Old Blue', the sole breeding female Black Robin *Petroica traversi* that brought that species back from the brink (p.146), and with the high public profile the species now has it is difficult to think that success will not come eventually.

THE RESPONSIBILITY OF THE HOLDERS

However, Juniper's book also reported some of the unapproved movements of captive birds between holders that led to the collapse of the CPRAA. One was the sale in 1999 of most of Hämmerli's stock, to do which Hämmerli had first to withdraw from CPRAA while still expressing a willingness to cooperate. He sold them to another Swiss, Roland Messer, who had been jailed in 1993 for organising a parrot heist. According to Juniper, Messer paid the equivalent of around US$230,000 for 15 birds but he quickly fell out with Hämmerli over the composition of this stock, since some of the birds were not the ones he was expecting. Next year, de Dios followed suit, selling two pairs to Sheikh Saoud Al-Thani in Qatar. Sheikh Saoud, celebrated for his collections of rare art, artefacts and animals, placed them in his aviaries at Al Wabra, where they have continued to breed. Although technically in breach of his agreement with CPRAA, de Dios hoped that Sheikh Saoud would himself be admitted to the committee. In fact these unauthorised transfers were the source of great concern, as the two holders who had been most successful at breeding the species, de Dios being the first to achieve second-generation breeding, appeared now to be prepared to make independent deals that would leave the committee increasingly unable to exert the necessary influence to maintain a coherent programme. On the subject of the Sheikh's cooperation with Brazil, Juniper considered the situation equivocal (Juniper 2002), but in 2004 IBAMA created a 'Working Group for the Recovery of Spix's Macaw', less formal and more flexible than the 'Permanent Committee', and the Qataris have been counted in, as Al Wabra Wildlife Preservation (AWWP). Indeed, their blue macaw specialist, Ryan Watson, is now the international studbook keeper for the species.

In any case, Messer's involvement was short-lived. In 2002 he turned four birds over to Sheikh Saoud and in 2005 seven more, and also in 2005 he sold a number of others to a new player on the scene, Martin Guth, a businessman based in Berlin (D. R. Waugh *in litt.* 2010). However, it is unclear how many birds Guth now controls. Birds in Switzerland require CITES permits to leave the country, and to date only three are believed to have been moved to Berlin, where Guth recently founded his Association for the Conservation of Threatened Parrots (ACTP). It is also a matter of speculation how many birds Hämmerli retains, or to whom he might have sold other stock. There is, moreover, a definite chance that other captive birds exist. The discovery in the USA of Presley, an ageing male Spix's living with a lady who apparently only realised very late in his life that he belonged to a Critically Endangered species (Fass-Holmes 2003), was remarkable evidence of this. Through the efforts of the World Parrot Trust the bird was swiftly repatriated to Brazil, although sadly he appeared to be too old to contribute genetically to the population. At the other end of the scale, there are hints and glimpses of illegality at a level too secluded ever to be able to gauge (let alone prevent), as when Anson Wong, a convicted trafficker based in Malaysia, told an undercover agent in 1995 that he could get him Spix's Macaws on the black market for $100,000 per bird, 'claiming he'd recently sold three' (Christy 2010).

In June 2009, the minimum count of Spix's Macaws known by members of the Working Group to be in existence was 68 (28 males, 38 females, 2 unknown), distributed at AWWP, Qatar, 52 (21, 29, 2 sex unknown); LPF, Tenerife, 8 (3, 5); ACTP, Germany, 2 (both females); Lymington Foundation, Brazil, 3 (2, 1) and São Paulo Zoo 3 (2, 1). This is certainly a more optimistic situation than the way things were seventeen years before, when the total known was 25. Breeding has taken place at AWWP and LPF, and recently through loans also at ACTP. But the situation is far from optimal: 43 extra birds in 17 years is only 2.5 birds a year, when the rate might easily be four times as high. Some of the Qatari birds have been found to have proventricular dilatation disease (PDD, also known as 'macaw wasting syndrome'), a serious viral infection that cannot be allowed to spread; the population at AWWP has therefore been split into those with (or having been exposed to) the disease and those not, but there are obvious consequences for the extreme caution that must be exercised in managing the population. Moreover, the birds that came from Manila all have dark irides and many have anthracosis, reflecting the high level of atmospheric pollution in the Philippine capital (the darkness of the eyes is caused by the accumulation there of heavy metals).

Nevertheless, exchanges between holders must continue to take place, in order to ensure a genetically and demographically viable population, although of course they need to be made according to recommendations made by the studbook keeper, with endorsement by the Working Group and approval by the Brazilian Government. No less important is the protection of the scarce suitable habitat that remains, especially by continuing to keep alive in the local community the aspiration that 'their' little blue macaw will one day return. To this end, land near to Curaçá (the adjacent Fazendas Concórdia and Gangorra) has been acquired by AWWP, Lymington Foundation, Parrots International and ACTP, and activities to support the local school are ongoing through Parrots International. Moreover, fieldwork to map other remaining patches of good habitat has been endorsed by the Working Group and is pending. Things are perhaps moving more slowly than they might, and the recovery of Spix's Macaw is still a very long way off; on the other hand, however, on present evidence so is the day when the last of its kind will roam the land, searching disconsolately for company.

Spix's Macaw chicks at the Al Wabra Wildlife Preservation in Qatar (AWWP).

Chapter 21
Madagascar Pochard *Aythya innotata*
CRITICALLY ENDANGERED

Isolation from the rest of the world for over 150 million years has meant that the wildlife of Madagascar is endemic at a higher taxonomic level than anywhere else. Madagascar has 11 endemic families of plants, whereas North America, forty-two times larger in area, has only two. The island supports three endemic bird families, the enigmatic mesites (Mesitornithidae), the ground rollers (Brachypteraciidae) and the asities (Philepittidae), and two others, the vangas (Vangidae) and the peculiar Cuckoo-roller (Leptosomatidae) that occur elsewhere only on the Comoros. Of 204 breeding bird species, 120 are found nowhere else. Many of these endemic species have very restricted distributions, probably the result of ancient climatic fluctuations (Wilmé *et al.* 2006). Because of these small natural distributions and the usual host of problems faced by island species, a high proportion of Madagascar's birds are threatened; with 22 bird species listed as Vulnerable, 11 as Endangered and two as Critically Endangered on the 2012 Red List, the majority of them endemic. In the last 500 years there have been several bird extinctions, involving the enigmatic Snail-eating Coua *Coua delalandei* and at least one species of elephantbird *Aepyornis*. At an estimated 454kg, *A. maximus* was probably the largest bird ever to have lived, and it may have survived into the seventeenth century (Goodman & Benstead 2003). More recently, the Alaotra Grebe *Tachybaptus rufolavatus* was declared extinct in 2010, more than 25 years after its last sighting, the victim of introduced predatory fish, monofilament nylon fishing nets, reduced water quality and hybridization with Little Grebes *T. ruficollis* (Hawkins *et al.* 2000). Of the two Critically Endangered species, the Madagascar Pochard *Aythya innotata* was until recently thought to be extinct and the Madagascar Fish-eagle *Haliaeetus vociferoides* has a dwindling population of perhaps fewer than 200 individuals.

Madagascar Pochard was feared extinct until a few birds were found in 2006, since when emergency conservation measures have been put in place (Pete Morris).

LOSS AND REDISCOVERY

Since its discovery in 1894, most records of the Madagascar Pochard have come from or near the huge Lake Alaotra at *c*.750m above sea level on Madagascar's central plateau (Salvadori 1894), which comprises 770km² of open water or flood zone and, since the early 1900s, rice fields (Collar & Stuart 1985, Wilmé 1994). The lake is surrounded by marshland, primarily papyrus *Cyperus madagascariensis* and *C. imeriniensis*, with reed *Phragmites australis* around the edge (Burgis & Symoens 1987, Langrand 1990). The Madagascar Pochard was considered common at Alaotra in the 1920s and 1930s (Webb 1936, Delacour 1956), but appears to have declined by 1960 (Wilmé 1994). Despite numerous subsequent attempts to find the species on Lake Alaotra (Dee 1986, Young & Smith 1989, Wilmé 1994), including a number of intensive searches backed up by major publicity campaigns to appeal for information, the only confirmed record was of a single male captured by hunters in 1991 (Edhem 1993, Wilmé 1994). This bird was held captive for a year, but with its death in 1992 many considered the species to be extinct. In 2004, following the failure of further surveys to locate any birds, the caveat 'Possibly Extinct' was added to the species' Critically Endangered classification (Butchart *et al.* 2006).

Red Lake, where the Madagascar Pochard was rediscovered in 2006 by a team of researchers looking for something else (Peter Cranswick, WWT).

Another Critically Endangered species on Madagascar is the Madagascar Fish-eagle Haliaeetus vociferoides, *now reduced to a few hundred individuals due to deforestation and the drainage of wetlands (Pete Morris).*

Fortunately, the species was not extinct. In November 2006, Lily-Arison René de Roland and The Seing Sam, biologists working for the conservation organisation The Peregrine Fund ('TPF), were surveying the biodiversity of a remote region in northern Madagascar named after the town of Bealanana. They had discovered the site earlier in 2006 while searching marsh and grassland habitat for the elusive Madagascar Harrier *Circus macrosceles* (Vulnerable). They found the harrier there (but few elsewhere across the entire island) and in the process they recognised the exceptional biological richness and diversity of the site, set in a spectacular, hilly landscape, a mosaic of rainforest patches among swathes of fire-dominated grasslands, with isolated marshes and lakes at the bottom of extinct volcanic craters. Where rainforest dominates the craters' edges the lakes are clear blue, but where grasslands dominate the lakes are filled with sediment, allowing a marsh flora and fauna to flourish. One lake, named Matsaborimena (Red Lake), among the four main lakes, large marshes and smaller sites that comprise the Bemanevika wetlands, is intermediate, with rainforest on about 80% of the cone and grassland and secondary shrub developing on the remaining 20%. The lake's edge is mostly forested and steep, but in places the water is shallow with reedbeds extending well into the lake's interior. It was here, while surveying waterfowl, that they rediscovered the Madagascar Pochard (René de Roland *et al.* 2007).

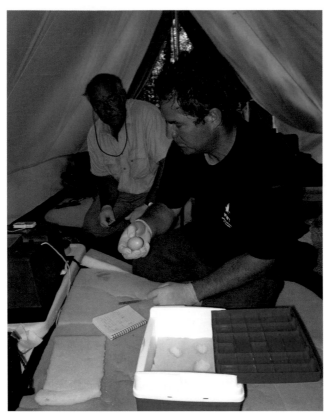

Emergency conservation in action. Above: Experts in captive breeding measure eggs taken from the first clutch of Madagascar Pochards in 2009 in makeshift accommodation on the shores of Red Lake (Martin Brown, WWT). Below: The eggs hatch shortly after, with the experts helping the chicks to emerge from the eggs (Nigel Jarrett, WWT).

EMERGENCY MEASURES

René de Roland instantly recognised the enormity of the find and the team spent several days crawling through the reeds to photograph and count the ducks to provide the proof they knew would be needed to satisfy any sceptics. Their counts suggested that the lake held nine adults and four young birds. Then they hiked their way back down the trail and on to the nearest town with an internet connection, two days' travel away, to spread the news. One of the first people they told was Glyn Young, a biologist from Durrell Wildlife Conservation Trust, who had been searching for the Madagascar Pochard for 15 years and had even named his daughter, Aythya, after the elusive bird. René de Roland and another TPF biologist Marius Rakotondratsima guided Young to the site the following month, where they counted around 20 adults and up to nine ducklings. The fact that the species not only survived but was still producing young was highly encouraging.

The immediate priority was to ensure the ducks were fully protected from any kind of human interference. TPF based a full-time team at the lake to monitor and respond to whatever human incursions might occur, and Seing Sam started biological studies on the ducks. Villagers from the local community guarded the site and were trained as eco-guides, and the local community quickly developed a strong commitment to the protection of the ducks and other wildlife in the area. Significantly, TPF also set about developing legal protection of the area under Madagascar's national protected areas system, taking advantage of the country's presidential proclamation to treble Madagascar's area of protected habitat by 2010. With habitat protection underway and the ducks protected from human interference, Seing Sam's study sounded a new alarm. In the autumn of 2008 he estimated 25 adult birds to be present. However, although at least 63 ducklings were produced that breeding season, none survived beyond a few weeks. With such a low rate of reproduction, the population was clearly in great danger.

Consequently, in late 2008, Durrell, the UK's Wildfowl & Wetlands Trust (WWT) and TPF started discussing options for reducing the extinction risk of the Madagascar Pochard. WWT has a long history of *ex situ* wildfowl breeding and became well known for averting the extinction of the Hawaiian Goose (or Nene) *Branta sandvicensis* through captive breeding and reintroduction as far back as the 1950s (Black 1995). In early 2009, the three organisations joined forces with the government of Madagascar's Ministère de L'Environnement, des Eaux et Forêts to develop a plan to pull the pochard back from the brink. Because of the very low population size and low survival of ducklings, a central aim of this plan was the development of a captive breeding centre in Madagascar, together with the fundraising and local capacity building needed to make this possible. In July 2009, a team including biologist Peter Cranswick and aviculturist Nigel Jarrett from WWT joined Young and his colleagues Felix Razafindrajao and Lance Woolaver in Madagascar to help local partners develop a detailed plan for setting up the breeding centre, and to assess any logistical problems associated with the collection and transport of eggs and the rearing of ducklings. During their visit to Red Lake they could find no more than 19 birds, of which only six were females. The low number of females, coupled with the fact that no ducklings had survived the 2008 breeding season, turned an urgent situation into a critical one. The partners decided that an emergency rescue plan was needed, and that rather than waiting until a breeding centre could be constructed in 2010, clutches should be taken in 2009, just a few months later.

Bringing forward the captive breeding strategy to avert the threat of extinction posed two very considerable logistical problems. First, access to the Red Lake involved travelling along 40km of dirt track in very poor condition, passable only with care in a 4×4 vehicle, and then only in the dry season. These were obviously less than ideal circumstances for transporting fragile eggs to a hatching and rearing facility. Second, no hatching and rearing facility yet existed! Instead, the team decided to take battery-operated incubators to the lakeside, find clutches and incubate and hatch eggs at the site, then transport the hours-old ducklings to a temporary rearing facility. Ducklings are far more robust than eggs, and very young ducklings survive without food and water for the first day or so of life by metabolising the egg yolk, which they absorb just before hatching. A hotel 90km but a tortuous eight hours drive from the Red Lake was found to act as a temporary rearing and holding facility, and the owners, who were sympathetic to the project's aims, agreed to make available a room for rearing the young birds and their grounds for housing fibre-glass ponds for the older birds. Temperature regulation during the early stages of the ducklings' life was to be managed by using heat lamps in an air-conditioned room at the hotel, and disease risk minimised by constant hygiene vigilance and daily care by experienced aviculturists. In mid-2009 it was agreed that an emergency rescue programme was feasible and the decision was taken to proceed.

No one doubted that the operation would be a challenge, but the team was soon to face unexpected problems. Staff at the lake monitored the behaviour of female pochards and estimated the onset of incubation, and hence the predicted date of hatching, of the first clutch that had been earmarked for captive rearing. This was the trigger for the UK aviculturists to begin. The incubators, bird food, fibreglass tanks and other equipment were sent ahead. Timing was critical as the team planned to spend a few days in Antananarivo (Tana), Madagascar's capital, to retrieve their equipment from customs, make final arrangements and source various other items needed. They would then travel to the hotel to set up the rearing facility before moving to the lake to ensure that the incubators were in place to receive and hatch the clutches before the ducklings were transported to the hotel. It was essential that the team was in position at the lake before the eggs hatched: if they missed this, the ducklings would leave the nest and there would be little chance of catching them subsequently. Accurate prediction of hatching date was therefore key to the success of the rescue programme.

As soon as news came through from the Red Lake in October 2009 that a female appeared to be incubating, the team calculated the probable hatching date and booked flights accordingly. Problems started when a violent electrical storm caused the plane to divert from Tana to Tanzania to refuel before returning to Nairobi. The team arrived in Madagascar two days later, and by then a number of its members had succumbed to the epidemic of swine influenza that was raging around the world. As they recovered, yet another problem arose with the closure of a major bridge on the road from Tana to the hotel where the ducklings were to be kept, causing further delays until

One of the first Madagascar Pochards to be hatched in captivity is weighed to assess its development (Martin Brown, WWT).

repairs were completed. Moreover, the equipment shipped earlier had been temporarily impounded by customs. Fortunately, the recovery team had had the foresight to carry a spare incubator in their luggage as a precaution, and they rapidly sourced a plastic tank that could be used for rearing the ducklings. All the time, the crucial hatching date was approaching. Thankfully, the bridge was repaired and the team arrived at the lake on the night before the eggs were predicted to hatch.

The next morning, the team waited at the lake for the arrival of the local mayor to observe the egg extraction. The local Malagasy villagers feel a strong level of ownership of their wildlife and are an integral part of the project, and the mayor was therefore a key observer who would relay events to the villagers. While waiting, the team walked out to a specially constructed raised platform that afforded a good view of birds on the lake. Within five minutes they watched in dismay as a passing Madagascar Harrier snatched what looked like a day-old Madagascar Pochard duckling from the water, then circled back and took another. It looked as though, after all obstacles the team had overcome, the eggs had already hatched and the team had arrived too late: the team's Critically Endangered pochard had been taken by a Vulnerable harrier.

Dispirited and exhausted, the team decided nevertheless to assess the state of any later clutches. Kassidi, the local Durrell field biologist based at the lake, had reported that two additional clutches had been laid, one with nine eggs and another with at least two eggs. On checking the nests, the team discovered that the clutch they had originally planned to take was still there, with several of its eggs already hatching, on the very day predicted; so three clutches existed. The ducklings taken by the harrier proved to be from an earlier, overlooked nest. The eggs from the target clutch were immediately moved into an incubator and, given the accuracy with which hatching date was predicted from Kassidi's field observations, the team called off their search for additional clutches in order to reduce disturbance.

Eight eggs hatched successfully in battery-operated incubators. The team had planned a convoy of two vehicles to transport the ducklings to their hotel accommodation, with the front vehicle scouting for large potholes and radioing back to warn the driver of the second vehicle containing the ducklings. However, a vehicle breakdown left the team and their precious cargo inching their way slowly to the hotel in one remaining vehicle with the ducklings in a cool-box on the front seat. On the way, the ducklings, among the rarest and most endangered animals on the planet, had their first swim and feed in a sandwich box filled with water.

During the next few weeks, the team managed to extract the additional two clutches and by December 2009, 23 Madagascar Pochard ducklings were being held, more than doubling the known world population. However, all was not plain sailing, as later that month the threat of local unrest forced a precautionary move of the birds to another temporary home 320km away at Durrell's turtle and tortoise breeding facility at Ampijoroa. Here, the ducklings grew into healthy yearlings, of which 16, fortunately, proved to be females. In 2010 the team searched for good sites to build a conservation breeding centre, but were slowed down by the many constraints of working in Madagascar at a time of political change. The site finally selected, Antsohihy, is the nearest large town to the lakes at Bemanevika. With a relatively reliable power supply and other services, good infrastructure and transport links, this was the logical site for an intensive propagation centre with a 'duckery' to incubate eggs, hatch and raise ducklings and aviaries to accommodate flocks of yearling, non-breeding and breeding pairs of ducks. In June 2011 a suitable building was found and refurbished to provide an incubation and rearing room, with ponds excavated and aviaries erected in the grounds. Based on the behaviour of the wild pochards, it was expected that the captive birds, now two years old and ready to breed but being held in temporary accommodation at Ampijoroa, could begin to lay as early as late summer, so the race was on to complete the aviaries and move the birds as soon as possible. While it was hoped that the birds would breed after their arrival at Antsohihy, they had other ideas, with a clutch laid in July and a burst of breeding activity in August. As conditions and equipment at Ampijoroa were far from ideal, birds and eggs were moved to the new facility at Antsohihy as soon as possible. On 1 September 2011, 11 eggs and the surviving 19 adult pochards were relocated to Antsohihy, and an egg from the first clutch hatched the next day; the project's first captive-bred duckling was fittingly named Voalohany, meaning 'first' in Malagasy. Adults released onto their new ponds were seen mating just two days after the move, a good indication of the suitability of the new facility, and in total 18 ducklings were produced from the first breeding season. During the 2012/13 breeding season the founder population was managed deliberately to produce 20 more eggs from seven pairs and by February 2013 all the eggs had hatched to produce healthy ducklings. Chick production was limited to 20 to ensure sufficient capacity in the facility to allow for the collection of a second batch of clutches from the wild population in 2013, to maximise genetic diversity in the captive stock. Meanwhile, the site is being expanded and aviaries will be built to house non-breeding adults and young birds prior to release.

Inevitably a wider programme of work will be needed before captive-raised Madagascar Pochards can be released to augment the wild population. One major obstacle is the lack of knowledge about the species' natural history, habitat requirements and historical distribution. To attempt to address the first two of these, a scientist was employed to coordinate an intensive research programme with participants from other partner organisations to gain a better understanding of the ecology and requirements of the species and investigate threats and possible causes underlying its decline. Initial results from research at the Red Lake and other lakes nearby suggest that the lakes are poor in insect food and that the ducklings may be dying of starvation. Although the wild birds hatched 58 chicks from 11 broods in 2011, all but one died before fledging. In 2012 the situation was slightly better with 100 ducklings produced from 20 broods, of which six fledged. Wild-born chicks birds showed severely delayed feather development and took longer to fledge compared to well fed chicks in captivity, and a wild duckling was found dead with an empty intestine and a body weight only half that of a similarly aged captive bird (A. Bamford, pers. comm.). Pochards are largely benthic feeders (i.e. they take food from the bottom of water bodies), and analysis of the soft, deep and loosely packed sediment from the bottom of the Red Lake found it to contain low invertebrate abundance, although fairly high diversity. Invertebrate density was far higher in the fringing vegetation. During their first two weeks of life, ducklings have been observed feeding by dabbling on the water surface around the reeds, before switching to the normal diving behaviour of adults as they became older. It is possible therefore that the ducklings can find sufficient food among the reeds but that the depth of the lake, which at around 3m is suitable for adults, may be too deep for growing ducklings to feed. The lake is steep sided and flat bottomed, which is not ideal for ducks. Adults can supplement their diet with plants and there are plenty of algae in the lake, whereas ducklings need the higher protein content of invertebrates. Invertebrate surveys were initially also undertaken at the three other lakes at Bemanevika, at three lakes to the east of the site and at Lac Alaotra, the species' former stronghold; a scarcity of invertebrates was a common feature. The three lakes east of Bemanevika also illustrated other potential problems such as deforestation, which can lead to excessive siltation of water bodies, and hunting of ducks.

The research programme helped to define the parameters that would need to be measured to assess the potential suitability of release sites and the team completed an exhaustive tour and survey of wetlands on Madagascar's central plateau from June to September 2012, looking for candidate sites. Surveys were restricted to the plateau area, as this is the origin of the majority of historic records of the species. Wetlands were identified using a range of methods including maps and satellite images to produce an inventory of wetland sites. The survey team visited 25 sites, at least one lake in each wetland area, to collect data on vegetation, depth, benthic invertebrates, sediment and water chemistry, and to talk to local communities. The results indicated that none of the visited sites away from Bemanevika appeared able to support Madagascar Pochards in their current state. A subsequent three-week expedition in November 2012 focused on the six most promising wetlands, with more detailed surveys of wildlife, vegetation, sediment and water quality, and collection of more detailed information about local communities and how they interact with their wetlands. Much wider stakeholder engagement is now being sought. All the sites identified as potential future release sites will require some restoration and have significant management issues associated with them. This next phase of the project will be challenging, but should provide, in addition to a Madagascar Pochard release site, more sustainably managed water catchments and wetlands that benefit local communities and other wildlife.

While it is believed to be endemic to the island of Madagascar, subfossil remains of an *Aythya* duck have been found on Réunion Island (Mourer-Chauviré *et al.* 1999), and these could represent rare Madagascar Pochard dispersal events, or the presence on Réunion of another closely related *Aythya* species (Young & Kear 2006). Within Madagascar, other than at Lake Alaotra, there are a few records from areas around Tana and elsewhere in the northern central plateau. These include the Lake Itasy area west of Tana in the 1930s (Lavauden 1937), a single record from Lake Ambohibao near Tana in 1970 (Salvan 1970, 1972), three birds collected from Maevatanana c.200km from Tana in 1915 (Benson *et al.* 1976, Wilmé 1994), a record from Antsirabe in 1930 (Rand 1936) and two birds at Ambadivato, 70km north of Alaotra in 1960 (Collar & Stuart 1985). Betsileo, the locality of the holotype, is an imprecise geographical area, but the Betsileo ethnic group is centred 300km south-west of Lake Alaotra (Wilmé 1994). Although the majority of historical records come from the Alaotra area, wetlands similar to the Alaotra basin were once widespread on the central plateau as far north as Bealanana, and the Madagascar Pochard may have occurred more widely throughout these wetlands, which today have all but disappeared.

THREATS TO THE WILD POPULATION

Although the causes of the Madagascar Pochard's precipitous population decline remain unclear, there are a number of candidate explanations, of which perhaps the most likely is habitat loss and degradation. The species appears to have been declining at Alaotra throughout the 1940s and 1950s, at a time when many of Madagascar's wetlands were being drained for agriculture, particularly rice. Large areas of Lake Alaotra's flood zone have been converted to cultivation and areas of marsh vegetation were regularly burnt around the lake, especially from September to November (Collar & Stuart 1985, Wilmé 1994), within what is now thought to be the species' breeding season. Vegetation burning during the dry season is now officially banned, but was widely practised and posed a major threat to the lake's wildlife. Papyrus burning was also undertaken, often by fisherman in an attempt to stop the spread of marshland vegetation caused by high levels of siltation (Young & Smith 1989). More recently, burning has enabled local people to collect the Asian Snakehead *Channa maculata*, a fish introduced in 1980 (Pidgeon 1996) which burrows into the underlying substrate during the dry season (Copsey *et al.* 2009). Many wetlands across Madagascar have been degraded through accumulation of sediment, as widespread deforestation of surrounding areas has resulted in soil erosion from water runoff. This is certainly true of Alaotra, where most of the surrounding hillsides have been deforested and the resulting siltation has considerably reduced water depth and with it, aquatic biodiversity (Wilmé 1994, Young & Kear 2006).

A second problem relates to the direct and indirect effects of exotic wildlife. The introduction of exotic plants and animals, especially fish, has almost certainly had an impact on water quality, food availability, vegetation structure and nesting habitat. Some of the introduced plants such as *Eichhornia crassipes* and *Salvinia* spp. have been associated with eutrophication (Wilmé 1994), and at least 28 species of fish have been introduced to Madagascan wetlands (Reinthal & Stiassny 1991). These include tilapia (Cichlidae), which feed primarily on plant material and invertebrates. Several tilapiine fish species were introduced to Madagascar in the 1950s, mainly to support commercial fishing, and these highly invasive species proliferated rapidly. Ducks in the genus *Aythya* generally feed on plant material, invertebrates and occasionally small fish (Kear 2005) and the Madagascar Pochard probably has a similar diet. It seems likely that tilapia have affected the pochard's potential food supply, and they are also considered responsible for dramatic declines in native fish species (Léveque 1997, Canonico *et al.* 2005). Predation on ducklings by introduced carnivorous fish, including Largemouth Bass *Micropterus salmoides*, apparently introduced to Alaotra in 1961 (Reinthal & Stiassny 1991, Pidgeon 1996), may have reduced productivity and introduced mammals such as rats could have increased nest predation (Collar & Stuart 1985, Pidgeon 1996).

It has also been suggested that hunting may have played a part in the decline (Collar & Stuart 1985, Morris & Hawkins 1998). Hunting is thought to be one of the reasons, along with hybridisation with Little Grebes *Tachybaptus ruficollis*, for the decline to extinction of the Alaotra Grebe *T. rufolavatus*. At Alaotra, commercial duck hunting, largely by fishermen driving and netting birds or killing moulting or sleeping birds, appears to have been intense in the past, particularly near rice fields when wildfowl were attracted to the ripening crops (Forbes-Watson & Turner 1973, Wilmé 1994).

The Red Lake is less than 3m deep and has not been particularly exploited by the local population; it possesses no fish, is unsuitable for rice cultivation and contains cold water. The lack of exploitation might have allowed Madagascar Pochards to cling on in this remote location. However, it is unclear whether Red Lake and surrounding lakes represent typical habitat for the species, and the results of recent research showing that the great majority of chicks starve suggest that the species is only just clinging on there. The limited historical records suggest the species preferred shallow freshwater lakes (the depth of Alaotra fluctuates seasonally from 2–4m, although today the depth is less than 1m in the dry season) and marshes with open water close to areas of dense vegetation (Langrand 1990, Wilmé 1994, Morris & Hawkins 1998). The Red Lake would seem to fit in terms of water depth and does have some stands of emergent vegetation, the habitat used exclusively by nesting pochard, although this is limited in extent.

Very little else is known of the ecology of the Madagascar Pochard. It appears to be sedentary, found singly or in pairs or trios (Edhem 1993), although there is one report of a flock of 20 birds from Alaotra in 1930 (Collar & Stuart 1985). It is not known to flock or to associate with other ducks (Kear 2005). Nesting at Red Lake takes place in dense papyrus stands at the lake edge, between May and January, and clutch sizes of six to nine eggs have been recorded. First broods were lost early in the three years when monitoring took place, but while the majority of birds laid second clutches in 2009 and 2012, this was curiously not the case in 2011. There is clearly still much to learn about the species. However, while many questions remain about the species' ecology, there are several reasons for optimism. Madagascar Pochards appear to be hardy and were bred in captivity before the 1940s, with captive collections spread across France, England and the Netherlands (Delacour 1959, Collar & Stuart 1985). Breeding took place at the Zoo de Clères, France, in May 1935 (Wilmé 1994) and Worcestershire in England (Young & Smith 1989), although the species disappeared from collections around the mid-1940s (Delacour 1959). Over the last 60 years, WWT has developed propagation methods for all *Aythya* species and the success seen with captive birds in Madagascar so far suggest that it may prove possible to produce enough birds to attempt trial releases to inform future conservation efforts. Also, the species still survives in the wild, and much has been learnt over the last few years from the detailed observations of birds at Red Lake and surrounding lakes.

Madagascar Harriers are extremely thinly distributed across Madagascar and numbers are declining (René de Roland *et al.* 2009). Their overall significance as a predator of young pochard ducklings is unclear, and it may be that predation in 2009 resulted from the destruction by fire of some of their normal feeding habitat that year. Indeed, observations in subsequent years suggested that they generally take few ducklings and that most ducklings disappear overnight, indicating a nocturnal predator. Half-starved ducklings would make easy pickings for any predator. Another possible predator of young Madagascar Pochards at Red Lake is a lone Nile Crocodile *Crocodylus niloticus*. It is unclear how this crocodile reached the lake, and whether it is present all year round, but in the apparent absence of fish, it is likely that its food will include waterbirds. Also, rats were suspected of taking eggs at several nests in 2007.

With the initial successes of the conservation breeding and research programmes, the Madagascar Pochard is one step closer to having a secure future. However a number of actions are needed to maximise the chances that a reintroduction of the species will be successful. Local community engagement is ongoing, and a wide range of outreach work is underway to raise the profile of the species and highlight the importance of its conservation and of sustainable wetland management. Asity, a Malagasy NGO and one of the project partners, has initiated community engagement and education work with local village associations in the Bemanevika area, and also with 3000 students from schools in 18 communes of the Bealanana district. The conservation breeding population is already well established and potential release sites have been identified. If all goes well, the next phase will involve the development with local communities and other stakeholders of sustainable livelihood practices and wetland management plans, possibly including habitat restoration, and trial releases of birds. The Madagascar Pochard is a classic example of a species for which adaptive management will be essential, with constant re-evaluation of the state of knowledge of its ecology and its responses to various conservation interventions. The final phase of its recovery will involve the establishment of self-sustaining populations in the wild, at enough sites and in sufficient numbers significantly to reduce its extinction risk. Close involvement of local communities will be essential if the species is to have a long-term future, and its recovery should benefit both local people and other wildlife.

The emergency conservation breeding programme is running in parallel with efforts to prevent the extinction of the small remaining wild population at Red Lake. The government of Madagascar has increased substantially its commitment to national conservation and is still identifying areas for protection, and the long process of gaining protected area status for Red Lake, initiated by TPF in 2007, is finally paying off. In early 2010, the first phase of a two-stage process was successfully completed, with temporary protection declared for 32,130ha of critical habitat,

A Madagascar Pochard at the conservation breeding facility established shortly after the species' rediscovery (Peter Cranswick, WWT).

including marshland and grassland and encompassing Red Lake, other nearby lakes and their surrounding forests. This probationary phase is required by law and is intended to test and hone the capacity of the local community associations to manage natural resource use and protect biodiversity. Provided the probationary period is navigated successfully, the site will be granted protection in perpetuity under a charter between government and the local communities, and the designated area would be then managed by the local community. This would not only help secure the future of the Madagascar Pochard, but also many other endemic and threatened species present in the area, including the Madagascar Serpent Eagle *Eutriorchis astur* (Endangered) and Madagascar Red Owl *Tyto soumagnei* (Vulnerable), two other species that were once feared by some possibly to be extinct until their rediscoveries in the eastern rainforest in 1988 and 1993 respectively.

Productive partnerships between the government, national and international NGOs and local people are essential to ensure that all interests are represented at Red Lake, within the captive breeding project and at future Madagascar Pochard reintroduction sites. Significant progress has been made so far and, if these partnerships can deliver their aims, the Madagascar Pochard may yet join the Black Robin *Petroica traversi*, Mauritius Kestrel *Falco punctatus* and many others on the list of species that were saved just in the nick of time.

Chapter 22
The lost and the found

Some species appear to straddle the dividing line between extreme rarity and extinction. Of the nearly 200 species listed in 2012 as Critically Endangered, 14 carry the extra proviso 'Possibly Extinct' (Butchart *et al.* 2006b), and others might merit this unfortunate caveat (Table 22.1). Several species have not been seen for decades; some of these may simply be awaiting rediscovery but others, like the Po'ouli *Melamprosops phaeosoma* (Chapter 14) are probably extinct. Yet every year one or two species that have not been seen for many years, sometimes centuries, are rediscovered, giving hope that no matter how long it has been since a species was last seen, it might still persist (Schaffers *et al.* 2011). This presents conservationists with a particular problem: in an uncertain and complex world, the distinction between extreme rarity and extinction cannot be treated as a clear divide but has to be regarded as a blurred uncertainty. This problem manifests itself in the allocation of resources: clearly, investing conservation's scant resources in looking for a species that is already extinct is wasteful, but balanced against that is the reality that not allocating time and money to a species on the brink of extinction simply because there is a perception that it is already lost may be wasteful of something beyond financial value. The key resource in the pursuit of these least-known species is knowledge: without the certainty of good information, there is barely an incentive even to begin the search, and in some cases bad information has been the worst disincentive possible.

DEAD OR ALIVE?

The history of the Cebu Flowerpecker *Dicaeum quadricolor* contains a stark warning about the problem of assuming a species to be gone forever. The flowerpecker, a forest-dwelling species, was believed to be extinct (King 1978–1979) because in 1959 its native Philippine island, Cebu, had been pronounced cleared of forest. This assertion, it later turned out, was made without reference either to sources concerning the island's protected areas or to the widely broadcast fact that the President of the Philippines himself had died in a plane crash in thick forest on the island just two years earlier (Collar 1998). Eventually, in 1992, Rob Timmins, a visiting birdwatcher (a great rarity in itself, given the presumption of the treelessness of Cebu), happened to reach a vantage point on the island from which he could make out a small patch of forest, decided to investigate, and by great good fortune, given the failure of many visitors following in his footsteps to see the bird, rediscovered the flowerpecker (Dutson *et al.* 1993). It turned out that not only was this forest adjacent to the site of the well-publicised plane crash but it was also within a national park established in the 1930s to protect a significant remaining tract of forest. The park, however, had never been adequately staffed, and by 1992 its few visitors (and even the official government documentation) believed it had been established as a memorial to the late lamented President Magsaysay. In the meantime, its forests, not believed to exist by outsiders and not known to contain anything of biological value to Cebuanos, had been cut back to practically nothing and the prospects for the flowerpecker's long-term survival had been profoundly compromised.

How things might have turned out if conservationists had known the true situation 20–30 years earlier is a matter for regretful speculation. The circumstance has been termed the Romeo Error (Collar 1998): Romeo's error is to assume that Juliet is dead, and this actually causes her to die. In conservation terms, premature assumption of extinction may divert efforts elsewhere at exactly the time the species is most in need of them. Fortunately, however, the great majority of other cases where birds have come back from the dead have not been haunted by such misfortune.

Table 22.1. *Species that are 'lost' and have a considerable chance of being extinct. CR = Critically Endangered, PE = Possibly Extinct, PEW = Possibly Extinct in the Wild. The seven species treated simply as CR in this list are included subjectively as belonging to the CR(PE) category.*

Species	Last seen	IUCN
Jamaican Petrel *Pterodroma caribbea*	1879	CR(PE)
Guadalupe Petrel *Oceanodroma macrodactyla*	1912	CR(PE)
New Caledonian Rail *Gallirallus lafresnayanus*	1890	CR
Samoan Moorhen *Gallinula pacifica*	1873	CR
Makira Moorhen *Gallinula silvestris*	1953	CR
Eskimo Curlew *Numenius borealis*	1981	CR(PE)
New Caledonian Lorikeet *Charmosyna diadema*†	1913	CR
Glaucous Macaw *Anodorhynchus glaucus*	(1951)‡	CR
Spix's Macaw *Cyanopsitta spixii*	2000	CR(PEW)
Jamaican Pauraque *Siphonorhis americana*	1860	CR(PE)
Turquoise-throated Puffleg *Eriocnemis godini*	1850*	CR(PE)
Imperial Woodpecker *Campephilus imperialis*	1956	CR(PE)
Ua Pou Monarch *Pomarea nigra*	1985	CR(PE)
Sangihe White-eye *Zosterops nehrkorni*	1999	CR
White-chested White-eye *Zosterops albogularis*	2000?	CR
Olomao *Myadestes lanaiensis*	1980	CR(PE)
Ou *Psittirostra psittacea*	1989	CR(PE)
Nukupuu *Hemignathus lucidus*	1996	CR(PE)
Oahu Alauahio *Paroreomyza maculata*	1985	CR(PE)
Po'ouli *Melamprosops phaeosoma*	2004	CR(PE)
Bachman's Warbler *Vermivora bachmanii*	1988	CR(PE)
Hooded Seedeater *Sporophila melanops*	1823	CR(PE)

* Only certain date (there may be later undated nineteenth century specimens)
† Already treated as extinct by King (1978–1979)
‡ The observation in this year open to question.

One of the most remarkable avian comeback stories took place on a tiny island some 2,000km north-east of Cebu half-a-century earlier. In 1945 the Japanese island of Torishima, way out in the north-west Pacific and the subject of more than a century of disputes between Japan and the USA, lay empty and desolate. This had less to do with the appalling ravages of human conflict, however, than with the appalling ravages of humans against nature. Torishima – 'Bird Island' – had been the largest and last breeding ground of the Short-tailed Albatross *Phoebastria albatrus*, and now the bird was gone. In the nineteenth century this distinctive species, largest of the three albatrosses that wander the northern Pacific, was extremely abundant. In 1892, when the demand for bird feathers (as much for down as decoration) was perhaps at its most intense around the world, the albatross colonies on Torishima and several other smaller islands were suddenly targeted, in an ornithological equivalent of a goldrush, as a major prize. In a 17-year period an estimated five million albatrosses were killed for their feathers. Numbers fell with dramatic speed: by 1929 only some 2,000 individuals were to be found on Torishima and by 1932 a few hundred. New laws to protect the birds were flouted: in 1933, in anticipation of proper enforcement, the poachers had a concerted drive to harvest as many feathers as they could (in other words, kill all the birds) before they were stopped (BirdLife International 2001). As a result, by 1945 Torishima was devoid of the birds from which it got its name, and the albatross was presumed to have gone forever (Austin 1949), a permanent victim of the unrestrained

The flightless Takahe Porphyrio hochstetteri *was rediscovered in a remote valley in Fiordland, South Island, New Zealand in 1948 and has since been translocated to a number of predator-free offshore islands, but remains listed as Endangered (Ray Wilson).*

greed that drove so many species to the brink during the fifty-year period when feathers of wild birds were a major international commodity. It was the horror of the feather trade that prompted the initiation of some of the world's first bird conservationist organisations including the RSPB, the foundation of which was laid in 1889 by a group of women in protest against the trade in wild bird feathers for the adornment of hats. Concern over the feather trade was not restricted to Europe: T. Gilbert Pearson, founder of the Audubon Society and of the International Council for Bird Preservation (later BirdLife International), was a staunch opponent of the trade. He estimated that France alone imported 50,000 tons of feathers (46 million kilos) between 1890 and 1929 (Pearson 1937).

But in 1951 a few Short-tailed Albatrosses were back on Torishima, and by 1955 there were 23 adults and three young, guarded with interest by the staff of the meteorological station set up on the island in 1947 (Hasegawa 1984). Surely no-one in the late 1940s could have dared to dream this might be possible, but in its showdown with extinction the albatross's exceptionally slow reproductive strategy, which put it at such a disadvantage when being caught and killed at the start of the century, had played a late trump card. Young albatrosses wander the oceans for several years without returning to their natal island. When they do come back, it is often simply to sit for just a few weeks, becoming familiar with the place, encountering other birds and beginning to form a pair-bond. It is a very slow process, and probably for well over a decade the few visitors to Torishima never noticed the short visits of the few prospecting youngsters. Today nearly 2,000 birds breed on Torishima and, unlike the great majority of other albatross species, the population is still rising.

Of course, there have other been cases where a presumption of extinction was plausible and reasonable in the light of the available evidence. The Takahe *Porphyrio hochstetteri* was known from just four specimens, all taken prior to 1898, until a tiny population was found in a then-unmapped valley on South Island, New Zealand, in 1948. The meat of the Bermuda Petrel or Cahow *Pterodroma cahow* sustained the first human colonists of Bermuda through the famine years that followed permanent settlement in 1612 and then became the subject of some of the earliest New World conservation legislation in 1616 and 1621. After the failure of this belated attempt to halt the decline in its numbers, the Cahow was presumed extinct for nearly three centuries, until a specimen that had been taken alive in 1906 was identified, a decade later, as the bird described in the early chronicles and given its scientific name. However, it took until 1951 for the all-important breeding site, without which nothing could be done for the species, to be discovered (Greenway 1958, Collar *et al.* 1992). Intensive conservation work involving close monitoring of breeding sites and the translocation of nearly-fledged chicks to artificial nest burrows on more secure islands has led to a substantial recovery in numbers to well over 100 mature individuals (Madeiros *et al.* 2012). Mark Twain's little quip, 'The reports of my death are greatly exaggerated', finds a happy echo in these stories, which have been repeated in various guises in more recent times. For example, the New Zealand Storm-petrel *Oceanites maorianus*, last found in 1850 and treated as extinct in 2000 (Brooks 2000), was photographed at sea in 2003; the New Caledonian Owlet-nightjar *Aegotheles savesi*, treated as extinct on the assumption that it had last been found in 1880 (King 1978–1979), was seen again in 1998; the Black Shama *Copsychus cebuensis*, treated as extinct in the 1970s (King 1978–1979) on the assumption that it had last been seen in 1956, is now known to be doing fairly well (BirdLife International 2001); and the São Tomé Grosbeak *Neospiza concolor* was rediscovered in 1991 after an absence of records for a century. Perhaps the most remarkable of these 'rediscoveries' are those of Gurney's Pitta *Pitta gurneyi*, for a time feared extinct but now known to survive in numbers in the thousands (Chapter 23), and of the Forest Owlet *Heteroglaux blewitti*, whose eventual relocation was hampered by a most bizarre case of fraud (Chapter 24). Over the last century or so, 'lost' bird species have been rediscovered at the rate of about one a year, and the rate of rediscovery has increased over time (Scheffers *et al.* 2011). The average number of years each rediscovered species went missing for is around 65 years.

PRESUMPTION *VS* PRECAUTION

Generally, conservationists tend to be optimistic about rediscovering 'lost' species, and the steady flow of seemingly unlikely rediscoveries supports this outlook. People who are deeply concerned for the survival of very poorly known species experience an inevitable tension between the hope that they survive, which leads them to resist listing them as extinct, and the fear that they may be doing very badly, which leads them to list them as more threatened than they actually might be. In general, of course, this pattern of behaviour is attributable to an entirely appropriate and sensible use of the precautionary principle. Nevertheless, the effect of not accepting a species as extinct may be to overpopulate the IUCN category Critically Endangered, and for this reason BirdLife International developed the qualification 'Possibly Extinct' (Butchart *et al.* 2006b). Table 22.1 lists the bird species in this subset, together with a number of others for which there can be comparatively little hope that they survive. The main effect of equating little information with likely endangerment is, of course, to overpopulate the entire IUCN Red List.

Evidence for these two effects is not hard to find, even before the formal establishment of the IUCN Red List and its categories. The history of bird conservation in the second half of the twentieth century is strewn with lazarine resurrections of species never actually listed as extinct but widely fretted over in the precautionary mind (Table 22.2). Conservation bodies and natural history museums, eager to enhance their profiles with the public, have always injected a sharp sense of wonder and delight into the press releases that cover these stories. The media gobble them up with enthusiasm, albeit not always with the seriousness they deserve: in 1984 a tabloid newspaper ran the story of Dick Watling's momentous rediscovery of the Fiji Petrel *Pterodroma macgillivrayi*, 129 years after the species was last seen, when a bird flew into his head one night on the island of Gau, under the headline: 'It's bird-brained Dick!'

A high proportion of these 'rediscoveries' could, of course, have been predicted. If a species is only known from one or two remote and rarely visited localities, for example, it might hardly be thought to count as a rediscovery when the rare visitor finds the species still in place. This is how the modest rediscoverers of the Silvery Woodpigeon *Columba argentina*, seen and photographed from a boat off the southern tip of Siberut island in the Mentawai Islands, Indonesia, in October 2008 (the first record since 1931), portrayed their encounter (Lee *et al.* 2009a). Indeed, with its myriad islands, Indonesia seems particularly suited to such stories. The Damar Flycatcher *Ficedula henrici* has the distinction – shared with very few other extant bird species – of not being seen by an ornithologist

Table 22.2. *Rediscovered species that, on balance, were perhaps unlikely to have become extinct, and for which intensive, species-specific action is probably not the highest priority. Almost all information in the table is derived from BirdLife online or published data sources. Other examples are discussed in the text. See p.11 for IUCN threat class abbreviations.*

Species	Last seen	Found	Years 'missing'	2012 IUCN threat class
Madagascar Serpent-eagle *Eutriorchis astur*	1930	1988	58	EN
Manipur Bush-quail *Perdicula manipurensis*	1932	2006	74	VU
Bruijn's Brush-turkey *Aepypodius bruijnii*	1938	2002	64	EN
Slender-billed Flufftail *Sarothrura watersi*	1930	1988	58	EN
Snoring Rail *Aramidopsis plateni*	1940	1980	40	VU
Invisible Rail *Habroptila wallacii*	1931	1981	50	VU
Austral Rail *Rallus antarcticus*	1959	1998	39	VU
Sakalava Rail *Amaurornis olivieri*	1962	1995	33	EN
Rufous-fronted Parakeet *Bolborhynchus ferrugineifrons*	1957	1985	28	VU
Seychelles Scops-owl *Otus insularis*	1880	1960	80	EN
Flores Scops-owl *Otus alfredi*	1896	1994	98	EN
Sulawesi Eared-nightjar *Eurostopodus diabolicus*	1931	1996	65	VU
Whitehead's Swiftlet *Collocalia whiteheadi*	1904	1993	89	DD
Royal Cinclodes *Cinclodes aricomae*	1931	1982	51	CR
White-browed Tit-spinetail *Leptasthenura xenothorax*	1915	1974	59	EN
Hoary-throated Spinetail *Synallaxis kollari*	1831	1956	125	CR
Orinoco Softtail *Thripophaga cherriei*	1899	1970	71	VU
Black-hooded Antwren *Formicivora erythronotos*	c.1870	1987	c. 117	EN
Rio Branco Antbird *Cercomacra carbonaria*	1831	1962	131	CR
White-masked Antbird *Pithys castaneus*	1937	2001	64	NT
Moustached Antpitta *Grallaria alleni*	1911	1971	60	VU
Brown-banded Antpitta *Grallaria milleri*	1942	1994	52	VU
Grey-winged Cotinga *Tijuca condita*	1942	1980	38	VU
Yellow-bellied Asity *Neodrepanis hypoxantha*	<1933	1988	>55	VU
Sooty Babbler *Stachyris herberti*	1920	1994	74	NT
Rusty-throated Wren-babbler *Spelaeornis badeigularis*	1947	2006	59	VU
Grey-crowned Crocias *Crocias langbianis*	1939	1994	55	EN
Large-billed Reed Warbler *Acrocephalus orinus*	1867	2006	139	DD
São Tomé Short-tail *Amaurocichla bocagii*	1928	1990	62	LC
Lompobatang Flycatcher *Ficedula bonthaina*	1931	1995	64	EN
Red-tailed Newtonia *Newtonia fanovanae*	1931	1989	58	VU
Yellow-throated Serin *Serinus flavigula*	1886	1989	103	EN
Sillem's Mountain-finch *Leucosticte sillemi*	1929	2012	83	DD
São Tomé Grosbeak *Neospiza concolor*†	1890	1991	101	CR
Golden-naped Weaver *Ploceus aureonucha*	1926	1986	60	EN
Banggai Crow *Corvus unicolor*	<1885	2007	>122	CR

† Treated as Extinct by King (1978–1979).

for the whole of the twentieth century, having been discovered in 1898 and only seen again in 2001, and the Black-chinned Monarch *Monarcha boanensis* was discovered in 1918 and next encountered in 1994. In both cases, the first and second dates, despite the lifetimes between them, simply represent the times of successive visits by an ornithologist to their tiny Indonesian islands, respectively Damar and Boano, and yet in both cases the new records were characterised as rediscoveries (Moeliker & Heij 1995, Shannaz 2001). So too was a recent encounter with the Lake Lufira Weaver *Ploceus ruweti*, found again in 2009 at the site of its original discovery in 1960 in the Democratic Republic of the Congo (Louette & Hasson 2008).

The danger is, of course, that these events suggest to the public and politicians that the world is a rosier place than it actually is. Worse, it can lead to accusations that conservation bodies have fallen down on their homework, and have been 'crying wolf' over the status of the species whose interests they are supposed to be serving. There is therefore considerable value attached to the proper and full documentation of threatened species, principally so that the most appropriate conservation response can be formulated based on the best available evidence (Collar 1996b). Unfortunately, in many cases the best available evidence is so limited that the conservation response is extremely difficult to decide: presumption cuts a deck of cards with precaution and, at another table, priority cuts a deck with price.

There are some very poorly known species that we can classify, crudely, according to probabilities determined by such factors as their range size, body size, level of crypsis, habitat selection, inherent vulnerability (for example, flightlessness), known threats and the number of failed recent searches for them. If there is a suite of species whose recent rediscovery could have been predicted with a moderate degree of confidence (Table 22.2), so there are those whose future rediscovery can also be predicted with similar cautious optimism (Table 22.3), owing mainly to evidence that their ranges are unlikely to be very restricted, their habitat is probably still fairly extensive, and their inherent vulnerability relatively low (particularly if they are continental rather than oceanic island species). As important is the issue of how easy it may be to encounter these species in the field. Birds in Table 22.3 include two owls, two nightjars, an antpitta and several other species that are extremely hard to detect in the field. All missing species are priorities, but these are perhaps less pressing ones, in that their conservation status would appear unlikely to be seriously compromised by their long absence from the attention of conservationists.

Table 22.3. Species that are 'lost' but probably extant and possibly not seriously at risk. See p.11 for IUCN threat class abbreviations.

Species	Last seen	IUCN threat class
Mayr's Forest-rail *Rallina mayri*	1966	DD
Manus Masked-owl *Tyto manusi*	<1914	VU
Congo Bay-owl *Phodilus prigoginei*	1996	EN
Itombwe Nightjar *Caprimulgus prigoginei*	1955	EN
Nechisar Nightjar *Caprimulgus solala*[*]	1990	VU
Schouteden's Swift *Schoutedenapus schoutedeni*	1972	VU
Coppery Thorntail *Discosura letitiae*	<1852	DD
Táchira Antpitta *Grallaria chthonia*	1956	CR
Black-lored Waxbill *Estrilda nigriloris*	1950	DD

* Publication of reported rediscovery in 2009 awaited; listed also in Table 22.6.

By contrast there are species which group together either side of the 'rediscovery' barrier either because their circumstances are known to be perilous (Table 22.4) or because of a reasonable expectation that if rediscovered, their circumstances will prove to be perilous (Table 22.5). The rediscoveries in Table 22.4 have been shown to have high levels of threat, and the great majority are Critically Endangered. The hoped-for rediscoveries in Table 22.5 have very plausible presumptions of threat associated with them, owing to various factors in various combinations, including small ranges, extensive fruitless searches, low levels of crypsis, and high levels of habitat loss and inherent vulnerability. These are the outstanding candidates for intensified emergency surveys and searches, redoubling the efforts that have so far been made on their behalf, a case in point being the last-ditch endeavour being put into the search for the Slender-billed Curlew *Numenius tenuirostris* in 2010 (Chapter 26). At a certain point, however, after resources have duly been spent without result, such efforts will have to be scaled back, and the resources redeployed. The species in question might then be transferred to another list where optimism no longer holds great sway, as with those in Table 22.1.

Table 22.4. *Species which when rediscovered proved to be genuinely very rare. Other examples are mentioned in the text. See p.11 for IUCN threat class abbreviations.*

Species	Last seen	Found	Years missing	2012 IUCN threat class
Madagascar Pochard *Aythya innotata*	1991	2006	15	CR
Fiji Petrel *Pseudobulweria macgillivrayi*	1855	1984	129	CR
New Zealand Storm-petrel *Oceanites maorianus*	1850	2003	153	CR
Chatham Island Taiko *Pterodroma magentae*	1867	1978	111	CR
Bermuda Petrel *Pterodroma cahow*	1621	1951•	330	EN
White-winged Guan *Penelope albipennis*	1877	1977	100	CR
Takahe *Porphyrio hochstetteri*	1898	1948	50	EN
Jerdon's Courser *Rhinoptilus bitorquatus* †	<1935	1986	>51	CR
Chinese Crested-tern *Sterna bernsteini*	1991*	2000	9	CR
Lear's Macaw *Anodorhynchus leari*	—*	1978	—	EN
Blue-throated Macaw *Ara glaucogularis*	1922*	1992	70	CR
Indigo-winged Parrot *Hapalopsittaca fuertesi*	1911	1989	78	CR
Sumatran Ground-cuckoo *Carpococcyx viridis* ‡	1916	1997	81	CR
Forest Owlet *Heteroglaux blewitti*	1884	1997	113	CR
Anjouan Scops-owl *Otus capnodes* ‡	1886	1992	106	CR
Honduran Emerald *Amazilia luciae*	1950	1988	38	EN
Black-breasted Puffleg *Eriocnemis nigrivestis*	1950	1980	30	CR
Recurve-billed Bushbird *Clytoctantes alixii*	1965	2004	39	EN
Stresemann's Bristlefront *Merulaxis stresemanni*	1945	1995	50	CR
Golden-crowned Manakin *Lepidothrix vilasboasi*	1957	2002	45	VU
Noisy Scrub-bird *Atrichornis clamosus*	1889	1961	72	EN
Niceforo's Wren *Thryothorus nicefori*	1945	1989	44	CR
Cerulean Paradise-flycatcher *Eutrichomyias rowleyi*	1873	1998**	125	CR
Cebu Flowerpecker *Dicaeum quadricolor* †	1906	1992	86	CR
Pale-headed Brush-finch *Atlapetes pallidiceps*	1969	1998	29	EN
Cone-billed Tanager *Conothraupis mesoleuca*	1938	2003	65	CR
Cherry-throated Tanager *Nemosia rourei*	1941	1998	57	CR
Gold-ringed Tanager *Bangsia aureocincta*	1946	1992	46	EN

*Dates of records from non-breeding areas or captivity (hence of little help to searchers).
† Treated as Extinct by King (1978–1979).
‡ These were long regarded as subspecies, so interest in relocating them may not have been great.
• 1951 was the year of discovery of the breeding grounds, 1906 the year of rediscovery of species.
** A sighting from 1978 is reported without comment by White & Bruce (1986).

Pale-headed Brush-finch Atlapetes pallidiceps *of Ecuador was not seen at all between 1969 and 1998, and is listed as Endangered (Jon Hornbuckle).*

The iconic Ivory-billed Woodpecker *Campephilus principalis* of the USA and Cuba stays on Table 22.5 as long as it remains, as for the time being, one of the most sought-after species on the planet. Once a moderately common bird, it declined in the face of forest clearance and heavy exploitation, although there are differing perspectives on which of these factors was the more decisive (Jackson 2006, Snyder 2007); the last generally accepted sighting in the USA was in 1948 and in Cuba in 1987 (Collar *et al.* 1992, Garrido & Kirkconnell 2000). Its placement in Table 22.5 takes no side in the recent controversy over whether the species was or was not rediscovered in Arkansas in 2004–2005, for the fact remains, on which all sides can agree, that the species needs to be rediscovered again if anything concrete is to be achieved for its conservation. The whole story has, however, been an object lesson in the evaluation and interpretation of evidence.

The evidence for the continued existence of this huge woodpecker came from two sources. First, reports of Ivory-bill-like woodpeckers in the Big Woods area of Arkansas in early 2004 led to a secret investigation during which a number of records were claimed and tracts of land acquired, and in April 2005 it was announced in one of the world's highest-ranking scientific journals, a measure of the seismic significance attached to the proclamation, that the species had conclusively been found alive there (Fitzpatrick *et al.* 2005). Testimony to its survival were some eyewitness reports, a number of tape-recordings of double-drums for which the species is known, and a split-second piece of blurry video footage of a bird flying away from behind a tree-trunk. Second, in a simultaneous development, the species was reported from the cypress swamps of the lower Choctawhatchee River in the Florida Panhandle, based on sightings and tape-recordings but, alas, no photographs except of 'bark scaling' and other foraging activities attributable to Ivory-bills (Hill *et al.* 2006).

The Arkansas reports, tape-recordings and video have all come in for reinterpretation (Jackson 2006, Sibley *et al.* 2006), and the Florida records, never substantiated, have not been repeated. Indeed, nothing has been seen of the species in the wake of these hugely publicised claims, and this is perhaps the single biggest cause to doubt that it does in fact still exist. Historical evidence and knowledge of related species indicate that this was a noisy and conspicuous bird, readily responding to the imitation of its double drum, but major team efforts have gone into the search, backed up by the deployment of hi-tech recording equipment to capture conclusive new evidence on camera, and all have so far failed. The researchers attribute this to the sheer size of the forests under investigation, and even the hardest-bitten unbeliever must still wish that their endeavours *will* eventually produce proof of sufficient quality to overturn all doubts. Nevertheless, with each passing year there is an uneasy crystallising consensus among the world's ornithologists that the Ivory-billed Woodpecker is not a Phoenix, and will not be rising again.

Table 22.5. Species needing rediscovery and probably immediate conservation intervention. See p.11 for IUCN threat class abbreviations.

Species	Last seen	2012 IUCN threat class
Himalayan Quail *Ophrysia superciliosa*	1876	CR
Crested Shelduck *Tadorna cristata*	1964	CR
Pink-headed Duck *Rhodonessa caryophyllacea*	1949	CR
Javanese Lapwing *Vanellus macropterus*	1939	CR
Slender-billed Curlew *Numenius tenuirostris*	2001	CR
Sulu Bleeding-heart *Gallicolumba menagei*	1891	CR
Thick-billed Ground-dove *Gallicolumba salamonis*[1]	1927	EX
Negros Fruit-dove *Ptilinopus arcanus*	1953	CR
Red-throated Lorikeet *Charmosyna amabilis*	2001	CR
Blue-fronted Lorikeet *Charmosyna toxopei*	1981	CR
Glaucous Macaw *Anodorhynchus glaucus*	1960	CR
Siao Scops-owl *Otus siaoensis*	1866	CR
Jamaican Pauraque *Siphonorhis americanus*	1860	CR
Bogotá Sunangel *Heliangelus zusii*	1909	DD
Ivory-billed Woodpecker *Campephilus principalis*	1987 †	CR
White-eyed River-martin *Eurychelidon sirintarae*	1978	CR
Semper's Warbler *Leucopeza semperi*	1961	CR
Pohnpei Starling *Aplonis pelzelni*	1995	CR

[1] Included here despite EX listing by BirdLife International, on grounds that (a) not all small islets within its general range may have been visited and (b) its situation is similar to that of Sulu Bleeding-heart.
† On Cuba; perhaps 2004 in USA (Fitzpatrick *et al.* 2005).

PROOF *VS* PROBABILITY

In becoming extinct, a species loses both its population and the range that its population occupied. Consequently, in attempting to measure declines towards extinction, the IUCN Red List criteria (IUCN 2001) allow assessments of the numerical and the spatial evidence not only in combination but also independently of each other, acknowledging that different kinds of species are more appropriately gauged by one measure rather than the other. Species declining for natural reasons often tend to contract towards the centres of their ranges. However, if the cause of these contractions is, as so often, a rising tide of human-driven habitat loss, it may well be that the range contracts in a directional manner, and that the last populations will persist in the more peripheral parts of the species' range, perhaps indeed in areas from which it has never been recorded (Channell & Lomolino 2000). Consequently, as a population declines and its range diminishes, the possibility of loss of human contact increases exponentially; and when a population becomes *really* small, so too do the chances of encountering any of its members. In 2009, as many as 118 bird species were classified under the IUCN criteria as having populations of fewer than 50 mature individuals, but for the great majority of these species this was simply informed guesswork, generated not by contact with them but by absence of contact.

The IUCN Red List criteria specify that a species should be entered into the Extinct category only 'when there is no reasonable doubt that the last individual has died', which in turn means 'only when exhaustive surveys… over a time frame appropriate to the taxon's life cycle and life form… in known and/or expected habitat, at appropriate times (diurnal, seasonal, annual), throughout its historical range have failed to record an individual' (IUCN 2001). This important formulation covers all the exits but, in reality, it asks for a level of scrutiny and comprehensiveness that is essentially undeliverable on any budget typically available to conservation bodies that are already hard-pressed with studying and securing those species that are known to survive. As the old saying goes, absence of evidence is not evidence of absence. It took years to reach the conclusion that the Aldabra Warbler *Nesillas aldabranus*, confined to an area of high dense scrub on one fragment of the atoll in the Indian Ocean from which it gets its name, was extinct. The area in question was just 50m deep and 9km in length, totalling less than half a square kilometre, although all records came from less than half this area and all but one record from just 10 hectares (Collar & Stuart 1985). However, despite possessing the smallest range of any bird species ever known (assuming that it occurs nowhere else: there is certainly nowhere else on Aldabra), it took at least four surveys, from 1968, when it was discovered, through to 1987, when five months were fruitlessly expended in its pursuit, before that point of 'no reasonable doubt' could be said to have been passed, and even then the verdict came in the form of a question (Roberts 1987). How in that case can extinction be demonstrated in a bird with a more usual range size, the Ivory-billed Woodpecker, for example?

In developing a model with which to examine the case of the Ivory-billed Woodpecker, researchers came to the conclusion that the search effort required in order to reach a high degree of certainty about a species' presence or absence becomes enormous once a population dips below ten individuals (Scott *et al.* 2008). Moreover, the surveys to which they refer are formally structured programmes of fieldwork involving either line transects, point counts or both, distributed over extended periods of time and extensive swathes of habitat: only then are the data amenable to statistical analysis. Given that within the Ivory-billed Woodpecker's range vast areas of potential habitat remain unsurveyed in the sense they indicate, they predict that 'hundreds of thousands of count periods or thousands of kilometres of transects' will be needed in order to furnish the data from which a conclusion can be reached on the likelihood of the bird's absence (whereas, of course, one sighting demonstrates its presence!). *Proof* of extinction in this case is simply not feasible, and the best that can be done is establish the highest degree of *probability* of extinction: in spite of the considerable search effort so far expended on the Ivory-bill, the verdict (for the USA, but doubtless equally applicable to Cuba) is that it is too little, but not yet too late (Scott *et al.* 2008).

The Aldabra Warbler had a range of less than 0.5km²; the Ivory-billed Woodpecker had a historical range in the USA of over 300,000km² (this excludes the range in Cuba), and it has proved extremely hard to demonstrate extinction in either of them. What possible hope can there be for achieving the level of statistical certainty of the type Scott and colleagues would find clinching for a giant and noisy woodpecker (in a country teeming with birdwatchers) for other species whose range states are significantly poorer in resources than the USA? A number of birds have defied rediscovery and, with it, reasonable doubt, and have gone down in recent years as extinct. They include the Bar-winged Rail *Nesoclopeus poecilopterus* (Fiji, last seen in 1973), Canary Islands Oystercatcher *Haematopus meadewaldoi* (1913), Thick-billed Ground-dove *Gallicolumba salamonis* (Solomon Islands, 1927), Choiseul Pigeon *Microgoura meekii* (Solomon Islands, 1904), Paradise Parrot *Psephotus pulcherrimus* (Australia, 1927) and Snail-eating Coua *Coua delalandei* (Madagascar, 1834), many of them inspiring last-gasp endeavours to see if they might, somehow, still survive. What characteristics do they show or share that might overcome the objections of those who require extensive, scientifically rigorous survey work before accepting they are extinct? Or how confidently can they be distinguished from some of the species in Table 22.1, still considered to have a slightly better chance of survival?

It is a very fine line. Two of them, at least, have had highly plausible explanations proposed for their disappearance. The Canary Islands Oystercatcher was simply out-competed by people for shellfish, and the species was discovered to science just as the last individuals were dying out (Hockey 1987). The Paradise Parrot was likewise starved of its primary grass-seed food by changes in fire regime and widespread heavy stocking within its range (Olsen 2007). Both, moreover, have repeatedly been searched for without success. In considering the others, however, things start to become a little less clear-cut. Thus a comparison of the circumstances of the Bar-winged Rail (listed as Extinct) and the New Caledonian Rail (listed by contrast as Critically Endangered; Table 22.1) reveals the following facts:

- The Bar-winged Rail is known from 12 nineteenth century specimens from Viti Levu (10,400km²) and Ovalau (100km²) in the Fiji group, and by sight records on Taveuni (435km²) in 1971 and Viti Levu in 1973; searches of mongoose-free Taveuni and Ovalau in 2002–2005 yielded no records, but two non-endemic rail species have disappeared from all three islands as a presumed consequence of predation by cats plus, on Viti Levu, mongooses.

- The New Caledonian Rail is known from 17 specimens taken on New Caledonia (19,100km²) in 1860–1890, and by unsubstantiated reports in 1960 and 1984; its closest relative fares badly in forest affected by pigs, and all forest on New Caledonia is affected by pigs, as well as rats and cats; it was not found in a major survey in 1998 and in 2004 local hunters reported they knew it but had not seen it since the 1980s.

BirdLife International treats one as dead and one as alive, but the line could scarcely be finer. Which was seen with certainty more recently? Which has several different islands on which to take refuge? Which occurs on an island that has not, apparently, been surveyed in the past 15 years? On the other hand, which has the larger range and therefore the greater chance of surviving in a pocket of habitat somewhere?

Very similar kinds of question can be asked of the Thick-billed Ground-dove (Extinct) and the Sulu Bleeding-heart *Gallicolumba menagei* (Critically Endangered):

- The Thick-billed Ground-dove is known from two specimens, one taken in 1882 on Makira (San Cristobal; 3,100km²), one in 1927 on Ramos (4km²), in the Solomon Islands; searches in the 1990s on Makira, which has introduced rats, pigs, cats and dogs, drew blank, as did a search on Ramos in 2004; the species 'may have been a tramp species of small islands'.

- The Sulu Bleeding-heart is known from two specimens, both taken in 1891 on Tawi-tawi (1,000km²) in the Philippines; there were two awareness campaigns in the 1990s and unconfirmed local reports in 1995; 'it might be a small-island specialist'.

In recent years the BirdLife Partner in the Philippines, the Haribon Foundation, has conducted searches for the Sulu Bleeding-heart, without success (Tabaranza *et al.* 2008), but both archipelagos in which the host islands sit are peppered with smaller islands. Have all these small islands been checked? If Makira is three times the size of Tawi-tawi, has it been surveyed as comprehensively? On the other hand, is it perhaps more likely that terrestrial pigeons in the Solomons (but not Tawi-tawi) evolved in the absence of ground predators and therefore are (or were) far more vulnerable to them when they arrived?

The Choiseul Pigeon, a bird so unusual in appearance that it was placed in its own genus, and whose loss is a cause of distress to all who know of it, provides strong corroborative support for the idea that terrestrial pigeons are particularly vulnerable (and therefore that the Thick-billed Ground-dove might better deserve its unfortunate classification as Extinct). It is one of a tiny number of species which only a single ornithologist has ever seen alive. In January 1904 the explorer A. S. Meek collected six specimens and an egg on the island of Choiseul and sent them to Walter Rothschild at Tring in the UK; this was the first and last encounter of a Western scientist with the species. A meticulous recent review of the evidence (Tennent 2009) comes down in favour of the presumption of extinction, taking the view that the bird's demise resulted from predation by cats brought to the island by missionaries. Rothschild's generic name *Microgoura* reflects the view that it was a small version of the huge, gorgeous ground-pigeons *Goura* that inhabit New Guinea, and which themselves evolved in the absence of carnivorous terrestrial mammals; despite the prefix *Micro-*, Meek's pigeon was a big bird that lived and even nested on the ground, characteristics that clearly indicate an evolutionary history devoid of encounters with animals with large sharp teeth. However, even for the Choiseul Pigeon there is also still a faint ray of hope, since Meek wrote to Rothschild in 1909: 'I should like to revisit the Solomons and collect on Malaita. I know the *Microgoura* pigeon occurs there, from the natives…' (Tennent 2009). Tennent himself has visited Malaita, another island in the southern Solomons of similar size to Choiseul, for entomological purposes, and states that 'even in the mid-1990s and early 21st century, [he] failed to venture far inland due to the reluctance or refusal of local guides to do so'. Apart from that, an earlier seeker after *Microgoura* spent two weeks on the island in 1968, probably in just one area, and did not find the bird. In the light of this information – Meek's report, the difficulty of travelling inland, the incomplete coverage of the island – Tennent's assumption of the species' extinction may be premature. Meek's letter to Rothschild has hitherto been unknown, and it is intriguing to speculate whether the shred of historical evidence it contains will be enough to cause a re-think on the classification of the Choiseul Pigeon as an extinct species.

A point of note here is the influence that unsubstantiated reports have on the way species are classified. Assessing the reliability of these reports – not just by local people, who might be politely trying to please the questioner, but also by officials, birdwatchers and expert witnesses of various types – is often impossible. The degree to which they might be genuine, erroneous or downright mischievous (as with certain claims about rare parrots) simply cannot be gauged, and the poor conservationist is left once again to make an appropriate use of the precautionary principle in a vacuum of information. 'Reports' keep our hopes for the Ivory-billed Woodpecker alive and are what kept, and in some minds continue to keep, the Snail-eating Coua on the conservation radar. This remarkable cuckoo, member of a genus endemic to Madagascar, is known from at least 13 specimens but the only certain locality for it is the long thin island of Nosy Boraha (Île Sainte-Marie) off the northern part of Madagascar's east coast. French naturalists living on Nosy Boraha in the 1830s mentioned its habit of consuming molluscs, for which, perhaps, its rather deep bill – markedly different from other members of the genus – was an adaptation. However, unsubstantiated reports scattered through the literature also placed the species on mainland Madagascar, just a few kilometres away at its closest point. An enigmatic plate in an old volume from 1876 actually mapped it in the eastern rainforests opposite Nosy Boraha, and in 1932 its survival there was averred by a 'very reliable native who knew exactly what bird was being referred to' (Collar & Stuart 1985). Careful investigations could substantiate none of these reports and possibilities, however, and pointed firmly to the conclusion that the coua was endemic to Nosy Boraha and had vanished with the island's forests (Goodman 1993). Even so, perhaps in part because the confinement of such a distinctive bird to such a slim little island so close to the mainland seems somehow implausible, some ornithologists still nurse the view that the hunt for the Snail-eating Coua has been called off too soon.

HISTORY AND MYSTERY

Almost all birds begin their taxonomic lives – their epistemological existences – as rarities. We know them from a few specimens and in most cases from a single locality, and this situation persists until new explorations bring fresh evidence of their occurrence elsewhere. Typically, over many decades of fieldwork, museums assemble specimens and journals publish records, so that in due course ranges can be postulated with reasonable degrees of confidence. The absence of records from explored areas contributes to the emerging picture. The tantalising possibility that the ranges of the Choiseul Pigeon and the Snail-eating Coua were (and perhaps still are) larger than known is only one aspect of this general process of hypothesis and verification. The patchwork nature of zoological exploration inevitably means that some species take a considerable time to emerge into the light of scientific day, even in this age of mass birdwatching and ecotourism. Inveterate skulkers in the historical undergrowth have included two birds from restricted parts of Brazil's devastated Atlantic Forest, the Fringe-backed Fire-eye *Pyriglena atra* (which was first found some time before 1825, then found again in 1913, and again only in 1968 and 1974, etc.), and the Slender Antbird *Rhopornis ardesiaca* (which was first found before 1831, then found again in 1928, and again only in 1974 and 1977, etc.). At least two species have actually had papers published announcing their rediscovery twice: Bruijn's Brush-turkey *Aepypodius bruijnii* (Meyer de Schauensee 1940, Mauro 2005) and the Yellow-green Bush-tanager *Chlorospingus flavovirens* (Griscom 1935, Hilty 1977).

Distributional uncertainty takes a particularly intriguing, and sometimes intensely vexing, twist in the cases of certain seabirds and birds in trade. The highly colonial behaviour of most seabird species packs them into very small areas when breeding, and while in many cases this makes them extremely conspicuous, it has also allowed colonies of certain species with apparently very low numbers and nocturnal habits to evade discovery. The result is a reversal of the pattern common to many terrestrial birds, which are typically most conspicuous on their breeding territories and least so away from them: these seabirds are known instead only from sightings made and specimens taken at sea, while nothing is known of the whereabouts of their nesting sites. Given that the historical rarity of a seabird is likely to be linked to problems on its breeding grounds, it is vital to find the areas in question as soon as possible; but the very remoteness of the places to investigate, small offshore islets or the forested or scree-strewn peaks of remote mountains, coupled with the costs of the endeavour and the uncertainty of success (owing to factors such as seasonality and nocturnal behaviour), means that many seabirds have taken or will yet take years to be pinned down to their breeding areas. In the case of the Magenta Petrel *Pterodroma magentae* of the Chatham Islands off New Zealand, 111 years (1867–1978) elapsed between the discovery of the species and the discovery of its breeding grounds (Crockett 1994). For the Fiji Petrel it took 129 years (1855–1984) (Watling & Lewanavanua 1985), Chinese Crested Tern *Sterna bernsteini* 139 years (1861–2000) (Liang *et al.* 2000) and Bermuda Petrel 330 or 45 years, depending on how one counts (it was thought extinct after 1621 until a specimen was found in 1906, but the breeding site was only discovered in 1951). Other seabirds, meanwhile, have been 'rediscovered', but only at sea: Beck's Petrel *Pseudobulweria becki* of Melanesia, known to science since 1928 and relocated in 2007 (Shirihai 2008) has yet to reveal its breeding grounds. The New Zealand Storm-petrel, known to science since 1850 but only rediscovered in 2003 (Saville *et al.* 2003), managed to evade all efforts to find its breeding grounds until early in 2013, when birds caught at sea and fitted with tiny electronic transmitters were finally tracked to their breeding grounds on an island just 50km from the city of Auckland.

Birds in trade have presented analogous challenges. Prime among them is Lear's Macaw *Anodorhynchus leari* (Endangered), named for the great English eccentric Edward Lear. In 1832 Lear published his first book, *Illustrations of the family of the Psittacidæ, or parrots*, including in it a beautiful illustration of what he (and everyone else at London Zoo) thought was a Hyacinth Macaw *A. hyacinthinus*. Twenty-four years later the engraving caught the attention of Prince Bonaparte, nephew of the once Emperor of France, who realised that it did not show a Hyacinth but a species new to science. However, nobody knew exactly where the bird Lear portrayed had originated, although in the century following Bonaparte's description a good number of living birds came into public and private collections in larger consignments of true Hyacinths shipped from Brazil. The great French aviculturist and explorer Jean Delacour, one of the co-founders with Gilbert Pearson of the International Council for Bird Preservation, possessed as many as seven birds in the late 1930s (Collar *et al.* 1992). Around 1950, a Brazilian ornithologist found a captive Lear's Macaw in Pernambuco state, and successive expeditions into the

Chinese Crested Tern Sterna bernsteini *was rediscovered in 2000, and is listed as Critically Endangered largely because its eggs are taken for food (Liao Pen-shing).*

The New Zealand Storm-petrel Oceanites maorianus *was not seen between 1850 and its rediscovery at sea in 2003; its breeding grounds were not found until 2013 (Ray Wilson).*

dry interior of the north-east of Brazil eventually narrowed down the options until, in December 1978, Helmut Sick and two students made the first contact by ornithologists with birds in the wild, near the Raso da Catarina in north-eastern Bahia (Sick *et al.* 1979). It is sobering, however, to think that were it not for trade Lear's Macaw could conceivably have remained undiscovered to this day.

Curiously, two of the world's three other all-blue macaws, the Glaucous Macaw *A. glaucus* (listed as Critically Endangered, but not seen since the 1960s) and Spix's Macaw *Cyanopsitta spixii* (Extinct in the Wild), had broadly similar histories to Lear's, both being known in Europe from small numbers of captive birds imported over many decades, always from unknown origins. Unlike Lear's, however, there were known localities for both species in South America. In the case of Spix's Macaw a single, moderately certain place, the type-locality, existed. For the Glaucous Macaw, which was described in 1816 from an account by a missionary written some years earlier, the construction of a putative area of origin was far more exacting, since everyone who had actually recorded the bird in the wild did so in near-complete ignorance of what they were seeing. It was only their published descriptions that allowed researchers, sometimes a century later, to work out that the birds in question were Glaucous Macaws. Sad to say, however, by the time these localities were revisited none of them held any birds, and of course with Spix's Macaw the return to the one known site was almost as depressing (Chapter 20). Another macaw, however, the Blue-throated Macaw *Ara glaucogularis* (Critically Endangered), followed a pattern midway between Glaucous and Lear's: several records of specimens, reports in the literature dating back to 1805 and, above all, birds in trade (sometimes in quite high volume) finally led researchers to the discovery of a wild population in 1992 (Jordan & Munn 1993).

Such was the trade in bird feathers as fashion items in the nineteenth century that certain taxonomists, including Walter Rothschild, would ask dealers to keep an eye out for unusual skins in markets, and several new species of bird-of-paradise were described as a consequence, only later being discovered in the wild by explorers. (The pattern is almost universal: economic exploitation first, zoological exploration second.) The most notable of Rothschild's feather-trade species, because the gap between discovery and rediscovery was longest, involved the Golden-fronted Bowerbird *Amblyornis flavifrons*, acquired from a plume dealer in 1895 but found in the wild in the Foya Mountains of Indonesian New Guinea only in 1981 (Diamond 1982). The most *notorious* of Rothschild's feather-trade species was his Intermediate Parakeet *Psittacula intermedia*, which he also described in 1895 from a number of skins bought from a dealer. The name he gave it acknowledged that in plumage it sat

239

MACROCERCUS HYACINTHINUS.

Hyacinthine Macaw.

Edward Lear's 1832 painting of what he thought was a Hyacinth Macaw, later identified by the nephew of Napoleon Bonaparte as a new species and named Lear's Macaw.

midway between two other species from India, but he stoutly resisted the implication that it was a hybrid. While subsequent taxonomic judgement dithered over its status, live birds occasionally appeared in private hands to fuel the belief that the species was out there somewhere, waiting to be discovered. Eventually, however, a breeder was found who had produced 'Intermediates' by crossing the two other species, and a detailed analysis of Rothschild's specimens confirmed, over a hundred years later, that all of them were hybrid in origin (Rasmussen & Collar 1999a). Precisely the same double exercise, incidentally, resulted in the taxonomic funeral of the Imperial Pheasant *Lophura imperialis*, known from specimens taken alive in Vietnam in the 1920s by Jean Delacour and long claimed to be a good (and Critically Endangered) species (Hennache *et al.* 2003).

Taxonomic conundrums like the Intermediate Parakeet used to be commoner than they are today. The past 30 years or more have witnessed a steady reduction in the number of forms of uncertain taxonomic status, typically known from a single specimen. Some have been shown to be valid (White-masked Antbird *Pithys castanea*, Rusty-throated Wren-babbler *Spelaornis badeigularis*, Cherry-throated Tanager *Nemosia rourei*, Cone-billed Tanager *Conothraupis mesoleuca*), others invalid, notably through the endeavours of Gary Graves scrutinising the hummingbirds (and publishing no fewer than 16 papers on the subject under the generic title 'Diagnoses of hybrid hummingbirds' between 1996 and 2006), but also others such as the Argus Bare-eye *Phlegopsis barringeri* (Graves 1992) and the Bulo Burti Boubou *Laniarius liberatus* (Nguembock *et al.* 2008). Some of the ones that remain either to be rediscovered or rejected are listed in Table 22.6.

An interesting recent case of validation involved the Large-billed Reed Warbler *Acrocephalus orinus*, originally described by Allan Hume in 1869 on the basis of a single specimen collected in the Sutlej Valley in northern India in November 1867. So like other reed warblers was this bird, apart from its rather long bill, that it was soon largely forgotten. Ali & Ripley (1968-1998) doubted its validity as a full species and thought it probably a form of Great Reed Warbler *A. stentoreus*, and it was left out of *Threatened birds of Asia* (BirdLife International 2001). Shortly afterwards, however, genetic analysis proved Hume right (Bensch & Pearson 2002) and within four years, in March 2006, Phil Round, rediscoverer of Gurney's Pitta twenty years earlier, extricated the first living specimen of *orinus* from a mist-net in Thailand (Round & Kennerley 2007, Round *et al.* 2007). This was hardly the most expected of places for a migratory bird from the Indian subcontinent to appear, but as if to make a point the very same individual turned up his nets two years later, shortly to be followed by a second individual (Nimnuan & Round 2008). This seemed to open the floodgates: researchers found another ten specimens misidentified as other species in various museums in the UK and USA, their label data providing clear evidence of a breeding distribution in southern Central Asia and a migration route along the Himalayas to South-East Asia (Svensson *et al.* 2008), and in June 2008 birds were found breeding in riverine scrub in easternmost Afghanistan (Timmins *et al.* 2009). Scarcely can a species have been lost for so long (139 years: Table 22.2) and then so comprehensively rediscovered!

Table 22.6. Species known only from one or two specimens and with no field observations. Their taxonomic status is sometimes queried. In the 'Species' column, the number in parentheses shows the number of specimens, and a question mark indicates published uncertainty over taxonomic status. In the 'Lost' column, the year is also often that when the taxon was found, as many taxa here are known from one specimen. See p.11 for IUCN threat class abbreviations.

Species	Lost	IUCN threat status	Key recent reference
Bryan's Shearwater *Puffinus bryani* (2) ?	1963	not listed	Pyle *et al.* 2011
Double-banded Argus *Argusianus bipunctatus* (1) ?	1871	EX	Davison & McGowan 2009
Siau Scops-owl *Otus siaoensis* (1)	1866	CR	BirdLife International 2001
Cayenne Nightjar *Caprimulgus maculosus* (1) ?	1917	DD	Cleere & Ingels 2004
Vaurie's Nightjar *Caprimulgus centralasicus* (1) ?	1929	DD	Leader 2009
Nechisar Nightjar *Caprimulgus solala* (1) ?	1990	VU	Safford *et al.* 1997
Bogotá Sunangel *Heliangelus zusii* (1)	<1909	DD	Kirchman *et al.* 2010
White-chested Tinkerbird *Pogoniulus makawai* (1) ?	1964	DD	Collar & Fishpool 2006
Rio de Janeiro Antwren *Myrmotherula fluminensis* (1) ?	1982	CR	Zimmer & Isler 2003
Red Sea Swallow *Hirundo perdita* (1)	1984	DD	Turner 2004
Liberian Greenbul *Phyllastrephus leucolepis* (1) ?	1984	CR	Fishpool & Tobias 2005
Blue-wattled Bulbul *Pycnonotus nieuwenhuisi* (2) ?	1937	DD	Fishpool & Tobias 2005
Blüntschli's Vanga *Hypositta perdita* (2) ?	1931	DD	Yamagishi & Nakamura 2009
Black-browed Babbler *Malacocincla perspicillata* (1)	c.1845	DD	Collar & Robson 2007
Hooded Seedeater *Sporophila melanops* (1)	1823	CR(PE)	Collar *et al.* 1992

On the other hand, taxonomic revisions of species limits occasionally throw up unexpected new enigmas. The distinctiveness of the Sumatran Ground-cuckoo *Carpococcyx viridis* had been completely overlooked, owing to the scarcity of museum specimens and the obscurity of texts accounting for them, but when it was finally recognised as being a different species from the Bornean Ground-cuckoo *C. radiatus* it emerged that the bird, first found in

1878, had not been seen since 1916 (Collar & Long 1996), and there was great uncertainty about whether or not it still survived. The answer came from an unexpected source early in the new millenium, when ornithologists examined photographs of various birds taken by mammalogists who had 'caught' them incidentally in camera traps set for mammals in Bukit Barisan National Park back in 1997. One of these birds was the missing ground-cuckoo (Zetra *et al.* 2002), and the species, listed as Critically Endangered, has now become one of the top targets for any birdwatching visit to Sumatra. In South America a slightly different scenario has played out: there the rediscovery in 2006 of the lowland Brazilian 'subspecies' *obrieni* (known from one specimen taken in 1926) of the rare Andean Rufous-headed Woodpecker *Celeus spectabilis* led to its recognition as a full species, Kaempfer's Woodpecker *C. obrieni*, and this too has immediately been classified as Critically Endangered (Santos & Vasconcelos 2007). Not all such taxonomic revisions result in rediscovery. A specimen of a small shearwater that was collected on Midway Atoll, Hawaii in 1963 and thought at the time to be a Little Shearwater *Puffinus assimilis* was re-examined over 40 years later and found to be a new species (Pyle *et al.* 2011). Given the name Bryan's Shearwater *Puffinus bryani*, this is North America's 'newest' species yet it awaits rediscovery and could conceivably already be extinct.

THE PROBABILITIES OF
EXTINCTION AND REDISCOVERY

It is extremely difficult to be certain of a species' extinction or to judge which 'lost' species are most likely to be rediscovered (Diamond 1987); each case seems so different that it is difficult to find generalities. However, statistical methods have been developed to attempt to quantify the likelihood that a given species is extinct, to estimate the likely date it succumbed, and to assess the likely validity of a recent record (Solow & Roberts 2003). The methods are based on two rather straightforward principles; first that the more recently a species has been sighted or collected, the greater are the chances that it is still alive today, second that changes in the frequency with which it is reported are likely to be related to changes in its status. Thus if a species was recorded every year for a hundred years, and then not at all for thirty years, there are better grounds for thinking it is extinct than if it had been recorded only once each decade for a hundred years, because then we would be less worried about a gap of several years without a sighting. The method presented by Solow and Roberts formularised the relationship between sighting records and extinction in an attempt to put dates on extinction events. For example, they used their method to estimate the actual date of the extinction of the Dodo *Raphus cucullatus*. The last living Dodo was seen in 1662 (Cheke & Hume 2008), some 24 years after the penultimate sighting. However the pattern of previous sightings suggested that extinction did not occur in the same year as the last sighting, but perhaps 30 years later, around 1690 (Roberts & Solow 2003, Solow & Roberts 2003). The same formula has been used as a test of the validity of recent claims of sightings of species such as Ivory-billed Woodpecker or Eskimo Curlew *Numenius borealis*, the results suggesting that recent reports did not match historical patterns and so were unlikely to be reliable, thus reinforcing the view that these species are already extinct (Roberts *et al.* 2010). Clearly, however, the accuracy of predictions based upon such methods cannot be assessed and they cannot be used as justification for writing off a species.

These methods might not help us in many of the cases discussed above. The problem is that the missing species are distributed very unevenly around the planet, resulting in an equally uneven search effort over time. Indeed, for many species there *is* no search effort. Many of these most elusive species have been highlighted as challenges for the more adventurous birdwatchers (Butchart *et al.* 2005a, Tobias *et al.* 2006, Butchart 2007). However, although the rediscovery of a species may be a moment of great triumph and publicity, it almost inevitably comes with a considerable price-tag and with a discouraging calculation of the odds. If nobody has gone in search of the Black-browed Babbler *Malacocincla perspicillata*, a bird that has not been seen since the collection of the type specimen somewhere between 1843 and 1848 (BirdLife International 2001), this is doubtless because nobody is very sure where to look for it: it was originally described – by Prince Bonaparte again – from Java, but a fuller reconsideration of its collector's itinerary in Indonesia led to the view that it was probably taken somewhere in south-east Borneo, perhaps near Martapura. If fewer people than expected have recently gone in search of the Himalayan Quail *Ophrysia superciliosa*, not seen since 1876 (BirdLife International 2001), it may be because the mustering of the necessary number of highly trained dogs to help flush the birds represents too complex and costly a challenge.

Then there is the disincentive supplied by the sheer inexplicability of the pattern of records shown by certain species, and by the too-high degree of randomness of one's chances of an encounter. What hope is there of ever encountering a Night Parrot *Pezoporus occidentalis* in the never-ending plains of central Australia? Sightings there certainly are (Garnett *et al.* 1993, Davis & Metcalf 2008), but at a frequency no higher than encounters with corpses resulting from collisions with motor vehicles and barbed-wire fences in very remote areas (Boles *et al.* 1994, McDougall *et al.* 2009). Where do we begin to look for that supremely bizarre creature the White-eyed River-martin *Eurochelidon sirintarae*, which was discovered at a large lake in central Thailand in 1968 – clearly not its usual habitat – and which soon afterwards disappeared again (Tobias 2000, BirdLife International 2001)? How much more effort, after three seasons of searching in 2003–2005, can realistically be put into the quest for the gloriously enigmatic Pink-headed Duck *Rhodonessa caryophyllacea*, last reliably recorded alive in 1949 but perhaps glimpsed on 1 December 2004 at Nawng Kwin in Kachin State, Burma (Tordoff *et al.* 2008)? Why is the Isabela Oriole *Oriolus isabellae* so patchily distributed in the forests of Luzon in the Philippines, to the point where no-one now knows where to look for it? What is it that makes the Blue-eyed Ground-dove *Columbina cyanopis* of south-central Brazil so extraordinarily rare? This is a bird hardly anyone alive has ever seen, for reasons that remain utterly unclear.

We know the answer in the case of another excruciatingly rare Brazilian pigeon, the Purple-winged Ground-dove *Claravis godefrida*: it is a bamboo specialist, and only ever seems to put in an appearance, albeit very rarely, at periodic bamboo flowering events in the more southerly reaches of the Atlantic Forest. In this case there may be a parallel with the Passenger Pigeon *Ectopistes migratorius*, which Enrique Bucher elegantly demonstrated to have been as much the victim of habitat loss as overexploitation (Bucher 1992): the Passenger Pigeon tracked masting events whose scale and location varied from year to year and were therefore patchy in both space and time, so that with increasing clearance and fragmentation of the eastern forests of the USA the spatial and temporal patchiness of the food resource simply became too extreme, and the last birds essentially starved to death. Fragmentation of the Atlantic Forest may steadily be doing the same thing for the Purple-winged Ground-dove but, when the species is so desperately elusive outside flowering events, the depressing question for conservation biologists is simply: how can it ever be studied in sufficient depth to enable us to determine the means of saving it from extinction?

The same question haunts many species whose appearances (and disappearances) are equally quixotic, surely indicating that we are indeed dealing with birds whose numbers are so low that their difficulty of detection represents a major obstacle to conservation. Even if they are found again, as everyone hopes they will be, birds such as the Kinglet Calyptura *Calyptura cristata*, Sangihe White-eye *Zosterops nehrkorni* and Cozumel Thrasher *Toxostoma guttatum*, all of them Critically Endangered, pose challenges to conservation to which we may never be able to rise, however strong the response and good the intention, simply because we do not have the information to guide our management decisions with sufficient accuracy. We can preserve their forest habitats, but if their rarity has causes other than habitat loss then the determination of its solution is likely to be as elusive as the birds themselves.

Nevertheless, as Emily Dickinson wrote, 'Hope is the thing with feathers', and over the past 30 years or so the number of avian 'rediscoveries', however one defines them, conveys several important messages, as does the small stream of discoveries of entirely new species of bird that the world continues to witness. In the past few years several new species have come to light, including the Vanikoro White-eye *Zosterops gibbsi* in the Solomon Islands (Dutson 2008), Limestone Leaf Warbler *Phylloscopus calciatilis* in Laos and Vietnam (Alström *et al.* 2010), Bare-faced Bulbul *Pycnonotus hualon*, a highly distinctive and apparently fairly common species in shrubby limestone karst forest of central Laos (Woxvold *et al.* 2009) and the 'Spectacled Flowerpecker', as yet without a scientific name, at Danum Valley's Borneo Rainforest Lodge (Edwards *et al.* 2009). The last is particularly noteworthy, since it was seen and photographed at one of South-East Asia's most visited birding sites and close to the Royal Society's research station, where ground-breaking work on tropical bird ecology has been done for many years. The number of rediscoveries made each year appears to be increasing, and many are of species that have not been recorded since their original description (Scheffers *et al.* 2011). The messages that these discoveries and in particular the rediscoveries hold for us are all positive, but with a distinct catch. They are telling us that we still have a chance, that the planet is still that bit richer in resources than perhaps we had imagined. But the most crucial lesson these birds are teaching us is not to allow ourselves to assume that we can afford to relax: this chance to save them will be the last.

Chapter 23
Gurney's Pitta *Pitta gurneyi*
ENDANGERED

Stunningly beautiful, extremely elusive and once considered perhaps the planet's rarest bird species, Gurney's Pitta has achieved an almost iconic status in the world of international bird conservation. It also has a particularly chequered history: first feared near-extinct, then rediscovered, then nearly lost again, before being found in unexpectedly large numbers in a country in which it had not been seen for nearly a century. The story of Gurney's Pitta gives hope that many other 'lost' species are still out there to be rediscovered.

The pittas, a family of around 30 species confined to Asia, Africa and Australasia, are celebrated for their startlingly gorgeous colours and patterns. Their closest relatives are the equally beautiful broadbills (Eurylaimidae), also of Africa and Asia, and the peculiar asities (Philepittidae) of Madagascar. This cluster of families is taxonomically interesting as it comprises the only Old World representatives of the suboscine passerines, a group of songbirds that dominate much of the New World. Suboscines lack the more complex syrinx of the oscine songbirds, so their vocalisations are simple by songbird standards, composed of short, stereotyped sounds. Despite their colours, pittas are generally shy and unobtrusive denizens of the tropical forest floor, but a few, such as Blue-winged Pitta *P. moluccensis* are more vocal and conspicuous and are able to occupy heavily modified habitats. The Eared Pitta *P. phayrei* is peculiar in lacking the dazzling colours that give the family the vernacular name 'jewel thrushes', but Gurney's Pitta exhibits all the characteristics of the group that so inspire birdwatchers, not least its highly secretive nature. Expert researchers in Thailand working on the species on a daily basis rarely see it even in the best areas, relying instead on its distinctive 'lillip' call to detect the presence of birds, yet because of the long fight to save it, Gurney's Pitta is one of the best known members of this enigmatic family.

Gurney's Pitta was first collected by William Ruxton Davison in southern Burma in 1875. Davison was working at the time as private curator and bird collector for the extraordinary Allan Octavian Hume (1829–1912),

Found, lost, found, nearly lost again and then found again in numbers that astounded the conservation world. Gurney's Pitta remains an iconic species in bird conservation and illustrates the ability with which even the most charismatic birds can 'disappear'. The top bird is a male, the lower a female (Nick Bray, Birdseekers).

among whose many notable achievements during a long personal crusade of social reform was the founding of the Indian National Congress, which eventually led India to independence in 1947 (Collar & Prŷs-Jones 2012). The manuscript notes of Hume's great handbook on Indian birds, the work of a quarter of a century, disappeared in unexplained circumstances just prior to its completion, their loss causing Hume to retire prematurely from ornithology and depriving the world of a classic study of the region's birds.

POPULATION DECLINE AND 'EXTINCTION'

Over the next fifty years or so, Gurney's Pitta was collected at a good number of sites in the narrow neck of the Thai-Burmese peninsula. Davison himself found it in Thailand for the first time either later in 1875 or during his next visit in 1877. The American explorer Dr W. L. Abbott, who had a booby and a babbler named for him, found it in southernmost Burma, and various collectors – English, French, Danish and Swedish – took specimens across the border in southern Thailand. The Singapore-based team of H. C. Robinson and C. Boden Kloss, working for the Raffles Museum, were particularly productive in the years 1909–1919 in exploring southernmost Thailand and establishing a clearer understanding the range of the species. From 1930 onwards, however, reports of the species rapidly and somewhat inexplicably dried up. In fact between 1930 and 1986 there were just two, one involving four birds (including the first known nestling) obtained in 1936 by Thai collectors on a mountain called Khao Phanom Bencha (Meyer de Schauensee 1946), and one involving a single specimen taken in 1952 and never published or even known about until 1986 (Collar *et al.* 1986). To all intents and purposes, the species had vanished.

By 1986, no living ornithologist appeared ever to have seen Gurney's Pitta in the wild, and there were reports that the area from which it was recorded had lost much of its forest habitat (King 1978–1979). A new edition of the international Red List – the Red Data Book – for birds was then under way, with Africa just finished (Collar & Stuart 1985) and the Americas about to begin (Collar *et al.* 1992). In an attempt to compensate for the neglect

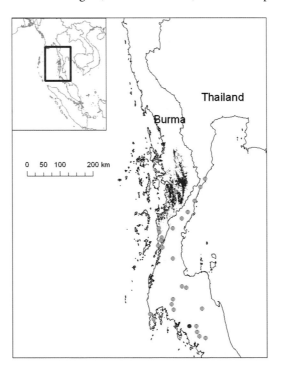

Approximate distribution of Gurney's Pitta in Burma (in red), derived from predictive modelling. The green dots indicate pre-1952 records (from BirdLife International 2001), and the red dot indicates the tiny surviving population in Thailand at Khao Nor Chuchi.

of Asia under this schedule, Gurney's Pitta, one of the most mysterious and exquisite Asian species, was selected for detailed investigation, and all the specimen evidence and information in the literature was assembled. This was sent to Philip Round, a British ornithologist resident in Bangkok since the early 1980s. Round had already been looking for Gurney's Pitta without success, and the compilation of evidence largely confirmed his suspicion that the species was confined to the lowlands of the Thai-Burmese isthmus. This was an important insight, because lowland primary forest, in Thailand at any rate, had almost entirely vanished, and what little remained was disappearing at terrifying speed. For example, in September 1984, after much searching, Round and his colleague Uthai Treesucon had found a tract of lowland forest some 150km² in extent within the range of the pitta, but by the time they returned in June 1985, equipped for a full survey, the entire area had been cleared for cucumber fields (Collar *et al.* 1986).

There was, however, one piece of evidence that did not fit the theory that the species was confined to lowlands. The 1936 records from Khao Phanom Bencha were from between 600m and 1,060m (Meyer de Schauensee 1946), far higher than any of the other specimen localities. This found an echo in the map of Gurney's Pitta provided in a book on the threatened wildlife of Thailand (Bain & Humphrey 1982) on which large areas were marked as part of the species' range. Careful examination showed that the book had simply marked in all remaining forested areas within the latitudinal limits of the pitta, on the assumption that, as a forest bird, it would be present throughout them. However, Round and Treesucon had spent many days in upland forests in peninsular Thailand and had never recorded the species. Could Khao Phanom Bencha somehow be different? Or might the records there suggest that more work in the uplands was needed? Round doubted either of these things. Meyer de Schauensee (1946) contained a number of other records of known lowland specialist bird species from unprecedented elevations. It was far more likely – and Round grew increasingly convinced of this as he read more of the Thai ornithological literature – that Meyer de Schauensee's collectors, in a curious parallel with the fraud by which Richard Meinertzhagen misled the searchers for the Forest Owlet *Heteroglaux blewitti* (another Hume species; Chapter 24), had simply decided to ignore his request to go up the mountain in the uncomfortable wet season. In order to pretend otherwise they appear to have marked a good number of specimens taken at the foot of the mountain with false altitudinal data (Round & Treesucon 1986, Round 1995).

Of particular concern was the uncertainty over whether the population in Burma, last recorded in 1914, still survived, or indeed whether it even bred there. Davison had reported that the species appeared there around mid-February, remained scarce until mid-April, became more numerous until the end of May and then disappeared with the onset of the monsoon (Hume & Davison 1878). From August to November the species was seemingly absent from southern Burma, and Davison speculated that it then migrated to breed 'probably to Siam [Thailand] or into the higher portions of the hills dividing Siam from Tenasserim [the southernmost region of Burma]'. If the species really was migratory, and if the bird were strictly a lowland species, then the disappearance of birds in Burma could be explained by the deforestation in Thailand. The urgency of finding and protecting a population in Thailand thus became critical. The biggest problem was simply finding an area of lowland forest.

TWO REDISCOVERIES AND THEIR CONSEQUENCES

In the mid-1980s it was not certain whether the species still survived, but occasional sightings of birds in markets and petshops in Bangkok since the 1950s were encouraging. Birds had even been imported to Britain and the USA in the 1960s and 1970s, and even bred, although this only emerged much later (BirdLife International 2001). The one keeper who did publish his observations described how his male escaped one winter night in the early 1970s and was last seen fluttering off across the rooftops of London (Vince 1980), an astonishing thing to contemplate in retrospect. In 1978 the head of Wildlife Fund Thailand actually kept a male as a pet. Philip Round photographed the bird in 1982 and made a tape recording of its call just days before it died in June 1985. The bird's death raised fears that this might have been the Thai equivalent of Martha, the last Passenger Pigeon *Ectopistes migratorius*, which died in Cincinnati Zoo in September 1914. Round continued to scour the bird markets of Bangkok in the hope of finding birds for sale, but without success.

The breakthrough came in May 1986, when Bruce Miller, a keen pitta breeder in the US who had helped with the compilation of the data on Gurney's, was called by a California dealer just back from Bangkok where he had seen a pair of birds in the back room of a petshop. The news was telexed to Round, who immediately resumed his visits to every likely shop until he struck lucky. The birds proved to have come from a dealer in an area that Round had already earmarked for investigation as one of the very last that might hold the species. Round took a train down to see the dealer, who told him that a trapper had brought in two birds that month. Round gleaned what information he could and identified the source as a patch of forest under a low mountain called Khao Nor Chuchi. There, after four tense days, he and Treesucon became the first living ornithologists to see Gurney's Pitta in the wild (Round & Treesucon 1986).

The rediscovery of this charismatic species sent a shiver of excitement around the ornithological world. Acting with commendable swiftness, the Government of Thailand gazetted part of the site as the Khao Phra–Bang Khram Non-hunting Area (NHA), and the International Council for Bird Preservation (ICBP, now BirdLife International), scraping together the living costs of a group of hastily assembled volunteers, established a small project to protect the site's remaining forest patches and to survey other areas. These surveys duly turned up tiny populations at three other sites, all of which were to be lost very shortly after they were found (Gretton *et al.* 1993), providing the most poignant proof that the rediscovery had taken place just in time. However, the species was very far from saved. Forest protection within the Khao Phra–Bang Khram NHA was not always strictly enforced and, worse, the protected area had excluded 30km² of key habitat (BirdLife International 2001). As a result of this omission, the initial small conservation project had to be developed into a full-blown programme in order to attempt to reconcile conservation with the disparate interests of the local communities. Many people living in the area were recent immigrants from other parts of Thailand who, although already owning lands in other parts of the country, were seeking to increase their wealth by clearing forest for growing cash crops.

The programme ran almost throughout the 1990s, but faced innumerable difficulties. Increasing numbers of immigrants eager to clear land for oil palm saw the project as a threat to their ambitions and some of those occupying land illegally launched a disinformation campaign against the programme. In addition, there was genuine confusion over land tenure rights, failure to enforce laws on logging and clearing, and a frequent change of leadership of the protected area, problems that continue to this day. Consequently, where at the time of rediscovery in 1986 the forests at Khao Nor Chuchi held some 44–45 pairs, by 2000, when Danish government backing for the work was withdrawn in the face of insufficient commitment from the Thai authorities, the forests had been so badly reduced that only some 12 pairs were estimated to remain (BirdLife International 2001). Even so, without these efforts the entire Thai population (which conservationists were at that stage compelled to consider as perhaps the entire world population) would surely have been wiped out. Time had been bought, and while the Thai and UK BirdLife partners planned a new initiative, the Oriental Bird Club (OBC), a volunteer-run non-profit organisation with a mission to help conserve Asian birds, stepped in with some timely small-scale interventions and support, petitioning the Thai government and senior officials. OBC helped by paying for training courses for forest rangers, supplying them with better equipment, liaising with key forest department personnel, establishing and supporting a tree nursery and starting a public debate in the Thai press about the importance of saving the species (Sykes 2000, Sykes *et al.* 2000, Browne *et al.* 2008).

While this bridging work was going on, a new conservation programme was being developed, this time a collaborative venture led by a Thai national NGO and BirdLife Partner, the Bird Conservation Society of Thailand (BCST) and their colleagues in the Thai government, supported by the RSPB in the UK and funded by the UK government's Darwin Initiative. The central element of this new initiative was to step up efforts to build consensus between local people, government agencies and conservation NGOs, and the first action was to hold a workshop that brought together representatives of all interests to agree the problems and identify solutions in the form of an action plan. The process was given weight by the presence of a Privy Councillor, representing the interests of the greatly revered royal family of Thailand.

Since then, there have been a number of very positive collaborations between NGOs, government and local communities, groups which previously had not always shared a common view and frequently misunderstood each other. Forest protection has been strengthened and the rate of loss of forest within the range of Gurney's Pitta greatly

Brian and Margaret Sykes of the Oriental Bird Club, long-time supporters of efforts to save the tiny Thai population of Gurney's Pitta, stand outside a tree nursery established with funding from the UK Government to help reforestation efforts at the site (Paul F. Donald, RSPB).

reduced (Donald *et al.* 2009). The Forest Restoration Research Unit (FORRU) of Chiang Mai University, again with funding from the Darwin Initiative, is undertaking forest restoration and runs the tree nursery, producing tens of thousands of saplings of local forest species each year for replanting and rehabilitating cleared areas. As a result of these efforts, the tiny population of Gurney's Pitta in Thailand has been stabilised at between 15 and 20 pairs (Donald *et al.* 2009).

As the finishing touches were being put to the new action plan in Thailand, news broke of the species' rediscovery in Burma. Round's work at Khao Nor Chuchi in the 1990s had led him to believe that Davison's view of the migratory behaviour of the species was mistaken: all that happens is that the birds become so unobtrusive when not breeding that they seem to disappear for months on end, so a search in Burma remained a priority (Round 1995). In May 2003, after several attempts to reach the politically unstable and strictly controlled region of Tenasserim in the south of the country, an expedition led by Jonathan Eames of BirdLife International and Htin Hla of the Biodiversity and Nature Conservation Association (BANCA), the BirdLife representative in Burma, heard and saw the first wild Gurney's Pittas recorded in that country since 1914, and subsequently recorded birds at a number of other widely separated sites (Eames *et al.* 2005). Clearly, the species was more widespread in southern Burma than it was in Thailand, and more numerous – perhaps as many as 8,500 pairs – than anyone had dared to hope (Eames *et al.* 2005). As a result of this rediscovery, the species was downlisted from Critically Endangered to Endangered in 2008, a reassessment that conservationists working to save the species in the 1990s could never have dreamed of. However, it was not until further expeditions were undertaken in 2007 and 2008, when the bird was recorded at sites up to 40km north of any previous records and at higher altitudes, that it became apparent just how widespread and numerous Gurney's Pitta is in Burma. Statistical models suggested a total range size in Burma of 3,200–5,800 km^2 and a population of some 20,000 pairs (Donald *et al.* 2009). Even this might be an underestimate, since surveys conducted throughout southern Burma by BANCA each year from 2010 to 2012 further increased the altitudinal and latitudinal range of records, and included sightings of the species up to 80km further north and at higher altitudes than it was ever recorded historically (BANCA, unpubl. data). What was for many years thought to have been one of the world's rarest birds was clearly far more widespread and numerous than anyone could have hoped.

SNAKES AND OIL PALMS

The research that supported conservation efforts in both Thailand and Burma not only generated new information on the pitta's population and distribution but also on its ecology and reproduction. In Thailand, researchers found over 20 nests and, if the nest was active, immediately mounted round-the-clock observations, not only to collect information on the breeding ecology of the species but also to protect the nest from predators. And predators there clearly were, in abundance. As with many tropical forest birds, the most significant despoilers of nests were snakes (Weatherhead & Blouin-Demers 2004). Snakes repeatedly attacked Gurney's Pitta nests in Thailand, almost always at night, and were it not for the quick actions of the dedicated researchers, all the nests under intensive observation would have been predated. At four guarded nests, a total of eleven snake attacks were intercepted, any of which would have led to the complete failure of the nest (Donald *et al.* 2009). Thanks to the vigilance of the Thai researchers, these few nests successfully fledged young, but the majority of unguarded nests must surely fail.

All the snakes observed were cat snakes of the genus *Boiga*, the genus that has invaded Guam and devastated the native wildlife there (Chapter 10). These reptiles tend to be common and widespread predators of human-modified landscapes, and it is entirely possible that those attacking Gurney's Pitta nests in southern Thailand enter forest fragments from the surrounding plantations. The high rates of nest predation, which may explain why the great majority of Gurney's Pitta nests are built in palms or rattans armed with fearsome spines, are offset to a certain

Surveying Gurney's Pitta in Burma is difficult because of the lack of roads and tracks, so researchers often have to wade along rivers to get into the forest (Paul F. Donald, RSPB).

Lowland forest clearance in southern Burma to plant oil palm. Oil palm represents a major threat to lowland forest birds in many parts of the tropics, and is a particular threat to Gurney's Pitta (Paul F. Donald, RSPB).

extent by the longevity of the birds, for tropical birds live far longer than their ecological equivalents in temperate zones (Johnston *et al.* 1997). However, the population in Thailand may be ageing and this might pose a threat to its survival. The remaining forest is now scattered and over half the birds are found in tiny forest patches isolated in a sea of plantations. The next challenges for conservationists working to save the Thai population are to reconnect isolated patches of forest by restoring or replanting the land between and to establish and agree a system of land tenure with other landusers in the area.

From the outset, it was recognised that the Gurney's Pittas in southern Thailand were associated not with the small patches of remaining lowland primary forest, but with scrubby, regenerating forest. This preference for regenerating secondary undergrowth was also observed in Burma, where forests inhabited by Gurney's Pitta have a structure more characteristic of disturbed or degraded forest, with a higher density of saplings, bamboo and smaller trees than forests where birds were not recorded (Donald *et al.* 2009). It therefore appears that Gurney's Pitta is a species of disturbed or naturally regenerating forest with abundant undergrowth, rather than of pristine climax forest, and that anecdotal reports of the species occurring in abandoned and overgrown oil palm plantations (Collar *et al.* 1986, Round & Treesucon 1986) might be reliable. The preference for disturbed forest might represent ecological separation from the more widespread and common Banded Pitta *Pitta guajana*, the other lowland forest pitta within the range of Gurney's in Thailand.

The ability of the species to tolerate, or even benefit from, some degree of forest disturbance raises hopes that recovery in Thailand might take place earlier than expected. Forest regeneration in wet tropical regions can be exceptionally fast, and early results from forest restoration work by FORRU in the area suggest that habitat suitable for Gurney's Pitta could be created on recently cleared sites within as little as ten years. The heavy and often illegal logging of certain trees in southern Burma, largely to feed the timber market in China, might not have as devastating an effect on Gurney's Pitta as previously thought, although it is likely to represent a severe threat to other species of the forests of the Thai/Burmese peninsula reliant on large trees in pristine forest, such as the Plain-pouched Hornbill *Aceros subruficollis*. A long-held view that more recent research is now challenging is that

Gurney's Pitta is strictly a lowland species, largely confined to flat forests below 100m in altitude. While the great majority of historical records and most recent records in Thailand do indeed come from lower altitudes, recent surveys in Burma have shown no decline in pitta numbers up to at least 230m, and there is evidence that the species may occur at higher altitudes in the politically sensitive border forests between Burma and Thailand (Donald *et al.* 2009), and the range of the species in Burma overlaps almost exactly with the only part of that country that is suitable for oil palm production. The absence of the Banded Pitta from these forests may allow Gurney's to exploit a wider range of altitudes than it can in Thailand.

The strongest economic driver of forest loss within the range of Gurney's Pitta in both Thailand and Burma is the spread of oil palm plantations. Practically all the forest loss within the range of Gurney's Pitta since its rediscovery in Thailand has been caused by the establishment of oil palm and rubber plantations (Donald *et al.* 2009). As part of the recovery project for Gurney's Pitta in southern Thailand, researchers undertook an assessment of the changes in bird communities that occur when forests are replaced by plantations (Aratrakorn *et al.* 2006). Within the range of Gurney's Pitta, conversion of forest to oil palm results in the loss of practically all forest species, their places taken by a small number of common and widespread generalists (Aratrakorn *et al.* 2006). Only one of the sixteen globally threatened or Near Threatened species recorded in forest patches was also recorded in the plantations, and that only once. Some groups of forest birds, such as woodpeckers, barbets and trogons, were entirely absent from plantations. While Gurney's Pitta can survive in degraded forest and perhaps even in long-abandoned oil palm plantations, it certainly cannot survive in intensively managed oil palm cultivation, which lacks any undergrowth. Similarly devastating losses have been documented in research on a wide range of animal and plant groups in forests and plantations around the world (Donald 2004, Fitzherbert *et al.* 2008, Danielsen *et al.* 2009).

The threat posed by oil palm to the world's tropical forests is likely to increase significantly as governments in the developed world aim to reduce emissions from fossil fuel use through increases in biofuels (Fitzherbert *et al.* 2008). Legal mechanisms and incentives are in place in many countries, particularly in the EU, to reach targets to replace fossil fuels with biofuels. Increases in the areas of oil palm and other bioenergy crops will have severe impacts on biodiversity where they result in loss of forests and other natural habitats. Although there is now plenty of evidence to show that the loss of tropical forests to plantation crops has catastrophic impacts on forest species, there are growing signs that the biofuels produced by such crops will not only fail in their aim of reducing global climate change but might actually contribute to it. This is because the loss of carbon to the atmosphere that occurs when forests are cut will probably greatly outweigh the carbon-saving benefits of biofuels: a recent assessment suggested that it would take a century or more before the greenhouse gases released by burning tropical forests to establish oil palm plantations would be compensated for by the biofuel produced (Danielsen *et al.* 2009). If the original forests were on peaty soils, as are many in the tropics, the break-even point would not be reached for 800 years.

Although they have had devastating consequences for the people of Burma, years of often brutal political repression by successive military dictatorships and resulting internal conflicts may explain why southern Burma retains large areas of lowland Sundaic forest, a habitat that has largely been lost elsewhere (Lambert & Collar 2002). Recent strides towards full democracy should be welcomed by all, but the country's return to the international fold will lead to an inevitable scramble by the world's largest oil palm companies to secure great swathes of lowland forest in southern Burma for conversion to plantations. A newly elected civil government would be hard-pressed to turn down the much-needed foreign capital that this will bring. The contagion of oil palm plantations that has so devastated southern Thailand's forests would inevitably follow. Unless ongoing efforts to designate national parks in southern Burma in advance of such destruction are successful, Gurney's Pitta might well one day return to the list of Critically Endangered species. It is for this reason that the continuing efforts to save the population in Thailand which, although small, is at least protected, remain important.

Chapter 24
Forest Owlet *Heteroglaux blewitti*
CRITICALLY ENDANGERED

'If this is a dream, it's the longest, most vivid, and best one I've ever had, and I don't want to wake up.' So said Dr Pamela C. Rasmussen to her companions on the morning of 25 November 1997, some hours after she and her fellow Americans Ben F. King and David F. Abbott had rediscovered the Forest Owlet in a small patch of woodland near Shahada, in Maharashtra, western India (King & Rasmussen 1998). Certainly there may be as much adrenalin and euphoria released by the rediscovery of a long-lost species as there is by the discovery of a new one, although the latter is probably every zoologist's private dream. Those lucky enough to find a new species are going to be elated and encouraged, but the event is likely to come without warning and therefore involve no preceding tension. Searchers after 'lost' species, by contrast, live in knowledge and hope, and their quest is racked by conflicting feelings of anticipation and anxiety rendered all the more acute as time runs out on their endeavours (Weidensaul 2002). Rasmussen's two-week expedition was already in its final days: she had been on the trail of the Forest Owlet, one way and another, for over a year and it had been one of the most tortuous trails that any searcher after lost species had ever had to take.

The Forest Owlet was described in 1873 by the great naturalist and administrative genius Allan O. Hume, who was well known within the British colonial establishment in the Indian subcontinent for his extraordinary ornithological expertise. On 14 December 1872, at 'Busnah-Phooljan' (Basna) in what is now Madhya Pradesh, one of his multitude of contacts, F. R. Blewitt, shot an owl he did not recognise and sent it to Hume, who recognised it as not just a new species for science but a new genus as well: he called it *Heteroglaux blewitti*. In February 1877 at 'Karial' (Khariar), a site some 100km to the south in present-day Orissa, an Irishman called Valentine Ball collected a second specimen and wrote about it in Hume's journal *Stray Feathers*, although he kept the skin for himself. Then in 1880 and 1881 James Davidson, clearly a keen and competent observer, collected three specimens at Taloda

The Forest Owlet was not seen for well over a century before its eventual rediscovery in 1997; efforts to relocate the species were hampered by a remarkable case of specimen fraud (Nikhil Devasar).

and Shahada in western Khandesh, some 900km to the west of the two previous localities; he thought they were Spotted Owlets *Athene brama* when he sent them to Hume, and wrote about them in a paper he prepared for *Stray Feathers* (Davidson 1882):

> All were shot in the heavy jungle below the Satpuras [a range of hills that runs west–east across India at around 22°N], and all were shot late in the morning sitting alone on the tops of thin trees. This being such an extraordinary position for *brama* I shot the birds to make sure, but not having specimens of *brama* to compare them with, stupidly took for granted they were only *brama*. They are not uncommon in this dense jungle, and I have repeatedly seen others sitting on exposed trees.

This was more or less all the information that ever came to light about the species not just for the rest of the nineteenth century but most of the following century too. The Forest Owlet simply disappeared. There were a few reports, and one or two claims of photographic evidence, but none of them bore scrutiny (Rasmussen & Collar 1999b).

Interest in the species only really resurfaced when Salim Ali and Dillon Ripley were preparing their monumental ten-volume handbook of subcontinental birds (Ali & Ripley 1968–1998). The third volume, published in 1969, dealt with the owls, and included their account of the Forest Owlet:

> Very like Spotted Owlet but larger though with shorter wings… Rare but apparently extending all along the Satpura mountain trend for over 1100km from Surat Dangs and W. Khandesh to eastern Madhya Pradesh and the Sambalpur area in Orissa. Since first described in 1873 less than a dozen specimens have been collected, the latest in October 1914 at Mandvi on Tapti river (21°16'N, 73°22'E), c.220km north of Bombay, by Meinertzhagen.

The authority of Ali and Ripley's great work remains unassailable but while the Forest Owlet is superficially similar to the Spotted Owlet, a more careful examination of the skins, some of which were then in London, New York and Harvard, would perhaps have shown them the errors of placing the bird in *Athene*, of naming it the 'Forest Spotted Owlet' and of describing it simply as a 'forest representative of the Spotted Owlet'. The most original item in their account of the species, however, was the publication of the record by Meinertzhagen. This was the first time it had surfaced in its by then 55-year history, but it was soon to have a significant impact on the history, study and conservation of the species.

Ali and Ripley, doyens of Indian ornithology and men of enormous distinction and influence, continued to ponder the fate of the Forest Owlet throughout the 1970s and into the 1980s. In 1975–1976 they made various attempts to rediscover the species, visiting forests near Blewitt's and Ball's localities and playing tapes of owls into the evening darkness in one year, doing the same again at Melghat Tiger Reserve (where the species was later to be discovered) the next, and finally despatching S. A. Hussain to Mandvi, Meinertzhagen's site, for a three-day search in April 1976 (Ripley 1976). Not giving up, Ripley then borrowed five specimens of *blewitti* and compared them to ones of *brama*, in order to obtain a better sequence of diagnostic characters than had appeared in the *Handbook*. In his descriptive evaluation he picked out the largely unspotted crown, a reduced and barely visible hind-collar, little if any spotting on back and scapulars, bolder white tail-stripes, a 'noticeable' dark transverse throat-bar (Hume thought this highly important), a well-defined continuous breast-band and a clear white central belly-patch, but the key he proposed to amend the *Handbook* entry did not register all these points, and the sketched illustration he commissioned continued to suggest the two owls were barely separable. This was clearly how Ali interpreted the new information (Ali 1978): in reproducing the sketch, he described the two species as 'almost identical' and 'so exceedingly similar in appearance… as to be easily confusable in the field, and casually even in the hand', and thus he concluded: 'the only leading clue remains the habitat preference of the two co-occurring species – *blewitti* in dense jungle, *brama* open country, cultivation and human habitations'.

While Ali encouraged the search for the Forest Owlet, with so little to go on by way of identification features it is perhaps hardly surprising that nothing appears to have been ventured. At any rate, there was no further news of the species, and a decade after writing his 'reconsideration' Ripley expressed the opinion that the bird was 'already extinct' (Clark & Mikkola 1989). After a second decade had almost passed, however, he was to make a decision that would happily lead him to revise his opinion. Having secured a considerable US government grant for the purpose of preparing a field guide to the birds of the Indian subcontinent, a work that would serve as a summation of his long involvement with the region, he needed to appoint someone who combined strong museum affinities, fine birding ability and a deep interest in the Indian avifauna, and he selected Pamela Rasmussen for the task.

THE CASE OF THE DISAPPEARING REPUTATION

Rasmussen's first task in preparing her guide (Rasmussen & Anderton 2005) was, inevitably, to produce a list of the species recorded in the region. It very soon became apparent that no fewer than 16 taxa were included in the subcontinent's avifauna on the sole evidence of Richard Meinertzhagen (1878–1967). This in itself might not have been a major concern, since during his lifetime and for many years afterwards Meinertzhagen was widely revered as a great naturalist. He had amassed a major collection of his own bird specimens and held high office in the ornithological establishment, he keenly supported the work of his niece – the world's leading expert on Mallophaga (feather-mites) – and he had written a series of books on birds. Meinertzhagen's dominance of British ornithological circles, achieved through a mixture of physique and mystique (he was a powerfully built, upper-class ex-soldier who cultivated the image of a ruthless spy), was such that the history of his relations with the British Museum (Natural History) remained largely unknown and rumours of his misdemeanours entirely unsubstantiated; and with the passage of time since his death these issues faded still further.

However, six years before Rasmussen's appointment, Mark Cocker had published a biography of Meinertzhagen in which the spectre of doubt about his probity was resurrected (Cocker 1989). In 1919, Meinertzhagen had been found leaving the British Museum with a number of specimens in his case. In 1935 he was investigated by the police for the theft from the museum of a paper on lice (Mallophaga), one of the more peculiar entries in the annals of criminology. Seven years after his death, an American museum scientist wrote to a member of staff at the British Museum which began: 'I can say *upon my oath* that Meinertzhagen's collection contains skins *stolen* from the Leningrad Museum, the Paris Museum, and the American Museum of Natural History and perhaps other museums…'. Cocker had even noticed a comment in an account (Collar & Stuart 1985) of the Raso Lark *Alauda razae* in which it was pointed out that Meinertzhagen's published claim to have seen the species was not substantiated by his unpublished diaries, according to which he had never set foot in the Cape Verdes.

If all this put a crack in the façade of Meinertzhagen's ornithological prestige, Alan Knox provided the seismic shock that rendered the whole edifice unstable (Knox 1993). He demonstrated conclusively that Meinertzhagen had been a thief: some of the specimens he had donated to the nation were in fact stolen from the very institution to which he had presented them; worse, he had relabelled them with new, false data on the time and place of their taking, rendering them virtually worthless as study material. 'The purpose of this paper', Knox concluded, 'has been to place on record specific examples of the shortcomings of the Meinertzhagen collection, as a warning to those who may use it'. As it happened, research staff at BirdLife International were poised to start gathering locality data from skins at the museum as part of their investigations into the distributions of threatened birds in Asia (BirdLife International 2001), where Meinertzhagen had spent so much of his time. A call was therefore made on the British Ornithologists' Union, which had published Knox's paper, to establish a committee to determine the extent of Meinertzhagen's fraudulence; this was chaired by Robert Prŷs-Jones, new head of the Bird Department at what was now known as the Natural History Museum (NHM) in England. Within a year and a half, Prŷs-Jones had interviewed several surviving key witnesses, confirmed Knox's findings by use of x-rays (which show up the internal preparation styles and materials of specimens, allowing comparisons to be made with specimens from other collectors), and been filled with serious doubts. Then he encountered Rasmussen, who was anxious to verify the 16 taxa for which Meinertzhagen was the sole authority for their occurrence in the subcontinent.

Working meticulously with skins and registers, Rasmussen soon proved that most of Meinertzhagen's unique records from the subcontinent were fraudulent (Rasmussen & Prŷs-Jones 2003). She then began a broader review of his material, as a subcomponent of her work on the field guide, and set aside dozens and in due course hundreds of specimens that she regarded with suspicion, and which Prŷs-Jones would send for x-ray analysis. However, because of its special interest as the most recent specimen to have been taken, her particular attention was turned

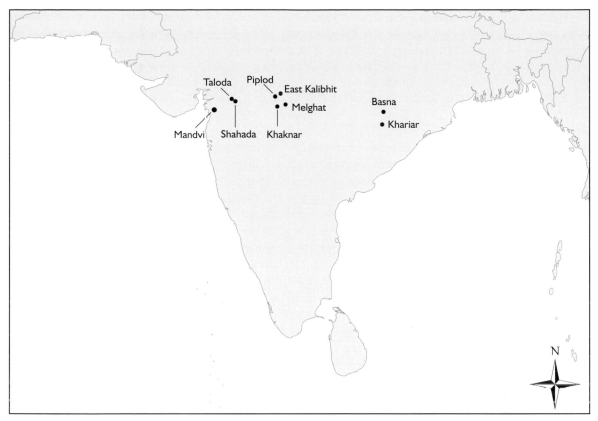

Key sites in India for the Forest Owlet, except Meinertzhagen's fictional Mandvi.

on the Meinertzhagen skin of the Forest Owlet from Mandvi in Gujarat. If this was also fraudulent, it could obstruct the species' conservation because it threw doubt on where conservationists should be looking for it; indeed, researchers had already invested time in searching for the species at Meinertzhagen's putative site. The published literature between 1969 and 1996 contained at least sixteen references to the record: its authenticity was established by simple repetition. It was this record, 100km west of Khandesh and at sea-level, that caused Ali & Ripley in 1969 to characterise the owlet's range as reaching the Surat Dangs in the west and therefore doubtless to presume it extended right through the Satpuras, an inadvertent misrepresentation of the evidence which in turn must have stood behind extraordinary statements in the literature such as that it was a montane species (Sibley & Monroe 1990). Moreover, coming 30 years after the last records, it perhaps made the sense of alarm at the owlet's disappearance just a little less acute.

The specimen was, inevitably, fraudulent (Rasmussen & Collar 1999b). When carefully inspected beneath the feathering, and when x-rayed alongside the other specimens of *Heteroglaux blewitti* in NHM (which included a further Davidson skin from 1883, not previously mentioned in the literature) plus Ball's bird (which had been traced to Dublin), it showed a series of tell tale signs of having been extensively 'remade'. It had ventral incisions and stitch-holes that had clearly been made after the skin had dried. There was no oiliness around the bill or legs such as accumulates after a decade or two in specimens of stockier birds like owls; instead there was a white deposit, vestiges of solvent that would only have been used if the constant handling of remaking required it. The skin of the neck had been compressed long after drying, so that it had buckled, to create a more natural-looking specimen. Parts of the skeleton, including the skull, had been removed to facilitate repositioning of head and limbs, the legs having been heavily twisted.

More to the point, Rasmussen discovered that Davidson frequently did two things to his specimens that are so unusual that they act as unintentional 'signatures'. He sometimes tied the wings together, to hold them close to the body, by stitching through the carpals and running the thread under the dorsal feathers. He also stuffed the wing-cavities (the area of the carpal joint) with cotton. When she checked Meinertzhagen's specimen, Rasmussen found traces of thread under the dorsal feathering where a wing-brace had been; and when the carpal joint was slit open on this and on a Davidson specimen, fat-yellowed cotton of precisely the same type was found in both. Rasmussen actually sent samples of this cotton to Douglas W. Deedrick, Head of the Trace Evidence Unit at the Federal Bureau of Investigation: Deedrick, who had worked on the OJ Simpson trial in 1994, found them indistinguishable. No other owl in Meinertzhagen's large collection had stuffing in the wing cavities or wings tied across the back.

Meinertzhagen kept a diary all his adult life. Although it is now abundantly clear that he edited and re-edited his diaries, particularly when they went for publication (Garfield 2007), they are likely to be more accurate in relation to his travels than some of the things he claimed elsewhere. The date on his specimen was 9 October 1914, ten weeks after the outbreak of the First World War. His diary has an entry for 6 October, when he was in Bombay: 'We have a great deal to do now. I am busy compiling an Intelligence Book for the troops…'; and next for 13 October, when he is still in Bombay: 'I have been kept very busy here with my Intelligence work…' It scarcely looks like he had time to slip away to Mandvi, several days away by train and several more hours on foot, simply in order to collect a single bird (his register has nothing for that day), an exceptionally rare one at that (which he never published) and return by the same laborious means.

Two mysteries remained. The Mandvi bird was clearly a Davidson specimen, but Davidson had given his specimens to Hume, who gave his specimens to the British Museum, and the catalogue accounted for all the Forest Owlets in the collection. So where *did* Meinertzhagen's bird come from? Rasmussen solved this conundrum by a mixture of diligence, vigilance and chance. Flicking through the massive museum catalogues one day while researching an entirely separate issue, she happened to notice an entry for *Carine noctua blewitti*, registered from a separate bequest from Davidson himself in 1925. Despite the somewhat misleading name, this was clearly a Forest Owlet. The entry indicated that Davidson had got the specimen on 4 December 1884, at Taloda in Khandesh. This could only be the bird that Meinertzhagen stole, and with the deletion of Gujarat from the range of the species, conservationists could now plan a thorough search targeting the places that could be relied on as valid: Basna, Khariar, Taloda, Shahada. This was the last mystery: was the Forest Owlet still alive?

THE CASE OF THE REAPPEARING OWL

Rasmussen was not a professional conservationist and did not expect to find herself undertaking the search for the owl, but the idea of an expedition rapidly took shape. She had worked on an exhaustive review of all records and claims, thereby establishing unequivocally the elevational range (150–500m) in which to search and the identification features to look for (Rasmussen & Collar 1998), and in King, author of a significant early field guide (King *et al.* 1975), she had a highly qualified and distinguished field ornithologist. The challenge could hardly be more exciting. Set against them was the fact that the species had not been seen for 113 years, it was (despite the habit noted by Davidson) presumed to be nocturnal, its call was unknown, it was not clear if any forest survived in the sites they were targeting, and indeed the sites themselves were far from exact or retraceable.

The rediscovery of the Forest Owlet in low hills close to Shahada was a triumph of dedication and scholarship. However, the party only found two birds for certain before their time ran out, and further information was needed on its habitat requirements, population and threats. Rasmussen raised the money for follow-up work to be conducted by the Bombay Natural History Society (BNHS), the BirdLife Partner in India, In the company of a young Indian researcher, Farah Ishtiaq, she gathered further information on the species, including its vocalisations, which were vital for future surveys (Rasmussen & Ishtiaq 1999). With support and guidance from Asad Rahmani, director of BNHS, and the Smithsonian, Ishtiaq continued to work on the ecology of the species for a year (June 1998 to June 1999), during which time she found just seven pairs: four at Shahada (Toranmal reserve forest) and three at Taloda. This study resulted in various discoveries of importance: that the owl breeds over an extended period in winter, from October to May, during which time it becomes highly territorial and responsive to tape playback; that it favours open parts of tropical dry deciduous forest, where it forages by day on terrestrial prey; that it appeared not to range above 500m, and that its habitat was under very strong pressure from landless tribes and people displaced by dam construction (Ishtiaq 1999, Ishtiaq *et al.* 2002, Ishtiaq & Rahmani 2005).

Armed with this information and now with additional backing from the Oriental Bird Club, Ishtiaq led the first full survey of the species at a series of sites across southern Madhya Pradesh and northern Maharashtra, obtaining new records at Khaknar forest range in the former and Melghat Tiger Reserve in the latter, and registering a total of 25 birds (Ishtiaq & Rahmani 2000). In 2001, with support from the Indian Ministry of Environment and Forests, Rahmani appointed Girish Jathar to lead a long-term study of the Forest Owlet (Jathar & Rahmani 2004) but, as interest and understanding about the species spread, a distinct element of citizen science began to emerge, particularly centred on Melghat. Independent observers reported the discovery of birds at Raipur, Malur and Jamodapadao inside Melghat and at Mahendri, 100km to the east, estimating that the tiger reserve might hold 50 birds, but warning that it was under dire threat from an irrigation project (Rithe 2003). Quite independently, other observers found the species at two separate sites in the reserve, one north of Malur village and one near the Jambukuwa waterhole (Kasambe *et al.* 2004), and inspired by this success they went on to discover no fewer than 48 birds at 16 different sites by mid-2004 and over 100 birds there by April 2005 (Kasambe *et al.* 2005).

Jathar also surveyed Melghat as part of a survey across northern Maharashtra. This resulted in the discovery of birds at just two sites: Toranmal reserve forest and Melghat. No birds were recorded at other sites, including Naranala, Van, Nagzira and Yawal wildlife sanctuaries, although three birds were found at Yawal later. As this work finished in Maharashtra, new surveys began in adjacent southern Madhya Pradesh in 2005–2006, when 24 birds were encountered in three forest ranges, namely Khaknar (6), Piplod (15) and East Kalibhit (3), the two latter sites being directly north-west of Melghat, where 20 birds were found in early 2006: nothing like as many as the hundred birds found the year before but doubtless finding more would be simply a matter of time and distribution of effort (Mehta *et al.* 2008). In fact, having drawn blanks in the states of Chhattisgarh, Orissa and Gujarat (not that any of these can yet be written off as lacking the species), the surveyors concluded that Melghat was possibly the most important site for the Forest Owlet, and it is clear that this reserve now merits a serious long-term study of the species, to map all its habitat and to arrive at a robust baseline population estimate (Mehta *et al.* 2008).

Meanwhile, Jathar's work has resulted in some valuable insights (Jathar & Rahmani 2004, Jathar 2008). Measurements of habitat variables in occupied and unoccupied areas of forest suggest that areas with taller trees appear to be favoured for nesting but that the owlet selects tracts with lower-than-usual tree densities and a higher representation of teak *Tectona grandis*. It avoids forest close to encroached and cleared land, and forages in habitats with a relatively reduced canopy cover, higher and denser grass/herb layer and thicker leaf-litter, a type of habitat which evidently generates higher prey densities. These prey are of various types, the majority being invertebrates (40%), then rodents (25%), reptiles (15%), shrews (7%), birds (6%) and unidentified (7%), although the seasonal variation in proportions remains to be evaluated (Jathar *et al.* 2005). Observations showed that the Forest Owlet is a diurnal hunter; one of the drawbacks of this is that its newly fledged young are highly vulnerable to a suite of raptors, notably the White-eyed Buzzard *Butastur teesa*.

However, human predation may be more important (and more feasible) to control. Two of the most striking findings of Jathar's study were that local tribal people use the body parts of owls for witchcraft and take the eggs for good luck. Moreover, interviews with villagers at Toranmal reserve forest, where Pamela Rasmussen made her rediscovery, discovered that 21% of them believed that owls feed on human souls. Major tasks lie ahead for conservation with these local communities, not simply in creating a more positive attitude among them towards owls but perhaps more importantly in managing their need for land. Clearance for cultivation, intrusions of livestock, firewood collection, teak removal for construction, and disturbance and disruption by hunting are all challenges to the integrity of the few remaining areas that hold the Forest Owlet. The species is still in the flush of goodwill and delight that followed its miraculous reappearance at the end of the last century, but the evidence suggests that the rediscovery came not a moment too soon.

Chapter 25
Slender-billed Curlew *Numenius tenuirostris*
CRITICALLY ENDANGERED

Eskimo Curlew *Numenius borealis*
CRITICALLY ENDANGERED
(POSSIBLY EXTINCT)

The curlews, eight species of wader (shorebird) in the genus *Numenius* that combine cryptic plumage with decurved bills, present a particular challenge for conservationists. Populations of most, if not all, of the world's curlew species are in decline, three are globally threatened and one, the widespread Eurasian Curlew *N. arquata*, is listed as Near Threatened. Two species in the genus must surely rank among the rarest and most enigmatic of all birds. The reasons for their extreme rarity continue to puzzle scientists, and although both were once common, recent efforts to find them have so far drawn a frustrating blank. The Eskimo Curlew of North America has not been seen on its breeding grounds for well over a century, and indeed has not been reliably reported anywhere at all since 1981 (Environment Canada 2007). No nests of the Slender-billed Curlew of Central Asia have been seen since 1924, and the last generally accepted sighting of the species was made in Hungary in 2001 (Oláh & Pigniczki 2010). However, a thin and unfortunately slowing trickle of tantalising but unsubstantiated sightings keeps alive hopes that both species might still survive in tiny numbers, and both species remain optimistically classified as Critically Endangered. The stories of the Eskimo Curlew and the Slender-billed Curlew provide some fascinating and intriguing parallels and illustrate the problems faced by conservationists when species become so rare and elusive that they have no known breeding or wintering sites.

THE VANISHING ASIAN CURLEW

In the turbulent years either side of the Russian Revolution, the ornithologist V. E. Ushakov made the first and, as it turned out, the last reliable observations of the Slender-billed Curlew on its breeding grounds (Gretton *et al.* 2002). Ushakov's first scientific article on the species, published in 1909, claimed that it was 'quite common' in the region south of Tara in south-western Siberia, and stimulated considerable interest among ornithologists eager to know the origins of this enigmatic species. However, in a subsequent paper published in 1912 he suggested that it was already becoming rare. A further paper published in 1916 described his exploits of two years previously, when he collected a single female and a clutch of four eggs. Ushakov's last published observation in 1925 described his discovery the previous year of 14 nests of the species near Tara, north of Omsk in south-western Siberia, close to the northern limit of the forest-steppe zone in the forest-bog transition (Gretton *et al.* 2002). He described the breeding habitat as an 'extensive quaking peatbog with a dense cover of sedge', and suggested that Slender-billed Curlews often nested close to each other and to Eurasian Curlews, a behaviour shown by other species of *Numenius*. Other species Ushakov recorded at this site included the Great Bittern *Botaurus stellaris* and the Jack Snipe *Lymnocryptes minimus*, giving an idea of how wet these areas were. Visits to the same site between 1989 and 1997 revealed that, apart from the absence of Slender-billed Curlews, parts of the area appeared little changed since Ushakov's day and Eurasian Curlews still breed there, although much of the original habitat in other areas identified from maps as being potentially suitable had been lost to agriculture (Boere & Yurlov 1998, Gretton *et al.* 2002). If these really were the main breeding grounds, it seems that loss of habitat there is unlikely wholly to explain the species' decline, since extensive tracts of apparently suitable habitat remain. Ushakov's site is the only

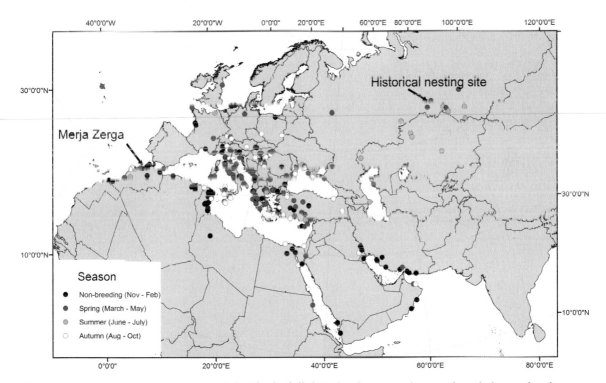

Distribution of generally accepted records of the Slender-billed Curlew by season, showing the only known breeding site in southern Russia and the last regular wintering site in Morocco (courtesy of the Slender-billed Curlew Working Group).

Very few photographs of the Slender-billed Curlew in the wild exist. These three form part of a remarkable series of images taken of a single bird in western France in February 1968, perhaps the best ever taken of the species (Michel Brosselin).

one for which incontrovertible evidence of breeding is available, but there are unsubstantiated claims of breeding at a number of other sites, mostly to the south of Tara but also to the west and east.

With so few reliable records of the species during the breeding season, it is difficult to know whether the habitat described by Ushakov was indeed typical of the species or whether it represented an unusual use of a habitat at the edge of a main breeding range that involved some other, unknown habitat. Certainly, the scattered distribution of largely unconfirmed nineteenth century records suggest that it might have bred north of Tara in the taiga zone, or to the south in the steppe zone (Gretton 1991, Danilenko *et al.* 1996, Gretton *et al.* 2002). Nineteenth century records suggest that the bird was seen throughout the breeding season in steppe between the Volga and Ural rivers, although breeding was never proved there (Dolgushin 1962). The rapid changes to the steppe zone that have so affected the numbers and distribution of the Sociable Lapwing *Vanellus gregarius* (Chapter 3) have raised suggestions that this is where the breeding grounds of the Slender-billed Curlew really lie, if for no other reason that this at least would provide a plausible explanation for its rapid decline (Belik 1994).

A long history of ornithology and hunting over large areas of Europe, North Africa and Asia means that there are a large number of records of the species away from the breeding areas. By piecing these together, it has been possible to identify the main migration routes and wintering grounds of the Slender-billed Curlew. The distribution of historical records, which also of course reflects the distribution of hunters and observers, suggest that the autumn migration took birds almost due west, principally to the shores of the Black Sea, particularly the Danube Delta, then to inland wetlands in eastern Europe (notably in Hungary) and on to northern Italy. Others seem to have taken a more south-westerly route and there are old records of birds in autumn along the coasts of the Red Sea and the Arabian Gulf. Winter records were widely scattered, but there were concentrations in northern Italy and, particularly, the northern shores of Africa. Although the species was claimed in the nineteenth century to be common in winter along the Mediterranean coasts of Spain and France, there are few substantiated records. However, it was clearly common in Italy, from where at least 141 specimens collected between 1828 and 1974 still survive in museums, the majority being spring passage birds shot in the south of the peninsula, but with winter records from both the north and the south (Baccetti 1995). The species appears to have been quite commonly sold in markets throughout Italy. Ominously, it appears that, during this period, the number of females started to diminish more rapidly than the number of males (Baccetti 1995), a common pattern in species heading towards extinction (p.33).

Apart from a few records in the Nile delta and along the Red Sea coasts, and a handful of intriguing inland records south of the Sahara, all wintering records in Africa since 1900 have been from Algeria, Tunisia and Morocco, most of them along the Mediterranean and Atlantic coasts (Buchanan *et al.* 2010). Since the last sighting of a single bird at the famous Merja Zerga site in Morocco in February 1995, there have been no confirmed records in Africa. The great majority of winter records, in Africa and elsewhere, were close to open water, and most were near the sea. Reliable records of birds migrating eastwards in spring follow a similar distribution to those of birds moving west in autumn, although sites in north-east Greece appear to have been more important. Like the Sociable Lapwing, the Slender-billed Curlew appears to be something of a wanderer, with substantiated records from sites as far apart as the Seychelles and Canaries. There are even unsubstantiated observations from as far west as Canada and as far east as China and Japan. On the basis of a possible but unconfirmed sighting in Gujarat in March 2002, it has been suggested that the species winters along the coasts of the Saurashtra Peninsula and on coral islands and reefs in the Gulf of Kutch (Khacher & Rughani 2006), a region previously suggested as a possible winter quarters for a wader with breeding grounds in south-west Siberia (Gretton 1991, Veen *et al.* 2005).

A problem dogging conservationists trying to piece together the history of the Slender-billed Curlew, and indeed hampering the evaluation of recent reports, is field identification (van den Berg 1988, Cleeves 2002). The eastern races of the Eurasian Curlew can be deceptively similar, and very detailed field descriptions or photographs are necessary to clinch a positive identification of Slender-billed Curlew. This might explain why the Slender-billed Curlew was only recognised as comparatively recently as 1817, when Vieillot described it from a bird shot in Egypt, and why there are few assessments of its numbers and distribution before 1900. However, the Slender-billed Curlew was clearly once a reasonably common and perhaps even abundant species. Henry Dresser described it in 1871 as being 'by no means uncommon in the countries bordering the Mediterranean'. The paucity of specific records of its numbers suggests that it was neither particularly rare nor particularly common (Gretton 1991). However, it appears to have been locally abundant at certain times of year and in certain places. In the nineteenth century it was described as being the most abundant species of curlew in Sicily, Malta, Morocco, Tunisia and Algeria, where it sporadically appeared in large numbers (Gretton 1991). On occasions, these were very large numbers indeed: one account from Algeria in 1870 described 'incredible flocks....as big as Starling flocks'. The reference to Common Starlings *Sturnus vulgaris* suggests that these flocks were not only large, but also dense.

Assessing the chronology of its descent towards extinction is difficult, not only because of the problem of identifying the species in the field but also because it breeds and winters in areas that historically have received little attention from ornithologists. However, by piecing together and critically assessing the validity of historical and recent records, a process undertaken by the Slender-billed Curlew Working Group building on Gretton (1991), it appears that the species started to decline around 1900. The efforts to which Ushakov went to find nests of this species in the second decade of the century suggest that by this time it was already becoming rare. By 1930 it was nowhere common, and a paper published in 1943 suggested that it might be heading towards extinction (Stresemann & Grote 1943). Perhaps because this important signal was published in German and in wartime, it was unfortunately never picked up by the international conservation movement that emerged early in the second half of the twentieth century, and consequently the species was omitted from the first two editions of the international bird Red Data Book (Vincent 1966–1971, King 1978–1979).

However, as late as the 1960s and even into the 1970s, claims of flocks numbering hundreds of birds continued to emerge from Morocco, although their validity remains controversial. The growth of birdwatching after 1980, the advent of good quality optics and a better understanding of the species' identification features produced a surge in the number of reliable records, although most were of small numbers of birds (Gretton 1991). What these and subsequent records showed clearly was that the decline in numbers noted before the 1940s was still continuing in the 1980s. In 1988, the year that the species was finally admitted to the Red List (Collar & Andrew 1988), a two-year international conservation initiative was launched by ICBP (now BirdLife International), but coordinated

The last generally accepted record of Slender-billed Curlew was made in Hungary in 2001, although the species might well still survive; this photograph was taken in 1995, the last year in which it was recorded at the previously regular site of Merja Zerga in Morocco (Chris Gomersall, RSPB Images).

surveys in that year could find no more than 36 birds, 22 of them in Greece, and in the following year fewer than half that number were found (Gretton 1991). After that, the number of reliable sightings fell rapidly.

The only site where birds were recorded regularly after 1950 was at Merja Zerga on the Atlantic coast of Morocco, where each year small numbers of birds were seen in winter until the last record in February 1995. In that same month, however, hopes were raised that a viable population might still exist when a flock of 19 birds spent several weeks and was photographed in Italy. The following year, 12 birds were recorded in Greece, but this was to be the last sighting of a flock in double figures. In May 1998, British birdwatchers reacted with a mixture of astonishment, elation and disbelief to the news that a Slender-billed Curlew was present in the UK, the only accepted record from this well-watched country (Cleeves 2002). Of particular significance was the fact that this was a bird in its first-year plumage, indicating that the species had bred successfully somewhere the previous year. In the spring of the same year, six birds were seen in Greece, where five were also recorded in 1999. Three birds in Oman in August 1999 were the penultimate record, and the last reliable sighting was made in Hungary on 15 April 2001 (Oláh & Pigniczki 2010), although there were claims, unfortunately not supported by photographs, of several birds by a respected observer in the Danube Delta in Romania in 2003 and 2004 (Zhmud 2005). A claim of another bird in the UK in 2004, accepted at the time by a number of experts on the species, proved the difficulty of identifying this species, since it was later proved by DNA analysis of a faecal sample to have been a small Eurasian Curlew. Dedicated searches for the species on the breeding grounds in Siberia in 1997 and on potential wintering grounds in Iran in 2000, in Tunisia in 2003 and in Libya in 2005 and 2006 all failed to find the species (Boere & Yurlov 1998, van der Have *et al.* 2001, Smart *et al.* 2006, Azafzaf *et al.* 2007).

The species' wintering distribution may have been larger than the database of historical records suggests. Just before his death in 1999, an old man called Pieter Mulder was interviewed at his home in The Netherlands by two renowned shorebird experts (Jukema & Piersma 2004). Mulder told the researchers that as a boy he had often prepared for the pot birds caught by his father, a professional hunter and one of the last of the 'wilsternetters', practitioners of an ancient hunting method that used nets to catch migratory shorebirds, particularly Eurasian Golden Plovers *Pluvialis apricaria*. He clearly recalled handling two types of curlew brought in by his father, the familiar Eurasian Curlew and a much smaller species that had a different name ('pikgulp', curiously similar to 'piskun', the local Siberian name of the species given by Ushakov). As this was in midwinter, the smaller species could not have been the Whimbrel *Numenius phaeopus*, the only other small species of curlew in Europe, as it winters in tropical Africa. The smaller species was apparently only ever found on saltmarsh and the intertidal zone, fitting well with what is known about the wintering habitat of Slender-billed Curlews elsewhere. The timing of Mulder's birds also fits well with the 11 accepted Dutch and Belgian records of Slender-billed Curlew, all of which were recorded in midwinter. Whatever it was, the smaller species disappeared abruptly in 1932 when the intertidal estuary of the Zuidersee that provided the hunting grounds of Mulder's father was turned into the enormous stagnant freshwater IJsselmeer by the completion of a dyke. Mulder's recollections suggest that Slender-billed Curlews might once have wintered regularly in estuaries around the North Sea, far to the north of the usual wintering grounds around the Mediterranean.

There has been much speculation on the causes of the demise of the Slender-billed Curlew, but there is little hard evidence. The most frequently cited reason is hunting, particularly on passage and on the wintering grounds. Several other species of curlew, being large and tasty, have suffered historically high hunting pressure, and hunting certainly provides the most obvious (though not necessarily the best) explanation for the collapse of the Eskimo Curlew of North America. Slender-billed Curlews were often found in meat markets in Italy and it is likely that many were killed for food and sport both there and in other passage and wintering range states (Gretton 1991). Interviews with an elderly hunter in Morocco in the late 1980s suggested that the Slender-billed Curlew was well known to bird-trappers, and that like other curlews it was readily attracted to decoys (Gretton 1991). During the 1980s, there is anecdotal evidence that French tourist hunters in Morocco shot a great many Slender-billed Curlews, after which records of the species there dried up. Unfortunately, the Slender-billed Curlew appears to have been more approachable than other waders, perhaps making it easier to hunt. Between 1962 and 1987, when the species was already one of the rarest in Europe, at least 15 were shot, two of them to provide scientific specimens for museums. Clearly the species' rarity proved no protection from hunting pressure.

THE VANISHING AMERICAN CURLEW

While the outlook for the Slender-billed Curlew seems unpromising, it is premature to consider it extinct. The same, alas, may not be true for the Eskimo Curlew, and while it remains optimistically classified as Critically Endangered, the depressing caveat 'Possibly Extinct' was added to its status in 2006 (Butchart *et al.* 2006b). Yet the Eskimo Curlew was once a very abundant bird, although reports of its numbers might have been exaggerated by its habit of migrating in large flocks that appeared regularly at certain times of year (Gill *et al.* 1998). The species' breeding habitat was Arctic tundra, particularly the habitat known as the Barrens, and the known range was located entirely within the Mackenzie District of the North-west Territories of Canada, although it probably also bred throughout much of the North-West Territories, possibly in the Yukon and Alaska, and perhaps even in extreme eastern Russia (Gill *et al.* 1998). The population before 1860 was estimated to be in the hundreds of thousands, if not in the millions, but it declined dramatically in the 1870s to 1890s, and the species was almost extinct by 1900 (Gill *et al.* 1998). The last record on its breeding grounds was in 1866, and numerous recent searches in the historical breeding range have failed to locate any birds.

The Eskimo Curlew had one of the longest migrations of any bird (Gollop *et al.* 1986). In autumn, birds left the high Arctic breeding grounds and headed east to the eastern coasts of Canada and the north-eastern USA, particularly Newfoundland and Labrador, where they fattened themselves up largely by feeding on berries, particularly crowberry *Empetrum nigrum* and blueberry *Vaccinium* spp., which they gorged on until they were stained purple from bill to tail by the juice (Gollop *et al.* 1986). During this brief fattening period they could apparently double in weight (Gill *et al.* 1998). The great naturalist and artist John James Audubon remarked that birds fed 'with a rapidity equalled by that of the Passenger Pigeon; in an instant all the ripe berries on the plant are swallowed and the whole country is cleaned of these berries'; indeed, the crowberry was known in Labrador as the 'curlew berry'. After this feast, birds then headed south-east over the western Atlantic and the Caribbean, often in the company of American Golden Plovers *Pluvialis dominica*, in a massive and apparently non-stop flight to make landfall on the north-eastern coasts of South America. They then appear to have crossed the Amazon basin on their way to the wintering grounds on the pampas of southern Argentina and Chile, some 15,000km south

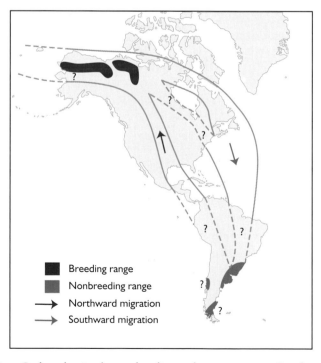

Migration routes of the Eskimo Curlew, showing known breeding and wintering areas. Based on Gill et al. *(1988).*

The only known photographs of the Eskimo Curlew in life were taken on Galveston Island, Texas, in 1962; this one has been hand-coloured. Up to four birds were present at the time. Just under 20 years later, the last generally accepted record of the species was made on the same island (Don Bleitz, courtesy of the Western Foundation for Vertebrate Zoology).

of the breeding grounds. Some even reached the Falkland Islands (Gollop *et al.* 1986, Gill *et al.* 1998). The long crossing of the western Atlantic even brought some storm-blown vagrants to western Europe, where four birds were recorded in the UK between 1855 and 1887 and one in Ireland in 1870 (Melling 2010). It has been suggested that the birds that Christopher Columbus followed southwards in October 1492, leading to his discovery of the island he called San Salvador (in what is now the Bahamas), were migrating flocks of Eskimo Curlews and American Golden Plovers (Tooke 1961).

The northward return migration in spring followed a more westerly overland route, taking birds over the Andes and up the Pacific coast of South America through Peru and Ecuador, then Central America, over the Gulf of Mexico to Texas and through central USA along the valleys of the Mississippi, Missouri and Platte rivers (Gill *et al.* 1998). Instead of migrating directly to the breeding grounds, they stopped off at regular staging points in the Great Plains, particularly in recently burned areas and areas disturbed by American Bison *Bison bison*, where they fed on a range of insect foods, particularly the eggs and young of locusts.

The large quantities of fat required to provide energy for these huge migrations made the species a delicacy (its colloquial name was the doughbird), and tens of thousands of birds were shot at the autumn jumping-off points in Newfoundland and Labrador, and at spring staging posts on the Great Plains. Contemporary accounts described the bird's flesh as 'far surpassing any of our English game in richness and flavour' and it was 'considered by epicures to be the finest eating of any of our birds' (Gollop *et al.* 1986). After their autumn fattening, the birds were 'white with fat'. Furthermore, the bird was very easy to hunt; like the Slender-billed Curlew it was very approachable, it occurred in large, dense flocks at predictable times and places, it was attracted to wooden decoys and it had the unfortunate habit of repeatedly wheeling back over the guns when some birds in a flock were shot, allowing hunters to keep blasting away until none was left. Single hunters could shoot hundreds of Eskimo Curlews in a day, and teams of hunters could shoot several thousand (Gill *et al.* 1998). The birds were transported, 300 to a barrel, to markets in large industrial cities right across North America, including Boston, Montreal, Chicago, Detroit, San Francisco, Philadelphia and New York. Hunting pressure increased greatly during the late 1870s and 1880s, when populations of another commercially valuable species, the Passenger Pigeon *Ectopistes migratorius*, started spiralling towards extinction. Hunters who relied on the pigeons for their income started to turn their attention to the migrating curlews, which from around this time became known as 'prairie pigeons' (Gollop *et al.* 1986). The species was not safe on its wintering grounds either, and birds featured regularly on the menus of the restaurants of Buenos Aires.

Declines in Eskimo Curlew numbers were noted very soon after this increase in human consumption. In the 1860s, contemporary accounts describe immense flocks of 'millions' of birds up to half a mile in length. In Texas, one observer noted immense flocks in 1875, a few small flocks in 1886 and just three birds in 1905. There were to be no further sightings in the state for another forty years (Gill *et al.* 1998). By 1900, the vast flocks that gathered along the Labrador coast prior to autumn migration had largely gone; in 1912, only 12 birds could be found along this whole coastline, all but one of which were shot. A collector of specimens for museums shot one bird in Labrador in 1926, four in 1927 and one in 1932. After this date, the number of reliable claims slowed to a trickle, and in 1956 a book, part fiction and part fact, was published describing in emotional terms the fates of the last few birds (Bodsworth 1956). The last wholly verifiable record was of a bird shot in Barbados in 1963 (Bond 1965), although a sighting of a flock of 23 birds in Texas in 1981 is generally accepted to be the final reliable record, and four records in Texas in 1987 appear credible (Gollop 1988). No Eskimo Curlews were found during extensive searches in historical wintering areas of Argentina and Uruguay in 1992 and 1993. Claims of sightings from Canada (1987 and 1996), Argentina (1990) and Nova Scotia (2006) are unsupported by photographic evidence but fuel hopes that the species still survives. The collapse of the species' population occurred largely before the advent of amateur photography, and only a handful of photographs of living birds exist, all taken by the late Donald Bleitz on Galveston Island, Texas, in 1962, showing one or two of up to four birds that were present (Bleitz 1962).

The Eskimo Curlew, like all large shorebirds, appears to have had a fairly low reproductive output, each pair producing only one or two chicks each breeding season, and surviving chicks did not breed until the age of two or three years. Because of this, it is likely to have been extremely vulnerable to even small declines in adult survival (Hitchcock & Gratto-Trevor 1997). However, a ban on hunting that came into force in 1916 after fears were raised that the species was on the verge of extinction (Swenk 1915) was not followed by a recovery in numbers, suggesting that the species was by then facing other problems, or perhaps was already too far down the road to extinction to stage a comeback (Gill *et al.* 1998). The intensified hunting pressure during the 1880s coincided with a period of cooler-than-average summers, perhaps reducing breeding success, and with stronger-than-average westerly winds during the southward migration over the Atlantic, which may have pushed migrating birds farther out to sea (Banks 1977); three of the five British records were recorded during this period. The conversion of pampas grassland to agriculture in its winter quarters in Argentina has greatly reduced the availability of habitat, although this happened some time after the main period of decline and is likely to be of secondary importance (Canevari & Blanco 1994). However, the loss of natural prairie habitats in North America to cultivation and the suppression of wildfire regimes happened at around the same time as the curlew started to decline (Gollop *et al.* 1986, Gill *et al.* 1998) and may have robbed it of a critically important staging post en route to the summer quarters, where the birds would have replenished reserves after a long northward migration and built up the necessary body condition for breeding. Only around 4% of the original prairie ecosystems remains today (Samson & Knopf 1994).

Directly related to the loss of spring stopover grasslands, and perhaps for the curlew the most crucial aspect of this change, was the unanticipated extinction of the Rocky Mountain Locust *Melanoplus spretus*. The eggs and young of this insect were an important food of the curlew on the prairies of the USA and southern Canada (Gill *et al.* 1998). The locust was a serious pest of the crops of pioneer farmers in western North America, to the extent that many were forced to abandon their land altogether. One famous swarm in 1874 covered over half a million square kilometres and contained an estimated 12.5 trillion insects with a combined weight of nearly 30 million tons, perhaps the largest aggregation of terrestrial animals ever recorded. However, a sighting of the locust in Canada in 1902 was to prove the last one ever (Lockwood 2004). The reasons for this unprecedented extinction are still unclear, but during the insect's non-swarming breeding phase it appears to have been confined to sandy areas along rivers, where the cultivation of natural prairie land may have driven numbers down to unsustainable levels (Lockwood & Debrey 1990). Farmers at the time recorded that the thousands of locust egg-cases they ploughed up attracted large numbers of Eskimo Curlews, and hunters, quickly seizing the opportunity, gathered in recently ploughed areas to pursue their relentless slaughter (Gill *et al.* 1998). Whether or not the extinction of the locust affected curlews directly, or whether the declines in both species were driven by the loss of prairie grasslands, is unclear, but the near-simultaneous disappearance of the Eskimo Curlew, the Passenger Pigeon and the Rocky Mountain Locust – the latter two respectively North America's, and perhaps the world's, most abundant bird and insect species – indicate the profound nature of the ecological changes that American pioneers wrought upon the continent at that time. Yet the great majority of the continent's species survived it, and it is curious that the animals to disappear were the most abundant. Superabundance, clearly no guarantee against extinction, perhaps actually carries its own additional risk.

HOW TO PROTECT GHOSTS?

The lack of recent records of both curlews means that little can be done to protect whatever birds remain. The Canadian recovery plan currently in force recommends that because repeated searches of the Eskimo Curlew's historic breeding and wintering grounds have drawn a blank, no conservation action can currently be undertaken other than the continued monitoring of reported sightings (Environment Canada 2007). Given the long absence of reliable records and the fact that the pattern of records suggests that the chances of the species surviving are very low (Roberts *et al.* 2010), this is perhaps an understandable approach. However, a premature presumption of extinction risks the Romeo Error, which is that it might cause conservation efforts, even if only in the form of searches for the last remaining birds, to be abandoned at exactly the time that they are most needed.

For this reason, in 2008 a major initiative was launched by a reinvigorated Slender-billed Curlew Working Group to give that species one last chance (Crockford 2009). The lack of recent records should not be taken to mean that the Slender-billed Curlew is extinct. Before a small number of satellite tags were fitted to Sociable Lapwings, this species had not been recorded in Africa for decades, but it is now known that hundreds and perhaps thousands of birds winter there each year, and presumably always have done. A colony of the large and unmistakable Northern Bald Ibis *Geronticus eremita* remained undiscovered in Syria for many years near Palmyra, an international heritage site that receives tens of thousands of visitors each year (Serra *et al.* 2004). The ability of small numbers of birds to disappear into the under-watched vastness of Africa and Asia should not be underestimated. Concerted surveys are now underway in a large number of countries where the species has been recorded in the past, their participants provided with detailed information on its identification and with a standardised recording form to ensure that all the necessary information is collected. A team of identification experts has also been established to judge the merits of any claimed sightings. If any convincing sightings emerge, a rapid reaction team of experts is standing by to rush to the site, catch a bird and fit it with a satellite tag, in the hope it might lead conservationists to the all-important breeding grounds. If these can be found, it would be possible to take action to help the species, for example by establishing a captive breeding programme.

All that is required now is for a bird to be found. Perhaps a search of the coast of Iran, from where there are a number of historical winter records, will locate some birds and reignite hopes that the species can be saved. Unfortunately, searching for potential breeding areas, without being led there by a bird carrying a satellite tag, remains more difficult, not least because of the uncertainty over where to focus on in the hugeness of Central Asia and Siberia. In an attempt to reduce the area of search as much as possible, conservation biologists are considering all the methods available to them, including trying to match the chemical composition (isotopic signatures) of feathers from specimens in museum collections to the areas where they were grown.

Clear parallels can be drawn between the declines to near, and perhaps final, extinction of the Slender-billed Curlew and the Eskimo Curlew. Both species have largely overland migration routes, whereas most other shorebirds use more coastal or marine flyways. Both appear to have suffered a steep population decline because of intensive hunting pressure, and both were particularly easy species to hunt; contemporary accounts indicate that hunters on both sides of the Atlantic were aware of this and capitalised upon it. However, hunting pressure alone may not be sufficient to explain their current rarity, as both species failed to recover when hunting pressure was reduced. The loss of habitat may have been a contributory factor, particularly if the Slender-billed Curlew really did breed largely in the steppe zone. If Ushakov's sites were indeed unusual, the almost complete loss of steppe to agriculture in southern Russia by 1900 provides more compelling evidence that habitat loss might have contributed to the species' demise. Perhaps the long-held assumption that the Slender-billed Curlew breeds solely in the habitats described by Ushakov has deflected attention from other potential breeding areas.

It is possible that both species were biologically incapable of recovering from low population sizes. As their numbers dwindled, so it must have become more and more difficult for potential mates to meet up and if birds depended on others of their species to protect breeding colonies or to lead and survive migration, their very rarity might have resulted in the emergence of a new range of problems unconnected to the hunting or habitat loss that reduced their numbers in the first place. The concept of the Allee effect (p.32) may be applicable to both species – once numbers fell below a certain level, extinction might have become inevitable even if the original problems disappeared. The last accepted records of both the Eskimo Curlew and the Slender-billed Curlew were made almost exactly a century after their respective periods of greatest decline, suggesting that extinction may be a penalty paid many years after the changes that made it inevitable. If so, these enigmatic species provide a particularly sobering lesson about extinction, which is that many of the species that survive today may already have travelled far down that same one-way street, without us yet realising.

Poignant and prescient, Audubon's depiction of a pair of Eskimo Curlews, one alive and one shot dead, was completed long before the slaughter of the species really took hold in North America.

Chapter 26
Rarity and extinction in the future

It is often said that we are in the middle of one of the planet's great extinction events, one that is predicted to take more species with it than any of the five previous mass extinctions documented by the fossil record (Raup & Sepkoski 1986). For birds at least, this bold statement hides some interesting patterns. It is undoubtedly true that since the start of the Holocene epoch around 12,000 years ago, and particularly within the last two or three thousand years of island colonisation, extinction rates have been several orders of magnitude higher than background rates (Pimm *et al.* 2006, Szabo *et al.* 2012b). However, they have not been uniform within this period. Were it not for the ecological catastrophe of Hawaii, extinction rates of birds during the last few decades might have been no higher than at any time in the last two thousand years. This is largely because many of the planet's most vulnerable species, such as flightless island birds, have already been lost, but also because of the success of conservation intervention targeted at the rarest species. It might therefore be more accurate to say that in the early twenty-first century we find ourselves in a trough between two waves of extinction. The first of these started when Polynesians populated the Pacific some two to three millennia ago and took with it perhaps thousands of bird species (Steadman 1995), making the 150 or so extinctions that have occurred in the last 500 years appear relatively modest. Many of these more recent extinctions can be attributed to similar waves of island colonisation by different groups of island settlers, particularly Europeans from the sixteenth century onwards, carrying with them a different and often more lethal complement of invasive species. The rate of extinction on islands is now slowing (Biber 2002), but a new wave is now approaching as increasing human pressure begins to push more and more continental species towards extinction (Ricketts *et al.* 2005). While islands continue to hold a disproportionate number of the world's rarest and most threatened birds, the spotlight of extinction is now shifting towards the continental landmasses, especially in tropical regions where the majority of the world's bird species are found (Szabo *et al.* 2012b). But where will rarity lie in the future, and what are the characteristics of those species that, without intervention, will appear in lists of the most endangered or even extinct species in fifty or a hundred years from now?

EXTINCTION RATES PAST, PRESENT AND FUTURE

Extinction can be seen as the final part of the evolutionary trajectory of all species (Purvis 2008) but all too often it strikes well before the end of their natural lifespans. There is little doubt that human activities have been the main, and perhaps the only, cause of the 150 or so bird extinctions that have taken place in the last five hundred years and they remain the key driver of elevated extinction risk to surviving species (Davies *et al.* 2006). The ease with which humans can drive species to extinction and the speed with which they can do this to seemingly secure species is chilling. Who would have thought in 1860 that the Passenger Pigeon *Ectopistes migratorius*, possibly the world's most abundant bird species at the time, would be extinct just half a century later? In the middle of the nineteenth century, flocks a mile wide and 300 miles long were recorded, forming the largest aggregations of birds ever known. So common were they that it is likely that their activities significantly altered woodland tree species composition, habitat dynamics and fire regimes across huge areas of the eastern USA (Ellsworth & McComb 2003). The species' demise, although poorly understood, is generally assumed to be linked to the terrible hunting pressure that the species was subjected to and to changes in the distribution of its key resources (Bucher 1992). Only marginally less dramatic has been the recent collapse in populations of vultures in southern Asia (Chapter

17). There are all too many other examples of formerly common birds being brought to the brink of extinction by our activities, intentional or otherwise.

By taking the number of known extinctions in the last 500 years and correcting it for the rate of discovery of the fossil remains of extinct species and the likely extinction of certain species that are still listed as surviving, we get an approximate extinction rate of one bird species lost per year, a rate one hundred times greater than that estimated for pre-human times (Pimm *et al.* 2006). Furthermore, it is likely to have fallen to less than 0.5 bird extinctions per year in recent decades, thanks largely to concerted conservation action that has prevented the extinction of at least 16 species (Butchart *et al.* 2006c). Without this action, the extinction rate would have been considerably higher. This may be a temporary respite, however, as the continued loss of forests is likely to push the rate up to 10–15 bird extinctions per year by the end of the century (McKinney 1998, Pimm *et al.* 2006) and if current fears about the impacts of climate change are realised, the extinction rate might greatly exceed this.

However, the prediction of future extinction rates is fraught with difficulty, not least because we have a far from perfect understanding of the factors that influence the extinction risks of species today. Previous attempts to predict estimates of extinction rates have turned out to be overly pessimistic, because the methods used to predict extinction tend to overestimate risk (Wright 1987, Gibbs 2001, Lomborg 2001). For example, it was predicted in 1986 that 12% of Amazonian birds would be extinct by 2000 (Simberloff 1986). In fact, none is known to have been lost by 2012. The actual rate of recent extinction of birds has been lower than that estimated by their IUCN risk status, but there has been a general movement of birds into increasingly high threat classes (Brooke *et al.* 2008). Although conservationists have a reasonable track record of preventing extinctions, there is a worrying build-up of species that require emergency intervention to prevent their imminent loss, and an increasing number of species are heading up the Red List. Clearly, if we can identify characteristics of species that will become rare in the future, we will be better placed to prevent further extinctions.

HIDDEN RISKS: THE EXTINCTION DEBT

Although recent rates of recorded extinction have not risen, and predictions made in the 1980s of the impending loss of many species were not realised, there is growing evidence for an insidious pattern in nature that masks the true risk of extinction: this is the considerable time-lag between the event that precipitates a species' extinction and the death of the last bird. The so-called 'extinction debt' might explain why the extinctions predicted in the 1980s have not yet happened (Wearn *et al.* 2012).

Between 1907 and 1913, a vast manmade lake was formed in Panama by the building of the Gatun Dam, part of construction work on the Panama Canal. Huge areas of rainforest were flooded, leaving only the tops of hills protruding. One of these newly created islands, Barro Colorado (15 km^2), became a nature reserve in 1923 and a research station was established there. Scientists have been recording the populations of birds on the island for over eighty years. Shortly after its isolation, they found the island to be 'supersaturated' with bird species – it had too many for its size, since birds displaced from the surrounding areas sought sanctuary there. Since then, however, species have become extinct on the island at the rate of about one per year (Robinson 1999). First to go were some of the forest's predators, other rare species and habitat specialists. Species are still being lost almost a century after isolation and the island has still not reached equilibrium in terms of the number of species it can support.

The idea of the extinction debt was first developed from work on islands and habitat fragments. For a long time, scientists have known that there is a relationship between the number of species found in any particular area and its size, the 'species-area relationship'. Darlington's rule of thumb (MacArthur & Wilson 1967) states that a tenfold increase in area is reflected by a doubling of the number of species it contains. Conversely, if a particular area is reduced to one tenth of its original size, half the species present initially are predicted to be lost. This relationship between species number and area holds for islands, continents, countries and regions and is one of the fundamental 'laws' of biogeography. Indeed, it has been used as the basis for a number of attempts to predict future extinction rates. When ecologists started to look at the effects of habitat loss on birds, it was found that they could predict the number of species that would be lost using Darlington's rule of thumb. However, not all the species that are to be lost from the remnant habitats are lost straight away – they go extinct over time, and some may hang on longer than others, as was seen on Barro Colorado. The extinction debt is a process whereby habitat that is being lost now will store up a cost in terms of extinctions in the future (Tilman *et al.* 1994). Because of this, it may take years, possibly decades, for the full impacts of habitat loss and fragmentation to become apparent (Sodhi *et al.* 2004), and many species currently not thought to be threatened might already be well down the road to extinction.

The Atlantic Forest of Brazil is one of the world's hottest hotspots of extinction risk. Because over 80% of the natural forests in this ecosystem have been cleared and the remainder is heavily fragmented (Ribeiro *et al.* 2009), the species-area relationship predicts that half its species should have been lost, yet so far none has been (Brooks *et al.* 1999). However, at this large spatial scale some species may take centuries to disappear, and even if deforestation ceases immediately their extinction in the wild is nevertheless almost inevitable. It is worrying that the number of species endemic to these forests that are predicted to become extinct under the species-area relationship is almost exactly the same as the number of endemic species currently listed as being globally threatened, providing evidence that the extinction debt is starting to bite. These potential future extinctions are likely to result from the factors that will reduce the survival of the very low populations that persist in reduced fragments. In three protected Atlantic Forest reserves over a quarter of the endemic species present had total population sizes of fewer than 100 individuals, even in fragments as large as 56km^2 (Marsden *et al.* 2005). When populations are so low, they become vulnerable to all sorts of pressures and may become extinct through local events, such as a fire, a storm or even just a few below-average breeding seasons.

Although poorly understood, the extinction debt might apply to birds under threat from factors other than habitat loss and fragmentation. Any changes that reduce productivity or survival by even a small degree might consign a species to extinction many years later. The most recent and perhaps the last ever sightings of the Eskimo Curlew *Numenius borealis* and the Slender-billed Curlew *N. tenuirostris* (Chapter 25) were made almost exactly a century after major declines were noted in their populations, after which the rate of sightings slowed to a trickle and finally to nothing. It may well be that many other species currently not considered to be at high risk already carry with them an extinction debt that may need to be paid off by intensive conservation action in the future. Thus the extinction debt poses a considerable challenge to conservation because it might serve to mask species' true likelihood of extinction (Kuussaari *et al.* 2009).

BACK TO THE FUTURE: THE CHARACTERISTICS OF VULNERABILITY

When looking to predict which species might be the ones to become extinct or to join the list of Critically Endangered species in the future, a first step is to examine the characteristics of those species that have already been lost. If people in Tudor times had been interested in bird conservation, they would have been able to predict with a fair degree of precision many of those species that were going to be lost in the next 500 years by looking at what had been lost already. Extinctions after 1500, like those in the preceding 500 years, were confined largely to islands, and some groups were over represented in both periods. Rails and related (often flightless) species, pigeons and Hawaiian honeycreepers all comprised similar high proportions of extinct birds before and after 1500. However, projecting future extinctions from patterns in the distant past might result in some serious inaccuracies. For example, parrots and songbirds (excluding those of Hawaii) suffered relatively few prehistoric extinctions, or at least we have no record of them doing so, but they succumbed in larger numbers after 1500 as part of a second wave of extinctions brought about probably as much by land use changes as by exploitation and introduced predators. There are no known precedents before 1500 for the collapse to extinction of superabundant species like the Passenger Pigeon.

Simply applying lessons from the past is therefore a fairly blunt tool with which to identify future conservation battlegrounds, particularly today when rates of change in the Earth's environment are so rapid. A more useful approach is to look at recent shifts in patterns of rarity and extrapolate from these. Perhaps the clearest lesson from

Table 26.1. The percentage of bird extinctions during the periods 500 to 40,000 years ago ('Prehistoric'), within the last 500 years and currently classified as Critically Endangered (CR) in selected bird groups.

	Prehistoric	<500 years ago	CR
Ostrich and related ratites	9	2	0
Ducks, geese and swans	12	6	4
Shorebirds, gulls and auks	6	4	6
Rails and related species	22	19	3
Petrels, shearwaters and other seabirds	6	3	9
Pigeons, doves and dodos	9	11	6
Parrots	4	11	11
Typical owls	9	5	4
Passerines (non-Hawaiian)	7	25	47
Passerines (Hawaiian)	14	14	9

such an analysis is that the spotlight of endangerment is shifting from islands towards continental landmasses, where the number of species listed as Critically Endangered is increasing. The current geographical and taxonomic distribution of the world's most threatened species differs from that of past extinctions, and suggests that the current extinction event is now creeping beyond the most sensitive species and places towards the planet's most biodiverse mainland regions (Ricketts *et al.* 2005). Indeed, when their range sizes are taken into account, mainland species may now be in greater jeopardy than island species (Manne *et al.* 1999). This only partly reflects the success of intensive conservation projects on islands.

The extraordinary efforts made to save island species reduced to tiny populations, particularly in New Zealand and on Indian Ocean islands, have undoubtedly prevented a number of extinctions (Butchart *et al.* 2006c). But other explanations for the shift in extinction risk from islands to continents are less encouraging. First, many of the most vulnerable island species have already been lost, leaving only those better able to survive alongside introduced predators and those whose existence depends on conservation intervention, so relative extinction rates on islands are bound to drop. Second, and more worrying, mainland birds are catching up because of massive land use and other environmental changes, particularly in South America and South-East Asia: there are now over 40 Critically Endangered bird species on mainland South America alone. The causes of rarity are also shifting; whereas island species declined largely through the impacts of invasive predators, mainland species are primarily threatened by habitat loss (BirdLife International 2008a,b).

Despite these considerations, the fact remains that some species, or groups of species, appear to be particularly vulnerable to the impacts of people on the planet. They may occur in areas where our own alteration of the environment has been particularly severe, or they may be inherently less able to cope with change. There has been much recent work trying to predict the species that will be most prone to extinction based on their evolutionary and physical characteristics and life history traits. If a formula or set of rules could be created that predicts species' vulnerability to environmental change based on their known attributes, it might be possible to identify the birds that will need to be monitored most closely in the future. Perhaps unsurprisingly, species in areas of highest human impact tend to be more threatened than those in less disturbed parts of the world (Davies *et al.* 2006). Because of the disproportionate human impact in the more easily cultivated lowlands, species at lower altitudes are at higher risk of extinction than species at higher altitudes (Manne & Pimm 2001).

However, there is growing evidence that the ability of different species to cope with these changes will vary, for there appear to be attributes of species' life histories that render some inherently more susceptible than others (Purvis *et al.* 2000a,b). Rarity and the risk of extinction are not spread randomly across the bird world but cluster within certain families (Bennett & Owens 1997, Russell *et al.* 1998, Lockwood *et al.* 2002). Groups such as the parrots, albatrosses and petrels, rails, cranes, cracids, megapodes and pigeons are already over-represented on the Red List and it seems likely that more members of these groups will appear there in the future. Large-bodied bird species and those with small clutch sizes also appear to be particularly likely to join the ranks of the threatened (Bennett & Owens 1997). Low fecundity predisposes certain lineages to extinction, since slow-reproducing species will take longer to recover if their populations are put under pressure. This might explain another pattern in the distribution of rarity and extinction risk in the world's birds, namely that species or families of greater evolutionary age, typically consisting of long-lived individuals with naturally low reproductive rates, are inherently more vulnerable than younger ones (Gaston & Blackburn 1997). Evolutionary history is important but so too is the shared history of birds and people, as the vulnerability of different species to future threats might well depend on the extent to which they have faced similar threats in the more recent past. Those that have suffered from changes wrought by humans even thousands of years ago appear to be better at withstanding further changes than species that have never been exposed to the pressures we place on the environment (Balmford 1996).

Other studies have searched within different bird families for factors that predispose certain species to rarity and extinction. Among the world's hawks, for example, threatened species again lay smaller clutches and show a greater degree of habitat specialisation than non-threatened species (Kruger & Radford 2008). Species in which different colour morphs occur are less likely to be threatened than species showing no variation, perhaps because this variability in appearance is a reflection of high genetic diversity. The pattern in hawks for more specialised species to be more threatened appears to be repeated in other groups of birds (Owens & Bennett 2000). Species whose ranges are highly fragmented, and which therefore survive in a number of small, unconnected populations, will be at greater risk of extinction than species whose populations are connected (O'Grady *et al.* 2004), and species whose populations fluctuate greatly are more at risk than species whose numbers show little change from year to year (Vucetich *et al.* 2000).

There are therefore a number of characteristics that can be used to predict which species will become threatened in future, and which might already be more threatened than current estimates suggest. An analysis of the world's parrots using basic life-history traits to identify extinction risk across the group picked out a number of species whose true extinction risk might be underestimated in the IUCN Red List (Jones *et al.* 2006). Parrot species with two or more subspecies tend to be less threatened than those with no distinct subspecies. Of the latter group, species that feed exclusively in the canopy tend to be more threatened than species that feed in a variety of niches, and among them those laying large eggs relative to female body size were the most threatened. Using these and other patterns of extinction risk in the group, a number of species were identified that clustered together in groups of highly threatened species but which were themselves not listed as being at high risk. These included the Henderson Lorikeet *Vini stepheni* (currently listed as Vulnerable), and the enigmatic Blue-bellied Parrot *Triclaria malachitacea* of the Atlantic Forest (Near Threatened), both of which exhibit life-history characteristics similar to those of species listed as Critically Endangered. These are candidates for more research as it may be that they might slide towards extinction relatively quickly and perhaps unnoticed. The analysis threw up some more surprising candidates for future conservation concern. For example, the Gang-gang Cockatoo *Callocephalon fimbriatum* of Australia has life history characteristics more typical of a Critically Endangered species than one of Least Concern, which is the category it currently occupies. Whether this reflects an imperfect correlation or the high degree of protection given to Australian parrots, or whether it fulfils these predictions and becomes threatened in the future only time will tell, but analyses like these can be used to draw up a list of species that conservationists should at least keep a particularly close eye on.

THE TAXON CYCLE, TAXONOMY AND FUTURE RARITY

Perhaps unexpectedly, scientists may be better able to predict which species will become naturally rare or extinct far in the future than they can predict those that our own actions will make rare in the near future. This is because of the existence in nature of an evolutionary process called the taxon cycle which goes some way to explaining the distribution of rarity in the natural world (Ricklefs & Bermingham 2002). Species on islands appear to go through a cycle of colonisation, expansion, specialisation, speciation and eventual extinction. Species arrive on an island as generalists and add competitive pressure to the species already present. The continual arrival of new species of competitors causes earlier arrivals to get pushed into progressively narrower niches, becoming less common in the process and eventually become extinct. As they move along this evolutionary conveyor belt, they tend to become first restricted-range subspecies, then endemic species and finally relics doomed to extinction.

The best-studied examples among birds of the taxon cycle are the species that inhabit the various islands of the Lesser Antilles in the Caribbean (Ricklefs & Bermingham 1999). Here, species such as the Grey Kingbird *Tyrannus dominicensis* are fairly common across the islands and not genetically differentiated from their mainland populations. The House Wren *Troglodytes aedon* on the other hand has been on the islands longer and occurs on most islands, but has endemic subspecies on some islands (e.g. St Lucia), and is at a later stage of the taxon cycle. Even further down the conveyor belt are single-island endemic species such as the St Lucia Warbler *Dendroica delicata* and the closely related Barbuda Warbler *Dendroica subita*. Several islands, including Dominica and Guadalupe, lie between these two relic populations and it is likely that populations of related warblers have already become extinct there. It may be a long way off but we might predict from the taxon cycle that the St Lucia Warbler will join the IUCN Red List and face extinction well before the Grey Kingbird does. Recent work has shown that taxon cycles are not just restricted to island species. In effect, every living species has a 'die-by' date, those with shorter remaining shelf-lives being most likely to become the threatened birds of the future. As with extinction debt, the taxon cycle suggests that some species may be further down the road to extinction than their current numbers suggest.

Although scientists continue to disagree on what constitutes a species and what a subspecies, they have available to them a growing armoury of sophisticated genetic tools and improved methods for identifying species based on measurements or vocalisations. Each year, new species are described both through the discovery of forms wholly new to science and through the realisation that what were formerly considered to be single species with a number of subspecies actually comprise two or more distinct species. The second of these two processes now accounts for more of the new species announced each year than the first (Isaac *et al.* 2004). In an age of extinction, the number of recognised species on the planet is actually rising as a result of this taxonomic reassessment (Silveira & Olmos 2007, Sangster 2009). The inevitable consequence of splitting a species into two or more new species is that the populations and ranges of each become smaller than that of the original form and so are more likely to be listed as threatened (Kemp 2001, Agapow *et al.* 2004). Some newly recognised species, such as the Antioquia Brush-finch *Atlapetes blancae* of Colombia, have moved straight into the Critically Endangered category and, even worse, others have not been recognised as full species until after their extinction. The Nuku Hiva Monarch *Pomarea nukuhivae* was last seen in the 1930s, at which time it was regarded as a race of the threatened Marquesan Monarch *P. mendozae*; only half a century after its extinction was the Nuku Hiva Monarch recognised as a full species (Cibois *et al.* 2004). If the current trend in taxonomic research to split subspecies into full species continues, there will inevitably be a steady flow of new additions to the IUCN Red List and a movement of species towards the more threatened end of this scale.

THE HUMAN FOOTPRINT

The natural rate of species loss pales into insignificance compared to the rate of loss that has resulted and will result from human impacts on the planet (Diamond 1989). The planet's human population will continue to rise in the immediate future, most predictions placing the number of people on the planet at well over nine billion by 2050. It would be easy to assume that there is a spatial link between the loss of biodiversity and increasing human populations, and there is certainly evidence that areas with high human populations have large numbers of threatened birds and other wildlife (McKinney 2001, McKee *et al.* 2004). The link is relatively strong in continental countries but human population size on islands does not influence the number of species present because the damage has already been done independently by introductions of predators and by other factors not necessarily linked to the size of the human population. Even on continental landmasses, human population size predicts only a small proportion of the variation in extinction risk to birds, suggesting that the problem is far more complex than one of population density alone (Manne & Pimm 2001). The clearest evidence of this is the parlous conservation status of the world's seabirds, many of which may never even land on a populated island.

Human population growth will not take place at a steady pace over time, nor will it be equal in different parts of the world. This variation is a further complication in any attempt to identify future extinction hotspots. Increasing numbers of extinctions are expected to take place in those countries or regions with large numbers of threatened species and high human population growth rates. These include places such as Cameroon, Colombia, Ecuador, India, Madagascar, Malaysia, Peru, Philippines, Tanzania and Venezuela (Vié *et al.* 2009). The number of bird and mammal species in each country that becomes threatened is expected to rise by 14% by 2050 (McKee *et al.* 2004) simply based on human population growth patterns. Overpopulation will become particularly acute in 'biodiversity hotspots' – those areas of the world that hold disproportionately high numbers of endemic species, but which are also, by definition, densely populated by people (Mittermeier *et al.* 1999, Myers *et al.* 2000a). In 1995, nearly 20% of world's human population were living within the hotspots, an area that comprises just 12% of Earth's land area, and population growth was higher in hotspots (1.8% per year in 1995–2000) than across the rest of the world (Cincotta *et al.* 2000). Similarly, human population density in and around African Important Bird Areas, many of them designated for the rare species they support, is around three times higher than the average for sub-Saharan Africa (Balmford *et al.* 2001, Buchanan *et al.* 2009). This is not simply a matter of chance, since the fertile, well-watered areas most suitable for agriculturalists are also particularly productive for biodiversity. Urbanisation too is likely to bring a new range of species under threat; for example, the average distance from a city to a protected area in eastern Asia is predicted to fall from 43km to 23km by 2030 as urban sprawl increases, and a number of key sites are likely to disappear under concrete altogether (McDonald *et al.* 2008).

It seems that in future, the fight to save the world's rarest birds will remain focused to a degree on Important Bird Areas, particularly those falling within biodiversity hotspots. However, new regions will require increasing attention from conservationists. Countries such as Bolivia, Papua New Guinea and Angola, and regions such as the Amazonian slopes of the Andes, currently have small but fast expanding human populations and would benefit from early conservation action before problems become too great (Vié *et al.* 2009). However, it is not impossible for conservationists to address threats on a far broader geographic scale than simply in hotspots. The loss of natural habitat to agriculture is a threat that will inevitably continue to place greater pressure on birds and drive many towards increasingly high categories of extinction risk. In developing countries, the area of agricultural land may increase by over 20% by 2050 to meet the needs of a growing population (Balmford *et al.* 2005). However, this could be greatly reduced if crop yields were to increase, thereby sparing more land for wildlife (Green *et al.* 2005). Conservationists may therefore find themselves in the unusual position of trying to save wildlife by encouraging increasingly intensive farming practices.

More important than human growth *per se* is the growth in impact or 'footprint' of increasing populations. The ecological footprint of a country, which can be quantified as the area of land required to provide the resources for and absorb the wastes of one person, varies massively between countries. Economically developed nations such as the USA (with a footprint of 12.2 hectares per person) and the UK (6.3ha) have a greatly larger footprint than economically developing countries such as Sierra Leone (0.7ha) and Bangladesh (0.6ha). Ecological footprints, therefore, give a rather different picture of human pressure on the world's lands and resources: the human population in a country with a small ecological footprint could double and still in no way match the outsize footprints left by people living in the gluttonous developed world. However, India (with a current footprint of 1.1ha) and China (1.8ha), which between them currently hold nearly 40% of the world's human population and are rich in threatened bird species, are enjoying rapid economic growth. Their economies are so large that their development will have enormous impacts in other countries, in much the same way that Western wealth building has had, and continues to have, huge humanitarian and environmental impacts in other parts of the world. A little simple multiplication shows that if the ecological footprints of India and China were equivalent to that of the USA, an understandable aspiration, simply meeting those two countries' needs would take up twice the land surface of the planet. Predicting the impacts on wildlife once these mega-economies mature and their ecological footprints increase is, arguably, one of the most important challenges to the conservation of birds in the future.

The prospect of many more people wanting more commodities may be bleak, but things can change in complex and unpredictable ways. As has happened in developed countries, many of which now export conservation expertise and resources to the developing world, increasing wealth brings with it an increase in the proportion of the population with the time, resources and education to care for wildlife. It is generally assumed that wildlife is safer in wealthier countries because these tend to have the most comprehensive and strictly enforced nature protection legislation and the strongest non-governmental lobbies, and for birds at least there is some evidence to support this (Naidoo & Adamowicz 2000). Corruption and ineffective governance, which are most prevalent in the world's poorer nations, often lead to the rapid loss of wildlife through unregulated land deals, greater illegal trade in endangered species, and a suppression of the civil society which forms the mainspring of conservation movements elsewhere (Smith *et al.* 2003, Smith & Walpole 2005). Increasing wealth and the better political governance it brings might therefore eventually produce positive changes in the resources available for conservation, although lessons from Europe and North America suggest that much will be lost before things start to improve.

There is therefore good reason to suppose that the changes brought about by economic development in the next 20–50 years will be negative or detrimental. The trend among the Chinese and Indian middle classes towards eating more meat and bread, for instance, is putting new pressure on agricultural land. The growth of large middle classes in formerly agrarian countries is likely to stimulate a greater demand for commodities such as coffee, and already large tracts of forest in South-East Asia are being eyed up by coffee companies to meet this demand. The growing popularity of ice cream among Asian youths means that they are not developing the lactose intolerance typical of older generations raised on diets free from milk, leading to the prospect of a large new generation of people with a desire for dairy products, the least efficient means of conversion of sunlight into food and a major driver of deforestation (Roberts 2009). At the same time, the massive demands that affluent lifestyles in developed countries put upon the environment overseas are not likely to diminish.

Increasing consumption, more in terms of the environmental footprint of food rather than its calorific value, is a natural progression for increasingly affluent people and something that cannot be avoided, but there are a host of other knock-on effects of this new wealth. For example, the growth in tourism places stresses on the environment. Air transport is a major concern for the planet's climate but there are also growing pressures on coastal land in many countries due to the desire for holidays by the sea and, more importantly, the ability to pay for them. The

The Restinga Antwren Formicivora littoralis *is now listed as Endangered, a victim of habitat loss caused by unsustainable tourism (Tasso Leventis).*

coastal zone of Rio de Janeiro and São Paulo states in Brazil is one such area where tourism is bringing considerable problems. Here, there is a fragile and short forest type called *restinga* that grows on sandy soil just behind the coast. These areas are in high demand for the building of weekend homes for people from the big cities inland and the Restinga Antwren *Formicivora littoralis* is now listed as Critically Endangered. In St Lucia in the Lesser Antilles, similar patterns of tourist development are adversely affecting many bird species such as the Endangered White-breasted Thrasher *Ramphocinclus brachyurus* (Young *et al.* 2010).

With human demands so easily met in the modern world, it is inevitable that threats will emerge of which conservationists can have no advanced warning. Who could have predicted in 1990 that populations of Asian vultures would be on the verge of extinction less than twenty years later, and who could have foreseen that their demise would be the result of a common veterinary drug? Rapid changes in the fortunes of birds can clearly have some unusual and wholly unpredictable causes. In the mid-1990s, large numbers of owls started appearing for the first time in the bird markets of Indonesia to meet a new market created by the tremendously successful Harry Potter children's books and films, as this verbatim informative internet discourse shows:

Q – Where could I buy a snowy owl for a pet? Are they good pets? I like harry potter alot and i would love to have a pet owl.

A – If you can afford it, you can perches a non-indigenous species from a breeder for about $5000 and up with out haveing to aquire a federal permit. Any digenous spieces requires federal permits even if perched from a breeder.

Such binge-buying of wildlife, be it a 'Nemo fish' or 'mutant turtles' (terrapins), is perhaps unlikely to drive a species to extinction, but it does show how quickly and unpredictably new threats can arise. In the same way, new crazes for certain foods can create unpredictable problems. In 2008, a shipment of dead birds en route from Malaysia to China was seized, and officials were astonished to discover among them the bodies of over 900 owls, some with unplucked heads to prove their identity, revealing a hitherto unsuspected and perhaps new demand for owls in food or traditional medicine (Shepherd & Shepherd 2009). A recent assessment identified a number of potential future threats to biodiversity as diverse as pollution by nanoparticles of silver, the development of synthetic meat, deoxygenation of the world's oceans and volcanic activity under polar ice sheets (Sutherland *et al.* 2010), and it is likely that many more equally obscure threats remain as yet undetected. All that conservationists can do is to keep scanning the horizon for new and emerging threats and act as quickly as possible to head them off.

CLIMATE CHANGE

It is now generally accepted that the planet is warming at a rate that greatly exceeds anything since records began, and perhaps anything that can be inferred from the geological record (IPCC 2007). The unprecedented rise in global average temperatures over the last fifty years is generally considered to be largely or wholly the result of the release of over fifty million of tons of greenhouse gases each day, largely through the burning of forests and fossil fuels, though other factors might also be at work. Whatever the causes, it is increasingly apparent that climate change has the ability to affect profoundly the world's natural systems and the species that depend on them, and indeed is already doing so (Parmesan & Yohe 2003). Perhaps the first vertebrate extinction caused by recent climate change took place before 1990, when the beautiful and once common Golden Toad *Bufo periglenes* disappeared from its only home at the summit of Monteverde in Costa Rica (Pounds *et al.* 1999). A number of recent estimates of the impact of climate change on biodiversity suggest that as many as one in ten of all species on the planet may become extinct during the next century, including perhaps one in twenty bird species (Thomas *et al.* 2004, Sekercioglu *et al.* 2008).

The models on which these estimates are based and their extrapolations to the real world are open to some doubt, as any attempt to predict what will happen under such complex changes inevitably must be, but even the most optimistic forecasts suggest a greatly heightened risk of extinction for hundreds of bird species (Jetz *et al.* 2007, Sekercioglu *et al.* 2008). In other words, while the rarest and most threatened birds – commonly those with the most restricted ranges – are likely to be particularly affected, the probability is high that a far larger number of species not currently treated as globally threatened will face a greatly increased risk of extinction (Pimm 2008). Conservationists will therefore need to brace themselves and indeed recruit considerable reinforcements, but with so much uncertainty surrounding the prediction of future change in climate and the effects they will have on birds, it is difficult to identify species, or groups of species, that might become rare in the future. Even so, some species' populations are already changing in exactly the way that have been predicted by these models (Green *et al.* 2008a, Seoane & Carrascal 2008, Gregory *et al.* 2009).

Perhaps the most profound change that will occur as a result of climate change is that species' ranges will change in size, shape and location, as birds move to track their preferred climates. This was the response of animals and plants to rapid climate change in prehistoric times, as the fossil record clearly shows (Huntley *et al.* 2005). Most predictions suggest that the distributions of birds will move towards the poles or will be pushed into higher altitudes than they currently occupy, where their ranges will inevitably become smaller as the land area decreases. Even if their only response to climate change is that species move uphill, extinction rates are likely to be greatly increased (Pimm 2009). An analysis of the possible future ranges of European breeding birds suggests that for several the climates within which they currently live will disappear altogether, at least over dry land, so they will have to adapt to new conditions or perish (Huntley *et al.* 2007). For example, if projections hold true Berthelot's Pipit *Anthus berthelotii* of the Canary Islands and Madeira will have to adapt to new climates throughout its small and fragmented range or it will die out (Huntley *et al.* 2007).

Migratory species will have to adapt to changes in both their breeding and wintering ranges, and migration distances between the two are projected to increase, placing them under increasing pressure (Barbet-Massin *et al.* 2009, Doswald *et al.* 2009). Furthermore, when they arrive back on their breeding grounds, they will face increased competition for food and nesting sites with populations of resident birds that will benefit from milder winters. Changing climates will also result in changes in the timing of events to which species need to respond (Carey 2009). For example, warmer springs in Europe have led to the earlier eruption of the swarms of moth caterpillars that many migratory species rely on to raise their broods. Birds that do not change their migratory habitats to arrive back on the breeding grounds earlier risk missing out on this vital glut of food, and there is evidence that migratory species that are not altering their arrival times in response to climate change are already suffering population declines (Møller *et al.* 2008, Jones & Cresswell 2010). Some species have recently changed their migratory behaviour by becoming resident or by travelling for shorter distances. For example, the Rook *Corvus frugilegus* used to be abundant in winter in the Iberian Peninsula, but it has largely ceased to migrate there since the early 1980s (Román & Gutiérrez 2008). Meanwhile, there is worrying evidence that the ranges of many bird species are already moving in the directions predicted by climate models (Tingley *et al.* 2009, Zuckerberg *et al.* 2009), and that populations of some migratory species are already starting to suffer (Sanderson *et al.* 2006).

The responses of birds to future climate change are likely to be far too complex to allow us to estimate extinction risks solely on the basis of projections of changes in their geographical distributions (Akçakaya *et al.* 2006). Climate change is likely to interact with existing threats to biodiversity, such as habitat loss, food availability and disease, to place increased pressure on a range of species (Brook *et al.* 2008). As species' ranges shift, they will come into contact with a range of other species, including predators, pathogens and invasive species, to which they are naive, raising the fear that they will suffer in the same way as island birds exposed to new threats. The beleaguered forest birds of Hawaii, whose tiny ranges have contracted uphill to the cooler altitudes avoided by malaria-carrying mosquitoes, will be forced even higher by climate change, or brought more into contact with the disease (Atkinson & LaPointe 2009). Avian malaria and other diseases are likely to spread into new regions as climates warm, raising the spectre of a continental equivalent to Hawaii, with birds increasingly forced into cooler highland refuges. Elsewhere in Hawaii, the Laysan Finch *Telespiza cantans*, already listed as Vulnerable, is at further risk of habitat loss through sea-level rise, as Laysan reaches a maximum height of just 12m above sea level (Baker *et al.* 2006). The Tuamotu Sandpiper *Prosobonia cancellata*, a strange and endangered shorebird, is now confined through the presence of introduced rats and cats to a few coral atolls in the Pacific, where it faces the added risk of sea-level rise that may eventually inundate its final refuges. Sea-level rise will threaten many of the planet's intertidal and littoral habitats with unpredictable impacts on coastal species such as the Critically Endangered Spoon-billed Sandpiper

Laysan Finch Telespiza cantans, *already listed as Vulnerable, is likely to become more threatened as sea-level rises inundate its island home. These two young birds are sitting on the carcass of a Laysan Albatross* Phoebastria immutabilis *(James Breeden).*

Eurynorhynchus pygmeus (Chapter 4). Greater climatic instability will result in an increase in the number of extreme weather events, such as tropical storms and hurricanes, and rising sea levels will exacerbate their effects on species inhabiting coastal habitats and small islands (Michener *et al.* 1997).

Species struggling to adapt to changing climates will need at the same time to adapt to massive changes to natural and modified ecosystems that will result from our own species' political, social and economic responses to changing climates. Already, efforts to reduce global warming through the planting of biofuels are causing untold damage to tropical forests, often with little reduction in levels of greenhouse gas emission and some even leading to increased outputs (Danielsen *et al.* 2009). The Brazilian cerrado and the lowland Sundaic forests of South-East Asia, together with the many threatened birds that occupy them, are coming under increasing pressure from habitat clearance for plantations of soybean and oil palm that are at least partly driven by misguided efforts to reduce fossil fuel use by growing feedstock for biofuels. The cerrado region is one of the world's biodiversity hotspots and holds some of the planet's most threatened birds. Crop failure, the spread of pests and diseases, drought and massive social upheavals will greatly compromise the ability of conservationists to try to mitigate the effects of climate change; in the most pessimistic scenarios, human society may come under such pressure that activities such as conservation are abandoned altogether as people fight for their own survival. By 2080, for example, nearly half a billion additional people may be at risk from malaria (Martens *et al.* 1999). How then will the world's governments justify spending money on the conservation of tiny populations of birds?

A few species already listed as being Critically Endangered, such as the Amsterdam Albatross *Diomedea amsterdamensis*, might actually benefit from climate warming through increased productivity (Rivalan *et al.* 2010). However, most projections suggest that the majority of species will have smaller ranges in the future than those they currently occupy. Since range size is a good indicator of extinction risk, this does not bode well (Schwartz *et al.* 2006). Species predicted to be at greatest risk from future climate change include tropical species that currently have small ranges, many of them already under intense pressure from habitat loss (Jetz *et al.* 2007), and species that are already marooned on islands or mountain tops. Single-brooded species, species with poor dispersal abilities, species with small current ranges and migratory species, particularly those unable to modify the time of their migration to changing climates or resources, may also be those most vulnerable to the effects of climate change, and in some parts of the world species showing these traits are already in decline (Lemoine & Bohning-Gaese 2003, Schwartz *et al.* 2006, Amano & Yamaura 2007, Jiguet *et al.* 2007, Møller *et al.* 2008). Even small changes in temperature might prove fatal to some species. The remarkable Ethiopian Bush-crow *Zavattariornis stresemanni* has puzzled scientists since its discovery in the 1930s. In particular, researchers have struggled to explain why this clever and adaptable species should be confined to a tiny area of unremarkable scrub habitat is southern Ethiopia. Only recently has this mystery been partly answered, when researchers seeking to understand its distribution realised that the bird appears to be confined to a small bubble of climate that is cooler and dryer than anything found nearby (Donald *et al.* 2012). The edge of the species' range is defined almost precisely by the 20°C isotherm – within this the species is common, but as one crosses the isotherm the species disappears abruptly and completely. Although the underlying mechanism of this limitation is not yet understood, the species seems likely to be particularly susceptible to any changes that threaten to upset its little climatic lifeboat.

Around 35% of bird species exhibit characteristics, particularly a reliance on a rare habitat and a poor ability to disperse and colonise new areas, that elevate their susceptibility to climate change impacts (Foden *et al.* 2009). Species already living near the poles are likely to suffer greatly as their climates warm and they have nowhere colder to move to, especially in the southern hemisphere, where the area of land decreases towards the pole. A recent study suggests that the Emperor Penguin *Aptenodytes forsteri*, currently listed as Least Concern, may be extinct by 2100 as a result of the loss of sea ice (Jenouvrier *et al.* 2009). King Penguins *A. patagonicus* are predicted to suffer a 40% decline in adult survival for each degree Celsius that the southern oceans warm, giving little hope for the species' long-term survival (Le Bohec *et al.* 2008). At the other end of the planet, populations of the Ivory Gull *Pagophila eburnea*, currently listed only as Near Threatened, are in severe decline, again possibly due to a loss of sea ice (Gilg *et al.* 2009). Areas that support many species that have small global ranges coincide with areas that have rare climates,

The Ethiopian Bush-crow (Endangered) is likely to be particularly susceptible to climate change, as its range appears to be confined within a small bubble of cool, dry climate (Paul F. Donald, RSPB).

Two species, neither currently listed as globally threatened, that are predicted to undergo severe declines, perhaps to extinction, because of climate change. Above: Ivory Gull Pagophila eburnea *(Rebecca Nason); below: King Penguin* Aptenodytes patagonicus *(Kevin Schafer).*

which are generally colder than surrounding climates. This might be because these climates have protected cold-adapted species from climatic warming in the past. Unfortunately, these distinctive climates are likely to shrink disproportionately under most scenarios of future climate change, placing increased pressure on species that are already limited in where they can live (Ohlemuller *et al.* 2008).

Meeting the many challenges posed by climate change will require a revolution in the way conservationists set their priorities and direct their resources (McClanahan *et al.* 2008), but the tools required are similar or identical to those already in use to address other threats (Mawdsley *et al.* 2009). The planet's existing network of protected areas will continue to function to reduce extinction rates, although it will need to be greatly expanded to reduce rising extinction rates (Jetz *et al.* 2007). The network of protected areas and Important Bird Areas in Africa will continue to support important populations of many threatened species under even the most extreme projections of climate change, since although some will lose the species for which they were designated, others will gain new species (Hole *et al.* 2009). Other conservation tools such as captive breeding, habitat restoration and legal measures will become increasingly important in addressing climate change (Mawdsley *et al.* 2009). The removal of predators from islands may help seabirds trying to track shifting climates over the oceans to survive in new homes if they can reach them.

MEETING FUTURE CHALLENGES

The future is unpredictable. In some respects, this is what makes the world such a wonderful place in which to live. But in terms of protecting bird species from the hidden menaces of the future, how will we do? Certainly, the conservation movement is better prepared now to identify problems and take actions than it was 50 years ago. In 2009, around 7,500 people were employed by the US Fish and Wildlife Service, which has a budget of hundreds of millions of dollars for nature conservation activities. In UK, the membership of the RSPB is now well over one million. The RSPB is just one of the bird conservation organisations that make up BirdLife International, which now coordinates its efforts in over more than a hundred countries. Many other large and successful bird and wildlife conservation organisations exist. These are welcome developments but such conservation resources are unlikely to grow at the same rate as the thunderclouds on the horizon.

Conservationists are now in the position of being able to predict some of the threats that will emerge in the future and can make educated guesses about which species are likely to become rare. They are also aware that some threats are almost wholly unpredictable, but they have the capacity and expertise to respond quickly to new threats, as the example of the Asian vultures shows. More important, they have a better understanding of exactly why people should want to protect birds in the future. Until the 1970s, few people cared about the conservation of birds in tropical countries (unless they were economically important). In the 1980s, the first truly global assessments of the extinction risk facing all bird species were produced. In the 1990s, conservationists started to think in terms of biodiversity, in which birds were included amongst a wealth of other animals and plants. At the start of the twenty-first century, ecologists started to talk of ecosystem services, placing a monetary value on intact forests and other habitats in much the same way that a rhinoceros can be given a value in dollars per year in attracting tourists to an African game reserve. The ecological services that birds provide are often greatly underestimated (Sekercioglu 2006). Scientists also started to soften the edge between wildlife and people by looking at the role of the environment in human well-being, for example finding that post-operative patients in hospitals set in green surroundings have faster recovery rates than those in urban settings (Maller *et al.* 2005). Making and maintaining these links between people and nature is crucial if people are to continue to care about birds. Just as our well-being as humans is linked to that of our environment and its wildlife, it is encouraging to note that the well-being of our governments and economies is also linked to birdwatchers. A report by the US Fish and Wildlife Service showed that 20% of all Americans are birdwatchers, contributing $36 billion to the economy in 2006 via their hobby (La Rouche 2009). In future, our interest in saving the world's rarest birds must be extended to helping other groups of animals and plants; to protecting land, habitats and the rights of people who depend on them, and most importantly to driving governments to address concerns about the future of the environment in the widest sense. Only then will further catastrophes like the extinction of the Dodo, the Passenger Pigeon and the Great Auk be averted.

REFERENCES

Abraham, E.R., Pierre, J.P., Middleton, D.A.J., Cleal, J., Walker, N.A. & Waugh, S.M. (2009) Effectiveness of fish waste management strategies in reducing seabird attendance at a trawl vessel. *Fisheries Research*, 95: 210–219.

ACAP. (2009) Species Assessment: Tristan Albatross *Diomedea dabbenena*. Retrieved October 2009, from http://www.acap.aq.

Acevedo, M.A. & Restrepo, C. (2008) Land-cover and land-use change and its contribution to the large-scale organization of Puerto Rico's bird assemblages. *Diversity and Distributions*, 14: 114–122.

Acharya, R., Cuthbert, R., Baral, H.S. & Shah, K.B. (2009) Rapid population declines of Himalayan Griffon *Gyps himalayensis* in Upper Mustang, Nepal. *Bird Conservation International*, 19: 99–107.

Adeney, J.M., Christensen, N.L. & Pimm, S.L. (2009) Reserves protect against deforestation fires in the Amazon. *PLoS ONE*, 4: e5014.

Afan, D.S., Ibañez, J.C., Bueser, G.L.L., Gatil, K.M., Ibañez, G.B. & Miranda, H.C. (2000) Notes on movement and behavior of a post-fledging Philippine Eagle in Mt. Sinaka, Mindanao Island. *Sylvatrop*, 10: 59–69.

Agapow, P.M., Bininda-Emonds, O.R.P., Crandall, K.A., Gittleman, J.L., Mace, G.M., Marshall, J.C. & Purvis, A. (2004) The impact of species concept on biodiversity studies. *Quarterly Review of Biology*, 79: 161–179.

Agreda, A., Krabbe, N. & Rodríguez, O. (1999) Pale-headed Brush-finch *Atlapetes pallidiceps* is not extinct. *Cotinga*, 11: 50–54.

Aguirre-Muñoz, A., Croll, D.A., Donlan, C.J., Henry, R.W., Hermosillo, M.A., Howald, G.R., Keitt, B.S., Luna-Mendoza, L., Rodriguez-Malagon, M., Salas-Flores, L.M., Samaniego-Herrera, A., Sanchez-Pacheco, J.A., Sheppard, J., Tershy, B.R., Toro-Benito, J., Wolf, S. & Wood, B. (2008) High-impact conservation: invasive mammal eradications from the islands of western Mexico. *Ambio*, 37: 101–107.

Akçakaya, H.R., Butchart, S.H.M., Mace, G.M., Stuart, S.N. & Hilton-Taylor, C. (2006) Use and misuse of the IUCN Red List Criteria in projecting climate change impacts on biodiversity. *Global Change Biology*, 12: 2037–2043.

Alagona, P.S. (2004) Biography of a "feathered pig": the California condor conservation controversy. *Journal of the History of Biology*, 37: 557–583.

Alcover, J.A., Sans, A. & Palmer, M. (1998) The extent of extinctions of mammals on the islands of western Mexico. *Journal of Biogeography*, 25: 913–918.

Ale, S.B. & Whelan, C.J. (2008) Reappraisal of the role of big, fierce predators! *Biodiversity and Conservation*, 17: 685–690.

Alexander, B. (1898) An ornithological expedition to the Cape Verde islands. *Ibis*, (7)4: 74–118.

Ali, S. (1978) President's letter: 'mystery' birds of India 3. Blewitt's Owl or Forest Spotted Owlet. *Hornbill*, 1978(1): 4–6.

Ali, S. & Ripley, S.D. (1968–1998) *Handbook of the birds of India and Pakistan*. Oxford University Press, Bombay.

Alström, P., Davidson, P., Duckworth, J.W., Eames, J.C., Le, T.T., Nguyen, C., Olsson, U., Robson, C. & Timmins, R. (2010) Description of a new species of *Phylloscopus* warbler from Vietnam and Laos. *Ibis*, 152: 145–168.

Amano, T. & Yamaura, Y. (2007) Ecological and life-history traits related to range contractions among breeding birds in Japan. *Biological Conservation*, 137: 271–282.

Andrade, R.D., Lins, L.V., Ribeiro, F. & Lima Neto, A. (2009) Ninhos do pato-mergulhão (*Mergus octosetaceus*) em cavidades em barrancos de terra na região da Serra da Canastra, MG. XVII Brazilian Ornithological Congress, Aracruz, Brazil.

Andreone, F. & Gavetti, E. (1998) Some remarkable specimens of the giant Cape Verde skink, *Macroscincus coctei* (Dumril & Bibron, 1839), with notes about its distribution and causes of its possible extinction. *Italian Journal of Zoology*, 65: 413–421.

Andreyeva, T.R. & Tomkovich, P.S. (1992) On the role of chick food items in the formation of population structure of tundra waders. In: Chernov, Y.I. (ed). *Cenotic interactions in tundra ecosystems*, 70–78. Nauca Publishers, Moscow.

Angassa, A. (2002) The effect of clearing bushes and shrubs on range condition in Borana, Ethiopia. *Tropical Grasslands*, 36: 69–76.

Angassa, A. & Beyene, F. (2003) Current range condition in southern Ethiopia in relation to traditional management strategies: the perceptions of Borana pastoralists. *Tropical Grasslands*, 37: 53–59.

Angassa, A. & Oba, G. (2007) Relating long-term rainfall variability to cattle population dynamics in communal rangelands and a government ranch in southern Ethiopia. *Agricultural Systems*, 94: 715–725.

Angassa, A. & Oba, G. (2008) Herder perceptions on impacts of range enclosures, crop farming, fire ban and bush encroachment on the rangelands of Borana, southern Ethiopia. *Human Ecology*, 36: 201–215.

Angassa, A. & Oba, G. (2009) Bush encroachment control demonstrations in southern Ethiopia: 1. Woody species survival strategies with implications for herder land management. *African Journal of Ecology*, 47: 63–76.

Angassa, A., Tolera, A. & Belayneh, A. (2006) The effects of physical environment on the condition of rangelands in Borana. *Tropical Grasslands*, 40: 33–39.

Angel, A., Wanless, R.M. & Cooper, J. (2009) Review of impacts of the introduced house mouse on islands in the Southern Ocean: are mice equivalent to rats? *Biological Invasions*, 11: 1743–1754.

Angulo, E., Deves, A.L., Saint Jalme, M. & Courchamp, F. (2009) Fatal attraction: rare species in the spotlight. *Proceedings of the Royal Society Series B-Biological Sciences*, 276: 1331–1337.

Anon. (2007) *Plan for the eradication of rabbits and rodents on Subantarctic Macquarie Island*. Parks and Wildlife Service, Department of Tourism, Arts and the Environment, Tasmania and Biodiversity Conservation Branch, Department of Primary Industries and Water, Tasmania, Hobart, Tasmania.

Antas, P.T.Z. (1996) The Brazilian Merganser (*Mergus octosetaceus*), the most threatened duck in South America. *Gibier Faune Sauvage*, 13: 799–800.

Aratrakorn, S., Thunhikorn, S. & Donald, P.F. (2006) Changes in bird communities following conversion of lowland forest to oil palm and rubber plantations in southern Thailand. *Bird Conservation International*, 16: 71–82.

Ardern, S.L. & Lambert, D.M. (1997) Is the black robin in genetic peril? *Molecular Ecology*, 6: 21–28.

Armenteras, D., Rodriguez, N. & Retana, J. (2009) Are conservation strategies effective in avoiding the deforestation of the Colombian Guyana Shield? *Biological Conservation*, 142: 1411–1419.

Armstrong, D.P. & Davidson, R.S. (2006) Developing population models for guiding reintroductions of extirpated bird species back to the New Zealand mainland. *New Zealand Journal of Ecology*, 30: 73–85.

Arshad, M., Chaudhary, M.J.I. & Wink, M. (2009) High mortality and sex ratio imbalance in a critically declining Oriental White-backed Vulture (*Gyps bengalensis*) population in Pakistan. *Journal of Ornithology*, 150: 495–503.

Aruch, S., Atkinson, C.T., Savage, A.F. & LaPointe, D.A. (2007) Prevalence and distribution of pox-like lesions, avian malaria, and mosquito vectors in Kipahulu Valley, Haleakala National Park, Hawai'i, USA. *Journal of Wildlife Diseases,* 43: 567–575.

Ash, J.S. & Olson, S.L. (1985) A second specimen of *Mirafra* (*Heteromirafra*) *sidamoensis* Erard. *Bulletin of the British Ornithologists' Club,* 105: 141–143.

Asner, G.P., Rudel, T.K., Aide, T.M., Defries, R. & Emerson, R. (2009) A contemporary assessment of change in humid tropical forests. *Conservation Biology,* 23: 1386–1395.

Atkinson, C.T. & LaPointe, D.A. (2009) Introduced avian diseases, climate change, and the future of Hawaiian honeycreepers. *Journal of Avian Medicine and Surgery,* 23: 53–63.

Atkinson, C.T., Woods, K.L., Dusek, R.J., Sileo, L.S. & Iko, W.M. (1995) Wildlife disease and conservation in Hawaii: pathogenicity of avian malaria (*Plasmodium relictum*) in experimentally infected Iiwi (*Vestiaria coccinea*). *Parasitology,* 111: S59-S69.

Atkinson, C.T., Dusek, R.J., Woods, K.L. & Iko, W.M. (2000) Pathogenicity of avian malaria in experimentally-infected Hawaii Amakihi. *Journal of Wildlife Diseases,* 36: 197–204.

Atkinson, C.T., Lease, J.K., Drake, B.M. & Shema, N.P. (2001) Pathogenicity, serological responses, and diagnosis of experimental and natural malarial infections in native Hawaiian thrushes. *Condor,* 103: 209–218.

Atkinson, I.A.E. (2001) Introduced mammals and models for restoration. *Biological Conservation,* 99: 81–96.

Aucca, C. & Ramsay, P.M. (2005) Management of biodiversity and land use in southern Peru: ECOAN's activities to help conserve *Polylepis* woodlands. *Mountain Research and Development,* 25: 287–289.

Austin, O.L. (1949) The status of the Steller's Albatross. *Pacific Science,* 3: 283–295.

Awkerman, J.A., Westbrock, M.A., Huyvaert, K.P. & Anderson, D.J. (2007) Female-biased sex ratio arises after parental care in the sexually dimorphic waved albatross (*Phoebastria irrorata*). *Auk,* 124: 1336–1346.

Azafzaf, H., Gretton, A., Kiss, J.B., Smart, M., Zenatello, M. & Feltrup-Azafzaf, C. (2007) Search for the Slender-billed Curlew (*Numenius tenuirostris*) in Tunisia in January 2003. *Ostrich,* 78: 505.

Azeredo, R.G.P. (1997) Projeto de preservação do *Crax blumenbachii*. In: Strahl, S.D. *et al.* (eds). *The Cracidae: their biology and conservation*, 146–147. Hancock House, Surrey, BC.

Azeria, E.T., Carlson, A., Part, T. & Wiklund, C.G. (2006) Temporal dynamics and nestedness of an oceanic island bird fauna. *Global Ecology and Biogeography,* 15: 328–338.

Baccetti, N. (1995) [Review of the Italian captures of a vanishing species: the Slender-billed Curlew *Numenius tenuirostris* (Aves, Scolopacidae)] (in Italian). *Ric. Biol. Selvaggina,* 94: 1–18.

Bain, J.R. & Humphrey, S.R. (1982) *A profile of the endangered species of Thailand, 1. Through birds (Report no. 4, Office of Ecological Services, Florida State Museum).* University of Florida, Gainsville, Florida.

Baker-Gabb, D. (2007) *The Black-eared Miner: a decade of recovery*. Black-eared Miner Recovery Team, Melbourne.

Baker, G.B., Double, M.C., Gales, R., Tuck, G.N., Abbott, C.L., Ryan, P.G., Petersen, S.L., Robertson, C.J.R. & Alderman, R. (2007) A global assessment of the impact of fisheries-related mortality on shy and white-capped albatrosses: conservation implications. *Biological Conservation,* 137: 319–333.

Baker, J.D., Littnan, C.L. & Johnston, D.W. (2006) Potential effects of sea level rise on the terrestrial habitats of endangered and endemic megafauna in the Northwestern Hawaiian Islands. *Endangered Species Research,* 2: 21–30.

Baker, P.E. (1998) A description of the first live Poouli captured. *Wilson Bulletin,* 110: 307–310.

Baker, P.E. (2001) Status and distribution of the Po'ouli (*Melamprosops phaeosoma*) in the Hanawi natural area reserve between December 1995 and June 1997. In: Scott, J.M., Conant, S. & van Riper, C. (eds). *Ecology, conservation and management of endemic Hawaiian birds: a vanishing avifauna*, 144–150. Cooper Ornithological Society, CA.

Balmford, A. (1996) Extinction filters and current resilience: the significance of past selection pressures for conservation biology. *Trends in Ecology & Evolution,* 11: 193–196.

Balmford, A. (2002) Selecting sites for conservation. In: Norris, K. & Pain, D.J. (eds). *Conserving bird biodiversity: general principles and their application*, 74–104. Cambridge University Press, Cambridge, UK.

Balmford, A. & Long, A. (1994) Avian endemism and forest loss. *Nature,* 372: 623–624.

Balmford, A. & Bond, W. (2005) Trends in the state of nature and their implications for human well-being. *Ecology Letters,* 8: 1218–1234.

Balmford, A., Moore, J.L., Brooks, T., Burgess, N., Hansen, L.A., Williams, P. & Rahbeck, C. (2001) Conservation conflicts across Africa. *Science,* 291: 2616–2619.

Balmford, A., Bruner, A., Cooper, P., Costanza, R., Farber, S., Green, R.E., Jenkins, M., Jefferiss, P., Jessamy, V., Madden, J., Munro, K., Myers, N., Naeem, S., Paavola, J., Rayment, M., Rosendo, S., Roughgarden, J., Trumper, K. & Turner, R.K. (2002) Economic reasons for conserving wild nature. *Science,* 297: 950–953.

Balmford, A., Gaston, K.J., Blyth, S., James, A. & Kapos, V. (2003a) Global variation in terrestrial conservation costs, conservation benefits, and unmet conservation needs. *Proceedings of the National Academy of Sciences of the United States of America,* 100: 1046–1050.

Balmford, A., Green, R.E. & Jenkins, M. (2003b) Measuring the changing state of nature. *Trends in Ecology & Evolution,* 18: 326–330.

Balmford, A., Green, R.E. & Scharlemann, J.P.W. (2005) Sparing land for nature: exploring the potential impact of changes in agricultural yield on the area needed for crop production. *Global Change Biology,* 11: 1594–1605.

Banko, P.C., Oboyski, P.T., Slotterback, J.W., Dougill, S.J., Goltz, D.M., Johnson, L., Laut, M.E. & Murray, T.C. (2002) Availability of food resources, distribution of invasive species, and conservation of a Hawaiian bird along a gradient of elevation. *Journal of Biogeography,* 29: 789–808.

Bankoff, G. (2007) One island too many: reappraising the extent of deforestation in the Philippines prior to 1946. *Journal of Historical Geography,* 33: 314–334.

Banks, R.C. (1977) The decline and fall of the Eskimo Curlew, or why did the curlew go extaille? *American Birds,* 31: 127–134.

Baral, H.S., Ram, A.K., Chaudhary, B., Basnet, S., Chaudhary, H., Giri, T.R. & Chaudhary, D. (2012) Conservation status of Bengal Florican *Houbaropsis bengalensis bengalensis* (Gmelin, 1789) (Gruiformes: Otididae) in Koshi Tappu Wildlife Reserve and adjoining areas, eastern Nepal. *Journal of Threatened Taxa,* 4: 2464–2469.

Baral, N. & Gautam, R. (2007) Socio-economic perspectives on the conservation of Critically Endangered vultures in South Asia: an empirical study from Nepal. *Bird Conservation International,* 17: 131–139.

Baral, N., Timilsina, N. & Tamang, B. (2003a) Bengal Florican *Houbaropsis bengalensis* in Royal Suklaphanta Wildlife Reserve, Nepal. *Oriental Bird Club Bulletin,* 34: 30–33.

Baral, N., Timilsina, N. & Tamang, B. (2003b) Status of Bengal Florican *Houbaropsis bengalensis* in Nepal. *Forktail,* 19: 51–55.

Barbet-Massin, M., Walther, B.A., Thuiller, W., Rahbek, C. & Jiguet, F. (2009) Potential impacts of climate change on the winter distribution of Afro-Palaearctic migrant passerines. *Biology Letters,* 5: 248–251.

Barbosa, M.O. & Almeida, M.L. (2010) Novas observações e dados reprodutivos do pato-mergulhão *Mergus octosetaceus* na região do Jalapão, Tocantins, Brasil. *Cotinga,* 32: 40-45.

Barker, F.K., Barrowclough, G.F. & Groth, J.G. (2002) A phylogenetic hypothesis for passerine birds: taxonomic and biogeographic implications of an analysis of nuclear DNA sequence data. *Proceedings of the Royal Society Series B-Biological Sciences,* 269: 295–308.

Barter, M. (2002) *Shorebirds of the Yellow Sea: importance, threats and conservation status. Wetlands International Global Series 9, International Wader Studies 12.* Wetlands International, Canberra.

Bartmann, W. (1988) New observations on the Brazilian Merganser. *Wildfowl,* 39: 7–14.

Basse, B., Flux, I. & Innes, I. (2003) Recovery and maintenance of North Island kokako (*Callaeas cinerea wilsoni*) populations through pulsed pest control. *Biological Conservation*, 109: 259–270.

Bataillon, T. & Kirkpatrick, M. (2000) Inbreeding depression due to mildly deleterious mutations in finite populations: size does matter. *Genetical Research*, 75: 75–81.

Bates, J.M. (2002) The genetic effects of forest fragmentation on five species of Amazonian birds. *Journal of Avian Biology*, 33: 276–294.

Battley, P.F. & Piersma, T. (2005) Body composition and flight ranges of Bar-tailed Godwits (*Limosa lapponica baueri*) from New Zealand. *Auk*, 122: 922–937.

Beadell, J.S., Ishtiaq, F., Covas, R., Melo, M., Warren, B.H., Atkinson, C.T., Bensch, S., Graves, G.R., Jhala, Y.V., Peirce, M.A., Rahmani, A.R., Fonseca, D.M. & Fleischer, R.C. (2006) Global phylogeographic limits of Hawaii's avian malaria. *Proceedings of the Royal Society Series B-Biological Sciences*, 273: 2935–2944.

Becking, J.-H. (2009) The Bartels and other egg collections from the island of Java, Indonesia, with corrections to earlier publications of A. Hoogerwerf. *Bulletin of the British Ornithologists' Club*, 129: 18–48.

Beissinger, S.R., Wunderle, J.M., Meyers, J.M., Saether, B.E. & Engen, S. (2008) Anatomy of a bottleneck: diagnosing factors limiting population growth in the Puerto Rican Parrot. *Ecological Monographs*, 78: 185–203.

Belik, V.P. (1994) Where on earth does the Slender-billed Curlew breed? *Wader Study Group Bulletin*, 75: 37–38.

Bell, B.D. & Merton, D.V. (2002) Critically endangered bird populations and their management. In: Norris, K. & Pain, D.J. (eds). *Conserving bird biodiversity: general principles and their application*, 105–138. Cambridge University Press, Cambridge, UK.

Bellingham, P.J., Towns, D.R., Cameron, E.K., Davis, J.J., Wardle, D.A., Wilmshurst, J.M. & Mulder, C.P.H. (2010) New Zealand island restoration: seabirds, predators, and the importance of history. *New Zealand Journal of Ecology*, 34: 115–136.

Bencke, G.A., Maurício, G.N., Develey, P.F. & Goerck, J.M. (2006) *Áreas importantes para a conservação das aves no Brasil: parte I-estados do domínio da Mata Atlântica*. SAVE Brasil, São Paulo.

Bennett, P.M. & Owens, I.P.F. (1997) Variation in extinction risk among birds: chance or evolutionary predisposition? *Proceedings of the Royal Society Series B-Biological Sciences*, 264: 401–408.

Benning, T.L., LaPointe, D., Atkinson, C.T. & Vitousek, P.M. (2002) Interactions of climate change with biological invasions and land use in the Hawaiian Islands: modeling the fate of endemic birds using a geographic information system. *Proceedings of the National Academy of Sciences of the United States of America*, 99: 14246–14249.

Bensch, S. & Pearson, D. (2002) The Large-billed Reed Warbler *Acrocephalus orinus* revisited. *Ibis* 144: 259–267.

Benson, C.W., Colebrook-Robjent, J.F.R. & Williams, A. (1976) Contribution à l'ornithologie de Madagascar. *L'Oiseau et R.F.O.*, 46: 103–134.

Benstead, P.J., Jeffs, C.J.S. & Hearn, R.D. (1998) Riparian bird densities along four tributaries of the rio Parana in north-eastern Argentina. *Hornero*, 15: 68–71.

Berec, L., Angulo, E. & Courchamp, F. (2007) Multiple Allee effects and population management. *Trends in Ecology & Evolution*, 22: 185–191.

Beresford, A.E., Buchanan, G.M., Donald, P.F., Butchart, S.H.M., Fishpool, L.D.C. & Rondinini, C. (2011) Poor overlap between the distribution of protected areas and globally threatened birds in Africa. *Animal Conservation*, 14: 99–107.

Bergin, A. (1997) Albatross and longlining – managing seabird bycatch. *Marine Policy*, 21: 63–72.

Berglund, H., Jaremo, J. & Bengtsson, G. (2009) Endemism predicts intrinsic vulnerability to nonindigenous species on Islands. *American Naturalist*, 174: 94–101.

Bergstrom, D.M., Lucieer, A., Kiefer, K., Wasley, J., Belbin, L., Pedersen, T.K. & Chown, S.L. (2009) Indirect effects of invasive species removal devastate World Heritage Island. *Journal of Applied Ecology*, 46: 73–81.

Best, H.A. (1984) The foods of Kakapo on Stewart Island as determined from their feeding sign. *New Zealand Journal of Ecology*, 7: 71–83.

Bester, M.N., Bloomer, J.P., van Aarde, R.J., Erasmus, B.H., van Rensburg, P.J.J., Skinner, J.D., Howell, P.G. & Naude, T.W. (2002) A review of the successful eradication of feral cats from sub-Antarctic Marion Island,

Southern Indian Ocean. *South African Journal of Wildlife Research*, 32: 65–73.

Bianchi, C.A., Brant, S., Brandão, R.A. & Brito, B.F. (2005) New records of the Brazilian Merganser *Mergus octosetaceus* in the rio das Pedras, Chapada dos, Veadeiros, Brazil. *Cotinga*, 24: 72–74.

Bianchi, C.A. (2008) Efforts in the recovery of the Alagoas Curassow (*Mitu mitu*). *Bulletin of the Cracid Specialist Group*, 26: 16–23.

Biber, E. (2002) Patterns of endemic extinctions among island bird species. *Ecography*, 25: 661–676.

BirdLife International (2000) *Threatened birds of the world*. BirdLife International and Lynx Edicions, Cambridge, UK and Barcelona.

BirdLife International (2001) *Threatened birds of Asia: the BirdLife International Red Data Book*. BirdLife International, Cambridge, UK.

BirdLife International (2004) *Tracking ocean wanderers: the global distribution of albatrosses and petrels*. BirdLife International, Cambridge UK.

BirdLife International (2008a) *State of the world's birds: indicators for our changing world*. BirdLife International, Cambridge, UK.

BirdLife International (2008b) *Critically Endangered birds: a global audit*. BirdLife International, Cambridge, UK.

BirdLife International (2009a) *Saving the Critically Endangered Spoon-billed Sandpiper. A report on conservation action – June 2009*. BirdLife International, Cambridge, UK.

BirdLife International (2009b) *State of the world's birds: indicators for our changing world*. BirdLife International, Cambridge, UK.

Black, J.M. (1995) The Nene *Branta sandvicensis* recovery initiative: research against extinction. *Ibis*, 157: S153-S160.

Blackburn, T.M., Gaston, K.J., Quinn, R.M., Arnold, H. & Gregory, R.D. (1997) Of mice and wrens: the relation between abundance and geographic range size in British mammals and birds. *Philosophical Transactions of the Royal Society Series B-Biological Sciences*, 252: 419–427.

Blackburn, T.M., Cassey, P., Duncan, R.P., Evans, K.L. & Gaston, K.J. (2004) Avian extinction and mammalian introductions on oceanic islands. *Science*, 305: 1955–1958.

Blackburn, T.M., Petchey, O.L., Cassey, P. & Gaston, K.J. (2005) Functional diversity of mammalian predators and extinction in island birds. *Ecology*, 86: 2916–2923.

Bleitz, D. (1962) Photographing the Eskimo Curlew. *Western Bird Bander*, 37: 43–45.

Blondel, J. (2000) Evolution and ecology of birds on islands: trends and prospects. *Life and Environment*, 50: 205–220.

Blumstein, D.T. (2006) The multipredator hypothesis and the evolutionary persistence of antipredator behavior. *Ethology*, 112: 209–217.

Bock, C.E. & Ricklefs, R.E. (1983) Range size and local abundance of some North American songbirds – a positive correlation. *American Naturalist*, 122: 295–299.

Bodsworth, F. (1956) *Last of the curlews*, Museum Press, London.

Boere, G.C. & Rubeck, G.D.A. (2002) Conservation policies and programmes affecting birds. In: Norris, K. & Pain, D.J. (eds). *Conserving bird biodiversity: general principles and their application*, 246–270. Cambridge University Press, Cambridge, UK.

Boere, G.C. & Yurlov, A. (1998) In search of the Slender-billed Curlew (*Numenius tenuirostris*). Preliminary results of an expedition to wetlands and waterbirds of the Baraba and Karasuk steppe in the south of West Siberia, Russian Federation, 17 May – 22 June 1997. *Wader Study Group Bulletin*, 85: 35–38.

Boessenkool, S., Taylor, S.S., Tepolt, C.K., Komdeur, J. & Jamieson, I.G. (2007) Large mainland populations of South Island robins retain greater genetic diversity than offshore island refuges. *Conservation Genetics*, 8: 705–714.

Boles, W.E., Longmore, N.W. & Thompson, M.C. (1994) A recent specimen of the Night Parrot *Geopsittacus occidentalis*. *Emu*, 94: 37–40.

Bond, M.W. (1965) Did a Barbados hunter shoot the last Eskimo Curlew? *Audubon Magazine*, 67: 314–316.

Bond, W.J. & Silander, J.A. (2007) Springs and wire plants: anachronistic defences against Madagascar's extinct elephant birds. *Proceedings of the Royal Society Series B-Biological Sciences*, 274: 1985–1992.

Bonheur, N. & Lane, B.D. (2002) Natural resources management for human security in Cambodia's Tonle Sap Biosphere Reserve. *Environmental Science and Policy,* 5: 33–41.

Bonier, F., Martin, P.R. & Wingfield, J.C. (2007) Urban birds have broader environmental tolerance. *Biology Letters,* 3: 670–673.

Bonnaud, E., Medina, F.M., Vidal, E., Nogales, M., Tershy, B., Zavaleta, E., Donlan, C.J., Keitt, B., Le Corre, M. & Horwath, S.V. (2011) The diet of feral cats on islands: a review and a call for more studies. *Biological Invasions,* 13: 581-603.

Bosso, A. & Gil, G. (2000) *Sobre la situación del Pato Serrucho (*Mergus octosetaceus*) en la Argentina.* Apunte preparado para el Taller sobre Pato Serrucho, São Roque de Minas, Brasil 18 a 22 de Septiembre 2000.

Bourne, W.R.P. (1955) The birds of the Cape Verde Islands. *Ibis,* 97: 508–556.

Bouzat, J.L., Johnson, J.A., Toepfer, J.E., Simpson, S.A., Esker, T.L. & Westemeier, R.L. (2009) Beyond the beneficial effects of translocations as an effective tool for the genetic restoration of isolated populations. *Conservation Genetics,* 10: 191–201.

Bowden, C. (2009) The Asian *Gyps* vulture crisis: the role of captive breeding in India to prevent total extinction. *BirdingASIA,* 12: 121–123.

Bowden, C.G.R., Smith, K.W., Bekkay, M.E.L., Oubrou, W., Aghnaj, A. & Jimenez-Armesto, M. (2008) Contribution of research to conservation action for the Northern Bald Ibis Geronticus eremita in Morocco. *Bird Conservation International,* 18: S74-S90.

Bowler, J. & Taylor, J. (1989) An annotated checklist of the birds of Manusela National Park. *Kukila,* 4: 3–30.

Bowman, M.J. (1999) International treaties and the global protection of birds: Part II. *Journal of Environmental Law,* 11: 281–300.

Boyd, C., Brooks, T.M., Butchart, S.H.M., Edgar, G.J., da Fonseca, G.A.B., Hawkins, F., Hoffmann, M., Sechrest, W., Stuart, S.N. & van Dijk, P.P. (2008) Spatial scale and the conservation of threatened species. *Conservation Letters,* 1: 37–43.

Boyer, A.G. (2008) Extinction patterns in the avifauna of the Hawaiian islands. *Diversity and Distributions,* 14: 509–517.

Bragin, V.A. (2006) [The Sociable Lapwing in Kostanai district in 2005]. *Kazakhstan Ornithological Bulletin,* 4: 176–177.

Brangenberg, N., McInnes, C., Connolly, J.H. & Rogers, L.E. (2003) Absence of Salmonella and Campylobacter species in fecal and cloacal swab samples from Kakapo (*Strigops habroptilus*) on Codfish Island, New Zealand. *Journal of Avian Medicine and Surgery,* 17: 203–205.

Braz, V.S., Abreu, T.L.S., Lopes, L.E., Leite, L.O., França, F.G.R., Vasconcellos, M.M. & Balbino, S.F. (2003) Brazilian Merganser *Mergus octosetaceus* discovered in Jalapão State Park, Tocantins, Brazil. *Cotinga,* 20: 68–71.

Brickle, N.W., Duckworth, J.W., Tordoff, A.W., Poole, C.M., Timmins, R. & McGowan, P.J.K. (2008) The status and conservation of Galliformes in Cambodia, Laos and Vietnam. *Biodiversity and Conservation,* 17: 1393–1427.

Bromham, L., Lanfear, R., Cassey, P., Gibb, G. & Cardillo, M. (2012) Reconstructing past species assemblages reveals the changing patterns and drivers of extinction through time. *Proceedings of the Royal Society Series B-Biological Sciences,* 279: 4024-4032.

Brook, B.W., Traill, L.W. & Bradshaw, C.J.A. (2006) Minimum viable population sizes and global extinction risk are unrelated. *Ecology Letters,* 9: 375–382.

Brook, B.W., Sodhi, N.S. & Bradshaw, C.J.A. (2008) Synergies among extinction drivers under global change. *Trends in Ecology & Evolution,* 23: 453–460.

Brooke, M. de L. (2004) The food consumption of the world's seabirds. *Proceedings of the Royal Society Series B-Biological Sciences,* 271: S246-S248.

Brooke, M. de L., Hilton, G.M. & Martins, T.L.F. (2007) Prioritizing the world's islands for vertebrate-eradication programmes. *Animal Conservation,* 10: 380–390.

Brooke, M. de L., Butchart, S.H.M., Garnett, S.T., Crowley, G.M., Mantilla-Beniers, N.B. & Stattersfield, A. (2008) Rates of movement of threatened bird species between IUCN red list categories and toward extinction. *Conservation Biology,* 22: 417–427.

Brooke, M. de L., Flower, T.P. & Mainwaring, M.C. (2010) A scarcity of females may constrain population growth of threatened bird species: case notes from the Critically Endangered Raso Lark *Alauda razae*. *Bird Conservation International,* 20: 382–384.

Brooke, M. de L., Flower, T.P., Campbell, E.M., Mainwaring, M.C., Davies, S. & Welbergen, J.A. (2012) Rainfall-related population growth and adult sex ratio change in the Critically Endangered Raso lark (*Alauda razae*). *Animal Conservation,* 15: 466-471.

Brooks, T. (2000) Extinct species. In: Stattersfield, A.J. & Capper, D.R. (eds). *Threatened birds of the world,* 701–708. Lynx Edicions and BirdLife International, Barcelona and Cambridge, UK.

Brooks, T., Lens, L., Barnes, J., Barnes, R., Kageche Kihuria, J. & Wilder, C. (1998) The conservation status of the forest birds of the Taita Hills, Kenya. *Bird Conservation International,* 8: 119–139.

Brooks, T., Tobias, J. & Balmford, A. (1999) Deforestation and bird extinctions in the Atlantic forest. *Animal Conservation,* 2: 211–222.

Brooks, T., Balmford, A., Burgess, N., Hansen, L.A., Moore, J., Rahbek, C., Williams, P., Bennun, L.A., Byaruhanga, A., Kasoma, P., Njoroge, P., Pomeroy, D. & Wondafrash, M. (2001) Conservation priorities for birds and biodiversity: do East African Important Bird Areas represent species diversity in other terrestrial vertebrate groups? *Ostrich, S15*: 3–12.

Brooks, T.M., Pimm, S.L. & Collar, N.J. (1997) Deforestation predicts the number of threatened birds in insular southeast Asia. *Conservation Biology,* 11: 382–394.

Brooks, T.M., Pilgrim, J.D., Rodrigues, A.S.L. & da Fonseca, G.A.B. (2003) Conservation status and geographic distribution of avian evolutionary history. In: Purvis, A., Gittleman, J.L. & Brooks, T.M. (eds). *Phylogeny and Conservation,* 267–294. Cambridge University Press, Cambridge, UK.

Brooks, T.M., Bakarr, M.I., Boucher, T., da Fonseca, G.A.B., Hilton-Taylor, C., Hoekstra, J.M., Moritz, T., Olivier, S., Parrish, J., Pressey, R.L., Rodrigues, A.S.L., Sechrest, W., Stattersfield, A., Strahm, W. & Stuart, S.N. (2004) Coverage provided by the global protected-area system: is it enough? *BioScience,* 54: 1081–1091.

Brooks, T.M., Mittermeier, R.A., da Fonseca, G.A.B., Gerlach, J., Hoffmann, M., Lamoreux, J.F., Mittermeier, C.G., Pilgrim, J.D. & Rodrigues, A.S.L. (2006) Global biodiversity conservation priorities. *Science,* 313: 58–61.

Brooks, T.M., Wright, S.J. & Sheil, D. (2009) Evaluating the success of conservation actions in safeguarding tropical forest biodiversity. *Conservation Biology,* 23: 1448–1457.

Brothers, N. (1991) Albatross mortality and associated bait loss in the Japanese longline fishery in the Southern Ocean. *Biological Conservation,* 55: 255–268.

Brothers, N., Cooper, J. & Løkkeborg, S. (1999) *The incidental catch of seabirds by longline fisheries: worldwide review and technical guidelines for mitigation.* FAO Fisheries Circular, No. 937. Food and Agriculture Organization, Rome.

Brown, J.H. (1984) On the relationship between abundance and distribution of species. *American Naturalist,* 124: 255–279.

Brown, J.H., Mehlman, D.W. & Stevens, G.C. (1995) Spatial variation in abundance. *Ecology,* 76: 2028–2043.

Browne, S., Collar, N. & Sykes, B. (2008) Editorial review: Gurney's Pitta and OBC. *BirdingASIA,* 9: 2–3.

Bruno, S.F., de Carvalho, R.B.A. & Bartmann, W. (2006) Reproductive rate and development of ducklings of Brazilian Merganser at Serra de Canastra National Park, Minas Gerais, Brazil, 2001–2005. *TWSG News,* 15: 25–33.

Bruno, S.F., Andrade, R.A., Lins, L.V., Carvalho, R.B.A. & Rigueira, S.E. (2010) Reproductive behavior of the Brazilian Merganser (*Mergus octosetaceus* Vieillot, 1817) with nest in a cavity of a tree in the Serra da Canastra National Park, Minas Gerais, Brazil. *Cotinga,* 32: 27–33.

Bryant, D.M. (2006) Energetics of free-living kakapo (*Strigops habroptilus*). *Notornis,* 53: 126–137.

Buchanan, G.M., Donald, P.F., Fishpool, L.D.C., Arinaitwe, J.A., Balman, M. & Mayaux, P. (2009a) An assessment of land cover and threats in

Important Bird Areas in Africa. *Bird Conservation International*, 19: 49–61.

Buchanan, G.M., Nelson, A., Mayaux, P., Hartley, A. & Donald, P.F. (2009b) Delivering a global, terrestrial, biodiversity observation system through remote sensing. *Conservation Biology*, 23: 499–502.

Buchanan, G.M., Crockford, N. & Gretton, A. (2010) The slender-billed curlew *Numenius tenuirostris* in Africa. *Bulletin of the African Bird Club*, 17: 202–206.

Buchanan, G.M., Donald, P.F. & Butchart, S.H.M. (2011). Identifying priority areas for conservation: a global assessment for forest-dependent birds. *PLoS ONE*, 6: e29080.

Bucher, E.H. (1992) The causes of extinction of the Passenger Pigeon. In: Power, D.M. (ed). *Current Ornithology, 9:* 1–36. Plenum Press, New York.

Bueno, B.A.D., Nunes, M.R. & Melo, C. (2011) Bills favor mining and threaten conservation of Brazilian Merganser (*Mergus octosetaceus*) at Serra da Canastra National Park, Minas Gerais, Brazil. *Natureza & Conservação*, 10: 64-71.

Bueser, G.L.L., Bueser, K.G., Afan, D.S., Salvador, D.I., Grier, J.W., Kennedy, R.S. & C., M.H. (2003) Distribution and nesting density of the Philippine Eagle *Pithecophaga jefferyi* on Mindanao Island, Philippines: what do we know after 100 years? *Ibis*, 145: 130–135.

Bull, L.S. (2007) Reducing seabird bycatch in longline, trawl and gillnet fisheries. *Fish and Fisheries*, 8: 31–56.

Bunce, M., Szulkin, M., Lerner, H.R.L., Barnes, I., Shapiro, B., Cooper, A. & Holdaway, R.N. (2005) Ancient DNA provides new insights into the evolutionary history of New Zealand's extinct giant eagle. *PLoS Biology*, 3: 44–46.

Burg, T.M. & Croxall, J.P. (2004) Global population structure and taxonomy of the wandering albatross species complex. *Molecular Ecology*, 13: 2345–2355.

Burgis, M.J. & Symoens, J.J. (1987) *African wetlands and shallow water bodies: directory*. Editions de l'Orstrom, Paris.

Burney, D.A., James, H.F., Burney, L.P., Olson, S.L., Kikuchi, W., Wagner, W.L., Burney, M., McCloskey, D., Kikuchi, D., Grady, F.V., Gage, R. & Nishek, R. (2001) Fossil evidence for a diverse biota from Kaua'i and its transformation since human arrival. *Ecological Monographs*, 71: 615–641.

Burnham, K.K., Burnham, W.A. & Newton, I. (2009) Gyrfalcon *Falco rusticolus* post-glacial colonization and extreme long-term use of nest-sires in Greenland. *Ibis*, 151: 514–522.

Burton, P.J.K. (1971) Sexual size dimorphism in *Alauda razae*. *Bulletin of the British Ornithologists' Club*, 91: 108–109.

Butchart, S.H.M. (2007) Birds to find: a review of 'lost', obscure and poorly known African bird species. *Bulletin of the African Bird Club*, 14: 139–159.

Butchart, S.H.M. (2008) Red List Indices to measure the sustainability of species use and impacts of invasive alien species. *Bird Conservation International*, 18: S245–S262.

Butchart, S.H.M. & Bird, J.P. (2009) Data Deficient birds on the IUCN Red List: what don't we know and why does it matter? *Biological Conservation*, 143: 239–247.

Butchart, S.H.M., Stattersfield, A.J., Bennun, L.A., Shutes, S.M., Akçakaya, H.R., Baillie, J.E.M., Stuart, S.N., Hilton-Taylor, C. & Mace, G.M. (2004) Measuring global trends in the status of biodiversity: Red list indices for birds. *PLoS Biology*, 2: 2294–2304.

Butchart, S.H.M., Collar, N.J., Crosby, M.J. & Tobias, J.A. (2005a) 'Lost' and poorly known birds: top targets for birders in Asia. *BirdingASIA*, 3: 41–49.

Butchart, S.H.M., Stattersfield, A.J., Baillie, J., Bennun, L.A., Stuart, S.N., Akçakaya, H.R., Hilton-Taylor, C. & Mace, G.M. (2005b) Using Red List Indices to measure progress towards the 2010 target and beyond. *Philosophical Transactions of the Royal Society Series B-Biological Sciences*, 360: 255–268.

Butchart, S.H.M., Akçakaya, H.R., Kennedy, E. & Hilton-Taylor, C. (2006a) Biodiversity Indicators based on trends in conservation status: strengths of the IUCN Red List Index. *Conservation Biology*, 20: 579–581.

Butchart, S.H.M., Stattersfield, A. & Brooks, T. (2006b) Going or gone: defining 'Possibly Extinct' species to give a truer picture of recent extinctions. *Bulletin of the British Ornithologists' Club*, 126: 7–24.

Butchart, S.H.M., Stattersfield, A.J. & Collar, N.J. (2006c) How many bird extinctions have we prevented? *Oryx*, 40: 266–278.

Butchart, S.H.M., Akçakaya, H.R., Chanson, J., Baillie, J.E.M., Collen, B., Quader, S., Turner, W.R., Amin, R., Stuart, S.N. & Hilton-Taylor, C. (2007) Improvements to the Red List Index. *PLoS ONE*, 2: e140.

Butcher, J.A., Morrison, M.L., Ransom, D., Slack, R.D. & Wilkins, R.N. (2010) Evidence of a minimum patch size threshold of reproductive success in an endangered songbird. *Journal of Wildlife Management*, 74: 133–139.

Butler, D. & Merton, D. (1992) *The Black Robin: saving the world's most endangered bird*. Oxford University Press, Auckland, New Zealand.

Butler, D.J. (2006) The habitat, food and feeding ecology of kakapo in Fjordland: a synopsis from the unpublished MSc thesis of Richard Grey. *Notornis*, 53: 55–79.

Butler, P.J. (1992) Parrots, pressures, people, and pride. In: Beissinger, S.R. & Snyder, N.F.R. (eds). *New World parrots in crisis: solutions from conservation biology*, 25–46. Smithsonian Institution Press, Washington, D.C.

Byers, A.C. (2000) Contemporary landscape change in the Huascaran National Park and buffer zone, Cordillera Blanca, Peru. *Mountain Research and Development*, 20: 52–63.

Cade, T.J. & Jones, C.G. (1993) Progress in restoration of the Mauritius Kestrel. *Conservation Biology*, 7: 169–175.

Cahill, A.J., Walker, J.S. & Marsden, S.J. (2006) Recovery within a population of the Critically Endangered citron-crested cockatoo *Cacatua sulphurea citrinocristata* in Indonesia after 10 years of international trade control. *Oryx*, 40: 161–167.

Calabrese, J.M. & Fagan, W.F. (2004) Lost in time, lonely, and single: reproductive asynchrony and the Allee effect. *American Naturalist*, 164: 25–37.

Campbell, K. & Donlan, C.J. (2005) Feral goat eradications on islands. *Conservation Biology*, 19: 1362–1374.

Canevari, P. & Blanco, D.E. (1994) *Literature search for the Eskimo Curlew*. Unpublished Report for US Fish and Wildlife Service and Conservation International.

Canonico, G.C., Arthington, A., McCrary, J.K. & Thieme, M.L. (2005) The effects of introduced tilapias on native biodiversity. *Aquatic Conservation-Marine and Freshwater Ecosystems*, 15: 463–483.

Capriles, J.M. & Bedregal, E.E. (2002) The economic, symbolic, and social importance of the 'kenua' (*Polylepis* spp.) during prehispanic times in the Andean highlands of Bolivia. *Ecotropica (Bonn)*, 8: 225–231.

Carboneras, C. (1992) Family Anatidae (ducks, geese and swans) In: del Hoyo, J., Elliott, A. & Sargatal, J. (eds). *Handbook of the birds of the world, Vol 1*, 536–628. Lynx Edicions, Barcelona.

Cardillo, M. (2003) Biological determinants of extinction risk: why are smaller species less vulnerable? *Animal Conservation*, 6: 63–69.

Carey, C. (2009) The impacts of climate change on the annual cycles of birds. *Philosophical Transactions of the Royal Society B-Biological Sciences*, 364: 3321–3330.

Carriker, M.A. (1932) Additional new birds from Peru with a synopsis of the races of *Hylophylax naevia*. *Proceedings of the Academy of Natural Sciences of Philadelphia*, 84: 1–7.

Case, T.J. (1996) Global patterns in the establishment and distribution of exotic birds. *Biological Conservation*, 78: 69–96.

Casey, T.L.C. & Jacobi, J.J.D. (1974) A new genus and species of bird from the island of Maui (Passeriformes: Drepanidae). *Occasional Papers of the B.P. Bishop Museum*, 24: 215–226.

Cassey, P., Blackburn, T.M., Duncan, R.P. & Lockwood, J.L. (2008) Lessons from introductions of exotic species as a possible information source for managing translocations of birds. *Wildlife Research*, 35: 193–201.

Castelletta, M., Thiollay, J.M. & Sodhi, N.S. (2005) The effects of extreme forest fragmentation on the bird community of Singapore Island. *Biological Conservation*, 121: 135–155.

Caughley, G. (1994) Directions in conservation biology. *Journal of Animal Ecology,* 63: 215–244.

Caut, S., Casanovas, J.G., Virgos, E., Lozano, J., Witmer, G.W. & Courchamp, F. (2007) Rats dying for mice: modelling the competitor release effect. *Austral Ecology,* 32: 858–868.

Caut, S., Angulo, E. & Courchamp, F. (2008) Dietary shift of an invasive predator: rats, seabirds and sea turtles. *Journal of Applied Ecology,* 45: 428–437.

Cha, W.M. & Young, L. (1990) Food of the Spoon-billed Sandpiper in Hong Kong. *Hong Kong Bird Report, 1990*: 192–193.

Chai, S.L., Tanner, E. & McLaren, K. (2009) High rates of forest clearance and fragmentation pre- and post-national park establishment: the case of a Jamaican montane rainforest. *Biological Conservation,* 142: 2484–2492.

Channell, R. & Lomolino, M.V. (2000) Trajectories to extinction: spatial dynamics of the contraction of geographical ranges. *Journal of Biogeography,* 27: 169–179.

Chaudhary, A., Subedi, T.R., Giri, J.B., Baral, H.S., Bidari, B., Subedi, H., Chaudhary, B., Chaudhary, I., Paudel, K. & Cuthbert, R.J. (2012) Population trends of Critically Endangered *Gyps* vultures in the lowlands of Nepal. *Bird Conservation International,* 22: 270–278.

Chaudhry, M.J.I., Ogada, D.L., Malik, R.N., Virani, M.Z. & Giovanni, M.D. (2012) First evidence that populations of the critically endangered Long-billed Vulture *Gyps indicus* in Pakistan have increased following the ban of the toxic veterinary drug diclofenac in south Asia. *Bird Conservation International,* 22: 389-397.

Cheke, A. & Hume, J. (2008) *Lost land of the Dodo: an ecological history of Mauritius, Réunion & Rodrigues.* T. & A. D. Poyser, London.

Chen, S.H., Chang, S.H., Liu, Y., Chan, S.B., Fan, Z.Y., Chen, C.S., Yen, C.W. & Guo, D.S. (2009) A small population and severe threats: status of the Critically Endangered Chinese crested tern *Sterna bernsteini. Oryx,* 43: 209–212.

Christidis, L., Leeton, P.R. & Westerman, M. (1996) Were bowerbirds part of the New Zealand fauna? *Proceedings of the National Academy of Sciences of the United States of America,* 93: 3898–3901.

Christy, B. (2010) The kingpin. *National Geographic,* 217: 78–107.

Cibois, A., Thibault, J.C. & Pasquet, E. (2004) Biogeography of eastern Polynesian monarchs (*Pomarea*): an endemic genus close to extinction. *Condor,* 106: 837–851.

Cincotta, R.P., Wisnewski, J. & Engelman, R. (2000) Human population in the biodiversity hotspots. *Nature,* 404: 990–992.

Clark, R.J. & Mikkola, H. (1989) A preliminary revision of threatened and near-threatened nocturnal birds of prey of the world. In: Meyburg, B.-U. & Chancellor, R.D. (eds). *Raptors in the modern world*, 371–388. World Working Group on Birds of Prey, Berlin.

Clavero, M., Brotons, L., Pons, P. & Sol, D. (2009) Prominent role of invasive species in avian biodiversity loss. *Biological Conservation,* 142: 2043–2049.

Cleere, N. & Ingels, J. (2004) Notes on the Cayenne Nightjar *Caprimulgus maculosus. Alauda,* 72: 281–284.

Cleeves, T. (2002) Slender-billed Curlew in Northumberland: new to Britain and Ireland. *British Birds,* 95: 272–278.

Clout, M.N. (2001) Where protection is not enough: active conservation in New Zealand. *Trends in Ecology & Evolution,* 16: 415–416.

Clout, M.N. & Merton, D.V. (1998) Saving the Kakapo: the conservation of the world's most peculiar parrot. *Bird Conservation International,* 8: 281–295.

Clout, M.N. & Russell, J.C. (2001) The eradication of mammals from New Zealand islands. In: Koike, F., Clout, M.N., Kawamichi, M., De Poorter, M. & Iwatsuki, K. (eds). *Assessment and control of biological invasion risks*, 127–141. Shoukadoh Book Sellers, Kyoto, Japan and IUCN, Gland, Switzerland.

Clout, M.N., Elliott, G.P. & Robertson, B.C. (2002) Effects of supplementary feeding on the offspring sex ratio of kakapo: a dilemma for the conservation of a polygynous parrot. *Biological Conservation,* 107: 13–18.

Cockburn, A., Legge, S. & Double, M.C. (2002) Sex ratios in birds and mammals: can the hypotheses be disentangled? In: Hardy, I.C.W. (ed).

Sex ratios: concepts and research methods, 266-286. Cambridge University Press, Cambridge, UK.

Cocker, M. (1989) *Richard Meinertzhagen: soldier, scientist and spy.* Martin Secker and Warburg, London.

Cockrem, J.F. (2002) Reproductive biology and conservation of the endangered kakapo (*Strigops habroptilus*) in New Zealand. *Avian and Poultry Biology Reviews,* 13: 139–144.

Cockrem, J.F. (2006) The timing of breeding in the kakapo (*Strigops habroptilus*). *Notornis,* 53: 153–159.

Coelho, G. & Silva, W. (1998) A new species of Antilophia (Passeriformes: Pipridae) from Chapada do Araripe, Ceará, Brazil. *Ararajuba,* 6: 81–84.

Cofre, H.L., Böhning-Gaese, K. & Marquet, P.A. (2007) Rarity in Chilean forest birds: which ecological and life-history traits matter? *Diversity and Distributions,* 13: 203–212.

Coimbra-Filho, A.F. (1970) Sobre *Mitu mitu* (Linnaeus, 1766) e a validez das suas duas raças geográficas (Cracidae, Aves). *Revta. Bras. Biol.,* 30: 101–109.

Coimbra-Filho, A.F. (1971) Tres formas da avifauna do nordeste do Brasil ameaçadas de extinção: *Tinamus solitarius pernambucensis* Berla, 1946, *Mitu mitu mitu* (Linnaeus, 1766) e *Procnias a. averano* (Hermann, 1783) (Aves – Tinamidae, Cracidae, Cotingidae). *Revta. Bras. Biol.,* 31: 239–247.

Colinvaux, P. (1980) *Why big fierce animals are rare: an ecologist's perspective.* Penguin Books, Harmondsworth, UK.

Collar, N.J. (1996a) Family Otididae (bustards). In: del Hoyo, J., Elliott, A. & Sargatal, J. (eds). *Handbook of the birds of the world, Vol. 3*, 240–273. Lynx Edicions, Barcelona.

Collar, N.J. (1996b) The reasons for Red Data Books. *Oryx,* 30: 121–130.

Collar, N.J. (1997a) The threat status of the Sidamo Lark. *Bulletin of the British Ornithologists' Club,* 117: 75–76.

Collar, N.J. (1997b) Species survival versus perpetuation of myth: the case of the Philippine Eagle. *Oryx,* 31: 4–7.

Collar, N.J. (1998) Extinction by assumption: or, the Romeo Error on Cebu. *Oryx,* 32: 239–243.

Collar, N.J. (2006) Parrot reintroduction: towards a synthesis of best practice. *Proceedings of the VI International Parrot Convention ('The Pleasure of Parrots')*, 82–107. Loro Parque Fundación, Puerto de la Cruz, Tenerife.

Collar, N.J. (2009) Conservation-driven changes in English bird names, and the case of the Liben Lark. *Bulletin of the African Bird Club,* 16: 245.

Collar, N.J. & Stuart, S.N. (1985) *Threatened birds of Africa and related islands.* International Council for Bird Preservation, Cambridge, UK.Collar, N.J. & Andrew, P. (1988) *Birds to watch: the ICBP world checklist of threatened birds.* ICBP and IUCN, Cambridge, UK.

Collar, N.J. & Long, A.J. (1996) Taxonomy and names of *Carpococcyx* cuckoos from the Greater Sundas. *Forktail,* 11: 135–150.

Collar, N.J. & Fishpool, L.D.C. (2006) What is *Pogoniulus makawai*? *Bulletin of the African Bird Club,* 13: 18–27.

Collar, N.J. & Robson, C. (2007) Family Timaliidae (babblers). In: del Hoyo, J., Elliott, A. & Christie, D.A. (eds). *Handbook of the birds of the world, Vol. 12*, 70–291. Lynx Edicions, Barcelona.

Collar, N.J. & Prŷs-Jones, R.P. (2012) Pioneer of Asian ornithology: Allan Octavian Hume. *BirdingAsia,* 17: 17-43.

Collar, N.J., Round, P.D. & Wells, D.R. (1986) The past and future of Gurney's Pitta *Pitta gurneyi. Forktail,* 1: 29–51.

Collar, N.J., Gonzaga, N.P., Krabbe, N., Madroño Nieto, P., Naranjo, L.G., Parker, T.A. & Wege, D.C. (1992) *Threatened birds of the Americas: the ICBP/IUCN Red Data Book.* International Council for Bird Preservation, Cambridge, UK.

Collar, N.J., Crosby, M.J. & Stattersfield, A. (1994) *Birds to watch 2 – the world list of threatened birds.* BirdLife International, Cambridge, UK.

Collar, N.J., Dellelegn Abebe, Y., Fishpool, L.D.C., Gabremichael, M.N., Spottiswoode, C.N. & Wondafrash, M. (2008) Type locality, habitat, behaviour, voice, nest, eggs and plight of the Sidamo Lark *Heteromirafra sidamoensis. Bulletin of the African Bird Club,* 15: 180–190.

Conant, S., Pratt, H.D. & Shallenberger, R.J. (1998) Reflections on a 1975 expedition to the lost world of the Alaka'i and other notes on the natural history, systematics, and conservation of Kaua'i birds. *Wilson Bulletin*, 110: 1–22.

Cooney, R. & Jepson, P. (2006) The international wild bird trade: what's wrong with blanket bans? *Oryx*, 40: 18–23.

Cooper, J., Croxall, J.P. & Rivera, K.S. (2001) Off the hook? Initiatives to reduce seabird bycatch in longline fisheries. In: Melvin, E.F. & Parrish, J.K. (eds). *Seabird bycatch: trends, roadblocks and solutions*, 9–32. Alaska Sea Grant Program, Fairbanks.

Coppock, D.L. (1994) *The Borana plateau of southern Ethiopia: synthesis of pastoral research, development and change, 1980–91*. International Livestock Centre for Africa, Addis Ababa.

Copsey, J.A., Jones, J.P.G., Andrianandrasana, H., Rajaonarison, L.H. & Fa, J. (2009) Burning to fish: local explanations for wetland burning in Lac Alaotra, Madagascar. *Oryx*, 43: 403–406.

Corfield, J.R., Gsell, A.C., Brunton, D., Heesy, C.P., Hall, M.I., Acosta, M.L. & Iwaniuk, A.N. (2011). Anatomical specializations for nocturnality in a critically endangered parrot, the Kakapo (*Strigops habroptilus*). *PLoS ONE*, 6: e22945.

Courchamp, F., Clutton-Brock, T. & Grenfell, B. (1999a) Inverse density dependence and the Allee effect. *Trends in Ecology & Evolution*, 14: 405–410.

Courchamp, F., Langlais, M. & Sugihara, G. (1999b) Cats protecting birds: modelling the mesopredator release effect. *Journal of Animal Ecology*, 68: 282–292.

Courchamp, F., Langlais, M. & Sugihara, G. (2000) Rabbits killing birds: modelling the hyperpredation process. *Journal of Animal Ecology*, 69: 154–164.

Courchamp, F., Chapuis, J.L. & Pascal, M. (2003) Mammal invaders on islands: impact, control and control impact. *Biological Reviews*, 78: 347–383.

Courchamp, F., Angulo, E., Rivalan, P., Hall, R.J., Signoret, L., Bull, L. & Meinard, Y. (2006) Rarity value and species extinction: the anthropogenic Allee effect. *PLoS Biology*, 4: 2405–2410.

Coutinho, L.M. (1982) Ecological effects of fire in Brazilian cerrado. In: Huntley, B.J. & Walker, B.H. (eds). *Ecology of tropical savannas*, 273–291. Springer-Verlag, Berlin.

Cowie, R.H. & Holland, B.S. (2008) Molecular biogeography and diversification of the endemic terrestrial fauna of the Hawaiian Islands. *Philosophical Transactions of the Royal Society B-Biological Sciences*, 363: 3363–3376.

Cristinacce, A., Ladkoo, A., Switzer, R., Jordan, L., Vencatasamy, V., Koenig, F.D., Jones, C. & Bell, D. (2008) Captive breeding and rearing of critically endangered Mauritius fodies *Foudia rubra* for reintroduction. *Zoo Biology*, 27: 255–268.

Cristinacce, A., Switzer, R.A., Cole, R.E., Jones, C.G. & Bell, D.J. (2009) Increasing use of exotic forestry tree species as refuges from nest predation by the critically endangered Mauritius Fody *Foudia rubra*. *Oryx*, 43: 97–103.

Crockett, D.E. (1994) Rediscovery of Chatham Island Taiko *Pterodroma magentae*. *Notornis*, 41: 49–60.

Crockford, N. (2009) [On behalf of the Slender-billed Curlew Working Group] Can you help find the Slender-billed Curlew? *Wader Study Group Bulletin*, 116: 62–64.

Croll, D.A., Maron, J.L., Estes, J.A., Danner, E.M. & Byrd, G.V. (2005) Introduced predators transform subarctic islands from grassland to tundra. *Science*, 307: 1959–1961.

Cronk, Q.C.B. (1997) Islands: stability, diversity, conservation. *Biodiversity and Conservation*, 6: 477–493.

Crooks, K.R. & Soulé, M.E. (1999) Mesopredator release and avifaunal extinctions in a fragmented system. *Nature*, 400: 563–566.

Croxall, J.P. (2008) The role of science and advocacy in the conservation of Southern Ocean albatrosses at sea. *Bird Conservation International*, 18: S13-S29.

Croxall, J.P., Butchart, S.H.M., Lascelles, B., Stattersfield, A.J., Sullivan, B., Symes, A. & Taylor, P. (2012) Seabird conservation status, threats and priority actions: a global assessment. *Bird Conservation International*, 22: 1-34.

Cruz, F., Carrion, V., Campbell, K.J., Lavoie, C. & Donlan, C.J. (2009) Bio-economics of large-scale eradication of feral goats from Santiago Island, Galapagos. *Journal of Wildlife Management*, 73: 191–200.

Cuddihy, L.W. & Stone, C.P. (1990) *Alteration of native Hawaiian vegetation: effects of humans, their activities and introductions*. Cooperative National Park Studies Unit, University of Hawai`i at Manoa, Honolulu, Hawaii.

Cunningham, A.A., Prakash, V., Pain, D., Ghalsasi, G.R., Wells, G.A.H., Kolte, G.N., Nighot, P., Goudar, M.S., Kshirsagar, S. & Rahmani, A. (2003) Indian vultures: victims of an infectious disease epidemic? *Animal Conservation*, 6: 189–197.

Cuthbert, R. & Hilton, G. (2004) Introduced house mice *Mus musculus*: a significant predator of threatened and endemic birds on Gough Island, South Atlantic Ocean? *Biological Conservation*, 117: 483–489.

Cuthbert, R., Phillips, R.A. & Ryan, P.G. (2003a) Separating the Tristan Albatross and the Wandering Albatross using morphometric measurements. *Waterbirds*, 26: 338–344.

Cuthbert, R., Ryan, P.G., Cooper, J. & Hilton, G. (2003b) Demography and population trends of the Atlantic Yellow-nosed Albatross. *Condor*, 105: 439–452.

Cuthbert, R., Sommer, E., Ryan, P., Cooper, J. & Hilton, G. (2004) Demography and conservation of the Tristan albatross *Diomedea [exulans] dabbenena*. *Biological Conservation*, 117: 471–481.

Cuthbert, R., Hilton, G., Ryan, P. & Tuck, G.N. (2005) At-sea distribution of breeding Tristan albatrosses *Diomedea dabbenena* and potential interactions with pelagic longline fishing in the South Atlantic Ocean. *Biological Conservation*, 121: 345–355.

Cuthbert, R., Green, R.E., Ranade, S., Saravanan, S., Pain, D.J., Prakash, V. & Cunningham, A.A. (2006) Rapid population declines of Egyptian vulture (*Neophron percnopterus*) and red-headed vulture (*Sarcogyps calvus*) in India. *Animal Conservation*, 9: 349–354.

Cuthbert, R., Parry-Jones, J., Green, R.E. & Pain, D.J. (2007) NSAIDs and scavenging birds: potential impacts beyond Asia's critically endangered vultures. *Biology Letters*, 3: 90–93.

Cuthbert, R.J., Taggart, M.A., Prakash, V., Saini, M., Swarup, D., Upreti, S., Mateo, R., Chakraborty, S.S., Deori, P. & Green, R.E. (2011a). Effectiveness of action in India to reduce exposure of *Gyps* vultures to the toxic veterinary drug diclofenac. *PLoS ONE*, 6: e19069.

Cuthbert, R.J., Dave, R., Chakraborty, S.S., Kumar, S., Prakash, S., Ranade, S.P. & Prakash, V. (2011b) Assessing the ongoing threat from veterinary non-steroidal anti-inflammatory drugs to Critically Endangered *Gyps* vultures in India. *Oryx*, 45: 420–426.

Cuthbert, R.J., Prakash, V., Saini, M., Upreti, S., Swarup, D., Das, A., Green, R.E. & Taggart, M. (2011c) Are conservation actions reducing the threat to India's vulture populations? *Current Science*, 101: 1480-1484.

Danielsen, F., Beukema, H., Burgess, N.D., Parish, F., Bruhl, C.A., Donald, P.F., Murdiyarso, D., Phalan, B., Reijnders, L., Struebig, M. & Fitzherbert, E.B. (2009) Biofuel plantations on forested lands: double jeopardy for biodiversity and climate. *Conservation Biology*, 23: 348–358.

Danilenko, A.K., Boere, G.C. & Lebedeva, E.A. (1996) Looking for the recent breeding grounds of Slender-billed Curlew: a habitat-based approach. *Wader Study Group Bulletin*, 81: 71–78.

Das, D., Cuthbert, R.J., Jakati, R.D. & Prakash, V. (2011) Diclofenac is toxic to the Himalayan Vulture *Gyps himalayensis*. *Bird Conservation International*, 21: 72-75.

Davidson, J. (1882) Rough list of the birds of western Khandesh. *Stray Feathers*, 10: 279–326.

Davidson, P. (2004) *The distribution, ecology and conservation status of the Bengal Florican Houbaropsis bengalensis in Cambodia*. MSc thesis, University of East Anglia, Norwich, UK.

Davies, R.G., Orme, C.D.L., Olson, V., Thomas, G.H., Ross, S.G., Ding, T.S., Rasmussen, P.C., Stattersfield, A.J., Bennett, P.M., Blackburn, T.M., Owens, I.P.F. & Gaston, K.J. (2006) Human impacts and the global distribution of extinction risk. *Proceedings of the Royal Society Series B-Biological Sciences*, 273: 2127–2133.

Davis, N.E., O'Dowd, D.J., Green, P.T. & Mac Nally, R. (2008) Effects of an alien ant invasion on abundance, behavior, and reproductive success of endemic island birds. *Conservation Biology*, 22: 1165–1176.

Davis, R.A. & Metcalf, B.M. (2008) The Night Parrot (*Pezoporus occidentalis*) in northern Western Australia: a recent sighting from the Pilbara region. *Emu*, 108: 233–236.

Davison, G.W.H. & McGowan, P.J.K. (2009) Is the Double-banded Argus *Argusianus bipunctatus* a valid species? *BirdingASIA*, 12: 94–97.

de Grammont, P.C. & Curaón, A.D. (2006) An evaluation of threatened species categorization used on the American continent. *Conservation Biology*, 20: 14-27.

de Juana, E. (2011) The Sociable Lapwing in Europe. *British Birds*, 104: 84-90.

de Juana, E., Suárez, F., Ryan, P., Alström, P. & Donald, P.F. (2004) Family Alaudidae (larks). In: del Hoyo, J., Elliott, A. & Christie, D.A. (eds). *Handbook of the birds of the world, Vol. 9*, 496–601. Lynx Edicions, Barcelona.

de Klerk, H.M., Crowe, T.M., Fjeldså, J. & Burgess, N.D. (2002) Patterns of species richness and narrow endemism of terrestrial bird species in the Afrotropical region. *Journal of Zoology*, 256: 327–342.

de Kloet, R.S. & de Kloet, S.R. (2005) The evolution of the spindlin gene in birds: Sequence analysis of an intron of the spindlin W and Z gene reveals four major divisions of the Psittaciformes. *Molecular Phylogenetics and Evolution*, 36: 706–721.

de Luca, A., Develey, P. & Olmos, F. (2006) *Waterbirds in Brazil: final report*. SAVE Brasil, São Paulo.

de Naurois, R. (1994) *Les oiseaux de L'Archipel du Cap Vert*. Ministério do Planeamento e da Administração do Território, Secretaria de Estado da Ciência e Tecnologia, Instituto de Investigação Científica Tropical Lisbon.

De Paula, G.A., Cerqueira Júnior, M.C. & Ribon, R. (2008) Occurrence of the Brazilian Merganser (*Mergus octosetaceus*) in the southern border of the Espinhaço Range, Minas Gerais, Brazil. *Waterbirds*, 31: 289–293.

Dee, T.J. (1986) *The endemic birds of Madagascar*. International Council for Bird Preservation, Cambridge, UK.

del Hoyo, J. (1994) Family Cracidae (chachalacas, guans and curassows). In: del Hoyo, J., Elliott, A.D. & Sargatal, J. (eds). *Handbook of birds of the world, Vol. 2*, 310–363. Lynx Edicions, Barcelona.

Delacour, J. (1956) *The waterfowl of the world, Vol. 2*. Country Life, London.

Delacour, J. (1959) *The waterfowl of the world, Vol. 3*. Country Life, London.

Delacour, J. & Amadon, D. (1973) *Curassows and related birds*. American Museum of Natural History, New York.

Deredec, A. & Courchamp, F. (2007) Importance of the Allee effect for reintroductions. *Ecoscience*, 14: 440–451.

Diamond, J. (1991) A new species of rail from the Solomon Islands and covergent evolution of insular flightlessness. *Auk*, 108: 461–470.

Diamond, J.M. (1982) Rediscovery of the Yellow-fronted Gardener Bowerbird. *Science*, 216: 431–434.

Diamond, J.M. (1987) Extant unless proven extinct? Or, extinct unless proven extant? *Conservation Biology*, 1: 77–79.

Diamond, J.M. (1989) The present, past and future of human-caused extinctions. *Philosophical Transactions of the Royal Society Series B-Biological Sciences*, 325: 469–477.

Dietrich, K.S., Meluin, E.F. & Conquest, L. (2008) Integrated weight longlines with paired streamer lines – best practice to prevent seabird bycatch in demersal longline fisheries. *Biological Conservation*, 141: 1793–1805.

Dietrich, K.S., Parrish, J.K. & Melvin, E.F. (2009) Understanding and addressing seabird bycatch in Alaska demersal longline fisheries. *Biological Conservation*, 142: 2642–2656.

Dolgushin, I.A. (1962) *The Birds of Kazakhstan, Vol. 2*. Institut Akademii Nauk Kazakhskoi SSR, Almaty.

Donald, P.F. (2004a) Biodiversity impacts of some agricultural commodity production systems. *Conservation Biology*, 18: 17–37.

Donald, P.F. (2004b) *The Skylark*. T. & A.D. Poyser, London.

Donald, P.F. (2007) Adult sex ratios in wild bird populations. *Ibis*, 149: 671–692.

Donald, P.F. & Brooke, M. de L. (2006) An unlikely survivor: the peculiar natural history of the Raso Lark. *British Birds*, 99: 420–430.

Donald, P.F., de Ponte, M., Groz, M.J.P. & Taylor, R. (2003) Status, ecology, behaviour and conservation of Raso Lark *Alauda razae. Bird Conservation International*, 13: 13–28.

Donald, P.F., Brooke, M. de L., Bolton, M.R., Taylor, R., Wells, C.E., Marlow, T. & Hille, S.M. (2005) Status of Raso Lark *Alauda razae* in 2003, with further notes on sex ratio, behaviour and conservation. *Bird Conservation International*, 15: 165–172.

Donald, P.F., Hille, S., Brooke, M. de L., Taylor, R., Wells, C.E., Bolton, M. & Marlow, T. (2007a) Sexual dimorphism, niche partitioning and social dominance in the feeding ecology of the critically endangered Raso Lark *Alauda razae. Ibis*, 149: 848–852.

Donald, P.F., Sanderson, F.J., Burfield, I.J., Bierman, S.M., Gregory, R.D. & Waliczky, Z. (2007b) International conservation policy delivers benefits for birds in Europe. *Science*, 317: 810–813.

Donald, P.F., Aratrakorn, S., Thun, T.W., Eames, J.C., Hla, H., Thunhikorn, S., Sribua-Rod, K., Tinun, P., Aung, S.M., Zaw, S.M. & Buchanan, G.M. (2009) Population, distribution, habitat use and breeding of Gurney's Pitta *Pitta gurneyi* in Myanmar and Thailand. *Bird Conservation International*, 19: 353–366.

Donald, P.F., Buchanan, G.M., Collar, N.J., Dellelegn Abebe, Y., Gabremichael, M.N., Mwangi, M.A.K., Ndang'ang'a, P.K., Spottiswoode, C.N. & Wondafrash, M. (2010) Rapid declines in habitat quality and population size of the Liben Lark *Heteromirafra sidamoensis* necessitate immediate conservation action. *Bird Conservation International*, 20: 1–12.

Donald, P.F., Gedeon, K., Collar, N.J., Spottiswoode, C.N., Wondafrash, M. & Buchanan, G.M. (2012) The restricted range of the Ethiopian Bush-crow *Zavattariornis stresemanni* is a consequence of high reliance on modified habitats within narrow climatic limits. *Journal of Ornithology*, 153: 1031–1044.

Donlan, C.J., Campbell, K., Cabrera, W., Lavoie, C., Carrion, V. & Cruz, F. (2007) Recovery of the Galapagos rail (*Laterallus spilonotus*) following the removal of invasive mammals. *Biological Conservation*, 138: 520–524.

Donlan, C.J. & Wilcox, C. (2008a) Diversity, invasive species and extinctions in insular ecosystems. *Journal of Applied Ecology*, 45: 1114–1123.

Donlan, C.J. & Wilcox, C. (2008b) Integrating invasive mammal eradications and biodiversity offsets for fisheries bycatch: conservation opportunities and challenges for seabirds and sea turtles. *Biological Invasions*, 10: 1053–1060.

Doswald, N., Willis, S.G., Collingham, Y.C., Pain, D.J., Green, R.E. & Huntley, B. (2009) Potential impacts of climatic change on the breeding and non-breeding ranges and migration distance of European *Sylvia* warblers. *Journal of Biogeography*, 36: 1194–1208.

Drechsler, M., Eppink, F.V. & Wätzold, F. (2011) Does proactive biodiversity conservation save costs? *Biodiversity and Conservation*, 20: 1045-1055.

Driskell, A., Christidis, L., Gill, B.J., Boles, W.E., Barker, F.K. & Longmore, N.W. (2007) A new endemic family of New Zealand passerine birds: adding heat to a biodiversity hotspot. *Australian Journal of Zoology*, 55: 73–78.

Duncan, R.P., Blackburn, T.M. & Worthy, T.H. (2002) Prehistoric bird extinctions and human hunting. *Proceedings of the Royal Society Series B-Biological Sciences*, 269: 517–521.

Duncan, R.P. & Blackburn, T.M. (2004) Extinction and endemism in the New Zealand avifauna. *Global Ecology and Biogeography*, 13: 509–517.

Dunn, E., Sullivan, B. & Small, C. (2006) *Albatross conservation: from identifying problems to implementing policy*. Symposium in Honour of Professor John Croxall held at the British Antarctic Survey, Cambridge, UK.

Dunn, R.R., Harris, N.C., Colwell, R.K., Koh, L.P. & Sodhi, N.S. (2009) The sixth mass coextinction: are most endangered species parasites and mutualists? *Proceedings of the Royal Society Series B-Biological Sciences*, 276: 3037–3045.

Dutson, G. (2008) A new species of White-eye *Zosterops* and notes on other birds from Vanikoro, Solomon Islands. *Ibis,* 150: 698–706.

Dutson, G.C.L., Magsalay, P.M. & Timmins, R.J. (1993) The rediscovery of the Cebu Flowerpecker *Dicaeum quadricolor,* with notes on other forest birds on Cebu, Philippines. *Bird Conservation International,* 3: 235–243.

EAAFP [Partnership for the East Asian-Australasian Flyway] (2011) Spoon-billed Sandpiper Task Force, News Bulletin No. 6, August 2011.

EAAFP [Partnership for the East Asian-Australasian Flyway] (2012a). Spoon-billed Sandpiper Task Force, News Bulletin No. 7, February 2012.

EAAFP [Partnership for the East Asian-Australasian Flyway] (2012b). Spoon-billed Sandpiper Task Force, News Bulletin No. 8, August 2012.

Eames, J.C., Hla, H., Leimgruber, P., Kelly, D.S., Aung, S.M., Moses, S. & Tin, U.S.N. (2005) The rediscovery of Gurney's Pitta *Pitta gurneyi* in Myanmar and an estimate of its population size based on remaining forest cover. *Bird Conservation International,* 15: 3–26.

Eason, D. & Moorhouse, R.J. (2006) Hand-rearing kakapo (*Strigops habroptilus*), 1997–2005. *Notornis,* 53: 116–125.

Eason, D.K., Elliott, G.P., Merton, D.V., Jansen, P.W., Harper, G.A. & Moorhouse, R.J. (2006) Breeding biology of kakapo (*Strigops habroptilus*) on offshore island sanctuaries, 1990–2002. *Notornis,* 54: 27–36.

Edhem, M. (1993) Lake Alaotra – in search of the Madagascar Pochard. *Wildfowl and Wetlands,* 109: 18–21.

Edmunds, K., Bunbury, N., Sawmy, S., Jones, C.G. & Bell, D.J. (2008) Restoring avian island endemics: use of supplementary food by the endangered Pink Pigeon (*Columba mayeri*). *Emu,* 108: 74–80.

Edwards, D.P., Webster, R.E. & Rowlett, R.A. (2009) 'Spectacled Flowerpecker': a species new to science discovered in Borneo? *BirdingASIA,* 12: 38–41.

Edwards, S.R. & Nash, S.V. (1992) Wild bird trade: perceptions and management in Indonesia. In: Thomsen, J.B., Edwards, S.R. & Mulliken, T.A. (eds). *Perceptions, conservation and management of wild birds in trade,* 93–116, TRAFFIC International, Cambridge, UK.

Eggert, L.S., Terwilliger, L.A., Woodworth, B.L., Hart, P.J., Palmer, D. & Fleischer, R.C. (2008) Genetic structure along an elevational gradient in Hawaiian honeycreepers reveals contrasting evolutionary responses to avian malaria. *Bmc Evolutionary Biology,* 8: 315.

Eichhorn, G. & Heinicke, T. (2000) Notable observations of the Sociable Plover *Vanellus gregarius* from the Tengiz-Korgalzhyn area, central Kazakhstan. *Wader Study Group Bulletin,* 93: 73–76.

Eichhorn, G. & Khrokov, V.V. (2002) Decline in breeding Sociable Plover *Chettusia gregaria* in the steppes of Naurzum and Korgalzhyn, Kazakhstan. *Sandgrouse,* 24: 22–27.

Ellenberg, H. (1958) Wald oder Steppe? Die natürliche Pflanzendecke der Anden Perus. *Die Umschau,* 21: 645–648, 679–681.

Elliott, G.P., Merton, D.V. & Jansen, P.W. (2001) Intensive management of a critically endangered species: the kakapo. *Biological Conservation,* 99: 121–133.

Elliott, G.P. (2006) A simulation of the future of kakapo. *Notornis,* 53: 164–172.

Elliott, G.P., Eason, D.K., Jansen, P.W., Merton, D.V., Harper, G.A. & Moorhouse, R.J. (2006) Productivity of kakapo (*Strigops habroptilus*) on offshore island refuges. *Notornis,* 53: 138–142.

Ellsworth, J.W. & McComb, B.C. (2003) Potential effects of passenger pigeon flocks on the structure and composition of presettlement forests of eastern North America. *Conservation Biology,* 17: 1548–1558.

Engblom, G., Chutas, C.A., Meza, G.F., Samochuallpa, E. & Palomino, W. (2002) The conservation of Polylepis-adapted birds at Abra Málaga, Cuzco, Peru. *Cotinga,* 17: 56–59.

Engen, S., Lande, R. & Saether, B.E. (2003) Demographic stochasticity and allee effects in populations with two sexes. *Ecology,* 84: 2378–2386.

Engilis, A. (1990) Field notes on native forest birds in the Hanawi Natural Area Reserve, Maui. *'Elepaio,* 50: 67–72.

Engilis, A., Pratt, T.K., Kepler, C.B., Ecton, A.M. & Fluetsch, K.M. (1996) Description of adults, eggshells, nestling, fledgling, and nest of the Poo-uli. *Wilson Bulletin,* 108: 607–619.

Environment Canada (2007) *Recovery strategy for the Eskimo Curlew (Numenius borealis) in Canada: Species at Risk Act Recovery Strategy Series.* Environment Canada, Ottawa.

Érard, C. (1975) Une nouvelle alouette du sud de l'Ethiopie. *Alauda,* 43: 115–124.

Ericson, P.G.P., Christidis, L., Cooper, A., Irestedt, M., Jackson, J., Johansson, U.S. & Norman, J.A. (2002) A Gondwanan origin of passerine birds supported by DNA sequences of the endemic New Zealand wrens. *Proceedings of the Royal Society Series B-Biological Sciences,* 269: 235–241.

Evans, S.R. & Sheldon, B.C. (2008) Interspecific patterns of genetic diversity in birds: correlations with extinction risk. *Conservation Biology,* 22: 1016–1025.

Ewen, J.G. & Armstrong, D.P. (2007) Strategic monitoring of reintroductions in ecological restoration programmes. *Ecoscience,* 14: 401–409.

Ewing, S.R., Nager, R.G., Nicoll, M.A.C., Aumjaud, A., Jones, C.G. & Keller, L.F. (2008) Inbreeding and loss of genetic variation in a reintroduced population of Mauritius Kestrel. *Conservation Biology,* 22: 395–404.

Fahrig, L. (2003) Effects of habitat fragmentation on biodiversity. *Annual Review of Ecology Evolution and Systematics,* 34: 487–515.

Fass-Holmes, B. (2003) An extraordinary find! *Parrots,* August: 20–23.

Faulquier, L., Fontaine, R., Vidal, E., Salamolard, M. & Le Corre, M. (2009) Feral cats *Felis catus* threaten the endangered endemic Barau's Petrel *Pterodroma baraui* at Reunion Island (Western Indian Ocean. *Waterbirds,* 32: 330–336.

Ferraro, P.J. & Pattanayak, S.K. (2006) Money for nothing? A call for empirical evaluation of biodiversity conservation investments. *PLoS Biology,* 4: e105.

Fiallo, E.A. & Jacobson, S.K. (1995) Local communities and protected areas: attitudes of rural residents towards conservation and Machalilla National Park, Ecuador. *Environmental Conservation,* 22: 241–249.

Fidler, A.E., Zwart, S., Pharis, R.P., Weston, R.J., Lawrence, S.B., Jansen, P., Elliott, G. & Merton, D.V. (2000) Screening the foods of an endangered parrot, the kakapo (*Strigops habroptilus*), for oestrogenic activity using a recombinant yeast bioassay. *Reproduction Fertility and Development,* 12. 191–199.

Fidler, A.F., Lawrence, S.B. & McNatty, K.P. (2008) An hypothesis to explain the linkage between kakapo (*Strigops habroptilus*) breeding and the mast fruiting of their food trees. *Wildlife Research,* 35: 1–7.

Fischer, K.N., Suryan, R.M., Roby, D.D. & Balogh, G.R. (2009) Post-breeding season distribution of black-footed and Laysan albatrosses satellite-tagged in Alaska: inter-specific differences in spatial overlap with North Pacific fisheries. *Biological Conservation,* 142. 751–760.

Fisher, I.J., Pain, D.J. & Thomas, V.G. (2006) A review of lead poisoning from ammunition sources in terrestrial birds. *Biological Conservation,* 131: 421–432.

Fishpool, L.D.C. & Tobias, J.A. (2005) Family Pycnonotidae (bulbuls). In: del Hoyo, J., Elliott, A. & Christie, D.A. (eds). *Handbook of birds of the world, Vol. 10,* 124–251. Lynx Edicions, Barcelona.

Fitzherbert, E.B., Struebig, M.J., Morel, A., Danielsen, F., Brühl, C.A., Donald, P.F. & Phalan, B. (2008) How will oil palm expansion affect biodiversity? *Trends in Ecology & Evolution,* 23: 538–545.

Fitzpatrick, J.W., Lammertink, M., Luneau, M.D., Gallagher, T.W., Harrison, B.R., Sparling, G.M., Rosenberg, K.V., Rohrbaugh, R.W., Swarthout, E.C.H., Wrege, P.H., Swarthout, S.B., Dantzker, M.S., Charif, R.A., Barksdale, T.R., Remsen, J.V., Simon, S.D. & Zollner, D. (2005) Ivory-billed Woodpecker (*Campephilus principalis*) persists in continental North America. *Science,* 308: 1460–1462.

Fjeldså, J. (1987) *Birds of relict forests in the high Andes of Peru and Bolivia.* Zoological Museum University of Copenhagen, Copenhagen.

Fjeldså, J. (2002) Polylepis forests: vestiges of a vanishing ecosystem in the Andes. *Ecotropica (Bonn).* 8: 111–123.

Fjeldså, J. & Krabbe, N. (1990) *Birds of the high Andes.* Apollo Books, Copenhagen.

Fjeldså, J. & Kessler, M. (1996) *Conserving the biological diversity of Polylepis woodlands of the highlands of Peru and Bolivia: a contribution to* sustainable natural resource management in the Andes. Nordic Foundation for Development and Ecology, Copenhagen.

Fjeldså, J., Krabbe, N. & Parker, T.A. (1987) Rediscovery of *Cinclodes excelsior aricomae* and notes on the nominate race. *Bulletin of the British Ornithologists' Club,* 107: 112–114.

Fjeldså, J., Lambin, E. & Mertens, B. (1999) Correlation between endemism and local ecoclimatic stability documented by comparing Andean bird distributions and remotely sensed land surface data. *Ecography,* 22: 63–78.

Fleischer, R.C., Tarr, C.L., James, H.F., Slikas, B. & McIntosh, C.E. (2001) Phylogenetic placement of the Po'ouli Melamprosops phaeosoma, based upon mitochondrial DNA sequence and osteological characters. *Studies in Avian Biology,* 22: 98–103.

Flint, V.E. & Kondratyev, A.Y. (1977) An experience of evaluating of total number of rare stenotopic species (Spoon-billed Sandpiper *Eurynorhynchus pygmeus* as an example). In: Voinstvenski, M.A. (ed). *7th All-Union Ornithological Conference, abstracts of talks. Part 2,* 250. Naukova Dumka, Kiev.

Foden, W.B., Mace, G.M., Vié, J.-C., Angulo, A., Butchart, S.H.M., DeVantier, L., Dublin, H.T., Gutsche, A., Stuart, S.N. & Turak, E. (2009) Species susceptibility to climate change impacts. In: Vié, J.-C., Hilton-Taylor, C. & Stuart, S.N. (eds). *Wildlife in a changing world ñ an analysis of the 2008 IUCN Red List of Threatened Species,* 77–87. IUCN, Gland, Switzerland.

Fonseca, D.M., LaPointe, D.A. & Fleischer, R.C. (2000) Bottlenecks and multiple introductions: population genetics of the vector of avian malaria in Hawaii. *Molecular Ecology,* 9: 1803–1814.

Forbes-Watson, A.D. & Turner, A.D. (1973) *Report on bird preservation in Madagascar, part 3.* International Council for Bird Preservation, Cambridge, UK.

Foster, J.T., Woodworth, B.L., Eggert, L.E., Hart, P.J., Palmer, D., Duffy, D.C. & Fleischer, R.C. (2007) Genetic structure and evolved malaria resistance in Hawaiian honeycreepers. *Molecular Ecology,* 16: 4738–4746.

Francis, J. & Shirihai, H. (1999) *Ethiopia: in search of endemic birds.* Privately published, London.

Frankham, R. (1999) Quantitative genetics in conservation biology. *Genetical Research,* 74: 237–244.

Freed, L.A. & Cann, R.L. (2009) Negative effects of an introduced bird species on growth and survival in a native bird community. *Current Biology,* 19: 1736-1740.

Freed, L.A., Cann, R.L. & Bodner, G.R. (2008a) Incipient extinction of a major population of the Hawaii akepa owing to introduced species. *Evolutionary Ecology Research,* 10: 931–965.

Freed, L.A., Medeiros, M.C. & Bodner, G.R. (2008b) Explosive increase in ectoparasites in Hawaiian forest birds. *Journal of Parasitology,* 94: 1009–1021.

Frenot, Y., Chown, S.L., Whinam, J., Selkirk, P.M., Convey, P., Skotnicki, M. & Bergstrom, D.M. (2005) Biological invasions in the Antarctic: extent, impacts and implications. *Biological Reviews,* 80: 45–72.

Fuller, E. (1999) *The Great Auk.* Harry N. Abrams, New York.

Galbreath, R. & Brown, D. (2004) The tale of the lighthouse-keeper's cat: discovery and extinction of the Stephens Island Wren (*Traversia lyalli*). *Notornis,* 51: 193–200.

Garfield, B. (2007) *The Meinertzhagen mystery: the life and legend of a collosal fraud.* Potomac Books, Washington D.C.

Garnett, S., Crowley, G., Duncan, R., Baker, N. & Doherty, P. (1993) Notes on live Night Parrot sightings in north-western Queensland. *Emu,* 93: 292–296.

Garnett, S., Crowley, G. & Balmford, A. (2003) The costs and effectiveness of funding the conservation of Australian threatened birds. *BioScience,* 53: 658–665.

Garrido, O.H. & Kirkconnell, A. (2000) *Field guide to the birds of Cuba.* Comstock Publishing Associates, Ithaca, New York.

Gartrell, B.D. & Reid, C. (2007) Death by chocolate: a fatal problem for an inquisitive wild parrot. *New Zealand Veterinary Journal,* 55: 149–151.

Gartrell, B.D., Alley, M.R., Mack, H., Donald, J., McInnes, K. & Jansen, P. (2005) Erysipelas in the critically endangered kakapo (*Strigops habroptilus*). *Avian Pathology,* 34: 383–387.

Gascoigne, J., Berec, L., Gregory, S. & Courchamp, F. (2009) Dangerously few liaisons: a review of mate-finding Allee effects. *Population Ecology,* 51: 355–372.

Gascoigne, J.C. & Lipcius, R.N. (2004) Allee effects driven by predation. *Journal of Applied Ecology,* 41: 801–810.

Gaston, K.J. (1994) *Rarity.* Chapman & Hall, London.

Gaston, K.J. & Blackburn, T.M. (1995) Birds, body-size and the threat of extinction. *Philosophical Transactions of the Royal Society of London Series B-Biological Sciences,* 347: 205–212.

Gaston, K.J. & Blackburn, T.M. (1997) Evolutionary age and risk of extinction in the global avifauna. *Evolutionary Ecology,* 11: 557–565.

Gaston, K.J. & Fuller, R.A. (2008) Commonness, population depletion and conservation biology. *Trends in Ecology & Evolution,* 23: 14–19.

Gaston, K.J., Blackburn, T.M. & Goldewijk, K.K. (2003) Habitat conversion and global avian biodiversity loss. *Proceedings of the Royal Society Series B-Biological Sciences,* 270: 1293–1300.

Gaveau, D.L.A., Epting, J., Lyne, O., Linkie, M., Kumara, I., Kanninen, M. & Leader-Williams, N. (2009) Evaluating whether protected areas reduce tropical deforestation in Sumatra. *Journal of Biogeography,* 36: 2165–2175.

Gibbs, W.W. (2001) On the termination of species. *Scientific American,* 285: 40–49.

Gilbert, M., Virani, M.Z., Watson, R.T., Oaks, J.L., Benson, P.C., Khan, A.A., Ahmed, S., Chaudhry, J., Arshad, M., Mahmood, S. & Shah, Q.A. (2002) Breeding and mortality of Oriental White-backed Vulture *Gyps bengalensis* in Punjab Province, Pakistan. *Bird Conservation International,* 12: 311–326.

Gilbert, M., Watson, R.T., Virani, M.Z., Oaks, J.L., Ahmed, S., Chaudhry, M.J.I., Arshad, M., Mahmood, S., Ali, A. & Khan, A.A. (2006) Rapid population declines and mortality clusters in three Oriental whitebacked vulture *Gyps bengalensis* colonies in Pakistan due to diclofenac poisoning. *Oryx,* 40: 388–399.

Gilbert, M., Watson, R.T., Ahmed, S., Asim, M. & Johnson, J.A. (2007a) Vulture restaurants and their role in reducing diclofenac exposure in Asian vultures. *Bird Conservation International,* 17: 63–77.

Gilbert, M., Watson, R.T., Virani, M.Z., Oaks, J.L., Ahmed, S., Chaudhry, M.J.I., Arshad, M., Mahmood, S., Ali, A. & Khan, A.A. (2007b) Neck-drooping posture in oriental white-backed vultures (*Gyps bengalensis*): an unsuccessful predictor of mortality and its probable role in thermoregulation. *Journal of Raptor Research,* 41: 35–40.

Gilg, O., Boertmann, D., Merkel, F., Aebischer, A. & Sabard, B. (2009) Status of the endangered ivory gull, *Pagophila eburnea*, in Greenland. *Polar Biology,* 32: 1275–1286.

Gill, J.A. (2007) Approaches to measuring the effects of human disturbance on birds. *Ibis,* 149: 9–14.

Gill, R.E., Canevari, P. & Iversen, E.H. (1998) Eskimo Curlew (*Numenius borealis*). In: Poole, A. & Gill, F. (eds). *The Birds of North America, No. 347,* The Birds of North America Inc., Philadelphia.

Gillespie, T.W. (2000) Rarity and conservation of forest birds in the tropical dry forest region of Central America. *Biological Conservation,* 96: 161–168.

Gilpin, M.E. & Soulé, M.E. (1986) Minimum viable populations: processes of species extinction. In: Soulé, M.E. (ed). *Conservation biology: the science of scarcity and diversity,* 19–34. Sinauer, Sunderland, Massachusetts.

Giraudo, A.R. & Povedano, H. (2005) Ameaças de extinção das espécies-bandeira na Mata Atlântica de Interior. In: Galindo-Leal, C. & Câmara, I.G. (eds). *Mata Atlântica: biodiversidade, ameaças e perspectivas,* Capítulo 16. Fundação SOS Mata Atlântica, Conservação Internacional e Centro de Ciências Aplicadas à Biodiversidade, Belo Horizonte, Brazil.

Gjershaug, J.O., Kvaløy, K., Røv, N., Prawiradilaga, D.M., Suparman, U. & Rahman, Z. (2004) The taxonomic status of Flores Hawk Eagle *Spizaetus floris.* *Forktail,* 20: 55–62.

Goerck, J.M. (1997) Patterns of rarity in the birds of the Atlantic forest of Brazil. *Conservation Biology,* 11: 112–118.

Goes, F.A. & Sam, V. (1999) The rediscovery of the Bengal Florican. *Cambodia Bird News,* 3: 22–31.

Gollop, J.B. (1988) The Eskimo Curlew. In: Chandler, W.J. (ed). *Audubon Wildlife Report,* 583–595. Academic Press, New York.

Gollop, J.B., Barry, T.W. & Iversen, E.H. (1986) *Eskimo Curlew: a vanishing species.* Saskatchewan Natural History Society, Regina, Saskatchewan.

Gonzales, R.B. (1968) A study of the breeding biology and ecology of the Monkey-eating Eagle. *Silliman Journal,* 15: 461–500.

Goodman, S.M. (1993) A reconnaissance of Ile Sainte Marie, Madagascar: the status of the forest, avifauna, lemurs and fruit bats. *Biological Conservation,* 65: 205–212.

Goodman, S.M. & Benstead, J.P. (2003) *The natural history of Madagascar.* University of Chicago Press, Chicago.

Gordienko, N.S. (1991) [Ecology and numbers of Sociable Lapwing in the Kustanai steppe]. *Ornitologiya,* 25: 54–61.

Gore, M.E.J. & Won, P.-O. (1971) *Birds of Korea.* Royal Asiatic Society & Taewon Publishing Company, Seoul, Korea.

Grant, P.R. (2001) Reconstructing the evolution of birds on islands: 100 years of research. *Oikos,* 92: 385–403.

Grau, E.T., Pereira, S.L., Silveira, L.F. & Wajntal, A. (2003) Molecular markers contribute to a breeding programme of extinct-in-the-wild Alagoas Curassow *Mitu mitu* and confirm the validity of the species. *Bird Conservation International,* 13: 115–126.

Graves, G.R. (1992) Diagnosis of a hybrid antbird (*Phlegopsis nigromaculata × Phlegopsis erythroptera*) and the rarity of hybridization among suboscines. *Proceedings of the Biological Society of Washington,* 105: 834–840.

Gray, T.N.F., Chamnan, H., Borey, R., Collar, N.J. & Dolman, P.M. (2007) Habitat preferences of a globally threatened bustard provide support for community-based conservation in Cambodia. *Biological Conservation,* 138: 341–350.

Gray, T.N.E., Collar, N.J., Davidson, P.J.A., Dolman, P.M., Evans, T.D., Fox, H.N., Chamnan, H., Borey, R., Hout, S.K. & van Zalinge, R.N. (2009a) Distribution, status and conservation of the Bengal Florican *Houbaropsis bengalensis* in Cambodia. *Bird Conservation International,* 19: 1–14.

Gray, T.N.E., Tarrant, M., Chamnan, H., Collar, N.J. & Dolman, P.M. (2009b) Sex-specific habitat use by a lekking bustard: conservation implications for the Critically Endangered Bengal Florican (*Houbaropsis bengalensis*) in an intensifying agroecosystem. *Auk,* 126: 112–122.

Grebmeier, J.M., Overland, J.E., Moore, S.E., Farley, E.V., Carmack, E.C., Cooper, L.W., Frey, K.E., Helle, J.H., McLaughlin, F.A. & McNutt, S.L. (2006) A major ecosystem shift in the Northern Bering Sea. *Science,* 311: 1461–1464.

Green, R.E. (2002) Diagnosing causes of population declines and selecting remedial actions. In: Norris, K. & Pain, D.J. (eds). *Conserving bird biodiversity: general principles and their application,* 139–156. Cambridge University Press, Cambridge, UK.

Green, R.E., Newton, I., Shultz, S., Cunningham, A.A., Gilbert, M., Pain, D.J. & Prakash, V. (2004) Diclofenac poisoning as a cause of vulture population declines across the Indian subcontinent. *Journal of Applied Ecology,* 41: 793–800.

Green, R.E., Cornell, S.J., Scharlemann, J.P.W. & Balmford, A. (2005) Farming and the fate of wild nature. *Science,* 307: 550–555.

Green, R.E., Taggart, M.A., Senacha, K.R., Raghavan, B., Pain, D.J., Jhala, Y. & Cuthbert, R. (2007) Rate of decline of the Oriental White-backed Vulture population in India estimated from a survey of diclofenac residues in carcasses of ungulates. *PLoS ONE,* 2: e686.

Green, R.E., Collingham, Y.C., Willis, S.G., Gregory, R.D., Smith, K.W. & Huntley, B. (2008a) Performance of climate envelope models in retrodicting recent changes in bird population size from observed climatic change. *Biology Letters,* 4: 599–602.

Green, R.E., Hunt, W.G., Parish, C.N. & Newton, I. (2008b) Effectiveness of action to reduce exposure of free-ranging California Condors in Arizona and Utah to lead from spent ammunition. *PLoS ONE,* 3: e4022.

Green, R.E., Barnes, K.N. & Brooke, M. de L. (2009) How the longspur won its spurs: a study of claw and toe length in ground-dwelling passerine birds. *Journal of Zoology,* 277: 126–133.

Greenway, J.C. (1958) *Extinct and vanishing birds of the world.* American Committee for International Wild Life Protection, New York.

Gregory, R.D. & Gaston, K.J. (2000) Explanations of commonness and rarity in British breeding birds: separating resource use and resource availability. *Oikos,* 88: 515–526.

Gregory, R.D., Willis, S.G., Jiguet, F., Voříšek, P., Klvaňová, A., van Strien, A., Huntley, B., Collingham, Y.C., Couvet, D. & Green, R.E. (2009) An indicator of the impact of climatic change on European bird populations. *PLoS ONE,* 4: e4678.

Gretton, A. (1991) *The ecology and conservation of the Slender-billed Curlew (Numenius tenuirostris).* ICBP Monograph 6. International Council for Bird Preservation, Cambridge.

Gretton, A., Kohler, M., Lansdown, R.V., Pankhurst, T.J., Parr, J. & Robson, C. (1993) The status of Gurney's Pitta *Pitta gurneyi,* 1987–1989. *Bird Conservation International,* 3: 351–367.

Gretton, A., Yurlov, A.K. & Boere, G.C. (2002) Where does the Slender-billed Curlew nest, and what future does it have? *British Birds,* 95: 334–344.

Griffiths, R. & Tiwari, B. (1995) Sex of the last wild Spix's Macaw. *Nature,* 375: 454.

Griscom, L. (1935) The rediscovery of *Chlorospingus flavovirens* (Lawrence). *Auk,* 52: 94–95.

Groombridge, J.J. (2009) Po`o-uli. In: Pratt, T.K., Atkinson, P.J., Banko, P.C., Jacobi, J.J.D. & Woodworth, B.L. (eds). *Conservation biology of Hawaiian forest birds: implications for island avifauna,* 487–498. Yale University Press, New Haven, CT.

Groombridge, J.J., Bruford, M.W., Jones, C.G. & Nichols, R.A. (2001) Evaluating the severity of the population bottleneck in the Mauritius kestrel *Falco punctatus* from ringing records using MCMC estimation. *Journal of Animal Ecology,* 70: 401–409.

Groombridge, J.J., Massey, J.G., Bruch, J.C., Malcolm, T., Brosius, C.N., Okada, M.M., Sparklin, B., Fretz, J.S. & VanderWerf, E.A. (2004a) An attempt to recover the Po'ouli by translocation and an appraisal of recovery strategy for bird species of extreme rarity. *Biological Conservation,* 118: 365–375.

Groombridge, J.J., Massey, J.G., Bruch, J.C., Malcolm, T.R., Brosius, C.N., Okada, M.M. & Sparklin, B. (2004b) Evaluating stress in a Hawaiian honeycreeper, *Paroreomyza montana,* following translocation. *Journal of Field Ornithology,* 75: 183–187.

Groombridge, J.J., Sparklin, B., Malcolm, T., Brosius, C.N., Okada, M.M. & Bruch, J.C. (2006) Patterns of spatial use and movement of the Po'ouli – a critically endangered Hawaiian honeycreeper. *Biodiversity and Conservation,* 15: 3357–3368.

Grossman, M.L. & Hamlet, J. (1964) *Birds of prey of the world.* Clarkson N. Potter, Inc, New York.

Grueber, C.E. & Jamieson, I.G. (2008) Quantifying and managing the loss of genetic variation in a free-ranging population of takahe through the use of pedigrees. *Conservation Genetics,* 9: 645–651.

Gupta, R.K. & Kanodia, K.C. (1968) Plants used during scarcity and famine periods in the dry regions of India. *Journal d'Agriculture Tropicale et de Botanique Appliquée,* 15: 265–285.

Hagelin, J.C. (2004) Observations on the olfactory ability of the Kakapo *Strigops habroptilus,* the critically endangered parrot of New Zealand. *Ibis,* 146: 161–164.

Hahn, I., Romer, U. & Schlatter, R.P. (2005) Distribution, habitat use, and abundance patterns of landbird communities on the Juan Fernandez Islands, Chile. *Ornitologia Neotropical,* 16: 371–385.

Hall, B.P. (1963) The status of *Spizocorys razae* Alexander. *Bulletin of the British Ornithologists' Club,* 83: 133–134.

Hansen, B.C.S., Seltzer, G.O. & Wright, H.E. (1994) Late quaternary vegetational change in the central Peruvian Andes. *Palaeogeography, Palaeoclimatology and Palaeoecology,* 109: 263–285.

Hardin, G. (1968) The tragedy of the commons. *Science,* 162: 1243–1248.

Hare, C.E., Leblanc, K., DiTullio, G.R., Kudela, R.M., Zhang, Y., Lee, P.A., Riseman, S. & Hutchins, D.A. (2007) Consequences of increased temperature and CO_2 for phytoplankton community structure in the Bering Sea. *Marine Ecology-Progress Series,* 352: 9–16.

Hartert, E. (1896) An account of the collections of birds made by Mr William Doherty in the Eastern Archipelago. *Novitates Zoologicae,* 3: 537–590.

295

Hasegawa, H. (1984) Status and conservation of seabirds in Japan, with special attention to the Short-tailed Albatross. In: Croxall, J.P., Evans, P.G.H. & Schreiber, R.W. (eds). *Status and conservation of the world's seabirds*, 487–500. International Council for Bird Preservation, Cambridge, UK.

Hawkins, F., Andriamasimanana, R., Sam, T.S. & Rabeony, Z. (2000) The sad story of Alaotra Grebe *Tachybaptus rufolavatus*. *Bulletin of the African Bird Club*, 7: 115–117.

Hayes, F.E. (1995) *Status, distribution and biogeography of the birds of Paraguay*. American Birding Association, Colorado Springs.

Hayes, F.E., Shameerudeen, C.L., Sanasie, B., Hayes, B.D., Ramjohn, C.L. & Lucas, F.B. (2009) Ecology and behaviour of the critically endangered Trinidad piping-guan *Aburria pipile*. *Endangered Species Research*, 6: 223–229.

Hazevoet, C.J. (1995) *The birds of the Cape Verde Islands*. BOU, Tring.

Heard, S.B. & Mooers, A.O. (2000) Phylogenetically patterned speciation rates and extinction risks change the loss of evolutionary history during extinctions. *Proceedings of the Royal Society Series B-Biological Sciences*, 267: 613–620.

Held, I.M., Delworth, T.L., Lu, J., Findell, K.L. & Knutson, T.R. (2005) Simulation of Sahel drought in the 20th and 21st centuries. *Proceedings of the National Academy of Sciences of the United States of America*, 102: 17891–17896.

Hennache, A., Rasmussen, P.C., Lucchini, V., Rimondi, S. & Randi, E. (2003) Hybrid origin of the imperial pheasant *Lophura imperialis* (Delacour and Jabouille, 1924) demonstrated by morphology, hybrid experiments, and DNA analyses. *Biological Journal of the Linnean Society*, 80: 573–600.

Herzog, S.K., Cahill M, J., Fjeldså, J., Kessler, M., Yensen, E., Tarifa, T., Capriles, J., Fernandez Terrazas, E., Hensen, I., Ibisch, P.L., Loayza, I., Renison, D., Dellacassa, E., Flores Bedregal, E., Cingolani, A.M., Lorenzo, D., Matthysen, E., Schinner, D., Soria A, R., Troncoso J, A., Stahl, B. & Vilaseca, A. (2002) Ecology and conservation of high-Andean polylepis forests. *Ecotropica (Bonn)*, 8: 93–95.

Hilker, F.M. & Westerhoff, F.H. (2007) Preventing extinction and outbreaks in chaotic populations. *American Naturalist*, 170: 232–241.

Hill, G.A., Mennill, D.J., Rolek, B.W., Hicks, T.L. & Swiston, K.A. (2006) Evidence suggesting that Ivory-billed Woodpeckers (*Campephilus principalis*) exist in Florida. *Avian Conservation & Ecology*, 1(3): 2.

Hilton-Taylor, C., Pollock, C.M., Chanson, J.S., Butchart, S.H.M., Oldfield, T.E.E. & Katariya, V. (2009) State of the world's species. In: Vié, J.-C., Hilton-Taylor, C. & Stuart, S.N. (eds). *Wildlife in a changing world ñ an analysis of the 2008 IUCN Red List of Threatened Species*, 15–41. IUCN, Gland, Switzerland.

Hilton, G.M. & Cuthbert, R.J. (2010) The catastrophic impact of invasive mammalian predators on the birds of the UK Overseas Territories: a review and synthesis. *Ibis*, 152: 443–458.

Hilton, G.M., Bowden, C.G.R., Ratcliffe, N., Lucking, V. & Brindley, E. (2001) *Bird conservation priorities in the UK Overseas Territories*. RSPB, Sandy, UK.

Hilton, G.M., Atkinson, P.W., Gray, G.A.L., Arendt, W.J. & Gibbons, D.W. (2003) Rapid decline of the volcanically threatened Montserrat oriole. *Biological Conservation*, 111: 79–89.

Hilty, S.L. (1977) *Chlorospingus flavovirens* rediscovered, with notes on other Pacific Colombian and Cauca Valley birds. *Auk*, 94: 44–49.

Hitchcock, C.L. & Gratto-Trevor, C.L. (1997) Diagnosing a shorebird local population decline with a stage-structured population model. *Ecology*, 78: 522–534.

Hockey, P.A.R. (1987) The influence of coastal utilisation by man on the presumed extinction of the Canarian Black Oystercatcher *Haematopus meadewaldoi* Bannerman. *Biological Conservation*, 39: 49–62.

Hockey, P.A.R. & Curtis, O.E. (2009) Use of basic biological information for rapid prediction of the response of species to habitat loss. *Conservation Biology*, 23: 64–71.

Hoffmann, M. *et al.* (2010) The impact of conservation on the status of the world's vertebrates. *Science*, 330: 1503-1509.

Hofland, R. & Keijl, G. (2008) *Syrian Sociable Lapwing survey: WIWO*

Report Series No. 85. Foundation Working Group International Waterbird and Wetland Research, Beek-Ubbergen, The Netherlands.

Hole, D.G., Willis, S.G., Pain, D.J., Fishpool, L.D.C., Butchart, S.H.M., Collingham, Y.C., Rahbek, C. & Huntley, B. (2009) Projected impacts of climate change on a continent-wide protected area network. *Ecology Letters*, 12: 420–431.

Holimon, W.C. & Montague, W.G. (2003) Reciprocal translocation reestablishes breeding status of Mississippi alluvial plain population of Red-cockaded Woodpeckers in Arkansas. *Journal of the Arkansas Academy of Science*, 57: 197–198.

Horrocks, M., Salter, J., Braggins, J., Nichol, S., Moorhouse, R. & Elliott, G. (2008) Plant microfossil analysis of coprolites of the critically endangered kakapo (*Strigops habroptilus*) parrot from New Zealand. *Review of Palaeobotany and Palynology*, 149: 229–245.

Houston, D. (1985) Indian White-backed Vulture (*Gyps bengalensis*). In: Newton, I. & Chancellor, R.D. (eds). *Conservation studies of raptors*. International Council for Bird Preservation, Cambridge, UK.

Houston, D. & Nager, R. (2009) Archaeology among the bird droppings: what does it tell us about raptor nest-site selection? *Ibis*, 151: 592–593.

Houston, D., McInnes, K., Elliott, G., Eason, D., Moorhouse, R. & Cockrem, J. (2007) The use of a nutritional supplement to improve egg production in the endangered kakapo. *Biological Conservation*, 138: 248–255.

Howald, G., Donlan, C.J., Galvan, J.P., Russell, J.C., Parkes, J., Samaniego, A., Wang, Y.W., Veitch, D., Genovesi, P., Pascal, M., Saunders, A. & Tershy, B. (2007) Invasive rodent eradication on islands. *Conservation Biology*, 21: 1258–1268.

Huang, C.Q., Kim, S., Song, K., Townshend, J.R.G., Davis, P., Altstatt, A., Rodas, O., Yanosky, A., Clay, R., Tucker, C.J. & Musinsky, J. (2009) Assessment of Paraguay's forest cover change using Landsat observations. *Global and Planetary Change*, 67: 1–12.

Huber, S.K. (2008) Effects of the introduced parasite *Philornis downsi* on nestling growth and mortality in the medium ground finch (*Geospiza fortis*). *Biological Conservation*, 141: 601–609.

Hughes, A.L. (1999) Differential human impact on the survival of genetically distinct avian lineages. *Bird Conservation International*, 9: 147–154.

Hughes, B. (2012) Spoon-billed Sandpiper *Eurynorhynchus pygmeus* conservation breeding project: the 2012 expedition to Russia. *BirdingAsia*, 18: 76–78.

Hughes, B., Dugger, B., Cunha, H.J., Lamas, I., Goerck, J., Lins, L., Silveira, L.F., Andrade, R.D., Bruno, S.F., Rigueira, S. & Barros, Y.M. (2006) *Action plan for the conservation of the Brazilian Merganser Mergus octosetaceus*. Ibama, Brasilia.

Hume, A.O. & Davison, W. (1878) A revised list of the birds of Tenasserim. *Stray Feathers*, 6: 1–524.

Huntley, B., Collingham, Y.C., Green, R.E., Hilton, G.M., Rahbek, C. & Willis, S.G. (2005) *Potential impacts of climatic change upon geographical distributions of birds*. Annual Spring Conference of the British Ornithologists' Union, Leicester, UK.

Huntley, B., Green, R.E., Collingham, Y.C. & Willis, S.G. (2007) *A climatic atlas of European breeding birds*. Lynx Edicions, Barcelona.

Ibañez, J.C., Miranda, H.C., Balaquit-Ibañez, G., Afan, D.S. & Kennedy, R.S. (2003) Notes on the breeding behavior of a Philippine Eagle pair at Mount Sinaka, central Mindanao. *Wilson Bulletin*, 115: 330–336.

Imansyah, M.J., Anggoro, D.G., Yangpatra, N., Hidayat, A. & Benu, Y.J. (2005) *Sebaran dan karakteristik pohon sarang Kakatua jambul kuning (*Cacatua sulphurea parvula*) di Pulau Komodo, Taman Nasional Komodo*. CRES Komodo Project. Laporan no 4.

Imber, M.J. (1992) Cephalopods eaten by wandering albatrosses (*Diomedea exulans* L) breeding at 6 circumpolar localities. *Journal of the Royal Society of New Zealand*, 22: 243–263.

Inchausti, P. & Weimerskirch, H. (2001) Risks of decline and extinction of the endangered Amsterdam albatross and the projected impact of long-line fisheries. *Biological Conservation*, 100: 377–386.

Inchausti, P. & Bretagnolle, V. (2005) Predicting short-term extinction risk for the declining Little Bustard (*Tetrax tetrax*) in intensive agricultural habitats. *Biological Conservation*, 122: 375–384.

Innes, J., Hay, R., Flux, I., Bradfield, P., Speed, H. & Jansen, P. (1999) Successful recovery of North Island kokako *Callaeas cinerea wilsoni* populations, by adaptive management. *Biological Conservation*, 87: 201–214.

Innes, J., Kelly, D., Overton, J.M. & Gillies, C. (2010) Predation and other factors currently limiting New Zealand forest birds. *New Zealand Journal of Ecology*, 34: 86–114.

Inskipp, C. & Collar, N.J. (1984) The Bengal Florican: its conservation in Nepal. *Oryx*, 18: 30–35.

Inskipp, T., Broad, S. & Luxmoore, R. (1988) *Significant trade in wildlife: a review of selected species in CITES Appendix II. Vol. 3. Birds*. International Union for Conservation of Nature and Natural Resources, Cambridge, UK.

IPCC (2007) *Climate Change 2007: Synthesis Report. Contribution of Working Groups I, II and III to the Fourth Assessment Report of the Intergovernmental Panel on Climate Change*. Intergovernmental Panel on Climate Change (IPCC), Geneva, Switzerland.

Isaac, N.J.B., Mallet, J. & Mace, G.M. (2004) Taxonomic inflation: its influence on macroecology and conservation. *Trends in Ecology & Evolution*, 19: 464–469.

Ishtiaq, F. (1999) The Forest Spotted Owlet *Athene blewitti* – an update. *Hornbill*, 1999(3): 26–28.

Ishtiaq, F. & Rahmani, A.R. (2000) Further information on the status and distribution of the Forest Owlet *Athene blewitti* in India. *Forktail*, 16: 125–130.

Ishtiaq, F. & Rahmani, A.R. (2005) The Forest Owlet *Heteroglaux blewitti*: vocalization, breeding biology and conservation. *Ibis*, 147: 197–205.

Ishtiaq, F., Rahmani, A.R. & Rasmussen, P.C. (2002) Ecology and behaviour of the Forest Owlet (*Athene blewitti*). In: Newton, I., Kavanagh, R., Olsen, J. & Taylor, I. (eds). *Ecology and conservation of owls*, 80–88. CSIRO Publishing, Canberra.

IUCN (2001) *IUCN Red List categories and criteria Version 3.1*. IUCN Species Survival Commission, Gland, Switzerland and Cambridge, UK.

Jackson, J.A. (2006) Ivory-billed Woodpecker *Campephilus principalis*: hope, and the interfaces of science, conservation, and politics. *Auk*, 123: 1–15.

Jahncke, J., Goya, E. & Guillen, A. (2001) Seabird by-catch in small-scale longline fisheries in northern Peru. *Waterbirds*, 24: 137–141.

Jameson, J.S. & Ramsay, P.M. (2007) Changes in high-altitude Polylepis forest cover and quality in the Cordillera de Vilcanota, Peru, 1956–2005. *Biological Conservation*, 138: 38–46.

Jamieson, I.G., Wallis, G.P. & Briskie, J.V. (2006) Inbreeding and endangered species management: is New Zealand out of step with the rest of the world? *Conservation Biology*, 20: 38–47.

Jankowski, J.E. & Rabenold, K.N. (2007) Endemism and local rarity in birds of neotropical montane rainforest. *Biological Conservation*, 138: 453–463.

Jathar, G.A. & Rahmani, A.R. (2004) *Ecological studies of the Forest Spotted Owlet Athene (Heteroglaux) blewitti*. Bombay Natural History Society, Mumbai.

Jathar, G.A., Talmale, S.S., Pradhan, M.S. & Rahmani, A.R. (2005) Mammalian prey species of the Forest Owlet *Heteroglaux blewitti* Hume. *Journal of the Bombay Natural History Society*, 102: 230–232.

Jathar, G.A. (2008) The Critically Endangered Forest Owlet. *Hornbill*, 2008(4): 19–23.

Jenkins, C.N. & Joppa, L. (2009) Expansion of the global terrestrial protected area system. *Biological Conservation*, 142: 2166–2174.

Jenouvrier, S., Caswell, H., Barbraud, C., Holland, M., Stroeve, J. & Weimerskirch, H. (2009) Demographic models and IPCC climate projections predict the decline of an emperor penguin population. *Proceedings of the National Academy of Sciences of the United States of America*, 106: 1844–1847.

Jepson, P., Brickle, N. & Chayadin, Y. (2001) The conservation status of Tanimbar corella and blue-streaked lory on the Tanimbar Islands, Indonesia: results of a rapid contextual survey. *Oryx*, 35: 224–233.

Jeschke, J.M. (2008) Across islands and continents, mammals are more successful invaders than birds. *Diversity and Distributions*, 14: 913–916.

Jetz, W., Wilcove, D.S. & Dobson, A.P. (2007) Projected impacts of climate and land-use change on the global diversity of birds. *PLoS Biology*, 5: 1211–1219.

Jetz, W., Sekercioglu, C.H. & Böhning-Gaese, K. (2008) The worldwide variation in avian clutch size across species and space. *PLoS Biology*, 6: 303.

Jiguet, F., Gadot, A.S., Julliard, R., Newson, S.E. & Couvet, D. (2007) Climate envelope, life history traits and the resilience of birds facing global change. *Global Change Biology*, 13: 1672–1684.

Jimenez, S., Domingo, A. & Brazeiro, A. (2009) Seabird bycatch in the Southwest Atlantic: interaction with the Uruguayan pelagic longline fishery. *Polar Biology*, 32: 187–196.

Johnson, J.A., Gilbert, M., Virani, M.Z., Asim, M. & Mindell, D.P. (2008) Temporal genetic analysis of the critically endangered oriental white-backed vulture in Pakistan. *Biological Conservation*, 141: 2403–2409.

Johnson, T.H. & Stattersfield, A.J. (1990) A global review of island endemic birds. *Ibis*, 132: 167–180.

Johnston, J.P., Peach, W.J., Gregory, R.D. & White, S.A. (1997) Survival rates of tropical and temperate passerines: a Trinidadian perspective. *American Naturalist*, 150: 771–789.

Jones, C.G. (2004) Conservation management of endangered birds. In: Sutherland, W.J., Newton, I. & Green, R.E. (eds). *Bird ecology and conservation: a handbook of techniques*, 269–301. Oxford University Press, Oxford, UK.

Jones, C.G. & Hartley, J. (1995) A conservation project on Mauritius and Rodrigues: an overview and bibliography. *Dodo*, 31: 40–65.

Jones, C.G. & Swinnerton, K.J. (1997) A summary of conservation status and research for the mauritius kestrel *Falco punctatus*, pink pigeon *Columba mayeri* and echo parakeet *Psittacula eques*. *Dodo*, 33: 72–75.

Jones, C.G., Heck, W., Lewis, R.E., Mungroo, Y., Slade, G. & Cade, T. (1995) The restoration of the Mauritius kestrel *Falco punctatus* population. *Ibis*, 137: S173–S180.

Jones, H.P., Tershy, B.R., Zavaleta, E.S., Croll, D.A., Keitt, B.S., Finkelstein, M.E. & Howald, G.R. (2008) Severity of the effects of invasive rats on seabirds: a global review. *Conservation Biology*, 22: 16–26.

Jones, M.J., Lace, L.A., Hounsome, M.V. & Hamer, K. (1987) The butterflies and birds of Madeira and La Gomera – taxon cycles and human influence. *Biological Journal of the Linnean Society*, 31: 95–111.

Jones, M.J., Linsley, M.D. & Marsden, S.J. (1995) Population sizes, status and habitat associations of the restricted-range bird species of Sumba, Indonesia. *Bird Conservation International*, 5: 21–52.

Jones, M.J., Fielding, A. & Sullivan, M. (2006) Analysing extinction risk in parrots using decision trees. *Biodiversity and Conservation*, 15: 1993–2007.

Jones, T. & Cresswell, W. (2010) The phenology mismatch hypothesis: are declines of migrant birds linked to uneven global climate change? *Journal of Animal Ecology*, 79: 98–108.

Joppa, L.N. & Pfaff, A. (2009) High and far: biases in the location of Protected Areas. *PLoS ONE*, 4: e4279.

Jordan, O.C. & Munn, C.A. (1993) First observations of the Blue-throated Macaw in Bolivia. *Wilson Bulletin*, 105: 694–695.

Joseph, S., Blackburn, G.A., Gharai, B., Sudhakar, S., Thomas, A.P. & Murthy, M.S.R. (2009) Monitoring conservation effectiveness in a global biodiversity hotspot: the contribution of land cover change assessment. *Environmental Monitoring and Assessment*, 158: 169–179.

Jukema, J. & Piersma, T. (2004) Were Slender-billed Curlews *Numenius tenuirostris* once common in The Netherlands, and do they have patches of powder feathers? *Ibis*, 146: 165–167.

Juniper, A. (2002) *Spix's Macaw: the race to save the world's rarest bird*. Fourth Estate Ltd, London.

Juniper, A.T. & Yamashita, C. (1990) The conservation of Spix's Macaw. *Oryx*, 24: 224–228.

Juniper, A.T. & Yamashita, C. (1991) The habitat and status of Spix's Macaw *Cyanopsitta spixii*. *Bird Conservation International*, 1: 1–9.

Kamp, J., Sheldon, R.D., Koshkin, M.A., Donald, P.F. & Biedermann, R (2009) Post-Soviet steppe management causes pronounced synanthropy in the globally threatened Sociable Lapwing *Vanellus gregarius*. *Ibis*, 151: 452–463.

Kamp, J., Koshkin, M.A. & Sheldon, R.D. (2010) Historic breeding of

Sociable Lapwing (*Vanellus gregarius*) in Xinjiang. *Chinese Birds*, 1: 70-73.

Kamp, J., Urazaliev, R., Donald, P.F. & Holzel, N. (2011) Post-Soviet agricultural change predicts future declines after recent recovery in Eurasian steppe bird populations. *Biological Conservation*, 144: 2607–2614.

Kamp, J., Siderova, T.V., Salemgareev, A.R., Urazaliev, R.S., Donald, P.F. & Holzel, N. (2012) Niche separation of larks (Alaudidae) and agricultural change on the drylands of the former Soviet Union. *Agriculture Ecosystems & Environment*, 155: 41-49.

Karels, T.J., Dobson, F.S., Trevino, H.S. & Skibiel, A.L. (2008) The biogeography of avian extinctions on oceanic islands. *Journal of Biogeography*, 35: 1106–1111.

Karl, B.J. & Best, H.A. (1982) Feral cats on Stewart Island: their foods and their effects on kakapo. *New Zealand Journal of Zoology*, 9: 287–294.

Kasambe, R., Pande, S., Wadatkar, J. & Pawashe, A. (2004) Additional records of the Forest Owlet *Heteroglaux blewitti* Hume, 1873, in Melghat Tiger Reserve, Maharashtra. *Newsletter for Ornithologists*, 1: 12–14.

Kasambe, R., Wadatkar, J., Bhusum, N.S. & Kasdekar, F. (2005) Forest Owlets *Heteroglaux blewitti* in Melghat Tiger Reserve, Distt. Amravati, Maharashtra. *Newsletter for Birdwatchers*, 45: 38–40.

Kattan, G.H. (1992) Rarity and vulnerability – the birds of the Cordillera Central of Colombia. *Conservation Biology*, 6: 64–70.

Kaur, J., Nair, A. & Choudhury, B.C. (2008) Conservation of the Vulnerable sarus crane *Grus antigone antigone* in Kota, Rajasthan, India: a case study of community involvement. *Oryx*, 42: 452–455.

Kean, J. & Barlow, N. (2004) Exploring rarity using a general model for distribution and abundance. *American Naturalist*, 163: 407–416.

Kear, J. (2005) *Ducks, geese and swans*. Oxford Universiy Press, Oxford, UK.

Keitt, B.S. & Tershy, B.R. (2003) Cat eradication significantly decreases shearwater mortality. *Animal Conservation*, 6: 307–308.

Kelly, D. & Sullivan, J.J. (2010) Life histories, dispersal, invasions, and global change: progress and prospects in New Zealand ecology, 1989–2029. *New Zealand Journal of Ecology*, 34: 207–217.

Kemp, A.C. (2001) The role of species limits and biology in the conservation of African hornbills. *Ostrich, S15*: 200–204.

Kennedy, R.S. (1977) Notes on the biology and population status of the Monkey-eating Eagle of the Philippines. *Wilson Bulletin*, 89: 1–20.

Kennedy, R.S. (1985) Conservation research of the Philippine Eagle. *National Geographic Society Research Reports*, 18: 401–414.

Kepler, C.B. (1967) Polynesian rat predation on nesting Laysan Albatrosses and other Pacific seabirds. *Auk*, 84: 426–430.

Kepler, C.B., Pratt, T.K., Ecton, A.M., Engilis, A. & Fluetsch, K.M. (1996) Nesting behavior of the Poo-uli. *Wilson Bulletin*, 108: 620–638.

Khacher, L. & Rughani, B. (2006) Slender-billed Curlew *Numenius tenuirostris* Vieillot – a probable new addition to Indian birds. *Journal of the Bombay Natural History Society*, 103: 99–100.

Khrokov, V.V. & Buketov, M.E. (2000) [The Sociable Plover in Kazakhstan: the situation causes alarm]. *Waders of east Europe and north Asia at the turn of the century: fifth meeting on issues concerning research and conservation of waders*, Working Group on Waders (CIS), Moscow.

Kilpatrick, A.M. (2006) Facilitating the evolution of resistance to avian malaria in Hawaiian birds. *Biological Conservation*, 128: 475–485.

King, B.F. & Rasmussen, P.C. (1998) The rediscovery of the Forest Owlet *Athene* (*Heteroglaux*) *blewitti*. *Forktail*, 14: 51–53.

King, B.F., Dickinson, E.C. & Woodcock, M.W. (1975) *A field guide to the birds of South-East Asia*. Collins, London.

King, W.B. (1978–1979) *Red data book, 2. Aves. Second edition*. International Union for Conservation of Nature and Natural Resources, Morges, Switzerland.

Kinnaird, M.F., O'Brien, T.G., Lambert, F.R. & Purmiasa, D. (2003) Density and distribution of the endemic Seram cockatoo *Cacatua moluccensis* in relation to land use patterns. *Biological Conservation*, 109: 227–235.

Kirchman, J.J. (2009) Genetic tests of rapid parallel speciation of flightless birds from an extant volant ancestor. *Biological Journal of the Linnean Society*, 96: 601–616.

Kirchman, J.J., Witt, C.C., McGuire, J.A. & Graves, G.R. (2010) DNA

from a 100-year-old holotype confirms the validity of a potentially extinct hummingbird species. *Biology Letters*, 6: 112–115.

Knight, A.T., Smith, R.J., Cowling, R.M., Desmet, P.G., Faith, D.P., Ferrier, S., Gelderblom, C.M., Grantham, H., Lombard, A.T., Maze, K., Nel, J.L., Parrish, J.D., Pence, G.Q.K., Possingham, H.P., Reyers, B., Rouget, M., Roux, D. & Wilson, K.A. (2007) Improving the key biodiversity areas approach for effective conservation planning. *BioScience*, 57: 256–261.

Knox, A.G. (1993) Richard Meinertzhagen – a case of fraud examined. *Ibis*, 135: 320–325.

Kock, K.H. (2001) The direct influence of fishing and fishery-related activities on non-target species in the Southern Ocean with particular emphasis on longline fishing and its impact on albatrosses and petrels – a review. *Reviews in Fish Biology and Fisheries*, 11: 31–56.

Komdeur, J. (1994) Conserving the Seychelles Warbler *Acrocephalus sechellensis* by translocation from Cousin Island to the islands of Aride and Cousine. *Biological Conservation*, 67: 143–152.

Komdeur, J. (1996) Breeding of the Seychelles magpie robin *Copsychus sechellarum* and implications for its conservation. *Ibis*, 138: 485–498.

Komdeur, J. & Pels, M.D. (2005) Rescue of the Seychelles warbler on Cousin Island, Seychelles: the role of habitat restoration. *Biological Conservation*, 124: 15–26.

Komdeur, J., Piersma, T., Kraaijeveld, K., Kraaijeveld-Smit, F. & Richardson, D.S. (2004) Why Seychelles Warblers fail to recolonize nearby islands: unwilling or unable to fly there? *Ibis*, 146: 298–302.

Krabbe, N. (2004) Pale-headed Brush-finch *Atlapetes pallidiceps*: notes on population size, habitat, vocalizations, feeding, interference competition and conservation. *Bird Conservation International*, 14: 77–86.

Krajick, K. (2005) Winning the war against island invaders. *Science*, 310: 1410–1413.

Kruger, O. (2005) The role of ecotourism in conservation: panacea or Pandora's box? *Biodiversity and Conservation*, 14: 579–600.

Kruger, O. & Radford, A.N. (2008) Doomed to die? Predicting extinction risk in the true hawks Accipitridae. *Animal Conservation*, 11: 83–91.

Krupa, R.E. (1989) Social and biological implications for endangered species management: the Philippine Eagle *Pithecophaga jefferyi*. In: Meyburg, B.-U. & Chancellor, R.D. (eds). *Raptors in the modern world*, 301–314. World Working Group on Birds of Prey, Berlin.

Kuehler, C., Lieberman, A., Oesterle, P., Powers, T., Kuhn, M., Kuhn, J., Nelson, J., Snetsinger, T., Herrmann, C., Harrity, P., Tweed, E., Fancy, S., Woodworth, B. & Telfer, T. (2000) Development of restoration techniques for Hawaiian thrushes: collection of wild eggs, artificial incubation, hand-rearing, captive-breeding, and re-introduction to the wild. *Zoo Biology*, 19: 263–277.

Kuehler, C., Lieberman, A., Harrity, P., Kuhn, M., Kuhn, J., McIlraith, B. & Turner, J. (2001) Restoration techniques for Hawaiian forest birds: collection of eggs, artificial incubation and handling of chicks, and release to the wild. *Studies in Avian Biology*, 22: 354–358.

Kummer, D.M. (1991) *Deforestation in the postwar Philippines*. University of Chicago Press, Chicago.

Kuussaari, M., Bommarco, R., Heikkinen, R.K., Helm, A., Krauss, J., Lindborg, R., Ockinger, E., Partel, M., Pino, J., Roda, F., Stefanescu, C., Teder, T., Zobel, M. & Steffan-Dewenter, I. (2009) Extinction debt: a challenge for biodiversity conservation. *Trends in Ecology & Evolution*, 24: 564–571.

Kuwae, T., Beninger, P.G., Decottignies, P., Mathot, K.J., Lund, D.R. & Elner, R.W. (2008) Biofilm grazing in a higher vertebrate: The Western Sandpiper, *Calidris mauri*. *Ecology*, 89: 599-606.

Kuwae, T., Miyoshi, E., Hosokawa, S., Ichimi, K., Hosoya, J., Amano, T., Moriya, T., Kondoh, M., Ydenberg, R.C. & Elner, R.W. (2012) Variable and complex food web structures revealed by exploring missing trophic links between birds and biofilm. *Ecology Letters*, 15: 347-356.

La Rouche, G.P. (2009) *Birding in the United States: a demographic and economic analysis*. US Fish and Wildlife Service, Washington DC.

Lafferty, K.D. & Gerber, L.R. (2002) Good medicine for conservation biology: the intersection of epidemiology and conservation theory. *Conservation Biology*, 16: 593–604.

Laich, A.G., Favero, M., Mariano-Jelicich, R., Blanco, G., Canete, G., Arias, A., Rodriguez, P.S. & Brachetta, H. (2006) Environmental and operational variability affecting the mortality of Black-browed Albatrosses associated with long-liners in Argentina. *Emu,* 106: 21–28.

Lamas, I.R. (2006) Census of Brazilian Merganser *Mergus octosetaceus* in the region of Serra da Canastra National Park, Brazil, with discussion of its threats and conservation. *Bird Conservation International,* 16: 145–154.

Lamas, I.R. & Santos, J.P. (2004) First description of the Brazilian Merganser *Mergus octosetaceus* nest in rock crevices, with reproductive notes. *Cotinga,* 22: 38–41.

Lamas, I.R. & Lins, L.V. (2009) Brazilian Merganser (*Mergus octosetaceus*) In: Schlenberg, T.S. (ed.) *Neotropical Birds Online,* Cornell Laboratory of Ornithology, Ithaca.

Lamas, I.R., Almeida, F.S., Andrade, R.D., Oliveira, L. & Silveira, L.F. (2009) *Confirmação da ocorrência atual de Mergus octosetaceus na região do Alto Paranaíba – MG.* Abstract presented at XVII Brazilian Ornithological Congress. Aracruz, Brazil.

Lambert, F.R. (1993) Trade, status and management of three parrots in the North Moluccas, Indonesia: white cockatoo *Cacatua alba*, chattering lory *Lorius garrulus* and violet-eared lory *Eos squamata*. *Bird Conservation International,* 3: 145–168.

Lambert, F.R. (1994) *The status of the Philippine Cockatoo* Cacatua haematuropygia *in Palawan and the Sulu Islands, Philippines.* IUCN Species Survival Commission, Gland, Switzerland, and Cambridge, UK.

Lambert, F.R. & Collar, N.J. (2002) The future for Sundaic lowland forest birds: long-term effects of commercial logging and fragmentation. *Forktail,* 18: 127–146.

Lamoreux, J., Akçakaya, H.R., Bennun, L., Collar, N.J., Boitani, L., Brackett, D., Brautigam, A., Brooks, T.M., da Fonseca, G.A.B., Mittermeier, R.A., Rylands, A.B., Gardenfors, U., Hilton-Taylor, C., Mace, G., Stein, B.A. & Stuart, S. (2003) Value of the IUCN Red List. *Trends in Ecology & Evolution,* 18: 214–215.

Langrand, O. (1990) *Guide to the birds of Madagascar.* Yale University Press, New Haven, USA.

Laurance, W.F. & Useche, D.C. (2009) Environmental synergisms and extinctions of tropical species. *Conservation Biology,* 23: 1427–1437.

Lavauden, L. (1937) *Supplement. Histoire physique, naturelle et politique de Madagascar, 12, Oiseaux.* Société d'Editions Géographiques Maritimes et Coloniales, Paris.

Lawler, J.J., White, D., Sifneos, J.C. & Master, L.L. (2003) Rare species and the use of indicator groups for conservation planning. *Conservation Biology,* 17: 875–882.

Lawton, J.H. (1993) Range, population abundance and conservation. *Trends in Ecology & Evolution,* 8: 409–413.

Le Bohec, C., Durant, J.M., Gauthier-Clerc, M., Stenseth, N.C., Park, Y.H., Pradel, R., Gremillet, D., Gendner, J.P. & Le Maho, Y. (2008) King penguin population threatened by Southern Ocean warming. *Proceedings of the National Academy of Sciences of the United States of America,* 105: 2493–2497.

Le Corre, M., Ghestemme, T., Salamolard, M. & Couzi, F.O.X. (2003) Rescue of the Mascarene Petrel, a critically endangered seabird of Reunion Island, Indian Ocean. *Condor,* 105: 387–391.

Leader, P.J. (2009) Is Vaurie's Nightjar *Caprimulgus centralasicus* a valid species? *BirdingASIA,* 11: 47–50.

Leberg, P.L. & Firmin, B.D. (2008) Role of inbreeding depression and purging in captive breeding and restoration programmes. *Molecular Ecology,* 17: 334–343.

Lee, M.T., Dong, D.L. & Ong, T.P. (2009a) A photographic record of Silvery Pigeon *Columba argentina* from the Mentawai Islands, Indonesia, with notes on identification, distribution and conservation. *Bulletin of the British Ornithologists' Club,* 129: 122–128.

Lee, T.M., Sodhi, N.S. & Prawiradilaga, D.M. (2009b) Determinants of local people's attitude toward conservation and the consequential effects on illegal resource harvesting in the protected areas of Sulawesi (Indonesia). *Environmental Conservation,* 36: 157–170.

Lee, W.G., Wood, J.R. & Rogers, G.M. (2010) Legacy of avian-dominated plant-herbivore systems in New Zealand. *New Zealand Journal of Ecology,* 34: 28–47.

Lemoine, N. & Böhning-Gaese, K. (2003) Potential impact of global climate change on species richness of long-distance migrants. *Conservation Biology,* 17: 577–586.

Lennon, J.J., Koleff, P., Greenwood, J.J.D. & Gaston, K.J. (2004) Contribution of rarity and commonness to patterns of species richness. *Ecology Letters,* 7: 81–87.

Lens, L., van Dongen, S., Wilder, C.M., Brooks, T.M. & Matthysen, E. (1999) Fluctuating asymmetry increases with habitat disturbance in seven bird species of a fragmented afrotropical forest. *Proceedings of the Royal Society Series B-Biological Sciences,* 266: 1241–1246.

Leonard, D.L. (2008) Recovery expenditures for birds listed under the US Endangered Species Act: the disparity between mainland and Hawaiian taxa. *Biological Conservation,* 141: 2054–2061.

Lerner, H.R. & Mindell, D.P. (2005) Phylogeny of eagles, Old World vultures, and other Accipitridae based on nuclear and mitochondrial DNA. *Molecular Phylogenetics and Evolution,* 37: 327–346.

Lévêque, C. (1997) *Biodiversity dynamics and conservation: the freshwater fish of tropical Africa.* Cambridge University Press, Cambridge, UK.

Levin, I.I., Outlaw, D.C., Vargas, F.H. & Parker, P.G. (2009) Plasmodium blood parasite found in endangered Galapagos penguins (*Spheniscus mendiculus*). *Biological Conservation,* 142: 3191–3195.

Liang, C., Chang, S. & Fang, W. (2000) Little known Oriental bird: discovery of a breeding colony of Chinese Crested Tern. *Oriental Bird Club Bulletin,* 32: 18–19.

Lindsay, K., Craig, J. & Low, M. (2008) Tourism and conservation: the effects of track proximity on avian reproductive success and nest selection in an open sanctuary. *Tourism Management,* 29: 730–739.

Lins, L.V., Andrade, R.D., Lima Neto, A., Hearn, R.D., Hughes, B., Dugger, B.D., Scoss, L.M., Ribeiro, F., Lamas, I.R. & Rigueira, S.E. (2010) Capture and marking the Brazilian Merganser *Mergus octosetaceus* in the Serra da Canastra region of Minas Gerais, Brazil. *TWSG News.*

Livezey, B.C. (1992) Morphological corollaries and ecological implications of flightlessness in the Kakapo (Psittaciformes, *Strigops habroptilus*). *Journal of Morphology,* 213: 105–145.

Lloyd, B.D. & Powlesland, R.G. (1994) The decline of Kakapo *Strigops habroptilus* and attempts at conservation by translocation. *Biological Conservation,* 69: 75–85.

Lloyd, H. (2008a) Influence of within-patch habitat quality on high-Andean *Polylepis* bird abundance. *Ibis,* 150: 735–745.

Lloyd, H. (2008b) Abundance and patterns of rarity of *Polylepis* birds in the Cordillera Vilcanota, southern Peru: implications for habitat management strategies. *Bird Conservation International,* 18: 164–180.

Lloyd, H. & Marsden, S.J. (2008) Bird community variation across *Polylepis* woodland fragments and matrix habitats: implications for biodiversity conservation within a high Andean landscape. *Biodiversity and Conservation,* 17: 2645–2660.

Lockwood, J.A. (2004) *Locust: the devastating rise and mysterious disappearance of the insect that shaped the American Frontier.* Basic Books, New York.

Lockwood, J.A. & Debrey, L.D. (1990) A solution for the sudden and unexplained extinction of the Rocky Mountain Grasshopper (Orthoptera, Acrididae). *Environmental Entomology,* 19: 1194–1205.

Lockwood, J.L., Russell, G.J., Gittleman, J.L., Daehler, C.C., McKinney, M.L. & Purvis, A. (2002) A metric for analyzing taxonomic patterns of extinction risk. *Conservation Biology,* 16: 1137–1142.

Lollback, G.W., Ford, H.A. & Cairns, S.C. (2008) Is the uncommon Black-chinned Honeyeater a more specialised forager than the co-occurring and common Fuscous Honeyeater? *Emu,* 108: 125–132.

Lomborg, B. (2001) *The sceptical environmentalist: measuring the real state of the world.* Cambridge University Press, Cambridge, UK.

Lorvelec, O. & Pascal, M. (2005) French attempts to eradicate non-indigenous mammals and their consequences for native biota. *Biological Invasions,* 7: 135–140.

Louette, M. & Hasson, M. (2008) Rediscovery of the Lake Lufira Weaver *Ploceus ruweti. Bulletin of the African Bird Club,* 16: 168–173.

Maas, B., Putra, D.D., Waltert, M., Clough, Y., Tscharntke, T. & Schulze, C.H. (2009) Six years of habitat modification in a tropical rainforest margin of Indonesia do not affect bird diversity but endemic forest species. *Biological Conservation*, 142: 2665–2671.

MacArthur, R.H. & Wilson, E.O. (1967) *The theory of island biogeography*. Princeton University Press, Princeton, New Jersey.

Mace, G.M. & Lande, R. (1991) Assessing extinction threats – towards a re-evaluation of IUCN threatened species categories. *Conservation Biology*, 5: 148–157.

Mace, G.M., Gittleman, J.L. & Purvis, A. (2003) Preserving the tree of life. *Science*, 300: 1707–1709.

Mace, G.M., Collar, N.J., Gaston, K.J., Hilton-Taylor, C., Akçakaya, H.R., Leader-Williams, N., Milner-Gulland, E.J. & Stuart, S.N. (2008) Quantification of extinction risk: IUCN's system for classifying threatened species. *Conservation Biology*, 22: 1424–1442.

MacKinnon, J., Verkuil, Y.I. & Murray, N. (2012) IUCN situation analysis on East and Southeast Asian intertidal habitats, with particular reference to the Yellow Sea (including the Bohai Sea). *Occasional Paper of the IUCN Species Survival Commission No. 47*. IUCN, Gland, Switzerland and Cambridge, UK.

Madeiros, J., Carlile, N. & Priddel, D. (2012) Breeding biology and population increase of the endangered Bermuda Petrel *Pterodroma cahow*. *Bird Conservation International*, 22: 35-45.

Mahood, S., Son Virak, Hong Chamnan & Evans, T. (2012) *The status of Bengal floricans in the Bengal Florican Conservation Areas, 2010/11 monitoring report*. Wildlife Conservation Society Cambodia Program, Phnom Penh, Cambodia.

Maller, C., Townsend, M., Pryor, A., Brown, P. & St Leger, L. (2005) Healthy nature healthy people: 'contact with nature' as an upstream health promotion intervention for populations. *Health Promotion International*, 21: 45–54.

Maloney, R.F. & McLean, I.G. (1995) Historical and experimental learned predator recognition in free-living New-Zealand robins. *Animal Behaviour*, 50: 1193–1201.

Malovichko, L.V., Fedosov, V.N., Kurochkin, E.N., Eltyshev, S.D., Sliníko, A.V. (2006) [New data on Sociable Lapwing *Chettusia gregaria* in Stavropol Region, Northern Caucasus, Russia]. *Information Materials of the Russian Wader Study Group*, 19: 45–47.

Manne, L.L. & Pimm, S.L. (2001) Beyond eight forms of rarity: which species are threatened and which will be next? *Animal Conservation*, 4: 221–229.

Manne, L.L., Brooks, T.M. & Pimm, S.L. (1999) Relative risk of extinction of passerine birds on continents and islands. *Nature*, 399: 258–261.

Maphisa, D.H., Donald, P.F., Buchanan, G.M. & Ryan, P.G. (2009) Habitat use, distribution and breeding ecology of the globally threatened Rudd's Lark and Botha's Lark in eastern South Africa. *Ostrich*, 80: 19–28.

Marie, C.N., Sibelet, N., Dulcire, M., Rafalimaro, M., Danthu, P. & Carriere, S.M. (2009) Taking into account local practices and indigenous knowledge in an emergency conservation context in Madagascar. *Biodiversity and Conservation*, 18: 2759–2777.

Markandya, A., Taylor, T., Longo, A., Murty, M.N., Murty, S. & Dhavala, K. (2008) Counting the cost of vulture decline – an appraisal of the human health and other benefits of vultures in India. *Ecological Economics*, 67: 194–204.

Markus, T., Stroeve, J.C. & Miller, J. (2009) Recent changes in Arctic sea ice melt onset, freezeup, and melt season length. *Journal of Geophysical Research-Oceans*, 114: C12024.

Marsden, S.J. (1992) The distribution, abundance and habitat preferences of the Salmon-crested Cockatoo *Cacatua moluccensis* on Seram, Indonesia. *Bird Conservation International*, 2: 7–14.

Marsden, S.J. (1995) *The ecology and conservation of the parrots of Sumba, Buru and Seram, Indonesia*. Manchester Metropolitan University, Manchester, UK.

Marsden, S.J. & Jones, M.J. (1997) The nesting requirements of the parrots and hornbill of Sumba, Indonesia. *Biological Conservation*, 82: 279–287.

Marsden, S.J., Whiffin, M., Galetti, M. & Fielding, A.H. (2005) How well will Brazil's system of Atlantic forest reserves maintain viable bird populations? *Biodiversity and Conservation*, 14: 2835–2853.

Martens, P., Kovats, R.S., Nijhof, S., de Vries, P., Livermore, M.T.J., Bradley, D.J., Cox, J. & McMichael, A.J. (1999) Climate change and future populations at risk of malaria. *Global Environmental Change-Human and Policy Dimensions*, 9: S89-S107.

Martin, J.L., Thibault, J.C. & Bretagnolle, V. (2000) Black rats, island characteristics, and colonial nesting birds in the Mediterranean: consequences of an ancient introduction. *Conservation Biology*, 14: 1452–1466.

Martínez, C. (2008) Distribution, density and productivity of great bustards *Otis tarda* in northwestern Spain: a regional approach. *Journal of Ornithology*, 149: 507–514.

Martins, T.L.F., Brooke, M. de L., Hilton, G.M., Farnsworth, S., Gould, J. & Pain, D.J. (2006) Costing eradications of alien mammals from islands. *Animal Conservation*, 9: 439–444.

Mateo, J.A., López Jurado, L.F. & Geniez, P. (2009) Historical distribution of Raso Lark *Alauda razae* in the Cape Verde archipelago. *Alauda*, 77: 309–312.

Mateo, R. (2009) Lead poisoning in wild birds in Europe and the regulations adopted by different countries. In: Watson, R.T., Fuller, M., Pokras, M. & Hunt, W.G. (eds). *Ingestion of lead from spent ammunition: implications for wildlife and humans*, 71–98. The Peregrine Fund, Boise, Idaho.

Mathews, F., Orros, M., McLaren, G., Gelling, M. & Foster, R. (2005) Keeping fit on the ark: assessing the suitability of captive-bred animals for release. *Biological Conservation*, 121: 569–577.

Mathot, K.J., Lund, D.R. & Elner, R.W. (2010) Sediment in stomach contents of Western Sandpipers and Dunlin provide evidence of biofilm feeding. *Waterbirds*, 33: 300-306.

Matson, K.D. (2006) Are there differences in immune function between continental and insular birds? *Proceedings of the Royal SocietySeries B-Biological Sciences*, 273: 2267–2274.

Mauro, I. (2005) Field discovery, mound characteristics, bare parts, vocalisations and behaviour of Bruijn's Brush-turkey (*Aepypodius bruijnii*). *Emu*, 105: 273–281.

Mawdsley, J.R., O'Malley, R. & Ojima, D.S. (2009) A review of climate-change adaptation strategies for wildlife management and biodiversity conservation. *Conservation Biology*, 23: 1080–1089.

Mayr, E. (1945) Bird conservation in the southwest Pacific. *Audubon Magazine*, 47: 279–282.

McCallum, H. & Dobson, A. (1995) Detecting disease and parasite threats to endangered species and ecosystems. *Trends in Ecology & Evolution*, 10: 190–194.

McCarthy, D.P., Donald, P.F., Scharlemann, J.P.W., Buchanan, G.M., Balmford, A., Green, J.M.H., Bennun, L.A., Burgess, N.D., Fishpool, L.D.C., Garnett, S.T., Leonard, D.L., Maloney, R.F., Morling, P., Schaefer, H.M., Symes, A., Wiedenfeld, D.A. & Butchart, S.H.M. (2012) Financial costs of meeting global biodiversity conservation targets: current spending and unmet needs. *Science*, 338: 946-949.

McClanahan, T.R., Cinner, J.E., Maina, J., Graham, N.A.J., Daw, T.M., Stead, S.M., Wamukota, A., Brown, K., Ateweberhan, M., Venus, V. & Polunin, N.V.C. (2008) Conservation action in a changing climate. *Conservation Letters*, 1: 53–59.

McDonald, R.I., Kareiva, P. & Formana, R.T.T. (2008) The implications of current and future urbanization for global protected areas and biodiversity conservation. *Biological Conservation*, 141: 1695–1703.

McDougall, A., Porter, G., Mostert, M., Cupitt, R., Cupitt, S., Joseph, L., Murphy, S., Janetzki, H., Gallagher, A. & Burbidge, A. (2009) Another piece in an Australian ornithological puzzle – a second Night Parrot is found dead in Queensland. *Emu*, 109: 198–203.

McEntee, J., Cordeiro, N.J., Joho, M.P. & Moyer, D.C. (2005) Foraging observations of the threatened Long-billed Tailorbird *Artisornis moreaui* in Tanzania. *Scopus*, 25: 51–54.

McGeoch, M.A., Butchart, S.H.M., Spear, D., Marais, E., Kleynhans, E.J., Symes, A., Chanson, J. & Hoffmann, N. (2010) Global indicators of biological invasion: species numbers, biodiversity impact and policy responses. *Diversity and Distributions*, 16: 95–108.

McGill, B.J., Etienne, R.S., Gray, J.S., Alonso, D., Anderson, M.J., Benecha, H.K., Dornelas, M., Enquist, B.J., Green, J.L., He, F.L.,

Hurlbert, A.H., Magurran, A.E., Marquet, P.A., Maurer, B.A., Ostling, A., Soykan, C.U., Ugland, K.I. & White, E.P. (2007) Species abundance distributions: moving beyond single prediction theories to integration within an ecological framework. *Ecology Letters*, 10: 995–1015.

McKee, J.K., Sciulli, P.W., Fooce, C.D. & Waite, T.A. (2004) Forecasting global biodiversity threats associated with human population growth. *Biological Conservation*, 115: 161–164.

McKinney, M.L. (1998) Branching models predict loss of many bird and mammal orders within centuries. *Animal Conservation*, 1: 159–164.

McKinney, M.L. (2001) Role of human population size in raising bird and mammal threat among nations. *Animal Conservation*, 4: 45–57.

McNab, B.K. (2002) Minimizing energy expenditure facilitates vertebrate persistence on oceanic islands. *Ecology Letters*, 5: 693–704.

McNab, B.K. & Ellis, H.I. (2006) Flightless rails endemic to islands have lower energy expenditures and clutch sizes than flighted rails on islands and continents. *Comparative Biochemistry and Physiology a-Molecular & Integrative Physiology*, 145: 295–311.

McPhee, M.E. (2004) Generations in captivity increases behavioral variance: considerations for captive breeding and reintroduction programs. *Biological Conservation*, 115: 71–77.

McWhinnie, S.F. (2009) The tragedy of the commons in international fisheries: an empirical examination. *Journal of Environmental Economics and Management*, 57: 321–333.

Medina, F.M., Bonnaud, E., Vidal, E., Tershy, B.R., Zavaleta, E.S., Donlan, C.J., Keitt, B.S., Le Corre, M., Horwath, S.V. & Nogales, M. (2011) A global review of the impacts of invasive cats on island endangered vertebrates. *Global Change Biology*, 17: 3503–3510.

Medway, D. (2004a) The land bird fauna of Stephens Island, New Zealand, in the early 1890s and the cause of its demise. *Notornis*, 51: 201–211.

Medway, D. (2004b) Taxonomic status of the Stephens Island piopio (*Turnagra capensis*). *Notornis*, 51: 231–232.

Mehta, P., Kulkarni, J. & Patil, D. (2008) A survey of the Critically Endangered Forest Owlet *Heteroglaux blewitti* in Central India. *Birding Asia*, 10: 77–87.

Meijaard, E., Sheil, D., Marshall, A.J. & Nasi, R. (2008) Phylogenetic age is positively correlated with sensitivity to timber harvest in Bornean mammals. *Biotropica*, 40: 76–85.

Meinertzhagen, R. (1951) Review of the Alaudidae. *Proceedings of the Zoological Society of London*, 121: 81–132.

Melling, T. (2010) The Eskimo Curlew in Britain. *British Birds*, 103: 80–92.

Menxiu, T., Liu, Z., Li, C., Zöckler, C. & Clark, N.A. (2013) The critical importance of the Rudong mudflats, Jiangsu Province, China in the annual cycle of the Spoon-billed Sandpiper *Calidris pygmeus*. *Wader Study Group Bulletin*, 119: 208–211.

Merton, D. (1992) The legacy of 'Old Blue'. *New Zealand Journal of Ecology*, 16: 65–68.

Merton, D.V., Morris, R.B. & Atkinson, I.A.E. (1984) Lek behaviour in a parrot – the Kakapo *Strigops habroptilus* of New Zealand. *Ibis*, 126: 277–283.

Meteyer, C.U., Rideout, B.A., Gilbert, M., Shivaprasad, H.L. & Oaks, J.L. (2005) Pathology and proposed pathophysiology of diclofenac poisoning in free-living and experimentally exposed oriental white-backed vultures (*Gyps bengalensis*). *Journal of Wildlife Diseases*, 41: 707–716.

Meuser, E., Harshaw, H.W. & Mooers, A.Ø. (2009) Public preference for endemism over other conservation-related species attributes. *Conservation Biology*, 23: 1041–1046.

Meyer de Schauensee, R. (1940) Rediscovery of the megapode, *Aepypodius bruynii*. *Auk*, 57: 83–84.

Meyer de Schauensee, R. (1946) On Siamese birds. *Proceedings of the Academy of Natural Sciences of Philadelphia*, 98: 1–82.

Michener, W.K., Blood, E.R., Bildstein, K.L., Brinson, M.M. & Gardner, L.R. (1997) Climate change, hurricanes and tropical storms, and rising sea level in coastal wetlands. *Ecological Applications*, 7: 770–801.

Milberg, P. & Tyrberg, T. (1993) Naive birds and noble savages – a review of man-caused prehistoric extinctions of island birds. *Ecography*, 16: 229–250.

Millener, P.R. (1989) The only flightless passerine: the Stephens Island Wren. *Notornis*, 36: 280–285.

Miller, H.C., Lambert, D.M., Millar, C.D., Robertson, B.C. & Minot, E.O. (2003) Minisatellite DNA profiling detects lineages and parentage in the endangered kakapo (*Strigops habroptilus*) despite low microsatellite DNA variation. *Conservation Genetics*, 4: 265–274.

Mills, M.S.L. & Ryan, P.G. (2005) Modelling impacts of long-line fishing: what are the effects of pair-bond disruption and sex-biased mortality on albatross fecundity? *Animal Conservation*, 8: 359–367.

Milner-Gulland, E.J., Kholodova, M.V., Bekenov, A., Bukreeva, O.M., Grachev, I.A., Amgalan, L. & Lushchekina, A.A. (2001) Dramatic declines in saiga antelope populations. *Oryx*, 35: 340–345.

Miranda, H.C., Salvador, D.I., Ibañez, J.C. & Balaquit-Ibañez, G.A. (2000) Summary of Philippine Eagle reproductive success, 1978–98. *Journal of Raptor Research*, 34: 37–41.

Mittermeier, R.A., Myers, N. & Mittermeier, C.G. (1999) *Hotspots: Earth's biologically richest and most endangered terrestrial ecoregions*. CEMEX and Conservation International, Mexico City and Washington, D.C.

MoEF. (2006) *Proceedings of the International Conference on Vulture Conservation*. Ministry of Environment and Forests, Government of India, New Delhi.

Moeliker, C.W. & Heij, C.J. (1995) The rediscovery of *Monarcha boanensis* (Aves: Monarchidae) from Boano Island, Indonesia. *Deinsea*, 2: 123–143.

Møller, A.P. & Legendre, S. (2001) Allee effect, sexual selection and demographic stochasticity. *Oikos*, 92: 27–34.

Møller, A.P., Rubolini, D. & Lehikoinen, E. (2008) Populations of migratory bird species that did not show a phenological response to climate change are declining. *Proceedings of the National Academy of Sciences of the United States of America*, 105: 16195–16200.

Monterrubio-Rico, T.C., Ortega-Rodriguez, J.M., Marin-Togo, M.C., Salinas-Melgoza, A. & Renton, K. (2009) Nesting habitat of the Lilac-crowned Parrot in a modified landscape in Mexico. *Biotropica*, 41: 361–368.

Mooers, A.O. & Atkins, R.A. (2003) Indonesia's threatened birds: over 500 million years of evolutionary heritage at risk. *Animal Conservation*, 6: 183–188.

Moores, N., Rogers, D., Koh, C.-H., Ju, Y.-K., Kim, R.-H. & Park, M.-N. (2007) *The 2007 Saemangeum Shorebird Monitoring Program Report*. Birds Korea, Busan.

Moores, N., Rogers, D., Kim, R.-H., Hassell, C., Gosbell, K., Kim, S.-A. & Park, M.-N. (2008) *The 2006–2008 Saemangeum Shorebird Monitoring Program Report*. Birds Korea, Busan.

Moorhouse, R.J. & Powlesland, R.G. (1991) Aspects of the ecology of Kakapo *Strigops habroptilus* liberated on Little Barrier Island (Hauturu), New Zealand. *Biological Conservation*, 56: 349–365.

Moreira, F. (2004) Distribution patterns and conservation status of four bustard species (family Otididae) in a montane grassland of South Africa. *Biological Conservation*, 118: 91–100.

Moreno, C.A., Castro, R., Mujica, L.J. & Reyes, P. (2008) Significant conservation benefits obtained from the use of a new fishing gear in the Chilean Patagonian Toothfish fishery. *CCAMLR Science*, 15: 79–91.

Morris, P. & Hawkins, F. (1998) *Birds of Madagascar: a photographic guide*. Pica Press, Robertsbridge, UK.

Mortensen, H.S., Dupont, Y.L. & Olesen, J.M. (2008) A snake in paradise: disturbance of plant reproduction following extirpation of bird flower-visitors on Guam. *Biological Conservation*, 141: 2146–2154.

Moulton, D.W. & Marshall, A.P. (1996) Laysan Duck (*Anas laysanensis*). In: Poole, A. & Gill, F. (eds). *The Birds of North America, No. 242*, The Academy of Natural Sciences, Philadelphis, PA, and the American Ornithologists' Union, Washington DC.

Mountainspring, S., Casey, T.L.C., Kepler, C.B. & Scott, J.M. (1990) Ecology, behavior and conservation of the Poo-uli (*Melanprosops phaeosoma*). *Wilson Bulletin*, 102: 109–122.

Mourer-Chauviré, C., Bour, R., Ribes, S. & Moutou, F. (1999) The avifauna of Reunion Island (Mascarene Islands) at the time of the arrival of the first Europeans. *Smithsonian Contributions to Paleobiology*, 89: 1–38.

Muñoz-Fuentes, V., Vila, C., Green, A.J., Negro, J.J. & Sorenson, M.D. (2007) Hybridization between white-headed ducks and introduced ruddy ducks in Spain. *Molecular Ecology,* 16: 629–638.

Muñoz-Fuentes, V., Green, A.J. & Sorenson, M.D. (2008) Comparing the genetics of wild and captive populations of White-headed Ducks *Oxyura leucocephala*: consequences for recovery programmes. *Ibis,* 150: 807–815.

Myers, N., Mittermeier, R.A., Mittermeier, C.G., da Fonseca, G.A.B. & Kent, J. (2000a) Biodiversity hotspots for conservation priorities. *Nature,* 403: 853-858.

Myers, J.H., Simberloff, D., Kuris, A.M. & Carey, J.R. (2000) Eradication revisited: dealing with exotic species. *Trends in Ecology & Evolution,* 15: 316–320.

Naidoo, R. & Adamowicz, W.L. (2000) Effects of economic prosperity on numbers of threatened species. *Conservation Biology,* 15: 1021–1029.

Naidoo, V., Duncan, N., Bekker, L. & Swan, G. (2007) Validating the domestic fowl as a model to investigate the pathophysiology of diclofenac in *Gyps* vultures. *Environmental Toxicology and Pharmacology,* 24: 260–266.

Naidoo, V., Wolter, K., Cromarty, D., Diekmann, M., Duncan, N., Meharg, A.A., Taggart, M.A., Venter, L. & Cuthbert, R. (2009a) Toxicity of non-steroidal anti-inflammatory drugs to *Gyps* vultures: a new threat from ketoprofen. *Biology Letters*: doi:10.1098/rsbl.2009.0818.

Naidoo, V., Wolter, K., Cuthbert, R. & Duncan, N. (2009b) Veterinary diclofenac threatens Africa's endangered vulture species. *Regulatory Toxicology and Pharmacology,* 53: 205–208.

Nardelli, P.M. (1981) La preservación del Paují del Nordeste Brasileño. *Memorias Primer Simposio Internacional de la Familia Cracidae, Cocoyoc, Noviembre 4–7, 1981,* 273–283. Universidad Nacional Autonoma de Mexico, Facultad de Medicina Veterinaria y Zootecnia, Mexico City.

Nardelli, P.M. (1993) *A preservação do mutum-de-Alagoas,* Mitu mitu. Zôo-Botânica Mário Nardelli, Nilópolis, RJ, Brazil.

Nel, D.C., Ryan, P.G., Crawford, R.J.M., Cooper, J. & Huyser, O.A.W. (2002) Population trends of albatrosses and petrels at sub-Antarctic Marion Island. *Polar Biology,* 25: 81–89.

Nelson, G.J. (1975) Review: Biogeography, the vicariance paradigm, and continental drift. *Systematic Zoology,* 24: 490–504.

Nelson, J.T., Woodworth, B.L., Fancy, S.G., Lindsey, G.D. & Tweed, E.J. (2002a) Effectiveness of rodent control and monitoring techniques for a montane rainforest. *Wildlife Society Bulletin,* 30: 82–92.

Nelson, N.J., Keall, S.N., Brown, D. & Daugherty, C.H. (2002b) Establishing a new wild population of tuatara (*Sphenodon guntheri*). *Conservation Biology,* 16: 887–894.

Nguembock, B., Fjeldså, J., Couioux, A. & Pasquet, E. (2008) Phylogeny of *Laniarius*: molecular data reveal *L. liberatus* synonymous with *L. erlangeri* and 'plumage coloration' as unreliable morphological characters for defining species and species groups. *Molecular Phylogenetics and Evolution,* 48: 396–407.

Nielsen, J. (2006) *Condor: to the brink and back – the life and times of one giant bird.* Harper Perrenial, New York.

Nimnuan, S. & Round. P.D. (2008) Further Thai records of Large-billed Reed Warblers *Acrocephalus orinus*. *BirdingASIA* 8: 10.

Nogales, M., Martin, A., Tershy, B.R., Donlan, C.J., Witch, D., Puerta, N., Wood, B. & Alonso, J. (2004) A review of feral cat eradication on islands. *Conservation Biology,* 18: 310–319.

O'Dowd, D.J., Green, P.T. & Lake, P.S. (2003) Invasional 'meltdown' on an oceanic island. *Ecology Letters,* 6: 812–817.

O'Grady, J.J., Reed, D.H., Brook, B.W. & Frankham, R. (2004) What are the best correlates of predicted extinction risk? *Biological Conservation,* 118: 513–520.

Oaks, J.L., Donahoe, S.L., Rurangirwa, F.R., Rideout, B.A., Gilbert, M. & Virani, M.Z. (2004a) Identification of a novel mycoplasma species from an Oriental white-backed vulture (*Gyps bengalensis*). *Journal of Clinical Microbiology,* 42: 5909–5912.

Oaks, J.L., Gilbert, M., Virani, M.Z., Watson, R.T., Meteyer, C.U., Rideout, B.A., Shivaprasad, H.L., Ahmed, S., Chaudhry, M.J.I.,

Arshad, M., Mahmood, S., Ali, A. & Khan, A.A. (2004b) Diclofenac residues as the cause of vulture population decline in Pakistan. *Nature,* 427: 630–633.

Oba, G., Byakagaba, P. & Angassa, A. (2008) Participatory monitoring of biodiversity in East African grazing lands. *Land Degradation & Development,* 19: 636–648.

Oestreicher, J.S., Benessaiah, K., Ruiz-Jaen, M.C., Sloan, S., Turner, K., Pelletier, J., Guay, B., Clark, K.E., Roche, D.G., Meiners, M. & Potvin, C. (2009) Avoiding deforestation in Panamanian protected areas: an analysis of protection effectiveness and implications for reducing emissions from deforestation and forest degradation. *Global Environmental Change-Human and Policy Dimensions,* 19: 279–291.

Ogilvie-Grant, W.R. (1910) The Monkey-eating Eagle. *Country Life,* 9 April: 531–532.

Ohlemuller, R., Anderson, B.J., Araujo, M.B., Butchart, S.H.M., Kudrna, O., Ridgely, R.S. & Thomas, C.D. (2008) The coincidence of climatic and species rarity: high risk to small-range species from climate change. *Biology Letters,* 4: 568–572.

Oláh, J. & Pigniczki, C. (2010) The first XXIst century record of Slender-billed Curlew (*Numenius tenuirostris*) in Hungary. *Aquila,* 114: in press.

Oldfield, S., Lusty, C. & MacKinven, A. (1998) *The world list of threatened trees.* World Conservation Press, Cambridge, UK.

Olmos, F. & Silva e Silva, R. (2003) *Survey of the Brazilian Merganser* Mergus octosetaceus *along the rivers Formoso, Corrente e Pratudão, Bahia, Brazil: results of a preliminary survey.* BirdLife Interntional – Programo do Brasil, São Paulo.

Olsen, P. (2007) *Glimpses of paradise: the quest for the beautiful parakeet.* National Library of Australia, Canberra.

Olson, D.M., Dinerstein, E., Wikramanayake, E.D., Burgess, N.D., Powell, G.V.N., Underwood, E.C., D'Amico, J.A., Itoua, I., Strand, H.E., Morrison, J.C., Loucks, C.J., Allnutt, T.F., Ricketts, T.H., Kura, Y., Lamoreux, J.F., Wettengel, W.W., Hedao, P. & Kassem, K.R. (2001) Terrestrial ecoregions of the worlds: a new map of life on Earth. *BioScience,* 51: 933–938.

Olson, S.L. (1975) Paleornithology of St Helena Island, South Atlantic Ocean. *Smithsonian Contributions to Paleobiology,* 23: 1–49.

Oppel, S., Schaefer, H.M., Schmidt, V. & Schroder, B. (2004a) How much suitable habitat is left for the last known population of the Pale-headed Brush-finch? *Condor,* 106: 429–434.

Oppel, S., Schaefer, H.M., Schmidt, V. & Schroder, B. (2004b) Cowbird parasitism of Pale-headed Brush-finch *Atlapetes pallidiceps*: implications for conservation and management. *Bird Conservation International,* 14: 63–75.

Orueta, J.F. & Ramos, Y.A. (2001) *Methods to control and eradicate non-native terrestrial vertebrate species.* Council of Europe Publishing, Bern, Switzerland.

Owens, I.P.F. & Bennett, P.M. (2000) Ecological basis of extinction risk in birds: habitat loss versus human persecution and introduced predators. *Proceedings of the National Academy of Sciences of the United States of America,* 97: 12144–12148.

Pacheco, J.F. & Silva e Silva, R. (2002) *The Brazilian Merganser* Mergus octosetaceus *in Jalapão, Tocantins, Brasil: results of a preliminary survey.* BirdLife Interntional – Programo do Brasil, São Paulo.

Packman, C.E. (2011) *Seasonal landscape use and conservation of a critically endangered bustard: Bengal florican in Cambodia.* University of East Anglia, Norwich UK.

Packman, C.E., Gray, T.N.E., Collar, N.J., Evans, T.D., van Zalinge, R.N., Son Virak, Lovett, A.A. & Dolman, P.M. (2013) Rapid loss of Cambodia's grasslands. *Conservation Biology,* 26: 245-247.

Pain, D.J., Cunningham, A.A., Donald, P.F., Duckworth, J.W., Houston, D.C., Katzner, T., Parry-Jones, J., Poole, C., Prakash, V., Round, P. & Timmins, R. (2003) Causes and effects of temporospatial declines of *Gyps* vultures in Asia. *Conservation Biology,* 17: 661–671.

Pain, D.J., Fishpool, L., Byaruhanga, A., Arinaitwe, J. & Balmford, A. (2005) Biodiversity representation in Uganda's forest IBAs. *Biological Conservation,* 125: 133–138.

Pain, D.J., Martins, T.L.F., Boussekey, M., Diaz, S.H., Downs, C.T.,

Ekstrom, J.M.M., Garnett, S., Gilardi, J.D., McNiven, D., Primot, P., Rouys, S., Saoumoe, M., Symes, C.T., Tamungang, S.A., Theuerkauf, J., Villafuerte, D., Verfailles, L., Widmann, P. & Widmann, I.D. (2006) Impact of protection on nest take and nesting success of parrots in Africa, Asia and Australasia. *Animal Conservation*, 9: 322–330.

Pain, D.J., Bowden, C.G.R., Cunningham, A.A., Cuthbert, R., Das, D., Gilbert, M., Jakati, R.D., Jhala, Y., Khan, A.A., Naidoo, V., Oaks, J.L., Parry-Jones, J., Prakash, V., Rahman, A., Ranade, S.P., Baral, H.S., Senacha, K.R., Saravanan, S., Shah, N., Swan, G., Swarup, D., Taggart, M.A., Watson, R.T., Virani, M.Z., Wolter, K. & Green, R.E. (2008) The race to prevent the extinction of South Asian vultures. *Bird Conservation International*, 18: S30-S48.

Pain, D.J., Fisher, I.J. & Thomas, V.G. (2009) A global update of lead poisoning in terrestrial birds from ammunition sources. In: Watson, R.T., Fuller, M., Pokras, M. & Hunt, W.G. (eds). *Ingestion of lead from spent ammunition: implications for wildlife and humans*, 99–118. The Peregrine Fund, Boise, Idaho.

Pain, D., Green, R. & Clark, N. (2011) On the edge: can the Spoon-billed Sandpiper be saved? *British Birds*, 104: 350-363.

Parkes, J. (2008) *A feasibility study for the eradication of house mice from Gough Island*. RSPB, Sandy, UK.

Parmesan, C. & Yohe, G. (2003) A globally coherent fingerprint of climate change impacts across natural systems. *Nature*, 421: 37–42.

Partridge, W.H. (1956) Notes on the Brazilian Merganser in Argentina. *Auk*, 73: 473–488.

Pattemore, D.E. & Wilcove, D.S. (2012) Invasive rats and recent colonist birds partially compensate for the loss of endemic New Zealand pollinators. *Proceedings of the Royal Society Series B-Biological Sciences*, 279: 1597-1605.

Pearson, T.G. (1937) *Adventures in bird protection*. D. Appleton-Century Company, New York.

Peet, N.B., Watkinson, A.R., Bell, D.J. & Sharma, U.R. (1999) The conservation management of *Imperata cylindrica* grassland in Nepal with fire and cutting: an experimental approach. *Journal of Applied Ecology*, 36: 374–387.

Peluc, S.I., Sillett, T.S., Rotenberry, J.T. & Ghalambor, C.K. (2008) Adaptive phenotypic plasticity in an island songbird exposed to a novel predation risk. *Behavioral Ecology*, 19: 830–835.

Phalen, D.N. & Groombridge, J.J. (2003) Field research on Hanawi: a story about working with the world's most endangered bird. *Journal of Avian Medicine and Surgery*, 17: 39–42.

Phillips, R.A. (2008) *Guidelines for eradication of introduced mammals from breeding sites of ACAP-listed seabirds*. Agreement on the Conservation of Albatrosses and Petrels (ACAP); downloaded from http://www.acap.aq on 30 January 2010, Hobart, Tasmania.

Pidgeon, M. (1996) Summary: an ecological survey of Lake Alaotra and selected wetlands of central and eastern Madagascar in analysing the demise of Madagascar Pochard *Aythya innotata*. *Newsletter of the Working Group on Birds in the Madagascar Region*, 6: 17–19.

Piersma, T. (1986) Feeding method of Spoon-billed Sandpipers on a mudflat in South Korea. *Journal of the Bombay Natural History Society (Supplement)*, 83: 206–207.

Pimm, S., Raven, P., Peterson, A., Sekercioglu, C.H. & Ehrlich, P.R. (2006) Human impacts on the rates of recent, present, and future bird extinctions. *Proceedings of the National Academy of Sciences of the United States of America*, 103: 10941–10946.

Pimm, S.L. (2008) Biodiversity: climate change or habitat loss – which will kill more species? *Current Biology*, 18: R117-R119.

Pimm, S.L. (2009) Climate disruption and biodiversity. *Current Biology*, 19: R595-R601.

Pimm, S.L., Diamond, J., Reed, T.M., Russell, G.J. & Verner, J. (1993) Times to extinction for small populations of large birds. *Proceedings of the National Academy of Sciences of the United States of America*, 90: 10871–10875.

Pimm, S.L., Moulton, M.P. & Justice, L.J. (1994) Bird extinctions in the central Pacific. *Philosophical Transactions of the Royal Society of London Series B-Biological Sciences*, 344: 27–33.

Pineschi, R.B. & Yamashita, C. (1999) *Occurrence, census and conservation of the Brazilian Merganser (Mergus octosetaceus) in Brazil with notes about feeding behaviour and habitat preferences*. VI Neotropical Waterfowl Symposium. Monterrey, Mexico.

Pinto, O. (1954) Resultados ornitológicos de duas viagens científicas ao estado de Alagoas. *Pap. Avuls. Dep. Zool. São Paulo*, 12: 1–98.

Pinto, O.M.O. (1952) Redescoberta de *Mitu mitu* (Linné) no nordeste do Brasil (est. de Alagoas) Provada a independência de *Mitu tuberosus* (Spix) como espécie à parte. *Pap. Avuls. Dep. Zool. São Paulo*, 10: 325–334.

Ploutkov, B.N. (1898) Ornithological survey of the surroundings of Yamyshevo, NE Kazakhstan. *Journal of the West-Siberian Branch of the Russian Geographical Society*, 24: 1–4 [in Russian].

Portenko, L.A. (1972) *Birds of the Chukchi Peninsula and Wrangel Islands*. Nauka Publishers, Leningrad Section, Academy of Sciences of the USSR, Institute of Zoology, Leningrad.

Porter, W.P., Vakharia, N., Klousie, W.D. & Duffy, D. (2006) *Po'ouli landscape bioinformatics models predict energetics, behavior, diets, and distribution on Maui*. Annual Meeting of the Society for Integrative and Comparative Biology, Orlando, Florida.

Posa, M.R.C., Diesmos, A.C., Sodhi, N.S. & Brooks, T.M. (2008) Hope for threatened tropical biodiversity: lessons from the Philippines. *BioScience*, 58: 231–240.

Poudyal, L.P., Singh, P.B. & Maharjan, S. (2008) Bengal Florican *Houbaropsis bengalensis* in Nepal: an update. *BirdingASIA*, 10: 43–47.

Pounds, J.A., Fogden, M.P.L. & Campbell, J.H. (1999) Biological response to climate change on a tropical mountain. *Nature*, 398: 611–615.

Powell, A. (2008) *The race to save the world's rarest bird: the discovery and death of the Po'ouli*. Stackpole Books, Mechanicsburg, PA.

Powell, A.N., Cuthbert, F.J., Wemmer, L.C., Doolittle, A.W. & Feirer, S.T. (1997) Captive-rearing piping plovers: developing techniques to augment wild populations. *Zoo Biology*, 16: 461–477.

Powlesland, R.G. & Lloyd, B.D. (1994) Use of supplementary feeding to induce breeding in free living Kakapo *Strigops habroptilus* in New Zealand. *Biological Conservation*, 69: 97–106.

Powlesland, R.G., Lloyd, B.D., Best, H.A. & Merton, D.V. (1992) Breeding biology of the Kakapo *Strigops habroptilus* on Stewart Island, New Zealand. *Ibis*, 134: 361–373.

Powlesland, R.G., Roberts, A., Lloyd, B.D. & Merton, D.V. (1995) Number, fate, and distribution of Kakapo (*Strigops habroptilus*) found on Stewart Island, New Zealand, 1979–1992. *New Zealand Journal of Zoology*, 22: 239–248.

Prakash, V. (1999) Status of vultures in Keoladeo National Park, Bharatpur, Rajasthan, with special reference to population crash in *Gyps* species. *Journal of the Bombay Natural History Society*, 96: 365–378.

Prakash, V., Pain, D.J., Cunningham, A.A., Donald, P.F., Prakash, N., Verma, A., Gargi, R., Sivakumar, S. & Rahmani, A.R. (2003) Catastrophic collapse of Indian white-backed *Gyps bengalensis* and long-billed *Gyps indicus* vulture populations. *Biological Conservation*, 109: 381–390.

Prakash, V., Green, R.E., Rahmani, A.R., Pain, D.J., Virani, M.Z., Khan, A.A., Baral, H.S., Jhala, Y.V., Naoroji, R., Shah, N., Bowden, C.G.R., Choudhury, B.C., Narayan, G. & Gautam, P. (2005) Evidence to support that diclofenac caused catastrophic vulture population decline. *Current Science*, 88: 1533–1534.

Prakash, V., Bishwakarma, M.C., Chaudhary, A., Cuthbert, R., Dave, R., Kulkarni, M., Kumar, S., Paudel, K., Ranade, S., Shringarpure, R. & Green, R.E. (2012a) The population decline of *Gyps* vultures in India and Nepal has slowed since veterinary use of diclofenac was banned. *PLoS ONE*, 7: e49118.

Prakash, V., Daemmgen, J.W., Cuthbert, R.J. & Bowden, C.G.R. (2012b) Gibt es doch noch Hoffnung? Indiens Gaier. *Der Falke*, 59: 372-378.

Pratt, H.D. (1992) Is the Poo-uli a Hawaiian Honeycreeper (Drepanidae)? *Condor*, 94: 172–180.

Pratt, T.K., Kepler, C.B. & Casey, T.L.C. (1997) Po'ouli (*Melanprosops phaeosoma*). In: Poole, A. & Gill, F. (eds). *The Birds of North America, No. 272*, The Academy of Natural Sciences, Philadelphia, PA and The American Ornithologists' Union, Washington DC.

Purvis, A. (2008) Phylogenetic approaches to the study of extinction. *Annual Review of Ecology Evolution and Systematics*, 39: 301–319.

Purvis, A., Agapow, P.M., Gittleman, J.L. & Mace, G.M. (2000a) Nonrandom extinction and the loss of evolutionary history. *Science*, 288: 328–330.

Purvis, A., Gittleman, J.L., Cowlishaw, G. & Mace, G.M. (2000b) Predicting extinction risk in declining species. *Proceedings of the Royal Society Series B-Biological Sciences*, 267: 1947–1952.

Pyle, P., Welch, A.J. & Fleischer, R.C. (2011) A new species of shearwater (*Puffinus*) recorded from Midway Atoll, northwestern Hawaiian Islands. *The Condor*, 113: 518-527.

Rabor, D.S. (1968) The present status of the Monkey-eating Eagle, *Pithecophaga jefferyi* Ogilvie-Grant, of the Philippines. In: Talbot, L.M. & Talbot, M.H. (eds). *Conference on Conservation of Nature and Natural Resources in Tropical South East Asia, Bangkok, Thailand, November 29-December 4, 1965*, 55–63. International Union for Conservation of Nature and Natural Resources, Morges, Switzerland.

Ralls, K. & Ballou, J.D. (2004) Genetic status and management of California Condors. *Condor*, 106: 215–228.

Rand, A.L. (1936) The distribution and habits of Madagascar birds. *Bulletin of the American Museum of Natural History*, 72: 143–499.

Rando, J.C., Lopez, M. & Segui, B. (1999) A new species of extinct flightless passerine (Emberizidae: Emberiza) from the Canary Islands. *Condor*, 101: 1–13.

Rasmussen, P.C. & Collar, N.J. (1998) Identification, distribution and status of the Forest Owlet *Heteroglaux* (*Athene*) *blewitti*. *Forktail*, 14: 41–49.

Rasmussen, P.C. & Collar, N.J. (1999a) On the hybrid status of Rothschild's Parakeet *Psittacula intermedia* (Aves, Psittacidae). *Bulletin of the Natural History Museum London (Zoology)*, 65: 31–50.

Rasmussen, P.C. & Collar, N.J. (1999b) Major specimen fraud in the Forest Owlet *Heteroglaux* (*Athene* auct.) *blewitti*. *Ibis*, 141: 11–21.

Rasmussen, P.C. & Ishtiaq, F. (1999) Vocalizations and behaviour of the Forest Owlet *Athene* (*Heteroglaux*) *blewitti*. *Forktail*, 15: 61–65.

Rasmussen, P.C. & Prys-Jones, R.P. (2003) History vs mystery: the reliability of museum specimen data. *Bulletin of the British Ornithologists' Club*, 123A: 66–94.

Rasmussen, P.C. & Anderton, J.C. (2005) *Birds of South Asia: the Ripley guide*. Smithsonian Institution and Lynx Edicions, Washington D.C. and Barcelona.

Ratcliffe, N., Monteiro, L.R. & Hazevoet, C.J. (1999) Status of Raso Lark *Alauda razae* with notes on threats and foraging behaviour. *Bird Conservation International*, 9: 43–46.

Rattner, B.A., Whitehead, M.A., Gasper, G., Meteyer, C.U., Link, W.A., Taggart, M.A., Meharg, A.A., Pattee, O.H. & Pain, D.J. (2008) Apparent tolerance of Turkey Vultures (*Cathartes aura*) to the non-steroidal anti-inflamatory drug diclofenac. *Environmental Toxicology and Chemistry*, 27: 2341–2345.

Raup, D. & Sepkoski, J. (1986) Periodic extinction of families and genera. *Science*, 231: 833–836.

Rayner, M.J., Hauber, M.E., Imber, M.J., Stamp, R.K. & Clout, M.N. (2007) Spatial heterogeneity of mesopredator release within an oceanic island system. *Proceedings of the National Academy of Sciences of the United States of America*, 104: 20862–20865.

Reaser, J.K., Meyerson, L.A., Cronk, Q., De Poorter, M., Eldrege, L.G., Green, E., Kairo, M., Latasi, P., Mack, R.N., Mauremootoo, J., O'Dowd, D., Orapa, W., Sastroutomo, S., Saunders, A., Shine, C., Thrainsson, S. & Vaiutu, L. (2007) Ecological and socioeconomic impacts of invasive alien species in island ecosystems. *Environmental Conservation*, 34: 98–111.

Redding, D.W. & Mooers, A.O. (2006) Incorporating evolutionary measures into conservation prioritization. *Conservation Biology*, 20: 1670–1678.

Reding, D.M., Foster, J.T., James, H.F., Pratt, H.D. & Fleischer, R.C. (2009) Convergent evolution of 'creepers' in the Hawaiian honeycreeper radiation. *Biology Letters*, 5: 221–224.

Reed, D.H., O'Grady, J.J., Brook, B.W., Ballou, J.D. & Frankham, R. (2003) Estimates of minimum viable population sizes for vertebrates and factors influencing those estimates. *Biological Conservation*, 113: 23–34.

Reed, D.H. & Hobbs, G.R. (2004) The relationship between population size and temporal variability in population size. *Animal Conservation*, 7: 1–8.

Reilly, S.E. (1998) Saving the Po`o-uli *Melamprosops phaeosoma*, the world's rarest bird. *'Elepaio*, 58: 17–18.

Reinthal, P.N. & Stiassny, M.L.J. (1991) The freshwater fishes of Madagascar: a study of an endangered fauna with recommendations for a conservation strategy. *Conservation Biology*, 5: 231–242.

René de Roland, L.-A., Sam, T.S., Rakotondratsima, M.P.H. & Thorstrom, R. (2007) Rediscovery of the Madagascar Pochard *Aythya innotata* in northern Madagascar. *Bulletin of the African Bird Club*, 14: 171–174.

René de Roland, L.-A., Thorstrom, R., Razafimanjato, G., Rakotondratsima, M.P.H., Andriamalala, T.R.A. & Sam, T.S. (2009) Surveys, distribution and current status of the Madagascar Harrier *Circus macrosceles* in Madagascar. *Bird Conservation International*, 19: 309–322.

Renison, D., Hensen, I. & Cingolani, A.M. (2004) Anthropogenic soil degradation affects seed viability in *Polylepis australis* mountain forests of central Argentina. *Forest Ecology and Management*, 196: 327–333.

Restani, M. & Marzluff, J.M. (2001) Avian conservation under the Endangered Species Act: expenditures versus recovery priorities. *Conservation Biology*, 15: 1292–1299.

Reynolds, M.H. & Snetsinger, T.J. (2001) The Hawai'i Rare Bird Search 1994–1996. *Studies in Avian Biology*, 22: 133–143.

Reynolds, M.H., Camp, R.J., Nielson, B.M.B. & Jacobi, J.D. (2003) Evidence of change in a low-elevation forest bird community of Hawaii since 1979. *Bird Conservation International*, 13: 175–187.

Reynolds, M.H., Seavy, N.E., Vekasy, M.S., Klavitter, J.L. & Laniawe, L.P. (2008) Translocation and early post-release demography of endangered Laysan teal. *Animal Conservation*, 11: 160–168.

Ribeiro, F., Lins, L.V., Gomes, V.M., Nery, F.H. & dos Reis, E.S. (2011) Dispersion and sexual maturity of *Mergus octosetaceus* (Vieillot, 1817) in the Serra da Canastra, Minas Gerais, Brazil. *Revista Brasileira De Ornitologia*, 19: 391-397.

Ribeiro, M.C., Metzger, J.P., Martensen, A.C., Ponzoni, F.J. & Hirota, M.M. (2009) The Brazilian Atlantic Forest: how much is left, and how is the remaining forest distributed? Implications for conservation. *Biological Conservation*, 142: 1141–1153.

Ricketts, T.H., Dinerstein, E., Boucher, T., Brooks, T.M., Butchart, S.H.M., Hoffmann, M., Lamoreux, J.F., Morrison, J., Parr, M., Pilgrim, J.D., Rodrigues, A.S.L., Sechrest, W., Wallace, G.E., Berlin, K., Bielby, J., Burgess, N.D., Church, D.R., Cox, N., Knox, D., Loucks, C., Luck, G.W., Master, L.L., Moore, R., Naidoo, R., Ridgely, R., Schatz, G.E., Shire, G., Strand, H., Wettengel, W. & Wikramanayake, E. (2005) Pinpointing and preventing imminent extinctions. *Proceedings of the National Academy of Sciences of the United States of America*, 102: 18497–18501.

Ricklefs, R.E. & Bermingham, E. (1999) Taxon cycles in the Lesser Antillean avifauna. *Ostrich*, 70: 49–59.

Ricklefs, R.E. & Bermingham, E. (2002) The concept of the taxon cycle in biogeography. *Global Ecology and Biogeography*, 11: 353–361.

Ricklefs, R.E. & Bermingham, E. (2007) The causes of evolutionary radiations in archipelagoes: passerine birds in the Lesser Antilles. *American Naturalist*, 169: 285–297.

Riley, J., Oaks, J.L. & Gilbert, M. (2003) *Raillietiella trachea* n. sp., a pentastomid from the trachea of an oriental white-backed vulture *Gyps bengalensis* taken in Pakistan, with speculation about its life-cycle. *Systematic Parasitology*, 56: 155–161.

Rios, S.S., Lloyd, H. & Valdes-Velasquez, A. (2011) Bird species richness, diversity and abundance in Polylepis woodlands, Huascaran biosphere reserve, Peru. *Studies on Neotropical Fauna and Environment*, 46: 69-76.

Ripley, S.D. (1976) Reconsideration of *Athene blewitti* (Hume). *Journal of the Bombay Natural History Society*, 73: 1–4.

Rithe, K. (2003) Saving the Forest Owlet. *Sanctuary (Asia)*, 23: 30–33.

Rivalan, P., Barbraud, C., Inchausti, P. & Weimerskirch, H. (2010) Combined impacts of longline fisheries and climate on the persistence of the Amsterdam Albatross *Diomedia amsterdamensis*. *Ibis*, 152: 6–18.

Robert, A. (2009) Captive breeding genetics and reintroduction success. *Biological Conservation*, 142: 2915–2922.

Roberts, D.L. & Solow, A.R. (2003) When did the Dodo become extinct? *Nature*, 426: 245.

Roberts, D.L., Elphick, C.S. & Reed, J.M. (2010) Identifying anomalous reports of putatively extinct species and why it matters. *Conservation Biology*, 24: 189–196.

Roberts, P. (1987) Is the Aldabra brush warbler extinct? *Oryx*, 21: 209–210.

Roberts, P. (2009) *The end of food*. Bloomsbury Publishing, London.

Robertson, B.C., Elliott, G.P., Eason, D.K., Clout, M.N. & Gemmell, N.J. (2006) Sex allocation theory aids species conservation. *Biology Letters*, 2: 229–231.

Robertson, B.C., Frauenfelder, N., Eason, D.K., Elliott, G. & Moorhouse, R. (2009) Thirty polymorphic microsatellite loci from the critically endangered kakapo (*Strigops habroptilus*). *Molecular Ecology Resources*, 9: 664–666.

Robertson, C.J.R. & Nunn, G.B. (1998) Towards a new taxonomy for albatrosses. In: Robertson, G. & Gales, R. (eds). *Albatross biology and conservation*, 13–19. Surrey Beatty and Sons, Chipping Norton, UK.

Robertson, I.S. (1995) First field observations on the Sidamo Lark *Heteromirafra sidamoensis*. *Bulletin of the British Ornithologists' Club*, 115: 241–243.

Robinson, S. & Milner-Gulland, E.J. (2003) Political change and factors limiting numbers of wild and domestic ungulates in Kazakhstan. *Human Ecology*, 31: 87–110.

Robinson, S., Milner-Gulland, E.J. & Alimaev, I. (2003) Rangeland degradation in Kazakhstan during the Soviet era: re-examining the evidence. *Journal of Arid Environments*, 53: 419–439.

Robinson, S.K., Thompson, F.R., Donovan, T.M., Whitehead, D.R. & Faaborg, J. (1995) Regional forest fragmentation and the nesting success of migratory birds. *Science*, 267: 1987–1990.

Robinson, W.D. (1999) Long term changes in the avifauna of Barro Colorado Island, Panama, a tropical forest isolate. *Conservation Biology*, 13: 85–97.

Rodl, T., Berger, S., Romero, L.M. & Wikelski, M. (2007) Tameness and stress physiology in a predator-naive island species confronted with novel predation threat. *Proceedings of the Royal Society Series B-Biological Sciences*, 274: 577–582.

Rodrigues, A.S.L. & Gaston, K.J. (2002) Rarity and conservation planning across geopolitical units. *Conservation Biology*, 16: 674–682.

Rodrigues, A.S.L., Pilgrim, J.D., Lamoreux, J.F., Hoffmann, M. & Brooks, T.M. (2006) The value of the IUCN Red List for conservation. *Trends in Ecology & Evolution*, 21: 71–76.

Román, J. & Gutiérrez, C. (2008) La Graja *Corvus frugilegus* deja de invernar en España: ¿Un nuevo caso de acortamiento en las migraciones? *Ardeola*, 55: 229–235.

Roques, K.G., O'Connor, T.G. & Watkinson, A.R. (2001) Dynamics of shrub encroachment in an African savanna: relative influences of fire, herbivory, rainfall and density dependence. *Journal of Applied Ecology*, 38: 268–280.

Rosa, K., Hopper, D. & Reilly, S. (1998) *Draft environment assessment for possible management actions to save the Po'ouli*. US Fish and Wildlife Service, H.D.o.L.a.N.R., Division of Forestry and Wildlife, Honolulu.

Rothschild, W. (1905) On extinct and vanishing birds. *Proceedings of the 4th International Ornithological Congress*, London: 191–217.

Rothschild, W. (1907) *Extinct birds*. Hutchinson & Co., London.

Round, P.D. (1995) On the seasonality and distribution of Gurney's Pitta *Pitta gurneyi*. *Forktail*, 11: 155–158.

Round, P.D. & Kennerley, P.R. (2007) Large-billed Reed Warbler *Acrocephalus orinus* back from the dead. *BirdingASIA* 7: 53-54.

Round, P.D. & Treesucon, U. (1986) The rediscovery of Gurney's Pitta. *Forktail*, 2: 53–66.

Round, P.D., Hansson, B., Pearson, D.J., Kennerley, P.R. & Bensch, S. (2007) Lost and found: the enigmatic large-billed reed warbler *Acrocephalus orinus* rediscovered after 139 years. *Journal of Avian Biology* 38: 133-138.

Rudel, T.K., Defries, R., Asner, G.P. & Laurance, W.F. (2009) Changing drivers of deforestation and new opportunities for conservation. *Conservation Biology*, 23: 1396–1405.

Ruiz-Gutiérrez, V., Gavin, T.A. & Dhondt, A.A. (2008) Habitat fragmentation lowers survival of a tropical forest bird. *Ecological Applications*, 18: 838–846.

Russell, G.J., Brooks, T.M., McKinney, M.M. & Anderson, C.G. (1998) Present and future taxonomic selectivity in bird and mammal extinctions. *Conservation Biology*, 12: 1365–1376.

Russello, M.A., Beheregaray, L.B., Gibbs, J.P., Fritts, T., Havill, N., Powell, J.R. & Caccone, A. (2007) Lonesome George is not alone among Galápagos tortoises. *Current Biology*, 17: 317–318.

Ryabov, V.F. (1974) [Changes in bird communities of the steppes of Northern Kazakhstan under human influence]. *Ornitologiya*, 11: 279–297.

Ryan, P.G. & Cuthbert, R.J. (2008) The biology and conservation status of Gough Bunting *Rowettia goughensis*. *Bulletin of the British Ornithologists' Club*, 128: 242–253.

Saenz, D., Baum, K.A., Conner, R.N., Rudolph, D.C. & Costa, R. (2002) Large-scale translocation strategies for reintroducing red-cockaded woodpeckers. *Journal of Wildlife Management*, 66: 212–221.

Safford, R.J. (1997a) Nesting success of the Mauritius Fody *Foudia rubra* in relation to its use of exotic trees as nest sites. *Ibis*, 139: 555–559.

Safford, R.J. (1997b) The destruction of source and sink habitats in the decline of the Mauritius Fody, *Foudia rubra*, an island-endemic bird. *Biodiversity and Conservation*, 6: 513–527.

Safford, R.J. & Jones, C.G. (1997) Did organochlorine pesticide use cause declines in Mauritian forest birds? *Biodiversity and Conservation*, 6: 1445–1451.

Safford, R.J. & Jones, C.G. (1998) Strategies for land-bird conservation on Mauritius. *Conservation Biology*, 12: 169–176.

Safford, R.J., Ash, J.S. & Duckworth, J.W. (1997) Sexual dimorphism, plumage variability and species determination in nightjars: the need for further examination of the Nechisar Nightjar *Caprimulgus solala* reply. *Ibis*, 139: 410–411.

Saint Jalme, M. (2002) Endangered avian species captive propagation: an overview of functions and techniques. *Avian and Poultry Biology Reviews*, 13: 187–202.

Salaman, P. (2006) A bright future for parrots in Colombia. *VI International Parrot Convention ('The pleasure of parrots')*, 147–152. Loro Parque Foundation, Tenerife.

Salaman, P., Coopmans, P., Donegan, T.M., Cortés, A., Hilty, S.L., Ortega, L.A. & Mulligan, M. (2003) A new species of Wood-wren (Troglodytidae: Henicorhina) from the Western Andes of Colombia. *Ornitologia Colombiana*, 1: 4–21.

Salvador, D.J.I. & Ibañez, J.C. (2006) Ecology and conservation of Philippine Eagles. *Ornithological Science*, 5: 171–176.

Salvadori, T. (1894) Remarks on the ducks of the genera *Anas* and *Nyroca*. *Bulletin of the British Ornithologists' Club*, 2: 7–8.

Salvan, J. (1970) Remarques sur l'évolution de l'avifaune malgache depuis 1945. *Alauda*, 38: 191–203.

Salvan, J. (1972) Statut, recensement, reproduction des oiseaux dulçaquicoles aux environs de Tananarive. *L'Oiseau et RFO*, 42: 35–51.

Samson, F.B. & Knopf, F.L. (1994) Prairie conservation in North America. *BioScience*, 44: 418–421.

Sanderson, F.J., Donald, P.F., Pain, D.J., Burfield, I.J. & van Bommel, F.P.J. (2006) Long-term population declines in Afro-Palearctic migrant birds. *Biological Conservation*, 131: 93–105.

Sangster, G. (2009) Increasing numbers of bird species result from taxonomic progress, not taxonomic inflation. *Proceedings of the Royal Society Series B-Biological Sciences*, 276: 3185–3191.

Santos, M.P.D. & Vasconcelos, M.F. (2007) Range extension for Kaempfer's Woodpecker *Celeus obrieni* in Brazil, with the first male specimen. *Bulletin of the British Ornithologists' Club*, 127: 249–252.

São Bernardo, C.S., Azeredo, R., Simpson, J. & Paiva, E.V. (2008) The reintroduction of the red-billed curassow at Reserva Ecológica de Guapiaçu, Rio de Janeiro state, Brazil. In: Soorae, P.S. (ed). *Global re-introduction perspectives: re-introduction case-studies from around the world*, 108–111. IUCN/SSC Re-introduction Specialist Group, Abu Dhabi, UAE.

Saunders, D.A., Hobbs, R.J. & Margules, C.R. (1991) Biological consequence of ecosystem fragmentation – a review. *Conservation Biology*, 5: 18–32.

Savidge, J.A. (1984) Guam – Paradise Lost for wildlife. *Biological Conservation*, 30: 305–317.

Saville, S., Stephenson, B. & Southey, I. (2003) A possible sighting of an 'extinct' bird – the New Zealand storm petrel. *Birding World*, 16: 173–175.

Sax, D.F. & Gaines, S.D. (2008) Species invasions and extinction: the future of native biodiversity on islands. *Proceedings of the National Academy of Sciences of the United States of America*, 105: 11490–11497.

Sax, D.F., Gaines, S.D. & Brown, J.H. (2002) Species invasions exceed extinctions on islands worldwide: a comparative study of plants and birds. *American Naturalist*, 160: 766–783.

Scales, B.R. & Marsden, S.J. (2008) Biodiversity in small-scale tropical agroforests: a review of species richness and abundance shifts and the factors influencing them. *Environmental Conservation*, 35: 160–172.

Scharlemann, J.P.W., Green, R.E. & Balmford, A. (2004) Land-use trends in Endemic Bird Areas: global expansion of agriculture in areas of high conservation value. *Global Change Biology*, 10: 2046–2051.

Scharlemann, J.P.W., Balmford, A. & Green, R.E. (2005) The level of threat to restricted-range bird species can be predicted from mapped data on land use and human population. *Biological Conservation*, 123: 317–326.

Scheffers, B.R., Yong, D.L., Harris, J.B.C., Giam, X. & Sodhi, N.S. (2011) The world's rediscovered species: back from the brink? *PLoS ONE*, 6: e22531.

Schmitt, C.B., Burgess, N.D., Coad, L., Belokurov, A., Besancon, C., Boisrobert, L., Campbell, A., Fish, L., Gliddon, D., Humphries, K., Kapos, V., Loucks, C., Lysenko, I., Miles, L., Mills, C., Minnemeyer, S., Pistorius, T., Ravilious, C., Steininger, M. & Winkel, G. (2009) Global analysis of the protection status of the world's forests. *Biological Conservation*, 142: 2122–2130.

Schwartz, M.W., Iverson, L.R., Prasad, A.M., Matthews, S.N. & O'Connor, R.J. (2006) Predicting extinctions as a result of climate change. *Ecology*, 87: 1611–1615.

Scott, J.M., Mountainspring, S., Ramsey, F.L. & Kepler, C.B. (1986) Forest bird communities of the Hawaiian islands: their dynamics, ecology, and conservation. *Studies in Avian Biology*, 9: 1–431.

Scott, J.M., Ramsey, F.L., Lammertink, M., Rosenberg, K.V., Rohrbaugh, R., Wiens, J.A. & Reed, J.M. (2008) When is an 'extinct' species really extinct? Gauging the search efforts for Hawaiian forest birds and the Ivory-billed Woodpecker. *Avian Conservation and Ecology*, 3(2): 3.

Seddon, P.J., Armstrong, D.P. & Maloney, R.F. (2007) Developing the science of reintroduction biology. *Conservation Biology*, 21: 303–312.

Sekercioglu, C.H. (2002) Impacts of birdwatching on human and avian communities. *Environmental Conservation*, 29: 282–289.

Sekercioglu, C.H. (2006) Increasing awareness of avian ecological function. *Trends in Ecology & Evolution*, 21: 464–471.

Sekercioglu, C.H., Daily, G.C. & Ehrlich, P.R. (2004) Ecosystem consequences of bird declines. *Proceedings of the National Academy of Sciences of the United States of America*, 101: 18042–18047.

Sekercioglu, C.H., Schneider, S.H., Fay, J.P. & Loarie, S.R. (2008) Climate change, elevational range shifts, and bird extinctions. *Conservation Biology*, 22: 140–150.

Seoane, J. & Carrascal, L.M. (2008) Interspecific differences in population trends of Spanish birds are related to habitat and climatic preferences. *Global Ecology and Biogeography*, 17: 111–121.

Serra, G., Abdallah, M., Assaed, A., Abdallah, A., Al Qaim, G., Fayad, T. & Williamson, D. (2004) Discovery of a relict breeding colony of northern bald ibis *Geronticus eremita* in Syria. *Oryx*, 38: 106–108.

Serra, G., Peske, L., Abdallah, M.S., al Qaim, G. & Kanani, A. (2009) Breeding ecology and behaviour of the last wild oriental Northern Bald Ibises (*Geronticus eremita*) in Syria. *Journal of Ornithology*, 150: 769–782.

Shannaz, J. (2001) Rediscovery of the Damar Flycatcher *Ficedula henrici*, Damar Island, Maluku, Indonesia. *Oriental Bird Club Bulletin*, 34: 38–39.

Sheldon, R.D., Kamp, J., Koshkin, M.A., Urazaliev, R.S., Iskakov, T.K., Field, R.H., Salemgareev, A.R., Khrokov, V.V., Zhuly, V.A., Sklyarenko, S.L. & Donald, P.F. (2013) Breeding ecology of the globally threatened Sociable Lapwing *Vanellus gregarius* and the demographic drivers of recent declines. *Journal of Ornithology*, 154: 501-516.

Shepherd, C.R. & Shepherd, L.A. (2009) An emerging Asian taste for owls? Enforcement agency seizes 1,236 owls and other wildlife in Malaysia. *BirdingASIA*, 11: 85–86.

Shirihai, H. (2008) Rediscovery of Beck's Petrel *Pseudobulweria becki*, and other observations of tubenoses from the Bismarck archipelago, Papua New Guinea. *Bulletin of the British Ornithologists' Club*, 128: 3–16.

Shultz, S., Baral, H.S., Charman, S., Cunningham, A.A., Das, D., Ghalsasi, G.R., Goudar, M.S., Green, R.E., Jones, A., Nighot, P., Pain, D.J. & Prakash, V. (2004) Diclofenac poisoning is widespread in declining vulture populations across the Indian subcontinent. *Proceedings of the Royal Society of London Series B-Biological Sciences*, 271: S458-S460.

Sibley, C.G. & Monroe, B.L.N.H. (1990) *Distribution and taxonomy of birds of the world*. Yale University Press, New Haven.

Sibley, D.A., Bevier, L.R., Patten, M.A. & Elphick, C. (2006) Comments on 'Ivory-billed Woodpecker (*Campephilus principalis*) persists in continental North America'. *Science*, 311: 1555.

Sick, H. (1980) Characteristics of the Razor-billed Curassow (*Mitu mitu mitu*). *Condor*, 82: 227–228.

Sick, H., Teixeira, D.M. & Gonzaga, L.P. (1979) A nossa descoberta da pátria da arara *Anodorhynchus leari* [sic]. *Anais da Academia Brasiliera de Ciências*, 51: 575–576.

Silveira, L.F. (2008) *Mergus octosetaceus*. In: Machado, A.B.M., Drummond, G.M. & Paglia, A. (eds). *Livro vermelho da fauna brasileira ameaçada de extinção*. MMA, Brasilia.

Silveira, L.F. & Bartmann, W. (2001) Natural history and conservation of the Brazilian Merganser *Mergus octosetaceus* at Serra da Canastra National Park Minas Gerais, Brazil. *Bird Conservation International*, 11: 287–300.

Silveira, L..F. & Olmos, F. (2003) Cracids in coastal Alagoas state, northeastern Brazil. *Annual Review of the World Pheasant Association*, 2002/2003: 49–52.

Silveira, L.F. & Olmos, F. (2007) How many bird species are there in Brazil? Species concepts, conservation and what is to be found. *Revista Brasileira de Ornitologia*, 15: 289–296.

Silveira, L.F., Olmos, F. & Long, A.J. (2003) The Alagoas Curassow: world's rarest cracid. *Bulletin of the Cracid Specialist Group*, 17: 31–34.

Silveira, L.F., Olmos, F. & Long, A.J. (2004) Taxonomy, history, and status of Alagoas Curassow *Mitu mitu* (Linnaeus, 1766), the world's most threatened cracid. *Ararajuba*, 12: 125–132.

Silveira, L.F., Olmos, F., Bianchi, C., Simpson, J., Azeredo, R., McGowan, P.J.K. & Collar, N.J. (2005) *Action plan for the conservation of the Red-billed Curassow Crax blumenbachii – a flagship species for the Brazilian Atlantic Forest*. World Pheasant Association and BirdLife Brasil, Fordingbridge, UK and São Paulo, Brazil.

Simberloff, D. (1986) Are we on the verge of a mass extinction in tropical rainforests? In: Elliott, D.K. (ed) *Dynamics of extinction*, 165–180. John Wiley, New York.

Simberloff, D. (1995) Habitat fragmentation and population extinction in birds. *Ibis*, 137: S105-S111.

Simpson, J.G.P., Azeredo, R.P.G. & Barros, L.P. (1997) The Red-billed Curassow Project in Brazil. In: Strahl, S.D. *et al.* (eds). *The Cracidae: their biology and conservation*, 472–473. Hancock House, Surrey, BC.

Sinclair, A.R.E., Innes, J. & Bradfield, P. (2006) Making endangered species safe: the case of the kokako of North Island, New Zealand. *New Zealand Journal of Ecology*, 30: 121–130.

Sizling, A.L., Sizlingova, E., Storch, D., Reif, J. & Gaston, K.J. (2009) Rarity, commonness, and the contribution of individual species to species richness patterns. *American Naturalist*, 174: 82–93.

Slikas, B., Olson, S.L. & Fleischer, R.C. (2002) Rapid, independent evolution of flightlessness in four species of Pacific Island rails (Rallidae): an analysis based on mitochondrial sequence data. *Journal of Avian Biology*, 33: 5–14.

Smales, I., Brown, P., Menkhorst, P., Holdsworth, M. & Holz, P. (2000a) Contribution of captive management of Orange-bellied parrots *Neophema chrysogaster* to the recovery programme for the species in Australia. *International Zoo Yearbook*, 37: 171–178.

Smales, I., Holdsworth, M., Menkhorst, P., Starks, J. & Brown, P. (2000b) Re-introduction of orange-bellied parrots, Australia. *Reintroduction News*, 19: 32–34.

Smart, M., Essghaier, M.F., Etayeb, K., Hamza, A., Azafzaf, H., Baccetti, N., Defos du Rau, P. & Dlensi, H. (2006) Wetlands and wintering waterbirds in Libya, January 2005 and 2006. *Wildfowl*, 56: 172–191.

Smith, K.F., Sax, D.F. & Lafferty, K.D. (2006) Evidence for the role of infectious disease in species extinction and endangerment. *Conservation Biology*, 20: 1349–1357.

Smith, K.W., Aghnaj, A., Bekkay, M.E.L., Oubrou, W., Ribi, M., Armesto, M.J. & Bowden, C.G.R. (2008) The provision of supplementary fresh water improves the breeding success of the globally threatened Northern Bald Ibis *Geronticus eremita*. *Ibis*, 150: 728–734.

Smith, R.J. & Walpole, M.J. (2005) Should conservationists pay more attention to corruption? *Oryx*, 39: 251–256.

Smith, R.J., Muir, R.D.J., Walpole, M.J., Balmford, A. & Leader-Williams, N. (2003) Governance and the loss of biodiversity. *Nature*, 426: 67–70.

Snyder, N.F. (2007) *An alternative hypothesis for the cause of the Ivory-billed Woodpecker's decline*. Western Foundation of Vertebrate Zoology, Camarillo, CA.

Snyder, N.F.R. (2004) *The Carolina Parakeet: glimpses of a vanished bird*. Princeton University Press, Princeton.

Snyder, N.F.R., Wiley, J.W. & Kepler, C.B. (1987) *The parrots of Luquillo: natural history and conservation of the Puerto Rican Parrot*. Western Foundation of Vertebrate Zoology, Caramillo, CA.

Snyder, N.F.R., Koenig, S.E., Koschmann, J., Snyder, H.A. & Johnson, T.B. (1994) Thick-billed Parrot releases in Arizona. *Condor*, 96: 845–862.

Snyder, N.F.R., Derrickson, S.R., Beissinger, S.R., Wiley, J.W., Smith, T.B., Toone, W.D. & Miller, B. (1996) Limitations of captive breeding in endangered species recovery. *Conservation Biology*, 10: 338–348.

Sodhi, N.S., Liow, L.H. & Bazzaz, F.A. (2004) Avian extinctions from tropical and subtropical forests. *Annual Review of Ecology Evolution and Systematics*, 35: 323–345.

Sodhi, N.S., Lee, T.M., Koh, L.P. & Brook, B.W. (2009) A meta analysis of the impact of anthropogenic forest disturbance on southeast Asia's biotas. *Biotropica*, 41: 103–109.

Solovieva, D., Vartanyan, S., Shokhrin, V. & Vartanyan, N. (2010) Artificial nest sites for Scaly-sided Merganser *Mergus squamatus* – a way to breeding habitat restoration. *TWSG News*.

Solow, A.R. & Roberts, D.L. (2003) A nonparametric test for extinction based on a sighting record. *Ecology*, 84: 1329–1332.

Songer, M., Aung, M., Senior, B., DeFries, R. & Leimgruber, P. (2009) Spatial and temporal deforestation dynamics in protected and unprotected dry forests: a case study from Myanmar (Burma). *Biodiversity and Conservation*, 18: 1001–1018.

Spiegel, C.S., Hart, P.J., Woodworth, B.L., Tweed, E.J. & LeBrun, J.J. (2006) Distribution and abundance of forest birds in low-altitude habitat on Hawai'i Island: evidence for range expansion of native species. *Bird Conservation International*, 16: 175–185.

Spielman, D., Brook, B.W. & Frankham, R. (2004) Most species are not driven to extinction before genetic factors impact them. *Proceedings of the National Academy of Sciences of the United States of America*, 101: 15261–15264.

Spottiswoode, C.N., Wondafrash, M., Gabremichael, M.N., Abebe, Y.D., Mwangi, M.A.K., Collar, N.J. & Dolman, P.M. (2009) Rangeland degradation is poised to cause Africa's first recorded avian extinction. *Animal Conservation*, 12: 249–257.

Spottiswoode, C.N., Olsson, U., Mills, M.S.L., Cohen, C., Francis, J.E., Toye, N., Hoddinott, D., Dagne, A., Wood, C., Donald, P.F., Collar, N.J. & Alström, P. (2013) Rediscovery of a long-lost lark reveals the conspecificity of endangered *Heteromirafra* populations in the Horn of Africa. *Journal of Ornithology*, 154: in press.

Stahala, C. (2005) Demography and conservation of the Bahama Parrot on Great Abaco Island. MSc thesis, North Carolina State University, Raleigh, USA.

Stattersfield, A.J., Crosby, M.J., Long, A.J. & Wege, D.C. (1998) *Endemic Bird Areas of the world: priorities for biodiversity conservation*. BirdLife International, Cambridge, UK.

Steadman, D.W. (1995) Prehistoric extinctions of Pacific island birds – biodiversity meets zooarchaeology. *Science*, 267: 1123–1131.

Steadman, D.W., White, J.P. & Allen, J. (1999) Prehistoric birds from New Ireland, Papua New Guinea: extinctions on a large Melanesian island. *Proceedings of the National Academy of Sciences of the United States of America*, 96: 2563–2568.

Steiger, S.S., Fidler, A.E. & Kempenaers, B. (2009) Evidence for increased olfactory receptor gene repertoire size in two nocturnal bird species with well-developed olfactory ability. *Bmc Evolutionary Biology*, 9: 117.

Stephens, P.A. & Sutherland, W.J. (1999) Consequences of the Allee effect for behaviour, ecology and conservation. *Trends in Ecology & Evolution*, 14: 401–405.

Strahl, S. & Schmitz, A. (1997) A taxonomic reference of the family Cracidae for common use by ornithologists. In: Strahl, S.D. *et al.* (eds). *The Cracidae: their biology and conservation*, 1–7. Hancock House, Surrey, BC.

Stresemann, E. & Grote, H. (1943) [Is *Numenius tenuirostris* heading for extinction?]. *Ornithologischen Monatsbericht*, 51: 122–127.

Stuart, B.L., Rhodin, A.G., Grimser, L.L. & Hansel, T. (2006) Scientific description can imperil species. *Science*, 312: 1137.

Suárez, F., García, J.T., Carriles, E., Calero-Riestra, M., Agirre, A., Justribó, J.H. & Garza, V. (2009) Sex ratios of an endangered lark after accounting for a male biased sampling. *Ardeola*, 56: 113–118.

Suárez, M.L., Renison, D., Marcora, P. & Hensen, I. (2008) Age-size-habitat relationships for *Polylepis australis*: dealing with endangered forest ecosystems. *Biodiversity and Conservation*, 17: 2617–2625.

Sugathan, R. (1985) Observations on Spoonbilled Sandpiper (*Eurynorhynchus pygmeus*) in its wintering ground at Point Calimere, Thanjavur District, Tamil Nadu. *Journal of the Bombay Natural History Society*, 82: 407–408.

Sutherland, W.J., Clout, M., Côté, I.M., Daszak, P., Depledge, M.H., Fellman, L., Fleischman, E., Garthwaite, R., Gibbons, D.W., De Lurio, J., Impey, A.J., Lickorish, F., Lindenmayer, D., Madgwick, J., Margerison, C., Maynard, T., Peck, L.S., Pretty, J., Prior, S., Redford, K.H., Scharlemann, J.P.W., Spalding, M. & Watkinson, A.R. (2010) A horizon scan of global conservation issues for 2010. *Trends in Ecology & Evolution*, 25: 1–17..

Svensson, L., Prys-Jones, R., Rasmussen, P.C. & Olsson, U. (2008) Discovery of ten new specimens of large-billed reed warbler *Acrocephalus orinus*, and new insights into its distributional range. *Journal of Avian Biology*, 39: 605–610.

Swan, G., Naidoo, V., Cuthbert, R., Green, R.E., Pain, D.J., Swarup, D., Prakash, V., Taggart, M., Bekker, L., Das, D., Diekmann, J., Diekmann, M., Killian, E., Meharg, A., Patra, R.C., Saini, M. & Wolter, K. (2006a) Removing the threat of diclofenac to critically endangered Asian vultures. *PLoS Biology* 4: 395–402.

Swan, G.E., Cuthbert, R., Quevedo, M., Green, R.E., Pain, D.J., Bartels, P., Cunningham, A.A., Duncan, N., Meharg, A.A., Oaks, J.L., Parry-Jones, J., Shultz, S., Taggart, M.A., Verdoorn, G. & Wolter, K. (2006b) Toxicity of diclofenac to *Gyps* vultures. *Biology Letters*, 2: 279–282.

Swarup, D., Patra, R.C., Prakash, V., Cuthbert, R., Das, D., Avari, P., Pain, D.J., Green, R.E., Sharma, A.K., Saini, M. & Taggart, M. (2007) Safety of meloxicam to critically endangered *Gyps* vultures and other scavenging birds in India. *Animal Conservation*, 10: 192–198.

Swenk, M.H. (1915) The Eskimo Curlew and its disappearance. *Proceedings of the Nebraska Ornithologists' Union*, 6: 25–44.

Swinnerton, K.J., Groombridge, J.J., Jones, C.G., Burn, R.W. & Mungroo, Y. (2004) Inbreeding depression and founder diversity among captive and free-living populations of the endangered pink pigeon *Columba mayeri*. *Animal Conservation*, 7: 353–364.

Sykes, B. (2000) Gurney's Pitta campaign update: November 2000. *Oriental Bird Club Bulletin*, 32: 41–43.

Sykes, B., Kohler, M. & Juniper, T. (2000) Gurney's Pitta campaign update: May 2000. *Oriental Bird Club Bulletin*, 31: 42–43.

Syroechkovskiy, E.E. (2004) The Spoon-billed Sandpiper on the edge: a review of breeding distribution, population estimates and plans for conservation research in Russia. *International Wader Studies*, 17: 169–174.

Syroechkovskiy, E.E., Zöckler, C. & Bird, J.P. (2009) Spoon-billed Sandpiper *Eurynorhynchus pygmeus*: last chance to save. *BirdingASIA*, 12: 109–111.

Szabo, J.K., Butchart, S.H.M., Possingham, H.P. & Garnett, S.T. (2012a) Adapting global biodiversity indicators to the national scale: a Red List Index for Australian birds. *Biological Conservation*, 148: 61-68.

Szabo, J.K., Khwaja, N., Garnett, S.T. & Butchart, S.H.M. (2012b). Global patterns and drivers of avian extinctions at the species and subspecies level. *PLoS ONE*, 7: e47080.

Tabaranza, B.R., Edrial, M., Tabaranza, D.G., Urriza, R., Guevarra, R., Almazan, A., Briones, E., de la Rosa, R. & Tabaranza, A.C.E. (2008) *A report on the search for the 'lost species', the Sulu Bleeding-heart* (Gallicolumba menagei) *in Tawi-tawi Island*. Haribon Foundation, Manila.

Tadena, D.O., Salvador, D.I., Miranda, H.C. & Aya-ay, A.M. (2000) Captive breeding by natural pairing, incubation and chick-rearing methods for Philippine eagles. *Sylvatrop*, 10: 45–58.

Taggart, M.A., Cuthbert, R., Das, D., Sashikumar, C., Pain, D.J., Green, R.E., Feltrer, Y., Shultz, S., Cunningham, A.A. & Meharg, A.A. (2007a) Diclofenac disposition in Indian cow and goat with reference to *Gyps* vulture population declines. *Environmental Pollution*, 147: 60–65.

Taggart, M.A., Senacha, K.R., Green, R.E., Jhala, Y.V., Raghavan, B., Rahmani, A.R., Cuthbert, R., Pain, D.J. & Meharg, A.A. (2007b) Diclofenac residues in carcasses of domestic ungulates available to vultures in India. *Environment International*, 33: 759–765.

Taggart, M.A., Senacha, K.R., Green, R.E., Cuthbert, R., Jhala, Y.V., Meharg, A.A., Mateo, R. & Pain, D.J. (2009) Analysis of nine NSAIDs in ungulate tissues available to critically endangered vultures in India. *Environmental Science & Technology*, 43: 4561–4566.

Tanner, E.V.J., Kapos, V. & Healey, J.R. (1991) Hurricane effects on forest ecosystems in the Caribbean. *Biotropica*, 23: 513–521.

TBI (2006) *Brazilian Merganser (*Mergus octosetaceus) *environmental education for the conservation of a critically endangered species*. Ref:195/07/04. Terra Brasilis Institute April 2006, Brazil.

Teixeira, D.M. (1986) The avifauna of the north-eastern Brazilian Atlantic forests: a case of mass extinction? *Ibis*, 128: 167–168.

Teixeira, D.M. (1997) A conservação do Cracidae no nordeste extremeo do Brasil. In: Strahl, S.D. *et al.* (eds). *The Cracidae: their biology and conservation*, 273–280. Hancock House, Surrey, BC.

Tennent, W.J. (2009) A cat among the pigeons! Known specimens and supposed distribution of the extinct Solomons Crested Pigeon *Microgoura meeki* Rothschild, 1904. *Bulletin of the British Ornithologists' Club*, 129: 241–253.

Tennyson, A.J.D. (2010) The origin and history of New Zealand's terrestrial vertebrates. *New Zealand Journal of Ecology*, 34: 6–27.

Terraube, J., Mougeot, F., Cornulier, T., Verma, A., Gavrilov, A. & Arroyo, B. (2011) Broad wintering range and intercontinental migratory divide within a core population of the near-threatened pallid harrier. *Diversity & Distributions*, 18: 401-409.

Terrazas, E.F. & Stahl, B. (2002) Diversity and phytogeography of the vascular flora of the Polylepis forests of the Cordillera de Cochabamba, Bolivia. *Ecotropica (Bonn)*, 8: 163–182.

Thibault, J.C., Martin, J.L., Penloup, A. & Meyer, J.Y. (2002) Understanding the decline and extinction of monarchs (Aves) in Polynesian Islands. *Biological Conservation*, 108: 161–174.

Thiollay, J.M. (1997) Disturbance, selective logging and bird diversity: a Neotropical forest study. *Biodiversity and Conservation*, 6: 1155–1173.

Thomas, C.D., Cameron, A., Green, R.E., Bakkenes, M., Beaumont, L.J., Collingham, Y.C., Erasmus, B.F.N., de Siqueira, M.F., Grainger, A., Hannah, L., Hughes, L., Huntley, B., van Jaarsveld, A.S., Midgley, G.F., Miles, L., Ortega-Huerta, M.A., Peterson, A.T., Phillips, O.L. & Williams, S.E. (2004) Extinction risk from climate change. *Nature*, 427: 145–148.

Thorsen, M. & Jones, C. (1998) The conservation status of Echo Parakeet *Psittacula eques* of Mauritius. *Bulletin of the African Bird Club*, 5: 122–126.

Tilman, D., May, R.M., Lehman, C.L. & Nowak, M.A. (1994) Habitat destruction and the extinction debt. *Nature*, 371: 65–66.

Timmins, R.J., Mostafawi, N., Rajabi, A.M., Noori, H., Ostrowski, S., Olsson, U., Svensson, L. & Poole, C.M. (2009) The discovery of Large-billed Reed Warblers *Acrocephalus orinus* in north-eastern Afghanistan. *BirdingASIA*, 12: 42–45.

Tingley, M.W., Monahan, W.B., Beissinger, S.R. & Moritz, C. (2009) Birds track their Grinnellian niche through a century of climate change. *Proceedings of the National Academy of Sciences of the United States of America*, 106: 19637–19643.

Tobias, J. (2000) Little-known Oriental bird: White-eyed River-martin *Eurochelidon sirintarae*. *Oriental Bird Club Bulletin*, 31: 45–48.

Tobias, J.A., Butchart, S.H.M. & Collar, N.J. (2006) Lost and found: a gap analysis for the Neotropical avifauna. *Neotropical Birding*, 2006: 4–22.

Tocher, M.D., Fletcher, D. & Bishop, P.J. (2006) A modelling approach to determine a translocation scenario for the endangered New Zealand frog *Leiopelma hamiltoni*. *Herpetological Journal*, 16: 97–106.

Tomich, P. (1986) *Mammals in Hawai'i*. Bishop Museum Press, Honolulu, Hawaii.

Tomkovich, P.S. (1992) Spoon-billed Sandpiper in north-eastern Siberia. *Dutch Birding*, 14: 37–41.

Tomkovich, P.S. (1995) Breeding biology and breeding success of the Spoon-billed Sandpiper *Eurynorhynchus pygmeus*. *Russian Journal of Ornithology*, 4: 77–91.

Tomkovich, P.S. (2003) Maximum life longevity of some waders in Chukotka. In: Tomkovich, P.S. & Shubin, A.O. (eds). *Information materials of the working group on waders, No. 16*, 55–56. Moscow.

Tomkovich, P.S. & Lebedeva, E.A. (2004) *International Single Species Action Plan for the conservation of the Sociable Lapwing* Vanellus gregarius. International, A.B., Moscow.

Tomkovich, P.S., Syroechkovskiy, E.E., Lappo, E.G. & Zöckler, C. (2002) First indications of a sharp population decline in the globally threatened Spoon-billed Sandpiper *Eurynorhynchus pygmeus*. *Bird Conservation International*, 12: 1–18.

Tompkins, D.M. & Gleeson, D.M. (2006) Relationship between avian malaria distribution and an exotic invasive mosquito in New Zealand. *Journal of the Royal Society of New Zealand*, 36: 51–62.

Tooke, A. (1961) The birds that helped Columbus. *Audubon*, 63: 252–253.

Tordoff, A.W., Appleton, T., Eames, J.C., Eberhardt, K., Thwin, K.M.M., Zaw, S.M., Moses, S. & Aung, S.M. (2008) The historical and current status of Pink-headed Duck *Rhodonessa caryophyllacea* in Myanmar. *Bird Conservation International*, 18: 38–52.

Towns, D.R. (2009) Eradications as reverse invasions: lessons from Pacific rat (*Rattus exulans*) removals on New Zealand islands. *Biological Invasions*, 11: 1719–1733.

Towns, D.R. & Broome, K.G. (2003) *From small Maria to massive Campbell: forty years of rat eradications from New Zealand islands*. 3rd International Wildlife Management Congress, Christchurch, New Zealand.

Towns, D.R., Atkinson, I.A.E. & Daugherty, C.H. (2006) Have the harmful effects of introduced rats on islands been exaggerated? *Biological Invasions*, 8: 863–891.

Traill, L.W., Brook, B.W., Frankham, R. & Bradshaw, C.J.A. (2010) Pragmatic population viability targets in a rapidly changing world. *Biological Conservation*, 143: 28–34.

Trevino, H.S., Skibiel, A.L., Karels, T.J. & Dobson, F.S. (2007) Threats to avifauna on oceanic islands. *Conservation Biology*, 21: 125–132.

Trewick, S.A. (1997) On the skewed sex ratio of the Kakapo *Strigops habroptilus*: sexual and natural selection in opposition? *Ibis*, 139: 652–663.

Trewick, S.A. & Gibb, G.C. (2010) Assembly of the New Zealand avifauna: a review of molecular phylogenetic evidence. *Ibis*, 152: 226-253.

Turner, A.K. (2004) Family Hirundinidae (swallows and martins). In: del Hoyo, J., Elliott, A. & Christie, D.A. (eds). *Handbook of the birds of the world, Vol. 9*, 602–685. Lynx Edicions, Barcelona.

Tweed, E.J., Foster, J.T., Woodworth, B.L., Monahan, W.B., Kellerman, J.L. & Lieberman, A. (2006) Breeding biology and success of a reintroduced population of the critically endangered Puaiohi (*Myadestes palmeri*). *Auk*, 123: 753–763.

Valqui, T. (2000) Rediscovery of the Royal Cinclodes *Cinclodes aricomae* in Bolivia. *Cotinga*, 14: 104.

van Auken, O.W. (2009) Causes and consequences of woody plant encroachment into western North American grasslands. *Journal of Environmental Management*, 90: 2931–2942.

van Balen, S., Nijman, V. & Prins, H.H.T. (2000) The Javan hawk eagle: misconceptions about rareness and threat. *Biological Conservation*, 96: 297–304.

van den Berg, A.B. (1988) Identification of Slender-billed Curlew and its occurrence in the winter of 1987–88. *Dutch Birding*, 10: 45–53.

van der Have, T.M., Keijl, G.O., Mansoori, J. & Morozov, V.V. (2001) *Searching for Slender-billed Curlews in Iran, January-February 2000*. WIWO, Zeist, Netherlands.

van Heezik, Y., Maloney, R.F. & Seddon, P.J. (2009) Movements of translocated captive-bred and released Critically Endangered-bred kaki (black stilts) *Himantopus novaezelandiae* and the value of long-term post-release monitoring. *Oryx*, 43: 639–647.

Van Riper, C., Van Riper, S.G. & Hansen, W.R. (2002) Epizootiology and effect of avian pox on Hawaiian forest birds. *Auk*, 119: 929–942.

VanderWerf, E.A. (2009) Importance of nest predation by alien rodents and avian poxvirus in conservation of Oahu Elepaio. *Journal of Wildlife Management*, 73: 737–746.

VanderWerf, E.A., Groombridge, J.J., Fretz, J.S. & Swinnerton, K.J. (2006) Decision analysis to guide recovery of the po'ouli, a critically endangered Hawaiian honeycreeper. *Biological Conservation*, 129: 383–392.

Vaurie, C. (1968) Taxonomy of the Cracidae (Aves). *Bulletin of the American Museum of Natural History*, 138: 131–260.

Veen, J., Yurlov, A.K., Delany, S.N., Mihantiev, A.I., Selivanova, M.A. & Boere, G.C. (2005) *An atlas of movement of southwest Siberian waterbirds*. Wetlands International, Wageningen, The Netherlands.

Vié, J.-C., Hilton-Taylor, C. & Stuart, S.N. (eds) (2009) *Wildlife in a changing world – an analysis of the 2008 IUCN Red List of Threatened Species*. IUCN, Gland, Switzerland.

Vince, C. (1980) *Keeping soft-billed birds*. Stanley Paul, London.

Vincent, J. (1966–1971) *Red data book. 2. Aves*. International Union for the Conservation of Nature and Natural Resources, Morges, Switzerland.

von Euler, F. (2001) Selective extinction and rapid loss of evolutionary history in the bird fauna. *Proceedings of the Royal Society Series B Biological Sciences*, 268: 127–130.

Votier, S.C., Bearhop, S., Fyfe, R. & Furness, R.W. (2008) Temporal and spatial variation in the diet of a marine top predator – links with commercial fisheries. *Marine Ecology-Progress Series*, 367: 223–232.

Vucetich, J.A., Waite, T.A., Qvarnemark, L. & Ibarguen, S. (2000) Population variability and extinction risk. *Conservation Biology*, 14: 1704–1714.

Walker, J.S. (2006) Resource use and rarity among frugivorous birds in a tropical rain forest on Sulawesi. *Biological Conservation*, 130: 60–69.

Walker, J.S. (2007) Geographical patterns of threat among pigeons and doves (Columbidae). *Oryx*, 41: 289–299.

Wallace, M. & Buchholz, R. (2001) Translocation of red-cockaded woodpeckers by reciprocal fostering of nestlings. *Journal of Wildlife Management*, 65: 327–333.

Walpole, M., Almond, R.E.A., Besancon, C., Butchart, S.H.M., Campbell-Lendrum, D., Carr, G.M., Collen, B., Collette, L., Davidson, N.C., Dulloo, E., Fazel, A.M., Galloway, J.N., Gill, M., Goverse, T., Hockings, M., Leaman, D.J., Morgan, D.H.W., Revenga, C., Rickwood, C.J., Schutyser, F., Simons, S., Stattersfield, A.J., Tyrrell, T.D., Vié, J.C. & Zimsky, M. (2009) Tracking progress toward the 2010 biodiversity target and beyond. *Science*, 325: 1503–1504.

Walther, G.R., Roques, A., Hulme, P.E., Sykes, M.T., Pysek, P., Kuhn, I., Zobel, M., Bacher, S., Botta-Dukat, Z., Bugmann, H., Czucz, B., Dauber, J., Hickler, T., Jarosik, V., Kenis, M., Klotz, S., Minchin, D., Moora, M., Nentwig, W., Ott, J., Panov, V.E., Reineking, B., Robinet,

C., Semenchenko, V., Solarz, W., Thuiller, W., Vila, M., Vohland, K. & Settele, J. (2009) Alien species in a warmer world: risks and opportunities. *Trends in Ecology & Evolution*, 24: 686–693.

Wang, M., Overland, J.E. & Bond, N.A. (2010) Climate projections for selected large marine ecosystems. *Journal of Marine Systems*, 79: 258–266.

Wanless, R.M., Ryan, P.G., Altwegg, R., Angel, A., Cooper, J., Cuthbert, R. & Hilton, G.M. (2009) From both sides: dire demographic consequences of carnivorous mice and longlining for the Critically Endangered Tristan albatrosses on Gough Island. *Biological Conservation*, 142: 1710–1718.

Wanless, R.M., Ratcliffe, N., Angel, A., Bowie, B.C., Cita, K., Hilton, G.M., Kritzinger, P., Ryan, P.G. & Slabber, M. (2012) Predation of Atlantic Petrel chicks by house mice on Gough Island. *Animal Conservation*, 15: 472–479.

Watkins, B.P., Petersen, S.L. & Ryan, P.G. (2008) Interactions between seabirds and deep-water hake trawl gear: an assessment of impacts in South African waters. *Animal Conservation*, 11: 247–254.

Watling, D. & Lewanavanua, R.F. (1985) A note to record the continuing survival of the Fiji (MacGillivray's) Petrel *Pseudobulweria macgillivrayi*. *Ibis*, 127: 230–233.

Watson, M., Wilson, J.M., Koshkin, M., Sherbakov, B., Karpov, F., Gavrilov, A., Schielzeth, H., Brombacher, M., Collar, N.J. & Cresswell, W. (2006) Nest survival and productivity of the critically endangered Sociable Lapwing *Vanellus gregarius*. *Ibis*, 148: 489–502.

Wearn, O.R., Reuman, D.C. & Ewers, R.M. (2012) Extinction debt and windows of conservation opportunity in the Brazilian Amazon. *Science*, 337: 228-232.

Weatherhead, P.J. & Blouin-Demers, G. (2004) Understanding avian nest predation: why ornithologists should study snakes. *Journal of Avian Biology*, 35: 185–190.

Webb, C.S. (1936) Collecting waterfowl in Madagascar. *Avicultural Magazine*, 5: 36–39.

Webb, T.J. & Gaston, K.J. (2000) Geographic range size and evolutionary age in birds. *Proceedings of the Royal Society Series B-Biological Sciences*, 267: 1843–1850.

Weidensaul, S. (2002) *The ghost with trembling wings: science, wishful thinking and the search for lost species*. Farrar Straus & Giroux Inc, New York.

Weimerskirch, H., Brothers, N. & Jouventin, P. (1997) Population dynamics of wandering albatross *Diomedea exulans* and Amsterdam albatross *D. amsterdamensis* in the Indian Ocean and their relationships with long-line fisheries: conservation implications. *Biological Conservation*, 79: 257–270.

Weldon, P.J. & Rappole, J.H. (1997) A survey of birds odorous or unpalatable to humans: possible indications of chemical defense. *Journal of Chemical Ecology*, 23: 2609–2633.

Western, D., Groom, R. & Worden, J. (2009) The impact of subdivision and sedentarization of pastoral lands on wildlife in an African savanna ecosystem. *Biological Conservation*, 142: 2538–2546.

White, C.M.N. & Bruce, M.D. (1986) *The birds of Wallacea (Sulawesi, the Moluccas and Lesser Sunda Islands, Indonesia): an annotated check-list*. British Ornithologists' Union, London.

White, T.H., Collazo, J.A. & Vilella, F.J. (2005) Survival of captive-reared Puerto Rican Parrots released in the Caribbean National Forest. *Condor*, 107: 424–432.

White, T.H., Collar, N.J., Moorhouse, R.J., Sanz, V., Stolen, E.D. & Brightsmith, D.J. (2012) Psittacine reintroductions: common denominators of success. *Biological Conservation*, 148: 106-115.

Whitehead, J., Case, B., Wilson, K.J. & Molles, L. (2012) Breeding variation in female kakapo (*Strigops habroptilus*) on Codfish Island in a year of low food supply. *New Zealand Journal of Ecology*, 36: 64-74.

Whitfort, H.L. & Young, R.J. (2004) Trends in the captive breeding of threatened and endangered birds in British zoos, 1988-1997. *Zoo Biology*, 23: 85–89.

Whittaker, R.J. & Fernández-Palacios, J.M. (2007) *Island biogeography: ecology, evolution and conservation*. Oxford University Press, Oxford, UK.

Widmann, P. & Lacerna Widmann, I. (2008) The cockatoo and the community: ten years of Philippine Cockatoo Conservation Programme. *BirdingASIA*, 10: 23–29.

Wikelski, M., Foufopoulos, J., Vargas, H. & Snell, H. (2004) Galapagos birds and diseases: invasive pathogens as threats for island species. *Ecology and Society*, 9: 5.

Wiles, G.J., Bart, J., Beck, R.E. & Aguon, C.F. (2003) Impacts of the brown tree snake: patterns of decline and species persistence in Guam's avifauna. *Conservation Biology*, 17: 1350–1360.

Williams, S.E. & Hoffman, E.A. (2009) Minimizing genetic adaptation in captive breeding programs: a review. *Biological Conservation*, 142: 2388–2400.

Williamson, M., Goodhart, C.B., Webb, D.A. & Cohen, J. (1989) Natural extinction on islands. *Philosophical Transactions of the Royal Society of London Series B-Biological Sciences*, 325: 457–468.

Wilmé, L. (1994) Status, distribution and conservation of two Madagascar bird species endemic to Lake Alaotra: Delacour's grebe *Tachybaptus rufolavatus* and Madagascar pochard *Aythya innotata*. *Biological Conservation*, 69: 15–21.

Wilmé, L., Goodman, S.M. & Ganzhorn, J.U. (2006) Biogeographic evolution of Madagascar's microendemic biota. *Science*, 312: 1063–1065.

Wilson, K.-J. (2004) *Flight of the Huia: ecology and conservation of New Zealand's frogs, reptiles, birds and mammals*. Canterbury University Press, Christchurch, New Zealand.

Wilson, R.J., Gutiérrez, D., Gutiérrez, J., Martínez, D., Agudo, R. & Monserrat, V.J. (2005) Changes to the elevational limits and extent of species ranges associated with climate change. *Ecology Letters*, 8: 1138–1146.

Witmer, G.W., Boyd, F. & Hillis-Starr, Z. (2007) The successful eradication of introduced roof rats (*Rattus rattus*) from Buck Island using diphacinone, followed by an irruption of house mice (*Mus musculus*). *Wildlife Research*, 34: 108–115.

Witt, C.C. & Lane, D.F. (2009) Range extensions for two rare high-Andean birds in central Peru. *Cotinga*, 31: 90–94.

Woodworth, B.L., Atkinson, C.T., LaPointe, D.A., Hart, P.J., Spiegel, C.S., Tweed, E.J., Henneman, C., LeBrun, J., Denette, T., DeMots, R., Kozar, K.L., Triglia, D., Lease, D., Gregor, A., Smith, T. & Duffy, D. (2005) Host population persistence in the face of introduced vector-borne diseases: Hawaii amakihi and avian malaria. *Proceedings of the National Academy of Sciences of the United States of America*, 102: 1531–1536.

Woolaver, L., Jones, C., Swinnerton, K., Murray, K., Lalinde, A., Birch, D., de Ravel, F. & Ridgeway, E. (2000) The release of captive bred echo parakeets to the wild, Mauritius. *Reintroduction News*, 19: 12–15.

Worthy, T.H., Tennyson, A.J.D., Archer, M., Musser, A.M., Hand, S.J., Jones, C., Douglas, B.J., McNamara, J.A. & Beck, R.M.D. (2006) Miocene mammal reveals a Mesozoic ghost lineage on insular New Zealand, southwest Pacific. *Proceedings of the National Academy of Sciences of the United States of America*, 103: 19419–19423.

Woxvold, I.A., Duckworth, J.W. & Timmins, R.J. (2009) An unusual new bulbul (Passeriformes: Pycnonotidae) from the limestone karst of Lao PDR. *Forktail*, 25: 1–12.

Wright, D.H. (1987) Estimating human effects on global extinction. *International Journal of Biometeorology*, 31: 293–299.

Wright, H.L., Lake, I.R. & Dolman, P.M. (2012) Agriculture - a key element for conservation in the developing world. *Conservation Letters*, 5: 11-19.

Wright, T.F., Toft, C.A., Enkerlin-Hoeflich, E., Gonzalez-Elizondo, J., Albornoz, M., Rodríguez-Ferraro, A., Rojas-Suárez, F., Sanz, V., Trujillo, A., Beissinger, S.R., Berovides, V., Galvez, X., Brice, A.T., Joyner, K., Eberhard, J., Gilardi, J., Koenig, S.E., Stoleson, S., Martuscelli, P., Meyers, J.M., Renton, K., Rodríguez, A.M., Sosa-Asanza, A.C., Vilella, F.J. & Wiley, J.W. (2001) Nest poaching in neotropical parrots. *Conservation Biology*, 15: 710–720.

Xu, H.G., Tang, X.P., Liu, J.Y., Ding, H., Wu, J., Zhang, M., Yang, Q.W., Cai, L., Zhao, H.J. & Liu, Y. (2009) China's progress toward the significant reduction of the rate of biodiversity loss. *BioScience*, 59: 843–852.

Yamagishi, S. & Nakamura, M. (2009) Family Vangidae (vangas). In: del Hoyo, J., Elliott, A. & Christie, D.A. (eds). *Handbook of the birds of the world, Vol. 9*, 142–170. Lynx Edicions, Barcelona.

Young, H.G. & Smith, J.G. (1989) The search for the Madagascar Pochard *Aythya innotata*: survey of Lac Alaotra, Madagascar October-November, 1989. *Dodo*, 26: 17–34.

Young, H.G. & Kear, J. (2006) The rise and fall of wildfowl of the western Indian Ocean and Australasia. *Bulletin of the British Ornithologists' Club*, 126A: 25–39.

Young, L.C., Zaun, B.J. & VanderWerf, E.A. (2008) Successful same-sex pairing in Laysan albatross. *Biology Letters*, 4: 323–325.

Young, R.P., Baptiste, T.J., Dornelly, A., Temple, H., Whitehead, H., Young, H.G. & Morton, M.N. (2010) Potential impacts of tourist developments in St Lucia on the Endangered White-breasted Thrasher *Ramphocinclus brachyurus*. *Bird Conservation International*, 20: 354–364.

Zavaleta, E.S., Hobbs, R.J. & Mooney, H.A. (2001) Viewing invasive species removal in a whole-ecosystem context. *Trends in Ecology & Evolution*, 16: 454–459.

Zetra, B., Rafiastanto, A., Rombang, W.M. & Trainor, C.R. (2002) Rediscovery of the Critically Endangered Sumatran Ground Cuckoo *Carpococcyx viridis*. *Forktail*, 18: 63–65.

Zhang, B., Fang, S.G. & Xi, Y.M. (2006) Major histocompatibility complex variation in the endangered crested ibis *Nipponia nippon* and implications for reintroduction. *Biochemical Genetics*, 44: 113–123.

Zhmud, M. (2005) Slender-billed Curlew: promising discovery in the Danube Delta. *Wader Study Group Bulletin*, 106: 51–54.

Zimmer, K.J. & Isler, M.L. (2003) Family Thamnophilidae (typical antbirds). In: del Hoyo, J., Elliott, A. & Christie, D.A. (eds). *Handbook of the birds of the world, Vol. 8*, 448–681. Lynx Edicions, Barcelona.

Zöckler, C. (2003) Neues vom Löffelstrandläufer *Eurynorhynchus pygmeus* und seinem alarmierenden Bestandsrückgang. *Limicola*, 17: 188–203.

Zöckler, C. (2006) *Spoon-billed sandpiper expedition Banladesh 2006*. ArcCona Consulting, Cambridge, UK.

Zöckler, C., Syroechkovskiy, E.E., Lappo, E.G. & Bunting, G. (2006) Stable isotope analysis and threats in the wintering areas of the declining Spoon-billed Sandpiper *Eurynorhynchus pygmeus* in the East Asia-Pacific Flyway. In: Boere, G.C., Galbraith, C.A. & Stroud, D.A. (eds). *Waterbirds around the world*, 147–153. The Stationery Office, Edinburgh.

Zöckler, C., Syroechkovskiy, E.E. & Bunting, G.C. (2008) *International Action Plan for the Spoon-billed Sandpiper*. CMS and BirdLife International Asia, Tokyo.

Zöckler, C., Syroechkovskiy, E.E. & Atkinson, P.W. (2010a) Rapid and continued decline in the Spoon-billed Sandpiper *Eurynorhynchus pygmeus* indicates imminent extinction unless conservation action is taken. *Bird Conservation International*, 20: 95–111.

Zöckler, C. Htin Hla, T., Clark, N., Syroechkovskiy, E., Yakushev, N., Daengphayan, S. & Robinson, R. (2010b). Hunting in Myanmar is probably the main cause of the decline of the Spoon-billed Sandpiper *Calidris pygmeus*. *Wader Study Group Bulletin*, 117: 1-8.

Zuckerberg, B., Woods, A.M. & Porter, W.F. (2009) Poleward shifts in breeding bird distributions in New York State. *Global Change Biology*, 15: 1866–1883.

Zydelis, R., Bellebaum, J., Osterblom, H., Vetemaa, M., Schirmeister, B., Stipniece, A., Dagys, M., van Eerden, M. & Garthe, S. (2009a) Bycatch in gillnet fisheries – an overlooked threat to waterbird populations. *Biological Conservation*, 142: 1269–1281.

Zydelis, R., Wallace, B.P., Gilman, E.L. & Werner, T.B. (2009b) Conservation of marine megafauna through minimization of fisheries bycatch. *Conservation Biology*, 23: 608–616.

INDEX